CW01249544

POETRY UNDERPINNING POWER

Poetry Underpinning Power

Vergil's *Aeneid*: The Epic for Emperor Augustus

A Recovery Study

Hans-Peter Stahl

The Classical Press of Wales

First published in 2015 by
The Classical Press of Wales
15 Rosehill Terrace, Swansea SA1 6JN
Tel: +44 (0)1792 458397
www.classicalpressofwales.co.uk

Distributor
I. B. Tauris & Co Ltd,
6 Salem Rd,
London W2 4BU, UK
Tel.: +44 (0) 20 7243 1225
Fax: +44 (0) 20 7243 1226
www.ibtauris.com

Distributor in North America
ISD,
70 Enterprise Drive, Suite 2,
Bristol, CT 06010, USA
Tel: +1 (860) 584-6546
Fax: +1 (860) 516-4873
www.isdistribution.com

© 2016 The author

All rights reserved. No part of this publication may be reproduced, stored in a retrieval system, or transmitted, in any form or by any means, electronic, mechanical, photocopying, recording or otherwise, without the prior permission of the publisher.

ISBN 978-1-910589-04-5

A catalogue record for this book is available from the British Library.

Typeset by Louise Jones, and printed and bound in the UK by Gomer Press, Llandysul, Ceredigion, Wales

---

The Classical Press of Wales, an independent venture, was founded in 1993, initially to support the work of classicists and ancient historians in Wales and their collaborators from further afield. More recently it has published work initiated by scholars internationally. While retaining a special loyalty to Wales and the Celtic countries, the Press welcomes scholarly contributions from all parts of the world.

The symbol of the Press is the Red Kite. This bird, once widespread in Britain, was reduced by 1905 to some five individuals confined to a small area known as 'The Desert of Wales' – the upper Tywi valley. Geneticists report that the stock was saved from terminal inbreeding by the arrival of one stray female bird from Germany. After much careful protection, the Red Kite now thrives – in Wales and beyond.

puellae carissimae doctissimae Giselae
semper amica mihi, semper et uxor.

CONTENTS

	Page
Preface	ix
Prologue	xi

PART I
PIOUS KING AENEAS AND HIS ETHICALLY FLAWED OPPONENTS

1	Augustan Vergil and the Political Rival	1
2	The Death of King Turnus	33
3	Aeneas the Warrior	109
4	Winning the Reader's Assent through Subliminal Guidance	163
5	Allocating Guilt and Innocence, I: Queen Dido, the Liberated Widow	183

PART II
CHECKS AND BALANCES OF A LITERARY INTERPRETATION: POLITICAL DETOURS OF POETIC TRAVEL ROUTES

| 6 | Before Founding Lavinium, Aeneas Inspects the Site of Rome | 251 |

PART III
TESTING A CRITICAL METHOD BY REPEAT APPLICATION: THE ANCIENT AUTHOR GUIDES HIS READER

| 7 | Allocating Guilt and Innocence, II: Turnus the Impious Opponent | 347 |
| 8 | Epilogue | 437 |

Bibliography	463
Index	475
Index locorum	487

PREFACE

Habent sua fata libelli: originally planned to be a timely sequel to the author's book on Propertius, the present project fell victim to the demands of professional life, especially on the Greek side of our field. But delay has not meant loss of perspective. Years of engaged teaching, especially in the Honors College with its inquisitive students, allowed thinking and rethinking the interpretation with an eye on clarity of presentation, as well as on reviewing the contents in the light of Greek literature. And so did the exchanges with audiences of many lectures in numerous countries, which acquainted the author with different ways of thinking and with immediate reactions one does not always learn from studying the secondary literature. It became clear that in today's literary-critical environment it might be difficult to convince readers of the integral role Vergil assigned the organizational coherence of his work. For that would involve acknowledging its (often less than welcome) political orientation.

So I decided to demonstrate, for doubters, the work's thoroughly Augustan perspective by complementing my independent interpretation with objective, non-literary, evidence. This involved many a summer month spent locating and identifying the archaeological remains of monuments alluded to in the *Aeneid*. It turned out that the evening stroll King Aeneas and King Evander take on the site of future Rome (Book 8), far from expressing the poet's personal nostalgia or romanticism over early Rome, leads the Julian ancestor to view three areas which, in the years Vergil worked on his *Aeneid*, were major construction sites. It was on these sites that Aeneas' greater descendant, the proud builder of Rome-in-marble, completed the program of Julianizing the cityscape, which his adoptive father, C. Julius Caesar, had begun.

Among those to whom I am indebted for their help a few should be named. First there is Mr James Wismer who took upon himself a truly Herculean labor, which I was no longer able to carry out myself. He not only checked all quotations and references, but also cut back a mammoth bibliography to "Works Cited", and arranged what remained in the order displayed in this volume.

I am much obliged to the Reader for the Press, Dr John Trappes-Lomax, whose meticulous observations prevented some foolish decisions of mine from appearing in print. To him – as to others – I owe an apology for my occasional stubbornness. Any remaining mistakes are truly my own.

Preface

Miss Margaret Hubbard read several early chapters, encouraging me to continue the project when I was still wavering. Her warm friendship and luscious hospitality are unforgotten. It pains me that she cannot see the completed book.

My greatest debt is owed to a fellow Vergilian scholar, Dr Anton Powell. A congenial editor, indulgent publisher, and never-failing friend, he stood by me in trying times, condoning delays and lending his support when I felt unable to continue. His advice has helped considerably to bring the book into the shape it displays now.

My preface should end with a warning to prospective readers. The book is not written for short distance readers of the *Aeneid*. I mean a group of interpreters who tend to break off pieces from the work of art and view them extra-contextually; some will even interconnect several such fragments to force an overall 'interpretation' (this group I also call "fragmentary interpreters".)

"Long distance interpreters", on the other hand, I call those who pay attention to the poem's overall rhetorical and logical organization (the existence of which it has lately been fashionable to deny). These interpreters will, while interpreting a specific passage or section, not lose sight of its place and function within the epic's whole.

A few sections published earlier have been, in part or wholly, integrated here. I thank the original publishers for permission to republish.

"The Death of Turnus: Augustan Vergil and the Political Rival", published in: *Between Republic and Empire. Interpretations of Augustus and his Principate*, edited by Kurt A. Raaflaub and Mark Toher, Berkeley 1990, pp. 174–211. (Sections of Chapters 1 and 2.)

"Göttliches Wirken und empirische Psychologie: Vergils karthagische Königin". *Gymnasium* 115, 2008, 309–330. (See Chapter 5. 1 and 2.)

"The Sword-Belt of Pallas: Holding a Quill for the Critic? Vergil, *Aeneid* 10. 495–500". *Würzburger Jahrbücher* 35, 2011, 7–31. (See Chapter 3. 2.)

Translations (except where otherwise indicated) are the author's.

Silvia Lai, of the University of Pisa, made the indices and helped expertly with the bibliography.

Pittsburgh, Pennsylvania, U.S.A
April 2015

PROLOGUE

> What offends modern sensibilities may be just what Vergil wishes his audience to appreciate. (See Chapter 5)

It is appropriate to start with twin precautionary statements. First, the prospective reader who fears to be confronted with yet another 'fresh reading' of the *Aeneid* may rest assured: the interpretation presented here does not claim to be new by the gauge of certain current critical endeavors. Rather, it aims at revisiting and reinstating into their dominant function those basic ancient laws of logic (and rhetoric) which underlie all highly developed Greek and Roman writing, laws and standards whose observation is a *condicio sine qua non* for any adequate reading. The result will, however, not mean a return to any fixed position of yesteryear.

Second, an apology is due to many whose names do not appear on these pages. Literature on Vergil has swollen to such a flood that I am no longer able to accompany the argument with the kind of running commentary on scholarship as was offered in the notes of my *Propertius. Individual and State under Augustus*, the preparatory antecedent and companion piece to the present volume. Also, a comprehensive commentary on scholarship might distract from the clarity of argument I am aiming at. The choice was either to write a limited number of sectional articles with full documentation and discussion of rival interpretations, or to offer an overall interpretation which establishes, secures, and emphasizes the consistency of the *Aeneid*'s artistic design and train of thought, with debate of opposing opinions restricted to critical moments of recent (and not so recent) scholarship.

For readers wondering at the mention of Propertius, a few results are here recalled from the detailed study published in 1985. That work showed the dilemma of the poet in a hierarchically structured, politically homogenized society; in order to make his voice heard (originally, a voice of independence), he was more and more forced into compromises toward the regime. The initial stance of the a-political love poet provided him with considerable protection. But, once drafted into the sphere of Maecenas, literary patron and guardian of Emperor Augustus' public image, he would also write regime-conforming pieces, which he sometimes balanced by a following palinode (e.g., 3. 4 and 3. 5). In the end, he announced an exclusively patriotic program (4. 1A), integrating even aspects of Vergil's *Aeneid*. But he immediately rescinded the presumed patriotic commitment by having an astrologer, Horus, remind him of his destiny as a love poet (4. 1B). In this last Book of his, he restates the old dilemma in an encoded form (4. 4): In a long monologue, Tarpeia, the treasonous Vestal, is allowed to

Prologue

voice her love for King Tatius, the country's enemy, and to revile Romulus (who is a central figure in the pro-Julian program of 4. 1A) as the nursling of the *"inhuman she-wolf"*, *inhumanae...lupae* (4. 4. 54). Though the opening and ending of the elegy duly condemn the treasonous Vestal, her tormented voice, which conceives of *love as treason*, is far from being silenced.

Propertius, as the references in elegy 4. 1A show, reads the *Aeneid* as a politically pro-Julian, pro-Augustan epic. His (tongue-in-cheek?) endorsement of Vergil's claim to writing something greater than Homer's *Iliad* (2. 34) is vociferously balanced by the love poet's own self-chosen political and social "worthlessness" (*nequitia* is the term he employs in 1.6 to characterize himself). Consequently, praising Octavian's civil war victory near Actium is not Propertius' pleasure, but is delegated to the poet of the *Aeneid*:

> May it be Vergil's pleasure to be able to sing of the shores of Actium
> that Phoebus guards,
> and of Caesar's brave ships,

> Actia Vergilium custodis litora Phoebi
> Caesaris et fortis dicere posse ratis,
> 2. 34. 61f.

Propertius' pleasure, by way of contrast, is "to lie relaxed among yesterday's garlands" (2. 34. 59).

Propertius' family had suffered expropriation and human sorrow during the civil war. The considerable reservations he early on displays toward Augustus as well as the distance he lays between his own poetry and the *Aeneid*'s support of the regime, reveal attitudes grown from personal, eye-witness experience. Present-day scholarship, when determining Vergil's political stance, does not take into account Propertius' testimony (though it is supported by ancient commentators), i.e., the contemporary's understanding of the *Aeneid* as serving the Julian family myth as well as praising the regime's coming-to-power. And yet – unless one deems the elegist an incompetent critic of the epic's underlying political affinity - by not listening to his voice, we as interpreters may deprive ourselves of an available premise that may *a priori* protect our work against a-historical literary constructs, such as the assumption of an anti-Augustan, 'subversive' *Aeneid*, or even the conceit (drawn not from historical evidence but from a modern layman's novel) that it was Augustus who, after the poet's death, 'appropriated' the *Aeneid* for his own political program.

Vergil, an extraordinarily gifted young poet of provincial background, proved the ideal choice for fashioning and promulgating the myth of the newly empowered dynasty, in a work that would become both the legitimizing manifesto of Augustus' authority and a blueprint for much of occidental Europe's hierarchically structured social order.

PART I

1

AUGUSTAN VERGIL AND THE POLITICAL RIVAL[1]

(1) Interpretative Premises

The main compositional division of Vergil's *Aeneid* offers its reader two halves: Books 1–6 and 7–12. The first half, describing Aeneas' travels from sunken Troy to the promised land of Italy, has – in view of the poet's claim to be the New Homer – not unfittingly been called his "Roman *Odyssey*", whereas Books 7–12, detailing the battles the hero has to "endure" (*passus* 1. 5) in Italy, amount to a "Roman *Iliad*." Vergil himself rated the second half more important, calling it, in a special second proem, his "major work," *maius opus* (7. 45). Given this weight distribution, it appears appropriate for today's interpreter to ascertain his procedural bearings by turning to the poem's second half first.

In recent decades, the bone of contention in Vergilian criticism has been the epic's final scene, in which Aeneas, mythical ancestor of Emperor Augustus, kills his opponent on Italian soil, Rutulian King Turnus: does Aeneas act with justice (as ancient commentators Servius and Donatus inform us), or has he turned into a merciless killer (as one 20th century school of interpretation assumed)? Little or no attention has any longer been paid to the answer which Vergil himself provides through (among other indications) the complex and consistent action line: gradually leading up to the final encounter, the poet early on sets (and continually reinforces) the parameters for weighing the eventual outcome. It may be a worthwhile enterprise to re-establish the epic's bearings by tracing the leads provided by its author, even if the resulting picture may not be so new – and may not recommend itself to modern tastes.

In light of present-day tendencies in literary criticism, it appears advisable to recall at the outset the role that logical (often combined with rhetorical) organization played at the peaks of developed ancient writing, prose as well as poetry. Whether we use terms such as story-line, plot-line, dramaturgy, literary architecture, or simply train of thought, as interpreters we face a twofold obligation: we should, on the one hand, both observe and trace the movement of thought through its interconnected sections, and we should, on the other hand, avoid violating the narrative sequence by arbitrarily lifting – and perhaps inter-connecting – links (or even isolated words) from the chain and then mistaking them for presumably self-contained, sovereign subunits (or indicators) of meaning – a procedure that in fact might run counter to the author's verifiable intention.[2]

Some premises for understanding the epic's final scene are actually established as early as the opening sections of the "Roman *Iliad*" in Book 7 of the *Aeneid*, and the movement of Books 7–12 is (notwithstanding a politically motivated excursus or two) organized as a coherent literary composition, which does not allow viewing the climactic final scene in isolation.[3] So the natural procedure for the interpreter would seem to be to begin with Book 7. However, this Book is traditionally seen to be burdened with special difficulties of interpretation that call for a comprehensive approach involving synopsis with Book 1 of the *Aeneid* and even with other authors. Starting out with a detailed reading of Book 7, then, might actually result in complicating access for today's readers rather than in clarifying the poetic design.

There is another reason, which likewise commends giving Book 7 a separate assessment. This is grounded in matters of content. The Book's first 600 lines, by describing the local reaction to Aeneas' landing in Italy, separate friend from foe. Aged King Latinus of Latium, in obedience to divine commands, welcomes Aeneas and offers him his daughter in marriage. Neighboring King Turnus, along with Amata, Latinus' consort, brazenly disregards the oracle's orders. Turnus insists on himself marrying the heiress to the Latin throne and declares war on Aeneas. Though this objectively puts Turnus in violation of divine will, a branch of scholarship has seen fit to (at least subjectively) exculpate him by arguing that peace-breaking Turnus is not his own self; rather, he – so the assumption goes – is subjected to heteronomy since being visited in a dream by a Fury who is sent by Juno, Aeneas' divine adversary. (The entailed question of Turnus' free will, however, is only superficially tackled in Vergilian scholarship and requires consideration in a special chapter – as does the case of Queen Dido.) This much, it seems, is safe to state at this point: Book 7 largely gives the psychological exposition of the characters' initial attitudes and responsibility with regard to coming events.

But it is also in the ensuing martial events themselves, narrated in the following Books, that the characters, through their specific actions and reactions, as well as through their general conduct, are presented to the reader as pious or impious, ethically flawed or distinguished, as humane or inhuman. Such valuations are found spread widely in the narrative of the later Books. Since they generally are in agreement with the psychological profiles drawn in Book 7, their interpretation may actually serve as a welcome confirmation later on when, in our Chapter 7, the investigation will focus on the exposition given in Book 7 and on the question of King Turnus' initial guilt or innocence. For the present purpose, it suffices by way of introduction first to highlight some political implications and parallels concerning the author's own time (as well as that of his contemporary reader) and then briefly to review the opening situation in Book 7.

In Vergil's version, Aeneas, ancestor of the Julian family, appears in Italy as a peaceful and peace-seeking newcomer. Perhaps one should better call him a home-comer, since the reader is being informed that his distant forefather Dardanus had emigrated from the region (*Aen.* 7. 206f.; 240; cf. 3.167). Through this feature (non-traditional, an apparent *ad hoc* invention of the poet), Vergil is lending additional legitimacy to Aeneas' claim to the land he is entering. His journey has been guided by Fate and by Jupiter, i.e., by Rome's highest religious authorities (1. 261ff.; 8. 381). He is sent under orders of Apollo, god of prophecy (and, in the reader's time, personal tutelary deity of Aeneas' descendant, Emperor Augustus), specifically to occupy the land between the rivers Tiber and Numic(i)us (7. 241f.), i.e., territory held by King Latinus' people and by the Rutulians of King Turnus. The ultimate purpose of Aeneas' arrival, according to divine revelation (7. 98–101; cf. 1. 268ff.),[4] is the worldwide rule Augustus will one day (i.e., in the time of Vergil's reader) peacefully exercise from this area.

Vergil does not spare his hero the saddening experience of resistance, raised by an increasing faction of the native population. There is, above all, the aforementioned King Turnus, oracle-defying and sacrilegious (cf. 7. 595ff.), who associates with such telltale characters as Etruscan King Mezentius, most cruel torturer of his own subjects (8. 485ff.) and "despiser of the gods" (*contemptor divum* 7. 648; cf. *contemptorque deum Mezentius* 8. 7);[5] another chief associate of Turnus is Messapus who, on the occasion of breaking a peace treaty, delights in killing a king in full regalia at the altar as, in his words "a better victim for the great gods" (12. 289–96). The pious Julian ancestor is, against his desire for peace, compelled to wage a holy war against aggressive and godless opposition.

His greater descendant had, in his own view, to face comparable problems. After the assassination of his adoptive father, C. Julius Caesar (the dictator), Octavian (the later Augustus) joined the second triumvirate and its mandate "to organize the republic," *rei publicae constituendae*. Octavian wishes his earthly achievements to be viewed as fulfillment of a divine mission – so much so that he would publicly spread the needed information. On a coin of his, one finds his public task, expressed by the three letters *r[ei] p[ublicae] c[onstituendae]*, superimposed on the outline of a tripod, i.e., on the symbol of Apollo, god of prophecy, whom he considered his personal tutelary deity.[6]

Octavian, as his *Achievements* (*Res Gestae*) inform posterity (*R.G.* 2), had to defeat the men "who butchered my father" (*qui parentem meum trucidaverunt* – the customary label for a dictator's assassins, we remind ourselves, would be "tyrannicides"); the assassins were, in Augustus' view, "raising arms against the republic", *bellum inferentis rei publicae*. True to his perception of his mission as serving the common weal of the republic, he calls his opponents a "faction" (*R.G.* 1), not dignifying them by mentioning a name.

To sum up, then: a just cause; executor of a divinely ordained mission; administrator of the nation's interests; facing irresponsible, godless, and criminal factionalism – these are features shared by the founder of the Julian family (as depicted by Vergil) and by his descendant (as his case is presented by Augustus himself).

It was the ancestor's task, according to the *Aeneid*, to prepare the road that would, in the distant future (i.e., in Vergil's own time), lead to Emperor Augustus. Now: since the portrait of the forefather was being painted at a time (29–19 BC) when the descendant had already completed (i.e., in 30 BC) the conquest of his 'unholy opposition', one can hardly *a priori* exclude that the epic on the ancestor may, at least in part, be designed to set the record 'straight' on the ethics and metaphysics of the descendant's career. My aim here is not to pursue "typological" correspondences between the two characters.[7] Nor do I subscribe to the hypothesis that the poetic ancestor was intended to enlighten the real-life descendant about his obligations as a ruler.[8] Questions more to the point appear to be: could any reader in the time of Augustus fail to notice the harmony between epic and present-day political pronouncements, e.g., the declared desire for peace and the unwelcome burden of having had to wage a holy war against sacrilegious rebels who threatened the peace of the community? Is the ancestor's enduring loyalty to his divinely directed mission not superbly helpful in guiding the reader and citizen when he ponders the presumed motivation of the latest Julian, his contemporary ruler (as well as that of his adversaries)? Repugnant as such rhetorical questions may sound to some modern students of the Augustan Age and of the civil war from which it grew, it would be rash *a priori* to posit that Vergil shares feelings and attitudes that are accepted in post-Enlightenment, democratically tinged societies.

The interpretation to be proposed here is to be derived from close literary analysis of the epic itself, especially its composition, which ranges over surprisingly long distances. But the approach does not foreclose a comparison with another author (or with historical references) when such a comparison may both illuminate Vergil's method and provide a wider background.

In Livy's *History of Rome from its Foundation*, we find King Turnus betrothed to Lavinia, daughter of King Latinus (1.2.1; see also Ovid, *M.* 14. 451). Upon Aeneas' arrival in Italy, Latinus withdraws his daughter's hand and reassigns Lavinia to Aeneas. Turnus reacts by waging war against both Latinus and Aeneas.

A widespread view in Vergilian scholarship wrongly assumes the same set-up for the *Aeneid*. In this case, readers would certainly be right in feeling sympathy for Turnus who could, through Books 7–12, be seen as trying to recover what is rightfully his. A close reading (as detailed in Chapter 7 below), however, reveals that Vergil was careful to avoid making the Julian ancestor a bride-snatcher.

Above all, Vergil's conception, when compared to Livy's, provides a different, more negative picture of Turnus. This is achieved by the timing (*tempora*, 7. 37) of events. Well before Aeneas arrives in Italy, an oracle (the one mentioned earlier, 7. 96–101) is made known throughout the cities of Italy (7. 104f.): Lavinia is destined not for a native suitor (7. 96f.) but for a son-in-law from abroad whose descendants will rule the world, etc.

In this way, Turnus' persistence in claiming Lavinia (i.e. the Latin throne) must be viewed, in the first place, as disobedience toward divine orders. His later political and military opposition to Aeneas, upon the Trojans' arrival in Italy, is secondary, both in time and in degree of impiety or even criminality.

One major achievement of Vergil can here be seen in the way he sets his markers. Far from being a foreign invader, the Julian ancestor from Troy is duly welcomed by pious Latinus as the carrier of a divine mission and as a home-comer; but then Aeneas is ruthlessly attacked by the oracle-defying head of a local faction (the opponent does not represent an Italian consensus).

This clearly spells out the negative role of Turnus. As scholars and literary critics, we should not uncritically allow ourselves to be led astray by our personal desire for fairness or humanity; nor should we (perhaps by imposing a label of greater "complexity" or "sophistication") disfranchise the poet's own design by introducing outside perspectives, e.g., Dante's programmatic, all-Italian view:

> Di quella umile Italia fia salute
> per cui morì la vergine Cammilla,
> Eurialo e Turno e Niso di ferute. *Div. Comm.* 1. 106–08.

Far from seeing in Turnus a hero dying for Italy (and far from granting him the same accolades as it grants to Camilla, Euryalus, and Nisus), the *Aeneid* presents Turnus as a rebel against the country's gods.[9]

Already, the service Vergil is rendering to his ruler is becoming clearer. By identifying Aeneas (i.e., the ancestor of Julian Augustus) with Fate and the will of the highest god, the poet is able to do two things. He can, on the one hand, disentangle Augustus from the (often gruesome) incidents of the recent civil war: Octavian (here we also recall the aforementioned coin) did not participate as yet another faction. He is the latest member of a family whose divine mission for Rome the *Aeneid* firmly anchors in a mythical past: the poet functions as ideologue of the ruler. Vergil is also, on the other hand, able to define – and in this he again agrees with the published position of Augustus – the political adversary as a criminal opponent of divine authority (a notion of lasting influence in Western history). Following this introductory orientation, I now proceed to trace King Turnus' later career in the epic, up to his death at the hands of Aeneas.

To facilitate elucidation of Vergil's complex plot, four strands that jointly lead up to the epic's final scene are analyzed separately:

(A) the contractual and strategic developments of Books 11 and 12, culminating in King Turnus' death (= Chapter 1, Section 2);
(B) the differing battlefield conduct of the leading characters (= Chapter 3, Sections 1 and 3); and
(C) the subliminal guidance provided to the reader in the tragic fate of Pallas, Aeneas' young disciple and ally (= Chapter 4, Section 1).

Special sections have been included to deal with pressing methodological questions:

Chapter 2, excursus 1 exemplifies types of circuitous reading.
Chapter 3, Section 2, offers a *Methodological Intermezzo*, dealing with the sword-belt of Pallas.

A special Chapter (7), as I indicated earlier, has been reserved for a fourth strand (D). It deals with a (if not *the*) main spring in the *Roman Iliad*'s unfolding of events: King Turnus' culpable decision (which defenders of Turnus like to transfer to the Fury Allecto) to issue his impious call for war and to attack the Trojans. The observant reader has been led to expect the death of Turnus ever since Book 7. When the Rutulian king and others, "against the prodigies", "against the fates", and "in perversion of the will of the gods" (7. 583f.), urge pious Latinus to raise war against Aeneas, the old king, full of presentiment, exclaims:

> For you, Turnus, (abominable event)
> the bitter death penalty
> will be waiting, and too late you will worship the gods with prayers.
>
> Te, Turne, (nefas!) te triste manebit
> supplicium, votisque deos venerabere seris. 7. 596f.

Aeneas himself, on his side, twice in Book 8 points to the broken peace treaty:

> What penalties will you pay me, Turnus!
>
> Quas poenas mihi, Turne, dabis! 8. 538.

And:

> Let them ask for battle and break the treaty!
>
> Poscant acies et foedera rumpant! 8. 540

His words, appropriate for Fate's proto-Julian emissary, combine the functions of judge (*poenas*) and executioner (*dabis*) in one and the same person.

(2) Toward the Single Combat of Aeneas and Turnus: a Tortuous Road, due to the Rutulian King's Evasiveness

Most clearly discernible of the *Roman Iliad*'s four major strands and, therefore, most easy to trace, is the development that leads up to the final battle in front of (and for) the city of the Latins, culminating in the duel between Aeneas and Turnus. The development is introduced by Aeneas' words at the opening of Book 11:

> Now our road leads to the king and the Latin walls.
>
> Nunc iter ad regem nobis murosque Latinos. 11. 17

However, this road will not be as straight as is suggested here. And the detours to a considerable extent are due to none other than King Turnus. In this context, as on other occasions, the poet contrasts Turnus' behavior with that of his greater counterpart, Aeneas.

In Book 11, the bodies of those who died in the great battle of Book 10 are buried. This necessitates some contact between the two warring sides (by asking for their dead, the Latins, carrying olive branches, acknowledge defeat), and thus "good Aeneas" (*bonus Aeneas* 106), the victor, is given a chance to show compassion (*miseris* 119) toward the fallen enemy and to emphasize that he would be only too happy to grant peace (*concedere* 111)

Chapter 1

also to the living. His intent is to avoid the war of the two nations, and, instead, by way of a deadly duel, to leave the decision to god or to personal valor (*vixet cui vitam deus aut sua dextra dedisset* 118). On the Latin side, it is not only Drances, the invidious opponent of Turnus, who, together with all those (*omnes*; cf. *uno...ore* 132) accompanying him, has an ear for Aeneas' suggestions (124ff.; 132). The reader is far from feeling increased sympathy for Turnus when the authorial voice, sharing (and confirming) Aeneas' sense of compassion, goes on to list further groups within the city (the details are well on target):

> The mothers here, and the *poor* daughters-in-law, the dear hearts
> of the *mourning* sisters, and the children, *bereft* of their slain fathers,
> they curse the abominable war and the wedding (plans) of Turnus:
> they say that he himself with his arms, he himself with his sword,
> should bring about the decision –
> he who demands the kingdom of Italy and the highest honors for himself.

> Hic matres *miserae*que nurus, hic cara sororum
> pectora *maerentum* puerique parentibus *orbi*
> dirum exsecrantur bellum Turnique hymenaeos:
> ipsum armis, ipsumque iubent decernere ferro
> qui regnum Italiae et primos sibi poscat honores. 11. 215–19.

At an earlier point already (9. 133–39) Turnus had been unwilling to see that, when encountering the fate-sent Aeneadae, one has to scale back one's political ambitions, even to give up one's most personal desires – in this case, his hopes for receiving the king's daughter as his bride (presumptuously, he already called her his "wife, snatched from me beforehand", *coniuge praerepta* 9. 138).

Now the reader, emotionally influenced by the sorrowful complaints of those bereft victims, is given reason to view Turnus' endeavor as a sort of private war which he is waging at the cost of his people to fulfill his personal goals. Thus at the beginning of Book 11 Turnus can by no means be seen exclusively to represent the interests of the Italians. Rather, he is found to have, by his ambition, maneuvered himself into considerable isolation. (There are, it is true, many voices in his favor, but the author confines them to three lines [222–24], and he mentions the influence of Queen Amata whom he has characterized as disrespecting and manipulating divine revelation [cf. 7. 367–72]).

It should be noted how, in this section, the reader's judgment is subliminally influenced by the author. Consciously, we first register the voices of Drances and of his fellow-ambassadors; then, later, the pitiful and heart-rending pleas of those who lost their loved ones in Turnus' war.

In between, Vergil inserts a description of the burials on both sides (182–214). In spite of the tears (191) and the unwillingness to part with the dead (201) on the Trojan side, there can be no doubt that the *pitiable* Latins (*miseri...Latini* 203), who pile up the "innumerable" (204) pyres and must burn a "huge pile" of anonymous, not individually honored, comrades (207f.), receive more sympathy from the writer's pen. This may, at first sight, seem to reveal impartiality on the poet's part, to express "Vergil's horror of war, and especially his sympathy for the unnumbered and unhonored dead."[10] But the authorial description of the sorrows experienced by the *miseri...Latini* has a less conspicuous function: it conditions the reader to accept as justified the invective that the *matres miseraeque nurus* etc. utter against Turnus. Far from representing what is presumed to be *Vergil*'s humanity, the appeal to the reader's sense of compassion serves (while on the surface favoring the Trojans' enemies over the Trojans themselves) to discredit Aeneas' Italian counterpart: Turnus, the feeling reader is supposed to conclude, is selfish at the cost of his miserable people's lives. An important facet of Vergil's literary (and rhetorical) technique is revealed here. At the same time, a critical reader may catch a glimpse of the potential which human compassion offers for subliminally creating political prejudice: an appeal to compassion may serve political partiality.

A new warning for Turnus and his followers occurs when the negative answer of the Greek prince Diomedes is received in the Latin assembly. Diomedes not only refuses to help, he even advises against fighting Aeneas (11. 225ff.). He insightfully interprets the losses encountered by the Greeks before Troy and on their way home as punishment for their attack on Troy (11. 255ff.; *supplicia et scelerum poenas* 258). Today he rates (and in doing so, he employs quite Julian standards) his own attack on Venus (in the *Iliad*, the first step in his escalating aggression against gods, which in that poem culminates in his wounding Ares, the war god, himself) as the climax (*et V̲eneris v̲iolavi v̲ulnere dextram* 277) of his own madness (*demens* 276). From personal experience (*experto* 283) he describes Aeneas' strength in fighting, even mentions a close combat he had with him (*contulimusque manus* 283) that is unknown to the *Iliad* (the *Iliad* passage only tells us of Aeneas' inferiority toward Diomedes: he had to be saved by his divine mother).[11] Vergil here not only upgrades the heroic status accorded the Julians' ancestor by Homer; he also re-programs Aeneas' Homeric opponent so that he now respects the greatness of the Julians' ancestral goddess.

King Latinus does understand the meaning of the message: one must not "wage war against the race of the gods and invincible [!] men" (*cum gente deorum / invictisque viris*, 305f.). When proposing peace, he is supported by Drances (the same man who had transmitted Aeneas' suggestion of a duel, 220f.): "Turnus, we, all of us, ask you for peace" (*pacem te poscimus omnes, Turne* 362f.) "Why do you throw the *poor* (*miseros*) citizens into the jaws of dangers?" (360f.) By openly implying Turnus' alleged hostility towards himself (364f.), he jeopardises the credibility his arguments deserve. His approach ("you source and cause of these sorrows for Latium!" 361) is anything but diplomatic. He suggests that the dowry (i.e., the kingdom) is more important to Turnus than the bride (369ff.).

Perhaps not surprisingly, by this appeal Turnus' notorious inclination to violence is kindled even more:

Talibus exarsit dictis violentia Turni. 11. 376

If he is standing in the way of the common weal (*si...bonis communibus obsto* 434–5), then, he says, he will accept the duel. Is he aware that Aeneas' call for him alone (220; 221) as a counterpart fighter represents an echo of his own earlier call (10. 442) for Aeneas' young ally Pallas as his own adversary (and his alone)? Probably not. But on the reader's ear this echo (which again appears repeatedly in Book 12) is not lost.

For me alone Aeneas is calling? Let him: that is my desire!

Solum Aeneas vocat? Et vocet oro. 11. 442

It certainly does not recommend Turnus to the reader if he now hopes to refute Drances' criticism concerning defeat by bragging (392ff.) that he has struck to the ground "the whole house" of King Evander. The truth is that senior fighter Turnus had unheroically killed (in unfair fight, as Section 1 of Chapter 3 shows) Evander's son Pallas, almost a boy still (*puer* 11. 42; 12. 943), on the young warrior's first (10. 508) day in battle. Similarly, he brags about his valor inside the Trojan camp (11. 396ff.) – whereas in truth his "unblessed leadership", to use Drances' words (*auspicium infaustum* 347), had cost his side the decisive victory. Had Turnus only opened the gates to let his fellow fighters enter the Trojan camp, that (the poet comments)

would have been the last day for the war and the (Trojan) race.

ultimus ille dies bello gentique fuisset. 9. 759

Turnus' erroneous estimation of his own rank is reflected in the 'tragic irony' ('comic irony' would be more fitting) of his words (11. 438–42): he will courageously face Aeneas, (a) even if the Trojan hero should be better than Achilles (he is, in Vergil's conception); (b) even if he should put on armour like that made by Vulcan (he does); (c) "to you and father-in-law Latinus I have dedicated my life" (Latinus is neither destined nor ready to be his father-in-law. And Turnus himself will fail to keep his solemn promise of *animam hanc...devovi*). If the Italian defeat conveys (as pious Latinus thinks, 233) the gods' wrath, *ira deorum* (443; cf. 233), then Turnus wants to be the one who atones for it with his life, not Drances (as in the alternative case Turnus himself, not Drances, shall win the glory of saving the situation, 443f.). It is characteristic of Turnus that he, though in the end offering his life, first bets on his *Victoria* (436) and on Chance (*Fortuna* 413; 427) in attempting to realize "so great a hope", *tanta...pro spe* (437ff.).[12] His mind is set on victory, not self-sacrifice. And he points to Italian reserves still available, among them warrior maiden Camilla and her female band (429–34). In short: Turnus, after the terrible defeat of Book 10, is willing to risk more Italian lives rather than to give his own.

Turnus' flaming outburst has kept the assembly from finding the peaceful solution old King Latinus had hoped for. When now the facts (Aeneas is reported to be approaching) overtake all further chances of deliberating – what is Turnus going to do now? Does he, according to his solemn offer, try to meet Aeneas in single combat when he, full of contempt, leaves the assembly and its talk of peace (460) and dashes out? Not at all. In a state of fury (*furens* 486) he arms himself and is exultant like a stallion finally (*tandem* 493) freed from his tether (*qualis...tandem liber equus* 492f.). To the maiden warrior Camilla, reinforced by the Latin and Tiburtine horsemen, he leaves the fight against Aeneas' advance horse. He himself, disregarding Camilla's urgent advice that he meanwhile use the foot soldiers and protect the walls of Latinus' city (506), moves to the mountains where Aeneas is on the move with his main troops – but not to ask for the duel, no: he plans to lay an ambush for Aeneas.

> A (tricky) stratagem I prepare in the hollow path of the forest, etc.
>
> furta paro belli convexo in tramite silvae, etc. 11. 515f.

Vergil could easily, if his plot-line required temporary removal of Turnus from the battlefield, have him slightly wounded (as he has Aeneas in Book 12). We must assume that a further characterization is intended if Turnus leaves the battle for a *ruse*.

In the eyes of the reader, the discrepancy between words and deeds certainly discredits Turnus. But author Vergil intensifies the negative impression further. His *ecphrasis* ascribes predicates of human deceit to the place of the ambush:

> There is a valley of curved course, fit for deceit
> and guile of arms, upon which on both sides the flank
> closes in, dark with thick foliage, where a slim path is leading {in}
> and the narrow pass guides, together with the malicious approaches.

> est curvo anfractu valles, accommoda fraudi
> armorumque dolis, quam densis frondibus atrum
> urget utrimque latus, tenuis quo semita ducit
> angustaeque ferunt fauces aditusque maligni. 11. 522–25

As already noted, the procedure of characterizing is indirect, but the reader can hardly avoid drawing conclusions from the quality of the landscape – *fraudi*; *dolis*; *maligni*; cf. *silvis...iniquis* 531 – regarding the character of Turnus who is familiar with the area (*nota...regione* 530) when planning his *furta...belli* (515).

The negative impression is not wiped out by the fact that Turnus' insidious intentions (*furta*) are not realized (he is prematurely called back to the city that is now endangered). As a matter of fact, it has been Turnus' absence which has made the city itself vulnerable (cf. 872f.), and fighting now erupts among Italians themselves, between those who seek protection by trying to get in and those inside who attempt to close the gates without regard for those bound to perish outside (883ff.). Camilla's dying words (825f.) repeat her earlier (506) demand that Turnus protect the city. His inconsistency and impulsive behavior have again cost his side immense losses.

Camilla has meanwhile paid for her provocation of the Trojans with "too cruel a death penalty" (to use the compassionate words of divine Opis – in the *Aeneid*, guilt does not exclude pity):

> too harsh a *penalty* have you paid
> as an *atonement*, (for) having undertaken to *provoke* the Trojans with war!
>
> nimium crudele luisti
> supplicium Teucros conata lacessere bello! 11. 841f., cf. 585f.

Divine Opis, we register by the way, *a priori* thinks along those lines which Diomedes, who professes to have learned from his experience, recommends: another confirmation of authorial guidance for the reader. In the *Aeneid*, *atonement* (*luisti*, cf. 1. 136) by *death penalty* (*supplicium*) is the result of raising hostilities against the Trojans, i.e., against Fate and the will of Jupiter. In the context of military operations, the death of the maiden warrior is clearly on the soul of Turnus who had turned a deaf ear to her urgent advice and left her alone to defend Latinus' city (this is true even if, on the level of individual empirical psychology, her death was caused, in Vergil's Roman male chauvinist accounting, by her 'female' [11. 782] interest in glitter).

Brave Camilla, painted by the poet in terms that lie outside the nefarious ambitions of a Turnus or a Messapus, nevertheless has, like all opponents of the Trojan (-Julian) mission, to pay for putting herself in the path of destiny, for unknowingly committing an ideological offense. This does not preclude that her malicious, dishonorable killer, too, "will make atonement

Augustan Vergil and the Political Rival

with death as he deserves", *morte luet merita* (849). It is worth noting that Vergil, when he wanted to portray an "innocent" leader on the Italian side (i.e., a leader not embroiled in the oracle-defying machinations of Turnus and his close associates) has chosen a fairy-tale figure.

Turnus, when receiving Camilla's last message, gives up his ambush – and moments later Aeneas with his main army of foot soldiers can pass through the gorge unimpeded. So both leaders are headed for the city (906) on different but parallel paths. But an instant clash of the two armies is prevented by nightfall. Both armies pitch camp outside the city.

On the next morning (we are now in Book 12), when Turnus sees the eyes and expectations of the disheartened Latins directed at himself, when he feels that fulfillment of his promise is "now (*nunc*) being demanded" (2), he no longer evades his responsibility but takes on a fighting spirit. A simile compares his mood-swing to that of a lion who, cornered and wounded by huntsmen, is finally stirred to fighting.

> Just as that lion in the Phoenicians' fields,
> wounded in his chest by a heavy wound of huntsmen,
> at this point finally moves to arms, and rejoices shaking
> the long mane from his neck, and, fearless, breaks the marauder's
> tightly embedded missile and roars with bloody mouth:
> no differently Turnus' violence grows, after he has caught fire.
>
>   Poenorum qualis in arvis
> saucius ille gravi venantum vulnere pectus
> tum demum movet arma leo, gaudetque comantis
> excutiens cervice toros fixumque latronis
> impavidus frangit telum et fremit ore cruento:
> haud secus accenso gliscit violentia Turno. 12. 4–9.

Long exploited in extra-contextual readings, the simile has taken on the function of a methodological touchstone. Pöschl saw the simile as an "introductory symbol" of Book 12, and viewed Turnus himself as wounded as the lion (*saucius* 12. 5), the wound symbolizing both his pain (*den Schmerz symbolisiert*) after his people's defeat, and (like Dido's love wound of 4. 1f.) the "passion of war as a consuming wound, a disease which tragically destroys its victim" (*die Leidenschaft des Krieges als eine zehrende Wunde, eine Krankheit, die ihr Opfer tragisch zerstört*); and he saw the simile as *symbolically* anticipating Turnus' fated death (*wird das Todesschicksal symbolisch vorweggenommen*),[13] pointing to his tragic resolve to die (*tragische Todesentschlossenheit*).[14] Here the momentary (and transient) flare-up of Turnus' resolve to fight is given tragic permanence. "Symbol" apparently permitted Pöschl to dispense with the simile's authorial context (the Latins' demands on their procrastinating leader following their defeat).

Chapter 1

M.C.J. Putnam's approach allowed him extra-contextually to equate the lion hunters with the Trojans and the *latro* with Aeneas as "leader of the hunters":[15] with the latter because *latro* means the same as *praedo*, and Aeneas is three times called a *praedo*. It did not trouble Putnam that *praedo* is used of Aeneas only by hostile partisans, not by the author: Queen Amata, disobedient to oracle and king (7. 362), Mezentius, "despiser of the gods" (10. 774), and the Latin mothers, following Amata's leadership (11. 484). Not minding the difference of authorial and partisan perspectives, Putnam claimed that the simile views Turnus "*through the poet's eyes* as a lion wounded" etc. (my italics), putting the emphasis on the lion's wound instead of (as grammar and the words *tum demum* would require) on his belated turn to action. And Turnus', the presumed lion's, wound is, by "metaphors", via Dido's love wound (*at regina gravi iamdudum saucia cura / vulnus alit,* etc., 4. 1ff.) boldly applied to "Turnus' relationship with Lavinia, his betrothed" (as was shown earlier and will be detailed in Chapter 7, there is, in the authorial narrative, no betrothal, except in Turnus' impious and ambitious hopes): "The verbal parallels between these lines [scil. 4. 1ff.] and the opening simile of Book XII are *precise enough to seem hardly fortuitous*" (my emphasis). Precise enough to take the simile's meaning from 'overdue fighting spirit' to 'deprived bridegroom'? For Putnam, the lion's wound additionally "hints at the literal outcome of the book, where Turnus does indeed fall *victim* to Aeneas' stroke" (my emphasis). I submit that it would be hard for any reader at the opening of the Book to catch such a prognostic 'hint' of what is going to happen 900 lines later.

The narrative context which the author illuminates through the simile of the lion's late turn to action is given short shrift: "Turnus is now the cynosure of all eyes", representing the routed Latins' "hopes for survival." No word about cornered Turnus feeling pressure that, after his evasive and injudicious conduct in Book 11, the Latins were now (*nunc*) exercising their due right to call in (*reposci*; see *OLD s.v.* 2.a) his promise (*promissa,* cf. 11. 434–42) of going to face Aeneas in single combat; that, marked out by his people's eyes or looks (*se* 3, reinforces the emphasized *sua*, 2), he prevents (as Servius rightly understands) any open accusations by, at his own initiative (*ultro*), now working up a courageous spirit (*attollitque animos* 4) that will lead to his peculiar *violentia* (9; Vergil uses this word – as well as the adjective *violentus* – only of Turnus: 11. 354, 12. 9, 45) – at the last moment, so to speak, in this like the wounded lion of the simile who "then finally" (*tum demum*) turns to fighting. Reliance on "verbal parallels" does not guarantee adequate observation of authorial context.

Whereas in Putnam's interpretation the Turnus of the narrative still survived minimally as the "cynosure", R. Thomas turns to a hypo-logical[16] principle of *counter*-contextual reading: "Simile, I will suggest, becomes a vehicle for subverting the epic's authoritative voice." Accordingly, Thomas, too, equates the lion wounded by the *latro* with Turnus later to be wounded by Aeneas, and also with Dido, the wounded doe (4. 68–73: lion=doe?), inferring: "It is difficult not to identify Aeneas with this *latro*, at least on some level." Which level is "some level"?[17] How is Turnus' non-existent wound to be explained? If the lion is wounded but Turnus is not, the wound can hardly be the *tertium comparationis*, the point of the comparison. Thomas states that "Any reader who identifies the *leo* as Turnus, as all readers surely do, and is then able to exclude Aeneas (cf.12. 14 *Dardanium*), works against the simile's Latin."[18]

But "the simile's Latin" tells it differently, viz. that the lion is *first* wounded (by *one* heavy wound, *gravi...vulnere*) and only "*then finally*" (*tum demum*, emphasized by the opening position in the hexameter line) turns to fighting and breaks the spear or arrow (*telum* again is singular) "left in his body by the ruffian who threw it" (David West's translation). But when Turnus mentions the "Dardanian" (=Aeneas) in 12. 14, this is, *pace* Thomas, no longer the simile situation of the lion changing from dodging to finally fighting, but here speaks the "new", post-simile, changed Turnus (characterized by his peculiar *violentia* 12. 9) who now (*tum*, 12. 10, marks the new stage) has been able to renounce his earlier procrastination: "*no delay* through Turnus", *nulla mora in Turno* (12. 11).

So, if one really wishes to extend the simile's meaning beyond its primary and logical function of showing Turnus shedding his procrastination and now honoring his grandiloquent promise, one would have to search for Turnus' presumed "wound" (but in the Homeric "model passage" Achilles is not wounded either, *Il.* 20. 164–73) in the immediate or preceding temporal environment. What preceded was Turnus' military loss (Camilla killed, the Latins fleeing, Latinus' city under attack) and "immense turmoil" (*ingentem...tumultum* 11. 897), which caused him to abandon, in a state of fury (*furens* 901), his un-heroic idea of ambushing Aeneas (11. 902) instead of dueling with him. On the other hand, the immediate situation, as explained earlier, is his awareness (*videt* 12. 2) that his people demand that he finally fulfill his promise and face Aeneas. So the hunters (*venantum*) would with greater probability represent the staring and demanding Latins, and the simile's *one* successful spear-thrower (or archer) might even be their speaker, Drances. (The sting of Drances' incendiary accusations [11. 343–75] will still rankle with Turnus personally as late as 12. 644.)

This explanation (if one indeed wishes to exploit the simile further, beyond its pointing to the late ending of Turnus' procrastination) is still a logically consistent interpretation that would well complement and by no means 'subvert' the authorial narrative of Book 11 as it has been traced in the present chapter.

But Thomas will have nothing of this. Pascal's correct understanding ("the immediate context shows that it is the Latins whom he [scil. Turnus] is facing down")[19] is to Thomas "an indication that *latro* bothers him".[20] How so? The *latro* becomes a contextual problem (instead of a merely lexicographical difficulty) only if one lifts him from the simile and introduces him as an agent into the narrative context. Admittedly, *latro* as "the huntsman" is "an unusual sense of the word, which normally means 'brigand'" (Williams *ad loc.*). *Thesaurus Linguae Latinae* assigns the word here, in Thomas' phrasing, "a separate class of meaning...*produced by a philological collective simply so we may avoid associating* 'Aeneas' and '*latro*', but that is what we must do, for it is what Vergil has done."[21] The motivation of *OLD*'s contributors hardly fares better : "The only basis for the *desiderated* meaning is the *need for an Augustan reading*; the grammarians and lexicographers struggle valiantly, but the effort fails to neutralize the complexity of the Virgilian word, and *the effort itself becomes revealing*".[22] Apparently, Thomas believes that he as an interpreter has the freedom to 'associate' (or mix) simile with narrative and that such commingling allows him authoritatively to decide "what Vergil has done", along the way casting doubts on the scholarly motivation of Pascal or a "philological collective" or "lexicographers".[23]

Thomas' methodological mistake is that he identifies what Vergil's precise Latin keeps separate: *ille...leo* corresponds to (but is *not identified with*) Turnus in one perspective: as the lion, once wounded, finally moves roaring to action, so (*haud secus*) Turnus, once set afire,[24] develops his peculiar *violentia* (line 9).

Destroying a simile's logical (explanatory or illustrative) function by detaching it from its context and then turning it into "a vehicle for subverting the epic's authoritative voice" turns out not to be a viable scholarly procedure. The attempt to establish that similes like the one discussed here "work against a simply Augustan reading of Turnus and Aeneas, ...by embedding disconsonant elements that work against the simply Augustan reading" has failed because it defies the laws of logic (in which Vergil was well versed). What is "disconsonant" is Thomas' (and his school's) endeavor "to de-Augustanize Virgil".[25] For it fails to do justice to the precise context of the complex authorial architecture which does not allow one "simply" to break off and arbitrarily realign structural parts (and a simile functions as a structural part) in the interest of "de-Augustanizing" (or "subverting") the whole. What results may be called a 'simile *dissimile*' that amounts to a *contradictio in adiecto*.

To sum up: the simile contains two stages, as does the main text in which it is embedded. (1) As the hunted lion, once he is wounded, finally turns to fighting, so Turnus, when feeling his countrymen's eyes demandingly directed at himself, seizes the initiative and, upon catching fire, raises his fighting spirits (*attollit...animos* 4). (2) As the lion joyfully tosses his mane, fearlessly breaks the stuck missile, and roars with bloody mouth, so (*haud secus*) in Turnus, once he is set ablaze, his peculiar violence develops. Or, in other words, the simile, setting out after Turnus' belated stirring (3b/4a), *first* presents the eventual stirring of the lion's will to fight (4b–6a); it *then* proceeds to paint the lion's joyful and roaring fervor (6b–8), which in turn illustrates Turnus' growing violence (9).

Vergil's precise grammar and logic leave no room for breaking loose single words (*vulnus*; *latro*) from their context and assigning them counter-contextual functions. The increasing license which segments of our discipline have taken toward text and context needs to be exemplified and illustrated in order to re-establish and secure an appropriate entrance into the *Aeneid*'s 12th Book.

"On his own initiative" (*ultro* 3), then, similar to the wounded Punic lion who, when cornered, at this point finally (*tum demum* 6) accepts the fight, Turnus, whom the narrative has established as an evasive procrastinator par excellence, announces: "No delay through Turnus", *nulla mora in Turno* (11), and he now asks King Latinus formally to conclude the treaty for the duel with Aeneas.

In doing so, Turnus describes his opponent in highly contemptuous words (*desertorem Asiae* 15), and he even states that "the cowardly Aeneadae", *ignavi Aeneadae* (12), cannot withdraw their "agreed" offer of a single combat: he *alone* (*solus*: his key word of 11. 442) – the Latins may sit down and watch – will blot out the stain of the defeat – or leave Lavinia and the Latins "defeated" (*victos*) to Aeneas (12. 15–17). His public appearance again is as courageous as it was in the assembly of Book 11.

Latinus now regrets the outbreak of the war in Book 7, even condemns it – and himself for having disobeyed Faunus' oracle (cf. 7. 96ff.):

I broke all bonds;
I snatched (my daughter) from the son-in-law to whom she had been promised [at 7. 267ff.], I took up impious arms (scil., against Aeneas),

vincla omnia rupi;
promissam eripui genero, arma impia sumpsi 30f.;

and he adduces compassion for Turnus' old father, 43f. But his arguments cannot calm down the *violentia* (12. 45; cf.9) of Turnus who wants to accept *death* in exchange for fame (*letumque sinas pro laude pacisci* 12. 49); but again,

Chapter 1

as before the Council in Book 11, he is confident: this time, Aeneas' mother won't be there to save her son when he flees (52f.). Nor is Queen Amata, threatening to commit suicide, able to change his mind – especially not because blushing Lavinia's presence perturbs him and fires him to war (70f.; Latinus, the reader recalls, had mentioned kingdom before bride, 22 and 24). His manly reply, solemnly (pompously?) mentioning himself in the third person, allows only one of the two enemies to live on (in the epic's final scene, he will change his mind on this point): "Turnus does not have the freedom to *postpone* (his) *death*", *neque enim Turno mora libera mortis* (74), and so his message to Aeneas is

> with our blood let us end the war:
> on that field Lavinia the wife shall be found!
>
> nostro dirimamus sanguine bellum:
> illo quaeratur coniunx Lavinia campo! 12. 79f.

(In the end, he will give up Lavinia, not for his blood, but to survive!)

There follows a scene where Turnus is arming himself for a dress rehearsal, so to speak, not yet for the final combat – though his vivid imagination makes him use the word *nunc* three times (95–97); and here readers again witness uninhibited Turnus as they have come to know him: he hopes to stretch Aeneas' body on the ground, to tear open the "effeminate Phrygian's" breastplate and to mar his crimped and perfumed hair in the dust (97ff.). He conducts himself like a bull trying "to vent his rage on his horns as he crashes against the trunk of a tree, and challenges the breezes" (Williams' rendering *ad loc.*) – his anger (cf. *irasci* 104) has no share in the kind of purpose that distinguishes Aeneas' fighting spirit (*Martem*) and anger (*ira* 108): far from being a purely negative term, *ira* in the *Aeneid also* characterizes the responsible warrior: as always, the context is decisive. It here requires Aeneas, too, to be ferocious, *saevus* (107). While Turnus is happy (*gaudet* 82) when seeing his snorting horses, Aeneas, feeling his responsibility and trying to console his saddened son as well as his fearful companions by referring to the course of fate – Aeneas is happy

> that the war is being settled by the offer of the treaty,
>
> oblato gaudens componi foedere bellum. 12. 109.

A similar sense of obligation is displayed by Aeneas at the time of the oath: in case of defeat (which he, too, equates with his own death) Iulus would withdraw with the Trojan forces (to Pallanteum – so the location of future Rome would not necessarily be lost to the Julian family). In case he himself should be victorious, he would *not* demand unconditional surrender (*non...parere iubebo* 189), but he would tie both nations to each other by a permanent treaty undefeated – a prospect that will be nullified by the breach of the present treaty, as will be Latinus' hope for the eternal duration of this peace and treaty (202). Aeneas would even leave Latinus (then his father-in-law, *socer*, 193) his army and his rule, while himself having his own city fortified, to be named after Lavinia (he would of course inherit, through Lavinia, Latinus' city and throne after the old king's demise or retirement 193f.).

Vergil marks the 'historical' (contemporary Augustan) importance of the duel's outcome for his contemporary readers by exhibiting both "Aeneas, origin of the *Roman* stock", in his super-human armor, and "Ascanius, the second hope of *great Rome*" (166f.). And, whereas King Latinus, father of the ancestral mother-to-be, appears on a four-horse chariot and crowned by the sun-god's golden rays, Vergil accords Turnus no more than two white horses and two spears: the author's lower esteem for the ultimately dispensable character is reflected also in the lack of stately appearance (161–5). Aeneas is shown to share this opinion when he sends his reply to Turnus' message (*mea dicta* 75) not to the sender but to the ruler of Latium (*regi...Latino* 111). Today's interpreter does well to observe the author's political emphases.

The solemn ceremony is summed up by the words *inter se firmabant foedera* (212), which are followed by Juturna's riot (instigated by Juno, who is prohibited from herself saving Turnus' life by Jupiter's stern injunction: 10. 622–27): the Rutulians, seeing Turnus' physical inferiority (*non viribus aequis*), his "youthful ("wasting" if you read *tabentes*) cheeks" (*pubentesque genae*) and the pallor on his youthful body (*iuvenali in corpore pallor* 221) at the altar, are – against Aeneas' pronounced intention – filled with fear that they will have to *dominis parere superbis* (236); so they arrive at the impious prayer

> they pray for the treaty
> not to be done
>
> foedusque precantur
> infectum 12. 242f.

Their troubled mood has already been building up for a long time (*iam dudum* 217), so the empirical conditions are ripe and waiting for the triggering spark provided by Juturna, Turnus' divine sister, in the shape of Camers, and by his rousing speech; s/he even weaves in base rancor against Turnus whose death would earn him eternal fame at the cost of his people (234–7, cf. Turnus' words at 11–17). Juturna's deceiving omen – a swarm of swans chases an eagle and makes him give up his prey – is sufficient for the Rutulian augur Tolumnius to see his wishes fulfilled and, disregarding

Chapter 1

the treaty, to throw the first spear. The underlying attitude apparently is to get out of the treaty obligation if only a chance is offered. Tolumnius causes a classic escalation. His spear hits one of nine Arcadian brothers. The remaining eight, in blind (*caeci* 279) reaction, dash forward against the Italians; whereupon the Laurentians, in turn, move forward, now to be met by the combined Trojans, Etruscans, and Arcadians. Quickly, general fighting arises.

To the shameful picture of Latinus, fleeing with his beaten gods *infecto foedere* (285f.), Vergil adds the other one showing the reader how warrior Messapus (on whom Turnus can always count), is "eager to destroy the treaty", *avidus confundere foedus* (290); he forces poor (*miser* 292) Etruscan King Aulestes, who is recognizably dressed in full regalia because of the solemn occasion (*regem regisque insigne gerentem* 289), to retreat so that he falls backward on the altar. Messapus, in killing him, derides him as "a better victim for the great gods", *melior magnis data victima divis* (296). Thus, the Roman reader's indignation about the broken truce is intensified by religious indignation about the blasphemy. The opponents of the Emperor's forefather are found deficient in basic standards of human and religious conduct.

Inevitably the question arises in the reader's mind: how do the two main characters react to the new development? Almost equally inevitable is the answer: *pius Aeneas* (311), his outstretched arm bared of weapons, his head unhelmeted (perhaps somewhat incautious, but idealistic and impressive in ranking right over reality), tries to check the situation on his side: "The treaty has already been concluded!" (i.e., it is valid), *ictum iam foedus!* (314). Demanding the duel, he reassures his people ("Give up your fears: it will be for *me* to make the treaty firm with my hand!" *auferte metus: ego foedera faxo firma manu* 316f.) – until he is (almost equally unavoidably, at least for a reader acquainted with Book 4 of Homer's *Iliad*) hit by an arrow from an unknown hand and forced to leave the field, a victim of his loyalty to the treaty in a counterworld of catch-as-catch-can: the ideal of a Roman hero and picture-book ancestor of the Princeps (whose loyalty to treaties was in need of some poetic enhancement).

It is worth noting that Aeneas insists on observing the terms of the treaty: "I *alone* have the *right* to clash with him... These rituals now *owe* Turnus to me" (315–7). For the reader, there is a literal allusion to Turnus' earlier words when he (see Chapter 3, Section 1) singled out Pallas, Aeneas' young ally, for a sure kill: "I *alone* storm against Pallas; to me *alone* Pallas is *owed*. I wish his father were here and watching!"(10. 442f.).[26] Whereas Turnus kills in order to hurt his victim's father, Aeneas, to end the war, acts on a right flowing from a treaty based on ritual, *haec...sacra* (317).

The anonymity of Aeneas' assailant gives the poet pause to ponder whether it was "chance or a god", *casusne deusne* (321) that provided such a great glory for the Rutulians. In Vergil's conception, the Julian ancestor apparently is sacrosanct, not a suitable target for human arms (except by chance, *casus*). Accordingly, his Jupiter will later censure Juno for the inappropriateness of the incident (executed by Juturna 813f):

Was it suitable that a divine person was hurt by a mortal wound?

mortalin' decuit violari vulnere divum? 12. 797

The boundary that separates the Julian ancestor from everyday humanity must not be blurred in the minds of Vergil's contemporaries.

And Turnus, on the other hand? A case of "déjà vu": when seeing wounded Aeneas leaving the field, he – *superbus* 326 – glowing in sudden hope (*subita spe fervidus* 325), allows himself to be carried away in un-Roman, un-Trojan fashion and causes, like *Mavors* himself (332), a bloodbath, insulting (*insultans*) even the miserably slain enemies (*miserabile caesis*), when the hooves of his horses splash through the blood (339f.). Here Vergil leaves his reader hardly a door open for sympathy toward Aeneas' opponent. Once again, as in Book 11 where he preferred an ambush over the single combat, the self-chosen obligation of the duel is shed the moment Turnus can hope to gain from its violation. He again turns to fighting as he did when Aeneas was absent (9. 6–13) or seemed to turn his back (*aversum...cedere Turnus credidit* 10. 647f.).

On the other side, Aeneas is quickly healed of his "undeserved pain" (411) by Venus' miracle (which counteracts Juturna's arrow) and again takes leave from his son, this time in the words of the suicidal (i.e., death-bound) Sophoclean Ajax (435ff.). One may expect that now Aeneas for his part too feels released from the treaty. (After all, his camp itself is in danger now: 405–10.) That kind of conduct at least seems to be what Turnus and the Rutulians are afraid of when seeing him and his army reappear – a fact that drives cold trembling deep into their bones,

gelidusque per ima cucurrit
ossa tremor; 12. 447f.

Aeneas, leading his troops in counter-attack, is likened to a terrible storm, causing devastation which "the poor farmers", *miseris...agricolis*, have anticipated long beforehand in their hearts, *praescia...corda*, 452ff. How else can we understand the comparison with the *foreknown* storm than that here the guilty conscience of the "poor" Rutulians finds an expression, i.e., their awareness of their king's and their own breach of the treaty as well as of their illegal rage, now yielding to justified fear? Elsewhere, too, in the

Aeneid, one finds compassion expressed – *o miseri*, 7. 596, cf. 8. 537 – for an erring and misguided people about to face the dire (and predictable) consequences of their – and their leader's – conduct. (We think also about the compassion expressed for fallen Camilla 11. 841f.; see above.)

Aeneas himself, however, does *not* justify the expectations of his rank-and-file enemies. He does not dignify (*dignatur*, 464) the fleeing Rutulians (among their dead is augur Tolumnius, first offender against the sanctified truce) with death at his own hand, nor does he deal with those willing to face him. "Alone" Turnus (here again, after 315, is the echo of Book 10. 442) is the one he is looking for, *solum...Turnum vestigat lustrans, solum... poscit* (466f.).

To keep his reader from overlooking Aeneas' thinking and conduct, directed even now at fulfilling the duel treaty, Vergil uses the rare verb *vestigare* three times (467; 482; 557). When divine Juturna, unsteady as a flying swallow, takes over as Turnus' charioteer and tries to abduct her triumphant (*ovantem* 479) brother, Aeneas follows that planless movement – and Vergil underlines his hero's exclusive focus by a fourfold alliteration –

> He searches for the man, and across the spread-out armies
> calls for him in a loud voice
>
> <u>v</u>estigatque <u>v</u>irum et disiecta per agmina magna
> <u>v</u>oce <u>v</u>ocat 12. 482f.

Turnus, of course, by not listening to his opponent's loud call, once more invalidates his very own words before the Latin assembly: "*Solum Aeneas vocat? et vocet oro*" (11. 442). The reader or hearer (I am not presently thinking of the Homeric or Vergilian scholar of the twenty-first century AD, but rather of the Roman boy or man who, in the new national epic, learns to admire his Emperor's ancestor), struck by Aeneas' unbending loyalty to the treaty, is frightened when he sees that bold Messapus (the same Messapus who made King Aulestes a "better victim" on the altar, 296) this time chooses even perplexed Aeneas himself for his target. He hits, it is true, only Aeneas' crest (because Aeneas is, by quick reaction, able to evade the attack); but finally (*tandem* 497), forced by this ambush (*insidiis*) as well as by Turnus' continuous evasive movements, and not without often invoking Jupiter and the altars because of the broken treaty (*multa Jovem et laesi testatus foederis aras*, 496) – *finally* Aeneas gives rein to his wrath and kills terribly, without discriminating any longer. His admirable patience and self-control were wasted, on this kind of enemy. His desperate question, *heu, quid agat?* (486 – as often, the reader is made to understand what is going through Aeneas' mind), has come down to only one of two answers: to abandon the vain pursuit of the duel, and to help his army.

Thus, a single word of comment, coming from the mouth of the author himself, is able to confirm to readers that they are on the right track with their understanding of the text. As the Punic lion Turnus "finally" – *demum* (12. 6) – was ready to accept the challenge of the duel (he is not necessarily a coward, no, he only takes the chance of evading whenever it is being offered), so Aeneas "finally" – *tandem* – (and formally: *Iovem...testatus* – by no means is he overcome by wrath or out of self-control) abandons the incredible self-discipline which he had imposed upon himself since entering into the treaty. *Tandem* in this context means that already, long ago, he would have had reason to state a breach of the treaty and act accordingly. But it also means that what follows is not a series of senseless killings on Aeneas' part but that he, when compelled by military emergency, is fulfilling his duty as a fighter in battle for his people: only he is better at it than others.[27] Fairness demands that we observe Vergil's statement that Aeneas' wrathful fighting here causes his fleeing Trojans to take a stand against the enemy (515f.; cf. 738).

However – the syncrisis continues – Aeneas (unlike Turnus, 511f.) would never decapitate enemies to attach their heads, "dripping with blood" (512), to his chariot: together with the different attitude toward the treaty goes a different attitude toward the dead enemy. Even when giving rein to his wrath, the Julian ancestor does not match the barbarous behavior of his rival. Modern interpreters have sometimes been dissatisfied with Aeneas' rage on the battlefield. But, when interpreting, we should place Vergil's context and the accents he sets ahead of our own expectations (or even desires).

This requirement applies also to the poet's question "Jupiter, did it please you that two nations, bound to live in eternal peace later on, clashed in so great a war?" (503f.). "The narrator is ultimately unable to commit himself to Jupiter's perspective, as his helpless question in the last book shows."[28] Not 'commit himself', but rather 'unable to fully fathom, to fully comprehend'. The poet here chooses to speak from the mortal perspective. Of course, the war did not 'please' Jupiter, as he (on an occasion when the poet showed himself privy to the divine sphere) had stated in no uncertain terms (*abnueram bello Italiam concurrere Teucris* 10. 8) in the council of the discordant gods. But Jupiter will not take away human freedom of decision by compelling the individual to act under heteronomy. Turnus has the freedom to honor a contract piously or to break it impiously – and consequently to be responsible for the renewed hostilities between the two nations, with all their sorrowful consequences. As in the cases of Dido and Amata, attitudes that result in hostility against the proto-Julians are freely chosen over clearly outlined standards of conduct (see Chapters 5 and 7).

Chapter 1

Returning to the *tandem* of 12. 497, it must be said that Vergil's guidance for his reader goes beyond this word. For even in the new turmoil Aeneas does not cease to search for Turnus: *vestigans* (for the third time this verb) *diversa per agmina Turnum* (557). While looking around for him, Aeneas' eyes fall on the city of the Latins, and so the futility of his pursuit finally leads him, presumably inspired by Venus (though Vergil as usual preserves the empirical mental process that progresses independently), to turn against the city itself – a new target not initially envisaged by him. But no longer can he now envisage the contracted peaceful coexistence of the two states – under the radically changed conditions he is forced to reduce the Latins to subjection:

> if they do not grant that they accept the rein and that, defeated, they obey
>
> ni frenum accipere et victi parere fatentur 12. 568.

The new twist in the plot is ingeniously designed by Vergil (it mirrors Roman political argumentation): if submission takes place, then it is originally unintended by the Trojan side. The assault upon the city – the "cause of the war", *causam belli* (567), "untroubled without being subject to punishment", *impune quietam* (559) – is understood to be the only way even now to force the enemy to observe the treaty (the second broken treaty, after all: *haec altera foedera rumpi* 582). Aeneas feels he can hardly be expected to wait until it pleases Turnus (*libeat...Turno*) to show up for the duel (570f.).

> This, my citizens, is the source, this is the essence of the godless war!
> Hurry to bring torches and *claim* {observance of} *the treaty* with flames!
>
> hoc caput, o cives, haec belli summa nefandi!
> <u>f</u>erte <u>f</u>aces propere <u>f</u>oedusque reposcite <u>f</u>lammis! 12. 572f.

Here the reader is being offered the ancestor of the Julians as an *involuntary attacker*, forced to assault the city by the perfidy of his enemy. (The *f*-alliteration in 573 underlines his loyal insistence on fulfillment of the treaty.) Once again we watch him proceed not without formally accusing Latinus, and not without calling upon the gods as his witnesses that he, following the second (after 7. 259f.; 283f.) breach of a treaty, is again (*iterum*) being *forced* to resort to fighting (580–82). Is it far-fetched to assume that the reader is supposed also to ponder the conduct and feel enlightened about the motives of Aeneas' greater descendant during the civil wars?

A large segment of late-20th-century scholarship has had difficulty with, and even distorted, the authorial portrait of Aeneas as the involuntary attacker. Boyle[29] speaks of "the *text*'s presentation of Aeneas' war in Italy as a repetition of the Trojan War itself – only this time Aeneas is Achilles". So Boyle paints Aeneas as an aggressor conducting 'his' war? Some of

Boyle's 'proof': "...notice the analogy between Aeneas' assault on Latinus' city at *A*. 12. 554ff., and Pyrrhus' attack on Priam's palace at *A*. 2. 469ff. (reinforced by verbal echoes: cf. *A*. 2. 479, 494 and *A*. 12. 579, 577)." It is faulty method to build an "analogy" on "verbal echoes", without verifying the authorial context. That gates are broken down and defenders killed is a common fact of all conquests, be they 'just' or 'unjust', and so is the feature of someone acting "among the first". But Pyrrhus, "himself among the first" attackers (*ipse inter primos* 2. 479) of Troy in Book 2, is portrayed in darkest colors: aged King Priam states that not even Pyrrhus' father, Achilles, behaved in such an abominable fashion (2. 540f.); whereas Aeneas in Book 12, standing "himself among the first", *ipse inter primos* (12. 579), stretching out his right arm, accusing treaty breaker Latinus and invoking the gods, is here shown to be the paragon of political restraint and religious correctness before resorting to use of military power. The contexts of the "verbal echoes" enhance a *contrast* rather between Aeneas and Pyrrhus than establishing an "analogy". But for Boyle (and he is not alone in this) "Aeneas not only resurrects the Trojan War in Italy, repeating the violence he had criticized in his narrative of Book 2, but becomes himself the 'other Achilles', *alius Achilles*, prophesied by the Cumaean Sibyl (*A*. 6. 89), a reincarnation in history of the paradigm of brutality (*saevum...Achillem*) he had observed in Book 1 (459f.)."[30]

Apart from distorting the fact that the Sibyl addressed her prophecy to Aeneas, warning him of a new Achilles in Italy (i.e., of Turnus) who again will be a deadly threat to the Trojans, Boyle also posits that "Vergil's transformation of the genre here and the demands he made upon his readers were so radical that the critique was largely misread." Are Boyle's readers perhaps supposed to feel sorry for poor Vergil because he had to wait for almost two millennia to be read adequately by the "verbal echo" industry of a-historical anti-Augustan scholarship? For reading Aeneas as a type of Vergil's war criminal, these scholars have to misrepresent a large number of "text" passages, among which passages like *Aen*. 12. 577 and 579 rank prominently. Sometimes their reader may feel reminded of the Chinese proverb, "Where there is a will to condemn, there is evidence."

Now that all valuations have been prepared (even if some perhaps are not yet quite explicit), the action quickly approaches its end. The city population is split (583f.) between advocates of defense and of surrender. Queen Amata's remorse (over having obstructed Lavinia's marriage to Aeneas) leads to an admission of guilt, which she under less stressful conditions would hardly have made, but in Vergil's concept any opponent of Aeneas has to confess to personal guilt before dying (the reader observes the emphasis of the *c*-alliteration):

Chapter 1

> she accuses herself as the cause, crime, and source of the misery
>
> se <u>c</u>ausam <u>c</u>lamat <u>c</u>rimenque <u>c</u>aputque malorum 12. 600

It is noteworthy how Vergil shapes the occasion of Amata's suicide: she is driven to take her own life not only in view of the enemy's assault on the city, but especially because she is confused by the sudden pain (*subito mentem turbata dolore* 599) over Turnus' presumed death on the battlefield, which she infers from his absence from the city (seeing *nulla agmina Turni* 597). In so acting, this semi-tragic character is true to her earlier declaration that she would not be willing to survive Turnus (and accept Aeneas as her son-in-law 12. 61–63). The irony, of course, is that Turnus is not yet dead: it is his *living* absence and pursuit of some stragglers "at the outer end of the battlefield", *extremo...in aequore* (614f.) that gave Amata her false impression. Under one aspect her death follows a feature of the warrior maiden Camilla, who likewise had been left alone by Turnus before the city in spite of her advice that he stay and guard the walls.

The noise and commotion drifting over from the direction of the city bring Turnus, already less happy about his 'success' on the field, to his senses. Now he is ready to go without further help from his divine sister, will no longer (*neque...amplius*) show himself indecorous (*indecorem* 679f.; cf. *dedecus* 641), and wishes to feel free from the reproach of cowardice (648f.). Now it hurts him to have watched Murranus, his dearest companion, die right before his eyes, calling for him:

> With my very own eyes I saw Murranus
> – no other one dearer to my heart survives –
> die while calling me in a loud voice,
> an enormous man defeated by an enormous wound.
>
> vidi oculos ante ipse meos me voce vocantem
> Murranum, quo non superat mihi carior alter
> oppetere ingentem atque ingenti vulnere victum. 12. 638–40.

The multiple *v*- and *m*-alliterations, together with the *ing...ing*-anaphora, provide the emotional ring to his insight of having failed his dying friend. (Murranus had been knocked from his chariot by a rock hurled from Aeneas' hand, then was run over by his own horses, 529–34).

Here, a surprising confession again places Turnus in an ambiguous light: "For long already" (*dudum*), ever since the breach of the treaty which she so skillfully brought about (*cum prima per artem foedera turbasti*), and since she joined the war (as his charioteer; *teque haec in bella dedisti*, 12. 632f.), he has recognized his sister, and now too (*et nunc*), he says, she does not deceive him. The reader recalls that Juturna's "sign" (*signum*) "confused" (*turbavit*) and "deceived" (*fefellit*) the "Italian minds" (*mentes Italas* 12. 245f.).

At 12. 633f. Turnus' words *per artem turbasti* and *et nunc nequiquam fallis* ("you skilfully brought about" and "now, too, in vain try to deceive") reveal that *he did not share the Italians' confusion and deception*. Does this not mean that Vergil has painted Turnus as having personally consented to the breach of the treaty *right from the beginning*, and as having willingly and consciously allowed himself to be abducted by his divine sister? The words *prima*, *dudum*, and *neque...amplius* (cf. also 646) give us from his own mouth what the word *demum* in the simile of the Punic lion expressed, viz.: Turnus has delayed, again and contrary to his corrective assurance given to Latinus: *nulla mora in Turno* (12. 11). And his reliance on Juturna will come to haunt him again.

Going into detail, one observes that Turnus' remorse here covers more than his most recent conduct, after the breach of the duel treaty. His wish to refute Drances' verbal attack (*dextra nec Drancis dicta refellam?* 644), which that man had launched before the assembly of Book 11 (see, especially, Drances' rhetorically dressed demand for the duel, *solum...solum* 11. 220f.) shows that Turnus is thinking also of his earlier evasive plan of ambushing Aeneas instead of following up on the grandiloquent answer he had given Drances: "Aeneas calls for me alone? I wish him to!" (11. 442). Recalling Drances' insulting words so late in the action of Book 12 makes it indeed somewhat more likely that the hunter's weapon that wounded Turnus (the late-acting 'lion' in the simile 12. 4ff.) was Drances' speech.

Turnus' admission of his twofold failure to face Aeneas in single combat reveals something about how Vergil conceived this character: by letting him start out on the path of heroism twice and then renege, the poet has made inconsistency and evasiveness his guiding characteristics. This feature is the more damaging to the Rutulian king's reputation because his attempts at valor show him being fully aware of the obliging heroic code that he fails to fulfill. (Chapter 5 will show a similar trait in the poet's portrait of Dido; cf. 4. 24–30.) Turnus is cognizant of his political and religious guilt resulting both from counteracting Faunus' forbidding oracle (as spread by King Latinus, 7. 102–5) and from incurring the aged king's condemnation for starting the war against Aeneas (7. 596f.: "too late you will worship the gods with prayers!"). Knowing therefore that the upper world is against him, he now turns to and invokes the spirits of his ancestors to assure them that he will not flee cowardly, but as "a soul ignorant of this guilt" (*anima...istius inscia culpae* 648) join the shades "never unworthy of my great ancestors" (*magnorum haud umquam indignus avorum* 649).

These are strong words after his earlier conduct. That Vergil is unrelenting in denying Aeneas' adversary consistent bravery, is revealed in the now ensuing *third* sequence of heroic upswing (motivated by remorse)

Chapter 1

followed in the very end by an ingratiating plea for mercy. (My count skips the situation, subordinate within the duel, where Turnus, before regaining sword and fighting spirit, "flees faster than the east wind", *fugit ocior Euro* 12.734. If one wishes to include this instance, the final plea for mercy would constitute the fourth not the third time Turnus dodges his self-chosen obligation.) It was perhaps almost predictable that modern (and post-modern) readers found it hard to accept (and thus tried to modify) the extent to which Vergil projects a partisan, pro-Julian position in delineating his characters. The state of denial in which late-20th-century scholarship liked to take refuge is once more well illustrated by Harvard's (see the self-identification on his 2001 title page) Richard Thomas who raised the accusation that the present writer's "procedure is to carry out a sustained attack on the character of Turnus," (etc.).[31] Apparently, it is deemed easier to assert character assassination, which would avert the imputed potential blame from Vergil to the irritating interpreter, than to refute the incriminated scholar's arguments in a scholarly manner,[32] – or even to face (and "deal with") the unwelcome prospect of a Vergil whose predetermined 'humanity' turns out to be partisan.

For now, then, Turnus is again determined to meet Aeneas in single combat and, bitter as it may be, to suffer death; no longer will his sister see him inglorious:

> It is my resolve to meet Aeneas in close combat,
> It is my resolve to suffer death whatever bitterness it means,
> And no longer, sister, will you see me indecorous
>
> stat conferre manum Aeneae, stat, quidquid acerbi est,
> morte pati, neque me indecorem, germana, videbis
> amplius. 12. 678–80

Meanwhile, a wounded messenger from the city conveys the bad news and the request: "Have pity on your people!" *miserere tuorum* (653). These were the exact words of Drances before the assembly (11. 365), and Vergil further enhances the repetitive situation by having the messenger report that the Latins' eyes are – as at the opening of Book 12 – looking to Turnus for their salvation (12. 656f.; cf. 12. 3). Now, immense shame, frenzy, love, sadness, rage, self-conscious virtue (667f.) drive him to the city, where he holds back his fighting companions:

> it is more appropriate that I alone
> for you atone for the [broken] treaty and decide with my sword.
>
> me verius unum
> pro vobis foedus luere et decernere ferro. 12. 694f.

The word that was heard earlier from divine Opis' lips (on the occasion of Camilla's death), *luo*, together with those mentioned just recently, *pudor* and *conscia virtus*, once more give away quite clearly Turnus' awareness of his status as one who has broken his commitment – a hint that is not unimportant for interpreting the final scene. "Father" Aeneas (*pater Aeneas* 697, Vergil here emphasizes his hero's caring, responsible conduct), on the other hand, *immediately* stopping all assault on the city in order to return to the idea of the duel, is again, as we saw him earlier (109), all joy, *laetitia exsultans* (700) – about the renewed prospect, of course, of avoiding genocide by solving the conflict according to the terms of the treaty, i.e., by a duel. Turnus, by emphasizing his personal (*unum*) responsibility, has come round full circle to his offer to Latinus (*solus* 16). Juturna, of course, had stirred the Latins by arguing they should not offer one single (*unam*) life for them all, strong as they were: *pro cunctis talibus unam obiectare animam* (229f.). Now they are desperate.

Notes

[1] A short preview of observations contained in chapters 1–3 was published in *Between Republic and Empire: Interpretations of Augustus and his Principate*, edited by Kurt A. Raaflaub and Mark Toher, Berkeley 1990, 174–211. Thanks are given to the University of California Press for permission to integrate the earlier material here.

[2] I am of course not addressing myself here to those 'unintentionalists' who wish to deny an author a design and an intention of his own, or to freewheeling spirits who, on the basis of denying the possibility of even an approximating interpretation, feel free to shed the obligation an interpreter has toward the organization of an author's work. On recent Vergilian criticism, see also the *Editor's Introduction* in Stahl 1998.

[3] Today's classicists often display helplessness when facing Vergil's complex and logically coherent composition. Richard Thomas may serve as an example of the prevailing incomprehension of the *Aeneid*'s literary organization. An approach which does indeed interpret the final scene as the culmination of the complex literary architecture (Stahl 1990) is characterized (and discredited) by Thomas (2001, 289) as one "which involves *diverting the critical focus...backwards, always away from the final act* and to the events that precede and precipitate that act." (My emphasis.)

Not happy with the *Aeneid*'s actual ending, Thomas dismisses the stringent organization and the poetic ascent of the preceding Books (one is tempted to ask, 'why then did Vergil bother to write his *maius opus*?'). He himself, however, forgoes a precise interpretation of what he calls "the critical focus" (i.e., a line-by-line explanation of the final scene and Aeneas' motivation within the Vergilian context).

[4] On the identity of Caesar (=Augustus) at 1. 268ff. see Stahl 1985, Chapter 5, n.46 (on p. 340, referring to p. 126).

[5] The desire to make Vergil appear more even-handed has led to desperate attempts to pry Turnus loose from the unsavory company of Mezentius: "The two never meet in the *Aeneid*" (Thomas 1998, 298 n.6). This disregards the fact that King Mezentius, when his maltreated Etruscans demand his extradition for capital punishment, has

found refuge with and is "defended by the arms of his host Turnus", *Turni defendier hospitis armis*, 8. 493. Does Thomas want his readers to believe that guest and host avoided seeing each other? His further argument, that the two "are at opposite ends of the Latin catalogue of *Aen.* 7.", does not prove either that "Vergil in fact keeps the two apart" (*loc. cit.*). Thomas misreads the rhetorical function of their physical separation in the poet's review of the Italian troops: "First (*primus*) to enter the war...is the despiser of the gods, Mezentius" (7. 647f.). The last leader mentioned (before the exceptional maiden warrior Camilla) is King Turnus (783ff.). The two leaders, united in their oracle-defying lust for war, are placed in polar position because, between them, they hold the doomed (and largely misled) Italian tribes.

[6] M.H. Crawford 1974, pl. LXIV, 6 = no. 538.2. This is a denarius issued in 37 BC by a mint "moving with Octavian," showing a "tripod with cauldron" (vol. I, p. 537). "Octavian's coinage of 37...for the first time introduces Apollo (or rather his tripod) as a type" (vol. II, p. 744). Trillmich (1988, 481, with Kat. 310 on p. 502) comments on the "...Verbindung Octavians mit Apollo" on this coin as follows: "Octavian legt, seine eigene Titulatur (IIIVIR ITER...) durchschneidend, die Aufgabe *rei publicae constituendae*...in die Macht des Gottes."

[7] See Binder 1971, 21.

[8] See Wistrand 1984, 198; Pöschl 1981, 713: "Virgil hat so dem Kaiser und seiner Nation und den folgenden Kaisern Leitbilder gegeben, die ihr Wirken prägen sollten." Renger 1985, 69: "Der Princeps sollte....zum selbstkritischen Vergleich angeregt werden." Lefèvre 1983, 40: "[Vergil] dürfte sich Augustus als Republikaner, nicht als Monarchen gewünscht haben und wies ihn deshalb auf Aeneas, der sich selbst überwunden und stets der res Romana untergeordnet hatte, zurück." Sometimes one cannot escape the impression that ivory tower professors yearn to advise active politicians.

[9] By taking its motto from Dante and by declaring Turnus "a young Italian defending his land and way of life", James' article (1995, 623) bases itself on a slanted, *a priori* un-Vergilian, premise, and the attempt to commingle distinct uses of the verb *condere* for upgrading Turnus and downgrading Vergil's *pius Aeneas* is doomed by this (post-Vergilian) perspective.

[10] R.D. Williams *ad* 11. 207–09; "a vivid and moving image of the desolation and meaninglessness of war", Gransden *ad loc.*

[11] For details see Stahl 1981, 173f.

[12] "mere gambler's philosophy", Gransden 1991, 34.

[13] Pöschl 1964, 199f.

[14] Pöschl 1964, 202.

[15] For the following quotes, see Putnam 1965, 153–7.

[16] To explain my use of the word "hypo–logical" I provide another pertinent paradigm of Thomas' procedure. In *Aen.* 6. 791–5, where Anchises for the benefit of his son Aeneas describes Augustus as the man "whom you often hear promised to you" as the founder of a new golden age in Latium (*hic est, tibi quem promitti saepius audis...aurea condet saecula qui rursus Latio...*), Thomas, drawing on a different meaning of *condere* in Lucretius (3. 1090: "bring to a close") finds a "profound ambiguity" and comments that what Vergil (to whom Lucretius is "an author of great familiarity") really means is "who will again *close out* ages of gold" (my emphasis). What kind of logic would make the disappearance of a golden age the object of a *promise*? The

obvious objection against Thomas' "ambiguity", viz. that immediate pre-Augustan Rome (after all, the age of civil war!) can hardly be called a golden age, is rejected by Thomas as "hyperlogical". (What does he mean? Perhaps "more than logical"? His escape clause of declaring "one man's golden age" "another's age of iron" logically violates the all-inclusive term of "age"). His reasoning both here (Thomas 2001, 2–7) and on *Aen.* 12. 4–9 (as well as elsewhere) appears to merit a classification of "hypo-logical".

[17] Thomas 1998, 288f.

[18] Thomas 1998, n.44.

[19] Pascal 1990, 268, n.50. See also Stahl 1990, 187.

[20] Thomas 1998, n.44.

[21] Thomas 1998, 289; emphasis mine.

[22] Thomas 2001, 97 (my emphasis).

[23] One way of dealing with the difficult *latro* (Servius does not help much) would be to see him from the lion's perspective (after all, we are told of the lion's emotion: *gaudetque...impavidus*; *movet arma* indicates an anthropomorphic perspective): the hunter who hit him as a marauder or perpetrator ("as a term of reproach", *OLD s.v.*, 2.b) or even as a predator (such as a hawk or a wolf are in human eyes, *OLD s.v.* 2.c).

[24] *accenso* in line 9, being perfect participle, in time *precedes* the word *gliscit* and picks up *ardet* of line 3. Thomas' translation of 12. 9 ("just so does violence *take fire and grow* in Turnus", 1998, 288; my emphasis) misses this fine point of Latin grammar: first Turnus catches fire (12. 3), then he develops his violence. (12. 9).

[25] Thomas 2001, XVIII.

[26] The poignant repetitions of "alone" (and "owe") at 10. 442f.; 11. 442; 12. 466; 467; 16 had been pointed out by Stahl (1990, 185; 200 with note 34). On "alone" at 10. 442, Stahl (1990, 200) comments that it is "emphasized twice in the same line: *solus ego...soli mihi*, 10. 442".

It is a misrepresentation when Thomas (1998, 276) offers the following (mis-)quote: '...Stahl notes ...that *Pallas' name* is "emphasized twice in the same line"' (my emphasis), then goes on to criticize that Stahl "has nothing on" the repetition of *Lausus' name* at 10. 809–10.

[27] The words of "killing indiscriminately" (*nullo discrimine* 498) have a negative ring to them for modern ears. Vergil uses them to contrast Aeneas' participation in the new *general* fighting with his preceding search for Turnus *alone*. His uncurbed wrath (*irarumque omnis effundit habenas* 499) results from Messapus' perfidious attack (*tum vero adsurgunt irae* 494) on Aeneas the supposed dueler. On the justification of Aeneas' wrath, see also Galinsky 1988, especially 329f.

[28] See Feeney 1991, 151–5.

[29] Boyle 1996, 91, with n.23; 86. My italics.

[30] Boyle 1996, 86. The Sibyl's prophecy, so clearly pointing to Turnus as the new Achilles the Trojans have to face in Italy, has proved to be a serious stumbling block for the Harvard school's interpretation (which would like Aeneas to be the Achillean victimizer, and Turnus his victim). It has further led to wishful contortions of grammar and text, based on presumed "intricacies of Vergilian intertextuality". Similar to Boyle, Thomas has squeezed "Aeneas himself" into the Sibyl's prophecy so he may share the vatic space with Turnus: by *alius* (*scil. Achilles*), he asks his readers to believe, the Sibyl means "potentially a third, rather than a second, *alter*", so that "the Sibyl of Cumae

Chapter 1

talks of yet another Achilles who comes into being in Latium" (and this Achilles is to be Aeneas, according to Thomas 1998, 278–81).

In fact, however, the Sibyl does *not* speak of *"yet another"* [see OLD s.v. *alius*, (7) (b)] Achilles who *"comes into being"* in Latium, but of "a new Achilles" who "has already been born in Latium", *Latio iam partus* (6. 89; also, he was born by a goddess, *dea*, not "a god", as Thomas has it).

Though the Vergilian Sibyl's words may be "wrapping truth in obscurity" (Thomas 281), she is hardly so entranced as both to forget her Latin grammar and to confuse the Trojans' pious defender with their impious neo-Achillean attacker on Italian soil. This, however, does not faze Thomas. By claiming, on the basis of Homeric passages, that Homer's Aineias is in the *Aeneid* represented by Aeolus who dies at *Aen.* 12. 542ff., Thomas declares the Homeric Aineias dead, to be substituted in the *Aeneid* from now on by the (presumably less attractive) Achilles-like Aeneas whom Thomas (like others of his school) foists upon Vergil, as "another" Achilles, i.e., "Aeneas himself". Discontinued identity as a critical tool? (The truth of the matter of course is that Vergil upgrades his hero – after all, his Emperor's ancestor – who in the *Iliad* had to be saved at least twice from Achilles, to the status of a new super-Achilles, who is now able to defeat the new Italian Achilles, i.e., Turnus – compensating for and erasing his Iliadic inferiority on the battlefield.)

By overriding the grammar of 12. 101–8 and extending a simile (Turnus like a bull) so as to cover Aeneas, too, Thomas ("in between is the bull, to whom both men are linked", 1998, 282) prepares the ground for seeing Vergil "equating the two adversaries" in the later simile of two bulls fighting for the herd (12. 715–22). (Of course there can be no talk of "equating" here beyond Vergil's rhetorical purpose of raising Aeneas' reputation by letting him fight and overcome an enemy of [almost] equal strength.) Having been caught in his self-built trap of equating (leveling the difference between) Aeneas and Turnus, Thomas (297) has no difficulty in following Boyle: "The destruction of the city [scil., of Latinus] takes us back to the assault on Troy", with Aeneas(-Achilles) taking over the role of Jupiter (who at 2. 617f. participated in the destruction of Troy) – of a Jupiter who, in the wake of Conte and Feeney, is a rapist and the enemy of Turnus; and Thomas' poor Turnus is left in the dark (he has no "skills" "to prognosticate", 295) about the cause of Jupiter's enmity. No word is lost about Latinus spreading Faunus' warning oracle all over Italy (7. 102–5; see Chapter 7) or about the aged King's dire prediction: "For you, Turnus, o abomination!, for you the death penalty will be waiting, and you will worship the gods with prayers that will be too late!" (7. 595ff.). Thomas' clueless Turnus appears to result from the interpreter's selective reading of the *Aeneid*, disregarding the literary organization that interconnects distant passages.

[31] Thomas 1998, 271.

[32] Thomas 1998, 273. "One could argue with Stahl's details." The only one of "Stahl's details" that Thomas here does "argue with" (in his note 6) in his endeavor to discredit the scholar who had mentioned Turnus' association with cruel King Mezentius, proves to be counterproductive, for Thomas reveals his selective acquaintance with the *Aeneid*: "The two never meet in the *Aeneid*" (298, n.6). According to Vergil (*Aen.* 8. 493), however, Turnus even played host to the expelled Etruscan king and defended him with his military. See note 5 above.

2

THE DEATH OF KING TURNUS

(1) The Duel, I: No Divine Support for Suppliant Turnus

The duel itself clearly consists of two phases. In the first (12. 697–790) Turnus loses the false sword (it breaks apart), Aeneas his spear (it becomes stuck in the stump of a tree). Jupiter's preceding act of weighing the lots of the two opponents points to the fact that the outcome of the duel has been destined by Fate (it opens the road that, in the distant future, will lead to the rise of Rome): the Iliadic elements (e.g., stag-like Hector being pursued by hound-like Achilles) have been thoroughly integrated into Vergil's own agenda. This is poetry claiming Homeric structure – but it aims at a new goal. The intention has been programmatically pronounced as early as the poem's first 7 lines which imitate details of the *Iliad*'s first seven lines (and of the *Odyssey*'s opening) but integrate them into a story-line that leads from the fall of Troy to the "high walls of Rome", i.e. the poet's contemporary city (*Aen.* 1.1–7).[1]

Before phase II, a conversation (motivated by Juturna's handing over the genuine sword to Turnus) takes place between Jupiter and Juno (12. 791–842).[2] Jupiter strictly forbids any further intervention on Turnus' behalf: "It has come to the end" (803). Juno admits that it was she who impelled Juturna to act, but not to the extent of shooting an arrow at Aeneas. Now she yields – Turnus' death is settled before the duel continues.

The dialogue helps the reader further to see the duel under the viewpoint of the epic future, i.e., it affords Vergil an opportunity to subsume his own time under the mythical norm: to show that today's conditions do not mean what their surface seems to indicate. The *aition* follows the fairy-tale pattern 'and that is the reason why today all ravens are black and not, as would be expected from our story, white.' To justify his implausible plot-line here (it is in the political sphere that he is most liable to violate the poetic *probabile*),[3] the poet puts a Stoic argument into Juno's mouth: in Chrysippean manner she asks for "what is fixed by no law of fate" (819). In similar fashion, Vulcan claimed that neither the "all-powerful father...nor fate" would have forbidden Troy and Priam to survive for another ten years, 8. 398f.). It is owed to Juno's pleading

Chapter 2

intervention that, after the peaceful fusion of the two nations, i.e. 'today', the Italians under (as Vergil's Jupiter calls him in Book 1) "Trojan" Augustus (*Troianus... Caesar*, 1. 286) do not speak Trojan but Latin, and have not remained Trojans but become Latins instead; that they do not dress in Trojan garb but in their own inherited way; that, together with the city itself, the very name Troy also has vanished.[4]

The Trojan component of the people is denied dominance by consenting Jupiter probably for two reasons. One is that, after all, 'Trojan'-Julian leadership itself had not reasserted itself in Roman history until fairly recently. The other reason is that in Vergil's time Rome and Italy are supposed to feel reconciled to the rule of the Trojan-Julian House, but not suppressed – reconciled as was Juno, protector of Italian Turnus, to the victory of Aeneas – and, after the Punic wars, to Roman supremacy. For us it borders on the ridiculous that Jupiter, in order to comply with the facts of Vergil's contemporary world, "voluntarily" (*volens* 833) agrees that the Trojans, for whose survival he has through twelve Books cared so much, "will sink to the bottom of the ethnic mixture" (835f.), losing their national identity. The modern reader compares the linguistic acrobatics by which in Book 1 the poet had Jupiter draw the line from Trojan (Ascanius-)*Ilus-Iulus* to (*Troianus...Caesar...*) *Iulius* (267f.; 286ff.). For Juno, of course, the disappearance of the Trojan element in the new ethnic mixture is, together with the promise of future worship, reason to be happy (*laetata* 841). But she says nothing about giving up her plans for Carthage (1. 13–18): that is another matter (as Jupiter himself states at 10. 11–14). At 12. 827 (Rome's power is to be based on Italian manliness) Juno's consent does not necessarily go as far down in history as to cover also the Punic Wars.[5]

The singular piety of the new melting pot population (12. 839f., cf. 836f.) should probably be understood as Trojan-Julian heritage. One recalls pious Aeneas' words about his contribution to the prospective union of the two nations: "I shall give rites and gods", *sacra deosque dabo* (12. 192). This has been his mission ever since Hector appeared to him in his dream in the night of Troy's fall (see also 1. 6):

> Troy entrusts to you its holy objects and its Penates
>
> sacra suosque tibi commendat Troia penatis. 2. 293.

Jupiter confirms Aeneas' religious mission once more by giving "custom and rites of sacrificing" to the new nation, *morem ritusque sacrorum adiciam* (836f). (This is in agreement with the advice given to Aeneas by the Trojan seer Helenus concerning a specific custom at sacrificing, which should be handed down to the "descendants", 3. 405–09; and it is, of course, in agreement with Augustus' religious restoration policies.)

The Death of King Turnus

All this helps the reader to a correct political classification of details before one reads about the final phase of the duel (887–952). Additional clarification is given immediately before the final phase when Jove sends down one of the *Dirae*,[6] who come together with *metus* and *letum horrificum* (850f.), fear and dreadful death.[7] Turnus' sudden weakness (cf. *metu, letumque*, 916; also 867 and 868) is, he claims, not founded in personal failure or in fear of Aeneas (who blames him because of the new delay, *mora* 889):

what frightens me are the gods and especially Jupiter my enemy

Di me terrent et Iuppiter hostis 12. 895.

Here finally we may be prepared to believe him that he now no longer wishes to evade his commitment, even if the deity, in spite of his eagerness, denies him the path of virtue (the boulder he tried to hurl falls short of its goal).[8]

Contemporary misinterpretation requires us here, at least in passing, to clarify the *Dira*'s function within Vergil's value coordinates. In Feeney's anti-authorial understanding, Jupiter "employs an agent whom we cannot but read as a creature of evil. Jupiter's force is Junoesque," etc. In saying so, Feeney invalidates Vergil's authorial description of the *Dirae* which includes that Jupiter, when wrathful,[9] sends them out "when he, *deum rex*, causes terrible death and diseases or frightens *deserving (meritas = guilty)* cities with war" (12. 851f.). It would be unreasonable to assume that human beings such as Turnus, when visited by a *Dira*, are less guilty in the author's estimate than cities he characterizes as guilty. But for Feeney, Jupiter's "is not a perspective from which problems disappear. In this *dismaying poem, most* readers want to find a vantage point of *comfort*, and it is therefore tempting to construct a 'high' Stoic position in the portrayal of Jupiter".[10] "Most readers": how does Feeney know? Since when did ancient poetics assign epic the task of providing "comfort" (perhaps even in a modern sense), thus allowing one to say that Vergil failed his assignment? Like the comfort-seekers of the so-called Harvard school, Feeney seems to think what is "dismaying" to himself must have been felt by Vergil and his contemporary readers to be dismaying. So, while eager to 'construct' a Vergil congruent with his own comfort level, he is even ready to 'deconstruct' Vergil's Jupiter who punishes guilty cities. The ancient author is made to comply with the demands of his modern reader. (However, since Vergil's Jupiter does act *justly* by frightening *deserving* humans, a closer look at the text might have persuaded Feeney that the high "vantage point of comfort" he is looking for does exist in the *Aeneid*.)

Another assumption found in recent criticism is that only now, in line 895, does Turnus become aware of Jupiter's hostility.[11] This, of course,

Chapter 2

would help to 'de-Augustanize' Vergil by allowing for a certain degree of innocence up to this point on the part of Aeneas' political rival. Already Pöschl, early champion of a basically innocent Turnus, saw Turnus here express his feeling that the gods have abandoned him, *daß ihn die Götter verlassen haben*.[12] This presupposes that the gods were with him earlier. The truth, likely to be overlooked by the short-distance reader, is (as was pointed out earlier) that Turnus ever since Book 7 has defied the widely publicized will of the gods. The reader especially recalls pious King Latinus' warning: "...too late you will worship the gods with prayers" (7. 597). Thomas calls lines 894f. "Turnus' realization of his desperate status", and, including lines 875b–78a (Juturna's reaction to the *Dira*), states: "Relevant here is the contrast between Turnus' final recognition and his delusion elsewhere in the poem."[13] This is again an attempt to exculpate Turnus (and to suggest that Vergil shares this view) by according him a sort of 'innocent' or less-than-conscious opposition against fate-carrying Aeneas.

The question, however, is hardly "whether Turnus is ever helped by divine signs",[14] but *whether he ever cares to observe divine signs* or to learn their meaning, as, for instance, Aeneas' father, Anchises, does in religiously correct fashion when seeing the flame on his grandson's head and asking Jupiter: *haec omina firma*, requesting an *augurium impetrativum* in addition to the *augurium oblativum* (2. 691). When Aeneas' ships are miraculously turned into nymphs, even (*ipse*) the less-than-pious (cf. 12. 293–96) Messapus is frightened, his horses are confused, not to speak of the Rutulians being dumbstruck; and the Tiber holds its flow. *But* – and this is the authorial voice speaking, emphasizing the contrast between Turnus and normal human, animal, and divine reaction by the strongly adversative word *at* as well as through heavy spondees – "*but* bold Turnus did not lose his confidence", *at non audaci Turno fiducia cessit* (9. 126). Accordingly, when giving his personal, autonomous (i.e., not advised by a competent interpreter or a divine confirmation) interpretation of the portent, Turnus in passing remarks that fate-carrying *responses of the gods do not scare him at all*, if the Trojans "brag" of having some in their favor,

> nil me fatalia terrent,
> si qua Phryges prae se iactant, responsa deorum. 9. 133f.

Though obviously referring to the *responsa* (sought by King Latinus and then spread around all over the Italian cities, 7. 92–106) about the destined son-in-law *from abroad*, Turnus autocratically claims to have his own, opposite "fate", *sunt et mea contra / fata mihi* (9. 136f.), viz. to take revenge for his "wife, snatched away beforehand", *coniuge praerepta* (138; i.e., pious King Latinus, obedient to the oracle, had offered Lavinia to Aeneas, not to

Turnus, 7. 268–71. On Turnus' knowledge of the oracle Chapter 7 will say more).[15]

So, in view of the authorial characterising of "bold" Turnus' singular confidence and of his expressed disregard for *responsa deorum* (referring back as far as Book 7), there is no way of maintaining that Turnus, when numbed and incapable after the *Dira*'s appearance, "has just realized that the cosmic order is against him."[16] The shoe fits better on the other foot, if only we are ready to accept Vergil's authorial guidance. Turnus has fought against the revealed divine order all along, and is aware that he now faces the final consequence of his impious conduct (as was pointed out earlier, on the occasion of Turnus, invoking the shades of his ancestors, 12. 646–49). And the interpreter inevitably faces the prospect of a Vergil who, by the laws of logic as well as of Latin grammar, is incapable of being 'de-Augustanized'.

> So, wherever Turnus tried to make his way by manliness,
> the dire goddess denied him the outcome.
>
> sic Turno, quacumque viam virtute petivit,
> successum dea dira negat. 12. 913f.

And thus, Turnus' feelings are conflicting (*pectore sensus / vertuntur varii*, 914f.; the *v*-alliteration echoes that of 913, emphasizing the change from *virtus* to changing sensations). His hesitation between fear of death and desire to attack appears *again* – the third time in Vergil's series – increasingly to be giving way to thoughts of flight (917a), especially when the reader sees him looking around for his divine sister (his charioteer) and the chariot that would save him (918). The mythological Dira has not changed Turnus' mindset (as it has so far manifested itself in the empirical terms of the authorial narrative). Turnus' conduct is painted in stark contrast with that of Pallas, his young victim (and Aeneas' disciple), who unflinchingly faced Turnus' incoming deadly spear (10. 459–85; see Chapter 3, Section 1).

In Turnus' hesitancy (*cunctatur* 916; *cunctanti* 919) Aeneas sees his chance (*fortunam* 920): it allows him to launch the decisive throw of his spear, piercing the thigh of Turnus. Under the echoing screams of his Rutulians Turnus collapses. Aeneas' missile, executing the first step on the road to Turnus' inescapable death (the epic's closure, as revealed beforehand by Jupiter to Juno and accepted by her, 12. 796–806), is termed *telum...fatale*, "acting as the instrument of fate, fateful" (OLD *s.v.* 4 (a) *ad loc.*).

And what now? It appears that Vergil has extended the instability or lack of consistency, which he repeatedly assigned Turnus, to its final consequence (I mark the stages of Turnus' wavering by numbers):

Chapter 2

(1) on the one hand as a suppliant (*supplex* 930) stretching out his right arm in a gesture of *request (dextramque precantem / protendens* 930f.),

(2) he on the other hand says that he is *not* asking for mercy (*nec deprecor*) but, in acknowledging his guilt (*equidem merui* 931), he tells Aeneas to utilize his fortune, i.e., to kill him (*utere sorte tua* 932). The reader here recalls the parallel confession of guilt uttered by suicidal Dido, the other major obstacle on Aeneas' fated course (4. 547ff.). However, Turnus proves not as determined as Dido.

(3) But abruptly (adversative asyndeton, 932) he again changes his position and appeals to the soft feelings Aeneas fosters toward his deceased father, Anchises. He adduces his own "pitiful" old father Daunus (*miseri* 932 – a word not usually part of Turnus' vocabulary, here used slyly to gain advantage through compassion), to whom he *begs* (*oro* 933) to be returned – he himself alive or

(4) his lifeless corpse. The latter (i.e., the heroic) alternative (hardly welcome to father Daunus; Servius remarks on its palliative intent) he immediately

(5) proceeds to exclude again by indicating that in his view the terms of the duel have already been satisfied as matters stand:

> yours is the victory and the Ausonians have seen the defeated
> stretching his hands: yours is Lavinia as your wife;
> do not strive to go beyond this in hatred.
>
> vicisti et victum tendere palmas
> Ausonii videre; tua est Lavinia coniunx,
> ulterius ne tende odiis. 12. 936ff.

So at 936 Turnus points back to earlier having raised his hands as a sign of defeat. This may be identical with *dextram precantem/protendens* of 930f.[17] In this case, *palmas* at 936 is a 'poetic' plural. Or stretching his arms may have occurred independently from that admission of defeat. One thing is clear: Turnus now uses the earlier gesture (for which he invokes his Ausonians as witnesses) as part of his argumentation for his own survival. By referring to his earlier gesture of request, he rescinds the heroic pose identified above in his speech as stages (2) ('I don't ask for mercy'; 'utilize your fortune') and (4) ('if you prefer, return me *dead* to my father'). Heroic pose and appeal to Aeneas' filial piety turn out to be rhetorical stratagems skillfully woven into the plea for survival.

There can be no doubt at all: Turnus who once gave himself the air of a hero "second to none"(11. 441); who "dedicated" his *life* (*animam*) to his people and his (hoped-for) "father-in-law" (11. 438–42); who for his declared bride – denied him by the gods – (and for becoming the prospective successor to the throne) was willing to risk his very existence in single combat (12. 79f.); and who, toward Latinus, was unwilling to listen to the argument of feeling pity for his own aged father (*miserere parentis / longaevi* 12. 43f.), has cunningly chosen the un-heroic alternative of survival, now allegedly for the sake of "pitiful" Daunus, his father. Can it surprise us at all that his soul – in the epic's often misinterpreted last line – is "resentful" or "indignant" (*indignata*, 952) when going down to the shades below? It certainly does not surprise the long-distance reader who remembers Turnus' repeated attempts to avoid the duel, and especially the author's comment on Turnus' lack of moderation (*servare modum*) following his un-heroic killing of Pallas ("the boy"), that Turnus would one day be happy to pay a high price for Pallas being unharmed, and that he then would hate the spoils taken from dead Pallas (10. 501–05). Well, that day has now come, and Turnus, as predicted in his creator's long-distance composition, resents facing the consequences. We shall return to the matter.

In parenthesis let it be said that the maiden warrior Camilla, with whom Turnus shares the same expression of indignation (11. 831=12. 952), did have a heroic reason for her departing soul's discontent (provided the line is designed to be more – i.e., Vergil's own *indignata* – than a mere Homeric-style formula; cf. *Il.* 16. 857; 22. 363), for she had been covertly stalked by her cowardly slayer. Or, does her dying indignation perhaps rather recall the fact that Turnus had let her down militarily (cf. 11. 825f.; 506; and our discussion earlier in this chapter)?

A special facet of Turnus' conduct merits fuller consideration. Before answering Amata's despairing words and informing her that the war is to be decided "by our [i.e., Turnus' and Aeneas'] blood"(*nostro dirimamus sanguine bellum* 12. 79) and that "on that field, Lavinia the wife is to be sought" (*illo quaeratur coniunx Lavinia campo* 12. 80), Turnus is not looking at his hoped-for mother-in-law, but, confused by his feelings of love, he fixes his eyes on the blushing maiden:

illum turbat amor figitque in virgine vultus 12. 70

And he once more makes clear that the encounter with Aeneas is going to be a deadly one: "Turnus is not free to postpone death" (*neque enim Turno mora libera mortis* 12. 74).

This is (except for the mention at the crisis point of his moral decision 12. 668) the only time that the reader is shown Turnus personally affected by feelings of love for Lavinia (elsewhere she is the political bride, heiress to the Latin throne). But it is an essential passage because Vergil shows Turnus willing to face death for winning his beloved.

Chapter 2

The more devastating is the effect of the final words the poet puts in Turnus' mouth:

Lavinia the wife is yours.
Don't go any further in hatred.

tua est Lavinia coniunx.
ulterius ne tende odiis. 12. 937f.

To survive, Turnus is not only willing to give up his political ambition, but also to acknowledge surrender of his love. His solemn (3rd person) statement that, for gaining Lavinia, "Turnus is not free to postpone his death" (74), has evaporated. With the political surrender, unforgiving Vergil has also included the personal betrayal. By including the private aspect (perhaps most appropriately to be weighed in Propertian terms, cf. Prop. 2. 7), he has added another character feature in which Turnus can first express commitment and then fail his self-proclaimed obligation.

The most remarkable fact (beside his confession of guilt) about Vergil's concept of Aeneas' political rival is that the poet denies him the courage of bravely facing the deadly blow. (The circumstance that Turnus' chest is turned toward Aeneas, *adverso...pectore*, 12. 950, can hardly be taken to be a heroic change from the earlier praying position of the man on bent knee 12. 926f.) The poet had granted the (at least partially, redeeming) feature of conscious acceptance even to the cruel tyrant Mezentius: *iuguloque haud inscius accipit ensem* (10. 907). Those who, in the service of "de-Augustanizing" the *Aeneid*, wish to upgrade Vergil's Turnus would do well to look at his last words in the light of Mezentius' bravery, as well as of young Pallas' heroism when he unflinchingly faced superior Turnus' oncoming spear (10. 482–5). Pallas, too, thought of his father, Evander. But he did so not in terms of a negotiating card to save his own life, rather to do him honor and earn his paternal recognition: death or victory, "my father is impartial to either lot," *sorti pater aequus utrique est* (10. 450). Victimizer Turnus falls below the heroic standard of his young victim.

As far as the reader's picture of Turnus is concerned, there is the aggravating circumstance that, in his skillful speech,[18] he rewrites his own earlier concept of the duel: earlier, he wanted to decide the war by bloodshed (which then could hardly be understood as thigh blood: *nostro dirimamus sanguine bellum* 12. 79); to mar "effeminate" Aeneas' perm in the dust (which can hardly point to a surviving enemy 12. 99f.); intended, with his right arm, to send the "traitor of Asia" "into Tartarus", *dextra sub Tartara mittam* (14) – as he bragged toward Latinus when he himself urgently asked for a formal duel: *fer sacra, pater, et concipe foedus* (13); above all, he declared himself prepared to accept *death* in exchange for fame: *letumque sinas pro laude pacisci* (49). No doubt, Vergil in the end again offers us his familiar Turnus who wants to escape the consequences of an obligation he had eagerly entered. Considering the *Aeneid*'s lasting influence on political thought and literature, some may see here an ominous precedent for later European attitudes toward non-conformist citizens in homogenized societies. In this context, it weighs heavy that, whereas, in addition to his evasiveness on the battlefield, Turnus' fear of death is depicted (12. 917), only rarely is the reader's sense of compassion for Turnus evoked (cf. 12. 221; 752f.; 881).

That the death of Turnus is largely modeled on Hector's death at the hands of Achilles is generally acknowledged. The more reason, then, for the interpreter to look out for any change that may point to Vergil's own agenda. Hector is wounded in the neck, but in such a way that his windpipe is not destroyed and Homer can believably have him deliver his last words before his certain death from the wound. Vergil has Turnus wounded *non-fatally* in the thigh. Why? Considering the history of Turnus' conduct in the *Aeneid*, it appears likely that Vergil wanted to continue his characterization of Turnus by providing him with the opportunity to un-heroically plead for his life. Dying Hector can only ask for worthy last rites (*Il.* 22. 338–40), which Achilles denies him. Wounded Turnus can ask for his life, and does receive a sympathetic hearing from the new Achilles (until a new aspect breaks into and changes the situation).

These findings, then, preclude the alternative interpretation favored by the Harvard school. The negative picture alone which Vergil draws of Turnus' unreliable character speaks against (to cite a leading representative of that school) Putnam's extra-contextual vision for Aeneas "of forgiving an enemy in order to reintegrate in peace a split society and not pursue divisive hatred further… Such is Turnus' proposal".[19] Hardly so. Rather, such had been the spirit of *Aeneas*' proposal at 12. 189–91. But by his recurrent treaty-breaking conduct as well as by his present deceitful speech, Vergil's Turnus has proved himself incapable of being harmoniously and beneficially integrated into a functioning society. The poet's long-term portrait does not support the thesis that "…the suppliant has offered *logical* and *reasonable* terms for *peaceful* community."[20] There is no "proposal" from a potential partner in stable statesmanship, only a sly plea for personal survival at all cost. Acknowledgement of defeat before the eyes of his Italians does not guarantee that Turnus would not again, as twice before, break a treaty. As interpreters, we must not exclude the long view taken by the author – or the short view either: by excluding the speaking gesture of stage (1) (i.e., lines 12. 930/31a: *dextramque precantem / protendens*) from his quotation and translation[21] (and, with it, the contrasting word-play on *precantem* and *nec deprecor*), Putnam has diminished Turnus' shiftiness and moved him closer to a genuine and trustworthy suppliant, thereby reducing not only the introductory impression of wavering vacillation depicted by the author in the sequence *precantem – nec deprecor – oro*, but also preventing the question from being asked, why would Turnus employ the gesture of request if he were sincere in telling Aeneas "...I am not asking for mercy" and "make use of your good fortune"?

In the context a related question arises: how far-reaching are Turnus' neighboring words *equidem merui* (12. 931)? It appears doubtful that the reason to be supplied with the words "I have deserved {death} and do not beg mercy" is limited to the idea 'because you defeated me in the duel.'[22] A long-distance reader can hardly exclude Turnus' history of broken treaties and evasiveness, his admitted awareness of having procrastinated ("*nulla mora in Turno*" 12. 11) and having shown himself *indecorem* (12. 679), the result having been the immense bloodletting of his own and of Aeneas' innocent people. In view of his long misconduct toward Aeneas, Turnus himself would hardly wish to restrict himself to only conceding him the victor's right to kill ("Siegerrecht", Wlosok); and this is especially true in view of his goal of securing his own survival with his plea – a *full* confession alone of his guilt and past trespasses might persuade Aeneas of the appropriateness of granting the request. (And if that should not suffice, there is of course the additional appeal to Aeneas' own devotion to his father Anchises, which for Roman ears would normally evoke an unquestionable obligation, were it not for its horrible misuse in the mouth of Turnus who had wished his young victim's father to be present to watch his son die (10. 443).)

(2) The Duel, II: Aeneas Enraged

And what about Aeneas? Let it be said *a priori* that Vergil has his attitude, too, presented as being complex, as developing in stages. Our point of departure must be that Aeneas, too, exactly like Turnus (12. 49; 79), had equated the outcome of the duel with the death of one of the two opponents. This is implied already in his very first suggestion, made to Drances (11. 118). This is also the motivation for the twofold good-bye to his son, the second time (12. 435f.) in the style of death-bound Sophoclean Ajax (*Ai.* 550f.). The author himself tells us during the fight that now the life and blood of Turnus are at stake:

> sed Turni de vita et sanguine certant. 12. 765.

One has to realize that Aeneas, after he successfully threw his spear, has naturally been contemplating the deathblow as his next step. Only in this way do we understand that his behavior *after* Turnus' request presents a counter-movement:

> Aeneas, fierce in his arms, stood without moving,
> rolling his eyes, and curbed his right arm.
> And gradually the speech had started increasingly to change his
> mind while he was hesitating, (when, all of a sudden, etc.)

> stetit acer in armis
> Aeneas volvens oculos dextramque repressit;
> et iam iamque magis cunctantem flectere sermo
> coeperat, (cum...) 12. 938–41.

Let us, for once, analyze Aeneas' situation under the definition his father laid down of the Roman's task in history:[23]

> fighting down the proud and pardoning those who comply

> parcere subiectis et debellare superbos 6. 853,

or under the comparable statement of Augustus

> Foreign nations that could be pardoned safely
> I have preferred to preserve rather than to extinguish

> Externas gentes, quibus tuto ignosci potuit, conservare
> quam excidere malui. *R.G.* 3.2

As shown above, Turnus cannot be "pardoned with safety", *ignosci tuto*. But to a degree the conditions outlined by Anchises apply also to him: called *superbus* earlier (326), he now is *humilis supplexque* (930; M's reading) and confesses his guilt (*equidem merui*). Consequently, one should not be surprised that Aeneas, against his original conception (cf. already 11. 118) and against the terms of the duel, but in agreement with his father's injunction of *parcere subiectis*, calls himself back from killing the enemy now that he has been defeated. Obviously, through the hesitation (*cunctantem*) of Aeneas the author lays claim to the principle of *clementia* for his hero, thereby taking him to the brink of a (as Vergil's reader has been led to see it) politically wrong decision. (The fact that Aeneas "checked his right arm", *dextramque repressit*, does not imply that he had fully made the decision to spare Turnus' life: the process of gradually "bending" [*flectere*] his mind had only begun, *coeperat*.)

Aeneas' receptive reaction toward Turnus' plea does not by any means flow from irrational emotion, from a sudden humanitarian impulse of compassion, but from soberly and rationally weighing the *sermo*, i.e., the argument of Turnus: that Aeneas, while listening, is "rolling his eyes",

Chapter 2

volvens oculos, is an expression of this slow (*iam iamque magis*), mind-changing (*flectere*) thought process – in the same way as King Latinus, *intentos volvens oculos* (7. 251), arrives in a slow process (cf. *tandem* 7. 259) at his conclusion about Aeneas' identity as that of the prophesied son-in-law from abroad. Aeneas dutifully, in agreement with his father's precept, reviews the potential validity of the reasons for clemency proffered by the defeated enemy (reminding the contemporary reader, of course, also of the ubiquitous Julian claim concerning *clementia Caesaris*). If Aeneas should not detect the inherent deception, that would not be detrimental to the portrait Vergil paints of his hero's character: in Book 2, also, it is anything but dishonorable that the decent Trojans, so far undefeated, fall for Sino's lies, *captique dolis* (2. 196), because they are "ignorant of crimes so great and of Greek trickery", *ignari scelerum tantorum artisque Pelasgae* (2. 106; see Stahl 1981).

One should observe that, with the appeal to Aeneas' own sacred bond that ties him as a son to his father Anchises ("if concern for a pitiable father can touch you": how could it *not* touch pious Aeneas? cf. 10. 824), Turnus adds the highest possible human component to the Roman-Augustan principle of right conduct (as defined by Anchises) toward a defeated enemy. On the other hand, as the reader knows, Turnus' invocation of Anchises, allegedly to spare grief to his own father Daunus, has been invalidated beforehand by Turnus' own grisly wish that his killing of young Pallas might be watched by Pallas' father, Evander, 10. 443. (See the details in Section 1 of Chapter 3.)

The aforementioned branch of Vergilian scholarship is mistaken in denying Aeneas here the feature of *clementia*:[24] it is present but in the end it is overruled and replaced by another obligation, one of higher priority. A close reading of the text shows that the development that would avoid the duel's preconceived ending and instead lead to mercy has clearly been set in motion, but then itself is interrupted by an unexpected third movement (its suddenness indicated grammatically by the so-called *cum inversum*, 941). The third movement is started by Aeneas' sudden perception that Turnus is wearing the sword-belt of "the boy" (*pueri* 943) Pallas.

This does not mean that up to now Aeneas has 'forgotten' Pallas. Recently (in terms of the epic's structure, through most of Book 12) his mind has been deeply engaged in (and preoccupied with) fighting on the battlefield to save his imperilled army (cf. 406–10) and enforcing a contracted duel to end the war between two nations destined to live in peace together. For a long time, he tried to prevent internecine destruction by pursuing Turnus alone, the enemy's evasive commander, to make him fulfill the terms of the treaty. He now (the duel element fulfilled) is thrown back to the earlier situation that demanded that he deal with the killer of

Pallas. The sight of the sword-belt, *saevi monimenta doloris* (945), brings back the original pain. But the fact that Aeneas will not allow Pallas' killer to be "snatched away from me" (*eripiare mihi* 948) confirms the parameters of the preceding narrative, by pointing to a long-standing resolve, revealing that in his mind the death of Turnus, killer of Pallas, had been a fixed matter all along (practically, ever since 10. 513–15). Only temporarily, because of large-scale communal emergencies and, in the end, by the diversionary speech of the contractual duel partner, had this aspect been relegated to the background. Similarly, in Book 2 Aeneas first thought of – and fought for – his country. But when this option was exhausted – Venus stopped him, pointing out that any further resistance would violate the will of the gods – the pious man turned to the task of saving his family.[25] It is a testimony to Vergil's artful composition that, for the long period of general fighting, and until the outcome of the duel has been decided, he is able to relegate the avenging of Pallas to the background, reserving it for the final climax of his work, and then to bring it back to the forefront by Aeneas' sudden recognition (an *anagnorisis*) of the sword-belt.

I do not agree with those who argue that Vergil (since supposedly failing to supply an express commendation of his hero's final action) considers Aeneas' wrath and rage, *ira* and *furiae* (946), to be a loss of his higher self. I have elsewhere and in preparation for the present interpretation shown that there does exist a *iusta ira* in the *Aeneid* (as there do exist *furiae iustae*, *iustae irae*, *iustus dolor*[26] as well as – without a qualifying adjective – the (laudatory) combination *pudor iraque* (9. 44), or (again meritorious) *iras* [plural] alone (10. 263).

In the same volume of my earlier demonstration, the editor in his *Introduction*[27] sought to obviate a positive meaning of *furiae* etc. in Vergil by claiming that *furiae* and *ira* "are given approving epithets only when mentioned in connection with a man of the most barbaric conduct", i.e., Etruscan King Mezentius, cruel torturer of his own subjects.

This argument misses Vergil's point. If it were only for Mezentius' (broadly painted) cruelty, no "approving epithets" would be necessary to justify morally the Etruscans' wrath and rage against their king. The problem that leads Vergil to emphasize the justice of their rebellious behavior ("finally" – *tandem*, the narrator's voice, 8. 489 – "all of Etruria" rises up and demands extradition of Mezentius from his host, King Turnus) is a sociological one: in the hierarchically structured world of the *Aeneid*, the top of the social pyramid is as a rule not called into question: King Priam, King Aeneas, King Helenus, even Queen Dido (at least, initially) among her own subjects, King Latinus. The poet's contemporary readers would easily find their bearings by being reminded of their own hierarchically structured society, specifically of Aeneas' greater descendant (their ruler) and his push for personal sacrosanctity for himself (as early as 36 BC), his sister, and his consort, as well as of its continuing consolidation in the widening application of the *maiestas* concept. In the epic on Augustus' ancestor, Vergil apparently feels, it needs special justification to demand extradition of a *king* to his *subjects* (*regem* at 8. 495 is emphasized by first-word-position in the line) for the *death penalty* (*ad supplicium* 8. 495). Of course, Turnus' hospitable association with (and military protection of) this human monster further contributes to discrediting the Rutulian king in the eyes of almost any reader.[28]

So the absence of an "approving epithet" does not automatically signal the author's disapproval of Aeneas' *ira* and *furiae* at 12. 946, but it is the context that must be taken into account in each individual case. On the contrary, a phrase such as *Furor impius* (1. 294; the personified rage of civil war) seems to imply that *furor* in itself can be neutral and that a 'disapproving epithet' (*impius*) is appropriate when Vergil wishes the word to clearly carry a negative connotation. Of course, when King Mezentius asks for protection against the *furor* of his maltreated citizens (*hunc, oro, defende furorem* 10. 905), he does not consider his insubordinate subjects' *furor* (although he is referring to the same instance of rage) in the morally positive terms of the *furiae iustae* invoked by King Evander (8. 494), or of the *merita ira* pronounced by the Etruscan *haruspex* (8. 501), or of the *iusta ira* affirmed by the authorial voice (10. 714). He would hardly share his citizens' (and the author's) perspective of himself as "committing unspeakable acts of (out-) rage" (*infanda furentem* 8. 489).

Certainly peace-seeking Aeneas, "happy that the war would be ended by the proposed (duel-) treaty" (12. 109), is not condemned by the narrator for working up his fighting spirit, *se suscitat ira* (12. 108) in preparation of the war-deciding duel; nor is the boxer who, after a fall returning to the fight with heightened ferocity, "works up with wrath (*ira*) his violence: then shame (*pudor*) and awareness of valour (*conscia virtus*) ignite his strength" (5. 454f.). So *ira* is found here in the company of *pudor* and *conscia virtus*; this kind of virtue must of course be distinguished from the wrath of those ignoring the single combat treaty whom Aeneas tries to curb, *o cohibete iras* 12. 314, or from Turnus' *ira*, when it is added to his "love of fighting", *amor ferri*, and his "*criminal* insanity of war", *scelerata insania belli* 7. 461f.: again it is the context that determines the moral value of *ira;* nor is Aeneas blameworthy when he, maliciously attacked (*insidiis subactus* 12. 494) during the duel truce, "at that point" (*tum vero*) allows his anger to rise (*adsurgunt irae* 12. 494); or when, seeing his duel partner's contract-breaking evasiveness, he repeatedly and formally invokes Jupiter and "finally" (*tandem* – the narrator's voice! – 12. 497) lets go "all the reins of his anger", *irarumque omnis effundit habenas* (12. 499). So it often depends on the situation in (or motivation under) which the wrath arises, to determine whether or not the resulting action or utterance carries the author's approval (a fact recent literary theory has often found hard to determine). When King Priam "spared neither voice nor wrath", *nec voci iraeque pepercit* (2. 534) in accusing his son's killer, there can be no doubt that his is to be seen as a *iusta ira*, considering the fact alone that the epic presents the Greek attack on Troy as a crime. On the other hand, even Turnus can, his impious motivation for once set aside, *as a fighter* show a lion's *ira* and *virtus*, wrath and courage (9. 795, cf. 798.). And *ira* can also characterize the (blameless) fighting spirit or anger that may characterize either Aeneas or Turnus in action (12. 527), as well as Aeneas' newly heartened soldiers when they see him returning to them (10. 263).

The picture does not change if one again includes rage, *furor / furiae*[29] (and the verb *furere*), but the perspective broadens. As the next Chapter (3) will show, Aeneas' responsive battlefield fury (*Dardanides* contra *furit* 10. 545) is a positive feature in the hero's portrait. (Fury, in this way much like *ira*, often is not more than a necessary condition for a warrior to engage in serious fighting, so also for Camilla or Penthesilea, 1. 491; 11. 709. In a different area, *furens* and *furiae* may characterize Dido's uncontrolled frenzy of love, e.g., 4. 69; 4. 376.) Denoting the prophetic frenzy of Cassandra (2. 345) or of the vatic Sibyl, Aeneas' guide to the underworld (6. 262, cf. 100), the verb lacks any negative connotation. And Cassandra's fate-driven frenzy, guiding Aeneas' voyage, provides an authoritative voice that even hostile Juno, albeit grudgingly, acknowledges (*fatis auctoribus* – esto- / *Cassandrae impulsus furiis* 10. 67f.; cf. 3. 183–7). On the other hand, when leading to an act of wrongdoing (the rape of Cassandra by the Lesser Ajax) and expressly associated with a term of blame (*ob noxam et furias Aiacis Oilei* 1. 41), the word *furiae* is unambiguously negative. Again, it is the context that makes the difference. The context will also have to guide the interpreter when considering Aeneas, *furiis accensus et ira / terribilis* (12. 946f.).

A much-favored hypothesis would like to turn the *Aeneid* into a sort of derailed *Entwicklungs-* or *Bildungs-Roman*: Allegedly Aeneas, irrational and uncontrolled in the beginning, later 'learns', especially under his deceased father's guidance during the encounter in the underworld, to control and perfect himself ("to spare the defeated and fight down the arrogant", *parcere subiectis et debellare superbos* 6. 853); but he is said in the end to lose or forget his 'education' when 'ruthlessly' killing suppliant Turnus. The hypothesis, by de-emphasizing the imperialistic *debellare* in favor of *parcere subiectis*, would of course help to include Vergil, presumed critic of his Aeneas, in a

Chapter 2

canon of anti-authoritarian or regime-critical literature of non-partisan humanity. However, its premise rests on a faulty translation.

In the night of Troy's fall, Aeneas valiantly tries to save the city (after all, Vergil can hardly have his Emperor's forefather sneak out of town without putting up a fight, as a less sympathetic strand of the tradition would have it):

> Out of my mind, I seize my arms; and yet, there is not enough of
> a strategic plan in (seizing) arms (alone),
> but my spirit burns to gather a band for fighting and hurry to the citadel
> with (these) fellow-fighters; *rage* and *wrath*
> rush my mind, and it seems a noble end to die in arms.

> Arma amens capio; nec sat rationis in armis,
> sed glomerare manum bello et concurrere in arces
> cum sociis ardent animi; *furor iraque* mentem
> praecipitant, pulchrumque mori succurrit in armis. 2. 314–17.

Again, one has to watch the context. Waking up and finding his town burning, invaded by a ruse (the Trojan Horse), the hero's passionate patriotic reaction is beyond reproach, especially convincing in terms of the Augustan Age since it culminates in the maxim of Horace, Vergil's fellow-Augustan poet, which pronounces *dulce et decorum est pro patria mori* ("it is sweet and honorable to die for one's country", *O.* 3.2.13). The context forbids the use of line 314 for disparaging Aeneas (as has actually been done) by morally equating defender and aggressor, Aeneas and Turnus, on the basis of two identical words (<u>arma amens</u> *fremit*, 7. 460, cf. <u>arma amens</u> *capio* 2. 314);[30] for Turnus' call to arms is (as mentioned earlier) driven by "*criminal* insanity of war" (<u>scelerata</u> *insania belli* 7. 461), leading to breaking the divinely ordained peace.

And yet, one has found fault with Aeneas because "thoughts of valour drive out *ratio*, and he is a victim of *furor* and *ira*" (R.D. Williams *ad* 2. 314f.). A "victim"? The text, as was shown above, suggests no such victimization. What then about "drive out *ratio*"? Here the commentator's ignorance of the Latin vocabulary helps him build up his (and his following's) untenable position: *nec sat rationis* is apparently taken to mean something like "not enough *rationality*"? But *ratio* (*OLD s.v.* 10: "a plan of action, scheme") here is a strategic concept: in seizing his arms (*in armis, scil. capiendis*, CN), there is "not enough of a strategic concept", but (*sed* 315) Aeneas needs military manpower to conduct an effective (even if ultimately doomed) defensive operation. So Aeneas' second thoughts, following his initial gut reaction (*arma amens capio*), are anything but 'irrational': spontaneous patriotic impulse is followed by awareness of the need for planning. Aeneas, upon gathering his group of desperate defenders, fires them, "hearts in vain so brave" (*fortissima frustra pectora* 2. 348f.), with the argument, "the only salvation for the defeated is to hope for no salvation"

una salus victis nullam sperare salutem 2. 354,

– an appeal by which "*furor* was instilled in the minds of the young warriors", *sic animis iuvenum furor additus* (355). Even in the hindsight of his report before Dido, Aeneas feels no blame for having defended Troy in a hopeless situation. On the contrary, he emotionally invokes "as witnesses" for his heroic conduct "the ashes of Troy and the final conflagration of my people" (*Iliaci cineres et flamma extrema meorum* 431).[31] Only the mistaken reading of *nec sat rationis in armis* ("thoughts of valour drive out *ratio*") is able to give a negative ring to the patriotic value of the *furor* that distinguishes brave Aeneas and his doomed band of fighters. Of course, the situation is quite different when Turnus' fighting frenzy, *furor*, is qualified by an addition: the strategically blind *furor* that drives "burning" (*ardentem*) Turnus inside the Trojan camp and obviates his side's victory, cannot have a positive meaning, especially since it is coupled with an "insane desire for slaughter" *caedisque insana cupido* (9. 760).

Having dismantled the faulty linguistic premise on which the thesis of Aeneas' derailed education in human self-control bases itself, I can more easily deal with its erroneous claims on the epic's closure. R. D. Williams mentions (*ad* 12. 887f.) "the fact" that "the reader expects Aeneas to show mercy and is profoundly disquieted when he does not". Killing his enemy "in a fit of fury...goes counter to all his efforts in the poem to overcome the *evil* effects of *furor* in himself and others" (my emphasis). "The reader" here apparently is an extrapolated R. D. Williams, who is "disquieted" when his expectations are not met by the ancient author, and his simplistic view of *furor* in the *Aeneid* hardly squares with the material I have detailed above.

So let it be stated unambiguously that Vergil's proto-Augustan hero does not have to be a follower of Immanuel Kant's *Kritik der praktischen Vernunft* to such an extent that dutiful acts are acknowledged only if they have been wrested from a resisting inclination. It is a misunderstanding to deny Vergil's concept of a hero *passionately* fighting or even hot patriotism (an attitude which Aeneas displays in the defense of Troy in Book 2 and which Vergil obviously wishes to be appreciated by his reader). Aeneas is supposed to be, among other things, *also* an Achilles (and a justified one, for that matter),[32] a Super-Achilles able to defeat the self-declared (9. 742) 'new Achilles' prophesied by the Sibyl (6. 89) who again threatens the Trojans' survival, this time on the soil of Italy as did the first one on the battlefield before Troy.

Nevertheless, one should be willing to examine the merits of the hypothesis that, in Vergil's eyes, Aeneas' retreat from the road of clemency

Chapter 2

at the sight of Pallas' sword-belt turns him "into a maniac, a terrifying addict of physicality and personal impulse", whose action is "a form of narcissism" which "never is made to reach out beyond individual self-gratification to any larger concerns", as Putnam, the most prominent interpreter of his school, put it.[33] After all, it is Putnam's merit to have most penetratingly attempted to prove that Vergil disapproves of his hero's final act.

Let us take up the question of "larger concerns" first. Here it must be emphasized that, according to convention, Aeneas is *obliged* to take revenge on Turnus,[34] especially so since Pallas' father had, from the grave of his son (so to speak), imposed on him the sacred duty. Evander solemnly spoke of Aeneas' "right arm...that, you see, owes Turnus to father and to son",

> ...dextera...tua..., Turnum gnatoque patrique
> quam debere vides 11. 178f.

Only a short-distance reader will, when reading the final scene, take the liberty of dispensing with the bereft father's forward-pointing words. Evander even said that Turnus' death was the only vacant spot on Aeneas' record of merits and success, and that he himself was alive waiting to take the news of the executed revenge down to his son (11. 176–81). Would Vergil have written such words for nothing? Those interpreters who chide Aeneas for his allegedly selfish and personal motivation in killing Turnus should also prove Evander's injunction to be without merit or influence. For otherwise they might incur the criticism of having ignored or suppressed their author's guidance in favor of an 'interpretation' that is more to their subjective taste. Evander's *mandata* (11. 176) can hardly be pushed aside as being the private emotion felt by a deprived father. Ever since offering hospitality and helpful guidance in Book 8, Evander has served as a mouthpiece of the authorial voice (see especially Chapter 4).

The assertion that "*pietas* toward Evander cannot claim a part in Aeneas' thoughts as he hesitates"[35] misses the critical moment: it is not during the hiatus of his hesitation (while listening to Turnus' pleading and gradually succumbing to his persuasion) that Evander's injunction would come back to Aeneas' mind (at that point, we showed, his mind is still set on the contracted duel's function as a means of ending the internecine war). But that he has never abandoned his intent of executing Evander's bidding and all along (ever since 10. 524f.) has had his sight set on punishing the killer of Pallas, is clear from several features, among which (as mentioned earlier) is first his use of the verb *eripere* at 12. 948: "are you to be *snatched away* (*eripiare*)" (scil., from me)? One does not see how use of this verb "furthers the impression of madness." Rather, its meaning points to Aeneas' long-standing resolve; and the metaphor hardly means that Aeneas' imagination now concretizes his "own possible instinct for *clementia*", perverting it "into a physical creature" (i.e., a body-snatcher or abductor). Vergil leaves the agent of the passive form *eripiare* undefined, and he gives no indication whatsoever that the reader should narrow down the agent to Aeneas' own "instinct for *clementia*". This reading would be inappropriate especially in view of the fact that the consideration Aeneas granted to Turnus' plea for mercy was based not on his gut reaction but on rationally weighing the possible validity of the reasons offered in Turnus' diversionary speech. Rather, one might think of the possible agent to *eripiare* as Turnus' forfeited argument of appealing to Anchises or to his own father's, Daunus', lonely situation.

Sparing the defeated enemy (it was shown above) was an appropriate consideration earlier when Turnus the conquered leader of the Italians asked for mercy. However, at this second stage, Aeneas' attention is drawn away from Turnus the defeated (and therefore, in Putnam's interpretation, pardonable) enemy toward Turnus the killer of the boy Pallas; when at this moment he sets (undeserved) clemency aside, his motive still need not be "private grief and private possessiveness"[36] – the name of Pallas, called out twice (12. 948), certainly brings back to long-distance readers the obligation so solemnly imposed by Evander – only short-distance readers would demand that Vergil here repeat the grieving father's solemn words.

Ancient commentators, Servius as well as Donatus, can still be correct in seeing Aeneas observing a twofold piety: he is *pius* while hesitating and contemplating mercy, and he shows *pietas* when obeying Evander's bidding and avenging Pallas' death (Serv. *ad* 12. 940). Donatus (*ad* 12. 947–49) emphasizes Aeneas' obligation of revenge owed *directly* to Pallas: *ecce servata est in persona Aeneae pietas qua volebat ignoscere, servata religio Pallanti*. It reveals something about ancient (as opposed to 'modern') attitudes that neither of these commentators, writing as late as the 4th/5th centuries AD (but possibly reflecting earlier material), views Aeneas as the mentally unhinged madman conceived by the latter half of the 20th century, but each bestows on his deed the highest praise of piety.

The question must be raised whether one may automatically assume that Vergil (or the authorial voice) shares modern-day feelings and demands for "someone soberly weighing alternative responses to *pietas* before performing the climactic action of his career – and of Vergil's epic."[37] With the answer to this question the hypothesis of a subversive, Rome-critical, or below-the-surface anti-Augustan (or whatever terms have been used) poet will stand or fall. Already, we saw that *pietas* is not so homogeneous and simple a concept that it is within the choice of the pious man to determine

Chapter 2

his 'responses'. For the complexity of *pietas* can place differing demands on its adherent, depending on the situations or cases under consideration.

Since there can be no doubt that Vergil's Aeneas is emotionally involved when exacting the blood penalty (*poenam* 12. 949) from Turnus, one will have to inquire how the text itself presents this involvement. First, we turn to Aeneas at the point of discovering Pallas' sword-belt on Turnus' shoulder (the point where we broke off our translation before, then only pointing to the *cum inversum* that at 12. 941 introduces the new, counteracting development), and later (in Chapters 3 and 4) we shall add and integrate more of the long view taken by Vergil in building his epic up to the closure of the final scene.

> (Aeneas had increasingly been persuaded by Turnus' pleading speech)
> when (suddenly) on top of the shoulder the luckless baldric struck his eyes
> and the belt flashed with the studs he knew,
> the belt of Pallas the boy whom, defeated with a wound, Turnus had struck down, and now he was wearing on his shoulder the trophy taken from the enemy.

> infelix umero cum apparuit alto
> balteus et notis fulserunt cingula bullis
> Pallantis pueri, victum quem vulnere Turnus
> straverat atque umeris inimicum insigne gerebat. 12. 941–44.

It is immediately obvious that Aeneas is undergoing a sort of *anagnorisis* as it is known from Tragedy. When the unlucky (*infelix*) shoulder-belt and, especially, the studs on the waist-belt strike his eyes (the studs are known, *nota*, to him, forming an *anagnorisma*), they bring up the association with its rightful owner, Pallas (*Pallantis*), and, next, the sorrow-raising fact that Pallas was so young, *a boy* (*pueri*) still, when he was set up and killed by the older and stronger Turnus in a fight of unequal powers (*viribus imparibus* 10. 459). This also brings back (as the reader together with Aeneas recalls) the bravery with which Pallas received the fatal wound in his chest (*vulnere*), unflinchingly facing mighty Turnus' oncoming spear (10. 478–85; details in Chapter 3).

Less immediately obvious to the modern reader are some of the details that shape this process of Aeneas' recognition. An obstacle to a correct understanding has been the prevalent opinion that *balteus* and *cingula* (plural) at 12. 942 refer to the same object, presumably a shoulder-belt or baldric. As the *Excursus* to the present chapter shows, *balteus* in the first place is (*pace OLD*) a *waist*-belt, as at *A*.12. 273f. Such a (leather) belt is traditionally decorated with rectangular plates that are riveted to the leather and embossed with cone-shaped elevations or mythological motifs (the *Excursus* cites the example of a plate with the Roman she-wolf and the twins, embossed within a circle of raised dots). Wealthier legionaries and horsemen (young Pallas was a horseman) would wear the belt over their mail coat (the prevalent type of armor in the *Aeneid*). So a *Roman* reader would, when reading of Pallas' *balteus* at 10. 496–98, naturally think of a waist-belt, and at 12. 941f. would need the addition of *umero* to be sure that here a *shoulder*-belt or band is addressed. The evidence submitted in the *Excursus* suggests that a Roman reader would take *cingula* at 12. 942 in its usual meaning of waist-belt or girdle. If the text is taken in this way, either term is allowed its distinct and specific meaning. It provides Turnus, who is wearing Pallas' equipment, with the type of sword suspension displayed by Pallas' father, Arcadian King Evander, who attaches (*subligat* 8. 459) his sword both to his side and to his shoulder. One may also think of the way in which Aeneas arranges the *tropaeum* of Etruscan King Mezentius (*ensem collo suspendit* 11. 11) and of the fact that Ascanius wears a sword-belt over his shoulder (9. 303). Though not changing my basic interpretation of Aeneas' thought process, the result of the *Excursus* adds significant details to its understanding.

The last word before the reader is introduced to Aeneas' perceptions is *infelix* (941): that the baldric is a source of misfortune, i.e., to Turnus, is not part of Aeneas' thoughts but is an objective comment by the author, pointing out the fulfillment of his earlier prediction (at 10. 502–505a) that a day will come when Turnus will hate these spoils, *spolia ista*. (Servius' interpretation, often repeated, *nullo domino felix*, misses the precise reference).

While Aeneas is still considering mercy, suddenly (*cum inversum*) the shoulder-band strikes his eyes. The word *umero* (we said) makes it clear to the Roman reader that *balteus* here signifies a band running over the shoulder, not the usual waist-belt. And *alto*, far from being a stopgap word, highlights the factual situation: Turnus, having collapsed *duplicato poplite* (927), must be considered being on his knees while delivering his crafty plea for mercy. In this position he offers to Aeneas' eyes first and foremost his head and shoulders. Following the sudden sight of the belt on top of the shoulder, Aeneas' eyes next follow it downward. At this moment, another sudden visual impression occurs (*et* in line 942 adds the new perception): the raised *bullae* on the plates of the waist-belt, reflecting the sun-light, flash (*fulserunt* is instantaneous perfect, used "in a punctual sense", *OLD s.v.* 1.b), and so trigger the mental process that results in recognizing the well-known (*notis*) pictorial representations. From what is detailed in the *Excursus*, one understands that Vergil's contemporary reader would assume the *bullae* to be embossed on the familiar rectangular belt-plates. Whether the flashes are produced by conical elevations, or by the raised pictorial presentations (such as in the *Excursus* exemplified by the she-wolf suckling the twins) themselves (pictorial plates that perhaps might alternate with the cone-plates), is a question that one would probably decide in favor of the pictorial *bullae*, considering two facts: (1) mere cones would hardly trigger Aeneas' *recognition*; and (2) the *impressum...nefas* of the slain bridegrooms (as it was described at 10. 497f.) is a crime that calls for punishment. In the eyes of the reader (as Chapter 3, Section 2 demonstrates in detail) the murdered bridegrooms symbolize and stand for young Pallas, so unfairly killed. The emotional effect that the sight of the *bullae* must have on Aeneas is easily understood by the reader who has followed the poet's guidance since the events in Book 10. It is true that Vergil at 12. 942f. does not once more mention the bloody decorations, but in view of the belt's predicted (10. 503–06) deleterious effect for Turnus – now about to be fulfilled – the representations of the murders cannot be discounted here in the final scene. Ancient (i.e., long-distance) readers, unlike some of their modern counterparts, would not fail to recall the reference contained in *notis* and would here apply the earlier description of the slain young men.

Recognizing the pictorial *bullae* is identical with being reminded of the rightful owner's unfair death. So it is the Danaid murders that, when recognized, lead Aeneas to recall the unfair way in which Pallas "the boy" was set up and killed. Here a third step is brought out in Aeneas' growing awareness: when raising his eyes again from the waist-belt to the kneeling man's shoulder (the double occurrence of the same word, *umero* in 941 and *umeris* in 944, marking steps I and III respectively, is far from being a careless duplication), he realizes that Turnus is wearing the band over his shoulder, that is, as a *mark of a military distinction or success*, as an *insigne*. (General Agrippa is wearing the *corona navalis* as a *belli insigne superbum* 8. 683.) The belt had belonged to Turnus' slain enemy, an enemy whom to have killed is of no great merit since the defeated was a boy still (*Pallantis pueri*) when struck down by the wound (*vulnere*).

The observation that Turnus is now unjustly wearing the sword-belt that is by right his enemy's (*inimicum*) raises a special point: against the *Aeneid'*s honor code, Turnus had appropriated his young enemy's belt for his own self-glorification (Pallas himself and pious Aeneas, on the other hand, were prepared to dedicate a slain enemy's armor to father Thybris or Mars Gradivus, 10. 421 and 542). Aeneas' sense of piety is here being reminded of a religious offense as well as of an act of injustice. (Likewise painful for Aeneas, the belt of course is only part of the equipment that was listed as missing from the funeral procession Aeneas had arranged for Pallas' corpse: *nam cetera Turnus / victor habet* 11. 91f.) Further, Servius is certainly right in emphasizing that Turnus took the belt for insult and bragging, not for a useful purpose (clearly he did not himself lack such a piece of equipment), *ad insultationem et iactantiam, non ad utilitatem* (ad 941).

So Aeneas is (as is the reader) further reminded not only of the unfair killing (as described in Book 10), but he is visibly confronted with the dishonorably acquired and arrogantly displayed symbol of victory (*insigne*) – another, newly perceived, instance of Turnus acting as a *superbus*. Already at 11. 394f. Turnus had pompously bragged that he had destroyed King Evander's "whole house with its progeny", *Euandri totam cum stirpe...domum* – not an incorrect claim, considering that aged Father Evander had called Pallas his "dear boy, my *only* and late joy", *care puer, mea sola et sera voluptas* (8. 581; cf. *spes et solacia nostri*, 8. 514).

Vergil has provided sufficient details to make his reader aware of an intensifying appeal to Aeneas' sense of empathy, piety and justice. However, the kind of action required as a response to *this* challenge and moral obligation would have to be different from the clemency he was just before contemplating toward the defeated and now submissive (*humilis* 930) enemy leader: the pardoning exemption would have to be annulled, and Aeneas would have, for long-standing, newly rekindled reasons, to act in a non-forgiving way (that would also amount to reinstituting the terms and the originally projected deadly outcome of the duel).

> After he had with his eyes taken in the memorial of savage pain
> and the spoil (the trophy), Aeneas, incensed with rage and terrible
> in his wrath {called out}: "You, dressed in the spoils of my close one(s),
> are you after this going to be snatched away from me? It is Pallas, Pallas
> who sacrifices you with this wound and exacts the penalty from your
> criminal blood."

> Ille, oculis postquam saevi monumenta doloris
> exuviasque hausit, furiis accensus et ira
> terribilis: "tune hinc spoliis indute meorum
> eripiare mihi?" Pallas te hoc vulnere, Pallas
> immolat et poenam scelerato ex sanguine sumit." 12. 945–49

Ille, as Donatus remarks, is Aeneas at the point of granting pardon. The 'changed', no longer forgiving, Aeneas grows out of (comes *after*, cf. *postquam* 945) the visual experience (*oculis*). That is, the poet expressly develops the new state of wrathful emotion out of the preceding process of recognition: *saevi monumenta doloris* in all likelihood refers to the belt displaying the Danaids' *nefas*; and the spoil (*exuvias*) recalls (provided – *que* does not merely add an explanation, "and that is") the next step in Aeneas' recognition, i.e., possibly the shoulder band alone, recognized before as a wrongful trophy, 944. (*Exuviae* as "trophy" [in the modern sense] is so common that already Cicero could use it figuratively as a personal victory adornment: *tu ornatus exuviis huius, Sul.* 50.) The verb *hausit* ("drank in") then draws together the detailed steps of Aeneas' recognition process.

Chapter 2

Why would the poet make his readers partake of the thoughts and feelings that go through the hero's mind before his final action? The savage pain; recollection of "the boy's" unfair death; the murdered bridegrooms seen on the belt; the outrage felt at the impious appropriation and triumphant display of Pallas' sword-belt, property of "the one(s) close to Aeneas". The word *meorum*, here referring to Pallas (and possibly to his father, Evander) is the same term (and reveals a comparable emotional value) Aeneas employed when calling upon "the ashes of Troy and the final conflagration of *my close ones*" (*Iliaci cineres et flamma extrema meorum* 2. 431) as witnesses (cf. *testor* 432) of his dutiful ultimate service to the country. (He then was defending himself against the potential accusation of having been remiss in defending the city.)[38] His father, Anchises, employed the word when he intended to hearten Aeneas by solemnly revealing to him "the (future) descendants here of *my people*", *hanc prolem cupio enumerare meorum* (6. 717). The same tone of kindred piety and national loyalty was sounded when Aeneas explained to Dido that, given the chance, it was not she who would be his first priority but

> I would first dedicate myself to the city of Troy and the sweet remnants of those close to me
>
> urbem Troianam primum dulcisque *meorum* reliquias colerem 4. 342f.

The word *meorum* at 12. 947 confirms that Aeneas has included Pallas in the circle of those who have an inviolable prior claim on his loyalty, for whom he must and will do whatever he can to act on their behalf. It is a grave misunderstanding to discount the moral obligation toward others that reverberates in *meorum*: 'Private grief and private possessiveness – hence his double emphasis on "mine" and "me" – now rule his actions.'[39] As in the night of Troy's fall, rage and wrath (about the enemy's un-heroic ruse) rushed his mind to noble deeds (*furor iraque mentem praecipitat*, 2. 316f.), so now he, incensed by rage (about Turnus setting up and unheroically killing "Pallas the boy", *Pallantis pueri*, 12.943) and terrible in his wrath, *furiis accensus et ira / terribilis* (12. 946f.; I have explained earlier that the value of *ira* as well as of *furiae* and *furor* depends on the context), must not allow Pallas' killer, dressed in the wrongfully appropriated spoils of his close one (*spoliis indute meorum*) to get away from Pallas' obligated avenger (*eripiare mihi?*); but, putting himself into the slain man's position, Aeneas renders the final service to his young ally who had not been able to defend himself against his superior attacker (it was the age difference that had saved Turnus from dying at the hands of Pallas, according to father Evander 11. 173–5):

> it is Pallas who sacrifices you with this wound, Pallas,
> who exacts the penalty from your criminal blood.
>
> Pallas te hoc vulnere, Pallas
> immolat et poenam scelerato ex sanguine sumit. 12. 948f.

So Aeneas feels he is acting vicariously: it is not alone he on his own behalf who does the killing here, but it is also Pallas (with Aeneas as his personally-involved avenging instrument) who performs a *sacrifice* and exacts the just punishment from Turnus' *criminal* blood. *Immolare* is also the word used when, after Pallas' death, Aeneas takes eight enemies prisoner to sacrifice them to the shade of Pallas, *quos immolet umbris* (10. 519). In a way, Turnus is being added to their number. One can hardly deny that it is, at least in Aeneas' own understanding, by all means a pious wrath that makes him strike the – in his feeling, deserved – death blow, and the correspondence of the avenging wound and the original one caused by Turnus is pronounced even in metrical symmetry (see below).

We must note that Aeneas' words are addressed to Turnus (*tu...te*, 947f.), *explaining* to him the changed situation: '{As the defeated (or, in the alternative interpretation, now submissive) enemy of my people, you had a claim on my consideration, which took me to the brink of pardoning you. But} this is a different case and a different situation: now it is *Pallas*, *Pallas the boy* so unfairly killed by you, who requires your punishment.' I have to emphasize the distinction between the two cases (well recognized by ancient interpreters. Their commingling has sometimes led modern readers to accuse Aeneas of denying a defeated enemy the pardon due to him according to the conventions of interstate warfare, as outlined to Aeneas by Anchises: *parcere subiectis*, 6. 853).

It has been pointed out that it is not Vergil's voice we hear at this moment but that of his main character, and it has been emphasized that the poet does not *expressis verbis* endorse his hero's reasoning and feelings.[40] Why then (to resume the question asked earlier) would the poet have taken his readers step by step into the depths of Aeneas' soul, his pain and his loyalty, the hurt to his sense of justice and piety, if not to make them understand his hero's motivation – and to persuade them to sympathize with it? Would it not have been counter-productive to detail the painful emotions that influence Aeneas' decision if the poet's intention had been to alienate his reader from Aeneas and to make us view his action as repulsive? Without having recourse to ancient theories of human wrath and fury, one can see that the text itself provides its reader with apposite standards of how to measure the hero's conduct. After all, the author has over a number of Books repeatedly informed his reader of Turnus' criminal behavior (*scelerato...sanguine* at 12. 949 is not an inappropriate characterization;

Chapter 2

one need only recall Turnus' initial *scelerata insania belli* of 7. 461), and, on the other side, Aeneas' wrath and rage are quite comparable to his laudable attitude in Book 2 where his death-defying fighting, guided by the same emotions (2. 316f.), would deservedly have earned him death at the hands of the invading Greeks (2. 433f.). If some miss an express authorial endorsement of Aeneas' final act, they should also accept that there is no reproach pronounced either on which they might base their own condemnation of Aeneas; but, if they cannot accept Vergil's portrait of Aeneas' emotions as depicted in the final scene (and of the details that arouse them), they should also provide convincing and detailed evidence from the text that would support an understanding hostile to Aeneas, and they should further take into account how much is said, in the Books leading up to the final scene, that favors Aeneas' position (including the obligation placed on his right arm by the victim's – i.e., Pallas' – father). It would be hard indeed, after the contrasting portraits of Turnus and Aeneas in Books 7–12, without any (con-)textual evidence to claim convincingly that the author in the final scene has reversed his valuations. It appears that the misreading of Aeneas in the epic's opening books (his Achillean attitude in Juno's storm at sea; his engaged heroism in defending Troy) favors the misreading of the hero's authorial characterization at the end.

And, though Aeneas is here concentrating on the obligation toward Pallas, the attentive reader will not have forgotten the larger context: Aeneas had long before threatened Turnus with the penalty for his breach of the peace (*quas poenas mihi, Turne, dabis*, 8. 538); and King Latinus, too, had threatened that for peace-breaking Turnus the death penalty would be waiting (7. 596f.). At least, even when setting the question of the author's position momentarily aside, one cannot deny that Aeneas himself, as depicted by his creator, subjectively feels he is executing a pious action, combining sacrifice with punishment (*Pallas te hoc vulnere.../ immolat* 12. 948f.).

Certainly, there is no "shifting of agency" from Aeneas to Pallas ("*Pallas te hoc vulnere, Pallas / immolat*") as if there were a de-personalization taking place and Aeneas would transfer his volition to Pallas ("his words curiously distance him from his deed"),[41] failing to show a will of his own. On the contrary, Aeneas' calling out the name of Pallas *twice* does not cancel out his personal involvement as it has unfolded in Vergil's detailed description of his *anagnorismos* and his savage pain: it is an act of even more intensely identifying himself with the lot of Pallas. For modern sensitivity it may be hard to accept Vergil's moral standard. But to assume that, as Augustus exercised personal power while claiming to rule through the republican institutions, so Vergil intends Aeneas' case to be understood as one of "private vengeance cloaking itself in legality, an act of judicial murder",[42] means circuitously carrying a later historian's (perhaps Syme's) terms of judging *Augustus* into the work of Augustus' *supporter*. The resulting "different reading of the end of the *Aeneid*" is bought at the cost of suppressing the climax of emotions Vergil ascribes to Aeneas. We shall have to return to Quint's way of constructing[43] a "different reading" because it is characteristic of some recent 'methodologies' that result in subverting the poet's text and, therefore, require attention in the context of dealing with the final scene.

What most irks moderns appears to be the unquestioned idea of retribution or revenge contained in that punishing sacrifice executed by Aeneas. But there is emphasis precisely on that "wound-for-wound" aspect, which strikes the reader's ear by metrical echo:

quem vulnere Turnus (12. 943)
te hoc vulnere Pallas (12. 948)

Those who take offense at Aeneas the avenger, not only (as shown earlier in this chapter) construct a Turnus who is far removed from Vergil's text. They also implicitly move Vergil out of his contemporary world for which (as likewise indicated earlier) *ultio* was an unquestioned given. Even the thought of "sacrificing" Turnus (often assumed by modern-day interpreters to be condemned by Vergil) is not alien to the *Aeneid*: it can be seen in line with Aeneas' capture of eight young enemy warriors in Book 10 who are to be sacrificed on the grave of Pallas. Chapter 3 shows in detail that Aeneas' conduct in Book 10, though often deplored (even hypothetically excised from the text) by Gentle Vergil interpreters, carries the author's seal of approval, and that human sacrifice is not so alien to Vergil's contemporaries as many 20th-century AD (and even some first-century BC) observers of Roman history liked to fashion it. (Even the killing of Pallas' slayer *at the end of the hostilities* finds a contemporary parallel in Octavian's hunting down and killing the last two surviving assassins of his "father" *after* his victory of Alexandria.)

There is no way around precise and detailed explanation of the text. Among scholars discussed here, Putnam deserved the recognition and deliberation due to his detailed involvement with the final scene, even if the present interpreter does not see fit to accept his results (or endorse his interpretative approach). But, after the explanation of *meorum* (12. 947) given above as involving obligation or duty owed to men of kindred status, and *mihi* (948) as involving the pious avenger, one will hardly see this "double emphasis" as a negative feature, pointing to "private grief and private possessiveness".[44] In addition it must be said that personal

Chapter 2

obligation does hardly, in Vergil's and his public's eyes, detract from the praise owed to the avenger, as ancient evidence documents.

A striking near-parallel combination of simultaneous public and private vengeance (here, however, without any thought of the clemency that Aeneas does contemplate toward Turnus) is found in Caesar's *de Bello Gallico* (1. 12). It throws light on Roman values, to which Caesar gears his presentation (Mutschler demonstrates the obligation of *pietas* which requires an act of *ultio* in favor of Caesar's killed predecessor).[45]

The circumstances are as follows: Caesar in a surprise attack kills the major part of the Tigurini (the rest flee into the woods), members of the tribe that in 107 BC had killed consul L. Cassius and sent his army under the yoke: so, through Caesar's action, the tribe "paid its penalty", *poenas persolvit*. In the same battle of 107 the Tigurini had also killed the grandfather of Caesar's father-in-law. *Qua in re Caesar non solum publicas sed etiam privatas iniurias ultus est* ("In this action Caesar has executed revenge not only for injuries committed against the state but also for private injuries", 1.12.7).

In view of Caesar's notorious endeavor of cultivating his public image, his combination of satisfying the requirements of public as well as of private *ultio* may indicate how Vergil could expect Aeneas' final action to be received by the Roman reading public: there would be no blame found in exacting a (semi-) private revenge in a situation in which Aeneas had initially considered pardoning the defeated enemy. One may even add that, in killing Pallas' killer, Aeneas not only avenged a personal loss (the private aspect being, moreover, overshadowed by the obligation Father Evander had placed on his "right arm"), but also the death of an allied leader (comparable to Caesar's *ultio* on behalf of consul L. Cassius). Strictly speaking, the killing of Turnus was less of a "private" act than Caesar's taking revenge for the grandfather of his father-in-law.[46]

It likewise is methodologically important not to introduce later, perhaps specifically Christian, ideas into the final scene. Lactantius blames Aeneas (and in doing so he is aiming his critique at Vergil himself), among other things, for acting *furiis accensus et ira* (*sic*! *D.Inst.* 5. 10. 8; cf. Vergil, *A*. 12. 948). However, Lactantius uses the passage outside its context, to blame Aeneas for killing suppliant Magus in Book 10 (cf. 10. 521–36; on Magus, see Chapter 3, Section 3 below). Even more careless, Lactantius protests that *bonus Aeneas haud aspernanda precantis* (11. 106) "*trucidavit*" (sic; *D.Inst.* 5. 10. 8), whereas Vergil's own text continues *prosequitur venia* (11. 107). He also, again without regard for the special situation, blames Aeneas for – in his wrath – disregarding an appeal to his father, Anchises. So, according to Lactantius, Aeneas is without any virtue, "because he flared up in fury like straw and was unable to curb his wrath, forgetful of his father's shade by which he was being implored", *qui et furore tamquam stipula exarserit et manium patris per quem rogabatur oblitus iram frenare non quiverit* (*D.Inst.* 5.10. 9). Lactantius' inference about Aeneas, *nullo igitur modo pius*, appears close to that of Putnam (Aeneas' killing of Turnus "could be seen, in fact, as the final *impietas*" [etc.]),[47] and so also Lactantius' condemnation of Aeneas, quoted by Lactantius as *furiis accensus et ira*, is close enough to Putnam's verdict: "No one *furiis accensus*, fired by furies, is acting contemplatively."[48]

At first sight, then, it may appear that what I would like to call the 'Gentle Vergil school' is in harmony with Lactantius: both view the enraged Aeneas as impious. But below the surface there is a fundamental and instructive difference. Whereas Putnam and other interpreters of his persuasion confidently assume that Vergil himself shares their feelings and therefore conclude that the poet must, as they do, abhor Aeneas' final action, Lactantius follows a different route: attacking Vergil for holding a mistaken (non-Christian) idea of piety, he views Aeneas as the mouthpiece and representative of the poet's own convictions; i.e., Lactantius blames *Vergil* for his mistaken belief that Aeneas' abominable actions are to be considered pious: *illud ipsum quod nefarie, quod detestabiliter fecit* [*scil., Aeneas*], *pietatis esse officium credidisti* (*Di.* 5. 10. 7). So, if taken at his word, Lactantius could be listed as understanding Vergil as the poet is interpreted in the present chapter (and consequently as detesting and condemning the *poet himself* and not only – as recent interpreters do – his protagonist).

If one prefers to understand the final scene in a context immediately contemporary with Vergil's own time, the closest widely known parallel is probably Augustus who in his *Res Gestae* (2; cf. 21) ascribes a considerable part of his bloody early career to his pious obligation to take revenge for his (adoptive) father's assassination. He liked to call himself C. Julius Caesar's "avenger" (so Horace addresses "Mercury"-Octavian in his temporary incarnation as *Caesaris ultor*, *O.* 1. 2. 41–44). Augustus, too, was both relentless and persistent in hunting down the killers of his adoptive father. Publius Turullius and Cassius Parmensis, the two last surviving assassins, were executed in 30 BC, fourteen years after the deed. The temple of Mars the Avenger was dedicated in 2 BC, four decades (!) after the occasion that it commemorated. If a contemporary Roman sought guidance in fathoming the emotions of a loyal avenger of the father-son relationship, Vergil's *Aeneid* would be able to provide him with what he needed: Fatherly Aeneas, stepping in for aged Father Evander, avenging Evander's son.

This opens access to the epic's closing (and we do mean *closing*) lines:

Chapter 2

> Seething, he with these words pushes his sword deep into the chest in front
> of him.
> But Turnus' limbs are loosened in a chill,
> and with a groan his life, resentful, departs to the shades below.

> hoc dicens ferrum adverso sub pectore condit
> fervidus; ast illi solvuntur frigore membra
> vitaque cum gemitu fugit indignata sub umbras. 12. 950–52

That Aeneas is 'seething', places him close to Trojan Pandarus who likewise is described as *fervidus* when trying to take revenge for his slain brother Bitias (*mortis fraternae fervidus ira*, 9. 736). The *Aeneid* hardly suggests censuring Aeneas for such feelings on behalf of his unfairly slain young disciple.

As mentioned earlier but worth recalling here, the maiden warrior Camilla shares with Turnus the same expression of indignation about dying (11. 831=12. 952); but: Camilla did have a heroic reason for her departing soul's discontent; for she had been covertly stalked by her cowardly slayer. In the case of Turnus, *indignata* points to the unheroic wish to live.[49]

Having traced Turnus' conduct ever since his tempestuous departure from King Latinus' *concilium magnum* in Book 11, the present interpretation gains an advantage over those readers who believe that dealing with the last scene (or perhaps even with the last thirty lines) of the *Aeneid* is sufficient for ascertaining the work's message. For it turns out to be a mistaken belief to suppose that Turnus' diversionary speech before his death is grounded in a serious heroic impulse. After three (four, if one includes 12. 734) times dodging the consequences of his boastful challenge, there is no authorial indication offered that Turnus can be seen at the last as experiencing a 'deathbed conversion' to genuine heroism. Such an inconsistency would be singular in Vergil's depiction of his characters. Even the monster Mezentius, in "knowingly" accepting the deathblow, does not leave the parameters of his career as a ruthless fighter.

(3) Excursus I
Circuitous Readings: Derivatives in Classical Scholarship
Intertextuality, Verbal Echo, Maphaeus Vegius, Psychoanalysis, Analogy, Topical Allusion

It would be gratifying if the reader deemed the present critical excursus superfluous because (s)he found the interpretation of the epic's climax as offered in the preceding section convincing by itself. However, the powerful vogue represented in the vast modern body of speculative and circuitous readings of the *Aeneid* makes the present writer doubt whether he has dissuaded his audience from assuming that a strictly text-based interpretation in itself would suffice.

Though complex and demanding, the work's climactic final scene does not lack guidance, both short-term and long-distance, for the reader who has been willing to track (and follow) the leads offered by the author. Where then to look for reasons that have led to frequent misunderstanding? The most pervasive (though less than scholarly, even if understandable on the human level) motive is found in a preconceived desire that Vergil may prove to be more humane than his contemporary fellow-Romans are usually judged to be by historians.

A (misleading) lead is often taken from Anchises' *parcere subiectis*, understood as "pardon the defeated", without much attention being paid to his *debellare superbos*, "fight down the proud", (or to *subiectis*) in the same line (6. 853). Anchises' pronouncement is preceded only a few lines earlier, in the same context of Roman expansion and domination, by his praise for L. Mummius (the widely decried plunderer of Corinth), *victor* over Achaea in 146 BC, "distinguished by <u>slain</u> Greeks", <u>*caesis* insignis Achivis</u> (6. 837), and for L. Aemilius Paullus, styled by *"pater"* Anchises (6. 854) as *avenger* of Rome's Trojan ancestors, *ultus avos Troiae* (6. 840) because of his defeat of Perseus, Achilleus' presumed descendant, at Pydna (168 BC). Obviously, 'pardoning' Father Anchises is not 'disquieted' (to use the present-day litcrit term) by the fact that Paullus, the (often called 'philhellenic') avenger, executed the enslavement and deportation program of 150,000 Epirotes (though, it is true, his clemency allowed Perseus to live on in captivity).

So Vergil's Anchises can by no means be cited in favor of an all-inclusive policy of pardoning the defeated (as has been done by way of an erroneous reference in the case of Aeneas avenging Pallas on Turnus).[50] The question, then, arises whether there exists a literary critical method providing credible evidence for a Vergilian voice of *non-partisan* humane import, beyond the imperial sentiment that reserves sympathy predominantly for the Trojan-Roman side while assigning guilt (and, therefore, *deserved* punishment) to the opposing party. Here the controversial sphere of possible Vergilian ambivalence (or even polysemy as well as polyphony) requires our attention. I shall satisfy this requirement by discussing in detail a small selection of representative cases *in concreto* rather than theoretically and comprehensively.[51]

My first example is taken from the area of intertextuality. Barchiesi, on the basis of intertextual Homeric "models", separates Aeneas the vengeful killer from the hesitating, merciful Aeneas – as if Aeneas, after his clement hesitation, distances himself from the death blow he is about to strike:

Chapter 2

"it is not I – whom you supplicate- who is about to kill you: it is Pallas", "*non sono io – quello che tu supplichi – ad ucciderti: è Pallante.*"[52] This of course disregards the textual emphasis, reinforced by the caesurae and by the counterbalance *tu...mihi* (12. 947f.), on Aeneas' personal involvement: *tune...eripiare mihi?* Are *you* to be snatched away from *me*?

Barchiesi objects to the opinion that intertextual analysis results in "a reading of the text that is reductive, formalistic, and mechanistic", "*letture del testo riduttive, formalistiche e meccanicistiche*".[53] But it does appear reductive as well as circular, to derive an interpretation of Aeneas' conduct in the final scene from Homeric "models", viz., from Achilles the (killing) avenger of Patroclus in *Iliad* 22 and from the (relenting) Achilles in Book 24 who listens to Priam appealing to his feelings for his father Peleus. Barchiesi claims that "the analysis of models presupposed by Vergil turns out to provide an *adequate* picture of the difficult dialectic between compassion and revenge", "*l'analisi dei modelli presupposti da Virgilio riesce a dare un'immagine adeguata della difficile dialettica fra misericordia e ultio*".[54]

The argument is far from being unobjectionable (and not only because it implicitly assumes that Vergil is unable to create a text whose message is intelligible in itself and on its own merit). Even if Turnus, like Priam addressing Achilles, uses the most effective argument known to ancient rhetoric by not only introducing his own "miserable" aged father Daunus but also by appealing to Aeneas' feelings for his father Anchises – this does not prove that Vergil here is making a genuine case for *misericordia* toward Turnus rather than characterizing the rhetorical craftiness of shifty Turnus. The unspoken premise of Barchiesi (as well as of others) is that the moral dilemma must be sought in Aeneas ("...the text of Vergil 'makes' Aeneas' choice 'difficult'" "...*il testo virgiliano 'rende difficile' la scelta di Enea*")[55] instead of in the (by the narrator's standards) immoral conduct of Turnus.

Once Aeneas catches sight of the sword-belt of Pallas, he no longer has the choice to exercise the forgiveness he increasingly contemplated toward the defeated enemy (*parcere subiectis*...): as explained earlier, Aeneas now is under a *different* obligation. There is no "difficile dialettica".

A methodological danger inherent in "intertextuality" exploration is that the author's very own agenda and train of thought may be subjected to and deemed determinable through supposed "models". This amounts to circuitous reading (and incorrect results).[56]

It appears far-fetched to maintain that through conflicting "models" Vergil leads his reader to a critical reflection on the tension between the two ideas.[57] A "precise intertextual effect"[58] can be claimed only by a short-distance reader ("this brief episode")[59] who (in addition to misreading Vergil's distinction between the two kinds of obligation) neglects the guidance that the poet has supplied on Turnus through all of Books 11 and 12 (not to say ever since Book 7). The long-distance reader, observing Aeneas on the verge of noble forgiveness, has been instructed by the author to see that in the case of Turnus clemency, if exercised, would be undeserved (and, besides, only lead to new breaches of peace , though this latter aspect has nothing to do with Aeneas' motive when killing Turnus).

Much modern scholarship has spun itself in a cocoon of denial with regard to the degree of violence (not to say brutality) accepted in the *Aeneid*. This has led to bizarre results: the affinity that Fascism and Nazism claimed with the *Aeneid*'s imperial ideology has been declared to be based on a total misunderstanding or misinterpretation. For those early-20th-century ideologies were not yet acquainted with the 'politically correct' interpretation of the *Aeneid* that was developed in the 20th century's latter half, an interpretation which sometimes (though not in the very beginning)[60] was viewed as a reaction to American imperialism and the military engagement in Vietnam, from which one wished to see the *Aeneid*'s spirit far removed, so that one might save Vergil's presumed (and obviously endangered) 'humanity'.[61] One more recent book (Thomas 2001), written in defense of the Harvard school, has in hindsight been reviewed under the headline "A Virgil for Vietnam".[62]

Dissatisfaction especially with the *Aeneid*'s actual ending has here led to circularly presuming a 2000-year pro-Augustan conspiracy that allegedly has suppressed an ambiguous, ambivalent poet: in short, the real Vergil. The alleged conspirators (poets as well as interpreters) have supposedly engaged in 'rewriting' and, so, have falsified the (supposedly true) Harvard Vergil, by unduly glorifying Aeneas (and blackening his opponent Turnus).[63] Some members of this allegedly misguided group are (roughly in the order in which they are discussed or listed by Thomas) Fascists and Nazis (with the shining exception of the refugee Broch [hardly an authority on Vergil][64] and the less shining anti-Fascist Sforza),[65] Syme, Maphaeus Vegius (a 15th century author of what is called the "thirteenth book of the *Aeneid*" – see below), Ariosto, Tasso, Stahl, Cairns, Galinsky, Milton – not to forget an earlier critique of Dryden.

Thomas, espousing what in recent decades has often been termed the "pessimism" of Vergil (Thomas himself has meanwhile dropped the term) repeatedly blames "Augustan" (or, as they are enigmatically called, "optimistic") interpreters for taking seriously the *Aeneid*'s panegyric passages and for not acceding to his school's thesis of Vergilian "ambivalence"; he has no patience with skeptical scholars who may not be persuaded that, e.g., Vergil "communicates a profound ambiguity" when saying that Augustus will found a new Golden Age. What the poet really means, Thomas (as shown earlier) speculates, is that Augustus – and this at the end of the dreadful civil wars! – "will again *close out* ages of gold".[66]

Modern-day unhappiness about the ending of the *Aeneid* has proved a strong motive in the search for ambiguity, and this search in turn has produced cases of intellectual *salto mortale* and of intertextual acrobatics, which, by their circular reasoning, tend to cloud a clear view of the *Aeneid* itself. It is significant that, e.g., Thomas himself forgoes a context-based, line-by-line interpretation (as offered in the present volume) of key passages in the final scene, instead pointing vicariously to another scholar's (viz., Quint's) as "one of the better recent treatments of the finale".[67] For himself, he 'exposes', in chapter after chapter, an alleged conspiracy of falsifiers who are deemed throughout history to have imposed "forced closure" on the allegedly open-ended epic (the standard of Thomas' literary judgement being the usual middle-to-late 20th century subjective feelings of "dissatisfaction", "uneasiness", or lack of "*comforting* ethical closure that is so lacking and *so yearned for*", in short: the yearning for a modern-day feel-good *Aeneid*).[68]

Those 'optimists' who are suspected of having as if by conspiracy *suppressed* the (supposedly) true, "pessimistic", (sub-surface) regime-critical Vergil are portrayed as *personally* holding a pro-Augustan, allegedly "optimistic" view: as if a pro-Augustan *Aeneid* were a cause for optimism, except in certain imperialistic scholarly (and political) quarters of the late 19th and early-to-middle 20th centuries. But for purposes of polemics, it apparently is considered profitable to take scholars' findings as an expression of their personal convictions, calling the scholars, too, "optimists" – a polemical labeling in which Thomas is far from alone. The underlying suspicion apparently is that scholars who arrive at different results cannot be motivated by an endeavor for objectivity but, like Thomas himself ("I decided to go looking for *my* Virgil elsewhere... I found him being suppressed and avoided..."),[69] are guided by a desire to find their personal views ("...my own views...were very much formed by reading Virgil in the context of a culture *troubled* by the exercise of power in Vietnam")[70] confirmed in Vergil and/or in the history of his reception. The result is a Vergil set off specifically against the spirit of Augustus' *Res Gestae* and Augustus' "shortcomings in the court of *humanitas* and *clementia*" – a Vergil who allegedly "remains unblinking in sustaining his focus on the exceptions, on those who lose and die, whether or not they ask for pardon – which incidentally Turnus did, thereby meriting the outcome that the author of the *Res Gestae* claims was the norm."[71] Thomas himself admits (note 8) that Augustus continues with "an escape clause" (available also to "the Augustan Vergilian") as follows: *externas gentes, quibus tuto ignosci potuit, conservare quam excidere malui* ("foreign nations that could be pardoned *safely* I preferred to preserve rather than to extinguish"). By banishing this quotation to his footnote, Thomas avoids discussing whether or not Turnus as portrayed by Vergil might have been pardoned "safely".

If so simple (not to say: simplistic) a moral formula of 'ask for pardon and be forgiven' is imposed on the complexity of the *Aeneid*'s nuanced narrative, the interpreter might indeed smoothly arrive at "a poem that constantly and powerfully confuses victor and victim".[72] Vergil's ideologically-colored horror story that reserves compassion mainly for 'victims' on the *Trojan* side (see, e.g., Nisus, Euryalus and the 'demoralizing' anti-war harangue of Euryalus' disconsolate mother at 9. 473–502), that, further, even uses compassion for the rank and file enemy in order to denigrate the enemy's leader (scil., Turnus) by portraying him as the unfeeling sacrificer of his own people for his personal goals (see what was said earlier about 11. 203–19) – such less than 'comforting' aspects of the *Aeneid* apparently exceed the range of Thomas' line of interpretation. These aspects also disprove the wishful picture of Vergil's non-partisan ethics as offered by the Compassionate Vergil School. Unpleasant as it may be, it is indispensable to keep in mind the political climate that Vergil's epic helped to engender. It probably was Hyginus (former slave of Augustus and writer of a commentary on the *Aeneid*) who contributed to the Emperor's concept of the *forum Augustum* with its fusion of Roman history and achievements of the Julian family, both represented on an equal footing (reflected in facing rows of statues pre-interpreted for the viewer by added *elogia* from the Emperor's hand or inspiration, with Romulus and Aeneas taking prominent positions at the distant flanks of Augustus). The pompous design of the temple of *Mars Ultor*, though ecumenically acculturated beyond the Graeco-Roman tradition and culminating in an apsis,[73] nevertheless concentrated on the Julians' divine connections. The *quadriga*, centrally placed in the *forum*, provided by a respectful Senate for the "Father of the Country", *Pater Patriae*, reinforced the central role assigned to the bringer of the new Golden Age, as Vergil had described him (*A.* 6. 792f.) (outdone only by the Savior of the World, *mundi salvator*, as Propertius had called him, 4. 6. 37). Considering the function of the *forum Augustum* as the official place for the highest military, civic, and imperial occasions, it is hardly an exaggeration to say that Hyginus, like a Roman Leni Riefenstahl (and the Forum's unknown architect like an Augustan Albert Speer) helped to design suitable 'parade' grounds for the physical display of the Emperor's ideology. There is no doubt that it was Vergil who (either under highest directive, as antiquity reports, or freely and all on his own, as the late 20th century liked to imagine the vatic poet's activity) helped to develop the original formula, especially in Anchises' 'parade of Roman heroes' (*A*. 6. 746–853). The main difference, as Zanker accurately saw,[74] is one of perspective: whereas the *Aeneid* looks forward from Aeneas' time to the future that will culminate in Augustus' Golden Age, the *forum Augustum*, now that the *Aeneid*'s pre-Roman prophecies are fulfilled, looks back to the ancestral foundations and their promise. Both perspectives are tied together in the idea of a fated mission (so ingeniously conceived in the *Aeneid*) that makes the coming of the Augustan Principate appear inevitable (and the recent civil war an unsavory aberration from the path of destiny and justice, perpetrated by the forces of impiety). It is, artistically speaking, one of the advantages of the unitarian perspective taken in the present volume that the 'body' of the *Aeneid* can be demonstrated to be in agreement with its grand prophecies. Anti-Augustan interpreters have found it necessary to try to break off the prophecies and isolate them as 'set pieces' with perspectives not endorsed by their author. They apparently do not realize that they may burden their author with a charge of opportunism.

It is helpful to keep the larger picture in mind when we now return to examples of the way reception history has been utilized to support and promote certain 'readings' of the *Aeneid*. One piece, proceeding by way of indirect defense and, so, advocating the existence of a presumably neglected "pessimistic" tradition, introduces itself with the words 'Historicizing the "Harvard school"' (Kallendorf 1999). This title aptly (though unintendedly) vocalizes the methodological dilemma underlying such purpose-driven, circuitous attempts at a *Rezeptionsgeschichte* that is asked to stand in for a close and methodologically adequate reading of the *Aeneid* itself: as if latter-day (mis-) understanding would gain in scholarly force and credibility if there had been numerous predecessors (a sort of self-perpetuating, scholastic argumentation comparable to pre-Copernican 'astronomy').

In the interest of a strict methodology, the present context requires me to deal more closely with this representative article. Kallendorf is guided by a desire to provide his bivocalist school with a long ancestry. He starts with Lactantius' condemnation of Vergil's Aeneas (as quoted earlier in this chapter: *nullo igitur modo pius*, "therefore, in no way pious"), without however mentioning that Lactantius' condemnation is aimed at the poet himself. He then focuses on "five scholars of the Italian Renaissance whose approach to the *Aeneid* shows affinities to the pessimistic approach of the 'Harvard school'".[75]

A key figure here is Maphaeus Vegius (1407–58), whose *Aeneidos Liber XIII* (today often quoted as the *Supplement*), written cento-like in Vergilian language, was for long attached to editions of the *Aeneid* (as it has been again by the Binders in their recent translation of the *Aeneid*). It 'completes' the epic by disregarding the Vergilian closure and compositional climax of the final duel in favor of naively narrating details (Turnus' burial, Aeneas' marriage to Lavinia, the building of his city [Lavinium], etc., etc.) that Vergil himself has either not described at all or artfully embedded in earlier predictions (e.g., in Jupiter's revelation to Venus in Book 1). As Schneider's *Similienapparat* documents, Vegius was himself accused of plagiarism by Pier Candido Decembrio[76] – well able "einzelne Motive und ganze Szenen der Aeneis Vergils für seine Zwecke dienstbar zu machen" ("to put individual motifs and whole scenes of Vergil's *Aeneid* into the service of his own ends").[77] But what Vegius needed for his own allegorical understanding of Aeneas' experience as a soul's journey through life's toils and temptations,[78] was Aeneas' final apotheosis, for which Ovid's *Metamorphoses* supplied classical models in Venus' deification of Aeneas (*Met.* 14. 607: *fecitque deum*, as predicted by Jupiter in *A.* 1. 259f. and 12. 794f.) as well as in her stellification of Julius Caesar's soul (*Met.* 15. 846–50). (The fact that Vegius adheres throughout to his project of using his classical model's language does not negate the allegorical *telos*.)[79]

A few examples suffice to illustrate how the *Aeneid*'s moral leanings are preserved in Vegius' continuation, especially the contrast between *bonus* (440; cf. *bonus Aeneas, A.* 11. 106), *pius* (406; cf. *pius Aeneas, A.* 1. 220, etc.), *magnanimus...Aeneas* (3; cf *A.* 1. 260) on the one hand and Turnus, treaty-breaker (*rupto...foedere* 32; cf. *polluta pace, A.* 7. 467; *foedera rumpant* 8. 540) and aggressor (35; cf. *A.* 7. 468–70; 577–84), on the other. Aeneas, as in the *Aeneid*, is personally opposed to war (46; cf. *A.* 11. 108–11) and, like a hen with her chicken, has *defended* his people against the kite (i.e., against Turnus, 107–20; *defendere* 47; cf. the situation at *Aen.* 10. 511f. and 604f.).

Aeneas addresses Turnus' corpse in similar fashion as Vergil's King Latinus chided the living Turnus: "Learn to worship Jupiter and to do what the gods order (*disce Iovem revereri et iussa facessere divum* 28) ~ Latinus: "the dire death penalty will be waiting for you, Turnus... and with (too) late prayers will you worship the gods; *te, Turne...te triste manebit / supplicium, votisque deos venerabere seris* (*Aen.*7. 596f.).[80] And Aeneas' reminder of Turnus' "...immense rage, with which you against right and loyalty troubled the Trojan race through breach of the treaty" (30–32: *tanti...furoris...quo contra iura fidemque Iliacam rupto turbasti foedere gentem*) reconfirms to (almost) any reader the *Aeneid*'s portrait of Fury-compatible Turnus[81] (*A.* 7. 445ff.) whose "criminal insanity of war" (*scelerata insania belli* 7. 461) causes the hostilities of *Aeneid* 7–12.

In view of Vegius' linear continuation of the *Aeneid*'s story-line and value judgments the reader may *a priori* raise the question: how can Vegius'

Chapter 2

"13th Book" be claimed for the Harvard school? It is precisely at this point that a branch of present-day literary criticism once more requires our methodological attention *in concreto*. Kallendorf's attempt challenges logic as well as evidence: the "very relentlessness" of Vegius' "black-and white interpretation" to Kallendorf "suggests that on some level, he *must have seen something else* in Virgil and been *disturbed* by it." To ambiguity-seekers even an unequivocally stated position apparently may, if felt to be expressed with "relentlessness", point to a hidden ambiguity. Vegius "*undoubtedly* felt that he was *only clarifying* what Virgil intended, but the decision that something needs clarifying is itself a recognition of ambiguity and complexity"[82] (a classic *petitio principii*, once you have turned Vegius' narrative continuation and completion into an act of "clarifying").[83]

Here Kallendorf is able to cite faith-based support from inside his school: "Richard Thomas also *believes* that Vegio wrote the *Supplement* as a response to a *disquiet* aroused by *some perception of pessimism* in the *Aeneid*."[84] *Belief* instead of evidence?

The next step in this bizarre literary critical enterprise is Thomas' apparent change of heart: later (2001) Vegius' continuation is "part of a literary critical collective"[85] that in Thomas' eyes apparently tries "to divert the reader from returning" to the epic's end and tries to "provide the *Aeneid* with the closure it lacks."[86] So, "loose Virgilian strings are tied off" ("loose"? So Vegius' plot-line does not follow and continue the path laid out in the model epic's predictions and prophecies?), "uneasiness quelled" ("uneasiness"? Is this Vegius', or the *ad nauseam* repeated 'disturbance' and 'disquiet' felt by some post-Roman, modern-day readers?).[87]

Vegius now (in the 2001 publication) is called (and Thomas hardly means this as a compliment) "a skillful rhetorician and organizer of facts", as he has his Aeneas "present the Trojans as liberators rather than invaders." Let's hold it here for a moment! "Liberators"? From whose oppression? One will look in vain for the word "liberators" in the lines of Vegius (24–35; and it is not found in the *Aeneid* either); "…rather than invaders"? Thomas' phrasing suggests that "invaders" would be the appropriate term for Vergil's Trojans. But Vegius' Aeneas in 24–35 is in complete agreement with the model poet's presentation in *Aeneid* 7, where the Trojans, arriving under divine guidance and announced by a revered local oracle, are welcomed by pious King Latinus who, obedient to the oracle, offers peace (*pacemque reportant* 7. 285) and even his daughter in marriage (7. 251–73). One apparently has both to subscribe to Thomas' rejection of Vergilian Aeneas' fated mission and to misread the organizational coherence in Books 7–12 (and instead endorse a Conte-type fragmentation of the epic with its resulting discrete, independent, individual spheres),

The Death of King Turnus

if one can see Vegius as an anti-Vergilian "skillful...organizer of facts" and Aeneas as an unwelcome "invader".

Let us check a few more of Vegius' (and Thomas') "facts". Vegius, beginning after Turnus' death, ("great-hearted Aeneas the victor was standing in the middle of the army, *medioque sub agmine victor / magnanimus stetit Aeneas*, 2f.), first describes the defeated Rutulians' pain and numbness, illustrated by a simile. Then (*tum*, 8) the Rutulians put down their arms, condemn the fighting and their own earlier "insane" love of the war (10: "insane". a cognate of the word Vergil used of their leader's, i.e., Turnus', "criminal insanity of war", *A*. 7. 461). They willingly accept the reins and yoke of captivity, asking for mercy, etc.

Vergil had compared the Italian and Trojan armies before the final duel to two herds watching the fight of their two leader-bulls, fearfully waiting "who will rule the forest, whom all the cattle will follow (*quis nemori imperitet, quem tota armenta sequantur, A*. 12. 719, cf. 12. 715–24). Vegius (13–22) picks up Vergil's simile and adjusts it to the post–duel situation of his own epic, elaborating on the Rutulians' newly found readiness to follow Aeneas' arms, their request for a peace treaty and for permanent quiet.

Only then (*tunc*, 23) does Aeneas, "standing close",[88] address Turnus' corpse "with a calm voice" (*placido ore*, 23). Obviously Vegius pictures kindly Aeneas, once Pallas has dutifully been avenged and the Rutulian army has surrendered, as seeing in Turnus once more the defeated enemy whom he was inclined to spare (*A*. 12. 938ff.) – in spite of his repeated treaty violations (recalled in Aeneas' address as excerpted above). During the extended capitulation and peace treaty negotiations (*Suppl*. 11 and 21f. especially) on the international level (i.e., outside the emotion-laden Pallas issue) Vegius apparently portrays Aeneas as Vergil's conciliatory statesman – the same who at the time he suggested the duel with Turnus emphasized that he was *not* waging war against the nation (*nec bellum cum gente gero A*. 11. 113; cf. 111–18). Vegius' account proves to be in agreement with the *Aeneid*'s sharp distinctions between personal/alliance obligation toward Pallas and interstate relations, as explained earlier in this chapter.

But to Thomas, Vegius, the "skillful rhetorician and organizer of facts", "in effect *contradicts Virgil*". How so? Because "in the *seconds* that follow his enraged killing of Turnus at *Aeneid* 12. 945–52", Aeneas "is here fully in control and addresses the corpse of Turnus 'calmly' (23, *placido ore*)"[89] – a charge Thomas repeats two pages later: "Where Virgil ended with Aeneas *furiis accensus et ira / terribilis*, Vegio *begins, some seconds later* in narrative time, not only with a placid Aeneas, but with the hero chastising the Italians for their *furiae*."[90]

Two objections must be raised:

(1) Seconds" later? It appears that it is Thomas who here (re-) organizes the facts by disregarding the intervening time in which (cf. *tum*, 8) the Italians lay down their weapons (8f.), condemn their earlier fighting (9f.) and "refuse neither the reins nor the yoke of captivity" (11f.), accept Aeneas' leadership (20f.), ask for a peace treaty (21f.) and for lasting quiet conditions without war (23). Only *then* (*tunc*, 23 – had Thomas only paid more attention to the indicators of time! Cf. *tum*, 8) does Aeneas "calmly" speak. After his speech, he immediately ("pronouncing no more", *nec fatus plura*, 49) leaves for the Trojan camp. So all the lengthy (time-consuming) negotiations etc. must have taken place *before* his address to the dead Turnus (and to the Italians), but not *"some seconds"* after the killing of Turnus.

(2) Once it is clear that Vegius has granted Aeneas ample time to calm down before his speech, another of Thomas' arguments collapses: after granting return of Turnus' corpse, Vegius' Aeneas 'then brilliantly shifts blame for his own actions to the Ausonians: "driven by *your* rage" (47, *vestris actus furiis*) – thereby suppressing his *own furiae*, so prominent at *Aeneid* 12. 946.'[91]

"Blame" for Aeneas' actions is here, of course, the blame proclaimed by Thomas and his school's affiliates, not by Vergil (who rather characterizes *Turnus* by "criminal insanity of war", 7. 461). Accepting Vergil's closure means for Thomas that "we remove the Virgilian Aeneas' final act from the sphere of human shortcoming."[92] In clinging to his school's orthodoxy that insists on indicting the Vergilian Aeneas, Thomas, too, commingles the two perspectives that (as demonstrated earlier in this chapter) are kept separate in the *Aeneid*: Aeneas' emotionally tinged revenge for his young ally and, on the international level, his defensive war against the Italians under Turnus' (the aggressor's) rage-driven leadership. The words "brilliantly shifts blame" impute a (textually not verifiable) shiftiness to Aeneas that is compatible with Thomas' mistaken judgement on Vegius' work: "Everything *conspires* to distract from Virgil's close."[93]

The term "conspires" perhaps reveals even more, viz. the recurrent concern about a suspected conspiracy steered by the aforementioned "literary critical collective".[94] After all, "two millennia of literature and scholarship have largely *tried to suppress*"[95] the meanings Thomas and his school seek to distill from the *Aeneid*. It is hardly conducive to fruitful scholarly discussion if repeatedly doubts are cast on the motivation ("skillful rhetorician and organizer of facts"; "brilliantly shifts blame for his own actions"; "suppressing his own *furiae*"; "tried to suppress") of divergent "literature and scholarship". Logically speaking, disproving (even if successfully disproving) opposing opinions does not yet establish correctness of your own position. (Some may even consider it damaging to your own position if your attack turns out to have misconstrued the object of the attacked person's endeavor and, along with it, the position of the attacked person himself.)

So far, then (as demonstrated also by Thomas' own shift between 1999 and 2001), 15th century AD Maphaeus Vegius can hardly be claimed with seriousness to support the Harvard school's negative reading of Vergil's Aeneas. On the contrary, Vegius has been shown by us conscientiously to continue the plot along the tracks laid down by his great model, and, so, it appears, cannot be listed as a member of an alleged truth-suppressing "collective". If Vegius is to be cited at all as a witness, his version speaks rather in favor of the detailed interpretation submitted in the present monograph than in support of Kallendorf (and Thomas) 1999 or even of Thomas 2001. Vegius will appear un-Vergilian only to readers who endorse the Harvard Vergil.

And yet, the attempts to provide proof by way of indirect and circular reading, so prevalent in current literary criticism, require at least one more example to be dealt with here, especially so since it offers a new (pro-Harvard) twist on Vegius, who – unlikely as it may appear – has by now been turned into an out-of the-way battlefield of Vergilian criticism.

In the *Introduction* to his 2004 translation of the *Liber XIII*, Putnam too has harsh words for the non-Harvardian poet: Vegius, in presenting Aeneas as a paragon both physically and mentally, is said to reveal a "latent but constant desire to alter his model hero, and therefore to change as well the model epic that describes him, in essential ways."[96] How does Vegius fulfill his alleged latent desire? By "building up the character of Aeneas while at the same time *denigrating* Turnus".[97]

Also, by using Vergilian passages in his own new context, Vegius is said – from the viewpoint of Putnam's reading of the *Aeneid* – "to alter, in ways immediate and less apparent, both Virgil's emphases and the reader's expectations".[98] The latter issue amounts to an arbitrary game: it both underrates the fact that Vegius uses Vergilian language for his specific agenda, viz. to continue the story to its prophesied end beyond the *Aeneid*'s narrative closure, and it would require a reader whose "expectations" endorse Putnam's reading of Vergil's epic. E.g., Putnam blames Vegius for connecting Turnus, not Aeneas, to *furor*[99] – in spite of Turnus' primary association with the Fury (Allecto) ever since Book 7.

Not unlike Thomas, Putnam (who has Vegius pick up Vergilian phrases to announce "a replay of the final book of the *Aeneid*")[100] reverses the course and direction of Vegius' continuation by projecting it back on the *Aeneid*'s ending: Vegius "carefully elides Virgil's troubling description of

Chapter 2

Aeneas", the enraged killer of *A.* 12. 945–47 and 953.[101] "*Carefully elides*"? Why in the world should Vegius present (repeat) to his reader a scene from the epic the narrative time of which precedes his project? But Putnam insists that "Vegio once more finesses a salient part of the conclusion of the *Aeneid*", because he has Aeneas' speech over Turnus' body deliver "the material that we might expect a rational Aeneas to convey before he offers the death blow to Turnus".[102] "*We*"? "*expect*"? One of Vegius' "purposes" in his concluding dialogue of Venus and Jupiter allegedly is "to eliminate the end of Virgil's epic" – which presupposes that Vegius would share Putnam's disapproval of "Jupiter's Fury" and of Turnus' "soul, indignant, making its way to the world of Shades".[103]

As regards the simile of the two bulls fighting for their herds (*A.* 12. 707–22), which (as I pointed out earlier) Vegius picks up showing the now completed outcome, Putnam comments: "And once again we are not shown the death scene of Turnus, only what happens in its wake."[104] One sees: Vegius is being blamed for defining his project the way he does (viz., as continuing and 'completing' the *Aeneid*'s narrative), without going back to the *Aeneid*'s final scene, as well as for failing to insist on Turnus' alleged goodness and Aeneas' presumed human shortcoming. Terms such as "finesse" and "finesses",[105] or "the *Supplement* suppresses"[106] (scil. the moment when Turnus prays Aeneas for pity) appear close to Thomas' "skillful rhetorician and organizer of facts" when flowing from the pen of a translator who, to his dismay, finds in Vegius' text "aspects…that *rehabilitate Aeneas*."[107]

From what has been exposed above it seems clear that Vegius cannot be claimed in support of the Harvard Vergil, not even by Putnam (who, so far, appears to go along with the converted Thomas of 2001). Or can he? Here comes the ultimate circuitous reading, performed by Vegius' translator.

In his *Astyanax* of 1430, Vegius describes the deplorable death of Hector's and Andromacha's young son, contrived by inexorable Ulysses: "a helpless victim and a sly, ruthless tyrant".[108] Andromacha (217f.) asking her son to pray (*precare*) Ulysses, now his master (*dominum*), "*supplex humilis*", reminds Putnam of Turnus, praying (*precantem*), "*humilis supplex*" before Aeneas (*A.* 12. 930f.), causing Putnam to ask: "Would Vegio, writing two years after the publication of the *Supplement*, now have us rethink his approach to the conclusion of Virgil's epic?"[109] It does not seem to trouble Putnam that Vegius' Astyanax does *not* follow his mother's submissive and less than heroic advice: unlike Vergil's praying Turnus, the brave little boy, after being dragged from his mother and taken to the high tower, unhesitatingly meets his death (*haud segni passu leto obvius ibat*), looking around like someone threatening (*similisque minanti*), his eyes noticeably untrembling (*intrepidamque aciem ostentans*). "On his own" (*ipse*) and "at his own initiative" (*ultro* – the reader observes the double emphasis), he jumps to his death (236–50), once more much unlike Turnus whose life goes down to the shades "groaning" (*cum gemitu*) and "resentful" (*indignata, A.* 12. 952). Is it then not more likely that the allusion contained in *supplex humilis* (if its function is more than that of a mere verbal echo taken from a classical author) would be intended to point to the *contrast* of Vegius' death-defying young boy and Vergil's life-seeking adult warrior? In that case, the intended comparison cannot be that between Aeneas and Ulysses (the latter is no longer mentioned in Vegius' death scene, where instead a compassionate crowd of weeping enemy [Greek] witnesses forms the setting). And if Turnus cuts a figure less shining than Astyanax, how can Aeneas, avenger of his brave young ally, be reflected in Ulysses, instigator of the murder of an innocent child? Obviously, a verbal echo or repetition alone, without regard for the situations in which it originally and later occurs, does not suffice methodologically to secure an interpretation. I shall have to return to the 'method'.

"Are there characteristics less noble than magnanimity to be found in Aeneas as he performs his final deed, characteristics that Vegio might have us sense in the implacable Ulysses?", Putnam asks.[110] Kallendorf uncritically chimes in: "If our sympathies are with Astyanax, who could and should be saved, shouldn't they also be with Turnus?" And though Seneca and Ovid are "the obvious sources" here, Vergil is said to provide "its *allusive emotional power*."[111] With even greater urgency, the methodological questions arise once more: What constitutes an allusion, and how does one secure its meaning? Apparently, if Kallendorf feels emotionally touched by a Vegius passage, he also feels free to go beyond "the obvious sources", and find emotional or intuitive confirmation for a desired reading of a Vergil passage in a contextually unverified verbal echo.

In the *Golden Fleece* (*Vellus Aureum*) of AD 1431, Medea, pursued by her father (Aietes) in her flight with Jason, kills and dismembers her brother, Apsyrtus, thus holding up her pursuer who grievingly cares for his son's remains. Here too Putnam finds Vegius "concerned with *commenting vicariously* on the end of the *Aeneid*".[112] Medea burying her sword in Apsyrtus' entrails and Aeneas his in Turnus' chest, both after a moment of hesitation, and both under the influence of "anger and fury", nevertheless reveal to Putnam a decisive difference: Medea acts "only after the intervention of the Fury Tisiphone, risen from Hell", whereas "the impetus for Aeneas' rage is self-generated",[113] after he catches sight of Pallas' sword-belt. "Primary *evidence*" for Vegius "commenting vicariously on the end of the *Aeneid*"?[114] "*Self*-generated" fury upon seeing the killer wearing, as a

Chapter 2

trophy, the killed friend's sword-belt? What does Putnam understand by *self*-generated, and what does "comment" mean to him? Are we to assume that Vegius wrote the story of the golden fleece because in it Medea makes a good commentary on Vergil's Aeneas? Obviously, the concept of "evidence" is different in different schools of literary criticism. For Kallendorf, it is once more clear that here "Vegio *comments intertextually* on the final scene of the *Aeneid*."[115]

When Aietes gives priority to gathering his sons's limbs rather than to pursuit of Medea, Vegius "mitigates the force of his Virgilian inheritance": Vegius, we are told by Putnam, "lets any propensity for a vendetta based on madness yield to a father's devotion to his son", viz. "by making Aeëtes' practice of *pietas* both possible and practicable."[116] The question is not even asked whether Vegius considered "vendetta *based on madness*" a conceivable reading of Vergil's Aeneas; after all, Aeneas acted also on behalf of a father *who had asked for revenge*. And Aietes' overriding concern for his son is hardly Vegius' invention in order to comment on Vergil, but part of the original story about Medea's successful escape. Yet once more, Kallendorf chimes in: "And, again, if here, why not in the *Aeneid*?"[117]

Kallendorf is obviously not aware that his rhetorical question may meet with an unexpected response: instead of 'of course', it would run: 'if Vegius had wished his Astyanax, Medea, and Aietes scenes to be understood as critical comments on Vergil's *Aeneid, why* did he *not* include clearly any such criticism already in his *Liber XIII*?' Putnam's assumption that such criticisms occurred to Vegius only *after* he wrote his *Supplement*, is obviated by a passage from Vegius' late (AD 1448) treatise *On Perseverance in Religion*:

> Then, before he [scil., Aeneas] attains to promised rest in Latium, he meets his enemy, *Turnus, that is, the devil*. The Latins, that is to say worldliness, wage war. Strife is had over Lavinia, who is to be interpreted as the soul. But Turnus is worsted, the Latins are put down, Lavinia is won. Aeneas rules at peace in Italy, and finally is made a god. This is the reward, this the goal, for the persevering hero.[118]

Even if in this explanation written for his sisters (both were nuns) the Christian-allegorical reading may appear over-emphasized, it is clear beyond any doubt that an understanding that views Aeneas as a mad killer and Turnus ("the devil") as a suppliant worthy and deserving of forgiveness is not compatible with Vegius' parameters.

This result – and here a major point of my long investigation is reached – not only again casts doubt on the method of 'intertextuality'; in the present case it actually refutes it. The circular and circuitous reading of Vergil via Vegius undertaken by Putnam, Kallendorf, and others fails to confirm or defend their interpretation of Vergil's *Aeneid* (i.e., the major concern underlying their enterprise). For Vegius' *Supplement* reveals a loyal younger later imitator and, so, ironically in the end can show up a modern misinterpretation of his 'model'. This, then, turns out to be a complementary other side of 'intertextuality' (and *Rezeptionsgeschichte*), in addition to the critique pronounced earlier (in my section on Barchiesi who used Homer to determine Vergil's meaning), which said that the securing of *similia* (be they single words or phrases or even situations) in an earlier author does not by itself guarantee access to the later author's meaning (*imitatio* may reuse earlier material, but the imitating author may very well be aiming at an agenda of his own, which may be independent of or even opposed to the inherited 'meaning').

My investigation not only exposes present-day literary criticism's logical laxity in establishing what it likes to call "evidence". Ironically, the specific case at hand even tries to support an erroneous interpretation of a classical Roman work by misreading an imitative work written almost a millenium-and-a-half later (but nevertheless faithfully preserving the ancient model's leanings): Putnam's examples from Vegius, says Kallendorf imperiously, "strike me as *important new evidence* that Vegio's understanding of the *Aeneid* is considerably more subtle than the simple black-and-white approach that I, and others, emphasized some years ago".[119] My own result shows that current literary critics' interest in Vegius is methodologically not justified. At the same time, it demonstrates again the necessity of Recovery Studies for (re-)gaining access to the *Aeneid* of *Vergil*.

Sometimes, we may now respond, the devil is not only in the detail, but he can in addition be in Turnus.

We are confronted by a contradictory situation. Faced with the same material, Thomas was led to changing his judgement: from welcoming Vegius' view of the *Aeneid* (1999), he moved to condemning it (2001). Putnam, on the other hand, went from harsh critique to critical approval – both of them on the basis of a method that appears unjustified to this interpreter. My earlier question, asked at the outset of this investigation, whether there is a critical method that would reliably establish a 'second' route of interpretation, viz. that of ambiguity, so far must, in view of unconvincing approaches and flawed, even mutually contradictory, results, be given a negative answer.[120]

The necessity of being selective allows me no more than a brief treatment of the role now firmly assigned to Maphaeus Vegius in Vergilian studies. Remarkable is the circularity with which one moves from the (unquestioned) Harvard *Aeneid* to the *Supplementum* and back to the "master text". Buckley, seeing Vegius discover the "holes in the *Aeneid* that fundamentally deny closure to the text", especially "the gap at the end", but also "other open-ended dissatisfactions",[121] unhesitatingly subscribes to the principle of reader's (dis-)satisfaction rather than to authorial organization of the Vergilian artefact. An interpreter appears free to state gaps (or "holes") wherever she would think more details to be appropriate, and wherever her own sense of "satisfaction" fails to understand how the author could have felt satisfaction about his work as he wrote it. So Vegius' first 300 lines "provide the Iliadic-style resolution afforded by burial ritual so *conspicuously lacking* in the *Aeneid* proper."[122] Did Vergil then perhaps, by (unlike Vegius) not filling in this alleged hole (scil., of Turnus' burial), wish to create a "conspicuous" ambiguity?

Though Vegius "quashes the moral ambivalence and disorientation of the *Aeneid*'s final lines to provide in its place soothing reconciliation, dynastic assurance and the perfect 'Christianized' finale, a soul in heaven" (i.e., Vegius can here not be claimed for the ambivalent, pessimistic, and disoriented Harvard Vergil), he nevertheless shows susceptibility to 'even modern critical notions of "supplementarity" and "closure"'.[123]

The inter- and intratextual evidence, however, is less than convincing, through which Buckley seeks to establish that Vegius' opening (by way of "allusion") "serves to encapsulate Virgil's final book", and "aims to pose as an integral part of the *Aeneid*". By his first line (*Turnus ut extremo devictus Marte profudit / effugientem animam*) Vegius is said to look back not only to the last two lines of the *Aeneid* (Turnus' life departing, 12. 951f., in itself, a neat continuation of *content*), but also to the first line of *Aeneid* 12 (*Turnus ut infractos adverso Marte Latinos / defecisse videt*): here Buckley comfortably switches from content-oriented intertextuality to intratextual (but a-contextual) recurrence of three words (*Turnus ut...Marte*; my reader recalls that the line 12. 1 looks back to the events of the *preceding* Book): 'In his first two lines Vegio <u>identifies</u> the <u>significant markers</u> of the final <u>book-division</u> of the *Aeneid* , <u>synthesizes</u> them in a <u>neat repetition</u> that <u>marks</u> the beginning of his own text, and assumes their "<u>authorizing</u>" <u>power</u> as the <u>basis</u> on which his own work will proceed.'[124] (My reader will find it sufficient that I have underlined the words that here appear pretentiously and pompously employed outside their precise customary English usage.)

Likewise, Buckley avails herself of present-day license (to be encountered repeatedly in the present chapter) in connecting words regardless of the context in which they are used. Vergil terms his epic's second (Iliadic) half his "greater work" (*maius opus*, *A*. 7. 45). Vegius uses the same phrase for a different context, viz. when describing how Aeneas assigns (exactly as he acted at the opening of *Aeneid* 11) *higher priority, maius opus* (*Suppl.* 57), to honoring the gods' altars over the likewise urgent task of burying the dead.

The Death of King Turnus

Tearing the words from their Vegian context, Buckley changes the meaning of Vegius' *maius opus* from 'precedence of sacrifice over burial' to a poetological statement on what she calls "post-*bella* epos": from Vergil's *horrida bella* (*A.* 7. 41) and even Horace's *tristia bella* (*A.P.* 73) as epic material, the *Supplementum* is said to move to "song concerned with war's aftermath, itself *as far as Vegio is concerned*, a *maius opus* (*Suppl.* 57, cf. *Aen.* 7. 45)."[125] Apparently it does not matter to Buckley that Vegius uses the words at *Suppl.* 57 to say something completely different from what the same words say in the *Aeneid* at *A.* 7. 45. No wonder, then, that in her belief Vergil's Aeneas is "*murdering* Turnus", but Vegius' Aeneas "*firmly shifts* the blame onto Turnus and the Rutuli for this war (*Suppl.* 24–48)".[126] Once more Vegius, while faithfully adhering to Vergil's unfavorable portrait of Turnus, faces the charge of distortion. So the *Supplement* is stylized into a negative foil for orthodoxy's *Aeneid*.

Here I offer a final instance of the *Aeneid* being distorted in the literary critical function which Buckley assigns to the *Supplementum*. According to her, Vegius annuls "the gloomy and morbid sentiments of the *Aeneid*'s end", by "creating for the *Aeneid* the happy ending hardly countenanced in the closing scenes of the Virgilian epic."[127] "Vegio shortcircuits the shocking cyclicity of Aeneas' actions", by in the end having Venus pick up Jove's predictions made to her in *Aeneid* 1, thus "running the events of the Virgilian epic backwards from the climactic death of Turnus".[128] However, one must object here, neither does the end of the *Aeneid* exclude or deny the better future (predicted with the greatest possible certainty by Jupiter, Anchises, Vulcan), nor does the *Aeneid* express 'shock' about Aeneas' "actions"(not to mention the posited "cyclicity"of the alleged plurality of "actions"), nor finally do "events" run backward: fulfillment is always later than prophecy (events *follow* but do not precede their announcement). If Vegius' Venus repeats to her son what she knows about his family's imperial future, and, at the very end, upon reminding Jove of the promised stellification of her son (cf. *A.* 1. 258–60), actually does stellify his soul, Vegius is not (in a "reversal") "running the events of the Virgilian epic backwards" – he only pedantically and ornately narrates what every un-forgetful reader of the *Aeneid* anyway expects to happen in the not-narrated future.

Vegius "restores to the poem a powerfully teleological drive which provides both the resolution so desperately needed to make sense of Turnus' death" (Buckley's admission of desperate incomprehension when looking for "teleological drive" in the *Aeneid* and when reading the *Aeneid*'s ending?) "and the look forwards to the apotheosis of Aeneas never more than hinted at or promised in the *Aeneid* proper" (so the interpreter feels free to reduce Jupiter's guarantee at *A*. 1. 258–60 to "never more than" a '*hint*' or unreliable '*promise*'?). This reader readily confesses his own incomprehension (marked by "[?]") when reading that, "in driving [?] the *Aeneid* back[?] to the point of the eternal future[?] [prophesied by Jupiter in *Aeneid* 1 and by Vegius in the *Supplement*], Vegio puts a frighteningly[?] accurate[?] choke hold[?] on the suggestive[?] ambiguities[?] that run through the epic as a whole[?]."[129] Especially the words "suggestive" and "ambiguities" of course are symptomatic of today's adumbrating vagueness so often employed to override the peculiar linguistic accuracy and precision of ancient literature, in order that the interpreter, unbridled by the onerous bonds of securing the textual evidence, may distill the vapors of a 'satisfying' meaning. Although it may be embarrassing having to put such current tendencies on display, their inflated bubbles have to be pricked open in the interest of (re-) opening access to the ancient literary artifice. It is only through detailed and thorough, but space-consuming analysis (which limits the number of cases to be studied here to a representative sample) that the futility of context-independent, ambiguity-hungry readings can be demonstrated.

There is one more claim to applicable methodology that requires detailing in the present context. According to Kallendorf, in Vegius' *Vellus Aureum* it is again Vergil who "provides the text with its allusive emotional power".[130] The concept of "allusion", omnipresent in current 'theory', suggests taking a look at another recent representative, Quint. Harvard's Thomas, while diverging from his own brevity in dealing with the *Aeneid*'s final scene, refers his readers to this representative of allusion who, he says, offers "one of the better recent treatments of the finale".[131] Quint (mentioned earlier in this chapter for his view of Turnus' death as a "judicial murder") also participates in the recent fashion of questioning the *Aeneid*'s "closure", so he may for more than one reason serve as a touchstone for the interpretation offered in the preceding chapter. Yet one must again be on guard against the danger that a method (as well as its practitioners) may emancipate itself from (or forcefully impose itself on) the text it purports to serve and interpret. It is only fair to give Quint's claims to critical correctness a detailed hearing since in his judgement the kind of interpretation presented in my preceding section "credits Virgil with *little ambiguity* of thought or feeling in the episode".[132] ("*Episode*"? "Ambiguity"?)

Professing his own toned-down derivative of poststructuralist New Historicism,[133] Quint claims to view a text both within its literary tradition and with regard to its "synchronous historical relationships" (the latter would, of course, be appropriate for analyzing the political *Aeneid*):

"My preference for *allusion* over analogy aims to establish *more precise* and *documentable* links between the text and its historical situation—for *more answerable criteria of evidence*".[134] This is an exciting and commendable claim to methodological accuracy, whose viability deserves to be tested. For Quint may seem finally to offer an answer to the present chapter's question whether there exists a literary critical method providing credible evidence of Vergilian ambiguity (and, implicitly, of a voice expressing a non-partisan position beyond the Trojan-Julian allegiance). "Topical political allusions and literary allusions that are themselves politically charged open up new perspectives on the poems' individual passages as well as on their larger structures and meanings."[135] Two potential problems, which one immediately senses to be inherent in this approach (as well as in similar theory-based approaches), are (a) how to verify what the text is 'alluding' to (and, by implication, that there actually *is* an allusion and not merely a relationship constructed by the interpreter), and (b) that, since especially a poem's "larger structure" itself provides "meanings" by virtue of its immanent coherence, such coherent meaning may be disfranchised when (part of) the structure is made subject to an assumed outside reference or influence not precisely identified in the text itself ("allusion").

If "allusion" may in itself appear to be a roundabout (and not easily verifiable) approach to securing meaning, Quint's approach is further complicated by his introduction of Freud's psychic *repetition compulsion*,[136] the two modes of which – (a): repeated re-enaction of one's victimization; (b): neurotic replaying of the trauma in a new version in which the former victim now masters and somewhat controls his psychic history – Quint coordinates with the *Aeneid*'s two halves, the Odyssean wanderings of the defeated Trojans in Books 1–6 and their eventually victorious fighting in the Roman *Iliad* of Books 7–12.

"The Trojans, *obsessed with their fallen city* in the first half of the poem, are *condemned to a futile repetition...*" (my emphasis). But are they in Books 1–6 really "*obsessed* with their fallen city" (i.e., their past) and not rather looking forward to founding a new beginning? "*Repetition*" (occasioned by obsession)? "*Condemned*"? Where is it said that they depend on "a repression or forgetting of the past"?[137] 'It is their victory...of the last six books that produces a "positive" repetition of their tragic past' (etc.).[138] Does the *Aeneid* in actual fact present the Trojans' victory in the second half as one "not so much over defeated external foes as over themselves"?[139] Where does *Vergil's text* say so? Quint does not offer any textual evidence that the *Aeneid* does bow to (comply with) the Freudian theory.

Quint further coordinates the two kinds of Freudian repetition with "two ideological imperatives" of "Augustan propaganda", which "can be assimilated to the personal virtues that Augustus claimed for himself" ("*assimilated*"?), i.e., of "*clementia* and *pietas*" (amounting to Quint's equivalents of Barchiesi's *misericordia* and *ultio*),[140] corresponding respectively to forgetting "a past of civil war (so as to stop repeating it)" and to demanding "that this past be remembered and avenged (and so be repeated and mastered)". Can one truly reduce the *Aeneid*'s essential story-line to a (post-) civil war epic, and ask that Vergil's Trojans now please rethink their heroic fight against the Greek attack in terms of a "past of civil war"?

Upon asking the (rhetorical) question concerning the killing of Turnus (obviously to be answered in the affirmative by the unsuspecting reader), "But will this revenge in fact be final...?", Quint states: "And in the killing of Turnus the *Aeneid* concludes with nothing less than an *image of civil war*, an ending that calls its own closure into question."[141] In reality, one must object, Vergil loyally excludes any hints of civil war, especially of – as Quint has it – *cyclic* civil war, from within the *Aeneid*'s story-line, by focusing on Turnus' personal guilt: with the death of the war-inciting and treaty-breaking individual, the obstacle to peace is removed. Here follows Quint's explanation for questioning "closure" and beholding "an image of civil war":

> For the repetition and reversal of Aeneas' Iliadic career in the final duel with Turnus not only constitutes the *hero's personal revenge upon his own past*, but it also makes the Turnus whom Aeneas defeats and kills a *mirror image of Aeneas himself*, the Aeneas who barely escaped Diomedes and Achilles at Troy.[142]

In an accompanying note,[143] Quint informs his reader that "Girard has provided a model for thinking about doubling, violence, and civil war". Here, Freud's *repetition compulsion* is apparently being augmented so the *Aeneid* may seem infused with notions of mirroring and civil war. The admission that here yet another outside "model" is being applied to (rather than derived from) the poem once more raises the question of its appropriateness. That Aeneas, in a situation where the evasive enemy leader finally honors the contract of the war-ending duel, should additionally have on his mind the idea of taking his "personal revenge on his own past" is not verifiable for the reader of the Latin text who has accompanied Vergil's hero through twelve Books (and, especially, since Book 10) of the *Aeneid*. Apparently aware of the missing verification, Quint resorts to *presumption*: "Aeneas himself *presumably shares*" the reader's "moment of déjà vu", when Turnus, like Diomedes in Homer's *Iliad*, lifts a boulder against Aeneas, so "both *he* [*scil.*, Aeneas] and the reader hold their breath."[144] Here presumption has easily and imperceptibly turned into a 'breath-holding' certainty (unknown to the *Aeneid*'s text and hero), so our interpreter can (his theory not depending on textual evidence) go on later to declare that Achilles and Diomedes "were Aeneas' *worst nightmares*"[145] (Vergil's Aeneas having nightmares?), and that Aeneas "enacts" towards Turnus, this deficient new (non-) Diomedes, "a therapeutic reversal of his earlier victimization".[146] Vergil's Aeneas on Doctor Freud's therapeutic couch?

The illogicality here is that the interpreter creates a meta-identity: it not only allows the literary character to feel an embarrassment (which neither the Vergilian protagonist nor his creator ever voices) because of the inferior role Aeneas plays in the *Iliad*, but it also gives him a chance to take his "personal revenge" on the earlier author's presentation of this character.[147] (The *Aeneid*, its reader recalls, through the mouth of Jupiter ascribes Aeneas' maternally assisted salvation from mortal danger on the battlefield – burning Troy; Diomedes – to his fated historical mission that will prepare the way for Roman world domination under Augustus: *A.* 4. 227–31; cf. 1. 286–88: *genetrix pulcherrima = pulchra...origine*.)

It appears advisable to check out *in concreto* a few more details of Quint's argument. This requires addressing in some detail another aspect of recent literary criticism and, with it, the problem of methodologies appropriate for the field of Classics. Quint continues, following the sentence I quoted on the "mirror image", as follows: "This doubling effect is reinforced by Vergil's use of internal echoes." Among Quint's "internal echoes" is line 12. 951, because its last three words about Turnus (*solvuntur frigore membra*) are also used of Aeneas' numbness in Juno's storm at sea in Book 1 (92):

extemplo Aeneae <u>solvuntur frigore membra</u> 1. 92
ast illi <u>solvuntur frigore membra</u> 12. 951.

In Quint's own words, this is "a phrase that, with *stunning poetic virtuosity*, recalls the very first appearance of Aeneas in the poem".[148]

Since, however, the narrative in Book 12 makes no reference whatsoever to the earlier situation, it is instructive to see how Quint uses the recurrence of the three words to support the thesis of "repetition and reversal". The lack of methodological precision that again reveals itself in the use of the associative term "recalls" is basically the same as demonstrated in our investigation in the previous chapter into what some interpreters make out of Vergil's use of *furor/furiae* or of *amens*. Again a truism must be repeated and emphasized against current litcrit practice: it rarely is the recurrence of a word or "phrase" alone that determines the meaning of a passage, but the context is decisive and must not be neglected by the interpreter. Both Turnus and Aeneas show signs of physical paralysis in extreme danger, it is true, but their mental reaction in comparable situations is *incomparably different*. Whereas Aeneas' Achillean[149] response in Book 1 was that he

Chapter 2

complained about being, by drowning, deprived of a hero's death (he would have preferred to fall gloriously before Troy among his fellow-fighters before the eyes of the acknowledging fathers), Turnus' soul goes down "resentful", i.e., he, unlike Aeneas, is unwilling to die the hero's death (and possibly, as Donatus suggests, to relinquish Lavinia [i.e., also, the throne of King Latinus] to Aeneas, *dolebat tamen se perdidisse lucem et Aeneae Laviniam reliquisse*). Turnus' resentful[150] departure is quite in agreement with his repeated earlier attempts to evade the responsibility he had claimed he was ready to shoulder, although this last time, i.e., immediately before the duel, he had (though to no avail, as it turned out) tried to convince his sister (and himself) that now he was truly ready to observe the terms of the duel treaty and not to show himself unworthy of his ancestors: "Is it so very miserable to die"? *usque adeone mori miserum est?* (12. 646–49). Augustan Vergil is not willing to grant Aeneas' chief adversary the heroic exit so intensely desired by Aeneas himself in Juno's storm in Book 1, an exit that the poet allows even cruel Etruscan King Mezentius (*iuguloque haud inscius accipit ensem*, 10. 907). In view of the different portraits the epic has painted of the two leading antagonists it appears more than far-fetched to declare Turnus the "double" of Aeneas by equating them as "victims" ("Turnus has completely assumed Aeneas' role as victim in the first half of the poem, and Aeneas thus kills his own double.")[151] and referring for proof to a recurring "phrase" that first has to be stripped of its defining context (not to mention that a contextual reference between the two passages is not verifiable; if there should be a connection, it would only prove once more what is brought out anyway all over the epic, viz. that the two characters react differently in similar situations. Awareness of this contrast can apparently not be achieved and accounted for by Quint's scheme of "internal echoes".

Thus it appears more fitting to apply the attribute "stunning poetic virtuosity" to Quint's own interpretative escapade that disregards the different contexts in which the same "phrase" occurs. The end pursued with such alleged "echoes" again (as indicated on an earlier occasion) leads to a grave misreading that subverts the actual text. For it declares the killing of Turnus by Aeneas "*an image of civil war*" (Quint's italics) that allegedly transcends the epic's end, whereas in reality (we said above) Vergil loyally excludes any hints of *cyclic civil war* from his story-line[152] by focusing on Turnus' personal guilt (with the war-inciting individual's death, the obstacle to peace will be removed, as Jupiter's prediction confirms). And, so, Quint sees fit to call the killing of Turnus "*an image of civil war*, an ending that calls its own closure into question".[153]

On the way to his denial of closure, Quint introduces another interpretative facet by arguing that "the killing of Turnus is itself contrasted in Book 12 with the settlement reached shortly before by Juno and Jupiter to let bygones be bygones".[154] "*Contrasted*"? Rather, it would be a correct statement to say that "the killing of Turnus is *in agreement* with the settlement". After all, already in his conversation with Hercules Jupiter had declared that Turnus' end was near (10. 471f.). And in his earlier conversation with Juno, Jupiter had made clear that he was granting no more than a delay of Turnus' death (10. 622–27). And before his final conversation with Juno in Book 12, Jupiter had used his scales to weigh the fates of Aeneas and Turnus (12. 725–27), so the final scene's deadly outcome (*letum*, 727) has in the reader's eyes been determined *a priori*. And this is also what Jupiter communicates to Juno, when he reproaches her for the wounding of Aeneas and the restoration of his sword to Turnus: "It has come to the end", *ventum ad supremum est* (803). "I forbid you to attempt anything further", *ulterius temptare veto* (806). In complying, Juno (though reluctantly) abandons her protégé Turnus, leaving him to his doom: *Turnum et terras invita reliqui* (809). There can be no doubt at all that among what Quint calls "the bygones" agreed upon in the settlement of Jupiter and Juno is the death of Turnus,[155] and the ambiguity of pardon and revenge that Quint imputes to the epic's closure is, it turns out, achieved at the cost of suppressing more than only one *unambiguous* advance announcement.

Upon constructing a (non-existing) contrast between the conversation on the divine level and the epic's ending, Quint adds the following sentence: "The poem, like the regime, has it both ways, but in the process it discloses the contradictions in the regime's ideology: its promise to pardon and avenge *at the same time*".[156] Apart from disregarding the fact that Jupiter in what Quint calls "the bygones" had unambiguously excluded a pardon for Turnus, Quint with this simplifying wholesale statement railroads the nuances also of the final scene itself by speaking of a *contemporaneous* coexistence where (as I have shown in the previous section and must now repeat) the reader is being offered two *different* aspects narrated *sequentially*. Turnus the defeated enemy king might, according to Anchises' motto of *parcere subiectis et debellare superbos* (6. 853), be pardoned. But the *following* recognition of Turnus as the killer of Pallas *changes the situation* by reinstating the obligation of *ultio* that had temporarily been relegated to the background by the necessities of the ongoing general Trojan-Italian fighting.[157]

Our investigation settles the question whether the Freud-based theory might correctly lay a claim to approaching a more apposite understanding of the *Aeneid*. The circuitous road has proved rather to be another cul-de-sac: the theory runs aground when *in concreto* confronted with the Latin text. Nevertheless, the discussion of Quint's work has so far not been fruitless insofar as its refutation has provided an opportunity to show the usefulness of a more detailed interpretation of key passages in Book 12. Even if it leads into a cul-de-sac, a theory has to be checked by scholarship in order to prevent it (and affiliated attempts) from putting down roots. So much, then, about what Harvard's Thomas calls (as quoted earlier) "one of the better treatments of the finale".

The key question of course has been whether or not Quint (and others, whose methods share a number of features with Quint's) succeeds in convincingly ascribing to the – allegedly, ambiguous – *Aeneid* an undercurrent of criticism toward the regime of Augustus. It is significant to see that no clear cases (clear, I mean, to the 'uninitiated', non-litcrit reader) are ever cited from the *Aeneid*'s text itself,[158] cases in which the author would *verifiably* negate or undercut his pro-Augustan position (as it is pronounced, for instance, in the three great prophecies of Jupiter, Anchises, Vulcan's shield) in the way Propertius in elegy 3. 5 for his own person retracted the earlier support for Augustus' Eastern campaign offered in elegy 3. 4; or disavowed his new political pro-Augustan commitment announced in 4. 1A, by means of the retraction that follows in 4. 1B.[159]

It turns out that the evasive and circuitous approaches that base themselves on intertextuality (Barchiesi, Quint), Freudian compulsion (Quint), presumed later reception (Putnam, Thomas, Kallendorf), etc., are not qualified to replace a strictly text-based interpretation of Vergil's poem (which, of course, must itself not claim to be free from potential errors).

The foregoing discussion, leading by way of a methodological excursus back to a renewed appreciation of Vergil's text precisely read, may serve as another demonstration of the difficulties present-day criticism incurs when encountering the strict logical (and rhetorical) organization of ancient literary works. Even an 'unsophisticated' voice like that of ancient Donatus, on the other hand, is able to point out how skillfully Vergil has built up his epic to the climax of the final single combat that takes place in isolation from the preceding general fighting and allows Aeneas himself to be the avenger of the injustice done to him, *ultor iniuriae suae*, etc.

The ending of the epic seems to disaffect primarily short-distance readers who, in search of an interpretation less 'disturbing' to modern tastes, concentrate on finding "ambiguity" by cherry-picking elements of the final scene (and de-contextualized "verbal echoes") while disregarding both the long-distance organization of the narrative (further detailed in the following chapter) and also Jupiter's consultation of his scales and his ensuing strict injunction to Juno that now the end has been reached.

It is a characteristic upshot of recent classical studies that, for (re-)opening access to and (re-)claiming Vergil's text, an interpreter has first to remove the simplifying schemata ("reversals", "repetitions", "doubling echoes", "topical allusions", etc., etc.) drawn from contemporary 'critical' theory and imposed on the poem. On the other hand, dealing with such circuitous and erroneous approaches may help to sharpen one's eyes for the complex but consistent organization of the text and its nuances.[160] It would, to repeat, be gratifying if the reader deemed the present critical chapter superfluous because (s)he found the interpretation of the epic's climax as offered in the preceding sections convincing by itself. However (as was said at the opening of this section) the vogue represented in the vast body of speculative and circuitous readings dissuaded this interpreter from assuming that a strictly text-based interpretation alone would suffice to convince a majority of today's readers.

(4) Excursus 2: *balteus* and *cingula* at *A.* 12. 942

A problem arises in *Aen.*12. 942: do the *balteus* (defined by *OLD s.v.* (1), "A shoulder band or baldric, oft. elaborately decorated, for supporting a sword, quiver, instrument, etc.") and the *cingula* (*cingulum* is explained in *OLD s.v.* not only (a) as "a band that is put round something, a belt or other binding", but also (b) "(spec.) a belt, often gilt or embossed, usu. as a sword-belt)" refer to the same object, and, if so, why would the poet mention it twice in the same line? *"Annon pleonasmus ridiculus?"*

Cucchiarelli (2002, 621f.), citing LaCerda's question, opts for a single object ("the *balteus* together with its periphrasis, the *cingula* and the *bullae*"), introducing "a definite emotive suggestion": the *bullae* on the *cingula* (*et notis fulserunt cingula bullis*, 12. 942), pointing to "a sort of ornamental bauble or pendant", represent "those distinctive markers, both for identification and good luck, that were worn around the neck to symbolize the wearer's youth". So the *bullae* would have to be distinguished from "the *impressum nefas* of the Danaids" (10. 495–500), which appears "wrought directly onto the belt" (scil. of Pallas). "For *pater* Aeneas, the infantile *bullae* inevitably bring with them the memory of the violated *puer* (*notis!*)" (etc.).

Though rightly emphasizing the emotional dimension, Cucchiarelli's analysis appears to disregard a factual detail (evidenced also in his own references to Cic. *Verr.* 2. 1. 152 and Plaut. *Rud.* 1171): the individual boy would wear only <u>one</u> *bulla* around his neck, not several. Cf. Propertius' autobiographical account at 4. 1. 131f.:

> Mox, ubi bulla rudi dimissa est aurea collo
>   matris et ante deos libera sumpta toga, (etc.)

Chapter 2

So one has to search elsewhere to find out how Vergil's contemporary readers might have understood the terms in question. Heinze (1965, 201–10) has repeatedly pointed out how Vergil, so that his contemporaries (and he himself) might better visualize the fighting scenes, has on occasion supplemented his Homeric models by introducing Roman national features and early (even contemporary) Roman equipment. At the outset it is useful to be aware of a certain ambiguity existent in modern English. *Webster's Dictionary* defines the word baldric(k) as both (1) "a belt worn around the waist, as the Roman cingulum or military belt", and (3) "a broad belt worn over the right or left shoulder, diagonally across the body, to the waist or below it, either simply as an ornament or to suspend a sword, dagger, or horn. ...The baldric was worn in feudal times," (etc.).

With definition (1), modern-day *Webster's* adds to the explanation for *balteus* as quoted above from the *Oxford Latin Dictionary*. And yet there is evidence also from antiquity to parallel *Webster's* account (though, of course, the sporadic character of literary as well as archaeological evidence does not always allow exact temporal and topical fixation).

A writer as late as Juvenal, in a passage incorrectly listed in *OLD* for the meaning "baldric", characterizes members of the soldier's profession as people "whom armor covers and the belt *encircles*" (*quos arma tegunt et balteus ambit, Sat.* 16. 48). Likewise incorrectly, *OLD* claims the meaning "baldric" for Caesar, *BG* 5.44.7, where a dart gets stuck in a centurion's belt, *verutum in balteo defigitur*. But a centurion's tombstone, "dating from before 42 BC", shows the man with no shoulder belt, his sword being held by the (single) belt that runs around his waist. The same is true about a Republican-era legionary from the altar of Domitius Ahenobarbus (both depicted in Bishop and Coulston 1989, 19, figures 6. 1 and 2. See also the pictorial reconstructions printed in Connolly 1998, showing a late Republican legionary [p.304] and a 1st century AD legionary as well as a centurion [p.305].) There is more: Vitruvius (3.5.7) applies the name *balteus* to the broad 'bands' which in circular fashion run around and seem to constrict (and tie in like a girdle) the central ('waist') part of the Ionian capital's *pulvinus* (visible in the side view of the volute-member). And Tertullian (*De spect.* 3) seems to use the word *balteus* for the circular walkways that separate the lower from the higher rows of seats in the Colosseum (whereas Vitruvius speaks of *praecinctiones* when mentioning the semicircular covered walkways in the theater, 5.3.4.). The girdle of the Amazons' queen, Hippolyte, embossed with gold (*caelatus balteus auro*, Ovid, *Met.* 9. 189), so coveted by Eurystheus' daughter, certainly was no shoulder belt. Nor was the 'charming' girdle of Venus that captured Iupiter (*ussit amatorem balteus iste Iovem*, Martial 14. 207. 2). In approaching Vergil, there is reason enough to expect the connotation "baldric" (i.e., shoulder belt) to be a specialized military option, while not losing sight of the pervasive and predominant meaning "belt" (or "girdle").

For the later part of the first century AD, Bishop and Coulston (1989, 35) state: "The belt of this period is frequently called the *cingulum militare*, but literary and papyrological evidence suggests that it was actually known as the *balteus*, the former term referring to the belt of the later Empire." An author as late as Hieronymus (*epist.* 64.12; cf. *TLL* II 1711. 55ff.) still confirms the basic (general) meaning: *tertium est genus vestimenti, quod...nos cingulum vel balteum vel zonam possumus dicere*. Closer to Vergil's time, Connolly (1998, 234; see also the above mentioned pictures on p. 305) formulates: "During the early first century AD the sword and dagger were suspended from two individual belts that crossed over at the back and front in cowboy fashion.... Later a single belt was substituted to which dagger and apron were attached, but the sword was suspended from a baldric on the right side". (See also figures 21 and 22, p. 232.)

It is worth pointing out that the *Aeneid*'s prominent heroes, like Homer's, handle (in addition to their spear) only the sword: they (in this like the above-mentioned Republican-era tombstone representations of a centurion and a legionary) have no use for an extra belt or girdle to hold a dagger (the Homeric ζωστήρ is a piece of defensive gear). A representation of a broad baldric in the shape of a shoulder belt with (two) *studs* (the natural meaning of *bullae* at *A*. 12. 942) and with a rectangular plate, on the tombstone of M. Aurelius Lucianus (Connolly p. 253), is too late to be of help for illustrating the sword belt of Pallas as possibly envisioned by Vergil's contemporary readers.

Another road may (or may not) lead further. Belt decorations in the form of rectangular bronze plates have been found at legionary sites as early as the 2nd century BC, and their use even goes back as far as the Villanova period (for a pierced plate from Altri, ca 7cm x 10 cm, see Connolly 93, fig.10). A line can be drawn all the way to Pliny (*N.H.* 33, 152) who censures the luxury of silver(ed) belt plates among contemporary soldiers. A first century AD rectangular plate with an embossed mythological theme (arranged inside a circle) shows the Roman she-wolf suckling the twins (Connolly 232 no. 17, = Bishop and Coulston1989, 36, no.5, from Risstissen in Germany). The mythological scene, as a motif type, of course takes us closer to the mythical crime of the Danaids embossed on Pallas' *balteus* (10. 496f.). Bishop and Coulston (35) report that the "very finely decorated, either with niello inlay or embossed designs", belt-plates of the first century AD "used decorative motifs derived almost entirely from classical art." And the fact that the she-wolf scene is arranged inside a circle (consisting of a ring of tiny raised dots in the metal plate) shows at least an affinity to round *bullae*. Some belt plates (Bishop and Coulston 36, figures 7 and 8) are decorated with non-pictorial, conical elevations that would definitely satisfy the term *bullae*, and there are also smaller studs, round and flat, riveted to the leather straps that, hanging from the soldier's belt, formed the (protective or merely jingling) 'apron' (Bishop and Coulston 36, figures 12–14; 16). Both types appear on the first century AD tombstone of Licaius (an "auxiliary infantryman"), where the raised rosette-like decorations on the belt plates take up almost the whole width of the (crossed) belts (Bishop and Coulston 11, figures 2 and 3). A curious sideshow is provided by the decorated bronze studs ("cabochons de bronze estampés du cingulum romain") discussed by Feugère (1985, 109–141), which, he believes, were given to soldiers on official occasions and were attached to the belt. Ranging in size from 1.6 to 4.3 cm, they have been found along the northern *limes* from Britain to Romania, displaying heads of Flavian emperors as well as naval emblems and chariots.

So at the least there is sufficient evidence of a lasting and broad Roman tradition that may have let Romans feel a degree of familiarity when reading of the bosses or studs and the pictorial decorations on Pallas' belt (*balteus*). It is worth keeping in mind that Vergil did not write *only* for literary connoisseurs who would easily recall from Homer either Aias' shoulder belts, crossed on the chest, for sword and shield (*Il.* 14. 404), or Heracles' "golden" shoulder belt (to support his quiver, not his sword, *Od.* 11. 609–12) with its gruesome battle scenes of manslaughter, or even Hektor's (undecorated?) present for Aias, consisting of a "sword with silver nails, together with the sheath and a *well-cut shoulder-belt*" (*Il.* 7. 303f.).

As Agamemnon wears the sword by a belt over his shoulder (*Il.* 2. 45; 11. 29), so does Trojan Prince Ascanius, his sword gilded (*A.* 9. 303f. His father, Aeneas, like the Roman legionary – or like Odysseus – [Heinze 1965, 203], lifts his new shield on his shoulder, *attollens umero* 8. 731). But Arcadian King Evander ties his sword to both his shoulder and his side, i.e., appears to have a combination set of baldric and belt (*lateri atque umeris Tegeaeum subligat ensem*, 8. 459). A hoplite on a Greek vase painting (500 BC; Connolly 1998, 58, figure 1) uses the shoulder belt to hold his sword, and so does Alexander on the mosaic in the House of the Faun in Pompeii (a copy of a ca. 300 BC painting). And soldiers of the Etrusco-Roman army of ca. 550 BC, their equipment fashioned on Greek models, apparently may, later development notwithstanding, be visualized with a sword belt around their hips or waists that is connected to a narrower band over their shoulders (visible in the reconstructions of spearmen of the classes II and III in Connolly 1998, 95, figures 2 and 3). A similar combination set of shoulder band-plus-belt (which would remove the *pleonasmus ridiculus* and satisfy the mention of both *cingulum* and *balteus* at *Aen.* 12. 942) is apparently not evidenced by archaeological finds before the late second century AD, as Bishop and Coulston state (1989, 47, with reconstruction, p. 48, figure 36, based on findings from Lyon). The archaeological as well as the literary evidence cannot provide certainty for determining the shape of Pallas' belt, in view of both Vergil's occasional mixture of Homeric and Italian elements (the latter of course predominantly concentrated in the "gathering of the clans" in Book 7) and the fact that archaeological evidence is scarcer for the 1st century BC than for the 1st century AD. Nevertheless, the material can lead us closer to gauging the perception of contemporary Roman readers for whom a *balteus* in the first place was a belt worn around the waist.

A further complicating factor is that the *Aeneid* itself is not consistent in using the two words. Whereas at 12. 942 the *balteus* appears on the shoulder, at 12. 274f. it must mean a waist belt or girdle since it is located "where the stitched *balteus* is rubbed by the belly and the clasp holds the connecting ends of the sides (*teritur qua sutilis alvo / balteus et laterum iuncturas fibula mordet*; line 275b perhaps open to different interpretations). On the other hand, when Euryalus fetches Rhamnes' *phalerae* (rings which a warrior wears on his chest) and his "belt, golden with studs" (*aurea bullis cingula*, 9. 359f.), he puts the *cingula* on his shoulder, *umeris...aptat*, 364. (Donatus understands *aptat* here as *apte componit* for carrying the objects more easily on the shoulder, but not everyone may agree with him, considering that *aptare* in the *Aeneid* is regularly used for arming oneself, cf. 2. 672; 12. 88; 2. 390.) However, when Penthesilea, the Amazon, fastens the golden *cingula* under her exposed breast, *aurea subnectens exsertae cingula mammae* (1. 492), she is most certainly not handling a shoulder belt (a "cincture" Austin calls it, *ad loc.*). For what it is worth, one may here add that Varro feels free to explain the *balteum* (*sic*) as a girdle with *bullae*, explaining its name because it was a leather (waist) belt studded with *bullae* (*balteum, quod cingulum e corio habebant bullatum, balteum dictum, L.L.* 5.116). To be on the safe side, then, one would, with a contemporary Roman reader in mind, wish to assume the meaning "baldric" or "shoulder belt" for *balteus* in the *Aeneid* only when a form of *umerus* accompanies the word, guaranteeing the meaning. (*TLL* is not of much help because it does not separately check for the meaning shoulder belt for either *balteus* or *cingulum*.)

Admittedly, the harvest to be reaped for *Aen.* 12. 942 at first sight may look meager. I see two possibilities.

(1) One resigns oneself to accepting the notion of Cucchiarelli and others that *balteus* and *cingula* at 12. 942 point to the same object, i.e.,

Chapter 2

the shoulder belt ("*balteus, cingula,* the two words refer to the same thing" – Williams *ad* 12. 941–4). In this case, the sentence following *et* in line 943 would best be taken to be explicative of *balteus*. Then, of course, the problem remains: why use a second noun to explain the attributes of the first? One does not see an artistic reason (nor a necessity of logic) that would be served by the *variatio* here. A hypothesis that would find the final hand of the poet missing would be unconvincing in light of the highly wrought character of the epic's final scene.

(2) The alternative would be to ask whether the material reviewed above can lead to a meaningful understanding of what at first sight looks like a *pleonasmus ridiculus?*

The point of departure should be the passage where the belt of Pallas appears for the first time, i.e., 10. 496–500. Whereas the far-reaching emotional effect of Pallas' death and spoliation (and the enhancement through the murder scene depicted on the belt) is dealt with in section 1 of Chapter 3, at this time the focus must be on the concrete shape, i.e., the *immania pondera baltei / impressumque nefas*, which King Turnus, setting his foot on dead Pallas, rips off the corpse. The evidence submitted above suggests that Vergil's contemporary reader, without any further specification, would take the *balteus* to be a waist belt (as at *A.* 12. 274 and as shown on the tombstones of the republican-era legionary and the centurion).

What also speaks in favor of this understanding is the "enormous weight" of the belt that points to the unbroken Roman tradition of attached (and decorated) belt plates, which, in the case of Prince Pallas' belt being made of gold, must render the piece exceptionally precious – and heavy. One will not demand that the 49 slain bridegrooms be depicted on as many belt plates (the less so since the symbolical meaning of the murders will reach beyond the present factual situation of the narrative), but rather expect an exemplification through a limited number of representative plates. (Mention of the artist's name, Clonus, is in line with epic custom of describing precious objects [cf., e.g., Ascanius' gilded sword, made by Lycaon of Cnossus 9. 303–05] and should not give rise to interpretative speculation.) The *enormous weight*, by the way, may not depend on the *balteus* alone, but the belt may be a sort of *pars pro toto* since, as the reader learns at 11. 91f., Turnus takes much more, leaving only the helmet and the spear (the latter having been cast by Pallas before his death): *nam cetera Turnus / victor habet*. That is, Turnus takes also the *lorica* (mentioned at 10. 485) as part of his booty. The poetic focus is on the balteus because of its symbolic long-distance meaning. (κατὰ τὸ σιωπώμενον *et alia eum sustulisse intellegimus, non tantum balteum,* S *ad* 11. 89).

If desirous of a more concrete idea of the belt, one may recall the raised scene of the she-wolf and the twins, arranged in a circle on the belt plate from Risstissen, and, so, imagine rectangular plates of gold riveted to Pallas' belt, embossed with similar circular presentations that, to accommodate a full scene, may likewise take the whole width of the belt plates as do the rosette-like belt buttons on the tombstone of Licaios. One may also picture the Danaid plates alternating with others that display non-pictorial conical or rosette-like buttons only, as detailed earlier.

Before moving on to the second passage that mentions what appear as Pallas' waist belt and the shoulder belt, one may ask whether a sword-holding waist belt may be considered at all possible in view of Vergil's Homeric models. It was (I said earlier) Heinze (1965, 204) who pointed out that Vergil, with no real idea of the Homeric heroes' armor, turned to the Roman armor he knew. Now a sword belt around the waist does not make much sense in the case of a muscled cuirass, except perhaps if the cuirass is exceptionally short, as one shown in Connolly 1998, 207. The officer on the Domitius Ahenobarbus altar (early first century BC), clad in a very short muscled cuirass, definitely has no shoulder belt to hold his sword, which he is wearing on his left side (attached to the sash on the cuirass?). Legionaries on the same altar (Connolly 1998, 226; cf. text 228), the *only* Republican sculpture of legionaries available, wear long mail shirts and carry their swords on a belt around the waist. (Because of its high cost, mail was originally available to aristocrats only, and slowly spread to wealthier legionaries.)

Now it is remarkable that, when Vergil provides specifics on *lorica* or *thorax*, the details mostly point to what is known as *lorica hamata* or *squamata*, i.e., mail or scale armor. On the Greek side, Neoptolemus' *lorica* is constructed with triple loops of gold (*loricam consertam hamis auroque trilicem A.* 3. 467) and so is that of another Greek, Demoleos, (*levibus...hamis consertam auroque trilicem / loricam*, 5. 259f.); but also that of an unnamed Italian shows the same construction (*auroque trilicem / loricam induitur*, 7. 639f.). Trojan Phegeus wears double-threaded mail (*bilicem / loricam*, 12. 375f.). But Trojan Bitias' cuirass has double layers of golden scales (*duplici squama lorica fidelis et auro*, 9.707). And so Turnus dresses in a cuirass reddish with bronze scales (*rutilum thoraca indutus aenis / horrebat squamis*, 11. 487f.; again at 12. 87f. but of different metals: *auro squalentem alboque orichalco / circumdat loricam umeris*), whereas that of his opponent Aeneas may rather be a muscled cuirass, "*unbending* (made) of bronze, blood-red, huge" (*loricam ex aere rigentem / sanguineam, ingentem*, 8. 621f. Apparently Vergil finds it worth noting that this cuirass, unlike others, is stiff.). Etruscan King Mezentius' armor may be expected to be an Etruscan muscled cuirass (see Connolly 100, with fig. 4), but the fact that it was pierced twelve times might speak in favor of the less rigid mail coat (12. 9f. Some Italians are said to have *thoracas aenos*, which are not defined more closely, 7. 633). Aeneas' attacker Thero is wearing mail armor (*aerea suta*, 10. 313, if this is not rather a belt with stitched-on plates, cf. CN *ad loc.*), in addition to his shirt with golden scales (*tunicam squalentem auro*, 10. 314).

How did Vergil expect his readers to picture the construction of Pallas', the horseman's, cuirass that proved not strong enough to hold off Turnus' spear (*loricaeque moras*, 10. 485)? We cannot know for sure, of course, but may conclude, from the majority of cases detailed in the epic, that his was no exception, i.e., that in all likelihood the reader envisioned Pallas wearing a mail coat. Archaeology perhaps offers some reassurance. The only Republican sculptures of legionaries available (those on the aforementioned altar of Domitius Ahenobarbus from the early first century BC) not only show three legionaries in mail shirts, their sword held by a waist belt over the shirt, but also specifically a "late republican horseman" clad in mail, his sword attached to a belt around his waist. The belt is articulated by what appear to be rectangular plates (Connolly 1998, 234, fig. 4. By contrast, fig. 2 shows a horseman from the later column of Trajan wearing his sword by means of a baldric over his mail shirt). See also a "Roman horseman from the monument of Aemilius Paullus at Delphi, 168 BC", clad in a mail shirt that is "split at the thigh so that he can sit a horse" (Connolly 133, fig. 8. Different is the relief of a Republican horseman from the *Lacus Curtius* in the Forum Romanum: he wears a short muscled cuirass, Connolly 133, fig. 9).

So there would be nothing extraordinary if Roman readers pictured Pallas' *lorica* in line with the other mail cuirasses described in the *Aeneid*, and nothing extraordinary either if they pictured him wearing his belt around the waist over his mail shirt as depicted on the archaeological finds mentioned above. The question then is whether this concept helps us in making sense of the terms *balteus* and *cingula* in 12. 942. Translating the terms by "high on the shoulder...the luckless *baldric*" and "the *belt* with its well-known studs" (Fairclough) or "das unglückselige *Wehrgehänge* oben auf der Schulter" and "der *Gürtel* des jugendlichen Pallas mit den vertrauten Knöpfen" (E. and G. Binder) does at least account for the two different terms by assuming two separate objects. However, why would Pallas (and, after him, Turnus) wear an additional belt if his sword is hanging by a baldric over his shoulder? I hypothesize a functional solution that accommodates both terms: as on the remnants from Lyons (end of

2nd century AD) and on the reconstructions of the Etrusco-Roman spearmen of the 6th century BC, the sword-holding waist belt is supplemented by an attached shoulder band that helps to carry (and, perhaps, keep in place) the *immania pondera baltei*. The only parallel from the *Aeneid* itself is the above-mentioned combination set of Evander, whose sword is tied to the shoulder and to the side (8. 459). Though not archaeologically evidenced as contemporary (unsurprisingly, since it is almost always the leather components that have not survived the onslaught of time, whereas the metal parts can still be found), such an arrangement of military equipment also remains well known in later times.

What does one gain from all this for understanding the context? A brief summary may here indicate how the results of the *Excursus* fit in with the interpretation I offer in the main text. First of all, one result of the *Excursus* allows us to dispense with the *pleonasmus ridiculus*, in which also CN acquiesced in the following words (*ad* 12. 942): "The second clause 'cingula bullis' brings the details of the 'balteus' more into relief".

Another result is that we become further aware of the steps in the recognition process that is taking place in the mind of Aeneas. For a reader who closely follows this step-by-step process (baldric – belt and *bullae* – baldric) also the double mention of "shoulder" (*umero*, 12. 941; *umeris*, 944) loses the odium of a meaningless stopgap duplication. And Aeneas' growing awareness appears well summarized in the verb *hausit* – Aeneas "drank in" the detailed reminders of his pains and the spoils.

The main result harvested from the detailed investigation, then, turns out to be of artistic importance. It further illuminates the effort Vergil has expended on taking his reader into the mind of his hero at the point when he makes the decision no longer to think of sparing the defeated enemy. Far from exposing the mind of a mad criminal, Vergil shows Aeneas being gradually made to recall the arrogant enemy's inhuman conduct that he is not entitled to forgive, but which to avenge is an obligation the victim's father had, in an unforgettable appeal to Aeneas' merits, placed upon his shoulders. Why would the poet introduce the "boy" victim, the unjust display of an unfairly acquired trophy, the gradual re-awakening of Aeneas' "savage pain", if not to make the reader appreciate – and share – his hero's rising rage? It would have been counterproductive if Vergil had detailed the factors that so understandably arouse Aeneas' emotion if he had intended his reader to be repulsed by the resulting action.

The last word before the reader is introduced to Aeneas' perceptions, is *infelix* (942): that the baldric is a source of misfortune, i.e., to Turnus, is an authorial comment, pointing out the fulfillment of the poet's earlier

Chapter 2

prediction (at 10. 502–505a) that a day will come when Turnus will hate these spoils, *spolia ista*.

This is the place also to answer the question why Aeneas has not recognized the belt earlier when confronting Turnus at 12. 711–14 (724f.): the answer is that Vergil reserves this recognition for the climax of the epic's final, climactic scene. There is no violation of the poetic *probabile* involved, since in the heat of that earlier close combat Aeneas hardly had the chance to look over Turnus' outfit. This chance occurred only when Turnus had collapsed *duplicato poplite* (12. 927).

Notes

[1] See Buchheit's forward pointing remarks (1963, 13–18). Griffin (1985, 195) feels that, e.g., Hector's death in the *Iliad* (Vergil's model) influences our reading of Turnus' death in the *Aeneid*: "...Hector is humanly an attractive figure, and his death is tragic. So too we feel that the death of Turnus is tragic." G. Williams (1983, 221) convincingly says that, beyond this, the model helps to define the difference, "thus modifying the sympathy." At this point especially, I feel justified in preferring wherever possible not to extend the use of Vergil's models in the interpretation of the *Aeneid* beyond the function that they are assigned by the Vergilian context. After all, we can neither forget all the guidance and distinctive leads Vergil has given his reader concerning Turnus' unattractive actions and character, nor should we wish to look for a standard of judgement outside of (and possibly alien to) the work of poetry to direct our 'responses'. The *limited* value of 'intertextuality' for interpretation is rarely reflected upon these days.

[2] The marital aspects of this conversation were ably analyzed by West 1998.

[3] See Stahl 1981, *passim*.

[4] Propertius, on the other hand, views Augustan Rome as Troy reborn, *resurgentis... Troiae*, 4.1.47; cf. *Troia, cades, et, Troica Roma, resurges*, 4.1.87; Aeneas about Latium: *illic fas regna resurgere Troiae*, *A*. 1. 206.

[5] For the extent of Juno's consent in the *Aeneid*, see E. L. Harrison (1984).

[6] On the *Dirae* (and how they differ from Furies) see Hübner 1970, 12–42; 110; also Hübner 1994. Furies such as Allecto activate, causing rage and disorder, whereas *Dirae* restrain, even numb (and restore order at Jupiter's bidding).

[7] I do not discuss in detail the moving scene when Juturna, recognizing the signs of her "poor" (*misero*, 881) brother's imminent death, raises her voice in lament. It is as the loving sister that she has been trying (and willing) to help, but as the sister she has never considered the possibility of her brother's being guilty. The sisterly voice of compassion and sorrow gives just enough human acknowledgement to Turnus' (self-forfeited) life to make Italian readers feel, if not reconciled to, at least integrated in the main course of events. (Vergil does not withhold compassion even where he states guilt.) Anyway, we saw, Turnus is fairly isolated and does not represent all Italians. Far off the mark appear Feeney's feelings about Jupiter here as "a god paralysing his lover's brother, laying him open for the kill" (1991, 151). It is Juturna's tragedy that she, innocent, is affected by the consequences of her brother's theomachic conduct (on which Chapter 7 will have to say more). Her sorrow is on the soul of Turnus.

⁸ This is an agreeable change Vergil engineered for the portrait of *his* Aeneas. In the *Iliad*, the boulder hurled at Aeneas (by Diomedes, Book 5) put him out of commission. His divine mother (and Apollo) had to save him by removing him from the battlefield. For the learned reader, here is a case where intertextuality can help to verify the poet's different intent.

⁹ Kleinknecht 1966, 443 (=1944, 78), with note 23, provides evidence that *saevus* in Vergil is almost a *terminus technicus* for divine wrath.

¹⁰ Feeney 1991, 155 (my italics). The nonchalance of basing an 'interpretation' on an only selectively read text has also helped E. Oliensis to contemplate the *contamination of Jupiter*: "The contamination of Jupiter by his seeming antithesis will culminate in Jupiter's dispatch of a Dira in Book 12, one of two, Vergil reports with shocking casualness, that have their residence *Iovis ad solium saevique in limine regis*, 12. 849" (Oliensis 2001, 42). In view of *meritas...urbes* 12. 852, one feels tempted to apply the label of "shocking casualness" rather to Oliensis herself and her attempt to unseat Vergil's Jupiter from his high seat of justice.

Misreading the crime-punishing Dira (and that is, Vergil's Jupiter) is almost obligatory among those interpreters for whom "It is no secret that there is a general dissatisfaction or uneasiness with this famous closure" (i.e., Turnus' death), as Johnson put it (1976, 115). For him, the Dira "represents not so much the will of Jupiter as the will of Juno" (127): the Dira, whom Vergil "boldly, even recklessly locates at the foot of Jupiter's throne" (128), "the satanic Dira at the throne of Jupiter"; "it is almost as if Jupiter himself had come under the spell of Juno" (14). When Johnson (l. c.) speaks of "the horror of this perversion of justice and the savagery of the Dira's attack on Turnus", he places himself in the long line of wishful and subjective 'interpretations', looking down on those who accept the end of the *Aeneid* with the punishment of Turnus as being Vergil's last word. Obviously unaware of his own circular reasoning, he comments, "a solution we would find banal in any ephemeral movie of our choice is found to be adequate in the hands of an acknowledged master of Western epic" (116). Refusing to face the possibility that Vergil may be "banal" and not "adequate", Johnson rather chooses to improve on him by appealing to a "general dissatisfaction" and dismissing *meritas*: in Vergil's imitation of Homer, "the justice disappears, leaving only a trace behind it" (1976, 129; here his translation does include *meritas...urbes*, rendered as "unrighteous cities": only a trace of justice?). The consensus of the dissatisfied apparently is: Turnus must not be guilty, and Vergil has to comply with their requirement if he wants to remain "an acknowledged master of Western epic".

¹¹ Thomas 1998, 291.
¹² Pöschl 1964, 235.
¹³ Thomas 1998, 291.
¹⁴ Thomas 1998, 292.
¹⁵ See also 7. 424 in addition to 7. 102–06, for Turnus' knowledge of the divine *responsa*, which the Trojans "parade", *prae se iactant* (9. 134). To exculpate Turnus, Thomas assumes (a) that Turnus had no certain information of the oracle that forbade Latinus to give him his daughter. (Would, in addition to divulging the oracle so that it was spread widely over the Italian cities [7. 103–05], Latinus not have mentioned the divine orders directly to the suitor he loved and who was favored by his wife? 12. 27–31 alone speak firmly against Thomas' construction); and (b) that by his words *si qua Phryges prae se iactant* (scil. *responsa deorum*) Turnus "is claiming they are false", "Trojan

propaganda." This is incorrect grammar as well as logic (see, especially, Turnus' *"et"* at 9. 136, and contradicts the seriousness with which the hoped-for father-in-law had treated the *responsa* of 7. 102 when he denied (cf. *abnegat* 7. 424) Turnus the marriage. *Aen.* 9. 134/5 cannot be claimed as an exception to Turnus' continuous theomachic conduct.

[16] Thomas 1998, 291.

[17] At 10. 595–8, stretching the arm accompanies begging for one's life (*miserere precantis*), and stretching the right arm conveys a request for peace at 11. 414.

[18] "His speech to Aeneas is full of equivocation: it is a cloak of nobility, courage, and piety concealing the reality of Turnus: it is meant to deceive or to seduce Aeneas into error" (Hornsby 1970, 139). The speech was analyzed with regard to its rhetorical *topoi* by Renger (1985, 90–95; see also Galinsky 1988, 324).

[19] Putnam 1981, 239 = 1995,158.

[20] Putnam 1995, 162f. My italics.

[21] Putnam 1995, 153f.

[22] Wlosok (1976, 231, note 16) sees here "kein Schuldbekenntnis, sondern die Anerkennung des Sieges durch den Besiegten, die den Spielregeln des Kampfes entspricht," ("not a confession of guilt, but the acknowledgement of victory by the defeated, which fulfills the rules of the duel").

[23] This, too, was a critical passage for the so-called Harvard school. Its members saw Aeneas here betraying his father's precept of mercy. See, e.g., Putnam 1995, 162: "His deed could be seen, in fact, as the final *impietas*, since he forgets his father's final utterance," etc. Putnam here missed another shift in Turnus' position, when he extra-textually took Turnus' calculating appeal to Aeneas' filial love for Anchises as an authorial reference, viz. to Anchises' precept of the Roman's clemency toward defeated enemies (6. 853, as cited in the text above): "It is no wonder that Turnus mentions Anchises to Aeneas. The last words father had uttered to son...were "spare the subjected and war down the proud" etc. (Putnam 1995, 154). The true authorial reference of Turnus' appeal to Anchises, however, is, as explained in the text above, to Turnus' callous intent of hurting father Evander by killing his young son, Pallas (10. 443; cf. 492). Suerbaum (1981, 142f.) endorsed measuring Aeneas by his father's demand for *clementia* while seeing the ethical judgement on Aeneas changing: "nicht einseitig als *pius*, sondern faktisch auch als *crudelis*" ("not one-sidedly as pious but practically also as cruel").That Anchises' rule of pardon is not all-inclusive will be argued later in this chapter. As explained in chapter 5, the translation of 6. 853 used by Putnam and others, who accuse Aeneas of violating his father's command, allows pardon also for the "arrogant", after being "defeated". The alternative – pardon the submissive and fight to the end (=kill) the arrogant – would see Aeneas as acting correctly when killing Turnus. The discrepancy of translations is moot for our interpretation here since King Evander's *ultio* command anyway obliges Aeneas not to pardon Turnus.

[24] "During the epic's last scene Aeneas grants his *supplex* Turnus no quarter" (Putnam 1998, 203). The sentence would adequately reflect the authorial voice if its subject "Aeneas" were exchanged for "Vergil".

[25] See Stahl 1981, 198.

[26] Stahl 1981, 166; see also 171 (cf. *Aen.* 8. 494 [King Latinus speaking]; 8. 500f. [the Etruscan *haruspex* speaking]; 10. 714 [the narrator's own voice]).

[27] Putnam 1981, 9–10 with note 8; see also Putnam 1995, 165 with note 33; Thomas 2001, 290.

[28] The association is significantly overlooked by Thomas 1998, 293, n. 6: "The two never meet in the *Aeneid*" etc.

[29] According to Horsfall (see 1995, 213, note 142, agreeing with R. Thomas 1991, 261) *furor* and *furia* are not distinct from one another, nor should *furiae* be taken as Furies rather than as *furiae*, "the mental state". For a comprehensive survey of proposed interpretations (in my own text above, I can only deal with select representative positions) see Horsfall's circumspect fourth chapter. Horsfall, however, appears hesitant to commit himself to a definitive reading of the final outcome (1995, 193; 216).

[30] Thomas (1998, 276), following Nethercut (1968, 87), cites the two passages among his examples "of the many ways in which Aeneas and Turnus are tied together, a procedure quite familiar to readers of Vergil," etc. "Tied together"? Hypological disregard of context here once more leads to isolating individual words and to turning a Vergilian contrast into an absurd affinity.

[31] For the fact that Vergil, in depicting Aeneas as the brave defender of Troy, is *ex silentio* countering a tradition less favorable to his hero (Aeneas the traitor), see Stahl 1981. – Williams' (1972) mistranslation of *nec sat rationis in armis* (2. 314) is preceded by Putnam (1965, 28: "...there is little purpose in weapons, but my heart burns to gather a band for battle," etc.). In 1995 (p. 141; a reprint of 1983), Putnam translates "nor is there sufficient reason in arms...", commenting that Aeneas "takes up arms not in defense of *pietas* but under the sponsorship of the *unthinking* use of force" (my emphasis).

[32] The point of Aeneas' rage was forcefully taken up by, among others, Galinsky: "The Attic orators...make it clear that anger is the essential component in the determination of the penalty." When the judge "is meting out the punishment, he should not do so without *orgé*" (1988, 326). "This concept continues in Rome." Since Turnus' guilt is clear, the "question is how to punish. To see Aeneas do so without the emotion of anger would have been repugnant to any ancient audience, except for the Stoics. ...the final scene is rooted...in real life, practice, and custom" (1988, 327). "In a situation like that the wise man, as defined by the Academics, Peripatetics, and even Epicureans, must act the way Aeneas does" (340). For the discomfort which members of the so-called Harvard school felt about the ending of the *Aeneid* see, e.g., W. Clausen (1987, 100): "Yet most readers find the violence and abruptness of the last scene disturbing." It would certainly be interesting to have a statistically reliable sampling of Vergil's readers, especially among his contemporaries. And the interpreter hardly has a right to claim that his own disturbance (or that of his entourage among interpreters) was also the poet's standard.

On the never-ending discussion of the "ethical issues" of the final scene, see also the more recent summarizing remarks by Morton Braund (1997, 214–16).

[33] Putnam 1995, 161f.
[34] See Burck 1979, 90.
[35] Putnam 1995, 159.
[36] Putnam 1995 159f.
[37] Putnam 1995, 159. He continues as follows: "No one *furiis accensus*, fired by furies, is acting contemplatively" (159).
[38] See Stahl 1981, 168.
[39] Putnam 1995, 159f.
[40] So Putnam 1995, 169, n.19; cf. n. 20.

Chapter 2

[41] Quint 1993, 95, referring (in note 51) to Greene: Aeneas "also reveals – the *impassivity* of the public executioner" (my emphasis).

[42] Quint 1993, 95.

[43] Quint (1993, 55) actually uses the verb "construct" when describing his method in terms of an "evident analogy" between the war-weary, wandering Trojans and Vergil's (civil) war-weary contemporaries: "...and we need to keep this analogy before us to *construct* a political reading of the *Aeneid*" (my emphasis). "*Construct*"? "*Evident analogy*"? If Vergil's text gives no indication of such an "analogy", how can it be "evident" (except perhaps self-evident to Quint?), and how can one verify that it does not amount to an arbitrary foreign importation into the poem (even an "allusion" would need a verifiable textual indicator of the relationship claimed by the interpreter)? Quint here comes dangerously close to a brand of ('postmodern') literary criticism that claims: "The role of the scholar or reader is in fact to create rather than recover meaning" (Laird 2003, 244), deferentially reviewing D. Fowler's "*Roman Constructions. Readings in Postmodern Latin*", and deploring that "for most philologists" this is not a viable road; that "conservatives" might object that this approach "could undermine or even destroy the practice of classical scholarship as we know it." Tragic irony?

[44] Putnam 1995, 159f.

[45] See Mutschler 2003, 101.

[46] The interpreter must be careful not to carry modern aversion against "senseless" revenge killings into a Roman context: "Virgil narrates a senseless vengeance-killing which is masked, in the words of the killer, as a sacrifice, but whose true nature many readers experience as quite other" (Hardie 1993, 21). Who are the "many readers" whose experience Hardie invokes, and what legitimizes their experience as apposite to the text? Whose standards does Hardie employ in declaring revenge "senseless"? What criteria does the text offer to determine that *pius Aeneas*' speech is "masked", and by what method is it that the (Vergilian) "true nature" of the killing can be revealed? What might have been Caesar's (or Augustus', or Vergil's, or a contemporary reader's) response when listening to Hardie's sentence?

[47] Putnam 1995, 162.

[48] Putnam 1995, 159.

[49] The resentful discontent (*indignata* 12. 952) of Turnus' departing life has been discussed in detail earlier. On the words *solvuntur frigore membra* (12. 951) and their earlier occurrence at 1. 92, and the extra-contextual speculations drawn from their repetition, see the next chapter.

[50] That Turnus' appeal to father Anchises (12. 933f.) is not meant to make the reader recall *parcere subiectis* (but is intended to remind the reader of Turnus' frivolous wish for father Evander's presence at his son's death) has been shown earlier in this chapter.

[51] For a broader account of tendencies in Vergilian Interpretation see my 1998 *Introduction*. For polyphony and polysemy see also Section 2 of Chapter (3).

[52] Barchiesi 1984, 111, with note 22.

[53] Barchiesi 1984, 120.

[54] Barchiesi 1984, 121 (my emphasis); see also 118.

[55] Barchiesi 1984, 111.

[56] In a chapter fashionably entitled "The Virgilian intertext", Farrell (1997, 238) sovereignly judges that Knauer (in his masterful comparisons of Vergil's *Aeneid* and Homer) "approaches his material somewhat mechanistically; but more recent work,

especially A. Barchiesi, ...treats Virgil's engagement with the literary past in a much more suggestive fashion." My reader will encounter the buzzword "suggestive" more often, wherever an interpreter, not only Barchiesi, feels freed from observing the linguistic and logical precision that organizes an ancient text.

[57] Barchiesi 1984, 119.
[58] Barchiesi 1984, 119, *preciso effetto intertestuale*.
[59] Barchiesi 1984, 106, *questo breve episodio*.
[60] See Clausen's *Appendix* in Horsfall 1995, 313f.
[61] See Stahl 1990, 179f.
[62] See Hardie in *TLS*, June 15, 2001.
[63] E.g., we read that Dryden transformed Vergil's Turnus by painting him, in terms inherited, as "animalized or diabolical", Thomas 2001,150. (Turnus the Devil is not found in Vegius' "thirteenth Book of the *Aeneid*" [Thomas 149] but in his *De Perseverantia Religionis* 1.5). Is Thomas aware that excesses of "Augustanism" in the Vergilian reception do not *per se* contribute to establishing the correctness of the alternative Harvard Vergil? Nor does the appeal of Vergil to Fascism, Nazism, etc. in itself constitute proof of misappropriation (see Thomas, Chapters 7 and 8), though it does show discrepancies with the Harvard school's view of Vergil.
[64] Broch (who at one time confused exiled Ovid and Augustan Vergil, or had Aeneas carried out of burning Troy by his father, Anchises, instead of vice versa) definitely was not interested in providing an interpretation (or "a reading") of the *Aeneid*, as Ziolkowski (1993, 203–22) documents: "Broch knew little and cared less about the historical Vergil, using him merely as a figure on which to impose his own views and concerns" (220). "Broch was not essentially concerned with Vergil at all" (221). "...he attempts in his appendix...to give the impression of competence and authority both in Vergilian studies and in Latin – and many students of Broch and his novel have taken him at his word" (218).
[65] "At least, Sforza's evidence existed, and in the text of Vergil"(in the eyes of Thomas). "He thus could not exploit ambiguity, insisting instead on open hostility" (scil., of Vergil toward Rome and Augustus). Thomas 2001, 274–75.
[66] Thomas 2001, 3ff. (my emphasis), on *aurea condet/ saecula, A.* 6. 792f.
[67] Thomas 2001, 281("my views, in as far as they are not already clear, will become so"), with note 7.
[68] See Thomas 2001, 292 n. 22; 285 (my emphasis). The 'critical' criterion of the reader's being pleased or displeased is, as has to be stated repeatedly, characteristic of the Harvard school and affiliated methodologies. See already Johnson (1976, 115f., my italics), on "those who are *content* to read the poem as an ethical melodrama." "Thus, a solution *we would find banal* in any ephemeral movie of our choice is found to be adequate in the hands of an *acknowledged master* of Western epic." The perfect *circulus vitiosus*: the "acknowledged master", once appointed, has to deliver to *our* satisfaction.
[69] Thomas 2001, xi (my emphasis), cf. xii.
[70] Thomas 2001, 224. My emphasis.
[71] Thomas 1998, 274.
[72] Thomas 1998, 275.
[73] For the "oikoumenische Akkulturation" ("ecumenical acculturation") see Ganzert's 2000 architectural study of the "Allerheiligste des Augustusforums".
[74] "Den Visionen Vergils folgend werden Mythos und Geschichte aufeinander

bezogen und als Heilsgeschehen gedeutet. Dabei ist der Blick aber – anders als im Epos – von der Gegenwart auf die Vergangenheit zurückgerichtet." ("Following the visions of Vergil, myth and history are seen in relation to one another and interpreted as salvation history. But differently from the epic, the viewing angle is from the present back to the past."): Zanker 1987, 198.

[75] Kallendorf 1999, 394. I refrain from discussing most recent publications that further elaborate this line of argumentation.

[76] See Schneider 1985, 17f., who even thinks "dass Maffeo überhaupt erst durch Decembrios Verse die Anregung zu seiner eigenen Aeneisfortsetzung bekam." ("that Maffeo received the first stimulus for his own continuation of the *Aeneid* from Decembrio's verses").

[77] Schneider 1985, 20, with note 43.

[78] See especially Brinton 2002, 24–26.

[79] See Putnam 2004, xviii; and also below.

[80] *Aen* 7. 596f. is much closer in *meaning* to Vegius' line 28 than the merely *verbal* echo from *Aen*. 6. 620 (*discite iustitiam moniti et non temnere divos*) listed in Schneider's *Similienapparat* and followed by Thomas (2001, 283).

[81] Chapter 7 demonstrates that the mythological figure of the Fury Allecto does not eliminate or even reduce Turnus' responsibility (as the Harvard school maintains with rather uncharacteristic unambiguousness. See, e.g., Clausen 2002, 187).

[82] Kallendorf 1999, 397f.; my emphasis. This reader admits that he does not know what to make of the logic in Kallendorf's next sentence: "We cannot say for sure how much of Virgil's pessimism Vegio saw, but once we note its absence in the *Supplement*, the decision to complete the *Aeneid* becomes considerably more comprehensible."

[83] Kallendorf 1999, 398.

[84] Kallendorf 1999, 398, note 22 (my emphases). In parentheses, Kallendorf adds "private conversation, 7 February 1997". The date will be recalled later.

[85] Thomas 2001, 280. See also the title of S. J. Harrison's review in *CR* 52, 2002, 292: "Virgil and the Conspiracy Theorists".

[86] Thomas 2001 281.

[87] Thomas 2001, 281. For the following quotations, see 283.

[88] This is S. J. Harrison's translation (1991, 33) of the same words (*super adsistens*) at *A*. 10. 490.

[89] Thomas 2001, 282 (my emphasis).

[90] Thomas 2001, 284 (my emphasis).

[91] Thomas 2001, 284 (Thomas' emphasis).

[92] Thomas 2001, 284.

[93] Thomas 2001, 284 (my emphasis).

[94] Thomas 2001, 280.

[95] Thomas 2001, xix (my emphasis).

[96] Putnam 2004, xiii.

[97] Putnam 2004, xix (my emphasis). In the accompanying note (19) Vegius is said to follow a "path...for the defamation of Turnus."

[98] Putnam 2004, xix. In note 20, Putnam mentions "recent readers" who (with Kallendorf and others) sensed in Vegius' consistent dark and shining portraits of Turnus and Aeneas respectively Vegius' "latent dissatisfaction with certain aspects of Virgil's text and especially with his portrayal of the irrational violence of the hero in the epic's

last moments." "Latent" as well as "dissatisfaction", once more, as a methodological concept to establish Putnam's mentally unhinged Aeneas also for Vegius?

⁹⁹ Putnam 2004, XX. The rage (*furiis*) of *A*. 12. 946 is, as was shown earlier, a transient, not a permanent affection of Aeneas.

¹⁰⁰ Putnam 2004, xix.
¹⁰¹ Putnam 2004, xx.
¹⁰² Putnam 2004, xx.
¹⁰³ Putnam 2004, xxi.
¹⁰⁴ Putnam 2004, xxii.
¹⁰⁵ Putnam 2004, xxvi; xx.
¹⁰⁶ Putnam 2004, xxvii.
¹⁰⁷ Putnam 2004, li, note 25 (my emphasis).
¹⁰⁸ Putnam 2004, xxvii.
¹⁰⁹ Putnam 2004, xxvii.
¹¹⁰ Putnam 2004, xxviif.
¹¹¹ Kallendorf 2004, 220 (my emphasis).
¹¹² Putnam 2004, xxxiii (my emphasis).
¹¹³ Putnam 2004, xxxivf.
¹¹⁴ Putnam 2004, xxxiii (my emphasis).
¹¹⁵ Kallendorf 2004, 220 (my emphasis).
¹¹⁶ Putnam 2004, xxxv.
¹¹⁷ Kallendorf 2004, 220.
¹¹⁸ The passage from *De Perseverantia Religionis* (1. 5) is quoted by Brinton 2002, 28 (my emphasis).
¹¹⁹ Kallendorf 2004, 220f. (my emphasis).
¹²⁰ I once more point to my *Propertius* (1985), especially Chapters vi–viii and xii, for a method of establishing and verifying an author's ambiguity.
¹²¹ Buckley 2006, 111.
¹²² Buckley 2006, 113 (my emphasis).
¹²³ Buckley 2006, 108; 110.
¹²⁴ Buckley 2006, 112.
¹²⁵ Buckley 2006, 113 (my underlining).
¹²⁶ Buckley 2006, 115 (my emphases). Is Buckley acquainted with *Aeneid* 7, or only with Thomas 2001 (see my earlier quote from his page 284: Vegius' Aeneas "brilliantly shifts the blame for his own actions to the Ausonians.")?
¹²⁷ Buckley 2006, 130.
¹²⁸ Buckley 2006, 128f.
¹²⁹ Buckley 2006, 129.
¹³⁰ Kallendorf 2004, 220.
¹³¹ Thomas 2001, 281, n.7. Likewise from Harvard provenance (Tarrant 1997, 187), the same book is viewed in a broader scope: "The links between the *Aeneid* and imperial ideology are viewed in a wider context by David Quint in *Epic and Empire*"(etc.).
¹³² Quint 1993, Chapter 2, note 52 (my italics), referring to Stahl 1990.
¹³³ Quint 1993, 14.
¹³⁴ Quint 1993, 15; my emphasis.
¹³⁵ Quint 1993, 16.

Chapter 2

¹³⁶ Quint 1993, 51f. If Vergil so appears as "a Freudian *avant la lettre*", then, on the other hand, "Freud's model of the psyche empowered by narrative", may, according to Quint, possibly be derived "from influential political narratives like the *Aeneid* in the first place" (1993, 52): circular reasoning to justify analyzing the *Aeneid* in Freudian terms?

¹³⁷ Quint 1993, 65.

¹³⁸ Quint 1993, 51f.

¹³⁹ Quint 1993, 52.

¹⁴⁰ Quint 1993, 52, with note 3, referring to Barchiesi's "very helpful" reading of the *Aeneid*'s ending.

¹⁴¹ Quint 1993, 79; Quint's emphasis. However, only in prophetic sections does the *Aeneid* refer to future civil war: 6. 826–35 (C. Julius Caesar vs. Gn. Pompeius); 8. 675 ("*Actia bella*") – 713 (Octavian, called – prematurely – "Augustus" [6. 787], vs. Antonius and Cleopatra: not at all a "civil" war in Augustan terms). In the *Aeneid*'s story itself, the war ends with Aeneas' and the Trojans' victory.

¹⁴² Quint 1993, 79 (my emphasis).

¹⁴³ Note 37 on p. 380.

¹⁴⁴ Quint 1993, 69; my emphases.

¹⁴⁵ Quint 1993, 74 (my emphasis).

¹⁴⁶ Quint 1993, 70 (cf. p. 74: "His victory over Turnus is a vindication both for himself and for his defeated Trojan nation."). This reader has difficulty imagining Aeneas' concomitant therapeutic thoughts of personal revenge, perhaps: 'My spear in your thigh, Turnus, is compensation for Diomedes' boulder that smashed my hip socket at *Iliad* 5. 305f.'? For Quint, Homer's ἰσχίον and Vergil's *medium...femur* (*A.* 12. 926) are the same: "In the *Iliad* Diomedes struck Aeneas in the thigh," etc. (1993, 71). To establish a stone-throwing parallel, Quint resorts to philological acrobatics: "Aeneas' flying spear is compared to stones – "saxa" – launched by a siege machine (921–22)". In the Latin text, the *sound* of Aeneas' flying spear is compared to the roaring sound (*fremunt*) of catapulted rocks, as well as to – a comparison conveniently dropped from Quint's account – the *sound* of crashing thunder (*crepitus*). The deadly spear in its flight (*volat...hasta*) is then compared to a dark whirlwind (*atri turbinis instar* 923). Only by way of this selective (and linguistically imprecise), cherry-picking reference ("saxa") can Quint maintain that "the action and language recall his [scil., Aeneas'] own wounding by Diomedes" (1993, 70f.).

¹⁴⁷ Switching characters' identities is now an accepted litcrit game. Thomas (1998, 278–80), claiming alleged "intricacies of Virgilian intertextuality", has Turnus, when killing Aeolus (*A.* 12. 542–47), kill the symbol of Homeric *Aineias* – an event that presumably "disrupts the closure" of a balanced passage. Who is the disrupter here?

¹⁴⁸ Quint 1993, 79 (my emphasis). The repetition of the three words is accorded significance also by Putnam (1965, 200f.) and Thomas (1998, 275). As is my practice, I here concentrate on one symptomatic, exemplary case.

¹⁴⁹ On Aeneas' Achillean attitude (misunderstood as past-oriented melancholy by Harvard's influential Clausen) right from the opening of the epic onwards, see Stahl 1981, 159–65. To turn Aeneas' preference for a glorious death in battle over inglorious drowning at sea into a "regressive death wish" (Quint 1993, 73; cf. Barchiesi's [1984, 103] "eroe esule e desideroso di morire") not only falsifies the epic's opening, but the tenor of the whole work: Aeneas does *not* (at 1. 94–101) desire "an anonymous

immersion into the waves of his native Simois", nor is it true that "the *Aeneid* must wage a campaign against this deathwish, drawing its hero away from the womblike waters of death", which allegedly represents "the greatest of Eastern temptations" (Quint 1993, 29). After all, the Latin text also incorporates Achilles' wish to have died on land at the hands of the greatest enemy warrior instead of in the water of a swollen river "like a swineherd boy" (*Il.* 21. 281–83).

[150] *Indignata*, "resentful", cannot – as Quint 1993, 31 has it – be replaced by "wrathful" (Turnus, 12. 952) or even "furious" (Camilla, 11. 831). On p. 23 he correctly translates *indignatus* (8. 728) by "resentful".

[151] Quint 1993, 79f.

[152] Last among Quint's dubious criteria for Vergil's presumed doubt in "the permanence of Augustus's achievement" (after all, according to the *Aeneid*, the return of the Golden Age, 6. 792f., and the end of wars as well as of civil war, 1. 291ff.) is his comment on river Tiber halting his flow to help Aeneas (8. 86–89): "But Virgil's Rome was well acquainted with the periodic disasters of the Tiber's floods." (Quint 1993, 30f.). The question arises whether "topical" allusion (see, e.g., Quint 1993, 14; 16) is a concept that satisfies the demands of (verifiable) logic employed in serious scholarship, as Quint apparently would have it. From the viewpoint of strict proof, Quint's "topical allusions" (1993, 28–30), both in terms of the Actian victory and of a presumably dark future, to this interpreter appear wildly associative, established by linkages of questionable value, such as "suggests" (a connection used repeatedly); "mirror"; "verbally recall"; "might seem to"; "may return to"; "echoes"; "look back to".

[153] Quint 1993, 79 (Quint's emphasis). Hardie, likewise viewing the *Aeneid* in a post-Augustan Age perspective, follows suit by taking over from Quint "the suggestion in the last scene of the possibility of an indefinite cycle of retaliatory revenge" (Hardie 1993, 15). Hardie maintains that, "as uncontrolled rage, revenge pure and simple rather than the judicial retribution envisaged by the terms of the treaty, it [sc., the killing of Turnus] retains its potential to repeat itself in fresh outbursts of chaotic anger (the dreary catalogue of vengeance-killings of Roman civil war)" (1993, 21). Nothing can be farther from the text than such an extra-contextually imputed "potential" (where does Vergil mention it?). On the erroneous commingling of duel treaty terms and revenge obligation, discussed earlier, see more also below.

[154] Quint 1993, 78.

[155] A comparable misunderstanding is found in Putnam's interpretation of the settlement scene (Putnam likewise views Aeneas' role when he kills Turnus as "reversed from victim to inflicter of fate", and Turnus "in the former role of Aeneas", i.e. as victim, 1995, 162). Putnam sees Jupiter and Turnus "equated as voices of moderation" (1995, chapter 8, note 24 on page 170) because of their use of the word *ulterius*: Turnus, asking for mercy, urges Aeneas not to go any further (*ulterius*) in hatred (12. 938), and Jupiter commands Juno not to go any further (*ulterius*) in her attempts to harm Aeneas [and to protect Turnus] (12. 806). This, Putnam concludes (in seeking support for his thesis of Aeneas as "the victim of rage"), places Aeneas and fury-dominated Juno together as "the impetuous forces needing restraint". He overlooks that Jupiter's *veto* (806) against any further attacks on Aeneas is designed to open the road to the killing of Turnus. Jupiter's voice here pronounces anything but "moderation" in favor of Turnus' survival. By forcing Juno to 'moderation' in her support of Turnus, Jupiter firmly aligns himself with Aeneas' imminent killing of

Turnus (and with fate). It appears impossible to view Jupiter (together with Turnus) as "opposing further violence". The methodological demand resulting from this example is once more: not to assume a meaningful verbal echo on the basis of one recurring word (here: *ulterius*) alone, but to respect the contexts in which it occurs (here requiring answers to the questions "*what* further action precisely is being discouraged by *ulterius*, and by whom?").

[156] Quint 1993, 78 (my emphasis).

[157] The inability to distinguish differing aspects or perspectives offered in the text is a characteristic of the Harvard school: with regard to "the vengeance" (i.e., the killing of Turnus in the final scene), Thomas (2001, 291) comments that "we are left with a sense that it might not have happened and therefore might not have needed to happen (*Aeneas' hesitation shows the reality of that possibility*)" (my emphasis). Like Quint (and Putnam), Thomas fails to distinguish the moment of "Aeneas' hesitation" toward the defeated enemy from the ensuing revenge for Pallas, triggered by a different motivation and a different obligation. And he ignores the four predictions of Turnus' death cited in the text above. If Thomas is "left with a sense that it...might not have needed to happen", his selective reading of Vergil's text has once more led him astray.

A comparative blurring of the text's distinction between the duel terms and the *ultio* obligation toward Pallas/Evander is found in Hardie (1993, 20): "...the resolution of the quarrel between Aeneas and Turnus...*should* have been regulated by...the *foedus* between Aeneas and Latinus described at 12. 161–215. But violence erupts once more to frustrate the terms of the treaty"(etc.). First: violence does not merely "erupt" impersonally but is perpetrated by the Italian side, and it is Turnus' evasive movements that render a return to the *foedus* terms impossible for a long time, despite Aeneas' endeavor to enforce the duel treaty. Second, when the duel finally takes place (Turnus eventually agrees to face Aeneas), it *does* – *cum pace* Hardie – follow the terms of the treaty – with the one exception that Aeneas does not kill the defeated enemy (as projected by the treaty participants: 12. 14; 38; 49; 74; 79; 110; 185; 646; 679; the author included: 765, not to mention here the passages involving Jupiter cited in the text above), but considers granting mercy and sparing Turnus' life. It is only when the *ultio* obligation is activated that the aspect of "sacrificing" is resumed from Book 10. Therefore, it is methodologically not admissible to connect the sacrifices that sealed the duel treaty (and their defilement by people like Italian Messapus) to Aeneas' act of "sacrificing" (*immolat*) Turnus. Hardie's assumption (1993, 21) of "an almost too neatly schematic dramatization of René Girard's theory of the 'sacrificial crisis'" turns out to be too neatly schematic itself.

[158] This applies not only to Quint. It is not convincing to argue (as Zetzel 1997, 200 does) that Vergil intended to undercut his panegyric of Augustus as the bringer of a new Golden Age by expecting his reader to object: "Golden ages had existed in the past, but they had not lasted." See also Zetzel on p.197 (my emphasis): "...and, above all, the idea that Romulus/Quirinus and Remus will rule together in harmony *clearly contradicts* the accepted legend of Romulus' murder of Remus." But in the context of 1. 291–96, Jupiter predicts that, *at the time and under the rule of* Augustus, Roman citizens (and/or leaders) will no longer engage in fratricidal strife, as it is known to Vergil's reader from the time of Rome's foundation. Jupiter's prophecy covers things that are not only future to his daughter Venus, but that can also be past or even present to the Roman contemporary of Augustus: Jupiter's information for Venus also contains

messages from Vergil for his reader, and in this perspective Romulus and Remus stand as cyphers for fratricidal citizens of past civil wars. What Zetzel calls (1997, 200) "discordant and disturbing elements" in the *Aeneid*'s three great prophecies, may not have been felt by Vergil (or his contemporaries) to be "discordant and disturbing". Like any intelligent author, Vergil was certainly not unaware of the message pronounced in Zetzel's concluding sentence, "Rome's past, and its future, are *what the reader will make of them*" (1997, 202; my emphasis), but that awareness apparently did not keep him from writing his panegyrical prophecies that culminate in Augustus and his 'golden' age. The influence of history's potential (or eternal) cyclicity ("The idea that history has an end is a false consolation; wars to end war are a hope, not a reality." Zetzel 1997, 202), so clearly formulated by Thucydides (1. 22. 4), can, in the case of Vergil, apparently be only *inferred or derived by reader's self-assured response*, but it cannot be documented by quotations from the work itself. Again and again we have seen Vergil's message of Augustus' Golden Age to be a stumbling block for the Harvard school's anti-Augustan interpretations ("One man's golden age" is "another's age of iron", Thomas 2001, 2–7).

[159] See Stahl 1985, chapters VIII, XI, and XII.

[160] Demonstrating *in concreto* the insufficiency and inadequacy of present-day theory to deal with Vergil's epic required me here to concentrate predominantly on one fashionable interpretation (Quint 1993), with a few other examples mentioned along the way. For a broader critique of tendencies in Vergilian Interpretation see Stahl 1990, 177–82 and 1998, XV–XXXIII.

3

AENEAS THE WARRIOR

(1) Battlefield Conduct: Vergilian Details, I

Section 2 of the preceding chapter has established how Aeneas feels: on the international or inter-ethnic level, he was, in consonance with his father's injunction of *parcere subiectis*, able to consider mercy to defeated Turnus, but not in matters of revenge for Pallas. The principal question of course deserves continued exploration beyond the scope of the final scene alone (where the reader obviously is asked to share Aeneas' position): has the reader been *prepared beforehand* for dealing with the sudden change from mercy to passionate revenge and, if so, by what means? Have the reader's thoughts and emotions already been 'tuned' or guided in a certain direction when we reach the final scene and read of Aeneas' reaction which, at the sight of Pallas' belt, makes him retreat again from the road of clemency just entered upon? The answer must observe Vergil's art of guiding his reader, which I would like to name by the Greek rhetorical term of *psychagogia*, – persuading the soul through guidance.

Since even those who believe that Vergil condemns Aeneas tend to admit that Aeneas' wrath and Turnus' death have their dramaturgical root in Book 10, it is appropriate to start looking there for the common ground that has evaded 20th-century interpreters. And it is there that the second of those strands begins which come together in the *Aeneid*'s final scene (i.e., the strand designated "B" in the survey offered in Chapter 1). In Book 10, too, the poet details the different battlefield conduct of the two leading warriors. (In Books 11 and 12 we found them predominantly characterized as contract-bound and duel-evading, respectively.)

From the general scope of fighting in Book 10 two scenes stand out: the death of young Pallas (Aeneas' apprentice, son of Arcadian King Evander, Aeneas' host at the site of Rome) at the hands of King Turnus, and the death of Lausus, young son of the tyrant Mezentius, at the hands of superior Aeneas. The fact that the latter event appears to be Vergil's own invention, makes the reader ask: if the death of Pallas[1] which eventually will rebound on his killer Turnus is Vergil's version of the death of Patroclus in Homer which eventually will rebound on the killer Hector (who falls under the avenging hand of Patroclus' stronger friend Achilles as Turnus will be killed by avenging Aeneas), to what purpose has Vergil *doubled* the scene of a superior fighter killing a young and inferior one?

In the case of Pallas (the case receiving by far the greater authorial attention) a first lead can be gained from the difference in age: in Homer, Patroclus was older than his avenging friend Achilles, and he had, in a sudden burst of self-glorification, acted against the express orders of Achilles by himself trying to take Troy on his own. In Vergil, Pallas is younger than his avenging friend Aeneas, almost a boy still (*puer* 11. 42; 12. 943), on his first day of battle ever (10. 507; 11. 155). This design from the beginning turns the scales of the reader's sympathy in favor of Pallas (as well as creating understanding for his avenger) and against his physically stronger and more experienced slayer.

At the end of a syncrisis of the two young heroes, Vergil points out that both will die equally "at the hands of a greater enemy", *maiore sub hoste* (438). That is, Vergil extends the comparison of the two young victims Pallas and Lausus to the two unequal main actors of the *Roman Iliad* and their conduct in a situation of manifest superiority. The most striking difference, to put it summarily, is that Aeneas kills only when being confronted, but Turnus actively seeks out and singles out his young and inferior victim with the intention of attacking him and executing a sure kill.

Again it proves helpful to take the compositional context into consideration, which here means the military development. Pallas' horsemen apparently have arrived overland (Pallas has come by sea on Aeneas' ship), and Turnus' intention is to keep them from linking up with the Trojan camp (10. 238–40). Turnus himself with his whole army (*totam aciem*) takes his stand on the shore to prevent Aeneas and his army from disembarking and gaining a foothold on land (308f.). Aeneas has an *aristeia* (310ff.), but the battle "right on the threshold of Italy" (*limine in ipso / Ausoniae* 355f.) is for a long time undecided, the forces on either side being, according to the simile of the fighting winds, "equal" (*viribus aequis* 357).

In another area, Pallas' horsemen, forced to fight on foot because of difficult terrain, are being routed by the Latins. Pallas rallies them, pointing out their choice between fleeing into the water and trying to reach the Trojan camp: *pelagus Troiamne petamus?* (378. The latter alternative is of course the one that Turnus wanted to see prevented.) Following up Pallas' address with a sweeping *aristeia* that culminates in the killing of Halaesus (who himself is built up by a mini-*aristeia* to be a worthy opponent for Pallas), Vergil crowns the young man's code-conforming attitude by having him vow Halaesus' arms to "Father Tiber", *Thybri pater* (421), as a *tropaeum*.

(How different will be Turnus' conduct when he kills Pallas and appropriates, among other pieces, his sword-belt!)

At this juncture, Vergil brings Mezentius' young son Lausus into the picture (426ff.). Lausus prevents his troops from panicking by executing a mini-*aristeia* of little more than three lines (427b–30), consistent with his lesser importance in the authorial concept. (Pallas' privileged focalization comprises sixty-four lines: 362–425. Also, the reader still has in mind the close emotional relationship of Evander, Aeneas, and Pallas, extensively described in Book 8 and earlier in Book 10). Nevertheless, as Aeneas and Turnus together with their armies were earlier set against each other "with equal strength" (*viribus aequis* 357), so now the two younger heroes' troops "clash with leaders and strength equal", *concurrunt ducibusque et viribus aequis* (431).

It is at this point that Vergil introduces the syncrisis of the two young men mentioned earlier. Almost equal in age, of eminent beauty, both are denied a homecoming. But "the ruler of great Olympus" (Jupiter = Fate, *sua fata*, or Vergil's dramaturgy) did not let them fight each other:

Soon their fate awaits them under a greater enemy.

mox illos sua fata manent maiore sub hoste. 438.

The word "soon" raises the readers' or listeners' expectation, forces us to be watchful when reading on. It is also at this point that the poet arranges the first of the two superior-against-inferior encounters, by moving Turnus from his section of the battlefield over to that of Pallas (in the case of the pair Aeneas-Lausus, he will, for good reason, proceed in the opposite way, by having the younger one approach and attack the experienced older warrior): Turnus' divine sister (a fitting *dea ex machina*) advises her brother to come to Lausus' aid (439f.).

Turnus, however, once reaching Lausus and his troops, does *not* join the din but does something unexpected, shouting: "It is time to stop the battle!" *tempus desistere pugnae!* (441). He has realized that here is his chance to execute a personalized vendetta against Pallas' father, King Evander, for having granted hospitality and support to Aeneas.

In fact, King Turnus even forbids all the others to go after Pallas and has the field cleared: he alone (emphasized twice in the same line: *solus ego...soli mihi*, 10. 442)[2] reserves for himself the right to kill the prey which is "owed" to him (*mihi...debetur*, 442f.). Why? Is he perhaps eager to have a duel? The reader's answer is clearly "no" because Pallas is no match for the *maior hostis*, as Vergil brings out when he describes the Arcadians' fear for their young leader (452) and Pallas himself when viewing the *corpus...ingens* (446) of Turnus. Like the superior lion coming down on the strong but doomed

Chapter 3

bull he has been stalking (*specula cum vidit ab alta*, 454),³ Turnus descends from his chariot toward Pallas, who, aware of his physical inferiority, sees his only chance (cf. *fors* 458) for this fight of *unequal powers* (cf. *viribus imparibus* 459) in hitting Turnus from a distance before he is drawing nearer. But the youngster's strength, though great (*magnis...viribus* 474) proves not sufficient: his spear can only graze Turnus' huge body (cf. *magno...corpore* 478), earning him nothing but a bullying and condescending, even schoolmaster-like, taunt (481) from his stronger opponent. When Turnus, long posturing (*diu librans* 480), hurls his own spear, he pronounces: "Look whether *our* missile has greater penetrating power!", *aspice num mage sit nostrum penetrabile telum* (10.481). Pallas, his sword now drawn for close combat (475), does not flinch but bravely awaits and faces the incoming missile: Turnus' spear penetrates Pallas' shield and chainmail and, still carrying deadly force, sinks into his chest, killing him (479–89). It definitely is a distorted understanding when a prominent modern representative of the anti-imperial interpretation three times tries to assure his readers: "...however much we pity Pallas, he met his death in fair fight...".⁴

With regard to the unequal situation resulting from the age difference, it is worth quoting Father Evander who later, in addressing the absent Turnus, states:

> You, too, would now stand, a huge trophy, in the fields
> if his (scil., Pallas') age were equal (to yours) and his
> strength were the same (as yours) based on his years,
>
> tu quoque nunc stares immanis truncus in arvis,
> esset par aetas et idem si robur ab annis, 11. 173f.

It is Pallas, on the other hand, who – erroneously – fosters noble ideas about the situation. He shows an honorable desire to encounter the superior opponent in single combat, either for the highest Roman (!) form of victory (cf. *spoliis...opimis* 449) or for a glorious death.

> "My father (scil. King Evander) is impartial toward either lot",
>
> sorti pater aequus utrique est (450).

The young man, even in the face of death, is concerned about what his father may think of him, wishing not to cause him dishonor. (The contrast with Turnus, who in the end will use his own father as a negotiating card for survival, is striking: *Dauni miserere senectae* 12. 934.) Pallas' father, the reader recalls, had sent his son out to learn from Aeneas as from a teacher (*magistro* 8. 515) the craft of a warrior. When accepting his enemy in order to achieve, in victory or in defeat, the highest honor of paternal recognition, Pallas proves himself a student worthy of his teacher. Aeneas, too, when facing certain death in Juno's storm at sea in Book 1, wishes he could rather have died fighting for Troy, like those fellow fighters who fell "before the eyes of their fathers, below Troy's high walls", *ante ora patrum Troiae sub moenibus altis* (1. 95).[5] In the same spirit, Aeneas will later refer to the honor code when trying to comfort Father Evander by saying that his son was "struck not by a shameful wound" (i.e., he was struck in the chest rather than in the back, 11.55f.).

Turnus, for his part, when seeking the mismatched fight, likewise thinks of Pallas' father (in fact, his taunt has in turn provoked Pallas' noble statement [*parens* 10. 443 ~ *pater* 450]):

> I wished his father himself were here and watched!
>
> cuperem ipse parens spectator adesset (443).

Worlds apart from Pallas (and from Aeneas in Juno's storm), Turnus (the lion stalking his victim, a predictable kill) has held the troops back not for an honest duel; rather, in claiming Pallas as his own prey and his alone, he primarily intends to hurt the father. In Vergil's conception, then, the death of Pallas is painted closer to a wilfull homicide or an assassination than to an honorable battlefield killing. Perhaps one should more appropriately say that Vergil paints Pallas' death as a pre-meditated killing, a murder.[6] And as Pallas' noble bravery can be measured by the gauge of Aeneas' death wish in the sea storm, so there is (as already Servius saw) a gauge to measure Turnus' frivolous wish for Evander's presence at his son's death: this is venerable King Priam accusing Pyrrhus, Achilles' son, of having made him an eye-witness to the killing of his son Polites,

> you polluted the father's eyes with his death,
>
> patrios foedasti funere vultus 2. 538f.

Consistently, Turnus addresses his final message to father Evander:

> As he has deserved him [i.e., dead], I am sending Pallas back to him
>
> qualem meruit, Pallanta remitto 10.492.[7]

And

> Not a small price is he going to pay for granting Aeneas hospitality
>
> haud illi stabunt Aeneia parvo hospitia 10. 494f.

The experienced warrior Turnus has not granted young[8] Pallas the dignity of taking seriously his courage on his first day (10. 508) of fighting on the battlefield. For superior Turnus the unequal fight was nothing but a welcome opportunity to make father Evander pay a price he "owed"

Turnus (cf. *mihi...debetur* 442f.), in other words: for Turnus Pallas' death was a commercial transaction, a payment in blood for hospitality granted to Aeneas.

Turnus' commercial vocabulary is resumed twice by the author in describing what follows. Aeneas refuses the ransom money offered by suppliant warrior Magus, who implores him by his father's, Anchises', shade and by his son, Iulus. For evaluating his refusal, three facts must be taken into account: first, Aeneas is by now informed of how Pallas was killed (510); second, before his inner eye are Pallas, Evander, their hospitality, the binding handshakes (515–17; this has already led to his taking prisoners as sacrificial victims, to be discussed by us in the next section); and, third, Magus has "craftily" (*astu*), as the authorial voice emphasizes, ducked and run under Aeneas' spear (522) to embrace his knees: instead of holding up his shield, he has cowardly avoided facing the warrior's death which Pallas so bravely and unflinchingly met. All this must be considered to have entered Aeneas' mind and to determine his response, given when Magus asks to be saved *for his son and his father*:[9]

> these commercial transactions of war Turnus was the first
> to abolish – then already when Pallas was killed.
>
> belli commercia Turnus
> sustulit ista prior iam tum Pallante perempto. 10. 532f.

So, for Aeneas' wishful thinking (his thinking is still under the fresh impression of what happened to Pallas) Turnus could have tried to take Pallas prisoner, alive, and release him for ransom (an idle thought, in reality incompatible with Pallas' – and Aeneas' own – honor code). Therefore Magus' appeal to Anchises and Iulus cannot help him:

> Thus feels the spirit of my father Anchises, thus Iulus.
>
> Hoc patris Anchisae manes, hoc sentit Iulus. 534.

The poet has created for Aeneas an opportunity to explain that Turnus' conduct has invalidated certain conventions that would allow for occasional exceptions even on the battlefield, and that it was Turnus who replaced the currency of ransom money with that of blood, and it was Turnus who, by violating and defiling the father-son relationship, has invalidated any appeal to Iulus and Anchises.

It is, Aeneas feels, as if someone has killed me in order to hurt Anchises, or my son Iulus in order to hurt me. Aeneas now acts as the avenger of this cruelly-treated relationship and feels that as such he must be inexorable. Releasing cowardly Magus would mean taking Pallas' heroic death lightly. "For from this deed (scil. your death at my hands) requital will extend to both, if both Evander's parental deprivation and the death of Pallas will be avenged.": *Ex hoc enim facto ad utrumque perveniet gratia, si orbitas Euandri vindicetur et interitus Pallantis* (Donatus). No word of criticism on excessive human behavior is heard from Vergil's lips here (if compared to his earlier comment on Turnus' conduct, when he appropriated Pallas' baldric instead of offering it to a divinity, 500–505). And if one takes into account the situation of utter need of Aeneas' men – Aeneas has meanwhile been informed (510–12) not only of Pallas' death but also of his own troops' defeat and flight, their need for his help and their being within "a hair's-breadth from death" (R.D. Williams' translation, *ad loc.*) – then Magus' arguments (528f.) that the Trojans' "victory"(!), *victoria Teucrum* (528), does not depend on this and that one single life does not make so great a difference, appear rather beside the point.

One observes two things here: first, that Aeneas has put himself in the place of grieving father Evander long before (in Book 11) Evander himself obliges him to take revenge for his son. Secondly, that Turnus, when in the final scene of the *Aeneid* he operates with his own aged father Daunus and appeals to Aeneas' feelings for Anchises, is using an argument the sanctity of which he himself has in the eyes of Aeneas compromised in the most horrible fashion, and so has forfeited the protection it would otherwise grant him. Viewed from Book 10, Aeneas' unforgiving final reaction at the end of 12 appears predetermined and inevitable, and his creator has gone out of his way to sympathetically acquaint the reader with Aeneas' reasoning and feelings.

The gesture that Turnus (after first appropriating the sword-belt of the slain) grandiloquently (*largior* 494) returns the body for burial, "whatever the honor of a tomb and whatever the consolation of burying is", should not be misunderstood as a sign of his humanity (or gentleness, "*Milde*," as Pöschl, pioneer of the 'tragic Turnus' interpretation, termed it);[10] the belittling[11] and derogatory statement,

> whatever the honor of a tomb, whatever the consolation of burying is
> I grant
>
> quisquis honos tumuli, quidquid solamen humandi est,
> largior 493f.,

proves that it is a small matter in which Turnus is willing to show magnanimity (if it is magnanimity at all and not cruel irony). For, as the main part and climax of his message, there follow the words about the high price he makes Evander pay. What he releases is small change, so to speak.

And it will be the visible reminder represented by Pallas' sword-belt that will trigger Aeneas' death-blow in the final scene of Book 12 (941ff.).[12]

Chapter 3

Therefore we understand the comment which the author adds in his own persona (thus emphasizing the plot-line) about Turnus exulting in the spoils: the human mind does not know moderation when uplifted by favorable circumstances (10. 501f.). (Pallas, after all, had promised the spoils of *his* last opponent to god Tiber, 421ff.; Aeneas will dedicate the arms of Mezentius to Mars, 11. 5ff. and not at all despoil the corpse of young Lausus, the opposite number of Pallas, 10. 827. But godless King Mezentius, acting like Turnus, also reveals his sacrilegious character in his intent to make his son a living trophy, *tropaeum*, by having him wear slain Aeneas' armour, 10. 774–76.)

> For Turnus, there will be a time when he will desire an
> un-touched Pallas bought at a high price, and when he will
> hate these spoils and this day.

> Turno tempus erit magno cum optaverit emptum
> intactum Pallanta, et cum spolia ista diemque
> oderit. 10. 503–05.

In this comment, Vergil not only establishes the causal nexus between Turnus' hybris and Turnus' death (thus bearing out Jove's indication at 471ff. with human motivation). Also, we here for the third time (in order of occurrence, it is the second time, cf. *magno* 503 ~ *haud...parvo* 494) meet a commercial vocabulary (cf. *belli commercia* 532), and see Turnus' metaphor of the price to be paid, and this time Vergil (not without irony?) turns the metaphor – less than ten lines have intervened – against Turnus himself. His predicted future desire for a high price to undo what he has done, especially when announced through the author's intervention, is a clear advance indication of Turnus' un-heroic desire to survive at the end of the work, and sufficient confirmation for the interpretation I offered earlier in the preceding chapter of his unwilling (*indignata* 12. 952) departure from this life.

Aeneas' ensuing refusal toward cowardly Magus' ransom offer, no longer allowing any *belli commercia* (10. 531ff.), then, can be seen in line with the authorial voice. Turnus has introduced the new currency of blood (494), Vergil points out the long-range consequence (503), Aeneas can no longer allow an exception and accept payment in the old currency (530ff.), for the father-son relationship has been cruelly mocked.

Vergil as the author even goes one step further and, confirming one of the alternatives mentioned by Pallas before the deadly encounter (449f.), in his own persona directly invokes dead Pallas:

> Oh you, about to return to your father as a cause of grief and a great honor!

> O dolor atque decus magnum rediture parenti... 10. 507.

These words pick up the father-son topic, which, like the price metaphor, can be seen to permeate all three passages considered here.

If thus the poet in his own persona, like his hero Aeneas, declares himself in sympathy with dead son and mourning father, where is his reader expected to stand now? After all, long ago the poet imbued his reader with a sense of fearful foreboding, ever since the moving departure scene when father Evander fainted while contemplating the possibility that his son might not return to him alive (8.572–84).

Let us also remind ourselves of the fact that even the father of the universe, recalling the death before Troy of his own son Sarpedon, cannot bring himself to watch the killing of Pallas:

oculos Rutulorum reicit arvis 10.473

The question of the reader's expected leaning has two answers, the first of which, concerning Turnus, can still be given within the framework of the present Section. Vergil has not left the reader with any option of finding Turnus' conduct acceptable once we have discovered his diabolic intentions. Killing a brave but physically inferior young man in order to exact a price of grief from his father is humanly so abhorrent (to Roman as to modern sensitivities) that the reader can no longer sympathize at all with the killer. One may hardly agree with Quinn's excuse for Turnus, that his repulsive wish is "a characteristic piece of braggadocio",[13] bragging. Partisan Vergil puts his reader here in the same position as he did when he presented to us the heart-rending lament of a Trojan mother (transferred from Sicily to Italy for rhetorical purpose) who must observe Turnus' Rutulians carrying on sticks the heads of her son and his friend (9. 481–97). He has not created a comparable situation to lend his art to an *Italian* mother's voice.

A further aggravating circumstance, let it be recalled, is that Vergil's Turnus, by triumphantly appropriating and donning the sword-belt, has committed an offense against the *Aeneid*'s honor code. Unlike Turnus, Lausus had promised the armor of his last opponent to river god Tiber; and Aeneas will dedicate the arms of Mezentius to war god Mars, and he will not despoil at all the corpse of young Lausus (the dramatic counterpart of Pallas) (10.827).

Repelled by Turnus' unethical, abominable conduct as depicted in Book 10, and won over to Pallas' (and his father's) case by the poet's sympathetic presentation, the attentive reader will feel asked to join Aeneas at the very end in opting for revenge for the killing of Pallas rather than for the consideration of mercy towards the defeated enemy. And such a reaction in favor of Aeneas is expected of the reader not only at the end, but also pertaining to his battlefield conduct immediately following the killing of Pallas, as will be shown in greater detail in Section (1) of Chapter 4.

(2) Methodological Intermezzo:
The Sword-Belt of Pallas – Holding a Quill for the Literary Critic?

First, however, and in parenthesis, we have to turn to an issue of determining force for the coming development. It concerns the role that the sword-belt of Pallas, so unethically, in violation of the *Aeneid*'s code of conduct, appropriated and worn by Turnus, plays for interpreting the scene of its original owner's death as well as for the epic's final scene. Again, we can draw on our earlier analysis of the compositional context.

Defenders of Turnus have sometimes viewed the "action of despoiling Pallas" as "the centre of Turnus' offence," as Lyne put it.[14] "Turnus' 'offence' turns out to be not so very large at all".[15] This estimation of course disregards the parameters of the preceding narrative, which has revealed the (in the authorial view) nefarious motivation of Turnus.[16]

Others have pointed to the bloody crime scene depicted on the sword-belt:[17] 49 sons of Aegyptus lie in their blood in their wedding chambers, slain by their 49 brides (In the myth, they have executed their father's orders; only one daughter, Hypermestra, spared her bridegroom. This latter feature is – understandably – not mentioned in the *Aeneid* passage). Here is Turnus in the act of appropriating the sword-belt:

> and, following such words, he pressed with his left foot[18]
> the deceased, snatching away the immense weight of the sword-belt
> and the wicked crime embossed on it: the band of young men foully slain
> in one night, their wedding night, and the bloody marriage chambers,
>
> et laevo pede pressit talia fatus
> exanimem rapiens immania pondera baltei
> impressumque nefas: una sub nocte iugali
> caesa manus iuvenum foede thalamique cruenti, 10. 495b–498.
>
> which Clonus, son of Eurytus, had embossed with much gold;
> in this spoil Turnus now exults and is happy possessing it.
>
> quae Clonus Eurytides multo caelaverat auro;
> quo nunc Turnus ovat spolio gaudetque potitus. 10. 499–500.

One can easily concur that the bloody scene on the sword-belt may have some bearing on the meaning of the context in which the poet has set it. But how to access that meaning? Now: the narrator has placed the taking of the spoil and this *ecphrasis* so as to follow, on the one hand, Turnus' heartless message for father Evander, that he will pay a high price for having granted hospitality to Aeneas (494/95a) but, on the other hand, so as to precede his own authorial comment on human lack of moderation in success and his prediction of Turnus' future willingness to pay a high price for having the killing of Pallas undone (10. 501–05).

If one takes into account this framing context together with the heavy sympathetic weighting of the preceding narrative in favor of slain Pallas, the nearest and most natural parallel to the murdered young bridegrooms would be Pallas whose death, we said, comes close enough to being murder.

The adverb *foede* (with its connotation of defiling), pointing to the nefarious character of the deed as well as of the doers, would likewise be appropriate for Turnus' wish to have father Evander present to watch his son dying – in the same way as the related verb *foedare* at 2. 539, as mentioned above, covers aged King Priam being forced to witness the slaughter of his son, Polites. One may also cite Juno's "foul" service, *foeda ministeria* (7. 619), of throwing open the Gates of War – a function which pious King Latinus refuses to provide for Turnus and his companions who want him to break the peace, declare war on the Aeneadae, and open the nefarious bloodshed of two nations destined to live in peace.

The phrasing *caesa manus...foede* does not ascribe any disparaging quality to the victims, but *caesa*, being a passive, requires an answer to the complementary question "(slain) by whom?". That is, the murderous Danaids find their complement in Turnus, slayer of Pallas. Precisely speaking, the scene on the sword-belt does not depict the act of killing but its aftermath, i.e., the slain corpses (*caesa manus*) lying in their bloodied (*cruenti thalami*) chambers. This exactly fits the present situation reached and depicted in the narrative: when "blood and life", *sanguis animusque* (487), leave him, Pallas touches the "hostile ground" "with bloody mouth", *ore cruento* (499). The sword-belt scene lets the reader perceive Turnus' crime multiplied 49 times, driving home the nefarious character of his action.

What about the wedding night, could it, too, have a reference to Pallas? One might think of the fact that Pallas was killed on his first day in battle ever (10. 508; cf.11. 155), right at the beginning of his career as a hero, and see a faint correspondence to the bridegrooms being cut down at the dawn of what is supposed to be a life-long relationship. If this comparison does not hit the mark, it at least brings us a step closer to another, more pertinent, parallel: the unsuspecting bridegrooms were as maliciously set up as Pallas, while fostering noble ideas of winning the *spolia opima*, was set up by experienced and superior fighter Turnus who ordered everyone else aside to have Pallas reserved for himself as a sure kill. Turnus has acted in a manner similar to the malicious and insidious way in which the *nefas*-planning daughters of Danaus entrapped their bridegrooms.

Taken in this way, the scene on the sword-belt confirms the tenor of the preceding narrative: Pallas' death was a premeditated homicide. So it is likely that the hideous (cf. *foede* 10. 497), sinful (cf. *nefas* 497) crime depicted on the sword-belt is supposed to give the reader confirmation on how to judge the slaying of its rightful owner. And it is the sight of this scene on the belt that will trigger Aeneas to switch from mercy to punishment in the epic's final scene (12.938bff.). Repulsed by Turnus' unethical, abominable conduct, and won over to the side of Pallas and his father by the poet's sympathetic presentation in Book 10 (and in Book 8), the attentive reader is to feel invited to agree with Aeneas' change of mind at the end of the work and to vote for revenge and punishment rather than for mercy.

My interpretation of the *ekphrasis*, being in agreement with and complementing the preceding narrative, further confirms the poet's negative portrait of Turnus. The Vergilian portrait, however, has proved unacceptable for members of the anti-imperial school, and so has its consequence, revenge, though it agrees with the contemporary concept of *ultio*.[19] In view of the (allegedly) merciless behavior of Aeneas toward Turnus, the (allegedly not respected) suppliant, one has (as was shown in the previous Chapter) felt "uneasiness"[20] or found the *Aeneid*'s final scene "disturbing",[21] even missed "the comforting ethical closure...so yearned for",[22] and so one has concluded, guided by uninhibited subjectivity and wishful thinking, that Vergil cannot have meant the end of his poem to be read as he wrote it.

However, what is needed methodologically for these interpreters is a Turnus in Book 10 who is presented very differently from the one I have explained from Vergil's text in the preceding Section. Contemporary literary critics located the quill for writing *their* Turnus – in the *sword-belt of Pallas*. I shall look more closely at three influential methodologies (considering the general fluency of their definitions I use names with some hesitation) as they have been applied to interpreting the belt: New Criticism, Semiotic theory, and a very different one, a combined philological-archaeological and political interpretation. All three have in common that they ascribe to the sword-belt's *ekphrasis* a meaning that lies outside its immediate context. As far as the literary critical scene is concerned, it is worth noting that, in addition to *ekphrasis*, today simile too is made to serve such extra-contextual purposes. Richard Thomas, for instance, in his endeavor to "de-Augustanize the *Aeneid*" (as he puts it),[23] presents the logic-defying thesis that the simile is "a vehicle for subverting the epic's authoritative voice".[24] One is inclined to name Thomas the inventor of the *simile dissimile*.

Putnam includes *ekphrasis* in the enterprise, claiming that both it and simile "are types of metaphor, offering us opportunities to *reinterpret the text* in which they are embedded, *to gain a new angle for the apprehension of its meaning.*"[25] So *ekphrasis* is viewed as offering another critical tool with which to interpret *against* the grain of the main text instead of in its support.

Though claiming to be concerned also with "context", Putnam compresses his summary of the author's preceding narrative into a few words: "Turnus has met and killed in single combat the young protégé of Aeneas." (Does "single combat" appositely render the author's compassionate focalization on young Pallas in recounting the killing?) Putnam further presents Turnus as "announcing...that *the defeated* got *what he* deserved" (my emphasis).[26] In truth, as was shown above, Turnus at 10. 492 gloats that he is sending Pallas home *as he* (i.e., *Father Evander*) *deserves* him, qualem *meruit*, i.e. dead. Both by this mistranslation (refuted already in Page's commentary of 1894–1900)[27] and by leaving out Turnus' announced intention of *killing the son in order to hurt the father* (*make him pay a high price*), Putnam has weakened the moral indictment which the authorial context had raised against Turnus. But the epic's narrative organization is not of high significance to the methodology of New Criticism, which allows verbal allusions and repetitions to be independent from plot development: "linearity" of story-line (which, Putnam admits, eventually leads from pious Aeneas to the golden age in the empire of Augustus), is said "in counterpoint"[28] to be complemented by "the poem's lyric or tragic dimension", which is assumed also to be found in the sword-belt's *ekphrasis*. The description of the sword-belt, Putnam claims, is supported and gains meaning *for the whole poem* through "circularity" and "repetition". In this way, the characterization of Turnus' act (defined as that of spoliation) by the words *foede* and *nefas* is acknowledged by Putnam, but the characterization is also transferred to the actions of Aeneas, who is said to develop, from being a suppliant before the Sibyl (in Book 6), to being a man who closes his eyes to suppliants, especially to Magus in Book 10 and in the final scene toward Turnus ("he symbolically...kills the Sibyl").[29]

In the method of New Criticism, no detailed investigation is needed of the individual contexts from which the so-called verbal allusions or repetitions are harvested. In the epic's final scene, Turnus is viewed "as a youth basely slaughtered"[30] (apparently, a "repetition" in the literary realm of "circularity", amounting to another Pallas *foede caesus*). *Some* shadow has even to be cast on Pallas (the earlier owner of the sword-belt, with whom Turnus the new owner accordingly shares "being in the position of a Danaid"!): "Vergil had given Pallas, too, before his death an *aristeia* with some *ugly* moments."[31] What *ugly* moments may Putnam have in mind? Vergil has painted the picture of an exemplary young leader whose rallying admonition (*monitu* 10. 397) turns his fleeing troops around and whose battlefield success the authorial voice characterizes by *praeclara...facta* (397f.), and Pallas himself as a *decus magnum* (10. 507), a "great glory" (transl. Harrison).[32]

Chapter 3

One sees: instead of the author's perspective, which offers one noble youth, one malicious killer, and, in the end, one justified avenger, we shall end up with two victimizers-turned-victims, both of less-than-perfect characters. Such sweeping and simplifying leveling does away with the moral nuances that distinguish the complex and varied focalizations developed in the authorial narrative context. But it helps to de-Augustanize the *Aeneid*. Bivocalism has here not developed a critical tool sufficient to establish what is often claimed to be a "second voice" in the *Aeneid*.[33] But it may be looked upon as helping along the road to de-Augustanizing the *Aeneid*.

Putnam emphasizes that Vergil bars features of *clementia* from his Danaid myth, such as Hypermestra sparing her bridegroom, Lynceus. The attentive reader of Book 10 feels like asking: how *could* Vergil have introduced clemency if Pallas shares the fate of the basely murdered bridegrooms and, unlike Lynceus, is *not* allowed to survive? But for Putnam Vergil may suppress clemency "just as Aeneas finally squelches any instinct to spare the suppliant Turnus". So he sees "Turnus as a youth basely slaughtered and...Aeneas as a type of Danaid enforcing the vendetta of her father."[34] Putnam indeed appears, by means of *circularity* and *repetition*, to transfer Vergil's picture of Pallas foully slain onto Turnus (while along the way assimilating Pallas to Turnus by assigning Pallas some – authorially uncorroborated – "ugly moments"), and Vergil's picture of Turnus onto Aeneas. By appropriating the sword-belt (if I understand Putnam correctly)[35] Turnus is also taking on the former owner's *role of victim*, and in the end the allegedly merciless Aeneas, "too, is a passive victim as well, *furiis accensus*, set aflame by inner demons."[36] Putnam indeed ends up with altogether three victimizers turned victims, the last one, however, being viewed as a merciless victim.

It does not take a leap of the imagination to see that, if a hypothesis – not to say: critical dogma – of "circularity" and "repetition" overrules plot-line and narrative foci, the causal nexus between Turnus' nefarious deed in Book 10 and Turnus' punishment (*Pallas...poenam scelerato ex sanguine sumit* 12. 948f.) is easily toned down and overlaid by "repetition" of the violent crime, this time committed by an allegedly merciless Aeneas himself. Such a reduction, however, invalidates the variety and simplifies the complexity of authorial perspectives that our interpretation of the narrative context has brought into evidence. To sum up: the *ekphrasis* on the sword-belt of Pallas does not appear to provide the interpreter with an appropriate critical quill on the road to establishing a non-Augustan dimension in the *Aeneid*.

Another prominent route of de-contextualizing the sword-belt's message is the one taken by Gian Biagio Conte. Applying Semiotic Theory, he especially availed himself of the concept of connotation, which claims that a word or expression suggests or even implies a further meaning. Conte tried, with Servius (*ad* 2.55), to limit the meaning of *foedus* in Vergil to "cruel" (*crudelis*), excluding the moral nuance of "foul" (*turpis*). Such exclusivity is sufficiently refuted by Juno's *foeda ministeria* (7.619), her opening of the Gates of War: breaking the divinely sanctioned peace is not just a cruel but it is a sinful, nefarious act.[37]

Defining a possible moral meaning of *foede* at 10. 498 as "with ignominy" or "with shame", "meaning that the young men died ingloriously" because "killed in bed and not in battle", Conte declares that such a meaning "would certainly be wrong". Right he is, but he is apparently not aware that it [he] is wrong in having transferred the adverb *foede* from the killers' action to their victims' suffering: "...the tone is set by 'foede' (barbarously): the poet's intervention is characterized by his *pity* and his *horror*", focusing on the bridegrooms' "tragic fate".[38] "Pity", of course, being an amoral concept, can be felt also toward victims of a crimeless misfortune. In truth the adverb *foede* characterizes the act of *caedere* (*caesa* requires as agents the complement *ab uxoribus*), not the passive humans who are the objects of the slaying so nefariously performed by their slayers. The moral turpitude is indeed not that the bridegrooms were slain "so barbarously", but that they were murdered nefariously, without a chance to live, *entrapped maliciously* in a way comparable to the manner in which Pallas was set up by Turnus in a hopeless, inescapable situation.

Having, by mixing up active killing and passive suffering, worked with a mistaken notion of the potential moral blemish indicated by *foede*, Conte gives the adverb the non-desecrating meaning of "so barbarously slain" (his translation of 10. 498): "*foede* refers to the ferocity with which the array of young men has been 'caesa,' and that is why this deed is a nefas."[39] "Ferocity" (of dying) instead of malice or nefarious murder?

Where Conte does admit a sense of defiling in *foede*, he misapplies the word, transferring it outside its Vergilian context. He refers to "the sullying profanation" associated in ancient culture "with the experience of having *seen* bloodshed."[40] This takes the focus away from the murderers' act to a (potential) viewer not mentioned in Vergil's description of the sword-belt scene. When Conte cites, e.g., aged King Priam who complains that Pyrrhus has made him watch his own son's death, *patrios foedasti funere vultus* (2. 539), the shamefulness still lies with the killer's act, not with the watching father who himself likewise is the slayer's victim. And Aeneas does not mean to say that he himself is being defiled (2. 501f.), when watching slaughtered Priam with his blood "defiling" (*foedantem*) his own altar fires. Conte's example here does not exemplify what he wished it to exemplify.

Chapter 3

The difficult *foede* having been transferred out of its murderous Vergilian context, Conte makes one more *contra-contextual* assumption (an addition of his own to Vergil's text): as the murdered bridegrooms must have been disappointed in their joyful expectations when suffering their premature death ("brutally betrayed in their illusion of happiness"), so Pallas, encouraged by success and victory, is said to be cut off in his "beautiful illusion": "Turnus' superior force destroys the confident hope that courage will suffice for victory."[41] This is extra-textual speculation: there was no confident hope (or "beautiful illusion") when Pallas, without flinching, faced the approaching superior 'lion' and decided to throw his spear first, before Turnus would do the same, in an attempt "if somehow chance would favor him in his daring, in the situation of unequal strength", (10. 458f. si qua = εἴ πως: "hope against hope", Harrison ad loc.).

Nor does it help Conte's case that, failing to distinguish different perspectives, he introduces father Evander deploring "the naïve, bold enthusiasm of a youth and the love of glory that had excited Pallas during his first experience to war". Evander is mistaken (11. 154–57): his son did not die in consequence of youthful, incautious (cf. *cautius* 11. 153) daring, but was maliciously sought out and attacked by a superior enemy in a pseudo-duel not of his own choosing; and, in clear awareness of his own inferior strength, he chose not to run away but met his death open-eyed, wishing not to be a dishonor to his father (10. 450). "Naïve, bold enthusiasm"? "Beautiful illusion"? Rather, courage in a hopeless situation.

But Conte, having eliminated the moral component in *foede* in favor of a general tragic horror, expands on his counter-contextual idea of "Deaths suffered with naïve confidence, with disenchantment." Finding that in Vergil's "own cultural reality" there is "a closeness" between "youths destroyed by *mors immatura* (death before maturity)" and "death before marriage"[42] (a "theme" richly evidenced in Greek as well as Roman literature), he pronounces "a creative mechanism whose significant elements have the same function in the anthropological system as in Virgil's text."[43] So Conte concluded that death-before-marriage represents a species of the genus premature death, and that the "proximity of Pallas' destiny to that of the young bridegrooms" is "a typical mechanism of literary connotation." So, then, if the sword-belt shows maliciously set-up and murdered bridegrooms, this means no more than "premature death", and by the "mechanism of literary connotation" we must retroactively understand Pallas' death also as tragically premature – and not in the first place as a nefarious killing, *impressumque nefas* (10. 497)? Like New Criticism's predilection for (allegedly) context-independent verbal repetitions, so the 'connotation' concept of Semiotic Theory does not protect its practitioner from doing violence to the text he claims to interpret. The consequence once more is an undifferentiated, generally tragic outlook of Vergil's epic, discounting the possibility that the authorial voice may be taking sides in matters of human compassion.

While Conte as an interpreter confidently claims that the philologist "simply assumes the function of the receiver programmed by the text of Vergil",[44] the guiding accents and rich nuances the poet included in his preceding narrative are lost, sacrificed to a leveling reduction. Even if Vergil utilizes such literary differentiations for the prerogative and benefit of the Trojan (i.e., ultimately, for a pro-Augustan) perspective, we as his interpreters do not have the right to discount such a bias.

However, if one is on the path to a "de-Augustanized" *Aeneid*, it is of course helpful to see, with Putnam, criminality deflected away from Turnus (declaring him, too, a victim) and attached to Aeneas (reading him as a merciless killer); or, one may (with Conte) interpret *foede* instead of as "nefariously" (scil., slain) as generally indicating a tragic situation of premature death suffered by the not-yet-married: this, too, takes away from the authorial depiction of Turnus' nefarious intent and will more easily allow him to be seen as a victim. Conte himself falls victim to his Semiotics-based theory of discontinuous 'foci' through which the poet allegedly grants equal rights and consideration to the perspectives of Aeneas as well as of Turnus (and of others: "Every point of view is a center of independent perception").[45] What Conte would wish to establish is that Vergil "introduces relativity",[46] offering the "multiplicity of relative truths coexisting in the text".[47] Conte's thesis that for Vergil "the norm was no longer absolute but relative"[48] requires him to devalue plot function (or dramaturgy) to the degree that "the dramatic component never goes deeper than the text's *surface structure*; it never affects the shaping of the deep content."[49] Vergil's "polyphonic way of writing"[50] producing a "text" that is "polycentric"[51] in a world where "the truth is no longer just one truth."[52] A similar fragmentation – and resulting leveling – of Vergil's hierarchical world-view was detected earlier (in Chapter 2, Section1) in Feeney's attempt to dethrone Vergil's Jupiter who, in the author's voice, punishes "deserving" (*meritas* 12. 892) cities, but, according to Feeney, must be considered unacceptable to Vergil because he (allegedly) lays his lover's brother open to the kill. Feeney, too, tries to exculpate Turnus, transferring guilt onto Jupiter. One sees: the epic's narrative architecture has to be declared unimportant or even non-existent so that the resulting fragments may be assigned each an independent value of their own.[53] A cogent example of the importance of the "dramatic compound" is found in Book 1, where Aeneas' role as that of protagonist is brought out by his postponed appearance before Dido due to the long-distance dramaturgy, taking its origin in Juno's storm which splits up Aeneas' fleet (see Chapter 5). Because of Conte's (and also Putnam's) widely ranging influence, it was necessary for once to expose the baneful consequences that arise from disregarding a narrative's artful imbalances produced by preferred (or less favoring) focalizations (as in the case of Pallas and Turnus; and also, as will be shown later, of Aeneas and Lausus *versus* Turnus and Pallas).

Though patently erroneous, Conte's treatment of Pallas' sword-belt has had followers.[54] Conte's American editor and promoter, C. Segal, recommended the chapter on Pallas' sword-belt as "sharply focused"(!), even maintained that "Here Conte's approach supplements the text-immanent reading that has dominated the American critical scene" (etc.), stating that "the representation of the murdered bridegrooms" is "the signal of a whole cultural code of mourning the premature death of the young."[55] Once again, an extra-contextual approach has proved misleading to the extent that it is out of touch with the authorial intent (and a clearly nuanced intent there is, as we have shown). Where "the application of contemporary critical and semiotic theory to literary texts" (to quote from the volume's jacket) supplants (rather than perhaps "complements") close linguistic observation of authorial text and meticulous tracing of context, a dangerous precedent is created. It applies not only to reading the remaining Books of the *Aeneid*, but to philologically and critically stringent interpretation everywhere. It is unfortunate (but eye-opening) that the late-20th-century critical scene required extensive and detailed analysis of erroneous and miso-logical (not to say: hypo-logical)[56] pseudo-methodologies for re-opening access to authorial intent (which, according to Glei,[57] is evidenced by the author's intent to communicate).

After interpretations affiliated with New Criticism and Semiotic Theory, two cases of a different approach of dealing with Pallas' sword-belt and its meaning for the *Aeneid* must at least be touched upon here. This type of approach (occasionally mixed with others) may fittingly be called the archaeological-philological and political one. It emanates from the philologist's habit of drawing together widely scattered bits of information and postulating an underlying connection of meaning.

From a number of sources (prominent among them is Propertius' elegy 2. 31) we know that the area of the temple of Apollo on the Palatine Hill (the location of the Emperor's residence, which was connected to the temple by a private covered ramp)[58] also held a Colonnade of the Danaids. In its *intercolumnia* statues were set up of the daughters of Danaus about to murder their young husbands (i.e., their cousins, the sons of Aegyptus, Danaus' brother); a statue of their father, his sword drawn, was nearby (see especially Ovid, *A.A.* 1.73f.). Definitely, those statues are not identical with the busts presently on display in the Antiquario Palatino.

Two questions posed by scholarship are of potential importance to the present investigation: first, the political meaning Augustus intended by including the statues within the wider temple area, and, second, the colonnade's relation to the Vergilian murder scene on Pallas' sword-belt.

First, then: "It goes without saying" (*Es versteht sich...von selbst*) that the temple area "was equipped with a sophisticated pictorial program" (*mit einem ausgeklügelten Bild-Programm versehen war*), "which mirrored the self-representation of the new ruler." The quotation from Lefèvre's opening section[59] outlines a basic premise shared by scholars who have investigated the colonnade for a possible Augustan meaning. Their results, however, vary widely. For the present purpose it suffices to identify only two.

Lefèvre himself, assuming that the Danaids were here understood to act in self-defense, refuses to judge the murderous action of the *Verteidigerinnen* (as he calls them) as a criminal outrage (*Frevel*); but how does this square with *miseris* and *ausae* in Ovid's description of the colonnade:

> where Belos' granddaughters dared to prepare death for their
> poor cousins,
>
> quaque parare necem miseris patruelibus ausae
> Belides... (*A.A.* 1.73f.)?

The words *miseris* and *ausae* seem to indicate sympathy for the poor victims rather than approval of Lefèvre's "revenge or self-defense" – *Rache oder Notwehr*. However, Lefèvre views the sons of Aegyptus (of whom there apparently were no statues set up) as attackers in their pursuit of their prospective brides, and as such believes them to be a symbol of the power (*Sinnbild der Macht*) which had recently threatened Rome and had been defeated by Augustus: the Danaids represent the triumph over Egypt (*über Antonius, Cleopatra und ihre Truppen*).[60] It is only consistent that Lefèvre interprets the statue of Danaus with his drawn sword as representing Octavian-Augustus.[61]

Second, Lefèvre's take on Pallas' sword-belt in the *Aeneid*. He assumes that Vergil, "presumably under the impression of the colonnade program (*wohl unter dem Eindruck des Programms der Porticus*)", understood the myth in the same way: Pallas, being outrageously attacked, is to be equated with the Danaids; whereas Turnus, the attacker whose deed is to be viewed negatively, corresponds to Aegyptus' sons "whose shameful action (*nefas*) has found an ignominious (*foede*) end (*deren schändliches Handeln (nefas) ein schmähliches Ende (foede) gefunden hat*)".[62] The message of the *balteus* then is that Pallas will be avenged (*Pallas wird gerächt werden*).

Lefèvre too has, though rightly seeing Turnus as the attacker, grammatically misapplied the words *foede* and *nefas*:[63] they cannot refer to any preceding misconduct of Aegyptus' sons (which supposedly would entail their disgraceful end, pointing ahead to Turnus' punishment). Rather, as was stated earlier by us, *nefas* is explained by the murder (*caesa*), and *foede* characterizes the malicious assault by which the Danaids killed their bridegrooms. Furthermore, Lefèvre's attempt to tie in Vergil's *ekphrasis* with his own evaluation of the temple area's archaeology amounts to an imported over-determination of a text that in itself displays an immanently consistent meaning. By exchanging victims and perpetrators of the Vergilian murder scene (Aegyptus' slain sons as actors, the killing Danaids as victims), he can assign to the *ekphrasis* only the function of pointing to future revenge rather than of elucidating the context at hand, i.e., the wrongful death of the sword-belt's rightful owner.

The other 'political' interpretation of the sword-belt to be cited here is by S.J. Harrison, who signed up to Conte's mistaken premature-death theory: "The primary emphasis in the text at *Aeneid* 10. 497–9 is on the tragic death of the victims, and the abomination of the death of unfulfilled youth, not on the criminality of the perpetrators."[64] So again: Vergil has apparently neglected to inform his readers of Pallas' wedding plans?

Comparing his interpretation of the Danaid myth to "its larger context in Augustan Rome", Harrison likewise moves from interpreting "the symbolic role" of the Palatine Danaid statues to, in a second step, once more considering the *ekphrasis* of the Vergilian sword-belt. Stating first that "In all Augustan allusions to the Danaids, their deed is condemned, as indeed in Vergil's *nefas*",[65] he proceeds to interpret the presentations on the temple doors of Palatine Apollo: the attacking Gauls in 278 BC being driven from Delphi by Apollo's lightning, and Niobe over her children's bodies (punished by Apollo and his sister for her *hybris*). Harrison finds a "clear" "link with Actium": "there too...Apollo took revenge on his enemies and supported his favourite Augustus." "Thus Palatine Apollo becomes the defender of civilization against barbarism," and the Danaids become "part of the scheme."[66] But, in contrast to Lefèvre, Harrison, supplementing an argument of Kellum, views the Danaids as standing not for Rome under Octavian, but for Cleopatra VII who married two younger brothers of hers and is said to have been involved directly in the killing of at least one of them. Danaus, who in Lefèvre's interpretation is equated with Augustus, in Harrison's scheme takes on the role of Augustus' adversary: "like Danaus, Antony urges a closely-linked female to barbarous deeds." All these associations, then, make the Danaids "a plausibly specific symbolic representation of contemporary enemies."[67]

As with Lefèvre's premise that the Palatine Danaids act in self-defense (or in revenge), so with the identifications Harrison suggests there is the problem that they cannot be proven. They even raise a practical question: if "the Danaids were taken from the cities and sanctuaries of the conquered" ("they may even have come from Alexandria itself"), how did the selection process work? Did Augustus give orders such as 'search Alexandria and get me a group of Danaids so they may represent my Egyptian adversary and her treasonous Roman associate?' This is hardly convincing. The Gauls and Niobe on the temple doors glorify the god's traditional punishment of human theomachic hubris – which may (or may not) 'symbolize' contemporary events. They may equally well be destined to support the new Augustan religiosity and the moral restraint it aims at.

But the case of Scopas' statue of Apollo as citharode[68] (not as the archer god!) definitely belongs to a different, wider context. Here I do not doubt that the statues of Apollo, Diana, and Latona (one of them even with a replaced head; Pliny, *Nat.* 36. 4; 24; 32) were sought out from different sources and assembled as a group. For by their configuration they show, as does Horace's *Carmen Saeculare* or the further dimension added by Vergil to his Actium battle scene (cf. *Aen.* 8.714; also Propertius 4.6.69–84), the post-Actium 'New Age' perspective of the 'Palatine Triad', which banishes civil strife (Vergil's fettered *Furor impius*, *Aen.* 1. 294f.) and restricts War to the external expansion of the Empire.

It appears methodologically dangerous to assume a securely interpretable "scheme" that would integrate every art object on the Hill to satisfy the desires of an unproved symboloscopy. What would under this assumption the sun god's chariot on the temple's roof stand for? Perhaps victorious Actian Augustus himself? What about the chandelier from Alexander's Theban booty that hung in Apollo's temple (Pliny, *Nat.* 34.8.14)? I shall return to the question below.

Returning to his own (Conte-influenced) take on the *Aeneid*'s sword-belt passage, Harrison finds that it does not fit the political propaganda he assumes (or rather: hypothesizes) for the Palatine Danaids: "The triumphalist discourse of post-Actian celebration, represented in the iconography of the Palatine complex, is reappropriated by Vergil to serve a more meditative and tragic view of war."[69] "Reappropriated"? Only through Conte's, linguistically imprecise, understanding of *Aen.* 10.498 can one arrive at a Vergilian correction of the alleged message issued by the Palatine Danaids. The underlying assumption again is that a passage one finds difficult to interpret may stand in reference to an extra-contextual message. So: an erroneous (since extra-contextually conceived) understanding of the sword-belt scene clashes with the presumed political meaning of the portico (to which Pallas' sword-belt *"very likely"* [my italics] "alludes")? Harrison himself appears to feel uneasy about the resulting contradiction-in-terms when he declares the poet critical toward Augustan propaganda, "though Vergil can of course turn on Augustan triumphalism when required (as on the Shield of Aeneas in *Aeneid* 8)".[70]

Obviously, Harrison is not aware that the idea of being "of course" able to "turn on" (or off) Augustan propaganda "as required" throws open a core problem of the bivocalist approach (to which his thinking here shows considerable affinity): if Vergil's alleged "second voice" is being construed in contradiction to his work's dominant story-line with its open propaganda (what Harrison calls "Augustan triumphalism"), and the second voice is claimed to be the poet's true voice, then the poet's 'turning on as required' of the first voice amounts to an opportunist's deportment, – hardly a compliment to a poet who received his share of official (including financial) support in his lifetime.

Another problem of bivocalism that is likewise breaking out into the open here is the critical misconception on which the idea of 'turning on' (or off) the propaganda faucet is based: it isolates propagandistic passages ("the Shield of Aeneas in *Aeneid* 8"; one may easily add Jupiter's revelation to Venus in *Aeneid* 1, or Anchises' vision of Rome's future in *Aeneid* 6 – all three culminating in Augustus) as if ideological passages are not part of the poetic design but can be broken loose and read in isolation from (even in contradiction to) the overall context. The underlying critical concept is a non-binding and, therefore, ultimately un-obliging story-line, studded on the one hand with propagandistic highlights and on the other hand with counter-indicative 'symbolic' or 'metaphorical' passages. It is a concept of compositional incoherence (not to say illogicality), which allegedly allows one to place those 'symbolic' passages outside the story-line and even to interpret them counter-contextually.

The error of such a 'concept' (if one may call it that) lies in underrating, even discounting, the compelling consistency of the surrounding narrative – three of the four examples I have analyzed (Putnam, Conte, Harrison) may be seen as attempts to evade the (apparently unwelcome) reality that would force the interpreter to acknowledge that the poet's voice is not impartial.

Though having taken my reader on what may seem to have been a long detour, I nevertheless hope to have confirmed and secured the principle of immanent consistency in reading the *Aeneid*. The three types of critical approach discussed (approximately identified as New Critical, semiotic, archaeological-philological-political) have in common that in their account they have not sufficiently observed Vergil's preceding (and, also, following) detailed narrative and its focalization(s). Instead, they each have imposed a foreign aspect on a contextually verifiable meaning. No case can be made here for authorial ambiguity (not to mention multivalence or polysemy) – as can be made, on a strictly logical basis, for many an elegy of Propertius, Vergil's regime-critical contemporary.[71]

Earlier, I remarked on the philologist's inclination to find common ground in widely scattered bits of information, which in the last two cases meant connecting a literary text to a hypothetically reconstructed and interpreted archaeological monument. It appears to me that the premise itself of a unified ideological design of the whole area surrounding temple and palace is not sufficiently secured. It is Ovid who (in addition to Propertius' description of the temple itself and its forecourt, 2.31) provides us with the most details of the palace area on the Palatine Hill. This is in the opening elegy of the third Book of his *Tristia*, where he also repeats almost verbatim a pentameter from his earlier description of the Danaid portico (*Tr.* 3.1.62 = *A.A.* 1.74). In the earlier passage, the portico ranks with others as an ambulatory space where the young man can look for girls. It must therefore have been a larger construction (perhaps on *substructiones*), probably extending the palace area toward the river (the exact blueprint is not known; see the details in Chapter 6).

The difficulty in attributing an ideological slant to the Danaid portico becomes apparent if one reviews content and context of Ovid's elegy *Tr.* 3.1.[72] This elegy, mouthpiece for its author, like others that try to induce the Master of Rome to issue a more lenient edict for the relegated poet, displays a thick adulatory tone, giving praise to many a prominent edifice or decorative detail on the Palatine. Augustus' palace is viewed as Jupiter's domicile (3.1.35ff.), the oak wreath over its door (the *corona civica*, awarded to Augustus for having saved the citizenry) taken as indicator of the god. The two laurel trees at the palace entrance are interpreted as signs of the ruling family's triumphs or, alternatively, as expressing the love of the "Leucadian god" (=Apollo, who is the victory-granting god with a famous temple on Leucas near Actium),[73] etc. (39ff.).

At lines 60ff., the visiting book (all the time standing in for its creator) is led up the stairs to the "unshorn god's white (marble) temple" (no explanation necessary because the political reference to the victory of the Leucadian god at Actium was already given in line 42 before). Then, without any comment added, there follows the purely topographical information (en route to the Palatine libraries, which are added by mere *–que*, 63):

> where the statues are, alternating with imported (marble) columns,
>
> Belus' granddaughters and their foreign father, his sword drawn.

> signa peregrinis ubi sunt alterna columnis,
>
> Belides et stricto barbarus ense pater, *Tr.* 3.1.61–2.

If there actually existed a well-known and publicly acknowledged association of the Danaid monument with the political parties involved in the Battle of Actium, would Ovid, considering the detailed adulatory character and monumental references of this elegy, have let the chance of further praise slip by unused?

It appears safe to say that the sword-belt of Pallas did hold his sword, but not a quill for critics who underestimate the logic and consistency of Vergil's thought sequence, action line, and narrative emphases. The *ekphrasis* cannot be decontextualized; it illustrates and, so, secures the narrative's focal point.

(3) Battlefield Conduct (Resumed): Vergilian Details, II

Before turning to the methodological "intermezzo" on how to interpret the sword-belt of Pallas, I had said that the reader is asked to react favorably to Aeneas' conduct not only at the end of the epic but also following the death of Pallas. Let us then at this point review Aeneas' battlefield activities after he receives detailed news of Pallas' death. (Later on we shall in greater detail also consider the longer-range emotional influence exercised upon the reader.) It has already been shown that the death of Magus (10. 521ff.) is not designed to alienate the reader from the epic's protagonist. On the contrary, Aeneas' engagement is viewed as a positive trait rather than a "rampage".[74]

Also, when blaming Aeneas for not sparing Magus, Gentle Vergil interpreters might wish to recall that the poet, at the time of Pallas' death, has placed Aeneas in an unambiguously defensive fighting situation. He faced the double task of first gaining a foothold on the shore, then trying to bring relief to the besieged Trojan camp (with his son inside). The battle, "right on the threshold of Italy" (*limine in ipso Ausoniae* 10. 355f.), between on the one hand, the landing Trojan-Etruscan allies and, on the other, the Italian attackers,[75] had been undecided for a long time (*anceps pugna diu* 359), as far as Aeneas' sector is concerned. In another sector (*parte ex alia* 362), Pallas had just restored the fighting spirit of his fleeing Arcadians. (The words *parte ex alia*, by the way, exculpate Aeneas from all modern imputations of guilt or negligence. As Aeneas' place was with his army, so that of Pallas was with his Arcadian contingent, which, having originally come by horse, had not yet united with landing Aeneas and his troops). After Pallas' *aristeia* (374ff.), Lausus had developed a comparable thrust on the Italian side:

> The armies clash with leaders and forces equal
>
> agmina concurrunt ducibusque et viribus aequis. 10. 431.

The death of Pallas had changed the situation completely. Aeneas was notified that his men (including those at the camp, we must assume) were now within "a narrow distance of death" (*tenui discrimine leti esse suos*), that it was "time to rush to help his fleeing Trojans" (*tempus versis succurrere Teucris* 511f.). Customarily such an emergency does not call for special treatment of individual members of the enemy forces, anyway. Rather, Vergil seems to suggest, it was extraordinary that, in this situation, his Aeneas even took the time to explain his moral reasoning concerning a specific case (i.e., that of Magus).

Likewise, Aeneas has been blamed for killing Apollo's (and Diana's) priest Haemonides, who was dressed in his full vestments. The argument works better when turned around: a priest of Apollo should rather have listened to the (widely spread: 7. 102–05) oracle of Faunus (7. 98–101) instead of misleading his flock by raising arms (*arma* 541) and carrying Apollo's (!) insignia against the prophesied successor to the Latin throne. It is Aeneas who piously offers the spoils to Mars (*rex Gradive* 542), after "sacrificing" (*immolat* 541) Haemonides. The verb *immolare*, from the author's lips, is either sarcasm (as at 393; 316f.) or it reflects the pious spirit of Aeneas (cf. 519). Or (and most likely), it is Vergil's judgment on the death of the disloyal priest: by being "sacrificed" (to Apollo?), the priest atones for his oracle-defying warfare.[76] (We recall that even Camilla had to "atone" for her warfare against the fated Trojans.) The *Aeneid* does offer the paradigm of another priest of Apollo, *arcis Phoebique sacerdos* (2. 319), and this one respects his duty: it is Panthus who, in the night of Troy's fall, carries the holy objects and the "defeated gods" (*sacra...victosque deos* 2. 320) to Aeneas (i.e., the *sacra* and *penates* of Troy which Hector's ghost had spiritually entrusted to Aeneas before, 293); so Panthus' action legitimizes Aeneas as the rightful heir to the kingship of Troy. Haemonides had to die because his disobedience to Faunus' well-publicized (7. 102–06) oracle violated the divinely sanctioned mission of the Trojan-Julian line. And his spiritual position should never have been at discord with that of Aeneas' guide, the vatic Sibyl, who like Haemonides himself was a servant of Apollo and Diana (*Phoebi Triviaeque sacerdos* 10. 537 = 6. 35). Unlike some present-day interpreters, no contemporary Roman would miss Vergil's point. The temple of Apollo, Diana, and their mother Leto on the Emperor's residential hill (for us described in Propertius' elegy 2. 31) was a widely visible reminder of the politically correct interpretation:

> Next, between his mother and his sister,
> the god himself in a long robe chants his songs.
>
> deinde inter matrem deus ipse interque sororem
> Pythius in longa carmina veste sonat. Prop. 2. 31. 15f.

On the whole, Aeneas' conduct following Pallas' death has incurred grave criticism: an uncivilized, rage-filled warrior and cynical killer who has lost all the moral polish which he (presumably) acquired earlier (see, e.g., R.D. Williams *ad* 10. 510f.).

Vergil's text does not support the accusation, though of course the hero's rage is not to be overlooked; it is made only too understandable to the reader who witnessed (339–506) Pallas' unfair death, caused by Turnus' unheroic deed, and who knows that Aeneas received a comprehensive report (510).

Earlier we pointed out that Aeneas does not rage blindly but concentrates on finding Turnus:

> Everything next to himself he mows down with the sword and,
> in his hot emotion, drives a wide path with iron through the army,
> looking for you, Turnus, you, proud of (arrogant in) your recent killing.
>
> proxima quaeque metit gladio latumque per agmen
> ardens limitem agit ferro, te, Turne, superbum
> caede nova quaerens. 10. 513–15.

Like the author himself (500), Aeneas observed the killer's arrogance. He is depicted as following a clear direction (a "path"), cutting down whatever lies between him and Turnus, i.e., he is by no means running amok, but forcefully trying to break through and reach the guilty one (who, of course, is also the leader of the presently victorious enemy troops) to punish him and to aid his own hard-pressed (512) people. This is what Vergil confirms by the narrator's intervention *te, Turne...quaerens*, and this guides the reader through Aeneas' *aristeia* (510–605). It is not supported by the text if R. D. Williams (*ad* 10. 510f.) maintains that "Aeneas totally loses that self-control which he has been striving to achieve all through the poem." Again, much-maligned Donatus is right on target: "And he slew those in his way not in a rage of killing (because he was in a hurry) but in his burning desire to get past" (scil., them, to reach Turnus): *et iste caedebat medios non occidendi adfectu, quoniam properabat, sed ardore transeundi.* Some more recent interpreters apparently think that Vergil criticizes his 'rampaging' hero for, when cutting a path to Turnus, not politely asking those in his way, "would you please step aside, I am trying to reach Turnus."

Those who get in Aeneas' way do not, we have seen, fare well. They are even cynically mocked. But recent interpreters do not give sufficient attention to the fact that Vergil presents Aeneas' sarcasm as springing from prior provocation. In the case of Caeculus and Umbro, the Trojan hero in his fury only *reacts* (*contra furit* 545) defensively to *their renewal of the fighting* (*instaurant acies* 543); and Anxur had spoken some bragging words of self-glorification (which *the author himself* mocks *in his own persona*: 547f.). Aeneas' Odyssean (*Il.* 11. 452f.) and Achillean (*Il.* 21. 122ff.) utterance, that his defeated opponent Tarquitus will be eaten by birds or fishes (*Aen.* 10. 559f.), is ironically addressed to *metuende*, "you hero to be feared" (557) – which answers Tarquitus' attack on Aeneas (*obvius ardenti sese obtulit* 552) and his jubilant (*exsultans*) posture in shining arms in Aeneas' path:

Tarquitus exsultans contra fulgentibus armis
...
obvius ardenti sese obtulit. 10. 550, 552.

And, as Harrison remarks (*ad loc.*), Aeneas refrains from having his taunts followed by the brutal actions of Achilles in the Homeric 'model' passage.

Is one really to assume that Vergil expected his Roman audience to blame Aeneas for (*over-*) reacting in a critical battlefield situation and so to sense that the author was censuring his hero for his conduct and wanted him judged as negatively as Turnus? It is to be feared that modern sensibilities and yearning for a non-partisan poet here add *Gentle Romans* as readers to their (supposedly) *Gentle Vergil*.

The gravest case of mockery might be considered Aeneas' joking disregard for the brothers Lucagus and Liger, who together attacked him (575–600). And nevertheless Vergil here calls him *pius Aeneas* (591). Does Vergil himself feel no pity for the brothers, for the plea "have pity on one who asks for mercy": *miserere precantis* (598)? R. Thomas, trying to build a case against Aeneas by summarily touching upon episodes some of which I have detailed, states that Aeneas' fighting "involves human sacrifice, decapitation followed by kicking of the headless trunk, sarcastic rejection of suppliancy, killing of brother before brother"[77] etc. Eager to paint Aeneas in colors as dark as the ones which the poet uses in painting his portrait of Turnus, Thomas simplifies, even reduces the complexity of Vergil's text by showing his reader one side only of the coin and leaving out the side of provocation. This procedure is especially misleading in the case of Aeneas' "killing brother before brother", and it self-defeats the Harvard school's desire to establish the poet's impartiality (on the underlying mistaken theory of epic – Conte, Feeney – see the next chapter).

Again, one has to read the provocation first. Liger, *on the attack* approaching together with his brother (*infert se* 575), had ridiculed Aeneas by reminding him of the two occasions where Aeneas, before Troy, had been (as Homer's *Iliad* tells) saved from certain death by divine interference

Chapter 3

(in the context of the Augustan *Aeneid*, the rescue is of course another sign of the Julian ancestor's chosen-ness and divinely guided mission [4. 227–30]), and he had told Aeneas he would fare differently (i.e., would be killed, i.e., not survive) here on Italian soil. *vesanus*, "mad" (583), is the word by which the poet in his own voice characterizes the provoker's taunt. Aeneas' spear hits Lucagus first, causing him to fall from the chariot death-bound; this earns him Aeneas' sarcastic remark about leaving his chariot at his own will and not thrown off by his own horses (as happened to Niphaeus just before, 573f.). Then Aeneas deals with previously-so-provocative Liger, who, now unhappy or miserable (*miser*), begs for mercy:

> Before, you didn't talk like this:
> die, and, as a brother, do not desert your brother!

> haud talia dudum
> dicta dabas. morere et fratrem ne desere frater. 10. 599f.

"Brutal words", indeed (though corresponding to Liger's prediction of Aeneas' death on Italian soil), leading Harrison to pronounce that "such scorn of family values ill befits *pius Aeneas*." But is (as we ask once more) the issue presented to the reader here "family values" and not rather response to a taunting (insulting) and death-threatening aggressor?

Magus, Tarquitus, Liger: Aeneas dispatches three suppliants, "disturbing the reader in departing from the Roman ideal of *parcere subiectis* (6. 853)" (Harrison p. 204 *ad* 10. 521–36). "Disturbing" which reader? When Magus invokes Anchises and Iulus, this "is a powerful appeal for the family-minded Romans and particularly for Aeneas, paragon of *pietas*, and his rejection is disturbing" (Harrison *ad* 524–5). But does the author not explain Aeneas' thinking, viz. as a reaction to Turnus' brutal violation of the father–son relationship, which ranks so highly among Roman "family" values? And besides, as shown earlier, Aeneas exposes cowardly Magus for wishing to avoid death on the battlefield at the cost of his sons' inheritance (531f.) It appears that we may have to withhold our own standards of judgement if we wish to follow the poet's leads and fathom his intentions, even if the Vergil who emerges in his own right should be deeply "disturbing" to our time and values.

Even the fact that Aeneas "victoriously spent his rage across the whole battlefield once his blade had become hot" (569f.) can hardly be understood as criticism of a warrior who fights to secure his community's survival (after all, the fleeing Trojans now need his help more than ever, 511f.); it even points back to his initial restraint.[78] Nevertheless, critics have tried to extract a condemnation if not from the narrative then at least from the simile Vergil employs at this point, when he compares Aeneas victoriously (*victor* 569) spending his rage on the battlefield to the way in which hundred-armed Giant Aegaeon (=Briareos) fought *against Jupiter's lightning strikes, Iovis...fulmina contra* (567). It has long been a dangerous (though fashionable) practice in literary criticism uncritically to extend a simile beyond the point of comparison (which here clearly and without grammatical ambiguity compliments Aeneas on his extraordinary strength and fighting power), so as to modify the meaning of the narrative which it illuminates, in our case so as to see "Aeneas...associated with Gigantic opposition to Jupiter" (Harrison *ad* 10. 565–70): "...it is difficult to avoid the notion that the equivalence of Aeneas and Aegaeon is somehow disturbing". What then about Horace's man of unwavering justice and constancy, whom "the great hand of *Jupiter when he hurls his lightning*" (*fulminantis magna manus Iovis*, *Od.* 3.3. 6) cannot shake (*quatit*)? Is his character then perhaps 'theomachic'? And what about Ovid's (*M.* 15. 871) 'impious' boast that Jove's wrath (*Iovis ira*) cannot wipe out his finished *opus*? In the case of the Aegaeon simile, there is one basic fact of logic alone which advises against extending its meaning beyond the narrative: Aegaeon did *not* defeat Jupiter, whereas Aeneas is called "victorious", *victor* (569) by Vergil (which can hardly be taken as "victorious against Jupiter").[79] "Had Vergil been seeking to deliver a ringing condemnation, less ambiguous means, I submit, lay open to him".[80]

Besides, there is an argument in favor of Aeneas' super-human, Aegaeon-like battlefield performance which short-distance readers have overlooked. At 10. 81f., in the divine council, Juno had teased Venus by pointing to her rescue of Aeneas from Diomedes' attack (in *Iliad* 5. 315ff.) – a potential stain on Aeneas' battlefield record that Vergil blots out by the *compliment* expressed in the Aegaeon simile.

To understand this, one must recall Jupiter's pronouncement in the same assembly that on this day of fighting he would not interfere but stay impartial (*rex Iuppiter omnibus idem* 10. 112) and let fate take its course (*fata viam invenient* 10. 113). The result has been Aeneas' victory and the relief of the Trojan camp. (Venus' defensive action of deflecting arrows from her son, 10. 330–32, does not *contribute to* his victorious advance.)

At this point Jupiter, taking the initiative (*ultro*), addresses Juno with exquisite irony:

> O my sister, and in the same person my consort most dear,
> as you believed – you are not mistaken in your opinion –
> it is Venus who provides support for the Trojan power,
> nor do men (i.e. mortals) have a right arm
> so strong in war and such fierce courage that endures the danger.
>
> o germana mihi atque eadem gratissima coniunx,
> ut rebare, Venus – nec te sententia fallit –

> Troianas sustentat opes, non vivida bello
> dextra viris animusque ferox patiensque pericli. 10. 607–10

Clearly, Aeneas' Aegaeon-like fighting has rendered Juno's earlier derogatory taunt void, and Jupiter's non-interference has proven Aeneas' military superiority – to the extent that now Juno for her part asks Jupiter's permission to remove Turnus from the battlefield (she tries to make a case for Turnus' "pious blood" [617] by pointing to his frequent offerings to Jupiter 619f.). Interpreters should not reproach Jupiter for allegedly breaking his commitment to non-interference. His point has by now been made (even Juno admits Turnus' imminent death – *nunc pereat* 617).

With the Aegaeon simile and its context Vergil has once more elevated the Julian ancestor beyond the role assigned him in Homer's *Iliad*, implicitly 'correcting' his forerunner. (The reader recalls that, on another occasion, Jupiter himself states that Venus saved Aeneas for his rule over fierce Italy and his family's world domination 1. 227–31.)

The observer of Vergil's long-distance organization (more than 600 lines have passed since Juno's taunt hurled at Venus) can only marvel at the short-circuited interpretative naiveté that, from an a-contextual reading of a simile, expects to gain support for its idiosyncratic reading of decontextualized slices of text: "His [scil., Aeneas'] behavior is well symbolized by the shocking comparison of Aeneas to Aegaeon, a hundred-armed Giant who fights *against* Jove (10. 565–70)"; this is followed by the adumbration that "metaphorically Aeneas has become a *contemptor divum*". Aeneas' 'behavior', allegedly leading him from *pietas* to *impietas*, is described as follows: "After Pallas' death he goes on a *vicious rampage* in which he seizes prisoners for human sacrifice (10. 517–20) and *kills* several *suppliant* enemies, including *a priest* (10. 537–41). Later he kills Lausus as Lausus *tries to defend his father* Mezentius",[81] etc. Kronenberg is entirely silent about the threat issued by Lausus against Aeneas, who is the one who has to defend himself against Lausus (as shown later on in the present chapter). Echoing Thomas' approach,[82] Kronenberg proceeds by regularly omitting the other side of the coin (on the human sacrifice see my next chapter), in this way turning the Aeneas of the narrative, vigorous defender of his threatened people, into "an impious Giant figure",[83] so "Aeneas steps into the role of the impious monster."[84] Enough for now of the errant ways of contemporary criticism.

Magus, Lucagus and Liger, Tarquitus: Vergil has made it clear that Aeneas' unforgiving conduct results from Turnus' action and evasiveness, and that his taunts are answers to preceding provocations. Even in hottest fighting, the reader is supposed to realize, Aeneas' sense of appropriate measure is not entirely blurred. Of doubters, the question may be asked:

what if Aeneas had granted mercy and survival? Would these warriors have left the fighting and gone home to sit at their hearth? Would Liger and Tarquitus, his haughty attackers, not soon have attacked him (or his fleeing troops) again? Did Vergil expect his Romans to be disappointed because Aeneas failed to say 'I don't mind your provocations: go, get a life!'?

Above all, the interpreter must not lose sight of the long-range strategic and political context: Aeneas the warrior does achieve what was asked of him (cf. 511f.), viz. to rescue his endangered people. His engaged fighting on the battlefield "finally" (*tandem* 604) results in relief both for the besieged camp and also (mentioned first, in agreement with Aeneas' – or Vergil's – priorities) for Ascanius, his son and prospective successor. Mention of Ascanius by name here also reinforces an important contextual aspect of political hierarchy. During the threatening siege, Ascanius had repeatedly been the object of privileged focalization, e.g., when distinguished as "the most justified concern of Venus" (i.e., of the Julians' ancestral goddess), *Veneris iustissima cura* (10. 132), or when being assisted by Jupiter (by Jupiter! 9. 630f.) with his first bow shot against the *taunts* of Turnus' brother-in-law (close enough to the top of the Rutulian hierarchy, considering that Turnus himself must remain reserved for Aeneas), or when being addressed by Apollo as offspring and ancestor of "gods" (9. 642, the latter pointing ahead to C. Julius Caesar and Augustus). Clearly, the dominant perspective of the narrative is that of the Trojans' plight and final relief.

Finally the boy Ascanius and the young crew, besieged in vain, break out and leave the camp.

tandem erumpunt et castra relinquunt
Ascanius puer et nequiquam obsessa iuventus. 10. 604f.

"Finally" (*tandem*) has a similar effect as when signaling the long overdue end of Aeneas' patience at 12. 497.[85] Turnus' attempt at cutting off the camp (initially, from the Etruscans and Arcadians, 10. 240, cf. 236) has finally been thwarted, and Aeneas, having rescued as the leader his troops and as the father his son (or as the king his successor), is now free to concentrate on hunting down Pallas' killer (661. In Book 12 too Aeneas [we recall the threefold use of the verb *vestigare*], after the treaty has been broken, concentrates – apart from helping his side – on facing the violator of fair fighting.)

Turnus, however, is removed by Juno's interference. (In the *Iliad*, we pointed out, it was Aeneas who was divinely saved. Now it is his opponent, called the "new Achilles" by the Sibyl at 6. 89, who must be rescued from Aeneas: Vergil is preparing a new role for his protagonist, viz., that of a new 'Super-Achilles'.) If Jupiter has granted Juno a postponement of Turnus' imminent death (*praesentis leti* 10. 622) at the hands of Aeneas, this does not change Vergil's portrait of Turnus. Juno fashions an effigy of Aeneas, which taunts Turnus, but turns to flight (*dato...tergo* 646) when Turnus throws his spear at it. "As soon as he believed that Aeneas turned away and retreated, he, confused in his mind, caught in an empty hope," [exclaimed]

> Where are you fleeing, Aeneas? Don't abandon your contracted marriage!
> With my right hand here you will be given the ground
> you sought across the seas.
>
> quo fugis, Aenea? thalamos ne desere pactos!
> hac dabitur dextra tellus quaesita per undas, 10. 649f.

As at the opening of Book 9 Iris could lure Turnus to battle with the bait of Aeneas' absence, so here his thoughts (they are revealing also by the admission of the marriage contract in Aeneas' favor) are brave as long (or as soon) as he believes Aeneas to be fleeing. (He will be everything but brave throughout Book 12 when the duel contract puts him under obligation to encounter Aeneas face-to-face.) This initial impulse toward phantom-Aeneas is not voided by his later embarrassment about Juno's life-saving tricks and his attempt at suicide (10. 666–86). Nor are his evasive movements in Book 12, helped by his divine sister, voided by his later feelings of remorse (cf.12. 637–41; 678–80). And even that remorse will again be superseded by renewed thoughts of flight (12. 917f.) – thoughts resulting in hesitation which will provide Aeneas with his chance, as was shown earlier in Chapter 2. The continuity of Turnus' character as drawn by the poet lies in his instability. Augustan Vergil does not grant the political rival of his Emperor's ancestor the heroic stature which even an inhuman tyrant such as Mezentius is allowed to display (to a degree). To modern readers, it may – understandably – be a 'disturbing' aspect of the *Aeneid* that human qualities are assigned or withheld according to partisan politics.

The many objections that have been raised against Aeneas' supposedly inhuman conduct in these sections are then not endorsed by the author. This is what counts for the present interpreter. That Aeneas can be called "pious" (or, perhaps better, "duty–bound") even in a context where he refuses a plea for mercy (591ff.), i.e., that his refusal is characterized by Vergil as being within the rules of acceptable battlefield behavior, may serve as a guide to the most hotly discussed action of Aeneas: that he takes eight young prisoners alive for future sacrifice. But this emotional issue (emotional for Aeneas as well as for today's readers, that is, though often for different reasons) is best considered later, within the context of the tragic death of Pallas.

For now I turn to reviewing the other scene where a younger warrior is killed by a superior older one: Aeneas' killing of Lausus. The most basic difference (unacceptable to contemporary orthodoxy) is that King Turnus actively seeks out his young victim whereas Aeneas is confronted and attacked by young Lausus and, so, is forced to react. Again, the overarching strategic situation must be a determining factor in reading Vergil's intent.

When Jupiter allows Juno to remove Turnus from the battlefield, he informs her that this is only a delay of Turnus' doom, and that any farther-reaching hopes would be in vain: *spes pascis inanis* (627). Jupiter here acts in agreement with Stoic doctrine, which allows minor deviations from fate's course without seeing fate's rule itself being invalidated. Vergil the poet likes to avail himself of this possibility when his dramaturgy is in danger of reaching a dead end. In Book 12, when the imminent Trojan victory seems to predict a future rule of the Trojans over Italy (a role that would flatly contradict contemporary conditions in the Italy of Vergil's reader), Juno asks her husband to grant that the Latins keep their name, language, and dress and not be called Trojans. Like a trained Stoic[86] she claims she is asking only for "what is held by no law of fate", *nulla fati quod lege tenetur* (12. 819). Elsewhere in the epic, Vulcan expresses the same principle when saying that he would have had the divine right (*fas nobis* 8. 397) to delay Troy's fall by ten years (one is reminded of the Pythia's words for Croesus, Hdt 1. 91.3) – neither the all-powerful father nor the fates forbade it (*nec pater omnipotens...nec fata vetabant A.* 8. 398).

In Book 10 Jupiter's fate-compatible delay is introduced like a *deus ex machina*, because otherwise Vergil's dramaturgy (and the *Aeneid* itself) would come to a grinding halt with Turnus' 'premature' death, according to a wide-spread opinion. (But it will be shown that Vergil uses Turnus' absence for another climax in Aeneas' *aristeia* that the figure of less-than-heroic Turnus could not provide.) Since Jupiter=Fate has proved his point of Trojan superiority when Fate is allowed to run its course, he can now, without incurring the charge of inconsistency (except from some Vergil scholars) interpose a limited delay. Accordingly, it is consistent that Etruscan King Mezentius, when succeeding to Turnus' place on the battlefield, should do so at Jupiter's admonition (*Iovis...monitis* 10. 689), though in this case the reader is not given any detailed description of how the admonition was delivered in the mortal sphere.

However (to resume the tracing of Vergil's context), Mezentius turns out to be more than a mere replacement. Turnus had shown no eagerness to encounter Aeneas. As a matter of fact, after first "from a distance" (*eminus* 645) throwing his spear at the exulting effigy Juno had fashioned of Aeneas, only when the effigy turned its back did he

Chapter 3

conceive an empty hope (*animo spem turbidus hausit inanem* 648) and turn to pursuing it.[87]

Mezentius, on the other hand, proves to be a different kind of enemy when he attacks the Trojans who, following Aeneas' successful relief action, are still triumphant (*ovantis* 690). His impressive *aristeia* takes up eighty lines (689–768). Having cut down Trojan Palmus, he – in violation of the heroic code – gives the armor as a present to his son Lausus instead of dedicating it to a divinity (700. After all, Vergil has fittingly designed this strongest counterpoint to *pius Aeneas* as a *contemptor divum* 7. 648). Mezentius' success leads to an equilibrium in the battle, so Aeneas' earlier victory is dissipated. Even the (partisan)[88] gods feel pity, when looking down at the suffering and the "vain fighting spirit" of either side (755–61).

A series of similes builds up Mezentius to superhuman format: first, he is compared to a rock (691–6) that, unmoved, withstands the onslaught of sky and sea: all the Etruscans together cannot move him. Next, he is compared to a boar (707–18) surrounded by hunters: none of the Etruscans, in spite of their justified wrath (*iustae...irae* 714) against their cruel former king, dares to go near him. Thirdly, he attacks like a lion (723–8), And fourthly, he is like the huge giant Orion who, while wading through the sea, has his shoulders above the water, or, when coming down from the mountains, has his head in the clouds. When Aeneas prepares to meet him, Mezentius blasphemously invokes his own right arm as his god (*mihi deus* 773) and, in confident anticipation, "dedicates" (*voveo* 774) to his son Lausus the armor of Aeneas, the "bandit" (*praedonis*, possibly so called because he "pirated" Mezentius' army). When his victim Orodes prophesies his imminent death, Mezentius coolly replies (I go with those who see irony here, quite in character): "Now die. Of me, 'the father of the gods and king of men' will take care" (743f.).

So ex-King Mezentius' military stature far exceeds that of King Turnus. In a way, he is the true battlefield counterpart to Aeneas, whereas Turnus' status as a hero will reveal itself as rather ambiguous because of his repeatedly evasive behavior. In fearless, unyielding Mezentius (*manet imperterritus ille* 770) the reader is given also a model by which to measure Turnus, and Aeneas, when moving to end the bloody deadlock and regain the advantage for the Trojans, faces the toughest battlefield opponent of all: this encounter will make or break the Trojans' chances of reaching beyond the bridgehead of their camp and fulfilling their mission (cf. 11. 17: "Now our road leads to the king [scil., Latinus] and the Latin walls"). By temporarily removing Turnus from the battlefield, Vergil has not only precluded a 'premature' ending of his epic, but also provided his hero with a victory far above his eventual encounter with Turnus, on an almost superhuman level (Orion versus Aegaeon, speaking in terms of the similes involved), but also with an opportunity to prove himself as a warrior whose *humane piety* is sharply contrasted with the conduct displayed by Turnus. The latter point has been hotly contested by the anti-Aeneas literature, so again I have to remove layers of misinterpretations in order to secure the text's meaning.

With the larger context in mind, one will hardly be tempted to interpret the following scene, as has been done, in isolation, by concentrating on Aeneas' killing of young Lausus alone.

The single combat is opened by Mezentius, whose spear, however, ricochets from Aeneas' shield and kills Antores, a follower of King Evander. When *pius Aeneas* (783) in turn throws his spear, it pierces Mezentius' shield but comes to rest in his groin without deadly force. "Happy" (*laetus*) to see the Etruscan's blood (is it really necessary to say that Vergil does not hint at Aeneas' bloodthirstiness, but at the joyful prospect of regaining the upper hand for the Trojan side?) Aeneas, hotly seething (*fervidus* 788) pulls his sword to follow up with the victory-promising deathblow; but Lausus (who had joined his father in exile) intervenes, motivated by "love for his dear father", *cari...genitoris amore* (789).

Using the emphasis of an apostrophe, the poet in three lines (791–3) lends his own voice to memorializing Lausus' distinguished deed and harsh fate. Remembering from the syncrisis of lines 433–8 that Lausus is one of the two young heroes destined to die at the hands of a greater enemy (*maiore sub hoste*), the reader also recalls the poet's three-line apostrophe (507–9) of Pallas, "pain as well as honor" for his father, and in addition Hercules' and Jupiter's pain at Pallas' death (465–73) as well as Turnus' code-violating appropriation of Pallas' sword-belt (495–500). Clearly, of the two young heroes Pallas receives the preferred focalization, corresponding to his greater importance for the plot-line (indicated also by the poet's prediction that Turnus will later regret having taken Pallas' sword-belt 10. 501–5): so Lausus' death simultaneously provides an opportunity for contrasting the two "greater enemies".

To return to the fighting: When Mezentius, hampered by the wound and by Aeneas' spear (which is stuck in his shield), slowly retreats, Lausus, jumping in, slips under Aeneas' sword, already raised for the final blow, and thus holds off Aeneas himself (*ipsum* 798). So the father is protected by the son's small shield (one notices the collocation *genitor nati parma protectus* 800). Lausus' companions from a distance aim their missiles at Aeneas, confusing him (*perturbant* 801).

Aeneas' reaction goes through three stages. First, finding himself under a massive missile attack and cut off from his all-important target, he rages

Chapter 3

(*furit*) and covers himself while not giving ground, *tectusque tenet se* (802): the alliteration and the rare monosyllabic line-ending drive home to the reader the surprising turn the fight has taken: from seconds-away-from-victory to a defensive situation. The sudden reversal is elucidated in an elaborate simile (803–808a) in which his plight is compared to "every" plowman, "every" farmer, and – no exception here! – "every" traveler seeking cover in a hailstorm, until they might continue their activity when the sun returns. So Aeneas endures "the cloud of war", *nubem belli* (809), "until it should completely expend its thunder": the storm of the simile re-appears as a metaphor (*nubem belli*) in the ensuing narrative; also, Aeneas' "bearing up" is expressed by the same verb as Lausus "holding" him "off" from killing his father (*sustinet* 810 ~ *sustinuit* 799), like effort versus effort; and, as the men of the simile seek shelter with the intent of resuming their activities afterwards (*ut possint sole reducto / exercere diem* 807f.), so Aeneas, though now "inundated with missiles from all sides" (*obrutus undique telis* 808), is taking shelter only preliminarily, with the intent of resuming his fight against Mezentius later (the subjunctives in *possint* [807] and *detonet* [809] are parallel and indicate final clauses of intent). So the simile not only exemplifies Aeneas' inescapably defensive situation, but through it Vergil also – as often when Aeneas is about to kill – takes his reader into the mental situation of his hero (see already *furit* 802).

Stage II in Aeneas' reaction is a warning issued to young Lausus (who apparently avails himself of the "hailstorm" of his companions' spears to move against pelted and hard-pressed Aeneas):

> Where are you rushing, bound to die, undertaking a daring deed greater than your strength?
> Your very own *pietas* [i.e., your loyalty to your father] misleads you into being off your guard (= being incautious).
>
> quo moriture ruis maioraque viribus audes?
> fallit te incautum pietas tua 10. 811f.

Aeneas' words in line 811 (*moriture*; *maiora*) of course are to remind the reader of the author's prediction that Lausus, like Pallas, will die at the hands of a greater enemy (10. 438). Recalling also that superior Turnus sought out his victim (everybody else had to stand back) to execute a sure kill like the lion felling a bull, the reader is impressed that Aeneas "chides Lausus and threatens Lausus" (the repetition of the name renders the warning even more intense, 810). Where else in the *Aeneid* does a fighter, when being confronted by another fighter, try to save the inferior one from his own rashness? It takes a *pius* Aeneas (the reader is asked to conclude) to show this kind of highminded conduct, which shines brightly when being compared to Turnus' less than noble intent when he assaulted Pallas in order to hurt Pallas' father.

That Vergil should spend, over hundreds of lines, so much of his artful composition on once more developing his black-and-white picture of Turnus and Aeneas, has driven a large group of scholars to take refuge in what amounts to interpretative acrobatics. Their school is not ready to trace and accept the evidence that the *Aeneid*'s author can hardly be called an advocate of humanity *in general* rather than exclusively the Julian partisan poet he actually is (a poet, as we have seen, who on occasion can appeal even to his reader's sense of compassion in order to drive home his partisan perspective).

One way of dealing with this (non-) issue has been to fiddle with Aeneas' vocabulary, by giving *increpitat* (810) the meaning of he "taunts" Lausus (Harrison *ad loc.*), in spite of line 830, where *increpat* (both words are *metri causa* used interchangeably, as Harrison *ad* 810 admits) undoubtedly means "rebuke". Why would Aeneas "taunt" the young man whom he warns of courting death (the "threat" in *minatur* of course points to the deadly consequences in case Lausus does not listen and does not desist from his dangerous behavior). Harrison points as a parallel to 10. 900 where Mezentius replies to Aeneas: "Bitter enemy, why do you *taunt* me and threaten death?"

> hostis amare, quid increpitas mortemque minaris?

What has to be taken into account when determining the meaning of the verb(s) is the context. Wounded and helpless Mezentius actually has been taunted by Aeneas ("Where is now fierce Mezentius and that wild force of his fighting spirit?" 897f.), and Mezentius responds by acknowledging the taunt with *amare*, "acrimonious". But it was Mezentius himself who had first provoked Aeneas' grim reaction, by three times loudly calling (*magna ter voce vocavit* 873) Aeneas to battle and sarcastically pretending to bring him "presents" (*haec tibi porto / dona* 881f.). So Aeneas had good reason to refer to "fierce" Mezentius and "the wild force of his fighting spirit" (897f.).

Similarly, at Livy 3.3.5 it is the context that provides the rebuke with the nuance of scorn, when consul Quinctius reminds the Romans that they are afraid of enemies who have already been defeated, *victos timeri increpans hostes*. Sometimes, to make sure that the nuance of scorn or indignation is understood, Latin authors add explanatory adverbs such as *superbe* (Flor. *Epit.* 1.7 [1.13.17]) or *contemptim* (Liv. 25.36. 10; both cited by OLD). No such context or adverb being present, there is no ground for burdening Aeneas at *A*. 10. 811f. with a condescending attitude toward the brave young man whom he is warning.

Chapter 3

In the *Aeneid* itself the two verbs are used about a dozen times. Apart from denoting different kinds of noises (rattling, snapping, etc.), the nuance of "taunting" is definitely indicated by the context of Turnus' condescending address to Lycus who in vain tries to escape:

> Victorious, he [scil., Turnus] taunts him with these words: Did you, madman, hope you could escape our hands?
>
> increpat his victor: nostrasne evadere, demens,
> sperasti te posse manus? 9. 560f.

In the majority of instances (e.g., 3. 454; 9. 127; [10. 278;] 12. 758), the situation warrants the sense "rebuke", "chide", as for instance also when Charon rebukes living Aeneas for approaching the realm of the dead (6. 385–01) or even when Queen Dido jokingly scolds Bitias, encouraging him to take a draft (1. 738). In sum, then, the Latin text at 10. 810 is unambiguous: Aeneas chides (and threatens) Lausus, while acknowledging his *pietas*. He cannot be made comparable to the taunting Turnus of 10. 481.

Nevertheless, scholars of the above-mentioned persuasion have here, too, believed to find a Vergil who denigrates Aeneas. Most significant among them is probably Putnam, who thinks that the poet here ironically turns the *epitheton ornans* (*pius*) against his hero, by having Aeneas interpret "in negative terms the abstract that had always been his".[89] An untendentious reader, I submit, will hardly accept that "the poet has him [scil., Aeneas] shout" (instead of "chide" and "threaten") in lines 811f. what amounts to "maddened words" (a maddened warning?). "If Lausus had been *cautus*, the hero implies, he would not have practiced *pietas* and would have escaped death."[90] By transforming the present indicative of lines 811f. into a past counterfactual case ('if ... had been ..., he would not have' etc.), Putnam changes the situation from a warning *before* killing to a determination or judgement *after* the fact.[91]

In truth Aeneas at the time of his warning does not know how the young man will react to the warning or that his fervor could be so great that he may disregard the mortal danger his behavior entails. It is only consistent with the warning issued before the fact that Aeneas should point out where Lausus' loyalty to his father will lead (*quo moriture ruis*) if he does not desist and throws caution to the winds.

But it is no longer *pietas* only that now motivates Lausus, as it did when "the father, protected by the son's (small) shield (*parma* 800), could make his departure" from the battlefield. Vergil paints a change in the young warrior's attitude – a change that, though decisive for understanding the scene, is regularly ignored by interpreters, including Putnam. Misreading his situation, Lausus, in spite of the warning, ("nonetheless" – *nec minus* 812) *challenges* his superior enemy (*exsultat* 813, a verb pointing to provocative, aggressive behavior and used, e.g., when Tarquitus moved against Aeneas, 643; cf. 550).[92] As line 817 (*minaci*[*s*]) shows, Lausus' demeanor even has answered (or preceded?) Aeneas' threat with a counterthreat of his own. No wonder then that the poet in his own voice makes clear that this new conduct amounts to madness (*demens* 813) – a word he (*cum pace* Putnam) does *not* apply to Aeneas' words of warning. The adjective is especially appropriate in view of the fact that Lausus' armor is described as light (he does not wear a cuirass).[93]

His well-meaning warning being met by aggressive provocation, Aeneas no longer has a choice if he is to restore the military situation he had brought about when liberating his camp and to eliminate the strongest (only temporarily neutralized) challenger who had annihilated Aeneas' victory and created a new equilibrium (755–57). It is only by disregarding Vergil's long-range composition that Putnam (and others) can ascribe to Aeneas the freedom to avoid killing madly aggressive Lausus. Should Aeneas perhaps withdraw and leave the field to son and to father, condemning his own people to losing Italy, their (in Vergil's terms) ancestral homeland? It is not without point that Vergil, in the next stage, calls his hero "the Dardanian leader" (*Dardanio...ductori* 814), thus placing Aeneas' killing of Lausus within the tenth Book's (or, rather, the *Aeneid*'s) larger context of winning Italy back for its destined leaders. And the reader experiences the Julian ancestor as an involuntary, reluctant slayer of an admirable youth – in this, too, unlike Turnus the eager slayer of Pallas. (Is the Julian ancestor's conduct perhaps designed to throw a positive light on his greater descendant's behavior in the civil war?)

This takes us, after stages I (defensive cover 801) and II (warning issued to aggressive Lausus), to the third stage in Aeneas' deportment. In reaction to Lausus' challenge, Aeneas' "fierce wrath rises higher", *altius irae...surgunt* (813f.), "and the Fates pick up Lausus' final threads" (814f.).

It would be wrong to see Aeneas' wrath as concentrating primarily on Lausus: the comparative "higher" (*altius*) points back to stage I, where Aeneas, thwarted, rages (*furit* 802) when forced to take cover (*tectusque tenet se*) against the "cloud" of spears cast by Lausus' comrades from a distance (*eminus*), instead of following up on his wounding of Mezentius – seeing whose blood had made him *happy* (*laetus* 787). It is true that Lausus' transformation from father's defender to defiant aggressor contributes to raising the level of Aeneas' anger, but clearly because Lausus' defiance interposes a further obstacle between Aeneas and his strategically most important target, which remains Mezentius.

So Vergil has skillfully placed his *pius Aeneas* in a situation where he kills a weaker young man in self-defense (how different from Turnus seeking out Pallas, the reader is to observe), i. e., where Aeneas has no choice if he wants to get back to Mezentius and save the Trojans. There is no "inner conflict between heroic passion and generalship on the one hand (which leads to his killing of Lausus), and a more 'enlightened' recognition of *pietas* on the other (which leads to his subsequent lament for the young hero)", as Harrison (*ad* 811–12) would have us believe, assuming "a crucial change in Aeneas", who "turns from heroic battle-rage to more civilized thoughts of sympathy, pity, and regret" (Harrison *ad* 821–2). "Regret"? This assumption (instead of a transition to pity or compassion alone) opens the door to a guilty (and perhaps feeling guilty) Aeneas along the Harvard school's extra-contextual lines of irrational rage followed by *pietas*.[94]

If there is a guilty one here, it is Mezentius who, in his 'conversion speech' (10. 846–56) following the news of his son's death, laments that he allowed his son to die in his place, *ut pro me hostili paterer succedere dextrae / quem genui* (847f.). As usual, Vergil is clear about the chain of cause and effect as well as about the moral implication. (Mezentius also laments that, through his crimes, he has deprived his son of the throne owed to him.)

The tendency to incriminate Aeneas is again most prominent with Putnam, whose Vergil has "Aeneas grimly see himself as an incorporation of a *pietas* that destroys in a particularly vicious manner because it kills the embodiment of a *pietas* that saves."[95] Myopia concerning the larger strategic context and disregard of textual detail (Lausus' suicidal aggressiveness) combine to create an un-Vergilian, *viciously* acting Aeneas – who is then even used as a methodological peg on which to hang the coat of generalization: "[…] the reader is left wondering about the depth of Aeneas' commitment to *pietas elsewhere*."[96] No wonder that in Putnam's eyes the poet apparently got his hero's *epitheton ornans* wrong: "Aeneas performs the greatest act of *impietas* by killing first the son who protects, then his *wounded* father."[97]

As this reading overlooks that Lausus at the moment of his death no longer "protects", but in a state of madness (*demens* 813) challenges (*exsultat* 813), even threatens (*minaci[s]* 817) his warner (Aeneas), so it also disregards that at the time of the final duel Vergil characterizes Mezentius no longer by his being "wounded", but by the superiority he has gained from on horseback encircling his enemy (who is on foot), planting in Aeneas' shield a "huge forest" (*immanem…silvam* 887) of spears, so that Aeneas, cornered and hard-pressed by the, in the author's words, "*unfair*" fight (*urgetur pugna congressus iniqua* 889) finally (*tandem* 890), upon reflecting on the possibilities open to him (*multa movens animo* 890), decides to kill the horse to bring its rider down to level ground (the unpredictable result being that Mezentius is pinned down by the falling horse). There is, speaking in the author's terms, no *impietas* in Aeneas' slaying of Mezentius (as the poet has the Etruscan himself concede: *nullum in caede nefas* 901).

And though Mezentius bravely accepts the death blow (907) and through his grief and guilty feelings over his son's self-sacrifice as well as over his own deportment as a ruler (846–56) has made the torture of his own people appear somewhat less prominent and himself somewhat less inhuman in the eyes of some scholars, there remains a remarkable inconsistency: in the end he asks Aeneas for the favor toward "defeated enemies" (*victis ... hostibus* 903), viz. to protect his corpse against his subjects' fury (*furorem* 905), and to bury him together with his son. This is unexpected, coming from the lips of the man who had not only impiously planned to make his son into a living *tropaeum* (775) dressed in slain Aeneas' armor, but who even intended to decapitate Aeneas' body and, while on horseback, carry his head back with him (like another Turnus, his close associate, cf. 12. 382; 511f.): *et caput Aeneae referes* (10. 863).[98]

Putnam's philologically indefensible approach, using passages that seem to support his thesis but neglecting awkward details that would force him to modify it, appears not dissimilar to Thomas' method (discussed earlier) of accusing Aeneas of excessive brutality while suppressing the provocations to which Vergil has his hero respond. By probing such misreadings we see the great care that Vergil employs to explain or even justify Aeneas' actions even in situations where a cursory reader might feel invited to see Vergil indict him.

At the same time a much more serious and fundamental result manifests itself: if Vergil does *not* (where latter-day orthodoxy likes to assert he *does*) criticize his *pius Aeneas*, then critics may be forced to face up to an unwelcome truth. Both the Aeneas of their readings (whom they dislike so much) and also the Aeneas whose portrait results from a non-tendentious reading of the text (whom they don't like either and who on occasion is the motive behind the litcrit acrobatics) inescapably do reflect and represent the author's (or, if you will, the 'implied' author's) position. So they perhaps ought to (as Lactantius did) direct their discontent against Vergil himself. This prospect, of course, is much more "disturbing" than the reassuring 'discovery' of a pro-Augustan readers' conspiracy of 2,000 years' duration.

Precise reading, then, has (re-) established that Lausus leaves Aeneas *no choice* but to respond to his challenge. That is, as in other cases of killing notable enemies, Vergil portrays his hero as re-acting, here clearly in self-defense. (It is a testimony to Vergil's rhetorical skill that here the stronger is presented as having no way of escaping a perilous situation except by killing the weaker.) This is the decisive difference from Turnus' conduct,

Chapter 3

who sought out his young victim for a sure kill, like a lion felling a doomed bull. Both fallen young warriors are addressed as "boy", *puer*, by Aeneas (even "pitiable boy", *miserande puer*, 10. 825 and 11. 42; the same emotionally laden words are used also by Anchises for death-bound young Marcellus, Augustus' son-in-law and prospective successor 6. 882), whereas Turnus insisted that he was sending Pallas back to his father "as he deserves him" (10. 492), i.e., dead. It is only by skipping relevant details of the text that one can repaint Vergil's black-and-white portrait so as to create an ethically ambiguous painting. For example, failure to observe Vergil's distinction of father's defender (stage I) and attacker of Aeneas (stage II) in Lausus' sequence of actions induces Putnam to see Aeneas "shifting the cause for Lausus' death onto Lausus' own practice of Aeneas' virtue."[99] So the emphatic *tua* (812: "your piety deceives you in your folly" [Putnam's translation]) in Aeneas' warning is assigned special significance insofar as allegedly "it also reveals a half-conscious awareness that he [scil., Aeneas] himself is blameworthy." (As in the case of Quint discussed earlier, one feels tempted to ask, "half-conscious" because not verifiable from the text?) Unhesitatingly Putnam once more adds a broader, generalizing smear on the Vergilian Aeneas by way of a (rhetorical) question: "How often, we ask, does Aeneas adhere to or reject *pietas* for subjective, even self-serving, reasons?"[100]

In view of critics' widespread tendency (I have chosen Putnam here as a representative – as well as a prominent – example) to offer 'interpretations' not based on the Vergilian text, it needed pointing out that neither the vicious killer Aeneas nor the Aeneas who is aware of his blameworthiness can be found in Vergil's text, if it is precisely and closely read. One may of course – with Putnam, interpreting Horace – suppose that "...it is our privilege as readers...to create our own dialogue with Horace and even to modify Horace's own chronologies, whether of books published of or lives spent, to suit our own fancy..."[101] This may be a "reader's" privilege, but such a "reader" can no longer justifiably claim to move within the boundaries of accountable scholarship – accountable both to verification by the community of fellow-scholars and to the author's intention as evidenced in his text. (I forego discussing here the thesis of 'unintentionalists' that the author has no intention in writing.)

Once the inescapability Vergil ascribes to his hero's situation is recognized, it is clear that Aeneas' angry (and necessarily harsh) response seals his young opponent's *fata* (10. 813–15): his sword pierces Lausus' small shield, ("light armor for one who threatened") and his shirt ("which his mother had woven with pliable gold thread" – in the poet's voice, the pathetic aspect rises), being pushed "through the middle of the young man's body", and his "life in sadness withdrew to the shades" (819f.).

"In sadness", *maesta*: Lausus certainly feels unfortunate to lose his young life, but – to glance ahead to the poem's ending (and back to our earlier discussion of that ending) – he is not "indignant" as unheroic Turnus (12. 952) is and as Camilla is (11. 831; she, however, has good reason to be indignant, ambushed by a spear hurled from afar).

With *at* (821, indicating, as often, a change of perspective) Vergil turns to Aeneas' feelings when looking upon the strangely pale face of dying Lausus. The linguistically and metrically highly elaborate lines are (as is generally acknowledged) among the most moving of the whole *Aeneid*. Aeneas, observing Mezentius' dying son, utters the same emotional groan that Lausus uttered when facing his wounded father: *ingemuit...graviter* (823 = 789), to which the poet adds Aeneas' feelings of pity: *miserans*, and the gesture of stretching out his right hand toward the deceased. By the boy's heroic conduct, the son of Anchises, *Anchisiades* (822), is reminded of his own loving loyalty to his father (this the meaning of *patriae...pietatis* rather than 'the father's love of his son' 824).

Recognition of this affinity leads Aeneas to view and honor the fallen in terms of his own piety:

> What can now, pitiable boy, in return for this glory,
> What can pious Aeneas give you that is worthy of so great an in-born nobility?
>
> quid tibi nunc, miserande puer, pro laudibus istis,
> quid pius Aeneas tanta dabit indole dignum? 10. 825–6.

"Now" meaning: when Lausus is no longer alive. Aeneas thinks of honoring the dead for his inborn and demonstrated bravery. There is no trace of irony, only respect for the fallen enemy in the words of Aeneas, who, solemnly speaking of himself in the third person (a feature appropriate to the top of the Vergilian hierarchy that should not be misread by moderns as self-aggrandizing), with *pius* points to his awareness of duty owed to the deceased. This duty is especially visible in the different treatment of the body: whereas Turnus tore off (*rapiens* 496) the sword-belt of Pallas, Aeneas continues as follows:

> Your very own arms, about which you were happy, you are to keep; and you {yourself} I am returning to the shades and ashes of your ancestors, if that concern means anything to you.
>
> arma, quibus laetatus, habe tua; teque parentum
> manibus et cineri, si qua est ea cura, remitto. 10. 827–8.

Again, there is the significant difference from Turnus' behavior, who condescendingly "grants" (*largior*) Pallas' father burial of his son's despoiled body, "whatever of a consolation there is in burying" (493).[102] Austin

Chapter 3

(*ad* 1. 78) has pointed out that the partitive genitive following *quodcumque* is depreciative, with parallels at Catullus (1. 8 *quicquid hoc libelli*) and Lucretius (2. 16). The same applies to Turnus' grandiloquence at 10. 493.[103]

On the other hand, there is the poet's own voice at 7. 1–4, paying tribute to Aeneas' wet-nurse:

> Still today honor paid to you guards your grave,
> and in Great Hesperia your name marks your remains, *if this glory means anything {to you}*.

> et nunc servat honos sedem tuus, ossaque nomen
> Hesperia in magna, si qua est ea gloria, signat.

si qua est ea gloria (7. 4), "a pathetic reflection" (Fordyce *ad loc.*). CN, in explaining 10. 828, quote 7. 4, "the doubt being whether the shades care for such things." Harrison (*ad* 10. 458) draws attention to 10. 827–8, explaining that the phrase *si qua* (= εἴ τις) expresses "a doubtful possibility, often 'hope against hope'". Aeneas at 10. 828 is aware that his sympathy is futile.

The fact that Aeneas wants Lausus to keep what was a source of joy in his lifetime shows an extraordinary approximation to the boy's mindset. If Vergil presents the hero so congenial to the youth, that is a significant hint for a correct understanding of the following lines:

> Nevertheless, with this you will console yourself, unfortunate one,
>   about your pitiable death:
> You fall by the hand of great Aeneas.

> hoc tamen infelix miseram solabere mortem:
> Aeneae magni dextra cadis. 10. 829f.

Again, one has to remove a layer of late-20th-century misunderstanding in order to regain access to the *Aeneid*'s meaning here. And again it is Putnam whose reading epitomizes widespread misconception. Ascribing Aeneas' slaying of Lausus to "a continued *desire for vengeance*" (instead of observing the contextual, i.e., the strategic necessity for Aeneas to deal as quickly as possible with the greatest danger threatening his people, which is Mezentius), Putnam writes that "the reader's disposition changes from understanding for Aeneas, about the sometimes violent task of establishing Rome, to compassion for his victims."[104] The fact that Aeneas himself shares the reader's compassion, at least for Lausus, can be disregarded only if one disallows him, in a situation where he defends himself against an attacker, the piety one allows him (and which he himself claims: 826) toward the now repelled and defeated opponent. In fact, it can be inferred that Vergil, by portraying Aeneas as compassionate toward the "pitiable boy" for whom the poet has elicited the reader's sympathy, succeeds in making a case for his hero's *humane* disposition – no small rhetorical achievement.

Unable to deny at least for lines 10. 821–4 that Vergil here endows his hero with moving human features, Putnam quickly returns to his creation of an impious Aeneas, who "will soon proclaim, with a *renewal of callousness*, that Lausus' consolation is his fall 'by the right hand of mighty Aeneas' (*Aeneae magni dextra*, 830)", etc.[105] "Renewal of callousness"? The interpreter appears to operate outside the *Aeneid*'s bearings. As the nurse (the *nurse*!) of the Julians' ancestor still "today" receives highest honor in Italy (7. 1–4), so it is to be considered a high honor to be defeated and slain in military battle by the Julians' ancestor. The *Aeneid*'s palaeo-Augustan hierarchy can hardly be approached in democratic terms, as the following examples show.

The consolation Aeneas offers young Lausus is the very same one Aeneas himself sought in Juno's storm when, threatened with the unheroic death of drowning, he prayed: "O, *bravest* of the race of the Greeks, son of Tydeus [= Diomedes], why could I not die on the fields of Troy and pour out this life under *your* right arm?" Aeneas is there modeled on the Homeric Achilles who wished not to die by drowning in the river "like a swineherd boy" (*Il.* 21. 282), but preferred death at the hands of the *best* hero on the Trojan side, i. e., Hector (ὃς ἐνθάδε...ἔτραφ' ἄριστος, *Il.* 21. 279). The same is true about Aeneas' self-estimation in *Aeneid* 1. Only "*the bravest* of the Greek race" (o *Danaum fortissime gentis* 1. 96) is worthy to offer him an alternative to drowning.[106] So there can be no doubt that Aeneas, greatest hero among the *Aeneid*'s Trojans, pays the highest tribute to deceased Lausus' bravery. Elsewhere in the *Aeneid*, one finds the same sentiment when the warrior maiden Camilla, during her *aristeia*, tells her defeated opponent, Ornytus:

> nevertheless, not as a light-weight fame
> will you carry this one back to your ancestors' shades: that
> you have fallen by the spear of Camilla.
>
> nomen tamen haud leve patrum
> manibus hoc referes, telo cecidisse Camillae. 11. 688f.

As Aeneas in Book 1 fashions himself (or rather, is fashioned by the poet) in the terms of the Iliadic Achilles, so he allows defeated Lausus to be measured by the same, his very own, heroic standard. It is far off the *Aeneid*'s scale to twist Aeneas' highest tribute into a "renewal of callousness". The attempts of recent decades to downgrade Aeneas and to ascribe such downgrading to Vergil himself proceed by neglecting the poet's own explicit parameters as he established them in his poem. No wonder they miss Vergil's emphasis on both his hero's humanity and on his code-conforming conduct. The wishful concept of a regime-critical poet is shattered by the harsh reality of the epic's precise logical and rhetorical organization.

I am now in a position to answer the question raised at the opening of Chapter 3: obviously, the death of Pallas at the hands of Turnus (which will later lead to Turnus' death at the hands of Pallas' stronger friend and ally, Aeneas) imitates the *Iliad*'s concatenation of deaths, in which Patroclus is killed by Hector but later avenged by Patroclus' stronger friend, Achilles. But why has Vergil doubled his first killing scene by adding to Pallas' death also the killing of Lausus by Aeneas? That the poet does want his reader to compare the scenes is (my reader saw) obvious from the syncrisis of the two young heroes and from the poet's comment that each would fall under the hands of a "greater enemy", *maiore sub hoste* (10. 438). An unbiased comparison cannot but state that Vergil has utilized this junction in his dramaturgy (when Mezentius, father of Lausus, fills in for Turnus) once more to demonstrate King Aeneas' moral superiority over his ethically (and religiously) flawed opponent, King Turnus. One may not like the criminalization of the political opponent in this black-and-white portrait (and the desperate attempts of interpreters in the 20th century's latter half, by means of so-called literary critical 'methodologies', to get around this conclusion, testify to such understandable abhorrence), but scholarship should not shrink from acknowledging unwelcome (even unpleasant and "disturbing") evidence. Nor should those disappointed by the evidence implicate the messenger (such as the present interpreter) by ascribing to him an affinity to the position he found to be Vergil's.[107]

Notes

[1] Even if Pallas shows some features of the Homeric Sarpedon, the place assigned to him in the chain of killings is undoubtedly that of Patroclus.

[2] This is echoed, as we saw, in Book 11 (442) and 12 (466, 467; cf. 16).

[3] For the comparison of Turnus to a lion stalking a bull, an example from art may serve as a precedent. In the Metropolitan Museum in New York, there is an Etruscan bronze tripod (identifier: 60.11.11, Fletcher Fund 1960), showing on the vertical rods: Hercules and Athena; the Dioscuri; two satyrs. On the arches, one sees: a panther felling a deer; a lion felling a ram; a lion felling a bull. The predictability of the kill seems to be clear in all three cases, with no exception. The simile is used in the *Iliad*, when Patroclus kills Sarpedon (16. 427–29). There, too, the lion's superiority is not in doubt (nor is the outcome: even Zeus cannot prevent the death of his son Sarpedon. See also *Aeneid* 10. 467–73: Jupiter cannot prevent Pallas' death from happening).

[4] K. Quinn 1968, 222; cf.227: Pallas was "killed in fair fight;" 18: "in fair fight."

[5] For the programmatic misunderstanding of Aeneas' prayer (and his contrary-to-fact wish for death before Troy) as homesick melancholy by members of the

anti-imperial school (W. Clausen, R. D. Williams) see Stahl 1981, 160f., and also the discussion in the previous chapter of the same misconception fostered by Quint (1993, 29).

[6] Critical indifference to the text's authorial nuances is well demonstrated by Harrison (1998, 227f.): "Turnus is only doing what all warriors are supposed to do ...: killing the enemy, and an important enemy commander at that, who has himself already killed many of Turnus' men earlier"... "if all killings with taunts are criminal, then any heroic killings will attract that label...killing an enemy who is weaker than yourself is not wrong either..." Does this not depend on where the author has channeled his reader's sympathy and placed the moral accents? "So Turnus' offence is to wear the sword-belt, not to kill Pallas; the death of Pallas is tragic and lamentable, but it is not in itself a crime." How might Harrison, if he chose to discuss its literary emphasis here, deal with Jupiter's compassionate sorrow (discussed by us in the next section of this chapter), which compels the highest god to turn his eyes away from the scene of Pallas' death (but he does not express pity at the death of Lausus)?

[7] Rightly Harrison *ad loc.* compares Pyrrhus' "equally vicious taunt" to Priam at 2. 547–50. For Putnam's mistranslation of 10. 492 see section (2) of this chapter.

[8] "Pallas the boy" Vergil will call him when he later brings back Aeneas' pain (12.943; see also Aeneas himself 11.42). "Look whether *our* spear has greater penetrating power" was older Turnus' schoolmaster-like taunt before the deadly throw (10.481).

[9] Donatus points out the refined argument of Magus: (1) an appeal to Aeneas' own obliging situation as a father and a son; (2) an artful suggestion of wealth (not specified, to avoid any impression of a possible shortage of funds), especially in silver and gold; (3) the Trojan victory does not turn on this one life.

[10] Pöschl 1964, 195.

[11] For the belittling character of the statement, compare Aeolus about his unenviable little kingdom (*quodcumque hoc regni* 1. 78, and Austin's comment *ad loc.*). On the other hand, compare Aeneas' utterance after Lausus' death, *teque parentum / manibus et cineri, si qua est ea cura, remitto* (10. 827f.) with Vergil's glorification of Aeneas' nurse Caieta, *si qua est ea gloria*, at 7. 4.

[12] As section (2) of this chapter will show, the ugly (cf. *foede* 10. 498), sinful crime (cf. *nefas* 497) depicted on the baldric is supposed to give the reader a hint on how to judge the slaying of its owner.

[13] Quinn 1968, 221.

[14] Lyne 1983, 193f.; see already W. Warde Fowler 1919, 155.

[15] Lyne 1983, 194.

[16] I myself had briefly outlined my interpretation in *Arethusa* 14 (1981), 158f. See also Stahl 1990, 203, n. 40. B. Otis came very close to Vergil's ranking of priorities in judging Turnus' offence: "The whole episode is thus designed to exhibit Turnus' *culpa* and character," (1964, 356, etc.).

[17] On this piece of equipment (important for precisely understanding the epic's final scene at 12.941–44), suffice it here to indicate that the *balteus* in all likelihood is a combination of waist- and shoulder-belt, the waist-belt traditionally decorated with rectangular plates that are riveted to the leather and embossed with cone-shaped elevations or mythological motifs. Vergilian scholarship usually intermingles the translations "baldric" and "sword-belt". See Excursus 2.

[18] On the action of setting one's foot on the defeated enemy, see the details in Stahl 1985, 29–31.

[19] Cf., e.g., Caesar, *B.G.* 1.12.6f., cited by Mutschler (2003, 103): See above, Chapter 3, Section 1.

[20] Thomas 2001, 290.

[21] Clausen 1987, 100.

[22] Thomas 2001, 285.

[23] Thomas 2001, XVIII.

[24] Thomas 1998, 288.

[25] Putnam 1998, 209. My emphasis.

[26] Putnam 1998, 189.

[27] "The explanation *talem remitto Pallanta qualem se remitti meruit* does violence...to the Latin, for, though *remitti* may be fairly supplied from *remitto* after *meruit*, the addition of *se* is arbitrary;" etc. Page *ad* 10. 492.

[28] Putnam 1998, 205.

[29] Putnam 1998, 204.

[30] Putnam 1998, 197.

[31] Putnam 1998, 193. My emphasis.

[32] Putnam elsewhere (1995, 209) expresses his "horror" at "Pallas' grisly plea" that dying Turnus may still perceive victorious Pallas stripping off his armor (10.462–63). Here we see the interpreter's subjective yearning at work for a de-Romanized "Gentle Vergil", but Pallas' "grisly" plea does not supply a methodologically sufficient reason to overrule the authorial apostrophe of the young hero, which at 10. 509 includes "huge piles of {killed} Rutulians".

[33] Putnam, unable (like Thomas 2001. 295, and others) to deny the Augustan *Aeneid*, vigorously fights against "any incontrovertible, secure interpretation" (1998, 210; cf. "variety" p. 212) in order to open a door for the possibility of an un-Augustan reading. Here literary theories are welcomed as tools to overrule logic of plot-line. Against interpreters' agnosticism that may easily be used to justify methodological subjectivism, the argument of scholarly approximation is still valid, as pronounced for Vergilian studies by Glei (1991, 33), viz., that a text's meaning "in einem zwar unabschliessbaren, doch approximativ weitgehend realisierbaren Prozess eruiert werden kann", ("can be determined in an unfinishable – it is true – process which however can widely be realized by approximation").

[34] Putnam 1998, 197. This of course underrates 12.939–41a, when Aeneas refrains from executing the deathblow. I have dealt in Chapter 2 with Putnam's substitution of Aeneas' "instinct" for the hero's weighing of obligations.

[35] Putnam 1998, 193.

[36] Putnam 1998, 206.

[37] Rightly *OLD s.v. foede* under (1) upholds the moral nuance for *Aen.* 10.498.

[38] Conte 1986, 187. My emphasis.

[39] Conte 1986, 187.

[40] Conte 1986, 187f. My emphasis.

[41] Conte 1986, 188f.

[42] Conte 1986, 190.

[43] Conte 1986, 192.

[44] Quotations in this section have been taken from Conte 1986, 190–94. It is

informative to see that the example Conte choses "to confirm this approach" is likewise misunderstood by him. He claims that Aeneas, while looking at the pictures of Juno's temple in Carthage, is absorbed by gazing at the warrior queen Penthesilea at the moment when Queen Dido appears, and that the "connotative power" of Penthesilea (later killed by her – potential – lover Achilles; but Vergil does not mention it) points to "the present context" of love and death (of Dido). Conte got his Latin grammar wrong, again: the truth is that Aeneas is not described as looking at *hanc...mirandam* but at *haec...miranda* (1. 494). This plural summarizes *all* the scenes from the Trojan War Aeneas has been viewing with so great emotion, and not the warrior queen only.

⁴⁵ Conte 1986, 161.
⁴⁶ Conte 1986, 152.
⁴⁷ Conte 1986, 162.
⁴⁸ Conte 1986,153.
⁴⁹ Conte 1986, 162; Conte's emphasis.
⁵⁰ Conte 1986, 157.
⁵¹ Conte 1986, 153; 157.
⁵² Conte 1986, 153.
⁵³ This aspect is eagerly seized upon by C. Segal, who in his *Foreword* (14) praises Conte for finding in Vergil "a new 'polyphonic' epic that not only incorporates multiple viewpoints but even allows contradiction *and incoherence as a fundamental part* of its multi-layered texture" (my italics). Logically and rhetorically trained Vergil incoherent?

Thomas (rendering Conte's message by saying "there is no overarching 'epic'" [Conte 187]) welcomes Conte's dissolution of the *Aeneid*'s architecture for his own vain endeavor to "de-Augustanize" (2001, XVIII) Vergil, specifically to level the poet's moral distinction between pious Aeneas and code-defying Turnus: "We can see the world through the eyes of...Aeneas, or *we can choose* to look from the very different perspective[s] of...Turnus. Either way of reading remains *an option*, and *Virgil impels us to neither*" (Thomas 2001, 296; my italics). How blunt would the narrator of Book 10 (and Book 12, for that matter) have to be to "impel" this Conte-follower to give up his belief in arbitrary interpretative "options"?

Another pillar for holding up Thomas' interpretative umbrella is taken from V. Pöschl's book (1ˢᵗ edition 1950, 2ⁿᵈ 1964; Thomas 2001, 295). Pöschl redeemed his own Nazi past (cf. *DNP* 15.2.314; 319; Wlosok 2001, 371f.; 375f.) by constructing, also against the "political delusion of the twentieth [century]" (!) a supra-national, even Christianized, poet of "mankind poetry" (*Menschheitsdichtung* 1964, 39); his directions for "the great geniuses of mankind" (*die grossen Genien der Menschheit* 175) are that they have to be "infinitely above" partisanship such as instantiated by "the derogatory interpretation of the Turnus-*Gestalt*" (*herabziehende[n] Deutung der Turnusgestalt* 175). This is material for Thomas of the Harvard school: by declaring Vergil a "great genius of mankind" (and who could contradict this classification?) one can, without reference to the text, *a priori* deduce Vergil's positive judgement of Turnus. The only thing still needed is a number of more or less decontextualized passages (see Thomas 1998). The present writer hopes to escape the accusation of being "hyper-logical" when pointing out circular reasoning (see also note 46).

⁵⁴ Among Conte's followers is even Horsfall (1995, 212): "I should like to believe

that Conte is right and that it [scil., the scene on the sword-belt] underlines the untimeliness of Pallas' end." See also Harrison 1998, 227: "The most influential recent interpretation... is justly that of Conte. He argues that the violent *mors immatura* of the young Pallas without the chance to marry is closely parallel to the fate of the sons of Aegyptus, similarly deprived of the hope of maturity and progeny through their murder by the Danaids, and that it is this which makes Turnus' action in killing Pallas a *nefas*." Instead of interpreting the sword-belt scene in light of the poet's narrative, Harrison imposes a (non-pertinent) element from the sword-belt upon the narrative, an element which the poet apparently 'forgot' to mention: in addition to being foully killed, Pallas might also have had wedding plans!

[55] Charles Segal in Conte 1986, 15.

[56] I use this term in response to Thomas' rationality-defying complaint about "hyper-logical" interpretation (i.e., an interpretation that respects historical facts; Thomas 2001, 7).

[57] Glei 1991, 18; 34.

[58] For a drawing of the ramp see Carettoni 1983, 48, *Abbildung* 6.

[59] Lefèvre 1989, 11.

[60] Lefèvre 1989, 12–14.

[61] Lefèvre 1989, 25.

[62] Lefèvre 1989, 16.

[63] As a matter of fact, Lefèvre has assigned *foede* a double function, by having the word refer both to the "schmähliches" end of the Aegyptids and to the "freventlich" killing of Pallas.

[64] Harrison 1998, 230.

[65] This quotation and the ones following have been taken from Harrsion 1998, 231–37.

[66] Harrison 1998, 232.

[67] Harrison 1998, 236.

[68] Harrison 1998, 236.

[69] Harrison 1998, 237.

[70] Harrison 1998, 237.

[71] On logically verifiable ambiguity in Propertius, see Stahl 1985, *passim*.

[72] On the problematic standing of this adulatory elegy among other, less regime-friendly, poems, see Stahl 2002, 273f.

[73] On the topographical difficulties, see Stahl 1998, 49–69.

[74] Putnam 1995, 174 calls Aeneas' conduct following Pallas' death a "rampage" (so also 1998, 203). On the preceding page (173) Putnam, summarily and cursorily dealing with Aeneas' taking of eight prisoners for sacrifice at Pallas' burial, his rejection of the suppliant Magus, and his killing of the priest Haemonides, states: "Loyalty to Evander, Servius' triumphant *pietas*, now produces some extraordinary results in the life of our precedent-setting hero." Why is the piety ascribed by Servius to Aeneas' final killing of Turnus called "triumphant", and why does Putnam alienate it from its context in Book 12 (the obligation to kill Turnus imposed on Aeneas by father Evander) and apply it to the different situations of Book 10 not referred to by Servius? Are we acting with correct method if we claim *our* revulsion as a standard for gauging Vergil's (or Roman) feelings? Because it suggests *uncontrolled* violence, the widely accepted phrase "Aeneas' rampage" (*sic* Lyne 1983, 193) appears to be used somewhat rashly.

⁷⁵ It is a grave misunderstanding to declare the Italians "defenders": they are aggressors and breakers of the peace concluded between King Latinus and Aeneas' ambassador, Ilioneus (7. 285: *pacemque reportant*). See Chapter 7.

⁷⁶ Donatus, quoted with approval by Renger (1985, 63), sees Haemonides punished for deserting his duties to Diana and Apollo: *qui, immemor officii sui Apollinem Dianamque deserens processit in campum, morte poenas exsolvit et templum dei bellatoris suis spoliis ornavit* (Don. *ad Aen*.10.540). "Sein *nefas* wird durch *immolatio* gesühnt" ("his nefarious deed is atoned for by his immolation", Renger 63). J.F. Miller, however, speaks of 'Aeneas' shocking "sacrifice" of the Italian *sacerdos* of Apollo and Trivia' (2009, 164), according to him a "troubling episode".

⁷⁷ Thomas 1998, 273. Quite in line with Thomas' selective reading is his teacher (Clausen 2002, 196), when he (excusingly?) refers to jubilant attacker Tarquitus as "a vain and foolish young warrior." Where did Clausen find information on Tarquitus' *young age* (which makes his death at older Aeneas' hands appear more cruel)? Aeneas' mention of Tarquitus' mother (557) hardly points to Tarquitus' youth...but to the fact that his mother, the immortal nymph Dryope (551), will survive and mourn him. (Being a son of Faunus, Tarquitus is a half-brother of King Latinus.) Why add the (likewise exculpatory?) notion of "foolish"? Putnam, too (1995, 173f.), withholds from his reader Tarquitus' provocative initiation (*exultans contra...obvius ardenti sese obtulit*, 10. 550–52) of his encounter with Aeneas, so once more Putnam's talk of Aeneas' "rampage" (in full: "the rampage on which Aeneas embarks after Turnus' killing of Pallas" 1995, 209) hardly represents Vergil's text to its full extent. J.F. Miller (2009, 161) states "Aeneas...tramples on familial values of *pietas*..."

⁷⁸ "But for the heating of his sword is required the stimulus of a great grief and wrong" (Otis 1964, 357). For the overall behavior of Aeneas after Pallas' death see also Renger 1985, 52–69.

⁷⁹ Hornsby (1970,109) makes the simile impose a moral warning on the Aeneas of the narrative: "But the simile also hints at dire consequences for such frenzy. Aegaeon finally succumbed to Jupiter's superior power and lies chained beneath Mount Aetna.... Aeneas, in book X, acts like a monster and specifically like an immortal one, and such presumption from even the great hero could not be long borne." The simile is asked to supply the moral condemnation that can complement and confirm the interpreter's misreading of the narrative ("Aeneas has descended into barbarism"). Cf. R.D. Williams (*ad* 10. 565f.): "It is very significant that Aeneas, given over as he now is to rage and frenzy, should be compared with a barbaric figure symbolizing violence and brutality." It rather appears 'very significant' that Williams replaces the simile's *tertium comparationis* of Aeneas' fighting power (*tot paribus strepere clipeis, tot stringeret ensis*, 568) with violence and brutality.

⁸⁰ Horsfall 1995, 114.

⁸¹ Kronenberg 2005, 406 (my emphasis). On the other hand, Vergil is said to transform (Epicurean) Mezentius "from a symbol of *impietas* to one of *pietas*" (2005, 405).

⁸² See R. Thomas in 1998, 273 and earlier in this chapter. Kronenberg (2005, 403) thanks Thomas, "who carefully guided the transformation of this paper...to a dissertation chapter."

⁸³ Kronenberg 2005, 403.

⁸⁴ Kronenberg 2005, 425. Her school's tendency of incriminating the Vergilian Aeneas even extends into straining the Latin vocabulary. When Mezentius hopes that

his victorious horse will carry back "the bloody spoils and the head of Aeneas", *victor spolia illa cruenta / et caput Aeneae* (862f.), Kronenberg (416) prefers, differing from *arma cruenta* at 10. 462, the reading *cruenti* (ably discussed by Harrison *ad loc.*), translating "bloodthirsty" Aeneas – a meaning listed in *OLD* for later authors, but which I cannot verify in the word's 25 occurrences in Vergil. Mezentius is hardly eager to characterize his enemy as bloodthirsty, but, bent on taking revenge for his slain son, he wants to see the slayer's blood; the same yearning is expressed in his desire to lay his hands on Aeneas' severed head (an "Epicurean" Mezentius?).

[85] "In einem Stoßseufzer (*tandem*) entlädt sich die ganze Spannung aus den vorhergegangenen Leiden und Gefahren" (Renger 1985, 59). Unlike the "Two Voices" school, Renger does view Aeneas' conduct in the context of his people's military plight: 56; 57; 59.

[86] See Heinze 1993, 238 (=1965, 296) and Chapter 5, Section 4 below.

[87] In the confusion of his sudden hope (*turbidus* 648), Turnus by a slip of the mind even admitted that Lavinia had been promised by Latinus to Aeneas (cf. 7. 268ff.), not to himself (see also his implicit admission *coniuge praerepta* 9. 138). His pursuit of the fleeing effigy of course parallels his attack of the Trojan camp during Aeneas' absence (Book 9).

[88] The divine pity displayed at 10. 757–61 can hardly be utilized to bolster the thesis (widely favored by Latinists) of the *Aeneid*'s "broader *humanitas*" when compared to the *Iliad*. It is highly doubtful that "the gods of Vergil feel pity for the sufferings of *all* the combatants" (Harrison *ad loc.*; my emphasis). After all, at least (see Harrison ad 10. 760) Venus and Juno watch from *opposite sides* (*contra* 10. 760): would Juno by now have given up her disregard of Trojan suffering as expressed in her speech at the opening of Book 1 and in the devastating storm (many Trojans drowned, feelingly described by the author through the eyes of Aeneas)?

On the other hand, the Homeric 'model passage' (*Il.* 11. 70–83) has its own context. And where in the *Aeneid* would one find a Jupiter who, like Zeus, pronounces that there is no living being on earth more miserable than man (*Il.* 17. 445–7)? The transnational humanity of Homer is perhaps best evidenced by the fact that the *Iliad* places its most moving scene, the encounter of Hector and Andromache and their little son, overshadowed by the ever-present threat of death, *on the Trojan side*, i.e., that of the Greeks' ('Achaians') enemies. See Stahl 2001, 87–89.

[89] Putnam 1995, 135.

[90] Putnam 1995, 135f.

[91] Also, by the proposition 'your piety misleads you to being incautious', Aeneas hardly means to logically reverse it into something like 'being cautious would mislead you to neglecting piety.'

[92] See Harrison *ad* 813: "a demeanour of confident aggression".

[93] Heinze 1993, 162f. (=1965, 204f.) views lightly-armed Lausus as "not yet strong enough for a full suit of armour".

[94] "Contemplation and madness, *pietas* and slaughter, would seem incompatible entities." Putnam 1995, 137.

[95] Putnam 1995, 135.

[96] Putnam 1995, 136 (my emphasis).

[97] Putnam 1995, 136 (my emphasis).

[98] Vergil leaves it to his reader to picture whether Aeneas could (and would) protect

the corpse against the Etruscans' *iustae ...irae* (10. 714; cf. *furiis iustis* 8. 494). His pierced armor (11. 9f.) seems to indicate at least *some* abuse; but the poet's decision not to pursue this matter any further hardly authorizes latter-day interpreters to attach yet another alleged flaw to Aeneas' record. To Vergil, obviously the religious priority observed by Aeneas is most important, *vota deum primo victor solvebat Eoo* (11. 4), even more important than the duty of burying his own fallen soldiers (11. 2f.).

Considering these expressly-stated priorities (to which are added the strategic one consisting in the urgent move against Latinus' city, 11. 17, and especially the care for Pallas' burial, cf. *primus* 11. 26), it appears bizarre *ex silentio* to find significance in (presumably) lacking information on the corpse of Mezentius, "whose fate hangs over the last lines of the... *Aeneid*" (Thomas 2001, 284). See also James (1995, 633) on the missing burials of Turnus ("an issue that hangs over the end of the poem") and Lausus: "The poet's *failure* or *refusal* to *erase doubt* on this issue...*suggests* that he wants to maintain a *mysterious silence* about it, thus leaving open the possibility that they [scil., Lausus and Turnus] receive no burial" (1995, 632; my emphases). What would James make of 10. 827f., "I send you back to the shades and ashes of your ancestors," if she cared to take notice of the lines?.

Freewheeling and non-differentiating bestowal of honorary titles ("piety") results in fancy readings of Vergil's original: "...in killing Mezentius, Mezentius' son, and Turnus, he [scil., Aeneas] overrules their claims for *pietas*, removes them from rule, and wipes out their political dynasty" (James 1995, 633). How would James deal with Turnus' 'claim for *pietas*' who brags to have (by killing Pallas) wiped out "Evander's whole house together with its progeny and the Arcadians, deprived of their armor" (11. 394f. The spoliation of course in the first place refers to Turnus' impious appropriation of slain Pallas' sword-belt)? Metaphilology indeed has mysterious ways of discovering silence and filling it with significance, thereby neglecting the priorities expressly stated by the author. (On a different way of reading silence, see my 2001 article "On the Sadness of Silence in Ancient Literature".) It is not without consistency that in James' article, too, at the end Vergil's valuations are stood on their head, when her reader is being offered "the original *conditor* of the Roman people stabbing a young man whose final thoughts and words are of concern and love for his father – the kind of *pietas* formerly so typical of Aeneas" (etc.; 1995, 636). Vergil's rhetorically skillful Turnus who, if only he can survive, slyly operates with his father's projected grief and is ready to bargain away even his sought-after bride apparently does not fit into the wishful picture and must be purged from the *Aeneid*. What is introduced instead is "the awareness that Rome was established with the sword – the sword that took the life of a young Italian, who was pleading for mercy, whose body may not have been given burial." So, at 10. 811–12 Aeneas "taunts Lausus for his deceptive *pietas* toward Mezentius", Lausus "whose *pietas* Aeneas had *derided*" (1995, 630, my emphasis).

[99] Putnam 1995, 136.
[100] Putnam 1995, 136.
[101] Putnam 2006, 411.
[102] Since Turnus is out to hurt father Evander, his words can hardly be taken in any other way than expressing cruel irony, and certainly not as Vergil's way of setting Turnus off positively against (negatively viewed) Aeneas, who "has explicitly denied to some, and implicitly to many more" (footnote: "Especially the eight sons of Ufens and Sulmo, whom he takes for sacrifice."), "return to their parents for burial, thus

Chapter 3

refusing them that minimal but crucial *comfort, which even Turnus granted to Evander*" (James 1995, 630; my emphasis).

It is likewise moot to state that Aeneas "returns Lausus not, *significantly*, to Lausus' father, Mezentius, but to his ancestors" (James, l. c.; my emphasis), What 'significance' is there in *not returning the body to the father* in the present situation? After all, Aeneas' most urgent task, dictated by the strategic necessity of saving his people by removing Turnus' stronger replacement, is to kill Mezentius, the father. In view of Mezentius' imminent death, Vergil has designed the most pious and honorable solution by having Aeneas return Lausus' body "to the shades and ashes of your ancestors", *parentum / manibus et cineri* 10. 827f. Once more, disregard of long-range composition and of philological detail are the premises of a distorting 'interpretation'.

[103] The linguistic evidence is sufficiently convincing, in spite of R. Thomas' protest at the 1996 *Aeneid* conference in Pittsburgh (on the conference, see Stahl 1998), where he denied the depreciatory meaning of Turnus' *quidquid solamen humandi est* at 10. 493.

[104] Putnam 1995,136.

[105] Putnam 1995,138 (my emphasis).

[106] Compare Stahl 1981, 163. See there also concerning Vergil's manipulation of the *Iliad* in order to make Diomedes the most prominent Greek hero (instead of Achilles, to whom Aeneas is clearly inferior, depending for his survival on god Poseidon *Il.* 20. 290). On the Harvard school's (Clausen's and others') misreading of Aeneas' heroic desire as a sort of nostalgic homesickness for Troy see the preceding chapter.

[107] See Thomas 1998, 271: "Stahl's *procedure* is to carry out a sustained attack on the character of Turnus", etc. On p. 272, Thomas recommends a German scholar (Pöschl) "writing before Vietnam, but, *more importantly*, after he had perhaps had time to reflect on the consequences of his own society's simplistically identifying, *sine humanitate*, enemies of the state" (my emphases). To protect Vergil against the charge of having portrayed Turnus unfavorably, Thomas claims the moral high ground by recommending to interpreters who do arrive at a negative reading of Vergil's Turnus the newly found moral bearings of a Nazi like Poeschl, an Austrian member of the *SS* (since 1933: see *DNP* vol.15.2, 314f.) before he, World War II having come to its end, reformed himself.

4

WINNING THE READER'S ASSENT THROUGH SUBLIMINAL GUIDANCE

(1) The Death of Pallas the Boy-Hero and Aeneas' Human Sacrifices

This now takes us to the second part of the answer to the question how Vergil wishes his readers to react to the killing of Pallas. For not only is the reader, as was shown above, being filled with sympathy for Pallas' noble courage and impregnated with abhorrence and antipathy against cruel, unheroic Turnus, he is also – and that through long-distance preparation – preoccupied so as to feel for Turnus' victim, Aeneas' young disciple and ally, Prince Pallas, and for Aeneas himself. Here, we encounter the third strand, designated "C" in the survey of Chapter 1 (p. 8) (it, too, will lead up to the epic's final scene). Now that we have reviewed Turnus' conduct before and during the duel in Books 11 and 12, and his killing of Pallas in Book 10 (and Aeneas' ensuing conduct on the battlefield), we may turn to the relationship of Aeneas and Pallas, and to the subliminal guidance Vergil provides for his reader.

Immediately before Pallas' death, we witness a sympathetic conversation on the divine level (a rare honor for a mortal in the *Aeneid*, revealing a privileged focalization). Divine Hercules, once (8. 188ff.) the savior of Father Evander's community and now invoked by Pallas for assistance but unable to help him, sheds tears over the young mortal's imminent fate. Hercules in turn is consoled by his father, Jove, who points to fate's inevitability, to the loss of his own son Sarpedon before Troy and to the fact that Turnus' own life will be coming to its end soon (10. 464–72). This is much more affection than will be granted to young Lausus when he is killed by Aeneas: Lausus' share of authorial sympathy is limited to the same kind of brief (but intense) apostrophe which the poet himself gave to Pallas (10. 507–09 ~ 791–93).

But it is not only the fact of divine compassion which is striking. Much more so is the *kind* of compassion. We already saw that Aeneas, when refusing to accept the ransom offered by Magus (531–34), for his part invokes the father-son relationship that unites him with both Anchises and

Chapter 4

Ascanius-Iulus, and that he seems to grant Pallas the place of a son in his feelings, standing in for Father Evander who had entrusted his son to him. The same is done by Jupiter when he renews the pain about Sarpedon's death (well-known from the *Iliad*) and has to turn his eyes away from the scene of Pallas'death.

> sic ait, atque oculos Rutulorum reicit arvis. 10. 473.

Gods cannot bear to witness the deaths of their favorite humans, as Diana (11. 593ff.) and Juno (12. 151) show in the *Aeneid*, Artemis in Euripides' *Hippolytos* (1437f.; cf. *Alc.* 22.).[1]

If Vergil has the divine ruler of the universe affected by pity for mortal Pallas, we may confidently say that this climax of compassion cannot be surpassed poetically.[2] The reader, seeing his own natural feelings sanctioned by the highest religious authority, cannot but feel an even deeper abhorrence at Turnus' disregard for the most basic human relationship (about whose ranking in Rome's male-oriented society no word need be said). Following the poet's guidance, the reader, too, will here feel grief for Pallas.

A reading which, perhaps even basing itself on the epic-crumbling influence of Conte,[3] suppresses the greater literary detail and higher emotional weighting the poet dedicates to Pallas (as compared to Lausus) by positing a kind of 'equal rights' focalization, is not in touch with the text it professes to interpret. It is a dangerous simplification to assign Lausus, Pallas, Turnus, Camilla (or Aeneas, Dido, Turnus, Mezentius) each their own independent right and perspective, for such a practice fails to grasp the *Aeneid*'s complex architecture with its different levels of priority and its all-encompassing idea of a fate-regulated justice (which does not necessarily comply with the justice of latter-day interpreters). There can be no doubt that Pallas is the recipient of a privileged focalization.

But how is the reader supposed to feel about Aeneas? In Chapter 3 we already saw his reputation to be established as that of an honorable warrior. And as one should not judge (or even condemn) Aeneas' wrath as it is let loose on the battlefield, especially after the death of Pallas, one ought also to take a look at the *Vorgeschichte* to which the poet adds the story of Pallas' valorous end as a continuation.

What is of interest here for us is that the reader views the death of Pallas through the eyes of Aeneas, the mature man and father who is close to Jove in his attitude, but not from the viewpoint of the suffering young man himself. We thus feel even more the pain (and rage) of Aeneas (which is sanctified by the parallel grief of Jupiter). This effect has been prepared for a long time.

The death scene contains an unmistakable reference to Book 8. Pallas, when praying to Hercules, reminds him of Evander's hospitality (10. 460). Now the same hospitality was granted to Aeneas too – on the day of the Hercules festival. It is not arbitrarily that I move Aeneas and Hercules together in their relationship to King Evander and his son Pallas. By accepting young Pallas as his apprentice, Aeneas had entered a relationship similar to the one which is ascribed to Hercules in Pallas' prayer.

But there is a difference and distinction. The relationship of Pallas and Aeneas is characterized by an emotional attachment of the younger to the older right from the beginning. The relationship even has its root in the distant past. Evander had, as a youth, met King Priam and Anchises, and felt great admiration – much greater, as a matter of fact, for the latter than for the king of Troy (he seems to have had a keen eye for those chosen, thus unknowingly furthering Vergil's agenda of the fate-directed branch of Anchises vs. the doomed line of Priam, 8. 161–163). When departing, Anchises gave young Evander a bow, a cloak, and a set of reins. The reins are now in Pallas' possession, kindling (we may assume) his youthful imagination. So, at the arrival of Aeneas at Pallanteum, Evander himself recalls the voice and features of venerated Anchises (8. 155f.), and Pallas is bound to be deeply impressed by the famous name (8. 121). He attaches himself to Aeneas as his father once did to Anchises (8. 124 and 164). His father wishes him to learn *grave Martis opus* (516) from Aeneas by watching and admiring him at an impressionable age (*primis...ab annis* 517). And on their way to Latium, sailing along the coast, we see Pallas sitting next to Aeneas' left[4] side – like a son, we would say, enjoying his superior father's presence – interrupting the worrying thoughts of the mature man by asking about the stars in the dark sky, about Aeneas' 'odyssey' (i.e., he becomes acquainted with some of what the reader knows from Books 1–6). Pallas himself does not know that his behavior characterizes his age, but the reader's impression is that of a bright kid to whose naïve curiosity the world and a great man are still new and exciting, and who is not burdened by his teacher's ever-present grave worries about the vicissitudes of war (*eventus belli varios*, 10. 160).

The reader cannot help being frightened by Pallas' interest in the world of the grown-up warrior because he has seen this promising young man departing from home under the foreshadowing cloud of aged Evander's fear: Vergil has anticipated the effect Pallas' death will have on his father by having the old king faint at the time of departure, after delivering a farewell speech the intensity of which borders on that of a funeral oration (8. 560–83). In invoking the gods and especially *Jupiter* with "the prayers of a father", *patrias...preces* (574), Evander touches the reader's heart with a human tone that will – in the light of paternal Jupiter's later inability

Chapter 4

to help – reveal itself as tragic irony. As Evander made it clear that his son is his life, so the reader cannot but feel sympathy.

The tragic atmosphere is intensified by the actual departure scene (8. 585–96). There the climax of the poet's description, even above Aeneas, was given to Pallas (*ipse...Pallas* 587), and in seeing him compared to Lucifer, most dear to Venus of all the stars (590), and to Lucifer's "holy face", *os sacrum* (591), we readers cannot but fear for his life almost as that of a member of Venus' and Aeneas' family.[5]

If thus Pallas is moved into the center of Aeneas' (and the reader's) emotional attention, taking on the value of a son in the usual father-son relationship, we must not be surprised that Iulus-Ascanius, Aeneas' real son, has been kept away from the scene. One may object that in Book 8 Iulus was left behind to guard the Trojan camp. But that was hardly Vergil's main motive. For (a) Aeneas does not usually leave him out of his sight for long (not even a farewell is mentioned), and (b) Iulus' role in defending the Trojan camp during his father's absence in Book 9 is, corresponding to his young age (cf. *puer* 9. 641; 656), limited. Depending for his survival on his father's return (9. 257), he can only participate in the call for help (224–313) and later make a token appearance on the battlefield which is incomparably less weighty and emotion-laden than the scenes in Book 9 granted to Nisus and Euryalus or to Turnus.

Iulus, too, however, is granted attention from the divine level (and that is, as exemplified in the previous section, privileged focalization from the author). Apollo sees to it that this 'early Julian' (cf. 1. 288) kills no more than one taunting Rutulian (again, a provocation cannot remain unanswered: Trojan action occurs as *re*action to a preceding provocation). He then addresses the "boy" as "descendant of gods and ancestor of future gods" (the latter being, according to Servius, C. Julius Caesar and Augustus), *dis genite et geniture deos* (9. 642), as being on his way to the stars (*sic itur ad astra* 641). This characterization comes from the lips of a competent divine source, indeed. Apollo, after all, is the personal tutelary deity of descendant-god Augustus (for the poet's contemporaries, of course, he is a god-to-be: 1. 289 [see Stahl 1985, 126 with note 46 on p. 340; cf. Hor. *O.*1.2.45: *sero in caelum redeas*]). Accordingly, Apollo does not fail to slip in a prophetic remark on peace and expansion at the time of Augustus (643ff.).

This clarifies Vergil's dramaturgy for us. While Iulus is removed from his father's immediate environment during Books 8, 9, and 10, his importance as a link in the chain of the Julian descent, i.e., the political *telos* of the *Aeneid*, must not be lost sight of by Vergil's reader.

But the circumspectly created vacuum in Aeneas' affection is temporarily (or up to the end of the epic, if one so wishes) filled by Pallas, and the reader's conception of this relationship is tinged by vivid presentations of the father-son relationships Jove-Hercules, Jove-Sarpedon, Evander-Pallas, Anchises-Aeneas, Aeneas-Iulus, even Magus and his son(s).

In observing Vergil's long-distance design here, we conclude that the reader is to view Aeneas at the time of Pallas' death like a bereft father, and even more: that the reader himself is by this time prepared to feel with him and to react along with him.[6]

The most critical answer to the question how far Vergil expects his reader to follow Aeneas is connected to the Trojan hero's capture (in the eyes of ancient commentators, another indicator of Aeneas' *virtus*)[7] of twice four prisoners so he may

> sacrifice them to the shades in the fashion of an offering to the dead
> and drench the flames of the pyre with their captive blood.
>
> inferias quos immolet umbris
> captivoque rogi perfundat sanguine flammas. 10. 519f.

It is worth mentioning that Pöschl (sometimes viewed by himself and others as inaugurating a post-imperial Vergil) saw fit to interpret even this act of "bitterness" (*Erbitterung*) as an expression of Aeneas' *compassion* (!), *Mitleiden*,[8] and other "Augustan" interpreters (as for instance, Büchner, Klingner, or Burck)[9] had little or no difficulty with this passage – if they at all touched on its (for many recent readers) problematical character. It does not change the general tone of awe and reverence in which one approached Vergil, the supposed representative of Western values. It seems that here a piece of Vergilian reality was (subconsciously?) being suppressed and excluded from the overall picture (or, alternatively, utilized by the succeeding orthodoxy for casting Vergil as an anti-Augustan).

On the other hand, there were those other 20th-century (mostly English-speaking) interpreters who sensed that Vergil subtly criticizes Aeneas' behavior. R.D. Williams, stating that in Vergil's source (*Il.* 21. 27f.; 23. 175f.) the human sacrifice is an "act of barbarity", feels that "in the *gentle* Vergil it seems *worse* still".[10] Others have tried to tone down the author's alleged criticism of his hero by pointing out that Aeneas will not be personally present at the sacrifice (Achilles performed the act himself) and that he grasps only eight victims (Achilles took twelve). One wonders whether Vergil's "gentleness" is not a modern postulate that fulfills a function similar to the supra-natural, universal human message accorded to the poet by the pro-imperial scholars of the earlier 20th century. Quinn writes that the readers for whom Vergil writes "cannot see Aeneas ...sink to this level without discomfort and regret."[11] Should one not perhaps, instead of using the standard of one's own personal "discomfort", rather

Chapter 4

follow the author's guidance and say "rise to this level" instead of "sink", in view of the long impregnation with sympathy for Aeneas that Vergil's readers have received so far? It is a wish-based hypothesis without probative value for Conway[12] to maintain that someone who views the poet as approving of such acts "is surely...blind to the deepest passion that molded Vergil's art – the passion of humanity." What do we know about the "passion" of rhetorically trained Vergil? So far, we have seen Vergil's 'humanity' in the service of the *Trojan* side, e.g., at 11. 203–21 in Section 2 of Chapter 1. And when Quinn refers to Mackail's comment about "Vergil's single lapse into barbarism"[13] and his hope "that the lines might have been cancelled in his final revision", he quotes another interpreter who clearly is personally dissatisfied with what Vergil has left us, but who would have to delete more from the *Aeneid* than this passage to make it acceptable to himself.

A comparison with Livy may prove helpful. M. Hubbard drew my attention to the fact that the cruel punishment of treasonous Mettius Fufetius, while reported with disgust and with emphasis on its un-Roman character by the historian (Livy 1.28.11), is dealt with in marked contrast by Vergil with his grim (and sarcastic) jussive (*Aen.* 8. 643) *at tu dictis, Albane, maneres*. At times, it indeed seems that, of the two, "gentle" Vergil is the one who is better able to stomach the gory aspects of his subject matter.

Significantly Aeneas sticks to the sacrifice of the prisoners long after the immediate rage of the battle is over (overlooked by Knight:[14] Aeneas, "as we must imagine, spares the captives". Why *must* we?). In Book 11, when describing the funeral procession which Aeneas prepares to have Pallas' body escorted to his father Evander, Vergil expressly mentions these sacrificial prisoners: Aeneas

> also had tied to their backs the hands of those whom he wanted to send as a sacrificial offering to the dead, intending to sprinkle the flames with the blood of the slain.
>
> vinxerat et post terga manus, quos mitteret umbris
> inferias, caeso sparsurus sanguine flammas. 11. 81f.

The almost identical wording confirms the former passage as undeletable. Rightly Ladewig-Schaper-Deuticke mention[15] that in Roman triumphal processions, too, the sacrificial victims formed a special part, and Thome adds that the victims were followed by the captured enemy leaders, the former to be sacrificed on the Capitoline Hill by the victorious general, the latter to be killed in parallel action in the Mamertinum at the Hill's foot: a clear trace and indicator of what were originally human sacrifices.[16]

Startling for modern readers is the fact that the later lines here confirm Aeneas' alleged act of raging battlefield barbarity, by matter-of-factly integrating the human victims into the vast arrangements he so considerately performs for his fallen ally's burial: these prisoners are added by mere *et* to the preceding booty of arms and horses (the horses, of course, likewise to be sacrificed on the pyre, cf. *Il.* 23. 171; 242), and they are followed (attached by serial *-que*) by tree trunks dressed up with the arms of slain enemies (i.e. *tropaea* 172): three groups of doomed, and the narrator adds nothing whatsoever to set the captives apart from the other offerings as a special feature. The tone of 81f. is almost one of indifference when compared to Aeneas' preceding personal grief expressed over the corpse of Pallas (see below). The narrator utters no word either on dire consequences (as when Turnus took the arms of Pallas, 10. 101–05) or of blame (in this, differing from Homer in the 'model' passage, cf. *Il.* 23. 176); and Father Evander (to the reader, ever since Book 8 a pious supporter of Aeneas' fated imperial mission) himself accepts the funeral arrangements expressly as they have been prepared by "pious" Aeneas:

> Yes, I for my part certainly do not deem you, Pallas, worthy of an other funeral than that by which *pious* Aeneas, the great Trojans, the Etruscan leaders and all the Etruscan soldiers honor you.
>
> quin ego non alio digner te funere, Palla,
> quam pius Aeneas et quam magni Phryges et quam
> Tyrrhenique duces, Tyrrhenum exercitus omnis, 11. 169–71.

There certainly is no voice of protest being raised against "pious Aeneas" and his human sacrifices within the world of the epic itself either, and it is clear that Mackail and many others have not only measured Vergil by, but even wishfully tried to mould him according to, their own modern standards, while disregarding the author's understanding and sympathetic portrait of his hero's state of mind. We shall return to this feature, after first taking a look at the author's Roman environment and its effect within the poem.

That human sacrifices were a Roman tradition is beyond doubt.[17] For those who wish to tone down the cruelty of Aeneas' action by viewing it as that of an *archaic* hero ("Aeneas auch ein Berserker..., ein Kämpfer aus mythischer Vorzeit, der nach archaischen Maximen handelt"),[18] there is the disquieting fact that it was less than seventy years before Vergil started work on the *Aeneid*, in 97 BC, that the senate outlawed human sacrifices, "finally" (*demum*), as Pliny says, and his comment (*Nat.* 30.3.12) is potentially ominous: "Down to that time the monstrous sacrifices were celebrated publicly (openly, without concealment), *palamque in tempus illut sacra prodigiosa celebrata.*

The text is uncertain,[19] and the question is whether *palam* (*scil. est*) means "obvious" as at 21.1.2, or (*scil., celebrata sunt*) points to the end merely of *public* practice (see *OLD s.v.*, 1 and 2). In other words, does Pliny want to emphasize the late end of human sacrifice performed *in public*, or does he wish to maintain that 97 BC is really the end of such practice altogether? The latter alternative appears less likely, since Pliny himself a few pages later (30.6.16) mentions Nero's penchant for human sacrifice (*nam homines immolare etiam gratissimum*).

Occasional recurrence even of *public* human sacrifice is evidenced by Dio Cassius: during a mutinous riot, C. Julius Caesar had one soldier killed right away, but two others were ritually sacrificed ("slaughtered") on the Campus Martius (their heads displayed at the *regia*) by the priest of Mars and the *pontifices* (Dio 43.24.4). This was in 46 BC, so that Livy's comment (22.57.6) on the human sacrifices of 216 BC (more than a hundred years before the senatorial interdiction!) as "highly un-Roman sacrifices", *minime Romano sacro*, sounds more like embarrassed whitewashing, especially in view of the fact that the premises of the sacrifices had "already before been drenched with the blood of human victims", *iam ante hostiis humanis...imbutum*, and that the sacrifices (unusual as they may have been) followed the guidance of the *libri fatales* (*loc. cit.*). Livy's enlightened skepticism is underlined by his remark *placatis satis, ut rebantur, deis* ("the gods having been sufficiently appeased, *as they believed*", 57.7). However, we cannot (as CN do, *ad Aen.* 10. 519f.) claim Livy's language at 7.15.10 as evidence of a general abhorrence toward human sacrifice in Vergil's "own day": Livy here emphasizes the national infamy that the Etruscans sacrificed 307 *Roman soldiers*; he speaks of the "hideousness of the *execution*" (*foeditate supplicii*) and calls it a highly remarkable "disgrace of the *Roman people*", *ignominia populi Romani*.

When, in the same year as his sacrifice of two soldiers on the Campus Martius (46 BC), C. Julius Caesar held games with a notion of commemorating his daughter Julia, they were accompanied near her grave by gladiatorial combats – gladiatorial shows serving, ever since the funeral of D. Iunius Pera in 264 BC, as a sort of refined (i.e., masked with pleasure, *voluptate*) human sacrifice to the dead, as Tertullian in *De spectaculis* (12.97; supported by Servius *ad* 10. 519) explains: "Thus they found consolation about death through homicides", *ita mortem homicidiis consolabantur*. The association of gladiatorial combat with human sacrifice at funerals is firmly rooted in custom.[20]

So Roman readers would hardly view Aeneas' sacrifice of prisoners to the shade of Pallas in terms of a distant 'archaic' past, but could without difficulty relate it to more recent memory (or maybe even to current non-public practice).

Perhaps, it has often been felt, the poet counted on an even more recent 'recollection' alive among his readers. Only six years after the sacrifice on the Campus Martius of C. Julius Caesar's two mutinous soldiers, viz. in 40 BC, his adoptive son and successor is reported to have sacrificed, at an altar erected to his adoptive father, a large number[21] of Roman knights and senators, who had unconditionally surrendered to him at his conquest of Perusia.[22] The Perusine town councilors were, according to one version, put to death as well.

The city of Perusia had been the focal point of republican opposition against the triumviral expropriation program executed in Italy by Octavian. Eighteen cities were affected, and the siege of Perusia, accompanied by famine, had a devastating effect on those caught inside the ramparts. Among contemporaries, Propertius (he lost a relative who had survived the siege but was killed on his way home) twelve years later published an uncompromising monument to his lasting pain, expanding the scope of the event from the personal to "the *country*'s graves at Perusia, ...*Italy*'s funerals in harsh times" (1.22.3f.).[23] Certainly, "Caesar's swords", *Caesaris enses* (Prop.1.21.7), had left their impression far beyond the merely local area. Scholars are divided on the historicity of the human sacrifices (Propertius does not mention any), and for methodological reasons it appears prudent to look upon the story with some skepticism.[24]

Kraggerud advises "interpreters of Vergil that they leave aside the dubious human sacrifice of Octavian in 40 BC if they wish to elucidate the indubitable human sacrifice of Aeneas in Vergil's epic."[25] But he concedes that "such fantasies...could well have found credence with many people both then and long afterwards."[26] The acknowledgment provides an important point for evaluating the historical background of the *Aeneid*. The executions following Perusia's surrender (Syme calls them "judicial murders") definitely were one of the climaxes in the bloody career of Octavian, who (we said earlier) liked to be called "the avenger of (C. Julius) Caesar", *Caesaris ultor*, and their reputation as acts of revenge was enhanced by the circumstance that only one man, a certain Lucius Aemilius, was granted exemption from execution: he had, as a juryman in Rome, voted in favor of the death penalty for Caesar's assassins and had encouraged his fellow-jurors to go along with him (Appian, *BC* 5.5.48). Octavian's (the "pious" son's) persistence in tracking down his (adoptive) father's assassins is well illustrated by the fact that the last two were killed only after the battle of Actium (31 BC), thirteen years after the event. So it is not far-fetched to assume that the human sacrifices were easily believed to be historical by Vergil's contemporaries, even without the later testimony of Seneca who warningly reminds the 19-year-old Nero of Augustus'

Chapter 4

pre-Actium (later hushed over) cruelty concerning, among other outrageous acts, "the altar of Perusia and the proscriptions", *Perusinas aras et proscriptiones* (*Cl.* 1.11.1). Belief in the sacrifices' historicity would hardly have first arisen as late as the time of Seneca's *De Clementia*. Rather, its origin would befit the time (and perhaps propaganda) of the civil war itself.

Rumor (or misinformed opinion) has its own historical reality and dynamics, as Thucydides recognized (6. 53–61),[27] and it cannot reasonably be excluded that Vergil felt he should counter its harshness by giving Aeneas' sacrifice of prisoners as persuasive a human motivation as possible. Ti. Claudius Donatus says of Vergil's treatment of the Aeneas figure: "...he admits those things that could not be denied, then removes the blame and turns it into praise, so that by extensive reasoning he makes Aeneas appear distinguished under aspects under which a disparagement could apply to him."[28] As Aeneas often personifies alleged positive qualities (and prefigures acts) of his greater descendant, it is methodologically justified to ask whether the human sacrifices, too, prefigure an act widely ascribed to Augustus by Vergil's contemporaries. Thus the founder of the Julian family would here again appear as an early practitioner of rites still familiar to the poet's audience. If the Princeps himself was supposed once to have practiced human sacrifice (as a sort of grim *Parentalia*), we may perhaps no longer be so surprised about Vergil's long-range interest in making his reader sympathize with Aeneas the avenger of Father Evander's maliciously killed son. After all, Augustus too viewed (and wanted to be viewed by others) a major part of the bloody career that brought him to power as performing the pious duty of avenging his (adoptive) father's assassination. Vergil's insistence on, and reference to, the sanctity of the father-son relationship, even in the case of the non-related pair Pallas and Aeneas, would, viewed in this context, find a convincing explanation (or application): the epic poet would point out the unrelenting sense of commitment and of duty (as well as the human attachment) which motivates a serious avenger. Exposed to Augustan propaganda with no 20th-century interpreter at his side, Vergil's contemporary reader would find here a ready network of references for sympathetically understanding the actions of his Emperor by reading about his Emperor's forefather.

The fact that Augustus' *Res Gestae* was published posthumously (AD 14) does not preclude that his wishful self-portrait was available earlier, communicated also through his (now lost) *Memoirs* and widely spread presentations in sculpture and architecture. Compare the (legally embroidered) statement of the 'pious son': *qui parentem meum trucidaverunt, eos in exilium expuli iudiciis legitimis ultus eorum facinus* (*R.G.* 2. "Those who butchered my father I drove into exile, taking revenge for their crime through legal courts" (i.e., by means of the ably orchestrated *lex Pedia*). Of course, "exile" does not imply survival.

Contemporary practice and political environment are a good foil for viewing Vergil's poetry in reference to historical reality. But his poem can and does speak for itself. Book 11 offers not only Father Evander's appreciation of Aeneas' funeral arrangements for Pallas, but allows the reader to learn about Aeneas' deepest emotions and, also, about the attitude his creator chooses to exhibit.

Only after first having offered due thanks to the gods for his victory over Mezentius (11. 2ff. – the Julian ancestor as always acts correctly in matters of religious requirements), Aeneas turns to the humanly pressing concern for the fallen comrades and allows his tears for Pallas to flow (29; 41; 59; 95); he prepares the cortège for the young lad's corpse. His address "*puer*" (42; cf. Evander at 8. 581: "*care puer*") and his resounding (but mainly restrained: *nec plura effatus*) Catullan good-bye: "*salve aeternum mihi, maxime Palla, aeternumque vale*" (97f.) are in harmony with the author's lyrical simile (again reminiscent of Catullus) of the prematurely dying flower (68f.) as well as with the epic feature of the crying horse (90). The intimate overall tone as well as the specifically added garment from Dido's hand (72ff.) make it clear that Aeneas' actions are expressions of his affection for the deceased "boy" whom he wishes to honor further both by the human victims (81f.; their sacrificial destination indicated by the fact that Aeneas ties their hands on their backs, says Donatus) and by the spoils of the slain enemy (83f.; the two items connected by mere – *que*, we said above, with not a hint of repulsion from the narrator's lips about the sacrifice). Above all, the flower simile (68–71), offered in the narrator's voice, makes it clear that here, too, any interpreter who disagrees with the funeral arrangements in general and the human sacrifice specifically, is not only quarreling with Aeneas but with the poet himself. In Vergil's hierarchically structured universe, the (Trojan-Julian) leaders and their associates are the ones who count.[29] We must not mistakenly expect of him (or read into his work) a (perhaps even democratically tinged) concern for the unaffiliated individual human being such as can be found in his independently-minded contemporary Propertius.[30]

Along with his care for the son, Aeneas is concerned also with the father's pride (no shameful wound, corresponding to Pallas' own words at 10. 449f.), his tears, his mourning, and a possible solace (62f.), and he expresses his deeply felt sympathy with Evander's pain:

Unhappy one, you will see your son's cruel funeral!

infelix, nati funus crudele videbis! 11. 53.

If Aeneas here deplores his own deficient reliability, *fides* (55), this should not be misunderstood as an admission of guilt (as we already explained on the basis of the battle situation). King Evander himself will expressly exclude any idea of possible blame (164f.). Nor should one believe that feelings of guilt keep Aeneas from facing Evander in person. For he has to stay and continue fighting: "The same horrible fate of war calls us from here to new tears" (96f.: *His is not a war of choice.*). It is not guilt but obligation and indebtedness (cf. *misero...debita patri* 63) that Aeneas feels toward Evander – as he does in his first emotionally tinged reaction to Pallas' death in Book 10 (514ff.): he owes it to his host that he goes after the killer of his son, Pallas.

Thus, Aeneas' utterances in Book 11 confirm our investigation of his conduct in Book 10. Paternal pain about the loss of Pallas is combined with awareness of obligations toward his host and deepest sympathy for the bereft father. The reader is certainly asked to acknowledge these qualities in the seemingly violent reactions of Book 10, to which we now return.

We saw that, right from the beginning, an apostrophe of Turnus from the author's own mouth (*te, Turne,...quaerens*, 10. 514f.) gives the reader an objective indication about the controlled direction of Aeneas' rage on the battlefield. In addition, as Vergil will do at important junctures, we are granted access to the hero's innermost feelings and thoughts at this moment. (This is comparable to the description of Turnus' mixed thoughts, increasingly of flight, in his moment of confused hesitation when Aeneas hits him with his spear, 12. 914–18.)

Before Aeneas' eyes (10. 515ff.) are Pallas, Evander, the handshakes (cf.8. 467) exchanged at the meeting in which the aged king entrusted his young son to Aeneas' guidance (8. 514–17), the hospitality he enjoyed upon arrival (*mensae*, 10. 516 recalls the *mensis* of 8. 110). The latter corresponds almost *verbatim* to the obligation of which Pallas in his prayer reminded Hercules:

Aeneas:
>mensae, quas advena primas
>tunc adiit, 10 .516f.

Pallas invoking Hercules:
>per patris hospitium et mensas, quas advena adisti, 10. 460

(Hercules, we recall, then turned to his father, Jupiter, who could only point to the death of his own son Sarpedon before Troy.)

It is manifest that Aeneas, in spite of pain and emotion, follows a *Leitbild*, a guiding concept which is based on and observes the moral obligations he has shouldered.[31] As readers, we are by these allusions made to recall those tender scenes of common worship, of friendship, of warmth and trust, in Book 8. His stay at Arcadian Pallanteum (in the poet's time, the site of Augustus' and Apollo's residences) was for Aeneas himself a visit in an idyllic enclave, a peaceful respite between past labors and imminent war. Now that Pallas, the "dear boy, the only and late joy" of Evander (*care puer, mea sola et sera voluptas* 8. 581) has been maliciously killed by Turnus in order to hurt Evander, there is no way that the perceptive reader's emotions are not with Aeneas when he cuts a path through the enemy to reach the killer Turnus (10. 513ff.).

Whereas the chain of outward events that leads to Turnus' death in Book 12 is triggered by Turnus' inhuman conduct in Book 10 as we have interpreted it, the other chain, that of *subliminal guidance* given to the reader's emotions and subconscious preoccupations, has begun much earlier, viz. in Book 8 where Vergil's pro-Julian partiality turns out to be much more effective (and efficient) and much more subtle than is perceived by those who like to discount it.

Likewise, Aeneas' role as the New Achilles who is bound to avenge the New Patroclus on the New Hector (richly documented in literature, e.g., by Klingner's comments on Book 12)[32] is rooted already in the beginning attachment of Pallas to him in Book 8, i.e., already at a time when the other "New Achilles" predicted by the Sibyl, viz. Turnus, is just beginning to unfold his formidable battlefield rage. For understanding the *Aeneid*'s design, it is indispensable to see that Turnus is called an Achilles only to the extent that he revives and repeats a past threat to the Trojans, but that he is *a priori* doomed to fall by the hands of an even greater hero, a new Super-Achilles, so to speak, who is Aeneas. The present-day situation of Vergilian scholarship suggests that we should once more point out Vergil's emphasis on Aeneas as a fully-developed ('Homeric') fighter, who, in avenging Pallas, himself takes on the role his poetic forerunner was denied in Homer's *Iliad*: that of Achilles, greatest of all.

(2) Results and Conclusion, Chapters 1–4

Thus, to summarize in concluding, our investigation has so far traced three (out of at least four) strands which come together in the final scene of the *Aeneid*.

(1) The breach of the treaty concerning the duel, concluded in Book 12, reaches its ultimate consequence. The development can be seen as starting much earlier if one observes that Vergil includes the promise given by Turnus – but not kept later – at the session of King Latinus' council in Book 11.

Chapter 4

In this area of political and international relations, Aeneas would be in a position to exercise *clementia* toward the defeated and now humble enemy, according to his father's advice, given to him in the underworld: *parcere subiectis*.

> (2) The dishonorable and unheroic killing of Pallas, committed in Book 10, finds its atonement. Here Aeneas is not free but *has* to (and eagerly does) avenge the killing, especially so since Father Evander has imposed the task on him as an inescapable, sacred duty (we recall the word *immolat*, 12. 949): "Your right arm owes Turnus to father and to son, as you see", *dextera...tua ..., Turnum gnatoque patrique quam debere vides* (11. 178f.).

In the area of revenge, Turnus has, even with his appeal concerning father Anchises and father Daunus, forfeited all claims to mercy, because *he himself* has horribly sinned against the sacrosanct father-son relationship by killing the son in order to cause pain to the father.

> (3) And, finally, the readers have, ever since Book 8, been circumspectly subjected to subliminal guidance up to the point where they are supposed to share Aeneas' savage pain at the sight of Pallas' sword-belt, the *saevi monimenta doloris* (12. 945). They share his feelings because the poet's artful psychagogy has taught them to love Pallas as Aeneas does and to see in him a sort of substitute Iulus.

The best key to a poet's partiality is found in those passages where he tries to influence the subconscious self of his reader.

This interpreter's conclusion then would be not only that Vergil fully agrees (and wishes to guide his reader to the same position) with Aeneas' act of killing Turnus, but views and presents it as the only morally justified solution to his epic. To what degree he is, even in this, loyally serving the Emperor who, even after his final victory, felt unable to show mercy toward the assassins of his adoptive father (as well as toward many others who had sided with their cause) is a question well worth pondering.

But first, since I initially pointed out that this book may not have to say anything basically new on the *Aeneid*, my reader will allow me once more to mention that the understanding presented here is consistent with and justifies two of the earliest interpretations of the final scene known to us. According to the ancient commentator Servius (*ad* 12. 940), the final scene serves the glory of Aeneas in two ways. He displays *pietas* because he thinks of pardoning Turnus, and he shows *pietas* because he observes Father Evander's bidding and kills Turnus. *Omnis intentio ad Aeneae pertinet gloriam*. Donatus' judgement moves along the same lines.

One may view the Servius quotation in connection with the suggestion of Propertius, Vergil's contemporary (2. 1. 42, quoted in the *Prologue* and at the opening of Chapter 3), that the epic is supposed to depict Aeneas in order to enhance (or give a foundation to) the fame of Augustus. Then it would be hard not to understand pious Aeneas' motives as a supposedly congenial guide to his descendant's feelings (and Aeneas' mythical opponents as giving, to contemporary Romans, guidance on how to judge the guilt of the historical adversaries Octavian had to face). Ultimately, this must remain speculation. But such a hypothesis goes a long way towards explaining Vergil's circumspect endeavor to make his readers appreciate conduct, feelings, moods, emotions, and motives of the Julian founding father even in those harsh situations which, to our time, might seem to allow (or require) more lenient handling or a different decision.[33]

Horace (*O.* 1.2.44) says that *Caesaris ultor*, "the avenger of (his adoptive father C. Julius) Caesar", is the name by which Mercury-Octavian allows himself to be invoked in his human manifestation. It appears that, when placing Augustus' forefather in a comparable (and complementary) context of revenge, Vergil wishes not only to win his reader over to seeing Aeneas' actions as just. Beyond this, he wants to convince us that, in order to protect the sacrosanct community of father and son, one may have to show oneself inexorable to any man or party that inflicts violence on either member of the relationship.

It is hard to picture Augustus not satisfied when listening to the new Roman epic and perceiving the kind of subliminal guidance the New Homer was giving the nation.

Over the years, the Emperor had, both in person and through Maecenas, shown an intense interest in the work's progress. The poet, at the time of his death, considered his epic unfinished and unpublishable in its existing form (he planned three more years of polishing).[34]

Nevertheless, Augustus personally saw to it that the work *was* published. He must have felt that his interest was sufficiently rewarded. This, at least, is the way Ovid understood the situation. In addressing Augustus (*Tr.* 2.533), he calls Vergil "the...author of *your Aeneid,* "*tuae... Aeneidos auctor*".[35]

Chapter 4

Notes

¹ See Stahl 2003b, 129f.

² Feeney will allow Jupiter to feel pity only on one occasion in the *Aeneid*, and even then not conclusively (i.e., not reported in the narrator's voice), viz. in the perspective of Anchises (5. 727), whereas he grants Juno two instances of pity (expressed through the verb *miserari*: 4. 693; 10. 686). About Jupiter Feeney states: "A god who can feel anger can feel pity, and this god appears to feel neither." By not considering Jupiter's fatherly feelings of pity for Pallas (did Feeney perhaps arrive at his strange omission by consulting not the epic's text but merely a concordance *s.v. miserari*?), Feeney not only fails the title of his own book ("The Gods in Epic") but also reveals a skewed approach to the *Aeneid* (Feeney 1991, 144 with note 61). It is not surprising that Feeney's Vergil (the "narrator") "is ultimately unable to commit himself to Jupiter's perspective" (1991, 155). See Chapter 2.

³ See, for instance, Thomas 1998 274: "G.B. Conte's formulation reminds us that we must always attend to individual focalizations in this poem: there is no overarching 'epic' or other point of view: 'The coexistence of the worlds of Aeneas, Dido, Turnus, Mezentius, and Juturna springs from the fact that Vergil allows each of them an autonomous, personal raison d' être' " etc. For details, see Chapter 3, Section 2.

⁴ "Left side", not just "side", so the difference in rank is preserved: "the side of respect and subordination", Harrison *ad* 10. 160–61.

⁵ Only adepts of Conte will need to be reminded here that no such intense and extensive attention is lavished on Lausus, the other young warrior to be killed by a superior older one. On the basis of a close (long-distance) reading of the text it would be difficult to dispute that some (pro-Trojan) characters are granted privileged focalization by their creator.

⁶ There have been attempts (e.g., Putnam 1985, Lloyd 1999) to view Aeneas' feelings for Pallas as homoerotic. This dimension seems alien to (and, if overly stressed, weakening) Vergil's tight dramaturgy in view of the divine and human reference parallels (all of which are defined as father-son relationships) as well as in view of a possible political implication concerning the *Caesaris ultor* component.

⁷ Both Donatus and Servius Danielis make it a point that Aeneas does not merely "abduct" or "capture" these victims but seizes them by military force: *in octo hominibus non abductis sed raptis quanta Aeneae virtus ostenditur! quantum obsequium propter honorandam memoriam mortui!* (Donatus). *emphasis virtutis quod multos, quod iuvenes, quod armatos, quod rapit: minus enim fuerat si dixisset 'capit'* (SD).

⁸ Pöschl 1964, 195. In a later article, he does pay tribute to the supposedly "alienating" features of Aeneas. See Pöschl 1983, 175–88.

⁹ Büchner 1961, 392; Klingner 1967, 575f.; Burck 1979, 76.

¹⁰ Williams *ad* 10. 519 (my italics). Quinn 1968, 18 calls Aeneas' "impulse" here "rather worse" (when compared to his impulse to kill Helen in Book 2), presumably "hard to forgive" (p.17).

¹¹ Quinn 1968, 225.

¹² Conway *CR* 46, 1932, 202.

¹³ Quinn 1968, 223 n. 3, quoting J. W. Mackail's commentary (Oxford 1930), p. XVI.

¹⁴ Knight 1933, 170.

¹⁵ Ladewig-Schaper 1973, 162f. (*ad* 10.519) and 185 (*ad* 11. 81f.)

[16] Thome 1979, 333f.

[17] Still useful on ancient human sacrifice, in spite of numerous factual errors, is F. Schwenn (1915). *OCD* of 1996, restricting human sacrifice among the Greeks to "only in myth and scandalous story", has nothing at all on this topic under "sacrifices, Roman" (the victims presumably being "always domestic animals").

[18] Renger 67; "...an act not incompatible with a vision of Aeneas as an archaic Roman warrior-hero", Horsfall 1995, 180.

[19] See the apparatus in Ernout's 1963 Budé and in Mayhoff's 1898 Teubner edition. Translators vary correspondingly; see Jones' 1953 Loeb vs. Bostock and Riley, London 1856.

[20] See also Schwenn 1915, 174, with note 1 on information from Varro preserved in Servius (*ad Aeneid* 3. 67).

[21] The number stated by Dio and Suetonius, viz. 300 (*trecenti*), "can mean, like 'sescenti' or 'mille', an indefinite large number" (Weinstock 1971, 398, n.10).

[22] The main passages about the human sacrifices are Suetonius, *Div. Aug.* 15; Dio 48.14.3–5; Appian *BC* 5.5.48; Seneca *Cl.* 1.11.1.

[23] On the effect of Perusia on young Propertius, according to his autobiographic poetic testimony, and on his later development see Stahl 1985, Chapter 5.

[24] Syme 1974, 212. Kraggerud (1987; he widely follows Appian's account, which apparently bases itself on Octavian's own memoirs, 5.5.45, cf. 4.14.110).

[25] Kraggerud 1987, 85f.

[26] Kraggerud 1987, 84.

[27] See Stahl 2003, Chapter 1, on civic disturbances at Athens in 415 BC that were caused by misinformed assumptions about domestic history. From recent memory one may recall that two years after the World Trade Center Towers were destroyed it was widely reported that 70% of Americans believed that Saddam Hussein of Irak had caused the destruction.

[28] ...*confitetur ista quae negari non poterant et summotam criminationem convertit in laudem, ut inde Aenean multiplici ratione praecipuum redderet unde in ipsum posset obtrectatio convenire*, p. 3 ed. Georgii (repr. Stuttgart 1969). I have shown that this technique can be verified in *Aeneid* 2, where Aeneas' brave (but unsuccessful) defense activities in the night of Troy's fall are designed to counter the story that Aeneas betrayed his city (alluded to by Turnus at 12. 15 when he calls Aeneas the "traitor of Asia", *desertorem Asiae*). See Stahl 1981, 167 with note 22.

[29] It must not be forgotten that the cortège is an expression not only of Aeneas' personal affection but also, since amounting to a sort of state funeral, of his imperial loss: Aeneas regrets that Pallas did not live to see *regna...nostra* (43f.) and that his death will mean loss of protection (*praesidium*) even for Ascanius, Pallas' contemporary, once Italy will be under Trojan sway (57f).

[30] See Stahl (1985) 127, 147, 155.

[31] Renger 1985, 76f., details Aeneas' obligation as flowing from the (inherited) *hospitium*, his participation in the Hercules festival, from his status as a relative (through Electra) which entails obligations of *pietas,* and from his *patrocinium* toward Pallas.

[32] Klingner (1967, 589ff.) outlines how Vergil in Book 12 combined the Menelaus-Paris theme and the Achilles-Hektor theme. See also Galinsky 1981, 999f. who, however, tends to discount political reasons of Vergil's presentation in favor of poetic ones.

Chapter 4

[33] More recently Powell (2008, 25–27 *et passim*), referring to Griffin, has built a strong case for viewing distinguishing character traits, according to Roman sociological thinking, as characteristic also of later descendants.

[34] The numerous (literary as well as 'scholarly') attempts to ascribe to the poet the intention of not merely finishing the form but of revising the *substance* of his work (perhaps even of retracting his pro-Augustan position) are not covered by the ancient information; they are rather part of the notorious late-20th-century endeavor to relocate the poet's bearings.

The so-called *vita Donati* (screened with healthy skepticism by Horsfall 1995; see especially pp. 22f.) reports that Vergil, in his 52nd year, went to Greece and Asia Minor to put the finishing touches (*summam manum*, 35) on his epic: for three years, he intended nothing more than to make corrections (*nihil amplius quam emendare*). Returning in the company of Augustus (whom he, upon setting out on his journey, had met in Athens) much earlier than planned, he fell sick and died at Brindisi. His deathbed wish to burn the *Aeneid* was not fulfilled, but Varius (who, together with Tucca, had been made heir of his published writings) published the *Aeneid* under Augustus' authority (*auctore Augusto*) "superficially corrected", *summatim emendata* (39–41). Another version let both Varius and Tucca do the corrections (*emendaverunt*) "at the order of Augustus", *iussu Caesaris* (37). Gellius, too, reports the poet's wish to burn the *Aeneid* "which he had not yet sufficiently polished", *quam nondum satis elimavisset* (17.10.7). On the historicity of events mentioned in the Donatus *Vita*, see now A. Powell's (forthcoming) paper in P. Hardie and A. Powell (eds), *The Ancient Lives of Virgil*.

Nothing in any of these (partly contradictory) bits of information points to a revision of content, but every relevant passage is concerned only with finishing touches or corrections: the verb *emendare* is used both of Vergil's intention for his journey and of his posthumous editor[s], *vita Donati* , 35; 37; 41. Nevertheless Thomas finds in sections 39–41 "one of the most stirring and troubling pieces of information we have about this poet", providing "a possible, and famous answer" to the question about Virgil's possible reaction when seeing his poem "converted to a text which could be put to uses he had not intended" (by such "uses," Thomas apparently means Vergil's epic being viewed as the work of a committed "Augustan" poet). Wavering between the words of 39–41 being "true or not" and "If they are indeed true", the scholar, ultimately deciding in favor the second alternative, in between invokes "the great work of Hermann Broch, in which the dying Virgil tries to prevent his masterpiece from falling into the hands of Augustus" (Thomas 2001, 53f. On Broch's ignorance in matters of Latin and Vergil, Chapter 2 has said enough.). (Un-) Scholarly imagination, no longer bound by textual evidence, here appears to move not only on thin ice, but to be in danger of trying to walk on water.

A similar line of approach is taken by Suerbaum: Quinn's assumption (even if it is only speculation) that Vergil's deathbed wish to see the *Aeneid* burned originated in his growing insight that he could not justify the war, "ist Vergils würdiger als die aesthetischen Skrupel eines Perfektionisten" ("is more worthy of Vergil than the aesthetic scruples of a perfectionist", Suerbaum 1999, 354). This is very close to the widespread mindset of "our Vergil". Powell (2008, 13) compares "the interpretation of sacred texts", which "tends to be defended with passion, in part because (consciously or not) their defenders are in effect defending a most precious thing, their own view of themselves."

[35] Thomas (2002, 76; cf. 35) wishes to persuade his readers that the *Aeneid* was appropriated by Augustus so that Ovid, long after the poet's death, would here refer not to the original *Aeneid*: "Virgil is the *auctor*, but it is *your* poem now." "But"; "Now"? Does Thomas emend the text by adding a *sed* and a *nunc*, or can his Latin do without such petty concerns as adverbs and conjunctions? It needs the fragmented, incoherent, and misological view of the *Aeneid*'s organization cultivated by Conte, Thomas, and others to arrive at this *cul de sac*: "Are all parts of the poem Augustus', or just the Augustan parts?" (Thomas 2002, 75). As far as the Ovid passage is concerned, see Stahl 2002, 271f. In Chapters 1–4 I hope to have been able to confirm in detail my preliminary 1990 sketch, while at the same time explicating the errant ways of much contemporary Vergilian scholarship.

5

ALLOCATING GUILT AND INNOCENCE, I: QUEEN DIDO, THE LIBERATED WIDOW

(1) Divine Theater and Human World: Parallel and Synchronized, but Unconnected

Shipwrecked Aeneas experiences the hospitality of Dido, Queen of Carthage, and enters into a love affair with his hostess. But then he leaves her, citing his mission and divine orders. Does he not behave like Theseus who accepted Ariadne's help in order to escape the dangers of the labyrinth, but then abandoned her on the island of Naxos? Or like Jason, who gained the Golden Fleece through the magic help of Medea, took her with him in alleged gratitude, but at Corinth dismissed her for a new wife? Does Vergil then not tell us that Aeneas' conduct, for once, is shabby, that at Carthage the hero stained himself with guilt, at least – if not by the way he ended it – by entering[1] into the relationship in the first place?

And, vice versa, is not Dido like abandoned Medea and abandoned Ariadne? (There are allusions in Vergil's text to literary models representing these heroines.) Apart from the fact that modern sentiment feels attracted to the idea of the abandoned woman (and of the faithless male lover), there also are scholarly positions involved. For, if Vergil allows his hero to become guilty (or at least to display a serious flaw), and if, on the other hand, Dido – representative of the city that was to become Rome's fiercest and most dangerous enemy in historical times – turns out to be a woman betrayed by her Trojan (i.e., palaeo-Roman) lover, then the poet's perspective appears less patriotic-nationalistic, and he is perhaps (like his main model, Homer) more interested in an account of the human experience in general. But the argument based on 'models' is as dangerous as it is alluring, as the Section on intertext of Chapter 2 (Excursus 1) has shown.

The same warning applies to imitation of poetic form. Book 4 of the *Aeneid* has frequently been characterized as a poetic unit in itself, the tragedy of Queen Dido of Carthage, so to speak. Its formal parts have been approached by reference to Greek tragedy and Aristotle's *Poetics* (and, even, Menandrian structure): opening dialogue as in the prologues of Euripides' *Medea* and Sophocles' *Antigone*, several 'monologues', *agon*, five 'acts', etc.[2]

But, even if helpful in determining compositional sections, the reference to the form of Greek drama and, especially, to tragedy, is latently detrimental to the objectivity of an interpretation. For it may predispose the interpreter to seeing the queen's character and fate likewise dominated by tragic features, whereas it is by no means *a priori* certain that, as far as Dido's errant ways are concerned, Vergil wishes to grant her the high status of a tragic heroine.

The problem is compounded when, as in Wlosok's 1976 analysis, Venus' (and Cupid's) interference in Book 1 (seemingly causing Dido to fall in love with Aeneas) is said to emphasize love's destructive and 'demonic' force,[3] and Dido's moral shortcomings are, at least partly, ascribed to temporary self-deception[4] and intellectual blindness (*Irrtum im Sinne der Verblendung; Illusion*), i.e., categories one can relate to Aristotle's *Poetics*. This amounts to a partial exculpation performed by the interpreter. In addition, Dido's initial *guilt* is connected by Wlosok with her non-legalized (*nicht legalisierten*) affair with Aeneas. The emphasis excludes any reference to potentially predetermining evidence offered in Book 1. And the other case (besides that of Venus and Cupid) in Book 1, of supernatural influence presumably exercised on Dido's mind (Jupiter sending Mercury to Dido in particular – *in primis regina* 303 – so that she may develop "a beneficent attitude" toward the Trojans) plays no part at all in Wlosok's account.[5] Is Jupiter's influence then to be considered less effective or less 'demonic' than Venus' and Cupid's? And vice versa, if Jupiter's influence can be disregarded with regard to Dido's character and decisions, may not the same be true about Venus' intervention?

The methodological problems raised by Wlosok's work are exemplary, making it imperative that we give full consideration to *all* the premises Book 1 contributes to the character of Vergilian Dido.[6]

Above all, the interpreter must not, perhaps guided by the contemporary reader's feminist interests, lose sight of the fact that the story of Dido is not related independently nor for its own sake but is tied into, and part of, the epic's action line which is primarily concerned with Aeneas' mission and experience. Through Aeneas' narrative of his labors and divinely guided travels (expounded for her ears in Books 2 and 3), the queen has been informed in detail about his target-oriented mission, so that her selfish and aggressive pursuit of her sexual desires in Book 4 in itself shows (at least) insensitivity to a life style which is dedicated to dutiful execution of higher orders. Vergil's contemporaries were well trained to see the point. (And to the Roman reader the point is valid independently of Aeneas' own conduct.) Modern readers who have perhaps been trained to see Dido through the tear-filled eyes of the boy Augustine (*Conf.*, 1.13), may find it difficult to adjust to the perspective of Augustan Vergil. (The adult Augustine moves closer to the Vergilian Aeneas, *Conf.* 6.15.)

The interpreter's first task, then, is to verify the story's premises and to trace how they are anchored in the plot-line of Book 1, which itself is advanced by three major impulses.[7]

The first thrust is caused by Juno. Eager to make her city of Carthage the capital of nations (even against the will of fate, 22), she has been persecuting pious Aeneas, ancestor of the competing Romans, relentlessly. When seeing him on the last leg of his travels, from Sicily to Italy, she, inappropriately[8] bribing the god of winds, causes a storm and devastates Aeneas' fleet, which, split into two groups, reaches the shores of Libya. Juno's motives, as revealed in her angry monologue (1. 37–49), are selfish, fate-defying, without regard for human piety: unbecoming a deity, the Roman reader is to conclude. Juno's role as a divine opponent of fate's will (and of *pius Aeneas*) is from now on fixed in the reader's eyes, up to her eventual change of mind and compliance with her husband's will in Book 12. When we include her other motives, i.e., female vanity (Paris' judgement, 1. 27) and sexual jealousy (Ganymedes, 1. 28), we see the representative deity of Carthage depicted as a foil and contrast to Roman male (chauvinist) virtues: a 'characteristically female' deity could never have represented Rome in Vergil's epic.[9]

Venus, seeing her son's plight, takes her worries to Jupiter. Subject to changing bursts of joy and fear, driven by a mother's (and grandmother's) cares, without a dominant concern for eternal necessities – fate is understood by her in the limiting terms of her descendants' well-being and her dynasty's political success, Venus is the most volatile, inconstant and, therefore, life-like of the *Aeneid*'s anthropomorphic gods. Aeneas' most recent misfortune has thrown her off balance, again (*re-mordet*, 261): 'What crime did my Aeneas commit? You promised us world domination! What made you change your mind?' To calm her anxiety (*cura*, 261), Jove reassuringly unrolls the plans fate has in store for her descendants: she will see Aeneas in heaven, will see Rome dominate Greece and the world, etc. Free from worries, *se-cura*, she will one day (*olim*) welcome in heaven her descendant[10] Julius Caesar (i.e., Octavianus Augustus),[11] "burdened with the spoils of the East" (289f.; Augustus took Egypt's treasure and made the country his personal province). That will happen at a time when world peace (i.e., the *pax Augusta*) is finally established (286–296).

The prophecy places Venus' release from anxiety in a far-away future (which is the presumably glorious present of Vergil and his contemporary audience) but seems to do little to calm her immediate concern – except that it assures her of Aeneas' eventual success in building his city and of his deification (258f.; his death is passed over quickly by Jove). Still, her father's revelation may perhaps be assumed to reassure Venus sufficiently so that she goes to see her son and confidently directs him toward the city of Carthage and its queen (389; 401).

Jupiter, however, in addition to revealing Rome's Julian destiny, takes some immediate action on Aeneas' behalf (and, though she – or the reader – has not been told so expressly within the long-range prophecy, Venus almost certainly would have become aware of this step), and, so, by giving the chain of events a new impulse (no. 2 in our count), he neutralizes the dangerous situation into which Juno's impulse had led the *Aeneadae*. Mercury is sent to Libya

> in order that the land and the citadel of young Carthage
> stand open in hospitality to the Trojans, to prevent
> Dido, in ignorance of destiny, fending them off her territory.
>
> ut terrae utque novae pateant Karthaginis arces
> hospitio Teucris, ne fati nescia Dido
> finibus arceret.   298–300

So far, two reasons for Dido's possibly inhospitable attitude seem to be indicated: first, concern for her newly founded city's safety may keep her from admitting outsiders into her territory. She herself will later on state this, to Aeneas' officer Ilioneus, as a reason for her men's hostility (*regni novitas*, 1. 563; cf. *novae*, 298). The "harsh situation", *res dura*, she simultaneously mentions refers mainly to the threat of being attacked by her brother, Pygmalion.

The other reason, her ignorance of fate, is unknown to herself and, so, more puzzling: would she, if cognizant of destiny's plans, be more inclined to offer hospitality? The answer can hardly be 'yes', since fate will one day allow Aeneas' descendants to destroy her city, 1. 19–22.

When acquainted by Ilioneus with the newcomers' target area (Italy and, specifically, Latium, 554), she willingly offers help and support so they may reach precisely "Hesperia and the Saturnian fields" (or their alternate choice, i.e., Sicily, 569f.). Jupiter's worry about her being "ignorant of fate", then, can concern only the urgent problem of immediate rescue, sustenance, and re-embarkation of the *Aeneadae* as the critical present part of their long-range destiny, but does not refer to long-range destiny itself.

Fati (299), then, is spoken in Jupiter's perspective: Dido will continue to be uninformed about fate, but for the short time during which she would be able to interfere she must be prevented from causing harm to Aeneas and his men. That is, her ignorance continues but her (and her people's) hostility to foreigners must be neutralized. So Mercury executes Jupiter's orders,

and, under the god's will, the Phoenicians lay off
their fierce temper.

> ponuntque ferocia Poeni
> corda volente deo. 302f.

The factual result of his intervention apparently is that the Phoenician guards on the coast will make an exception to their rule of hostility toward strangers and allow Ilioneus' part of the fleet to send an embassy (*cunctis... lecti navibus*, 518) to the queen (Aeneas' part of the fleet, hidden in the natural harbor, remains undetected). In empirical terms, the guards' decision would come as natural and be quite understandable without any divine intervention. For what they have been ordered to protect their shores against is the threat of an invasion (especially by Phoenicians of Pygmalion) but hardly the arrival of a destitute group of – obviously peaceful – shipwrecked men.

> and especially the queen receives (accepts)
> a tranquil mind toward the Trojans and a beneficent attitude.
>
> in primis regina quietum
> accipit in Teucros animum mentemque benignam 303f.

If one takes these words at face value, they seem to indicate a change of mind (which Dido "receives" or "accepts"), against the queen's usual or normal attitude. Is this a case of a human mind being re-programmed by a heterogeneous force, as has been assumed?[12] It is much easier to understand how, say, Queen Amata in Book 7 would be stimulated by Juno's agent, Fury Allecto, to revolt against accepting a son-in-law she does not want to see in the family anyway. There the Fury seems only to intensify a pre-existing attitude.

But does in Dido's case the text not indicate an about-face? Is her often cited magnanimity, then, a basically alien and temporary feature? (Some of her later behavior might favor this interpretation.) Or are we dealing here, too, with a natural feature, prevented from realization by adverse circumstances?

In support of the latter alternative one might cite the fact that, in the empirical world, it will need no more than a slight trigger (Dido grants Ilioneus permission to speak, 520) for the break-through: Ilioneus' moving speech before the queen (522–558) successfully appeals to her sympathy, reinforcing a long-standing respect for the Trojans, a respect which Aeneas finds expressed in the temple murals (461–463) and Dido herself will profess to have fostered since the days of her father's rule (619–626). (According to 1. 755, this would have been about six years ago, but *tempore iam ex illo* [623] makes it sound at least subjectively like a longer period of time).

Chapter 5

So Jupiter's (and Mercury's) influence could be seen to be limited to making the queen lend her ear to the shipwrecked Trojans. The rest of her friendly reaction could follow on the basis of natural sympathy and of an attitude that was acquired long ago, part of it apparently even during the time she considers still her formative years. This part of her reaction, then, might be covered by *quietum...animum*: a calm, unconcerned, not disquieted willingness to listen to Ilioneus' case.

But at this point precisely the same argument concerning *Dido's* decision can be made as in the case of the guards: realizing at once that a delegation which submissively requests indulgence (*orantes veniam*, 519) represents destitute people rather than an army of dangerous invaders, she has no reason to be concerned and to refuse them their hearing. In the present case, the circumstances which, according to her own words, "force" her (*cogunt*, 563) to protect her borders with harsh measures, do ostensibly not apply. There is no trace of divine intervention found in her granting Ilioneus permission to speak.

But certainly *mentem...benignam* seems to cover more? Does it not signify a positive, new attitude toward the "Teucrians", an attitude not previously experienced? Does this then prove divine influence and remove responsibility from Dido for her own ensuing actions? Not necessarily so. When considering lines 303f., one must not forget that Dido has been a long-time admirer of the Trojans. Since we can hardly assume that Jupiter and Mercury did not know this, we obviously have to change our focus in reading these lines.

As the words *fati nescia* (299) reflect Jupiter's perspective, so the name *Teucros* (304) serves as an identifier for the *reader*. What the brachylogy means is that Dido is made to assume a generous attitude toward the Teucrians *qua shipwrecked strangers*, in other words: toward the shipwrecked people who turn out to be Trojans, i.e., toward the arriving group of Trojans.

In the empirical world this means that, once their identity is established (*Troes te miseri...oramus*, 524f.), her well-known longstanding respect for Troy can take over. Even the minimal understanding of Jove's direct influence (putting Dido's defensive hostility at rest, and letting beneficent generosity toward people in need take over and prevail), then, does not show interference with the empirical context outlined in Book 1 – unless one is unwilling to attribute to Dido a natural compassion for destitute people whom she has been respecting all along anyway. (If one were, one might wish to ascribe her willingness to listen to a – perhaps concerned – curiosity on the part of the country's ruler rather than to find Jove's influence attested here.)

As a matter of fact, the foregoing considerations suggest that no real change of mind has to take place at all: so far, harsh circumstances have prevented Dido from looking upon strangers in a non-military context. Mercury's intervention is consonant with the empirical cessation, vis-à-vis a non-threatening situation, of an alien mental block, freeing Dido now to follow her natural inclination (or concerned curiosity) and her long-established sympathy for the Trojans:

> Who would be ignorant of the race of the *Aeneadae*, who would not know
>   the city of Troy,
> its brave deeds and men...?
>
> Quis genus Aeneadum, quis Troiae nesciat urbem,
> virtutesque virosque...?   565f.

Viewed in this way, her case no longer appears inconsistent with, but rather parallel to, that of Queen Amata mentioned above: in the case of either woman, supernatural intervention would seem in the empirical world to be equivalent to a breakthrough or intensification of a pre-existing condition, or to the actualization of an inherent potential.[13] And since Dido does give an account of her motives and her decision to grant assistance, there can be no question about her being fully responsible for her actions. One should take note that, so far, this interpretation has not found a case of pure altruism, but that knowledge of the Trojans' national character plays an important part in Dido's attitude. Lines 565f. articulate an essential factor in Dido's decision. (The emphasis placed on the name *Troy* appears enhanced by violation of Marx's law, which simultaneously underlines the anaphora of the two rhetorical questions.)

But would such an empirical interpretation do justice to Mercury's intervention, undertaken at the order of the highest god of the Roman universe? Perhaps one has to recall that, ever since Homer's *Iliad*, divine interventions in epic need not (though they not infrequently do) interfere with normal human psychological processes. As Chapter 7 will show in greater detail, the intervention of Zeus, highest god of the Greek universe, was not really needed to explain King Agamemnon's deceptive dream at the opening of Book 2. Aged Nestor had warned Agamemnon not to alienate Achilles, his "bulwark in battle", but Agamemnon did not listen and continued the quarrel with his strongest ally to the breaking point. In the dream, Nestor reverses himself and now suggests that Agamemnon can finally conquer Troy on this very day – without the help of Achilles, of course. If the warner reverses himself, then the royal advisee has been right instead – this is the ego-padding stuff of which wishful dreams are made. In order to occur, such dreams hardly depend on the intervention of a

Zeus. Empirical psychology is what the epic tradition also requires of the audience for understanding the king's dream.

Do then in the *Aeneid* divine theater and human world perhaps operate in precisely parallel and synchronic fashion, with the divine causation not being verifiable within the empirical world because the latter consistently runs according to its own immanent premises?[14] A consequence would be that, unless told by the poet, we as humans (characters as well as hearers) do not and cannot know that, and how, empirical processes participate in affairs of the divine theater. This hypothesis might be corroborated by looking in even greater detail at Dido's psychology.

(2) The Queen Offers Permanent Residency: Divine Inspiration or Conscious Decision?

Before the queen, Ilioneus complains about the "barbaric" (*barbara*, 539) country where "we are kept from the hospitality of the beach" (*hospitio prohibemur harenae*, 540), by being forbidden to sit down "on the most outlying rim of the land" (*primaque vetant considere terra*, 541).[15] He asks for permission to pull the battered ships ashore (*quassatam...liceat subducere classem*, 551 – apparently, the boats are still out there on the water at the time of the embassy to Dido) for repairs and cutting oars, by using wood from local forests. Their goal is, if Aeneas and Ascanius (and their other companions, 553) are found alive, to go to Italy and, specifically, Latium; alternatively (555f.), they want to return to King Acestes in Sicily (553–558).

To this request Dido responds (we saw) positively, and she does so in three steps. First, with some embarrassment (*vultum demissa*, 561) she apologizes for having her territory protected: she cites dangerous circumstances for her young realm (cf. *regni novitas* 563); second, she points to the ubiquitous fame of Troy, its brave men (565/66a), and "the conflagration of so great a war", *tanti incendia belli* (566b). In the next line, she in asyndetic fashion juxtaposes the Phoenicians' sympathetic attitude to precisely the fiery catastrophe by which Troy was consumed:

We Phoenicians are not so insensitive in our hearts

non obtunsa adeo gestamus pectora Poeni[16]   1. 567

The phrasing is very close to the description of Mercury's alleged inspiration: *ponuntque ferocia Poeni / corda volente deo*, etc. (302f.), and especially the words *non obtunsa...pectora* may remind us of *mentem...benignam* (304). So one may believe that we finally grasp the critical moment where Dido speaks under direct divine influence – were it not for the fact that she herself consciously deduces both her awareness of and her compassion for Troy's fate from the general, wide-spread information about Troy's final fiery calamity. There is no room in this tightly knit logical and emotional sequence for outside divine intervention, and we find ourselves again thrown back on our earlier result: that Dido is herself fully responsible for her thoughts, decision, and actions – even when what she arranges fulfills Jove's wish that she open her land (*ut terrae...pateant*, 298). Freely she offers help and supplies for the Trojans' voyage to Italy and Latium (or, alternatively, to Sicily, 1. 569–571).[17]

The search for *verifiable* divine influence on Dido's mind must, then, concentrate on the third step of her response. The queen now even proceeds to make an offer for which no preceding request has been made by Ilioneus:

> Also,[18] would you like to settle together with me in this kingdom?
> The city which I am building is yours: pull up your boats.
> Trojan and Tyrian will receive no different consideration from me.
>
> vultis et his mecum pariter considere regnis?
> urbem quam statuo, vestra est: subducite navis.
> Tros Tyriusque mihi nullo discrimine agetur.   1. 572–574

Coming, as it seems, totally out of the blue, does the queen's invitation finally demonstrate Mercury's influence? After all, if the Trojans are admitted into the city, this also fulfills Jupiter's intent that "the citadel of young Carthage stand open in hospitality to the Teucrians" (298f.).

To evaluate the queen's motive for her surprise invitation, one should have in mind what Book 1 so far has told its reader about this extraordinary woman. Most of the information comes from Venus' lips (338–368) when she, apparently happy about Jupiter's revelation and assistance,[19] prepares her son for his meeting with Dido,[20] – yes, even directs him to her city (399; 401).

Dido was a virgin when she was formally given in first marriage by her father to Sychaeus, a rich Phoenician, for whom she developed a deep love. Her brother Pygmalion nefariously murdered Sychaeus in front of an altar, keeping the truth from his sister for a long time. But Sychaeus appeared to his wife in a dream, disclosed the crime, and advised her to leave the country, financially supported by a huge treasure the location of which he described to her.

The next step is that Dido gathers followers from those who hate or fear her brother, the "tyrant". They commandeer boats that happen to lie ready and leave. "Leader of the undertaking is a *woman*" (*dux femina facti*, 364) – a piece of information which certainly impresses Aeneas (there is an affinity to his own role as a leader of refugees) as well as the reader. We begin to see why Venus calls Dido's community a "kingdom" (*regna*, 338) and an "empire" (*imperium*, 340), over which she "rules" (*regit*, 340). "Huge walls and the rising citadel of young Carthage" (365f.) are the result of her leadership (appealing to Aeneas' own desire to found his own city, cf. 437), even of her and her followers' sharply calculating minds: they "bought as much territory as they might be able to surround with a bull's hide" (368: they cut the hide into a long strip, of course).

Next, we see (421–437), with the eyes of admiring Aeneas, the immense size, variety (ranging from harbor to theater), and orderly construction process of Dido's city (compared to a hard-working and well-organized community of bees). The impression is rounded out and crowned by the huge and rich temple, which "Sidonian Dido" had built for Juno (447).[21] Its murals (453–493) show familiarity with the Trojan War, even a degree of sympathy for the Trojan side (this is – and rightly so, as it will turn out later – reassuring for the beholder Aeneas, 461–463).

Finally, again with Aeneas looking on, the reader is being directly acquainted with "most beautiful Dido" (496), who turns out every inch a queen (*regina*, 495; for *incessit*, 496, compare Venus' movement, *incessu*, 405). Surrounded by a large number of young men, she is compared by the poet to Diana directing her choruses of mountain nymphs (later, in Book 4, Aeneas will be compared to Diana's brother, Apollo). While happily (*laeta*, 503) moving through the crowd, she presses on the work-in-progress, i.e., her "kingdom-to-be" (*regnis...futuris*, 504); then, upon taking her seat on the throne in the center of the temple she built for Juno, lays down legal decisions and laws; equalizes work loads or, alternatively, distributes work by lot (so no one will feel burdened unfairly by design; 496–508).

To sum up, then, and to integrate essential features: Queen Dido is presented to Aeneas and to the reader as a widow (it was her first marriage, arranged by her father) and as the sister of a treacherous king. To protracted injustice (*longa est iniuria*, 341) she responds by taking her life into her own hands. Like a man gathering malcontents from her brother's realm, she does not mind commandeering his fleet or availing herself of his financial resources: *navis.../...onerant...auro. portantur avari / Pygmalionis opes pelago* (362f.).[22] Nor does she, when acquiring her new territory, shrink from executing a questionable practice in making her deal (the bull hide trick). Her hand is excellent at ruling sovereignly and assigning burdens to her subjects without causing bad feelings. She is happy in concentrating on building her empire. She (in this, similar to the Julians) derives her authority from Juno, in whose magnificent temple the queen's throne is placed in the center, near the cella door (*foribus divae, media testudine templi*, 505). In short, an able, commanding, future-oriented leadership figure, with a firm grip on the available resources of her rule, but also in constant fear of an attack from outside (563f.).

We may now return to the queen's invitation that the Trojans who lost their king join her (subjects) "side by side". Does it need a Jupiter and a Mercury to stimulate an empire-planner and -builder like Dido, who lives in fear of outside attacks, into offering hospitality to leaderless and homeless men of fighting age and proven *virtutes* (cf. 566)? And could her motives be exclusively altruistic? Though we already know that Troy's fate has long stirred the queen's compassion, both questions can safely be answered in the negative. The bull hide deal has shown her ability to take care of her advantage even in a way her business partners may not suspect. Later on, when the complicating presence of Aeneas has changed Dido's personal perspective, Anna, her mind-reading sister (her *second self*, so to speak), will (to make consummation of the queen's love for Aeneas socially acceptable) adduce precisely this argument: adding the Trojans to her empire is imperative for strengthening its position against outside threats (4. 35–49). Clearly, Anna there counts on Dido's own political instinct, if not on her sister's own earlier arguments. In the situation of Book 1 and according to Dido's characteristic given therein, we cannot expect the queen not to have noticed the advantage her endangered young state would draw from the accretion.

It is time to correct a long-standing, romanticizing misunderstanding. Well-meaning (not to say predisposed) interpreters have assigned to the queen more magnanimity than Vergil himself has. Her words, "Also, would you like to settle with me side by side in my kingdom?"(572) are being understood as an offer to the Trojans to settle down "mit mir zu gleichen Rechten" (Binder), "on equal terms with me" (Austin), or "with me on an equal footing" (West), "with me on even terms" (Fairclough).

The correct translation of *pariter* is "together with me", "side by side with me",[23] i.e., more fully expressed

> Also, do you wish to settle with me in this kingdom side by side?

That the queen does not yield an inch of her sovereignty is shown by her words "in this...kingdom", *his...regnis*, i.e., "together with me *as my subjects under my rule*"; two lines later she makes this more than clear:

> Trojans and Tyrians will be considered no differently by me
>
> Tros Tyriusque *mihi* nullo discrimine agetur.   1. 574

So, *cum* in 572 may well carry one of its nuances listed in *OLD s. v*, 4 b) "under the command of (an officer)", or even, considering the military threat Dido feels she lives under, "on the side of, supporting" (*OLD s. v.* 2). Applied to the Trojans' prospective position, this means nothing less than subordination under the queen's rule ("with me", i.e., "under my command"). Far from making her city over to the Trojans, the regal and lapidary words *urbem quam statuo vestra est* (473) offer the strangers a home and a part in *her* community. E. Fraenkel's admiration and over-interpretation overlooks the limitation and subordination expressed in her offer, when he comments: "In magnanimous trust she makes her proud foundation over to the strangers", etc.[24] ("In grossherzigem Vertrauen eignet sie ihre stolze Gründung den Fremdlingen zu und erläutert den Sinn ihrer Gabe mit den Worten *Tros Tyriusque mihi nullo discrimine agetur*"). Fraenkel does not seem to sense the limitation and subordination imposed by *mihi*. Terms like "Gabe" (gift) and "zueignen" (make over) veil the queen's expectation of subordination under her rule. The ably calculating ruler of Carthage trusting blindly? Austin narrows and romanticizes Vergil's multi-layered perspective when he comments on her offer of line 572 by saying "Dido's warm magnanimity finds clear expression here".[25] Elsewhere he even speaks of her "disinterested idealism".[26] It appears that Vergil's sovereign female ruler still today has the power to make romantically inclined scholars (and not only Aeneas) fall in blind love with her.

Political advantage *and* sympathy go together in Dido's positive response to, and her surprise offer beyond, Ilioneus' request. No trace can be verified of Mercury's (Jupiter's) alleged intervention.

There also is a contemporary aspect to the queen's offer, an aspect which no Roman reader would overlook, because the friendly gesture amounts to a national insult. That the ancestors of the Romans should as subjects join the empire of a *queen* (a woman in the role of a ruler!) would be bad enough in itself. (It took the rebellious spirit of a Propertius [Elegy 3. 11] to upset the Augustan cliché of male turpitude resulting from a Roman serving a foreign queen.[27] Vergil, however, firmly follows the official Augustan concept of "Roman" conduct.) But, even worse, that the invitation comes from the ruler of *Carthage* (it would take three wars to fight down this "arrogant" city) is an intolerable thought, hurting the dignity of any Roman. Vergil would count on his readers: they would scrutinize any invitation extended by the earliest representative of *fides Punica*.

The *Aeneid*'s first divine intervention directed at changing a human mind must leave the modern reader puzzled. Whereas Juno apparently can cause a devastating storm, Jupiter effects nothing extraordinary in the soul of his "target", nothing that would interfere with empirical psychology and its verifiable processes. (But Juno's storm may no longer appear to be so extraordinary either, once we learn that it apparently took place at the beginning of the stormy season, 4. 52f.; cf.1. 535).

There is, of course, a level on which Jove's intervention is needed independently from human motivations, namely the level of the divine theater, in the dimension pertaining to the political future of Rome. As Juno, defying fate, caused the storm, so Jupiter has to neutralize its results to guide the fated train of events back into its prescribed course. In an unexpected fashion, then, human hospitality and meteorological phenomena occupy comparable positions on the coordinates of events (as do Aeolus' stirring up of the weather and Mercury's calming of Phoenician fierceness). It is evident that, under these circumstances, consistency of interplay between divine and empirical world is not always easy to achieve for the poet. Occasional concessions or subtractions on one level or the other are unavoidable.

But he often succeeds, as an example may show. When Neptune causes Juno's storm to recede, he threatens the rebellious wind gods and their unreliable jailer (King Aeolus) and is said to smooth the waves in the way that a man of dignity and merit calms a seditious mob.[28] The simile (1. 147–153) has been, by Pöschl and others, taken to demonstrate an Augustan principle of order imposed on a chaotic world. But what it communicates above all is the message that the storm, to the human eye a 'natural process', should be understood also in terms of a divine revolt: what appears as a storm to its human victims (one may think of Ilioneus' uninformed description as given to Dido, where "Orion" is nothing more than a metonymy, instancing an event of the stormy season, 535–538; cf. 4. 52f.), is in the divine perspective a stirring of sea and waves caused by the rebellion of anthropomorphic gods against Jupiter's fate-observing orders. (Apparently, the meritorious citizen's admonition of the mob must be seen in parallel to Neptune's scolding of the wind gods.)

Consequently, the simile points out that Jove's (and his brother's) world order is restored after a rebellion (132–134) of the former chaotic powers under the leadership of Jove's and Neptune's unruly 'Saturnian' (cf. 23) sister (cf. *fratrem*, 130; also *et soror et coniunx*, 47). The simile helps the mortal reader understand how the higher level was involved in the way the turmoil was started and ended, and what was at stake. As far as its origin and containment are concerned, the audience is asked *not* to understand the storm only in terms of a "natürlicher Vorgang."[29] So the simile, taken from the human sphere, reminds the reader in terms understandable to a mortal that what has been happening to pious Aeneas is also the reflection of a power struggle in the divine theater. (The fact of a divine clash of wills of course adds distinction to the cause of that human party which has fate on its side.)

Chapter 5

To demonstrate human ignorance of divine activity, one may cite not only (as was done above) the uninformed description of the storm which Ilioneus gives to Dido (535–538) or Aeneas' own un-illuminated impression (88–117). The irony of human ignorance is especially poignant when Aeneas explains to his divine mother (unrecognized by him as such – she had just gone to ask Jupiter for help against the result of Juno's storm) that what has driven him to Libya's shores has been "a storm with its peculiar chance" (*nos...forte sua...tempestas appulit*, 375ff.). Like the reader, he could benefit from the help of the poet as of a guide familiar with the issues and forces behind the earthly scene.

So there definitely is an attempt on the poet's part to enliven the divine theater by utilizing its anthropomorphic constituents, and to make its presence felt so as to impress it on the reader. Information the poet provides allows the reader to see human events within the larger context of fate and of history, and also in terms of the harm or good they contribute to the cause of the *Aeneadae* and to future Rome. But, though running parallel to (synchronized with) conflicts of the human sphere, the divine is not therefore automatically the empirically verifiable cause of human actions. The human sphere functions as a circuit closed in itself.

If so far Jupiter has been seen not to interfere with empirical psychology, the picture is hardly any different when Aeneas visibly enters the scene. (As a matter of fact, unknown to all he has been present, hidden in his mother's cloud, ever since Dido entered the temple.) At the end of her response to Ilioneus' request, i.e., immediately upon offering the Trojans settlement in her city side by side with her subjects, the queen expressly desires that Aeneas himself be present: she even will have the remotest shores of Libya searched for him (576–578).

Dido does not say what Aeneas' projected role would be, but she has no reason to assume that he would stay for any length of time. From Ilioneus' oration she knows that, should Aeneas (and the missing comrades with him, 553) be found alive, the Trojans intend to resume their voyage to Italy (and if not, to return to Sicily). Her offer to settle in Carthage was made to the surviving group who lost their king and comrades. So far, one can only assume that she intends to extend her offer of assistance also to their king himself (*rex ipse*, 575) whose praises Ilioneus has sung before her (544f.). It is not until later that she will reveal her longstanding acquaintance with Aeneas' personal fame (*nomen...tuum*, 624). But still at the time of the banquet, her toast describes the Trojans as *guests*, i.e., as temporary visitors (731; this is in agreement with Jupiter's intention: *hospitio*, 299).

Dido's desire to see Aeneas also serves a special purpose. As in Book 7 King Latinus wishes Aeneas himself to be present (*ipse modo Aeneas...*

adveniat, 7. 263ff.) and not only his ambassador Ilioneus, so here King Aeneas need not suddenly impose his presence but is made to feel invited (*atque utinam rex ipse.../ adforet Aeneas*, 1. 575f; cf. *coram quem quaeritis adsum* 595). In this an important feature of Augustan etiquette becomes apparent, repeated (as we shall see) in Book 4 and elsewhere: the highest-ranking person (and there can be no doubt in any contemporary reader's mind that Emperor Augustus' forefather ranks higher than the queen of Carthage, both by gender and by fated political weight) appears last on the scene, desired by and welcome to his Carthaginian counterpart.

As a matter of fact, the storm caused by Juno (impulse I, by our method of counting), by splitting the Trojan fleet into two parts, also serves the dramaturgical function of letting Aeneas' "ambassador" Ilioneus appear in advance and pronounce his king's fame (so especially 1. 544f.) as well as the warm respect he enjoys from his men (*te, pater optime Teucrum*, 555) before the king himself takes the floor.[30] In this way Aeneas, beautified by his divine mother to be god-like (589–593; the traditional simile uses only the most precious ingredients: gold, silver, marble, ivory) and suddenly (cf. *repente*, 594) released from her protective cloud, can "steal the show" in this theatrical scene. If anywhere, then here the climax in the plot makes clear who is protagonist and who is destined to play second fiddle – an important advance hint for interpreting Book 4 appropriately (and a serious pointer to the importance, denied by Thomas, Conte, and others, of dramaturgy, i.e. the long-distance organization, for understanding the work's message).

Aeneas' address to the queen (595–610), of highest eloquence and of most elevated vocabulary, is – naturally, considering the perspective of one who suddenly finds help in greatest need – full of gratitude: her "singular" sympathy for Troy's sufferings (597; the reader also recalls Aeneas' justified relief when seeing the temple murals, 461–463) and her generous hospitality (the words *urbe, domo socias*, acknowledge her offer to settle in Carthage, 600) cannot be sufficiently rewarded by all the remaining Trojans scattered over the world: may the gods do so, in regard for her piety, justice, and awareness of what is right. In eternity her praises will be sung, "whichever countries are calling me," *quae me cumque vocant terrae* (610). The closing words make it unmistakably clear that Aeneas is not here to stay. Even if further detours (we notice the plural *terrae*) are his lot, he will follow fate's calling: he is not in a position to accept the invitation of permanent residence she extended to his men. Nobody who has heard (or read) the resounding coda of this address will be able to say that he did not reveal the conditions of his presence openly, and right from the beginning. Again, here is found an important premise for an adequate reading of Book 4. (And that Dido for her part has achieved a correct understanding of

Chapter 5

Aeneas' plans, is clear from the toast she later pronounces at the banquet, cf. *hospitibus*, 731.)

Dido is numbed, first[31] (613) by the man's visual appearance (as described at 588–593), then (614) by his vast misfortune (described at 596–599). She can hardly believe she has that famous Aeneas (*tune ille Aeneas...?* 617), son of Venus and Anchises, before her eyes. She remembers from her earlier days, in the time of her father's rule in Sidon, Teucer's praise for the Trojan enemy (he 'liked' to be of Trojan origin himself, 625f.), the fate of Troy, "your fame", and the Greek kings (619–626). *Nomen...tuum* (624) points to a degree of individual respect, even admiration – the same as on the murals in the temple she built for Juno (where Aeneas had seen himself depicted fighting "with the highest-ranking Greeks", 488).[32]

Dido has made clear that her sympathy and respect for the Trojans antedate Ilioneus' speech by a considerable number of years, so that in her invitation ("Therefore, come, enter under our roofs", 627) the logical conjunction "therefore," *quare* (i.e. 'because of the heroic qualities I just mentioned'), makes good sense.[33] The same coherence of thought shows in her pity. Impressed by the famous man's vast sufferings (*casu...viri tanto*, 614) as he has described them (597–599), she senses (628–630) a reflection of her own (*me quoque*) "similar" (*similis*) misfortune with its "many sufferings" (*multos...labores*, cf. Aeneas' words, citing Trojan *infandos...labores*, 597), and with her own experience of being driven about (*iactatam*, 629; she is referring to Aeneas' words *terraeque marisque omnibus exhaustos iam casibus*, 598f.).

So, in addition to her longstanding admiration, it is (she feels and concludes) the similarity of negative experience – of suffering – which incites her to grant the help she herself once was in need of:

> Not ignorant of misfortune, I am learning to assist those in need.
>
> non ignara mali, miseris succurrere disco.   1. 630.

Longstanding admiration and long personal suffering lead to the present decision in favor of support for the Trojans. There is no gap in Dido's continuous chain of reasoning, and there is no critical juncture at which Jupiter or Mercury can be seen to implant (or even be observed doing so) into her "a calm mind toward the Trojans and a beneficent attitude" (1. 303f.). As the destitute condition of the strangers allowed her to lift standing military precautions, so the striking discovery of their Trojan nationality activated her long-fostered sympathy and admiration, and so also their sufferings have struck a chord of affinity. Dido's psychological process as presented by the poet is seamless in itself. So, the divine theater here appears synchronized, but like an unconnected layer superimposed without evidencing, in the minds of humans, the effects its agents (Jupiter and Mercury) set out to stimulate. Knowledge of the divine affairs acquaints the reader with the larger context. It does not force us to revise our view of empirical processes presented in the narrative. The question (to be answered later) arises: what is the intended consequence of an intervention-free empirical psychology?

Though, of course, every instance of divine intervention has to be investigated separately and individually, our first case already grants some specific (if negative) insight, by showing that such reported divine activity need not add any outside, perhaps even 'demonic', element to the human psychology. (*A priori* exempted from this statement are, of course, instances of directly given divine directions, such as the ones Aeneas receives from the god at Delphi in Book 3.)[34] This result allows a more open-minded approach to Venus' ensuing intervention in Book 1 than would Wlosok's and Austin's conceptually predisposed interpretations (introduced earlier *exempli gratia*), which declare love in Vergil "a destructive, demonic power by which man is seized and possessed";[35] its "impulse" coming "from something outside her control."[36]

I shall maintain that a seamless empirical development can be observed also on the occasion of Amor's alleged influence on Dido later in Book 1 as well as in the case of King Turnus' encounter with the fury Allecto in Book 7 (Chapter 7). Interpreters, who believe that they can pass over in silence Jupiter's inefficient role as the alleged founder of human hospitality in Book I, run the risk of overestimating the role of Amor, and the degree of awareness and responsibility which the poet has accorded Queen Dido.

(3) Dido Falls in Love: Inefficient Cupid Aided by Female Weakness

So far (i.e., up to line 630), there has been no trace of an erotic perspective in Dido's conduct. And this does not change during the preparations for the banquet through to the opening toast. As a matter of fact, it is Aeneas who (unknown to himself?) initiates the first move in this direction. Among the presents he has taken to Dido ("presents snatched from the ruin of Troy", 1. 647), there are, especially described in elaborate detail (six lines out of nine), a cloak and a veil which Helen had brought from Greece when she sailed for Troy "and an illegitimate wedding," *inconcessosque hymenaeos* (651). How Helen's garments were saved in the night of Troy's fall (Aeneas or somone else finding the time to go through her closet?) is a question better not asked by the reader. This is not the only time that Vergil somewhat heavy-handedly violates the poetic *probabile* in order to secure a degree of political symbolism.[37] What is being indicated by the tainted gifts is that Aeneas himself is on the brink of entering an illicit affair which may run counter to his mission and to his family's Roman destiny. The hint is confirmed by the poet's later remark that Dido is being stirred (*movetur*, 714) in equal fashion by "the boy" (*puero*, i.e., Amor in the guise of Ascanius) and by the gifts (*donis*): cloak and veil again receive special mention by being *the only ones* of all the *munera* to be there precisely identified.

That Aeneas' choice of gifts is extraordinarily infelicitous is indicated by their geographical origin: they are said to have been brought to Troy not perhaps by "Menelaus' wife from Sparta" but by "*Argive* Helen from *Mycenae*" – the latter city, at a later stage called "savage" by Ilioneus (*saevis*), being the place of origin for the "storm" which flooded Troy (7. 222f.), and the two names being selected by Jupiter for a fated punishment of servitude under Troy's successor, i.e., Rome (*Mycenas*; *servitio*; *Argis*; 1. 284f.)[38] Unknowingly to himself (but intelligibly to the reader who has heard Jupiter's prophecy being given to Venus) or perhaps just carelessly, Aeneas dresses Dido up as another threat to Trojan national survival.

A similarly gloomy note is struck by the gift of Ilione's scepter, necklace, and crown (653–655; see Austin *ad loc.*). Ilione was King Priam's unlucky daughter. Her husband, Thracian King Polymestor, murdered Priam's youngest son (cf. 3. 19–68). Ilione killed her husband and/or herself – either case a dire omen for the recipient of the gifts. (Would Dido symbolically "kill" Sychaeus when entering a relationship with Aeneas?)

Since Aeneas at the time of giving does not know the effect he himself will have on Dido (or the full effect she will have on himself), the foreground question arises of *why* did he include Helen's *ornatus* (1. 650) with Ilione's scepter, necklace, and crown? The likely answer is that he thought Dido would be impressed – and Vergil later (714) confirms that his hero's guess was right.

The reason why Aeneas wanted to impress the queen is open to the reader's conjecture. One possibility is that he wanted to express his gratitude in a way she would personally appreciate; another, that he already felt sufficiently attracted to let her know that he'd like to see her wrapped in the enhancements of a beautiful woman. Either way, the feature added to Dido's portrait here is the usual male cliché of a woman whose judgement is affected (she "catches fire by viewing", *ardescitque tuendo*, 713) by presents – especially presents that flatter her vanity.

But in the second case (Aeneas feeling attracted to Dido) is his choice of the compromised gifts conscious or not? Notoriously, Vergil gives his reader little information on his hero's emotions (restricted by genre, Roman code of male conduct, and hesitancy to compromise the Julian ancestor).[39] Thus, one may perhaps not be over-interpreting when seeing Aeneas here inclined, willing and ready to start an extra-curricular affair.

It is not only the disproportionate number of highly styled lines Vergil spends on describing cloak and veil which points to the importance he ascribes to the queen's receptive attitude towards such presents. There is a contrasting case in Book 7. Aged King Latinus weighs Aeneas' request for land, conveyed through the same ambassador Ilioneus[40] and accompanied once more by some truly royal gifts: Anchises' golden sacrificing vessel; King Priam's ceremonial objects, his scepter, and his tiara. (Aeneas is portrayed by Vergil as the true heir and legitimate holder of Troy's royal insignia.)[41] But aged King Latinus, a pious man obedient to oracles and portents, is more impressed by a prophecy about a son-in-law coming from abroad:

> neither the embroidered purple
> stirs the king nor stirs him Priam's scepter as much
> as his thoughts concentrate on marriage and wedding of his daughter,
> and in his heart he ponders *Faunus' prophecy*.

> nec purpura regem
> picta movet nec sceptra movent Priameia tantum
> quantum in conubio natae thalamoque moratur,
> et veteris Fauni volvit sub pectore sortem.   7. 251–254

The poet's use of the same verb (*movere*) in both passages makes the contrast even more poignant. Not so much influenced by the royal gifts as by divine guidance: the pious Italian king; subject to influence by gifts that flatter her vanity: the queen of Carthage. The fact that the *Aeneid* knows and obviously approves of a greater reserve toward gifts than the reaction displayed by Dido makes her weakness even more obvious. Early on already, the Roman cliché of female instability (a woman being subject to influence) is called up in the reader here, long before Mercury will warn Aeneas about Dido: "A woman is something that is different and subject to change all the time" (4. 569f.). In view of the early subliminal message one will be cautious about declaring Dido a tragic heroine. More useful may be a working hypothesis which lets Dido slip not by a one-time error but by a decision compatible with a permanent trait inherent in her character (or gender) – a feature (i.e., her instability) which increasingly surfaces with changing outward circumstances. The question of continuity of character traits will have to be addressed again in the case of King Turnus, Aeneas' other major opponent.

Chapter 5

Whatever the symbolic implication intended by Vergil when introducing Ilione, there is one more result to be deduced from a comparison of the presents. Whereas Latinus, pious supporter of the Trojans' fated progress, receives gifts from the possessions of the former king of Troy, Phoenician Dido is presented with the derivative royal insignia Ilione received (probably) from her (in Roman eyes, barbaric) Thracian husband. This depends not merely on the difference of male/female recipient, for Vergil (or his Aeneas) could easily have chosen a gift formerly owned by Trojan Queen Hecuba. Such a high honor, however, was more than a Queen of Carthage could be accorded. Aeneas' (or the poet's) deck of cards appears *a priori* stacked against Dido – as may indeed be expected in view of the relations between Rome and Carthage in historical times.

With the Trojans having been welcomed in Carthage, the ill effects of the storm have been largely undone. The *Aeneadae* are now free to realize their intention of repairing their boats and resuming their voyage to Italy. On the divine level, the state of affairs may be described as follows: Jupiter has restored the fated course of events by neutralizing Juno's intervention. As far as plot-line is concerned, impulse I (which, in addition to the forced detour, also enabled the poet to let Aeneas' arrival at Carthage be prepared before the Julian ancestor himself appeared in the limelight) has been neutralized by impulse II so that the original thrust of the action (i.e., before Juno's intervention) seems ready to resume.

At this point, impulse III sets in, apparently starting on the divine level. Venus, originally introduced as rather sad (*tristior*, 1. 228), had seemed reassured by Jove's prophecy, even cheerful (*laeta*, 416) under his calming influence (see also *serenat*, etc., 254–256). So the reader watched her confidently sending her son into the city of Carthage (389; 401). But by nightfall "her anxiety returns" (*cura recursat*, 662; cf. *cura remordet*, 1. 261). The thought of fierce Juno and of the Phoenicians with their forked tongues (the reader has seen two cases of Punic double talk in Book 1) triggers a burning fear in her heart (661f.). Jupiter's guarantee is forgotten, and the memory of Juno's storm lets Venus expect similar harm for her son inside Juno's city. The sequence of thought and of feelings is typical for a concerned mother (and grandmother) whose irrational love is driven to panic by imminent danger, real or imagined, to her family's well-being. Consistently with her emotional instability, she will upset the equilibrium Jupiter achieved by generating Carthaginian hospitality. Her plan is to make Dido fall in love with Aeneas – a loving woman will not harm the man she loves. That such a transformation of the guest/host relationship may in the long run have consequences alien to those she desires, apparently lies outside Venus' present perspective.

Her shortsightedness again goes well with her earlier behavior. This life-like person shows none of the static antithesis which characterizes Juno and Jupiter in their relationship (though both "women" share a lack of imperturbability).

In particular, her plan is to replace Ascanius (just about to be taken to the city together with Aeneas' gifts for Dido) with her own son Cupid/Amor, who then is

> to kindle the queen to passion with the presents
> and to sink the fire into her bones
>
> donisque furentem
> incendat reginam atque ossibus implicet ignem.   1. 659f.

What presents is Cupid to use for his amatory purpose? Manifestly, they are the same ones which Aeneas has already chosen *before* Venus develops her plan and which he has ordered to be brought to Dido. According to the information given by Venus to Cupid, Ascanius

> ...is, following his dear father's call,
> about to go to the Sidonian city,
> ...carrying presents that have survived the sea and the flames of Troy.
>
> accitu cari genitoris ad urbem
> Sidoniam puer ire parat...
> dona ferens pelago et flammis restantia Troiae.   1. 677–679

Later Cupid is said to bring, led by Achates, "the royal presents", *dona...regia* (695f.), also called *dona Aeneae* (709). Apparently there is absolutely nothing Venus or Amor is going to add to this side of the process which Aeneas has already set in motion by picking Helen's cloak and veil – the gifts that, "together with the boy", *puero*, himself, help to kindle Dido's love (714).

What then about Venus' other weapon, i.e., Cupid in the guise of Ascanius?

Is there any evidence that *he*, at least, adds and exercises some indisputably divine influence on Dido's heart, though his means are said to be Aeneas' presents? (*donis* at 659 is *ablativus instrumenti* – as it is at 714, there together with *puero*). Venus' directions to Cupid are as follows:

> You impersonate by guile his shape for not more than one night
> and, a boy yourself, put on the boy's well-known features,
> in order that, when Dido most happy receives you on her lap,
> during the royal banquet and the wine of the Loosener of Worries,
> when she gives you embraces and attaches sweet kisses to you,
> you breathe the hidden fire into her and, without her being aware of it, apply
>   your charm.[42]

> tu faciem illius noctem non amplius unam
> falle dolo et notos pueri puer indue vultus,
> ut, cum te gremio accipiet laetissima Dido
> regalis inter mensas laticemque Lyaeum,
> cum dabit amplexus atque oscula dulcia figet,
> occultum inspires ignem fallasque veneno.   1. 683–688.

At least the word "inspire", "breathe into", appears here so that we may finally believe we verify an act of direct divine influence on a human mind. (But what is meant by the application of Cupid's charm remains hard to picture – unless one takes it on the human level of a "charming boy.") On the other hand, however, the situation Venus is projecting here could be taken right out of Ovid's *Ars Amatoria*: wine, banquet, and a happy mood prove to be the climate where, the instructor says, love likes to blossom. With Vergil's *laetissima Dido*, compare *A.A.* 1. 359f.:

> mens erit apta capi tum, cum *laetissima* rerum
> ut seges in pingui luxuriabit humo.

With Vergil's *regalis...mensas* and *laticem...Lyaeum*, one may compare *A.A.* 1. 525f. and 229–252, especially 229f.:

> dant etiam *positis* aditum *convivia mensis*;
> est aliquid praeter *vina* quod inde petas.

This distich is followed by the wrestling match of *Bacchus* and *Amor*, which leaves *Cupido*, sprinkled with *wine*, temporarily unable to leave the scene.

So far, we see in the *Aeneid* passage a pre-established context of purely empirical ingredients on which the divine sphere superimposes itself (not to say: into which it injects itself) without changing any of them or the situation they constitute. A non-concrete understanding is suggested by Venus' own words. When she addresses Cupid as "Son, my powers, my great force...on my knees I request your divine might" (664–666), she seems, prayer-style, to speak to an abstract concept of herself. It is as if Vergil's Venus, when contemplating and projecting an intervention in the world of mortals, can conceive of herself and describe her son's efficacy down there only in terms which humans would call allegorical. *In actu*, then, she lacks and loses those lively and concrete 'human' traits the poet has assigned her when he allows us to watch her in her celestial life and anxieties. (In the case of Amor, too, human traits go with his divine personality: we think of his having boyish fun when imitating Ascanius' gait, *gaudens*, 690; cf. *laetus*, 696.)

As far as matters on earth are concerned, Venus' control appears restricted to predicting that empirical development which is detailed in the author's narrative of the events at Carthage. She herself does not appear at all, and her 'son' must take on and act the role of a human boy, without displaying any trace of divinity or immortal power. By all accounts, he acts in the same way as the person he replaces, and his effect on Aeneas (715f.) and his hostess is no different from the effect the real Ascanius would have. The way Amor is taken care of by Dido (*gremio fovet*, 718) is identical with the motherly way in which Ascanius is said to be cared for by Venus (*fotum gremio*, 692). And, so far, Dido is being captivated, while *she* embraces and kisses the boy: her involvement is active, her capture simultaneous (coincident) with her activity (*cum dabit...atque...figet*, 687).

The reduction which takes place in the goddess' lively literary personality, when she is dealing with and contemplating application of her power, is even more striking. It is found side by side with the credible rekindled fear she feels as a mother. The fear is unjustified. It ascribes to "Junonian hospitality" (*Iunonia...hospitia*, 671f.) what Jupiter, god of hospitality, has arranged. And it attributes to Dido an attempt to delay Aeneas with "flattering words" (*blandisque moratur vocibus*, 670f.), when Dido so far has shown only admiration and readiness to help.[43] Panic rules her motivation but abstract symbolism (if not mere allegory) her action.

Again it seems, then, that the reader is being directed to distinguish between the affairs on the well-illuminated divine stage and the closed system of human experience in the narrative terms of which the divine does not appear with even a trace of interference. (Again the proviso is made that there are, of course, cases where the divine presence does make itself felt because it wants to, as does the god of Delphi, when speaking to Aeneas in Book 3).

Under these conditions, it is imperative that the reader closely trace the process of Dido's falling in love. When arriving at the palace, (Pseudo-)Ascanius first embraces Aeneas and hangs on his neck, gratifying the father's love; then he

> makes for the queen. She, with her eyes, she, with her whole heart
> holds on to him and in between caresses him on her lap, Dido,
> not knowing how great a god is, to her misery, sitting on her. But
> he, mindful of his Acidalian mother, begins step by step to efface the
>   memory of Sychaeus,
> and he attempts to preoccupy with love for a living man
> her mind, sluggish for a long time already, and her disaccustomed heart.

> reginam petit. haec oculis, haec pectore toto
> haeret et interdum gremio fovet inscia Dido
> insidat quantus miserae deus. at memor ille
> matris Acidaliae paulatim abolere Sychaeum
> incipit et vivo temptat praevertere amore
> iam pridem resides animos desuetaque corda.   717–722.

Chapter 5

What in this description can be unambiguously identified as, and ascribed to, the intervention of a god? Frankly, nothing. For all means and purposes employed and achieved in this section, the presence of the real human Ascanius will do. That the queen is enchanted by the boy any Roman would consider a most natural reaction for a woman in her situation (she was never allowed to raise her own in union with her husband). Later, at the time of her guest's departure, she will, when contemplating her future loneliness (*deserta*, 4. 330), deplore not having herself a "little Aeneas" playing in the palace whose face might remind her of his departing father ("bring him back", "reproduce him"):

> si quis mihi parvulus aula
> luderet Aeneas, qui te tamen ore referret   4. 328f.

The lines show that Vergil conceived of his Dido as potentially being a mother and – more important for the passage in Book 1 (though probably self-evident to any reader) – that she could picture her affectionate feelings as gliding from son to father, i.e., as seeing the father in the son. The latter feature is confirmed by 4. 84f., where the situation is as good as identical with that of the welcoming banquet in Book 1. Dido has given yet another in the series of banquets for Aeneas, Ascanius, and the retinue (*eadem* at 4. 77 points to the same set-up as on the first evening, *nunc...nunc* to the frequent repetitions), and "again has, out of her mind, hung on the lips" of Aeneas when she made him tell the events of Troy's suffering over again (77–79). Now the guests have left (*digressi*, 80), and it is late in the night. But longing Dido, lying on the abandoned couch, "mourns, being alone in the empty house." She imagines the guests being present, "sees and hears" absent Aeneas; at another moment, she even, trying to deal with her "unspeakable" love, imagines that she "is holding on to Ascanius on her lap, captured by the picture (likeness) of the father" which the son offers, *genitoris imagine capta* (84f.).

The fact that Dido pictures herself as having Iulus on her lap (*gremio*, 4. 84) when recognizing Aeneas in his son's features, forms an exact parallel to the situation at the welcoming banquet in Book 1, where she also holds the boy whom she believes to be Ascanius-Iulus on her lap, caressing him (*gremio fovet*, 1. 718). It establishes a firm premise for concluding that, within the parameters of Vergil's empirical psychology, the real human Ascanius suffices to intensify and direct Dido's growing feelings for Aeneas, even without the added-on presence of Amor the god. If it is the similarity to his father which endears Ascanius to Dido, one understands why Venus insists on Amor taking on Ascanius' figure and, especially, features: *notos pueri puer indue vultus* (1. 684). Apparently, the poet wants the empirical side of the process to be consistent in itself. Why? An answer will have to be provided later on. For now let it then be stated about the situation in Book 1 that, in addition to the aforementioned *dona*, *mensae*, and *latex Lyaeus*, the *puer* on the lap, be he Amor or Ascanius, would, by his similarity with Aeneas, waken her dormant feelings and give them direction, so that the memory of Sychaeus begins to pale.

In parenthesis let us add that there is, in the two passages quoted from Book 4, a third ingredient, in addition to Dido's being potentially a mother and to her feelings' being guided from son to father. This is Dido's loneliness which is (though it will be intensified and adjusted to those later occasions) also prefigured and hinted at already in Book 1 when the poet remarks on her "disaccustomed" heart.

The only straight hint of divinity given in the passage 1. 717–722 is that Dido does not know "how great a *god* is sitting (on her lap), to her (later) misery." In other words: she does not yet know into how great a love her present feelings will develop and what misery the development will bring her. So far, nothing has been said about any exclusively and peculiarly divine activity exercised by Cupid/Amor on the human level.

It was Heinze who pointed out that Vergil, though indebted to Apollonius Rhodius, introduces an important change.[44] Medea, hit by Eros' arrow, falls (young girl that she is) in love *immediately* when seeing Jason for the first time (*Arg.* 3. 275–288). Dido's heart is won over *gradually* (*paulatim*, *Aen.* 1. 720), during the course of the night. And here Amor is indeed said to be at work, beginning (an unexpected verb) to wear away *gradually* the memory of her first husband and *trying* (another unexpected verb for a god's activity!) to preoccupy the disaccustomed heart with love for the living Aeneas. Compared to Apollonius' sharpshooter god Eros, Vergil's Cupid, "trying" and working his way ahead "step by step", *paulatim*, for a whole night,[45] must be called a failure – and is of course calculated to be recognized as such. Thus, when the poet's dual track concept encounters an incompatibility, the necessary compromise is allowed to materialize and take place on the divine side rather than on the level of human psychology.

Amor's inefficiency (comparable to the Fury's, Allecto's, initial failure to arouse King Turnus in book 7) is the poet's way of accommodating the thesis of alleged divine influence (i.e., a feature of the divine theater) to the empirical process in which the mature widow re-awakens to emotions that have gone to sleep long ago. The process (cf. *interdum*; *incipit*; *temptat*), in addition to the elements we enumerated earlier, emerges and is drawn out through the stages of the evening. First, there is the queen's toast, still invoking Jupiter as protector of *guests* (she is still *inscia* [cf. 718] about her developing condition) and ominously hoping for Phoenician-Trojan friendship even in later generations (728–735); this is followed by Iopas' song on cosmology (740–746); then by a conversation on various topics (*vario...sermone*, 748), this one prolonged by the queen, "who was, to her misfortune, drinking a (life-)long love"[46] (749; here "love", *amorem*, is no longer to be identified with the boy-god of love, *Amor*, as he appeared even as recently as 689; rather, the narrative now in poetic terms accounts for the empirical process of her falling in love); and, finally, there is Aeneas' heroic narrative (= Books 2 and 3): his features, his family background, his speech, and his manliness – all of them purely empirical features! – are said to have impressed themselves firmly into her heart (4. 2f.).

(4) Intellectual Background: Stoic Philosophy at Rome

Under the conditions outlined above, the result of Venus' intervention parallels that of the preceding impulse, issuing from Jupiter, in regard to being not verifiable as such within the framework of the earthly events and of human developments as established by the narrative. The reader is *being told* that divine influence is being exercised on a human mind – and we need to be told so, for, from the character's reactions to the situation as described to us, we would never guess so. The psychological process again manifests itself in a circuit closed in itself, and its elements again receive priority over consistency in the intervention of the divine theater.

Our earlier question, then, returns with greater urgency: what advantage did the poet believe he gained when, in his epic, he made human (empirical) psychology run independently from (and occasionally even at the expense of) the divine interventions he took such pain to report? At least a hypothetical answer should be formulated to guide us (and to be tested) when we approach Dido's psychological dilemma in Book 4.

A good way of accessing the problem is to look, at least briefly, into the school of thought and of intellectual inquiry which forms an important undercurrent in Vergil's poem. Several strands are worth taking into consideration, all of them related to Stoic philosophy.[47] First then let us recall that Stoicism exercised a strong voice in Rome already around the middle of the second century BC when Panaetius (himself a Greek of aristocratic background) had the ear of the leading political class, above all through a warm personal relationship with Scipio Aemilianus (scil., *Africanus Minor*, the destroyer of Carthage and conqueror of Numantia in Spain). Panaetius, whose stewardship opened what is today considered the middle period of the Stoa, saw fit to offer a philosophical justification of Roman imperialism – the morality of leadership provided. So he gave an originally supranational and cosmopolitan doctrine a Roman note, keyed to the top layer of society.

Another strand of Stoicism that has found its way into the *Aeneid* concerns religion and fate (both no strangers to early Roman epic, in any case). Panaetius had influenced Roman religion, too: his *tripartita theologia* was used for a defense of state religion by the Pontifex Maximus of 115, Q. Mucius Scaevola. The resulting distinction between popular polytheism and religion of the educated (the latter would understand the individual gods as diverse forms of the all-comprehensive Stoic deity) has been applied to interpreting the *Aeneid* – as if it was Vergil's goal to retain or exhibit as much of Stoic philosophy as could be accommodated in a poem: "To execute these tenets with absolute purity is, however, not possible in the poem...concessions are unavoidable" ("Diese Dogmen in voller Reinheit durchzuführen, ist freilich im Gedicht nicht möglich... Konzessionen sind unvermeidlich").[48] Here the question has to be asked whether Vergil would even have *wanted* and *intended* to stay as close to the Stoic system as poetry would allow. As an artist, it must be said, he wanted to be first of all the Roman Homer, i.e., a *national poet* of highest rank, not a popularizer or interpreter of Stoic theory.

But pointing out that the poet had his own agenda when borrowing from Stoicism is not to imply that he is less systematic as a thinker (and a thinker he is, not only a poet). Destiny, pressed into the service of the Augustan ideology, in the *Aeneid* takes on a teleological character, guiding events, from the fall of Troy, first to the founding of Rome (*Aen.* 1. 1–7; cf. *fato*, 2), and eventually, as revealed by Jupiter (*fatorum arcana movebo*, 1. 262) to the rule of Julian Augustus over the known world (287). At that time, the *pax Augusta* proves to be the return of the Golden Age: *Augustus Caesar...aurea condet saecula*, etc. ("Augustus Caesar will found golden centuries" 6. 792f.). The *Aeneid*'s identification of destiny with the rise of Julian power amounts to yoking Stoic philosophy to the bandwagon of a personalized political program – originally, we recall, Stoicism was quite cosmopolitan in character, though in the second century BC it was already claimed for Roman imperialism. Jupiter, the highest Roman god, is in Vergil's construct not restricted to being only the mouthpiece of fate. In decisive aspects, he *sets* fate, especially when, in the opening Book's grandiloquent prophecy, he tells Venus that, as for the Romans,

> *I am setting* no boundaries in history and no fixed period for them;
> *I have granted* them empire without end.
>
> his *ego* nec metas rerum nec tempora *pono*:
> imperium sine fine *dedi*. 1. 278f.

And, in reassuring his daughter, he states: "...the *fates* of your descendants remain unmoved...no opinion has changed *me* [*scil.*, as you suspect, cf. 1. 237]" (*manent immota tuorum fata...neque me sententia vertit*, 1. 257–260).

In the understanding of Vergil's contemporaries, this means that the empire of Augustus will prove eternal, even after its founder's future deification (envisaged by Jupiter at 1. 289f.). This is not poetry serving philosophy but philosophy (and religion) being employed to help establish political power through ideology.

There are several obvious advantages Vergil gains from his construction. One is (and this has proven consequential for the European tradition of hierarchically structured authority versus the rights of the individual) that political opponents of the ruling regime can be classified as sinners against the country's highest god and thus against fate (this is an aspect we shall have to deal with especially when reviewing Turnus' dream in Book 7). Another, repeatedly to be cited later on, is that the recent development of Augustus' personal rise to power has no longer anything accidental about it since it fulfills fate-inspired prophecies made many centuries ago. A third advantage is that an epic which represents Augustus' rule as the outcome of inexorable destiny serves the imperial ideology much better than, say, an epic which directly praises Octavian's (debatable) military successes (i.e., his civil war record).

As a poet, then, Vergil was hardly out to win new territory or even converts for Stoicism. Rather – to rephrase what was said above – he utilized the ever-present Stoic background to impress on his fellow Romans the political message of his epic, i.e., the idea that the nation's well-being was tied to the Julian leadership which fate had been aiming at ever since the fall of Troy.

And lastly, fate and its ramifications also offered him a point of contact where Homeric mythology of the epic tradition could be tied in fruitfully with the Julianized Stoic concept. Homer's Zeus had to live with the fact that his fellow-Olympians now and then tried to evade sneakily his orders. (But Zeus was hardly in charge of fate: he is more characterized by a situation where he himself would consult a higher authority.) In Vergil's construct, headstrong and insubordinate gods, though unable to prevail in the long run, might be seen as availing themselves of the leeway which Stoicism sometimes allowed within the range of fate: not all things are predestined, some have been left in suspense. So Juno may ask Jupiter for concessions in the area of "what is not being held by any law of fate," *nulla fati quod lege tenetur* (*Aen.* 12. 819).[49] In Book 7 she knows that, by unchangeable fate, she cannot keep Aeneas from getting the Latin throne, and that Lavinia will be Aeneas' wife – but she can delay this result by starting a war and destroying the two kings' people (7. 313–316). Vulcan at 8.398f. maintains that King Priam could have survived another ten years without interference of Jupiter or Fate.

It has been obvious since antiquity that the idea of temporary deviations from fate's appointed course, even if they are kept within certain limits, throws the Stoic system open to objections. Seneca's statement (*N.Q.* 2. 37), "so this does not run against fate, but is itself too within fate," (*ita non est hoc contra fatum sed ipsum quoque in fato est*), shows awareness of the necessity to deal with the problem. But it is equally obvious that, for the poet, the concept offers a chance to add life and its vagaries to his fate-directed plot-line.

One may, for the purpose of illustration, compare how in the *Iliad* "Zeus' will", aiming at Agamemnon's temporary defeat (so that sulking Achilles' honor may be restored), is constantly being counteracted by divine (combined with human) interventions. The resulting picture is that of a 'normal' war, with its usual ups and downs for either side. In a similar fashion, the *Aeneid*'s dramaturgy, where it is lively, springs from the tension between the fated course of history and the actions of those, be they gods or humans, who defiantly pursue their own agenda and their personal goals. In the resulting clashes, the *Aeneadae* act in agreement with the fated purpose of the universe (as long as they do not fail their sacred mission, as Aeneas does in Carthage). Their opponents, to the extent that they avail themselves of the latitude fate allows for such activities, also incur guilt (or, in the case of a deity, at least moral blemish), and they forfeit the support, favor, or clemency of the highest god.

In Homer, Zeus' will temporarily leans toward the Trojans, until Achilles' honor is restored; then, the fated movement resumes which will lead to the fall of doomed Troy. This zigzag development is a far cry from the *Aeneid*'s metaphysical teleology. As a matter of fact, offenders against the will of fate were, certainly in the eyes of politically correct contemporaries, writing their own sentence and their own condemnation: how can anyone avoid incurring the charge of an objective transgression who impedes the fated development which leads to the return of the Golden Age at the time when (in the words of Jupiter's prophecy)

> grey-haired Faith and Vesta [guarantor of Rome's survival], Quirinus
> in harmony with his brother Remus, will give laws,
>
> cana Fides et Vesta, Remo cum fratre Quirinus
> iura dabunt,

and when (civil) war will be abolished (1. 292–294)? The label of objective transgression applies whether fate's opponents act knowingly, as does

Juno, when she, in spite of knowing fate's will (1. 22), persecutes a man distinguished by his piety (1. 10), or unknowingly, as would be the situation of *Dido* (cf. also *fati nescia* 1. 299). In her case, however, the additional question will have to be raised and answered as to whether she has perhaps incurred guilt in the subjective sense, i.e., in an area where she is not *nescia*. There may even be the question whether someone like Venus (as she is depicted in Book 1), acting from panic but in goodwill toward the *Aeneadae*, is still deserving of Jove's indulgence when counteracting his line of action as he has expounded it to her.

The relationship of fate and gods of mythology as depicted in the *Aeneid* can give literary critics an important clue for their work. Deviations from Jupiter's orders, however they may be motivated, are immediately recognized by the observant reader as signposts supplied by the author. For instance, interventions in the prophesied course of events, whenever they are initiated by Juno and her immortal agents (e.g., Aeolus in Book 1; Iris in 5; Allecto in 7) or her human protégés (Dido in Book 4; Turnus in 7–12), tend to signify a threat to the *Aeneadae*'s mission and to history's Julian fulfillment.

It is good to remind oneself of these basic data. Awareness of the skeleton of Vergil's construct protects the interpreter against the lure of "polyphonic" voices, allegedly enjoying 'equal rights', as erroneously heard in the epic by many a critic in the 20th century's latter half.

After dealing with fate in the *Aeneid* with an eye on its interplay with imperialism, religion and Homeric mythology, we now turn to ethics. That Stoicism's strongest influence at Rome undoubtedly lay in the field of ethics is generally acknowledged and need not be established anew here. It is sufficient to remind ourselves in passing how much Vergil's *pius Aeneas*, with his obedience toward Fate's revelations and instructions, his sense of duty, and his endurance, owes to the Stoic ideal of the man of virtue who accepts fate into his will.[50] By the same token, it will hardly have surprised the Roman reader to find Aeneas' Carthaginian counterpart ('eclectic' as she may be in choosing her arguments) *in theologicis* espousing tenets of Epicureanism (4. 379f.), the philosophy that was (allegedly) so alien to Roman virtuousness. (It may be good not to forget that Vergil himself had once [*Geo.* 2. 477ff.] aspired to the Lucretian kind of song which in the *Aeneid* [1. 740–747] arouses the Carthaginians' applause.) Under these circumstances, we have to take special care when approaching the phenomenon of erring Dido, fate's unknowing opponent, and the question of why Vergil presented her thinking and her feeling as uninfluenced by those divine interventions, which he also reports.

The field of ethics is the area where the Stoic dilemma of assumed detours from the course of inexorable fate is felt most severely, and the problem many ancient critics had with Stoicism was that complete determinism (every event being both the consequent of an antecedent and a cause for a consequent), moving like "the unwinding of a rope" (*rudentis explicatio*, Cicero, *Div.* 1. 127), takes away freedom of action, leaves nothing "within our power", *in nostra potestate* (see, for instance, *Fat.* 11. 25). As a consequence, reward and punishment would be meaningless. Thus the morally dangerous "do-nothing" argument (ἀργὸς λόγος, *ignava ratio*, Cicero, *Fat.* 12. 28f.) has to be met.

One can easily see how devastating this argument would be for viewing the Julian ancestor (and, by implication, for viewing his latest descendant): since the outcome of history is fated, it would seem that the rise of the Julian empire from Trojan origin is guaranteed whatever labors Aeneas may or may not take upon his shoulders. The notorious loyal passivity displayed by Aeneas as a poetic character may be rooted precisely in the fact that important steps on his path through the epic are pre-defined by fate.[51] Readers' excitement is caused more often by those who oppose destiny's will than by those who fulfill its demands. But the toils of Aeneas are certainly not a matter of indifference to the author of the *Aeneid*. Nor must they be to its readers.

The problem must have been one of great urgency for Vergil. How can man's actions be free, so humans can be held responsible for their actions? This is a question Vergil's reader, too, would certainly like to be able to answer unequivocally in the case of, for instance, Dido.

The Stoics' attempts to deal with their critics have been under scrutiny up to this very day. A.A. Long, in a penetrating analysis, has pointed to the Stoic "bifocal lenses" of God's perspective and of the human viewpoint. "Possibility exists to the extent that, but only to the extent that, men are ignorant of the future... To God only what will take place is possible."[52] In the end Long states that "doubtless the Stoics were too ready to keep their cake and eat it."[53]

So Vergil inherited a potential vulnerability whose consequences he would certainly wish to debar from his epic. Doubt falling on his characters' freedom of action would be an undesirable corollary. We have already seen (and more will have to be said in chapter 7) that the intervention of Homer's gods could at times be taken as the poet's way of externalizing human psychological processes. When Athena comes to Odysseus and tells him to rally the troops and keep them from going home in their boats, she basically does nothing but reinforce what he is inclined to do anyway: he is the only one who has not participated in the general drive for departure but is standing at his boat in disapproval of what is going on around him.

Chapter 5

So his epic model did allow Vergil to use divine interventions as epic's peculiar way of presenting mental processes to one's audience. Amor's presence, at his mother's request, on Dido's lap during the animated hours of the banquet, with lively conversations and Aeneas' narration, might well be compared to Athena's intervention in *Iliad* 4: like Odysseus, Dido does nothing which could not count as her natural reaction in this situation.

But, since Vergil has admitted fate into his work in a much more systematic position than Homer, he has to guard his characters against the possible misunderstanding that they are mere puppets whose strings are pulled by fate or by powers which are granted temporary leeway within fate's large scale scheme. He also might wish to prevent his readers from thinking that it is Dido's nature which forces her to react as she does. If the stone, once released, cannot not fall, then Dido's situation might, once she has been exposed to Amor's nightlong influence, be seen to be that she cannot not fall in love. In other words, the critique generally leveled at the Stoics might rub off on Vergil's own work.

Above all, then, one should not expect the poet to deal with this problem in a manner alien to either his medium or his subject matter. (That Vergil is not something like a Stoic counterpart to Epicurean Lucretius our earlier discussion has shown.) It may be helpful to review how a fellow countryman of his, who wished to give philosophical concepts a home in a Roman setting, handled the specific problem posed by human action.

Cicero's position is that something can't be which ought not to be. If our individual inclinations result from natural antecedent causes, it cannot mean that also the stirrings of our will (our volitions) and our consent to desires are the result of natural antecedent causes. "*For* if this were true, nothing would be in our power." *Nam nihil esset in nostra potestate, si ita res se haberet* (*Fat.* 5. 9). Character flaws can result from natural causes, it is true; but they can be eradicated so that even the person who has a propensity toward vice can call himself off. "This (scil. the ability of calling oneself off) is not grounded in natural causes but in will, endeavour, and discipline." *non est id positum in naturalibus causis sed in voluntate studio disciplina* (*Fat.* 5. 11). "But those who introduce an eternal chain of causes, deprive man's mind of free will and tie it by the necessity of fate." *At qui introducunt causarum seriem sempiternam, ii mentem hominis voluntate libera spoliatam necessitate fati devinciunt* (*Fat.* 9. 19). The opinion that everything happens through fate (*fato omnia fieri*) is to Cicero simply unbearable (*haec vero non est tolerabilis*, 10. 21).

The difficulty Cicero sees the Stoics run into is of a kind Vergil would certainly wish to avoid. Of course we are not entitled to draw inferences concerning Vergil's position from Cicero's stance in *De Fato*. But we can very well learn about the kind of objections that were current against the thesis *omnia fato fieri*, and, from them, we can picture in which areas Vergil would wish to be on his guard. After all, what both writers have in common is a strong sense of obligation concerning the present condition of their society (different as their respective ideals may have been about what the desirable form of the state ought to be) and the applicable standards of morality.

This leads to the last two of the passages to be considered here, taking us back to the point of departure (cf. *Fat.* 6. 11). Against Stoic Chrysippus' thesis of multiple co-fated constituents of a situation, Cicero introduces Carneades' objection (in which "he did not employ any fallacy", *nec ullam adhibebat calumniam*). In an abbreviated form, Carneades' argument runs like this: if all things happen through fate, i.e., everything results from anteceding causes, it ultimately follows that nothing lies "within our power" (*in nostra potestate*). "But there does lie something within our power. (...) So it follows that not all things happen through fate" (*Est autem aliquid in nostra potestate.[...] non igitur fato fiunt quaecumque fiunt, Fat.* 14. 31).

One may object that Cicero's Carneades here, in order to puncture the all-pervasiveness of Chrysippus' fate, bases his refutation on a mere postulate. But that is exactly my point. Cicero goes along with Carneades, *because* he ranks the free choice of moral action so highly. The issue comes up again later, where the dire consequences are being considered. The opponents of an all-pervasive fate argue that, if everything is determined by fate and antecedent causes, then "neither the assents nor the actions lie within our power. And from that it follows that neither praise nor blame is justified, and neither honors nor punishments." *Ex quo efficitur, ut nec laudationes iustae sint nec vituperationes nec honores nec supplicia.* And again, there follows a sort of *a priori* rejection: "*But since this result is faulty*, they believe that one can with probability draw the conclusion that not all that happens happens through fate." *Quod cum vitiosum sit, probabiliter concludi putant non omnia fato fieri, quaecumque fiant* (*Fat.* 17. 40).

Looking at Stoicism in general and especially at Cicero's (a committed Roman citizen's) reaction to its moral implications, has brought us close to the problems Vergil must have faced when adapting the system to his own purposes of eternalizing the Julian claim to leadership over Rome and its empire by basing the claim on a mission guaranteed since primeval time by Jupiter and destiny. It certainly was inconceivable that the founders and builders of Roman power should have been acting out of an inner necessity which was predetermined by antecedent causes, without having the choice of freely giving assent to their own roles and actions. The whole catalogue of future Roman heroes reviewed by Anchises and Aeneas in Book 6 would lose its moral appeal if they all were merely puppets waiting to be pulled by the strings of fate. ("αἰτία ἑλομένου· θεὸς ἀναίτιος", "God is not guilty [not the cause]. The guilt is that of the one who chooses". This was Plato's answer, supplied to the pre-natal souls, *Rep.* 10. 617e 4f.). On the other hand, Rome's rise to Julian world domination must not be the result of chance, but had to be based on the unchangeable will of the highest authority in the universe. The contradiction inherent in the Stoic system was just what Vergil needed.

And so the same catalogue also bears out the Vergilian collocation of fate and individual personal achievement, by explaining the shades' destined future roles to Aeneas (including his very own *fata*, 6. 759) as well as dishing out praise by indicating the men's respective *gloria* (767), *pietas* (769; 878), bravery (*armis egregius*, 769f.), distinction by civic crown (*civili...quercu*, 772), *amor patriae* (823), *fides* (878) – to mention only a selection of the praise (sometimes interspersed with criticism).[54] That the poet does *not* consider the concept of praise, honors, and rewards invalidated by his employment of fate can also be seen from so simple a context alone as Aeneas' distribution of prizes and rewards at the games he establishes in honor of his deceased father (Book 5). Here Vergil is found on the same side as Cicero.

The matter gets more complicated, however, when his poetry delves into *details of psychological processes*, because in this area his acceptance of stoically tinged fate puts him under obligation to make clear that a character follows her/his own choice and not predetermining antecedent causes alone. This obligation is probably felt by him even more strongly where he deals with motives and actions of Aeneas' leading opponents. Is it Turnus' inborn ferocity (represented by the Fury Allecto) that makes him start a war against Aeneas, or is he responsible for his action? Is it Dido's nature that makes her inescapably fall in love once she meets attractive Aeneas? Does she act like the released stone or like Chrysippus' rolling drum which (in one interpretation), once pushed, keeps rolling on account of its nature?

Knowing already that Vergil, like Cicero, upholds the principle that blame and praise are justified, we may ask the question: what means are at the poet's (as opposed to the philosopher's) disposal to let his reader know that, in spite of (fated or fate-opposing) divine intervention, a character's actions are his or her free moral choice and responsibility?

Part of the answer, as far as Dido is concerned, has already been given earlier in this Chapter when the poet was found to emphasize a seamless process of empirical psychology. In spite of Jupiter's and Mercury's intervention, Dido credibly bases her decision to offer the Trojans assistance on premises she calls up from autobiographical experience. In spite of Venus' and Amor's reported influence (which, though not in accordance with fate, nevertheless would represent another instance of divine intervention in a human soul), the psychological process of Dido falling in love is based by the narrator on premises which are given in (are ingredients of) the human situation also without the presence of Amor; yes, Amor the god here proves unable to overpower the mortal queen by a one-shot-action (unlike the model case of Apollonios' Medea where his arrow causes love-at-first-sight); rather, he must work (in ways not communicated by the narrator and therefore unintelligible to the reader) on his victim for a whole night, initiating a *gradual* process.

The other part of the answer lies, of course, in cautiously tracing the leads provided to the reader at the time when the loving queen actually embarks on a relationship with her guest. Is she, at this point, under the control of "divinity," or does she know what she is doing and make a decision for which (and for the consequences resulting from which) she is held responsible by her creator? Only a precise reading of the text can tell.

(5) Dido in Love: The Liberated Widow in Action

Having left the queen at the end of Book 1 when she was drinking in "a long (-lasting) love" (749), the reader meets her again at the end of Aeneas' report on Troy's fall (Book 2) and on his own travels (Book 3). One should not forget that it was she herself who had asked for the report, and that her self-centered insistence may even have bordered on tactlessness. She paid no attention to Aeneas' protests that it was getting late in the night (2. 8f.), or to his pleading words "unspeakable the pain you bid me renew, o queen" (2. 3). Knowing his obligation toward a hostess who had just saved him and his men from total destruction, Aeneas complied, but not without at least hinting at the inappropriateness he sensed in her curiosity:

> But if your desire is so great to get acquainted with our misfortunes
> and to hear briefly the ultimate suffering of Troy,
> I shall, although my mind shudders to remember and shrinks back
> in mourning, begin.
>
> Sed si tantus amor casus cognoscere nostros
> et breviter Troiae supremum audire laborem,
> quamquam animus meminisse horret luctuque refugit, incipiam.
> 2. 10–13

Little did Aeneas realize (or had he perceived the impact that "boy as well as presents" had had on the queen? [cf.1. 714]) that it was his person at least as much as the story he had to tell which caused the queen to pose her request.

When the poet changes our perspective (*at*, 4. 1) from Aeneas' narrative to that of "the queen," he informs us of the fact (unbecoming her regal status, as Servius indicates) that she, "for a long time already wounded by the heavy pain, nourishes the wound with her blood and is consumed by invisible fire." Since Amor has not been shown to shoot an arrow (or use any other bloodletting implement), there is no way to take (as Pease assumes) the "wound" as the result of a concretely conceived activity of the god. Moreover, the stylistic variation of the consuming fire in line 2 proves beyond doubt (no such thing as an incendiary arrow has been indicated) that "wound" and "fire" are here the usual metaphors for the pain of unfulfilled love. One may, for instance, recall Propertius' warning to his friend Ponticus about the "fire" (*igni*) to come (1. 9. 17) or Lucretius' Mars who, though powerful in arms and ruling over war, often seeks solace with Venus, when he is "defeated by the eternal wound of love," *aeterno devictus vulnere amoris* (1. 34; no arrow-shooting Amor appears in the context, since here all love is caused by Venus herself, cf. 1. 19f.).

As a matter of fact, by the end of Aeneas' report and the end of the banquet, god Amor has unnoticeably made his exit from the poem, and the reader is once more left to deal with a markedly empirical perspective. Recalling her guest's manly courage, the high rank of his descent, his features, and his words, the queen, agitated by her love, *cura*,[55] is unable to find rest: she is struck by positive impressions in all four areas which traditionally (as the parallels cited in Pease's commentary *ad* 4. 11 demonstrate) are considered to lead a woman to falling in love with a man she meets.

It is important to note that in lines 1–5 the poet details Dido's condition in his own voice. Apparently Vergil himself, before letting Dido speak, wishes to convey to his reader the notion that Dido's fascination with Aeneas should be understood in the traditional terms of *virtus, gentis honos, vultus verbaque* (manliness, distinguished family, face, speech, 4. 3–5); i.e., any idea of supernatural influence is now kept out of sight. Fate, as well as any possible influence of supporters or opponents on the divine stage, has been removed from view once the reader is made to witness a psychological process on the human level. As Dido earlier accounted for her compassion toward the shipwrecked Trojans in autobiographical terms by referring to her personal experience (Jove's and Mercury's intervention seemed to play no part whatsoever in her decision to offer help), so in Book 4 too she will account for her feelings toward Aeneas exclusively in those same traditional empirical terms which the poet uses in his opening description of her condition in 4. 1–5. A few lines into Book 4 already, the absence of divine control lets the reader see a Dido who is herself responsible for her actions and decisions.

On the morning after the banquet, Dido, no longer of sound mind (*male sana*, 8), reveals to sister Anna, her 'accordant' or 'unanimous' second self, that she is in a state of anxiety and is being frightened by dreams. What does she have to fear? If what follows gives some guidance, she would be frightened by the prospect of undergoing punishment for wavering in her loyalty toward her deceased husband. The cryptic line (9; we shall return to it) is followed by a series of exclamations. In them, she both restates her earlier compassion (*heu...fatis* 13f.; cf. 1. 614–616) and expresses her admiration for the high qualities of her "guest" (*hospes*, 10). The words *ore, forti pectore et armis, genus...deorum* (speech, brave fighter, divine family background,11f.) recall the terms Vergil used in 1–5 to describe her condition. According to her own words too, then, Dido experiences herself as being affected by Aeneas' presence as a woman naturally would when falling in love (see Pease *ad* 4. 11). The label of "guest" is beginning to appear unrealistic.

Consequently, one may expect a clear-cut confession to follow. (The function of the *asyndeton* after line 14 would then be causal.) Instead, we are offered two negating conditions (*si...non....si non*, 15 and 18) which supposedly prevent any realization of the possibility that "perhaps I could succumb to this single instance of guilt" (19). The treacherous main clause delivered by line 19 is more revealing when one understands (following a suggestion by Miss M. Hubbard) that in it Dido corrects and redirects her contemplated line of thought. The first word in line 19, *huic*, makes the listener, within the given context, expect a continuation by a *male* noun or name (i.e., she could have succumbed to Aeneas) for which she then, hesitating and rephrasing her thought, substitutes *culpae* (emphasized last word in line 19).

The surprise turn offered by line 19, then, is that her wish to avoid (*ne vellem*, 16) a new marital bond (*vinclo...iugali*) not only protects Dido against possibly having again to experience immeasurable sorrow ("after my first love failed me, cheated by death", *postquam primus amor deceptam morte fefellit* 17), but her wish not to enter a second marriage also *observes the moral imperative* which ought to rule her life anyway. On *culpae*, Austin remarks: "...here it is used of Dido's 'weakness' in her passion for Aeneas, which she knows is wrong – the 'tragic flaw' in her character." The question arises whether her awareness (Austin's "she knows") does not require a stricter interpretation than 'tragic flaw' or 'weakness'.

If taken as "sexual misconduct" (a translation offered by *OLD*) or as

219

Chapter 5

"the crime of un-chastity" (*LS ad locum*), *culpae* also goes a long way to explain the fearful aspect of her dreams[56] (we now resume discussion of line 9): in her dreams she has gone farther than she would allow herself to proceed when being awake – the latter being a state in which succumbing would entail manifest guilt. The present tense *terrent* leaves it perhaps open whether the frightful aspect appeared in the dreams themselves (the warning shade of Sychaeus – Pease) or reveals itself to, and affects, her agitated condition (*suspensam*, 9)[57] in the clear light of the new day (*Aurora...dimoverat umbram*, 4. 7).

The second alternative, i.e, of understanding the fear as generated by bad dreams (9), is the more likely one, considering not only the present tense (*terrent* 9) and the parallel from Book 2 (728f.), but also the situation after last evening's growing infatuation and the ensuing dreams of the night. Dido, in taking stock of her situation, is now frightened by the drift of her feelings – the moral consequences of which she is slow to admit (see the postponed or even substituted *culpae*). We should perhaps not always cling to the cliché that dreams are bad because their contents are experienced as bad at the time when the dreams occur.

In themselves, the two conditions which prevent Dido from giving in to her feelings might appear to be exclusively such as to serve her self-protection: first, her "firm and unchangeable" decision not to marry again "after my first love failed me, cheated by death;" second, consecutively and more specifically, a weariness of marriage: both point to the same fear of possibly having once more to go through sorrow.

Indeed, it is the mention of *culpa* which reveals the *moral* character of her dilemma and which makes a confession (*fatebor*, 20) of her following pronouncement that, after the death of "Sychaeus, my husband", at her brother's hand, Aeneas alone has affected her feelings and driven her mind (i. e., the organ of her firm resolve she referred to earlier: *animum*, 22 ~ *animo*, 15) to wavering (*labantem*, 22): "I recognize traces of the old flame" (23).

The admission contained in these words is so close to revoking her former "firm and unchangeable" attitude/position that, when restating that position in a powerful self-curse (to take effect in case she should fail her ideal), she cannot continue by saying "and so" or "therefore". Realizing the contrast between the two states, she introduces her movement from her present condition back to her longstanding resolve by "but," "however" (*sed*, 24). Below the surface of her 'public' stance, she has already slipped to the opposite position.

This slippage is also the cause for the twofold message of the self-curse: she wishes that Jupiter with his lightning drive her to the shades in the underworld, before, o Chastity, I violate you or dissolve your laws.

ante, Pudor, quam te violo aut tua iura resolvo. 4. 27

Pudor, the characteristic of chastity (also of married women of high moral standing), is elevated by Dido to the rank of an obliging divinity; it lessens the moral appeal if one renders the term by the subjective "(guilty) conscience". Of course the self-curse signals her desperate attempt to hang on to her high moral standard, to free herself from being *labans*. But it also conveys to the reader the fact that Dido is aware of the moral imperative, i.e., she is to be held responsible because she *knows* the "laws" (*iura*) she should follow. Her transgression will not be a guiltless 'tragic error', but involve a conscious decision. This aspect is enhanced by her following words:

> That one who as the first joined me to himself
> Carried my love away. He is to keep it and hold it safe with himself in the grave.
>
> Ille meos, primus qui me sibi iunxit, amores
> abstulit; ille habeat secum servetque sepulcro. 28f.

Dido does know that Sychaeus should be the only man in her life. The reader recalls that it was her father (*pater*) who gave her, a virgin (*intactam*) still, to her husband with the *formal auspices* of a *first* wedding: *primisque iugarat / ominibus* (1. 345f.): especially the term *ominibus* shows that the reader is supposed to view the arrangement – and judge Dido – by well-known *Roman* (and not by any alien 'Phoenician') standards. (In comparable fashion Vergil for his Roman audience makes the Greeks in Book 2 leave Troy for Mycenae allegedly to take the "auspices", *omina* [2. 178] over again.) This means that, in spite of her political independence from the traditional role of a woman (*dux femina facti*), Dido was far from claiming for herself the sexual freedom of Propertius' Tarpeia, the traitorous (her treason motivated by love, that is) Vestal virgin who "herself picked the day she wanted for her marriage!" (*nubendique petit quem velit ipsa diem* Prop. 4. 4. 88).[58]

The ideal Dido here professes to follow is, of course, that of the conventional Roman *univira,* the woman who is married to only one man in her life. In spite of Augustus' later impositions on widows (and widowers) for remarriage, the ideal is alive and well around Vergil's lifetime – in official representations of women of high social standing. A striking example is provided by the same Propertius in a politically-correct, adulatory court poem (hierarchically minded critics have called it the "Queen of Elegy") on Augustus' deceased stepdaughter from his wife's earlier marriage. In it, Cornelia is represented defending her impeccable lifestyle before the judges of the underworld. But her approval rating is of course enhanced also by more worldly (and-more-than-worldly) 'judges': not only her weeping mother's, Scribonia's, praise and the city's lament but even Augustus' groaning (*gemitu Caesaris*) – yes, one could even see him, "the god", shed tears, *lacrimas vidimus ire deo* (4. 11. 55–60).

In addition to providing another pointer to the "god's" supernatural inviolability (historically cultivated during the two preceding decades through the claim of *maiestas* initially granted him and his sister) and to the aura steeped in which Vergil's *Aeneid* (and Aeneas) must be seen, Cornelia's plea specifically refers to her virtue of having stayed *univira*:

> On this stone let it be read that I have been married to *one* man <only>.
>
> In lapide hoc uni nupta fuisse legar.   11. 36, cf. 45f.

Historical hindsight may see involuntary irony when the poet makes Augustus think that Cornelia has lived "a worthy sister of his own daughter", *sua nata dignam vixisse sororem* (59), the corresponding "sister" being Augustus' daughter Julia whom he later exiled because of her licentious lifestyle – a reproach that, to a degree, Vergil will raise also against Dido (as well as against Aeneas, 4. 193f.; 211).

At any rate, Propertius' Cornelia is so sure of her reputation that she advises her daughter by saying,

> you, my daughter, born a model of your father's censorship,
> see to it that you, by imitating me, hold on to <only> *one* man!
>
> filia, tu specimen censurae nata paternae,
> fac teneas *unum* nos imitata virum!   11. 67f.

So, Vergil lets his Dido profess the highest (patrician) standard of Roman womanhood, on the one hand to show her struggle of holding herself up to the ideal of the *univira* (of course there has to be a considerable degree of moral worthiness for the concubine of the Emperor's ancestor), and on the other hand to demonstrate that her decision to give in to her love is definitely a conscious choice, made in full awareness of the applicable standards (no room here for the customary excuse of love's "demonic" force).[59] A further purpose is that Vergil's readers should not feel any doubt about the standard by which they, too, should measure the Carthaginian queen.

The last point is enhanced by the following advice given to Dido by her sister Anna who enumerates the arguments that might rationally as well as irrationally justify overthrowing Dido's "firm and unchangeable" decision (4. 15); among them is the point that Dido should not forego Venus' rewards, i.e. having "sweet children"; that the dead in their graves don't care (what an un-Roman thought!), etc. The political arguments point not only to the existing threat from brother as well as neighbors mentioned by Dido herself earlier (1. 563f.), but also to the military reinforcement a joined Trojan army, hers by marriage (*coniugio*) with Aeneas, would contribute to "Carthaginian...glory" (*Punica...gloria* 4. 49). The latter argument was not pronounced (but in all likelihood, as we showed, taken into account) by Dido when she offered the Trojans permanent settlement "side by side" with her own subjects. (Anna says more than she knows because her suggestion of proto-Romans serving under an African queen is, in terms of Augustan propaganda, to make contemporary Roman readers shudder in memory of very recent history: Octavian's fight against Antony and Cleopatra and their troops would come to their minds.) Anna's further point, that the Trojans have arrived with the gods' and especially Juno's blessing (again, she is unaware of her words' full meaning) who should be asked for indulgence with sacrifices, tips the scales of Dido's wavering mind "and dissolved her chastity" (*pudorem* 55, the key word of line 25): according to her own self-curse, Dido now implicitly condemns herself to the underworld shades (26), the decision of course being hers not Anna's.

Not unlike Herodotus' Croesus who believed he could bribe Apollo's oracle by repeated gifts, Dido, unmindful that she is asking the divine guardian of marriage to help break her loyalty to her first marriage by a new union, now makes repetitive sacrifices,

> above all to Juno (to) whose concern are the marital ties
>
> Iunoni ante omnis, cui vincla iugalia curae. 59

"With her own hand" (*ipsa*) "most beautiful Dido" (*pulcherrima Dido* 60 – how unbecoming her beauty!) pours from the sacrificial bowl, gapes over the opened breasts and consults the (still) fuming innards. The narrator leaves no doubt that her conduct is inappropriate. But unhappy (*infelix* 68; cf. 1. 712) Dido, afire (*uritur* 68) and in a frenzy (*furens* 69), roams through the city like a doe hit by the hunter's lethal arrow. (Did Aeneas aim at her intentionally – with his presents that, together with Cupid in Ascanius' shape, "moved" her 1. 714, or did he unwittingly cause her "wound", *vulnus* 4. 67? The reader is never told.)

Dido repeats the symposia, asks Aeneas again to tell of Troy's sufferings, hears and sees him whether he is present or absent,

> or she would hold Ascanius back on her lap, taken by his similarity with his father,
> attempting whether she might overcome ("deceive") the love she must not profess

> aut gremio Ascanium genitoris imagine capta
> detinet, infandum si fallere possit amorem. 84f., cf.76.

The point interesting for my investigation is here that the situation almost equals that in Book I when she holds Cupid/Ascanius (717–19) on her lap, the difference being that no attempt is made here by the poet to transcend the empirical sphere: no divinity is needed to account for Dido's desire to hold Aeneas' son on her knees.

Dido's moral decline is so thorough that she even abdicates her queenly duties and allows the construction sites in her city (once the essence of her pride) to lie idle.

It is significant for my thesis of Dido's empirical responsibility that Juno does not intervene until her 'victim' has on her own reached the state of no return:

> As soon as Jove's dear wife realized that she was in the grip of such a plague and that her reputation was not standing in the way of her frenzy,

> Quam simul ac tali persensit peste teneri,
> cara Iovis coniunx nec famam obstare furori, 91f.

she turned to Venus, mocking her that *two* gods (scil., Amor and Venus) had defeated *one* woman (93–95).

Action on the mythological level, we said, for the reader often indicates the historical and political dimension. So here: Juno's allegedly conciliatory suggestion to Venus, that a marriage of Aeneas and Dido would bestow on Venus' Trojan son the rule over Carthage, is deceptive. It would, if executed, turn the proto-Julian away from his destined goal in Italy (4. 106) and serve the goal of Juno, the rebel against Fate, of making *her* city the *regnum* over nations (1. 17ff.). That is, paralleling Dido's individual decisions and fortunes, we face a pivotal point in world history: here the future deadly struggle of the two mighty cities might have been *a priori* avoided and decided in pre-historical time in favor of Carthage – another insult to Roman ears. To what extent the concerns of Vergil's contemporaries are being touched upon here is perhaps not hard to determine. At any rate, Octavian's propaganda countered the Romans' fear of being subjected to an Alexandrian queen who financed and enabled a Roman triumvir's assault on his country (in the *Aeneid* duly condemned, 8. 685–88): Octavian, while only in his thirties, built his gigantic mausoleum on the Tiber (this, too, duly incorporated in a panegyric section of the *Aeneid*, 6. 873f.), ostensibly to show that he would not relocate the nation's capital to Alexandria but end his days residing in Rome.[60] Juno's proposal, dressed in mythological garb, might then also point to the undesirable alternative outcome of very recent history. But this lies in the realm of conjecture, from which my investigation wishes to abstain.

Since Dido no longer thinks of her reputation (4. 91), Juno's plan (smilingly endorsed by sly Venus: 'You are Jupiter's wife, it is your part to deal with the problem of his consent to the union of the two nations') is simple: on a hunting party bring Aeneas and love-sick (*miserrima* 117) Dido together in a tempting situation, and "I will join them in stable marriage" (126 – an intention fulfillment of which Fate will not allow) "and make her his very own" (this should please Venus, Juno thinks; cf. *Phrygio servire marito* 103). True to her unprincipled ways (see for instance her ungodly persecution of *pius Aeneas* 1. 19f.; 69f.), it is Juno, supposedly the divine guardian of marriage, who turns out to have less scruples than human Dido when abandoning the idea of the *univira* in order to bind the widow in a new, politically consequential, "stable" (*stabili*) marriage. The fate-defying plan of making Carthage into the world power at the cost of future Rome involves the divine level but far exceeds the parameters of mortal Dido's understanding (compare how Jupiter intervenes, so *fati nescia Dido* at 1. 299 cannot derail the fated course of history – but the decision will be completely Dido's own, made within *her* mental and intellectual framework).

On the morning of the hunt, Dido is broadly portrayed with all the accoutrements of splendid royalty (as is Agamemnon on the morning after his deceitful dream of victory in *Iliad* 2, but there the poet himself openly lifts the veil of specious splendor: νήπιος 2. 38). Her magnificent appearance has deceived many a commentator. While "the first of the Phoenicians" are waiting outside the palace, she herself hesitates (*cunctantem* 4. 133) inside. Why? Hardly because the poet wishes to give his audience a multivalent artful foreshadowing of her misfortunes-to-come.[61] The truth lies in Augustan diplomatic etiquette. As in Book 1 Aeneas did not make his theatrical entrance on the stage until his presence was expressly desired by the queen, so here Aeneas has to be the second to appear on the scene and join the waiting inferior monarch. This feature also confirms Dido's disgraceful condition: unable to wait any longer for the arrival of the man she loves, she finally (*tandem* 4. 136) gives away her queenly status to the proto-Julian by coming out before he arrives. Her conduct sets the scene for the proper (Augustan) encounter: being expected and waited for, "most beautiful" Aeneas, like a second Apollo (in Book 1, majestic Dido was likened to Apollo's sister Diana, that likeness being no more than a surface status now), comes to join her company as her *socius* and to join his retinue to hers:

> Ipse ante alios pulcherrimus omnis
> Infert se socium Aeneas atque agmina iungit. 141f.

Chapter 5

Austin's comment on 4. 142, "the two splendid figures join their companies into one", misses the decisive social nuance of the set-up.

During the hunt, Juno (also goddess of the clouds) causes the planned (122ff.) thunderstorm, and the two principal characters find themselves together seeking shelter in the cave Juno had picked (*speluncam...eandem* 165, cf. 124). The resulting union of the two lovers has caused considerable scholarly disagreement regarding the authenticity of this "marriage". But not only should the howling nymphs as bridesmaids and wedding torches in the form of lightning (etc.) make the reader suspicious of this underground substitute for a 'wedding' (after all, Dido knew from her first marriage to Sychaeus how a proper wedding is performed, 1. 345f.). Above all, one should not neglect that the union is created with the intent of preventing the birth and rise of the Roman empire. That intent alone, in the eyes of Roman readers, must assign this 'wedding' with all its eerie imitative features to the realm of pseudo-legality.

Besides, the poet validates this judgement in objective words pronounced by the third person narrator:

> That day as the source[62] was the cause of death, as the source the cause of misfortune: *for* Dido is neither motivated by appearance or reputation, nor does she any longer think of a stealthy affair: she calls it marriage, with this term she embroiders her guilt.

> Ille dies primus leti primusque malorum
> causa fuit; neque *enim* specie famave movetur
> nec iam furtivum Dido meditatur amorem:
> coniugium vocat, hoc praetexit nomine culpam.   4. 169–73.

There can be no doubt that *culpa* here means guilt. But it is no longer alone the guilt of adultery, i.e., of violating the ideal of the *univira*, which she feared to incur when falling in love with Aeneas (4. 19). If she actively mantles ("embroiders") the developed relationship by falsely assigning it the name of a legal union[63] instead of keeping it a "stealthy affair", her guilt in addition lies in her willful and open disregard for reputation (*fama* 170; cf. *famam* 91) and decorum required of her status as the queen *as well as* the widow of Sychaeus. So her guilt here has a double nuance. This understanding will be confirmed later when Dido accounts for her reasons for choosing suicide (550–52; see later on in this chapter). In the quotation above and in my translation I have put *enim* = "*for*" in cursives because the logical particle establishes the *reason why* Dido will decide she has to die: as usual, Vergil's logic is impeccable.

Dido's awareness of what she is (actively) doing has been hard to accept by her modern-day advocates. R. D. Williams turns the narrator's objective report on the weird circumstances of the 'wedding' into a subjective expression of Dido's contorted intellectual understanding: "...a parody of a wedding, *a hallucination* by which the *unhappy Dido is deceived*". "The 'lightning flashes' (*fulsere ignes*) *seem to Dido* to be wedding torches" (Williams *ad* 4. 166f.; my cursives). This exemplifies the textual distortions (and contradictions with earlier and, as we shall show, later passages) to which the commentator is led by his desire to confirm a bi-vocalist Vergil who would allow for an excusable Dido. So the commentator disregards the ensuing authorial comment in favor of the preceding fantastic description. *De facto* he, without any authorial indicator, transposes the narrative from the mythological level into the soul of a character. But the reader has not forgotten that Dido's 'wedding', after all, is arranged by Juno *after* the goddess has seen the mortal stumbling. The drive to ascribe to Dido's action, if possible, a high extent of passivity, is perhaps best exemplified by the analysis of Wlosok who first categorically declares: "For Vergil...love is an *incurable* disease, a destructive, demonic power by which a human being is *seized and possessed*."[64] Later, when dealing with 4. 169–72, she says:

> According to Vergil's opinion, by violating *pudor,* Dido has burdened herself with guilt in the not legalized love relationship with her guest, about which [scil. the *culpa*] however she *deceives herself* through the fiction of legal marriage. Thus her transgression has a moral and a noetic component, is moral guilt and *misconception* in the sense of *delusion*.[65]

"Dido, however, deceives *herself*": Really? Does the text here, at 169–72, not rather say that she consciously (see the active voice) abandons the status of a secret liaison and tries to deceive *her environment* by applying the label of marriage (a sort of damage control to benefit appearance and reputation, *species* and *fama*, cf.170)? Is the adjective "noetic" justified by the text, and does Vergil's wording suffice to add "misconception" and "delusion" to the precise moral term of *culpa*? The passage under discussion addresses the initial act in the area of public relations, regardless of the question whether Dido may perhaps have later on, in the course of the relationship, tried to persuade herself, too, that she was married to Aeneas. The 'noetic' defense of Dido, allegedly supported by reference to Greek tragedy and Aristotle's *Poetics*, fails since it bases itself on circular reasoning: 'Dido's love is tragic, so it can be illuminated in Aristotelian terms, which confirm that she is a tragic heroine.' The possibility that Vergil might *a priori* not have granted the queen of Carthage a tragic status, has been excluded *a priori*.

The story-line appears to back up my interpretation: it continues (4. 173ff.) by describing the *public* effect that Dido's disreputable act of "embroidering" her liaison has on the surrounding world. Evil *Fama* (Rumor), multi-tongued and sleepless, whose nature it is to grow while it ("she"), swift-footed and on nimble wings, is spreading, persistent messenger of truth as well as of fiction (190), "fills the nations with manifold talk", singing "alike of things done and not done" (190 – so the reader can verify): Dido deems it worthy to join herself to Trojan Aeneas (true); they spend the long winter together captured by shameful desire and unmindful of their kingdoms (true).

Right away Libyan King Jarbas, rejected suitor of Dido and son of Jupiter, out of his mind (*amens animi* 203), invokes the Almighty (*Omnipotens, scil. Jupiter* 220), even expressing doubts about the effectiveness of the son's rich offerings to his father's altars. Result: *Omnipotens* (who, after all, in good Stoic fashion, cannot have his eyes everywhere at the same time) now turns them to

> the royal walls
> and the lovers who are forgetful of their better reputation.
>
> ad moenia torsit
> regia et oblitos famae melioris amantis.   4. 220f.[66]

Jupiter, upset by what he now gets to see, sends his son Mercury to Carthage with strict orders for Aeneas. But he also includes words not intended for Aeneas but for the reader's ears, namely that Aeneas was rescued twice by his mother from Greek swords not to while away his time "in a hostile nation" (*inimica in gente* 235: historically speaking, the correct political coordinate) but for his imperial mission in Italy.

Rescued twice: the first time from Diomedes' attack before Troy (*Iliad* 5), the second time inside burning Troy (*Aen.* 2). As through the description of Aeneas' brave but unsuccessful fighting in the night of Troy's fall in Book 2, the poet's side intent here is to counter the impression that the Emperor's ancestor was a weakling or coward who had to be rescued by his unwarlike mother: such rumors (or even worse ones, cf. Turnus at 12. 15) do not know the fated intent of the rescue. Jupiter outlines the purpose of Aeneas' survival: to be the man "who would rule Italy, pregnant with empires and roaring with war, ...and would subject the whole earth under laws" (229–31). It is worth quoting R.D. Williams' comment on the passage: "This is one of the *finest* expressions in the poem of the Roman mission; first to conquer in war, and then to bring laws and civilisation" (my cursives) – testimony to two thousand years of Vergil's survival into European colonialist thought.

Mercury finds Aeneas, dressed up (*jaspis*-studded sword, purple cloak interwoven with gold) by "rich Dido", *dives...Dido* (263), supervising the construction work that was once supervised by the queen herself (1. 503f.). Clearly, the situation of luxury has seduced the homeless indigent.

The lover (or "husband", in Dido's terms, cf. 4. 171) acts at the bidding of his mistress. No wonder then that Mercury sarcastically, to drive home the point, addresses Aeneas as "wife-pleaser", *uxorius* (266; cf. Hor. *Od.* 1. 2. 19f.). The word *uxorius* here cannot, as some have taken it, be an indicator of Aeneas actually being married to Dido. That would mean that his later denial before Dido (4. 338f.) would be a cheap lie and that he could – conveniently for a certain school of readers – be portrayed as the *deserting husband*. Interpreters should take into account that the ambassador of Jupiter, guarantor of Rome's world rule, would never endorse Dido's interpretation of the relationship.

Another feature here is extraordinary, comparable to the way Apollo in Book 3 (94ff.) addresses Aeneas directly without an intermediary. Mercury's interference could easily be seen as reflecting the pangs of Aeneas' own guilty conscience (and, indeed, some of Mercury's arguments the hero will later before Dido present as his own, 351–55), but the narrative as well as Aeneas' later recollection (356ff.) is apt to remove any possibility of doubt in the god's actual appearance in this world before Aeneas' eyes. At this point this feature may appear to be in contrast with Jupiter's and Venus' attempts in Book 1 to influence Dido (and her guards), which are not verifiable in the natural world. I am inclined to ascribe this exceptional emphasis to the fact that Aeneas in the *Aeneid* has (semi-)divine status as son and grandson of divinities and is the chosen carrier of the will of fate that has to be executed by highest ordination. (His moral autonomy will be revealed in his strict obedience to divine orders.) There may also be a contemporary component insofar as descendant Augustus enjoyed similar privileges in his communications with Apollo, his neighbor on the Palatine hill, accessible from the imperial palace through a covered walkway. The exceptional real-life appearance of Mercury is convincingly explained by the fact that Jupiter "*himself...himself*", *ipse...ipse* (268; 270), ruler of the gods and the universe, is the sender of the orders, his orders even in part word-for-word – in epic breadth – repeated before Aeneas. At this pivotal point of world history (Rome or Carthage the future world ruler?) the mythological level has to be employed at full force. This persuasively contrasts with the rather cursory way in which earlier the dispatching of Mercury, purportedly to influence Dido and her guards, has been reported. When Mercury later once more appears to Aeneas, it will be 'only' in a dream (*in somnis* 557). Then, however, he does not bring a message from Jupiter but tries to wake up Aeneas, who, soundly asleep, apparently has already gotten over his separation pangs (he is unmindful of the fact that "a woman is always unstable, subject to change", *varium et mutabile semper / femina* 569f. – supposedly unlike a man such as Aeneas. The male

Chapter 5

chauvinism is apparently shared by Aeneas' men when from the sea they see the fire of her pyre, knowing "what a woman in a frenzy is capable of", *notumque furens quid femina possit* 5. 6).

Aeneas is stunned by Mercury's appearance but immediately obeys and

> burns to depart in flight and to leave the sweet country
>
> ardet abire fuga dulcisque relinquere terras. 4. 281

"Flight": he has to free himself from the 'imprisonment' (or 'enslavement') in "sweet" Carthage. But this does *not* mean that he intends to desert Dido without explaining to her the necessity he is placed under. On the contrary, in his loving concern for her he only wishes to find the "softest" hour when the inescapable news will least hurt "best Dido", *optima Dido* (291), who does not "expect so great a love to be broken", *tantos rumpi non speret amores* (292). Meanwhile, he asks his men (to their delight) to prepare the fleet for departure without revealing the true reason.

But Dido, "fearing everything safe", (i.e., safe on the surface: she is of course aware of her fictitious marital status) and informed by "the same wicked *Fama*" (298: the same monster that spread the rumor about her upgrading her relationship to 'marriage', 173ff.), anticipates what is going on and enters a state of Bacchant-like frenzy. Finally she addresses Aeneas at her own initiative (so preventing Aeneas from executing his intention of approaching her: the classic premise for a Euripidean altercation scene, including the dramatist's famous sigmatism, 305f.).

> Did you even expect, unfaithful one, that you can hide so great a crime and in silence leave *my* country?
>
> Dissimulare etiam sperasti, perfide, tantum
> posse nefas tacitusque mea decedere terra? 305f.

Of course, as the reader knows, she is mistaken in her assumption, pronounced in proud royal sovereignty (*mea...terra; cf. nostris inluserit advena regnis* 591).

Her tone quickly changes when she, "bound to die" (*moritura*), appeals to "our (mutual) love" and "the right hand given" (307f.). Given in a promise of marriage? For that the poet has not provided any indication or even confirmation to his reader. (Parallel are the handshakes given to 'fiancé' Turnus, 7.336, as Chapter 7 explains.)

> Even for Troy, your home, you would not, if it still existed, set sail in this the stormy season (310–13).

In ever more intensely moving words she infers: "Are you fleeing from *me*?" (*mene fugis?*) and implores Aeneas "by our marriage, by the marriage we entered upon" (why the imploring repetition? Why "entered upon"? Because she knows there is no formal "marriage"? 314ff.).

Because of *you*, neighboring rulers and my own people are hostile to me, because of *you* it is that "*pudor* has been extinguished" – a sentence she does not complete (scil., *a me*); later she will try to ascribe her moral breakdown to her sister's influence 549f.; cf. 55; it is grammatically not justified to replace the passive meaning of *extinctus* by "I have lost", as West does (320–26). Looking for guilt in others does not remove the blame from the wrongdoer (as she will later come to admit).

My guest (whom I can no longer address as "husband", cf. *coniuge* 324), to whose whim (my brother's? my rejected suitors'?) are you abandoning me death-bound? Claiming the role of a deserted Ariadne, she returns to the official-sounding language of her welcoming toast (*hospes* 323 ~ *hospitibus* 1. 731) while giving up the 'embroidering' (cf. *praetexit* 172) term that defines a lasting intimate bond, i.e., marriage.

Her speech ends on a note of pure despair and personal loneliness (it is quite credible that Vergil read this passage to Augustus *ingenti adfectu*, as Servius tells *ad* 323): "If at least... I had a tiny Aeneas playing in my court, who nevertheless [i.e., in spite of your physical absence] would bring you back by his face" (...I would not be so utterly alone and deserted) *saltem...si quis mihi parvulus aula/ luderet Aeneas, qui te tamen ore referret...* 327–29. The underlying idea is the same as in Book 1 when Cupid in Ascanius' shape stirs her feelings (715–22), or as earlier in Book 4 when she holds Ascanius back after a party, "captured by his likeness with his father" (84). Her emotions are totally centered on Aeneas.

Regarding Aeneas' reply it must be prefaced: in spite of its *agon*-like character the exchange, with its point-to-point rebuttal, should not be mechanistically milked for viewing Dido as another Medea (and Aeneas as another Jason). Too often Vergil could be shown to follow his own agenda even when availing himself of predecessors whose art he wishes to rival.

Aeneas' reaction to (and during) her speech? Under "Jupiter's admonitions", *Iovis monitis*, he does not move his eyes and suppresses his worrying emotion (*curam* 331, also the word for loving affection). He displays obedience to the highest Roman divinity's personally conveyed orders – an obedience that can hardly be subsumed under "Aeneas' fall from *pietas*"[67] (about Aeneas' empirically verifiable motivation, see later on). In Vergil's concept, there *is* a higher standard beyond the realm of human desires, a clearly stated fact one has to take into account if one wishes on Vergil's terms to judge Aeneas' reply, thought by some to reveal "the cold and formal rhetoric of an attorney".[68] *What offends modern sensibilities may be just what Vergil wishes his audience to appreciate.*

Chapter 5

That Aeneas will never deny what she has done for him nor ever regret to remember "Elissa", is in agreement with his words of everlasting gratitude "whichever lands are calling me", words spoken when she took in him and his companions (1.609f.) – hardly a "very different Aeneas" (Austin *ad* 335) then and now. That he addresses her as "queen", *regina* (334), is not a sign of cold-hearted distance but of respect owed the local sovereign. Even when not being in her presence, he thinks of her as "the queen" (*reginam* 283), and even in the underworld he will address her shade in this dignifying way (*regina* 6.460). His status in relation to her is both that of a paramour and, socially speaking, of an attendant or subordinate companion who only too willingly (cf. Mercury's rebuke *uxorius* etc., 265ff.) functions as her stand-in when she neglects her ruler's duties (4. 260f.). His feelings for her are deep, which however does not prevent him from being, by divine authority (as well as by his own conscience), called back to the path of duty without any undue resistance. To have entered a temporary liaison is by Roman standards hardly extraordinary, not even for a husband. But, as Vergil has prudently arranged his situation, Aeneas is 'between wives': his first wife is dead (no adultery involved for him as for Dido the *univira*), a fact confirmed to him by the appearance of Creusa's shade (2.788f.); in Roman good taste, Vergil has made Creusa personally predict her successor wife in Italy (*regia coniunx* 783, a possibility envisaged without any blame also by Cornelia, the *univira* of Prop. 4. 11). The serious potential objection, which might result from the admonishing presence of his father, the poet has circumspectly removed by the end of Book 3 (710): Anchises can appear to his son only in a dream (4. 351) or express his concerns *post factum* later in the underworld (6. 823). The poet has carefully set the parameters of Aeneas' erotic detour (Jupiter's blame concerns the shameful neglect of his political mission inherent in the affair, 227–31, not his conduct towards Dido).

Turning to his own behavior, Aeneas states two points first: she should not falsely (*ne finge* 338) accuse him of planning a furtive flight. In this he is correct: though he had ordered his men in silence (*taciti* 291) to prepare the boats for sailing, his motive for this measure was his loving concern for *optima Dido* (289), to whom he wished to broach the harsh but inescapable news as sparingly as possible, waiting for a "soft" hour, *mollissima fandi/ tempora* (293f.). This caring intent has been nullified by her early discovery of the goings-on. Second, the reproach of breaking their 'marriage': *never* (*nec...umquam* 338) has he performed the rites of a *husband, coniugis*, carrying the wedding torches. It was she, the reader recalls, who "embroidered" the affair, arbitrarily calling their subterranean union "marriage", *coniugium* (172), though she fully well knew how a formal marriage bond ('formal' even satisfying Roman standards) is established (1. 345f.). Aeneas has never entered into "this kind of contract", *aut haec in foedera veni* (339). So the claim she has put forward on a legally valid relationship (324) is in Aeneas' eyes without merit: 'no insurance contract – no damage claim'. It is not likely that by this time she has persuaded herself that her initial mislabeling reflects reality. Her constant distrust of anything "secure" (298) does not seem to support the interpretation of self-delusion (put forward, we saw, by Wlosok and others).

Aeneas' next point must come as a shock to her because his primary (*primum* 342) loving concerns (*curas* 341), if he were free to act on his own initiative, would be tending Troy and "the sweet remains of my loved ones" *dulcisque meorum reliquias* (cf. my discussion of *meorum* at 12. 947 in Chapter 2), and even Priam's palace would stand re-erected. "But now", *sed nunc*, Apollo of his home area orders him to go to Italy, i.e., Dido would not even be his second concern (not even his plan B, so to speak): *Italy,*

> this (here[69]) is my love, this is my country
>
> hic amor, haec patria est. 4. 347

Clearly, love is here being subordinated to country, causing Austin (*ad* 331–61) to state that Aeneas' speech is "the *Roman* answer to the conflict between two compelling forms of love" (my italics). But "Roman" is a partisan generalization performed by the 20th-century commentator who, trained in traditional imperial thought, equates "Roman" with "Augustan", to the exclusion of non-Augustan ("less Roman"?) voices. Propertius, poet of love elegies and contemporary of Vergil, who knew a lot about the growing *Aeneid* (see my *Prologue* to this volume and my *Propertius*, Chapter VII), and whose family had during the civil war suffered grievously from the party of Octavian the later Lord of the "Augustan Peace", frequently raises his voice to oppose the kind of position expressed by Aeneas. Should his stance then perhaps be labeled "un-Roman"?

Most significant testimony is perhaps Elegy 2.7,[70] where the poet says he would rather have his head cut off than betray his love and, forced by a (meanwhile repealed!) Augustan law to marry another woman, breed future soldiers for the country's triumphs. (Augustus had not long ago celebrated a *triple* triumph, and his marriage legislation was to emphasize its purpose as "for the sake of producing children", *liberorum creandorum causa*). Octavian may be great – in war (*in armis*), but defeated nations do not count in love (*in amore* 2.7.5f.; a frequently employed Propertian paronomasy). The loving individual, in contrast to the country's defeated enemy, is not subject to the Emperor's power: his is the freedom to choose death over subjugation. Love counts more than 'patriotism', than allegiance to the victor of the

Chapter 5

recent civil war, whose swords (*Caesaris enses* 1. 21.7) threatened the poet's family and are responsible for many civil war deaths, symbolized by the "graves of Perusia" (*Perusina...sepulcra* 1. 22. 3) close to Propertius' home area of Assisi.

One can see how an exclusive phrasing like "the *Roman* answer to the conflict between two compelling forms of love" is still steeped in a long European tradition whose origin was forcefully 'legalized' by Augustus and whose mythological blueprint was persuasively put into words and given perennial validation by his court poet. In Vergil's partisan underworld there are found, along with "the usual" criminals, also those "who pursued impious war and had no qualms deceiving their masters' hands", *quique arma secuti / impia nec veriti dominorum fallere dextras* (6. 612f.), i.e., probably runaway Roman slaves who joined Sextus Pompey against 'the country', i.e., against the 'pious avenger' of his "butchered" father (*R.G.* 1) as whom the murderous young Octavian presented himself during the civil war.[71] For poets of his own ilk Vergil reserves the "blessed locations", *sedesque beatas* (6.639), using the Augustan code words "chaste *priests*", *sacerdotes casti* (6. 661) and "pious seers who have sung poems worthy of Phoebus" *quique pii vates et Phoebo digna locuti* (663), i.e., poems worthy of the emperor's personal tutelary deity. For comparative evidence one need only look at Propertius' late (and flattering) elegy 4. 6, where the ([truly?] converted) poet has *Apollo* address the Actium victor as "the world's savior", *mundi servator* (37; for *vates*, see also lines 1 and 10 *ibidem*). The historical and mythological message of the *Aeneid* was for later times (and is still today) often made palatable by the posthumous Christianization of Vergil (the *anima naturaliter Christiana*) who in his 4th Eclogue predicted the birth of a child and could become Dante's guide in the *Divina Comedia*. The Christianization even extended to Vergil's Emperor, to whom, upon his consultation of the Tiburtine Sibyl, the Virgin and Child appeared on the Capitoline Hill – as still today commemorated there by a 12th-century altar in St. Helen's Chapel of the church *S.a Maria d'Aracoeli*.[72] Vergil's partisan world-view could without too much difficulty be absorbed into European societies' continuing imperial and hierarchical framework (see Chapter 8).

The outgrowths I selected above (and similar ones) might by now be locked up in the cabinet of History's curiosities, had not the traditional view of Vergil in the latter half of the last century rankled with an increasing number of (mostly young) scholars, not a few of them in opposition to America's war in Vietnam. They opposed the predominant Christian-European pro-imperial understanding of the Augustan epic and set out to discover a "second voice" in the *Aeneid*, i.e., a voice of *non-partisan, general* human compassion for the victims of Roman imperial expansion.[73]

(One may speak here of a continuing Christianization minus the imperial strain). By locating the counter-position to Augustan Vergil in Vergil's own work, they desired to eat their poet and keep him, so to speak – or, to say it pointedly: they were not aware that they were reading the sorrows of a Propertius (and other, non-conformist and mostly forgotten victims of the regime) into the partisan *Aeneid*. As Section 3 of Chapter 2 (on derivatives in Classical Studies, with special reference to Maphaeus Vegius) has shown, even Reception Studies have been – and still are – employed (i.e., alienated from their task or misused) to fortify an 'interpretation' that cannot be verified by a precise reading of the text's logic- (and rhetoric-)based organization. One can see why this escapist branch of Vergilian Studies must be interested in seeing the traditional Augustan (called "optimistic") Vergil as counterbalanced or even put to rest – a position that also entails disregard for the testimony offered by the poems of a contemporary Roman such as Propertius.

By the end of the 20th century, this fact-free (or, perhaps rather, text-free) "binarism"[74] of pro-Augustan "optimistic" vs. "pessimistic" anti-Augustan 'readings' (supposedly an "unanswerable"[75] antithesis) had even been illustrated through the binarism of pacifism vs. militarism – a position taken again with scant regard for surviving contemporary Roman testimony and its cautious opposition to the pro-Augustan political bias of the *Aeneid*, but again importing contemporary politics. Farrell cites the recent past of an allegedly parallel Cold War "binary logic of Manichean character".[76] He illustrates his approach to the contrast of pro- and anti-Augustan readings through his own rigid partisan self-identification: "…I am quite willing to declare myself a pacifist, but *I am not willing to go on arguing the point against my militarist friends: I want to talk about something else*",[77] using a rhetorical stratagem not infrequently embraced by scholars of the "pessimistic" side.[78] The 'argumentation' (whenever, that is, it exists) on occasion seems not dissimilar to present-day combat waged by Creationists against Darwinists. In particular the dogmatic refusal to present to the other side the arguments for one's position, by verifiable tools of textual interpretation, amounts to a declaration of intellectual bankruptcy.

Since in Farrell's 'pacifism' last century's scholarly controversy has come to a head, it is worth recalling a few facts. Vergil's "peace", of course, is often preceded by bloody conquest to the bitter end (i.e., death) for the "arrogant" (i.e. those who do not comply), while the submissive may find pardon, according to the stern message Anchises has for the Romans (*tu, Romane memento!*): *parcere subiectis et debellare superbos* 6. 853. (This is the predominant interpretation; see, e.g., *LS s.v. subiectus*, "submissive". The alternative, offered by *OLD s.v. subicio*, 5, takes the word as *p.p.* of "make subject", amounting to "fight the arrogant (i.e., the non-compliant) all the way [*de-*] to the end and spare them after subjection". The latter one is the version preferred by scholars who blame Aeneas for not pardoning Turnus, see Chapter 1). And Vergil's fate-like Jupiter has granted the Romans "empire without end" in time and space, *imperium sine fine dedi* (1. 279). For Aeneas this includes "*smashing* fierce people" (263f.) in Italy. The *Georgics* are crowned by homage to "great Caesar", *Caesar...magnus*, who strikes his lightning "in war", *bello*, around the faraway area of deep Euphrates, and who after victory, *victor*, gives laws across "*willing*" nations, *volentis* (how pleasant it must have been forcefully to come or return under Roman central control, taxation, and jurisdiction! 4. 560ff.).[79] And on Aeneas' divinely manufactured shield Augustus, after his triple triumph, is pictured sitting on the threshold of his new Apollo temple, accepting the homage of innumerable, multilingual, faraway, "defeated" (*victae*) nations (*Aen.* 8. 714–28). In an earlier chapter I have already pointed to Father Anchises' penchant for triumphant L. Mummius, "distinguished by slaughtered Greeks", *caesis insignis Achivis* (6.837). The sheer endless list of the *Aeneid*'s bellicose-cum-panegyric passages on its own makes it *a priori* hard to believe the tale of a pacifist Vergil, and to accept that "the debate...whether geopolitical goals should be pursued by military or pacific means"[80] has anything to do with a Vergilian context. The state of Vergilian studies makes one ever more urgently demand that denials of the pro-Augustan bias (which, as shown in Chapter I, reaches even into the partisan presentation of human compassion) be supported by a sound analysis of the work's coherent organization.

In the poems of Propertius there can often be found clearly-mouthed contradictions of his own panegyric concessions. In my *Prologue* I have already pointed to the opposition of the elegist's own preferences and Vergil's 'pleasure' of being able to sing of Octavian's Actium war (2. 34). One of the seemingly strongest pro-regime poems is elegy 3.4, where Propertius speaks in the garb of a priest blessing Augustus' troops when they are about to leave for a campaign against 'India' and Parthia, and asks Venus to preserve in eternity the descendant (i.e., Augustus) of her son (i.e., of Aeneas). Line 1 starts out "War (plans) God Caesar", *ARMA DEUS CAESAR* (*meditatur*). This is countered by a word play in the programmatic first line of 3.5: "Of peace, Amor is the god", *PACIS AMOR DEUS* (*est*), *PACEM VENERAMUR AMANTES*, "peace is what we lovers worship". And the poem goes on distancing the poet from any violent acquisition of war booty, instead delivering a diatribe against the ambitions of us humans who "connect new war to war" *armis nectimus arma nova* (3.5.12) and announcing for his poetry's post-love period enlightened scientific themes (no epic on Augustus!) through to the very end of his life. "But you who prefer war, bring home Crassus' standards [lost in Parthia 53 BC]!" (47f.) No such open distancing from Augustus' war and personal profession of peace can be found in the *Aeneid*, needless to say. One understands why promoters of a "pacific" Vergil have to suppress the contemporary evidence offered by 'un-Roman' (?) Propertius, the self-declared author of peace poetry (*quod pace legas* 3. 1. 17).[81]

Back to Dido and Aeneas! In her total dedication to her love, the queen has even run the risk of sacrificing her political achievement and will still be running it when she will consider (but then reject as not viable) accompanying departing Aeneas (4. 537–43). Her attitude is not so very different from that of the young love poet who, feeling victimized by the victorious party of the civil war, counts himself among those many who "have perished gladly in a long-lasting *love*" (*longinquo perire in amore libenter* 1.6. 27), and who contrasts with his friend, the regime-bound Tullus, whose "concern has always been the fatherland *in arms*" (*semper at armatae cura fuit patriae* 22): In the terms of powerless and regime-critical Propertius, Dido would be far more leniently judged than she can be by her partisan literary creator.

The contrast between Vergil's Aeneas and the young elegist is even intensified by what follows. It is as if Propertius' poem 2.7 has been written in response to the nascent *Aeneid*. After next asking Dido that she grant him the same political fulfillment of founding his own settlement in Italy that she herself has achieved in Carthage (347b–50), Aeneas continues by saying that, in his sleep, his father's troubled image is admonishing and frightening (*terret* 353) him. Also, the injustice he is doing to his dear (*cari*) son frightens him, whom he is "defrauding" of his "kingdom of Hesperia" and "the destined lands" (354f.). Aeneas makes clear to his lover that the political mission of his family's line (which, the reader knows, will in the far future extend to the Julians and to Augustus 1. 286–88) is more important to him than she can ever be. Pious Aeneas defines his life's task to be: serving in the family chain as the link between his father and his son.

Quite differently Propertius: upon assuring his lover that she is his only love and expressing his anxious desire that he be her only lover (to his sorrow, he can never be sure, almost like Dido fearing 'everything safe'), he states:

This love will be worth even more than the bloodline of my forefathers.

Hic erit et patrio sanguine[82] pluris amor.   2.7.20.

No stronger contrast can be imagined to Aeneas' statement (and his "*hic amor, haec patria est*" of *Aen*. 4. 347). Most poignantly expressed is Propertius' socially revolutionary position perhaps in the last couplet of the preceding poem (by some editors even read as the first couplet of 2.7):[83]

> Never will a wife, never a mistress take me away from you:
> You will always be my mistress, always also my wife.
>
> Nos uxor numquam, numquam seducet amica:
> Semper amica mihi, semper et uxor eris.   2.6.41f.

Philologists tend to classify statements like these as expressing no more than traditional sentiments of love poetry. But by suppressing and excluding the important ties to contemporary politics, one unduly limits the poet's voice (and the interpreter's task). When one-sidedly excluding Propertius' choice from the "Roman" answer to the dilemma of personal versus pro-regime commitment, one may perhaps think one is securing for the *Aeneid* space for the often-claimed "private" or "second" voice,[84] but one would do so at the heavy cost of silencing the historical 'private' voice of the victim of the civil war (however much he later may reluctantly have on occasion complied in order to keep audible his literary voice).[85]

There is also an aspect to Aeneas' self-defense that deserves mention for the *Aeneid*'s wider context. In earlier observing the unusual physical reality ascribed to the appearance of Mercury, I explained that the intervention of Rome's highest god, at the decisive point when the tracks are set for the future world rule of either Rome or Carthage, deserved an exceptional emphasis on the epic's mythological level. Does the divine intervention exclude a free decision on the part of Aeneas and make him a marionette pulled by the strings of Fate? This kind of question was earlier answered by us in the negative, and will have to be so again here.

After mentioning his first (*primum* 342) obligation to Priam and Troy, Aeneas had next (*sed nunc* 345) listed Apollo's orders. Asyndetically added to his following appeal to Dido's sympathy as a fellow-ruler and -colonist, he then extensively and emotionally bared his feelings of guilt (following him into his dreams) towards father and son "whom I am defrauding of his kingdom of Hesperia and the lands destined (for him) by Fate" (355). Undeniably Aeneas' conscience has for some time already, during daytime as well as by night, been burdened by the guilt of abandoning his family's fated mission. There can hardly be any doubt about the eventual decision that would result from this psychological process. In the given context, the (first) visit by Jupiter's messenger then amounts to no more than a final addition: "*Now even* (*nunc etiam* 356) the gods' messenger, sent by Jupiter *himself*"; "in clear daylight I saw the god with my own eyes"; "I swear" (etc.) – words spoken to convince Dido of the fateful inescapability of his situation: "Stop burning me and you with your laments – it is not by my own will that I follow the call to Italy" (360f.; he will stand by this statement even when meeting her shade in the underworld 6. 460.).

Aeneas' decision process falls into place following the pattern observed earlier: Jupiter's orders to Mercury to soften the queen's heart toward the arriving foreigners was preceded by Dido's longstanding admiration for Troy and Aeneas. Cupid had to share his slowly growing influence on the widow's feelings with the presents previously selected by Aeneas. Jupiter's Mercury now amounts to no more than a mythological-level add-on, awe-inspiring in appearance but crowning a long-running psychological development on the human level whose outcome appears in any case inescapable. For the reader who was impressed by Mercury's divine presence (apt for conveying the situation's historical significance) and by Aeneas' stunned original reaction, it comes as somewhat surprising that Aeneas in hindsight describes the god's effect as only the last step ("now even the messenger of the gods, sent by Jupiter himself", *nunc etiam interpres divum Iove missus ab ipso* 356).

An important conclusion must be pointed out: if Aeneas does not leave Dido voluntarily (361), this does not mean that he acts under heteronomy, i.e., under some influence he would not be conscious of (as the Phoenicians and Dido were initially introduced as acting unaware of Mercury's influence on them 1. 302–04). On the contrary, by letting him consciously obey Jupiter's orders, delivered "in bright daylight", and by making him, at the same time, follow the longstanding demands of his guilty conscience, Vergil has his hero act upon a freely given consent. Again, divine and empirical levels, though working toward the same end, are clearly separated so as to preserve human freedom and responsibility. This result is an important premise for answering the difficult question, reserved for the last chapter, how to assess King Turnus' war against the arriving Trojans.

It remains briefly to trace unhappy Dido's saddening downward spiral toward suicide, which has made many a reader, overwhelmed by compassion, overlook the moral component, so clearly stated by the author. Her first enraged reaction to Aeneas' defense speech is spiked with unfair accusations: no tears, no look or pity for her (370; but see his hard-won composure 331f.). Like a textbook Epicurean,[86] she ridicules his mention of Apollo, Jupiter, Mercury: "*That*, of course, is the business of the high ones, *that* concern troubles them in their state of tranquility" (379f.). The excited reference to divine imperturbability reveals the unbridgeable chasm between her and stoically depicted, duty-bound Aeneas. Pious Aeneas (*pius Aeneas*), though wavering under his love and desire to console her, nevertheless obeys the divine orders (*iussa...divum* 396). Later appeals, conveyed through sister Anna, he withstands like an oak tree battered by

Chapter 5

storms (441–49). Vergil repeatedly shows his hero's suffering and human warmth: in his Aeneas there is nothing of the cold-hearted divorce lawyer often imputed by modern readers.

Dido's guilty conscience manifests itself, among other occurrences, at night when she hears her rightful husband's voice calling her from the shrine she built for him, and her despair is revealed in her dreams of being, helplessly alone, pursued by Aeneas (457–73). Vergil, appealing to his audience's theater experience (the *Aeneid*'s narrator is always the reader's contemporary), compares her condition to Euripides' frenzied Pentheus and to Orestes, Aeschylus' demented matricide (as if she metaphoriclly killed Sychaeus?). Deciding to die, she deceives her sister about her true intention by pretending to free herself from Aeneas by burning on a pile the things Aeneas left behind, together with "the marriage bed on which I perished" (*lectumque iugalem, quo perii* 496f.). A last review of solutions possibly open to her (all must be rejected) ends in self-condemnation:

> Yes, die, as you have deserved, and end your pain with the sword!
>
> Quin morere ut merita es, ferroque averte dolorem.   547.

As you have deserved: we here see the same confession of guilt that can be observed in Turnus when he faces death from Aeneas' hand (*equidem merui* 12.931) – and, as an aside, that also defines another opponent of Aeneas, oracle-twisting Queen Amata when she commits suicide (12. 600; see Chapter 7). However, the "deserved" death Dido chooses for her transgression, though it may end her pain, will be judged excessive punishment (4. 696), and it does not detract from her greatness, which she herself is proud to see accompanying her to the underworld (4. 654).

Abruptly, she tries to put the blame for her condition on Anna, her sister – though admitting that her sister acted out of love for her: "You, *overcome by my tears*", *tu, lacrimis evicta meis*, you early on burdened me frenzied one with this misfortune and threw me before the enemy (*hosti*). "Frenzied", *furentem* (548): another implicit admission. Anna's political argument, that a marriage (*coniugio* 48) with Aeneas would strengthen Carthage, had provided the welcome pretext that fired Dido's love even more with the prospect of fulfillment. So allegedly it was Anna who "dissolved" her chastity, *solvitque pudorem* (55), i.e., the external, publicly displayed side of chastity, which Dido subsequently abandoned to the extent of calling her extra-marital liaison "marriage", *coniugium vocat* (172). The other aspect of violating her chastity, her potential betrayal of her husband Sychaeus, had been incurably battered already, in spite of her self-curse in case she should violate *Pudor* (24–29). And it is the latter aspect that she turns to now.

Lines 550–53 have been endlessly discussed by commentators, sometimes without sufficient regard for the overall context as reviewed above. The opening *asyndeton* should not be understood as a causal question ("Why was it not allowed me?" *CN*), but has logical function (Dido draws a conclusion concerning her conduct):

> It was not permitted, then, outside marriage to lead my life
> without blame in the way of a wild animal, nor to involve myself in such emotional pains.
> (For) the faithfulness promised to the ashes of Sychaeus has not been kept.
>
> Non licuit thalami expertem sine crimine vitam
> degere more ferae, talis nec tangere curas;
> non servata fides cineri promissa Sychaeo.   4. 550–52

Dido, "who feared all things safe" (*omnia tuta timens* 298), must now realize that the big lie about her "marriage" to Aeneas (172) has fallen apart, and concludes that she deserves blame (*non...sine crimine*): the life of an animal of the wild who chooses her mates freely, without regard for the bonds of human convention, is not permitted to her. The words *non licuit* acknowledge the general moral law and are not to be watered down by an addition to the manuscripts of the words "*per te*" (Austin: "You [scil., Anna] would not let me"). The above interpretation of *thalami expertem* would be unacceptable to Williams (see *ad loc.*), because it would be "contrary to Dido's *convinced view* that she was not out of wedlock" (my cursives). Is Dido really "convinced" that her act of "embroidering her guilt" by "calling it marriage" (172) has changed reality? Why then her constant fear? Williams must be listed together with those (I earlier mentioned Wlosok) who seek a degree of innocence for 'their' Dido – who hardly is Vergil's. And so must Austin (*ad loc.*), who "cannot think that Dido is concerned with indicting her passion for Aeneas as adulterous." But for him, she now also is "almost delirious". Above all, it must be acknowledged that "marriage" (*thalami*) here does not refer to her animal-like (cf. 550f.) liaison with Aeneas but to her unbreakable marriage to Sychaeus.

The logical *asyndeton* at 551/52 presents a causal brachylogy (confirming my reading of 550–51): 'my behavior has not been blameless, *for <it entailed that>* the faithfulness promised to the ashes of Sychaeus has not been kept.' "Promised to the ashes of Sychaeus". This means that Dido has come full circle, returning to her initial proclamation of the (Roman, as we showed) *univira* ideal: the man who "as the first (scil. Sychaeus) joined me to himself...is to keep it (scil., my love) and hold it safe with himself in the grave" (4. 29). At that time she called Jupiter's lightning upon her head in case she should violate "your laws, o *Pudor*" (24–27). We then said that by

Chapter 5

this self-curse Vergil ensures that the reader views Dido, when entering upon the liaison with Aeneas, as being *fully aware that she is guilty of violating the moral standard pertinent to her personal situation.* She is showing undeniable greatness and consistency when she now acts upon the terms of her self-curse. (But of course, a mistress of the proto-Julian has to display a certain degree of greatness to be worthy of his companionship – especially so since many a contemporary reader may feel reminded of another African queen who more recently played a similar role in the life of the Emperor's adoptive father. She likewise, according to the official version accepted and spread by Augustan poets, chose a heroic ending).[87]

Her broken promise may for Vergil's contemporaries even be an example of the *fides Punica* that is given such a prominent role in Livy's nationalistic infotainment books. This would go well together with her increasing de-humanization once she, now hate-filled, has confessed the impiety of her actions (*facta impia* 596): not only does she predict eternal war between the two nations and the coming of her avenger (i.e., Hannibal, 624), thus fulfilling the political *telos* of Book 4; she also wishes she could have torn to pieces Aeneas' body and dispersed its parts on the sea (as Medea did to her brother Apsyrtos), and even have killed Ascanius to serve his flesh to his father (another Thyestes' meal, 600–602). Vergil has picked, as his models for Dido's revenge desires, from the most exquisite examples of criminal cruelty known from Greek literature. Adding her vain wish to have extinguished by fire Aeneas, Ascanius and the whole race (605f.), one wonders if Vergil wanted to paint Dido as a figure who, once his influence is gone, could be as excessive in her hatred of Aeneas as earlier in her love of him. This consideration appears endorsed by the generic characteristic pronounced on the divine level by the same Mercury when he now, *deus ex machina*, in a dream visits Aeneas. The guileless Trojan hero is soundly asleep after preparing for departure, apparently far from concerned about any ambush or dire crime (*dolos dirumque nefas* 563) planned by his former lover: "A woman is unbalanced and always changing", *varium et mutabile semper femina* (569f.) – a lesson *pius* Aeneas, stable in his own mindset (!), is apparently learning only now in his – also empirically explainable – dream... (But the Trojans, when from the sea they look back and see the smoke rising from Dido's pyre, do know "what *a woman* in rage is capable of when a great love has been desecrated" 5.5f.; Vergil's male chauvinism accompanies his Dido beyond her life's end.)

We come to the end of Book 4 and to Dido's death. Two arguments might conceivably point to her being free from guilt: the fact that at the orders of "almighty" (*omnipotens* 693) Juno, who takes pity (*miserata*), divine Iris can release Dido from the agony of her slow death; and one of the two reasons why (*quia*) Proserpina had not yet consigned Dido to the underworld:

> for because she was dying *neither* by fate *nor* by a death she deserved, but in misery before her (allotted) day
>
> nam quia nec fato merita nec morte peribat,
> sed misera ante diem   696f.

On the divine level, Juno might well feel pity when her anti-Roman plan to 'marry' Dido to Aeneas (103f.) has backfired with so cruel an outcome for her protégée; so she may understandably interfere on the human level by shortening Dido's dying process (that, empirically speaking, would end no differently anyway). But taking pity does not necessarily mean acquittal, and the pro-Carthaginian deity (who does not shrink from attempting to kill proto-Julian Aeneas and his men: *disice corpora ponto* 1.70) can hardly be taken to stand for the author's view. Juno's range of action is limited to alleviating Dido's passage to the underworld.

The reason why Dido is still alive lies outside Juno's prerogative: for (*nam*) Proserpina has not yet consigned her to the underworld because of (*quia, etc.*) objective facts (see the change of agent from Juno to delaying Proserpina and compare the final subjunctive in line 695 with the indicatives of 696–99). For Vergil's action line, Juno's mitigating intervention is necessitated by ancient belief that would temporarily withhold access to the underworld from those suffering a violent death "before their allotted date".[88] That the phrase *nec fato* (and, together with it, *ante diem*) must be seen as opposed to *merita nec morte*, is well illustrated by Gellius' (13. 1. 1–8) interpretation of our passage. He contrasts a θάνατος *naturalis et fatalis* (a natural and fated death) that is *nulla extrinsecus vi coactus* (brought about by no outside force), with that of Dido *quae mortem per vim potita est* (who achieved her death by force).

Which leaves us with the phrase *merita nec morte*, a death not deserved (earned). Does *it* acquit Dido from *any* guilt? Hardly, for it only shows that Dido is not guilty of a crime that deserves capital punishment: the phrase *morte...merita* is used of those punished for criminal acts. E.g., Ovid says that the assassins of C. Julius Caesar now lie in a death they deserve, *morte iacent merita* (*F.* 3.707), thanks to the first act of revenge rightly taken by Augustus in favor of his assassinated father. So Vergil here makes clear that Dido cannot be grouped with criminals like Caesar's assassins and those criminals who are cruelly punished in Vergil's Augustanized[89] Tartarus: for her offense amounts in no way to an equivalent of murder, and, indeed, the reader will find her in the underworld grouped not with the criminals but with those who died from wounds of love (6. 450).

What then can be meant by the phrase? Perhaps one should think of Dido's undeserved death in the contemporary terms of Augustan marriage legislation.[90] We know as good as nothing outside an elegy of Propertius (2.7). The poet laments about a law that would have separated him and Cynthia, had it not been repealed. Even if Propertius maintains that he would rather have his head cut off than marry another woman (2.7. 7f.), one will hardly conclude that disobedient lovers were threatened with the death penalty. The (later) criminalization of adultery, though including the possibility of public prosecution, apparently did not involve the death penalty either: the two adulterers could be punished by loss of property and find themselves on different islands. Too little is known of the law about curbing adultery (*lex Iulia de adulteriis coercendis*) of 18 BC and its alleged success in restoring the purity of marriages as it is touted by Horace in his *Secular Hymn*, produced at the Emperor's *Secular Games* of 17 BC. What one definitely can take away from the information available is that in the 20's BC, when Vergil was writing his *Aeneid*, the topic of marriage and marital fidelity was very much in the political air at Augustan Rome. My suggestion then is that Dido did not deserve to die because her offense was not considered a crime deserving capital punishment. The fact that she committed suicide even bestows on her the degree of greatness that Horace (grudgingly) concedes another African queen, the one eager to control contemporary Rome: suicidal Cleopatra, a "woman not humble" *non humilis mulier*, who "seeks to die more nobly" *generosius perire quaerens* (*O.* 1. 37. 21–32).

However, does the fact that Dido did not deserve to *die* rid her of the guilt she incurred by *knowingly* violating the obligation she owed her societal obligations and her status as the *univira*? Definitely not, as both the poet's analysis of her mental processes and resulting decisions has made overwhelmingly clear and the objective fact (of religious importance) that the wine she offers on the altars now turns into blood (*Aen.* 4. 455). We saw that Dido cannot be seen as "the truly tragic victim of powers beyond her control".[91] But what then to make of the extensive and sympathetic description of her pain and despair, which have influenced many a reader to believe that the narrator is siding with Dido? Here another principle of Augustan Vergil – a principle that will reveal itself again in Vergil's treatment of King Turnus (and also, of Queen Amata) – comes to light: '*compassion and pity – yes; acquittal – no!*'

One may, on the other hand, also think of the fact that the (in-) famous *clementia Caesaris* (decried already by Cicero as no more than a political slogan employed by Gaius Julius Caesar)[92] would of course not be granted by the father, or by the adoptive son, without an 'offense' that might be 'forgiven'.

Notes

[1] See Heinze 1965, 124 (continuation of note 1 from p. 123): "...liegt die Schuld in der Anknüpfung, nicht in der Auflösung des Verhältnisses." For Pease, Vergil intended "Aeneas' sin...to lie in his staying so long with her as he did" (45).

[2] Wlosok (1976, with more literature), especially 231–233 with note 28.

[3] Wlosok 1976, 229; see already Pease, 39: Vergil "conceived of her as the truly tragic victim of forces *beyond her control*" (italics mine).

[4] "sich...hinwegtäuscht"; "Dido täuscht sich über den wahren Charakter ihrer Verbindung mit Aeneas". Wlosok (1976) 242f.; cf. 247f. Later Dido allegedly "erkennt einen Irrtum ihrerseits" (247) and "gelangt...zur Einsicht in ihren Irrtum und ihre Schuld" (246). "Die Schuld ist jetzt ins Bewusstsein gelangt" (246, *ad* 4. 550–552).

[5] No word is said about Mercury's mission to provide Dido with *mentem...benignam* (1. 304). "Dido wird bei ihrem ersten Auftritt eingeführt als die *edle* Königin von Karthago: schön, gerecht und...*menschlich*" (Wlosok 1976, 238; italics mine); "die *gewährende* Fürstin" (op. cit. 234; italics mine).

[6] "Die Exposition dieser Tragödie ist im ersten Buche in der Ausführlichkeit gegeben, die ein Vorrecht des Epikers vor dem Dramatiker ist" ("The exposition of this tragedy is offered in Book 1 in the kind of detail which is the privilege of the epic as compared to the dramatic poet"). Heinze 1965, 119.

[7] For a more detailed analysis of Book 1 (used with modifications in the present investigation), see Stahl (1969). On the three *impulses* see especially 348.

[8] For Juno's inappropriate conduct, see Büchner (1961) c. 318.

[9] The case is different with Venus because she was the only access to divinity the Julian family traditionally could lay claim to. And even here, her connection to Jupiter is stressed by Vergil.

[10] That her descendant is said to be "from beautiful origin" (286) is a compliment to Venus (cf. 4. 227) and, indirectly, to the Julians.

[11] At the time of C. Julius Caesar's, the adoptive father's, death, there will be no occasion for her to feel *se-cura*. Regarding the identity of *Caesar...Iulius* at 1. 286ff. as *C. Iulius Caesar Octavianus Augustus*, see Stahl (1985) 340 (= note 46 to Chapter V). Jupiter's *tum* (291) answers Venus' *nunc* (249; 240).

[12] "It is made clear that the impulse which ended in tragedy came from something outside her control," Austin *ad loc.*, pointing to G. Williams, p. 367.

[13] Whether this applies also to the Phoenician guards on the beach we are not told. The ultimate decision rests, of course, with their queen.

[14] "Everything in the story could have happened without a god lifting a finger. Yet Vergil marks every crisis of the drama by the action of a god." Irvine (quoted by Pease, 51, n. 398) *ad* 4. 90–128.

[15] Later on in his speech (541f.; cf. 526), Ilioneus will invoke divine law for the protection of the shipwrecked. Precisely as in Ilioneus' later speech before King Latinus in a parallel situation (see Chapter 7 below), Vergil maneuvers the Trojans' prospective hosts into a potential position of inhumane impiety, should they decide not to accede to the newcomers' requests for help. The reader, his own compassion having thus been channeled into a pro-Trojan direction, will hardly make the rational connection that Dido unwittingly seals the fated destruction of her nation at the hands of Rome (1. 22).

[16] In a chiasmus, the following line (568) refers back to the earlier-mentioned ubiquity

of knowledge about Troy (*quis...nesciat*, 565): nor is our Tyrian city so far out of this world that we would not have heard of you (568). One should not be surprised that Dido uses terms like "Hesperia," "fields of Saturn," and "the territory of Eryx" (569f.) in a context where she wishes to display the Phoenicians' knowledge of geography.

[17] Austin's comment (*ad* 303, quoted earlier) "that the impulse which ended in tragedy came from something outside her control," should now be modified. Isn't it (when viewed from the human perspective) rather so that natural human behavior can be here depicted as an integral factor of a divine plan?

[18] See LS *s.v. et*, II. H: "To connect an idea as either homogeneous or complementary to that which precedes," etc. In line 572 the second nuance applies.

[19] cf. *laeta*, 416, and see Stahl (1969) 359 (establishing the cause-and-effect sequence); also 352f. (on Venus' sequence of moods in Book 1, which renders her more 'human' than divinely tranquil).

[20] Dramaturgically parallel is the information Dido receives about Aeneas from Ilioneus, in addition to what she has learned in earlier years: so both royal characters have been prepared for each other when they, at the climax of Book 1, finally meet face to face.

[21] For the pluperfect meaning of imperfect *condebat* (447), cf. *vastabat* (470 and 622).

[22] It seems best to take *Pygmalionis* as a genitive of possession: as king (346f.) of the country, he automatically is the owner of the treasures hidden in its ground.

[23] I owe this insight to Dr. J. Heverly who drew my attention to 4. 241: Mercury's winged sandals carry the god "side by side with the rapid wind", *rapido pariter cum flamine portant*. Numerous parallels can be cited from the *Aeneid* itself. In 2. 205 the two snakes glide side by side toward the shore, *pariterque ad litora tendunt* (cf. 10.222). 3.560 emphasizes the cooperation of the men rowing in unison side by side: *o socii, pariterque insurgite remis*. At 10.865 Mezentius predicts to his horse Rhaebus their joint death (side by side): *occumbes pariter*. "Side by side victors and defeated slew and fell, *"caedebant pariter pariterque ruebant/ victores victique* (10.756f.; cf. 11. 673; 8.545). See also *pariter gressi* (they walked "side by side") 6.633.

[24] E. Fraenkel 1954, 158.

[25] Austin *ad* 1. 572. Nor does her invitation show "a charming diffidence".

[26] Austin 1971, xviii.

[27] See later on in this Chapter and, for details of Propertius' unconventional position, see Stahl, 1985, Chapter 10.

[28] Miss M. Hubbard pointed out to me that Vergil uses the simile in a non-traditional manner: it is not so that a mob is likened to the sea but the winds are the mob here.

[29] Pöschl 1964, 38, where he assumes "dass im Neptungleichnis ein natürlicher Vorgang durch einen politischen gedeutet wird". The *princeps rei publicae* with whom Pöschl operates is actually not mentioned by Vergil.

[30] See Stahl (1969) 348.

[31] For *primo aspectu...deinde*, 1. 613f., see Stahl (1985) Chapter 2, note 12 on pp. 311f. (directed against Austin's "it was her first sight of Aeneas"). More material is discussed in the preceding notes and on pp. 26–28 in Stahl 1985.

[32] No names are mentioned. (Those of Achilles or Diomedes would hardly support the picture.) As is his manner in cases lacking literary or historical documentation,

Vergil assigns prominent 'Julians' non-specific (or even invented) military prowess. Cf. 3. 286–288 and Stahl 1998, 67f. ; 6. 879–881.

[33] Though occasionally close to being formulaic, the juxtaposition *quare agite* (or *age*) has its full justifying force also at 7. 130 and 429.

[34] On the topic of "direct contact between hero and supernatural" see also Webb (1978–80).

[35] Wlosok (1976) 239 (my translation): "Für Vergil" "die Liebe" is "eine zerstörerische, dämonische Gewalt, von der der Mensch ergriffen und besessen wird."

[36] Austin *ad* 1. 303.

[37] See Stahl (1969) 350f. with notes 1 and 2 on p. 351; Austin's assumption ("The poet in Vergil allowed him to ignore the practical problem", etc.) at this point perhaps confuses "poet" and "politically engaged writer."

[38] The name of Argos is of course closely associated also with hostile Juno, who had waged the war against Troy *pro caris...Argis*, 1. 24; cf. 7. 286f. In Chapter 7, we shall see that misguided Queen Amata falsely believed that Turnus' Mycenean background might qualify him for the position of her daughter's fated husband.

[39] For some of these restrictions, see Heinze (1965) 123 with his note 1.

[40] On the similarity of the opening scenes of Books 1 and 7 see already Büchner 1961, 372–374.

[41] Placing Anchises' golden vessel next to those of King Priam is another case of parasitic publicity: the reader never learns how and by what Trojan right Anchises' son, Aeneas, received the title *rex*, – his 'right' (by default) being that he is the family's only ranking survivor – except for resigning Helenus. See Stahl (1998) 44–46.

[42] *OLD s.v. venenum*, 2, assume here (as they do at Propertius 2. 12. 19) the meaning "poison", "w. ref. to Cupid's arrows." However, Amor will *not* (as does Eros in the *Argonautica* of Apollonius Rhodius) use an arrow. Rather, he is supposed to influence Dido *by being the boy* Ascanius. This is the meaning of *ut* (685), introducing an intended effect of his disguise. *LS* are right (*s.v. venenum*, 2. b), listing for our passage "charm, seduction"; to *veneno*, they add: "i.e., *amoris*." At Propertius 2. 12. 19, a reference to Amor's arrows (assumed by *OLD*'s listing, *l.c.*) is highly doubtful. *LS*, perhaps more appropriately, list it, too, under "charm, seduction."

[43] In view of Venus' irrational, changing moods in Book 1, it is not advisable to take her panicky accusation of Dido as an objective indication by which the poet would intend to give his reader insight into any sinister motives harbored by the Carthaginian queen.

[44] Heinze (1965) 122; 124.

[45] Venus' words "for not more than one night," *noctem non amplius unam* (683), must not be misunderstood as perhaps pointing to the surprisingly short period of time within which Cupid will accomplish his task. No, Venus, who has submissively been approaching her son, wants to make her request palatable to him by pointing out how *little* this task will take of his precious time. The fact that she projects it can't be done in less than one night supports the argument made in the text above for gradual and empirical development of Dido's feelings for Aeneas.

[46] Servius, referring to Anacreon for the metaphor of "drinking" love, points to the sympotic context (instead of wine, Dido drinks love); he explains *longum* (749) as either "over-ripe" or as "not to be ended except by her own death", i.e., life-long.

Chapter 5

At 3. 487 *longum...amorem* refers to Andromache's lasting affection for the boy Ascanius. Austin settles on "drinking in long draughts of love."

[47] On the Stoa in general, see A. A. Long's survey (1986, Chapter 4, for the non-specialist); still useful for the classicist is M. Pohlenz' chapter on "Die Stoa in Rom" (1947, 257–76).

[48] Heinze 1965, 295; cf. 292: "An undisguised confession of Stoic pantheism cannot be expected <to appear> in the *Aeneid*" ("Ein offenes Bekenntnis zum stoischen Pantheismus ist in der Aeneis nicht zu erwarten.") My translations. The translators of the 1993 English edition seem to have mixed up German "offen" (here = "undisguised") with "öffentlich" ("public").

[49] For further examples and discussion, see Heinze 1965, 295f.; Heinze, perhaps the most 'pro-Stoa' among (many) interpreters, quotes Seneca, *N. Q.* 2. 37, where the gods are said to have left certain things open so they can provide a positive outcome if mortals are approaching them in prayers: *quaedam a diis immortalibus ita suspensa relicta sunt, ut in bonum vertant si admotae diis preces fuerint, si vota suscepta.*

[50] For the Stoic features of Aeneas, see, most forcefully among many voices, Heinze 1993, 240f. and *passim*.

[51] Most sarcastic on this point is probably Grönbech (1953, 37): Aeneas "goes through events with a strange heroic obstinacy of a mule... What is destined to happen, does happen, and Aeneas is always present." ("...geht er durch die Begebenisse mit einer seltsamen heroischen Maultier-Hartnäckigkeit... Was geschehen soll, geschieht, und Aeneas ist immer mit dabei.")

[52] Long (1971) 189; cf.176. On the likelihood that Chrysippus' reconciliation of all-pervading fate and moral responsibility took place "at the cost of confusion generated by his ambiguous use of the idea of cause", see Inwood (1985) 70.

[53] Long (1971) 193.

[54] On the aspects of contemporary politics that motivate Vergil in his "peopling of the underworld", see Powell 2008,133–47.

[55] *Cura* (4. 5) closes a compositional ring back to *cura* (4. 1) which has by now been explicated for the reader.

[56] or of her dream, if *insomnia* is a poetic plural.

[57] One may compare how agitated Aeneas, when frightened in a situation of his waking life, *terrent...suspensum*, 2. 728f.

[58] On Propertius' sympathy for the straying Vestal virgin (whom he in the poem's setting dutifully condemns) see Stahl 1985, Chapter XII.

[59] Wlosok; Pease.

[60] See von Hesberg 1994, 55 (but he overlooks Vergil's tribute to the mausoleum).

[61] Segal (1990, 1–12) misses the precise obvious reason – in itself fraught with enough grave consequences – for Dido's hesitation, while extolling that Vergil "can condense many meanings into a small compass" (1) and while filling in the story's "gaps" and "indeterminacies" (12) of Vergil's "complexity" (12).

[62] Austin translates *primu*s by "in the beginning", pointing to what he labels as "adverbial" use of the word. Cf. 1. 1 and 613; add *Prop*. 1. 1, with Stahl 1985, 26ff.

[63] On the *de facto* frequent interchangeability of *conubium* and *coniugium* in different cases, apparently for reasons of meter, see Austin ad 4. 126.

[64] "Für Vergil ist...die Liebe eine *heillose* Krankheit, eine zerstörerische, dämonische Gewalt, von der der Mensch *ergriffen und besessen* wird." Wlosok 1976, 239 (my cursives).

[65] "Dido hat nach der Meinung Vergils durch die Verletzung des *pudor* in dem nicht legalisierten Liebesverhältnis zu ihrem Gast Schuld auf sich geladen, über die sie sich aber durch die Fiktion des Ehebundes hinwegtäuscht. Ihre Verfehlung hat somit eine moralische und eine noëtische Komponente, ist sittliche Schuld und Irrtum im Sinne der Verblendung." Wlosok 1976, 242.

[66] The reader may ask here: Was perhaps the possibility that Jupiter might have his eye on Libya the motive for his fate-defying consort to choose a subterraneous place for the encounter of the two lovers? Vergil does not tell us, but it would fit the circumstances.

[67] Monti (1981) 78.

[68] Page, xviii.

[69] For *hic* possibly being an adverb here, cf. 7.122. But within the given political context it hardly means that Aeneas wishes to point to his prophesied future wife in Italy, as G. Knauer orally suggested to me. For *hic* in the meaning of our "there" see Chapter 6, Excursus 3.

[70] A thorough discussion of this programmatic elegy and its relation to the *Aeneid* is found in Stahl 1985, 140–55.

[71] See Powell 2008, 136; 139; 141. Norden's huge but historically silent commentary has nothing but stylistic observations to 6.612f.

[72] Rich information on the Christianized Augustus may be found in Dahlheim's *Augustus* (see especially pp. 360–84); pertinent material also in Tanner's *The Last Descendant of Aeneas*.

[73] A very brief account sketching the two scholarly camps may be found in Stahl 1990, 177–81. See also the surveys, e.g., in Harrison 1990, Glei 1991, Perkell 1991, and my own review of some pertinent tendencies in Vergilian criticism in Stahl 1998 A.

[74] Farrell 2001, 19, n.15 uses the term binarism.

[75] Farrell 2001, 23.

[76] Farrell 2001, 17.

[77] Farrell 2001, 23. (My italics).

[78] The evasive scheme runs like this: 'One could argue against scholar X's thesis (but I am going to turn somewhere else...)'. See, for instance, Thomas 1998, 273.

[79] On the alleged 'happiness' experienced by the recipients of Roman jurisdiction, see Stahl 1985, 83–87.

[80] Farrell 2001, 19.

[81] For details on Propertius' pacifist position see the excerpted chapter in Stahl 2012, 235–72 or *Propertius* 1985, Chapter VI.

[82] In my *Propertius* (1985, 152) I explain why the manuscript reading *sanguine* is correct (as compared to modern extra-contextual conjectures).

[83] On Prop. 2.6.41f., see Stahl 1985, 144f.

[84] Probably most vociferously claimed by Parry (1963) and Lyne (1984; he later even came up with "further voices in the *Aeneid*", 1987).

[85] See Stahl 1985, Chapters XI and XII on Propertius' slow surrender.

[86] On Dido's Epicurean tenets, see also Pease 36f.

[87] For a suspicion about Cleopatra's 'suicide', see A. Powell 2013, 184–95.

[88] Normally the souls of those prematurely killed are barred from entering the underworld until the time allotted them by fate is fulfilled. For ancient traditions of classifying violent deaths and assigning the shades in the underworld their appropriate

Chapter 5

locations see Pease *ad* 4. 696 and, especially, Norden 1957, 11–13. Though in general following inherited classifications, Vergil, as often observed by us, so here breaks the mould for his own purposes. To reunite Dido in the underworld with her former husband, he allows murdered Sychaeus' soul to enter the "mourning fields" of perished lovers instead of joining those violently killed (see Norden *ad* 6. 442). That is, Vergil upholds the Roman value system beyond this life by reuniting Dido with her former (rightful) husband (in mutual love!), in this way restoring the status that Dido as a *univira* should have observed:

> coniunx...pristinus illi
>
> respondet curis aequatque Sychaeus amorem. 6.473f.

[89] See Powell 2008, chapter 4, on Vergil's criminalization of Octavian's civil war enemies.

[90] On the scarcity of chronologically-reliable information about the tendency and effect of Augustus' marriage legislation see the *ad hoc* survey in Stahl 1985, 142–44.

[91] Pease 1935, 39.

[92] For instance, "I am afraid this whole 'clemency' is being accumulated only for the purpose of that (imminent) cruelty", *metuo ne omnis haec clementia ad unam illam crudelitatem colligatur, Att.* 8.9a.2; "this man's tricky 'clemency'", *huius insidiosa clementia, Att.* 8.16.2.

PART II
CHECKS AND BALANCES OF A LITERARY INTERPRETATION: POLITICAL DETOURS OF POETIC TRAVEL ROUTES

6

BEFORE FOUNDING LAVINIUM, AENEAS INSPECTS THE SITE OF ROME (*AEN.* 8)

(1) Introduction: Political Stop-overs on Aeneas' Travels

Any reader is of course free to form his or her personal opinion and understanding (his or her "reception") of the epic. But the scholar who interprets Vergil for a modern-day audience is under obligation to verify and explain the *Aeneid*'s message by observing, analyzing and respecting clues which the author has embodied in his work to indicate its purpose. (Scholars of course have a right to state their agreement or disagreement with the author. But, while giving the reasons for their position, they will always try to separate clearly their position from the interpretation proper.) To do justice to the author's priorities, it is still necessary to view "*Vergil's Aeneis im Lichte ihrer Zeit*", in the light of its own time, as an investigation of 1901 (one still worth reading today) put it.[1] The concern that our historical approximation may never be complete does not release us from the obligation to undertake our best effort.

Vergil's Augustan position can be exemplified directly by reference to programmatic passages such as Jupiter's prophecy of Augustus' rule in Book 1 or Vulcan's fate-informed pictorial decoration on Aeneas' shield in 8. It can also be demonstrated more indirectly from the different ways in which the *Aeneadae* and their Greek, Carthaginian or Italian counterparts are characterized through their conduct. Analysis of plot-line adds another helpful and fairly reliable tool. Chapters 1 through 5 provide examples hereof. But it is also in this field of literary interpretation that scholarship has been led to diverging results, sometimes setting contemporary theory against the epic's dramaturgy or against its divine prophecies, and thus arriving at a position which attributes contradictory perspectives or "voices" to the poet, even denies him his intention. It is good to recall that the problem is a modern one. Ancient commentators, from Donatus to Servius, never found any reason to doubt Vergil's loyalty to Augustus.

For the reader who feels discomfort in the face of such divergent interpretations, and who has not been wholly (or even partly) convinced by the argument in the five preceding chapters, it will be a welcome realization that there exists a fourth area, besides programmatic prophecies, character depiction, and plot organization, which allows verification of the epic's original political message; here, scholarship proceeds by reference to hard evidence. The area in question is mainly that of archaeological remains (though written evidence from outside the *Aeneid* is, of course, not excluded). Yet, since Vergil does not always refer by name to what was clear to his contemporary reader, this dimension requires painstaking registration of the historical monuments (and, occasionally, of historical events as well) to determine the role which they play in the poem's design. The goal of my undertaking is purely literary. Apart from a very few cases, no claims are made in this Chapter of new findings or contributions to existing controversies in the field of archaeology. The purpose will be considered achieved if the effort is deemed worthy by readers who desire independent confirmation of the *Aeneid*'s overall tendency.

Methodologically speaking, it will be worth the effort, too. A road is being opened to greater objectivity if one investigates the use the *Aeneid* makes of those contemporary stone monuments which archaeologists often refer to under the name of "the building program of Augustus." If it turns out that the epic supports the ideological aspects of this program, then an independent measurement has been found by which the methodological quality of a literary interpretation may be tested.

In a 1998 study, entitled "Political Stop-overs on a Mythological Travel Route", I showed that Aeneas' seemingly Odyssean travel route alludes to political facts of the author's own time. Thus, the fact that Aeneas and his men feel (temporary) relief upon arriving at Actium when they have escaped from Greek territory, is based on the fact that they have now left the territory held by Antony during the civil war. That nearby they practice "inherited" (i.e., Trojan) athletic contests (called by the Greek word *palaestra*!), supplies the mythical precedent to Augustus' splendid revival of the Anactorian games in his newly founded "Victory City" (Nikopolis). That Aeneas leaves behind an arch (?) and, sign of a victory (not recorded in the *Iliad*), attaches a shield to the posts of the edifice, supplies the mythical precedent for Augustus' gigantic Actium victory monument (the largest monument he built outside Italy) as well as for the *clupeus virtutis* (accorded Augustus by the Senate and set up on display in the senate house) and for the shields, evidenced for us on coins, with which he decorated both his Actium arch on the *forum Romanum* and his mausoleum. That Aeneas leaves behind an inscription (the only time he does so in the whole epic) on his victory monument predates the inscription his greater descendant set up on his own victory monument, declaring himself savior of the republic. The shield Aeneas affixes to his memorial also responds to the decorations of Augustus' Nikopolis monument, i.e., to the huge rams taken from Antony's defeated fleet affixed to it; they were echoed on the *forum Romanum* by the smaller Actium rams, set up by Augustus in front of the new *Divus Iulius* temple opposite the republican *rostra* from the battle of Antium. And so on.

From the precedents located in the mythical time after the Trojan War, the reader is to conclude that the achievements of Augustus are preordained. It is important to see that it is not the historical moment of the Actium victory (as praised at the end of Book 8) which is important to the poet here, but the way in which the Actium battle is being memorialized and eternalized by the victor in the twenties BC. I would confidently assert that by reference to the Augustan monuments the pro-Augustan bias of Aeneas' travel route has been safely established: Vergil blows the horn of Augustan propaganda.

But, of course, this kind of approach is itself not uncontested. D. Fowler (1998, 155f.) maintained that grounding an interpretation on public monuments of Augustan Rome is a (vain) attempt at "escape from the shifting sands of textuality" and, in general, that the use of parallels depends on "what one *wants to do with them*" (my italics*).* Yes, but what if the interpreter has no biased intent and does not want "to do" anything with parallels except to find out what the references in the text mean? Obviously that would have been hard to accept for Fowler, a committed polysemy-seeker, who was also able to discover that, on the occasion of pious King Latinus' oath (12. 198), "Vergilian ambiguity...celebrates [*sic*] Latin duplicity" (note 36).

If an interpreter's results agree with Vergil's use of (and perspective on) contemporary stone monuments, then the method employed can be called commensurable with the epic. If not, we may feel that the interpreter has bitten on stone.

Another case in point is the meaning one can or cannot extract from Aeneas' visit at the site of future Rome in Book 8. To prepare us for the investigation, it is useful first briefly to look at the Book's seemingly erratic overall movement.

Chapter 6

(2) A Twisted Plot-Line: Going up the River to Reach the Coast

Threatened by the alliance of Rutulians, Latins and other Italians under Turnus' bloodthirsty leadership, Aeneas, guided by the advice of Father Tiber (8. 49–56), turns to King Evander for help. The king, on his part following divine guidance (8. 334–336), has settled his Arcadians on the site of future Rome: more precisely, on the Palatine Hill, close to (if not actually on) what in the reader's day are the grounds of Augustus' residence. Moreover, in Vergil's concept he has been an admirer of Aeneas' father Anchises from his early youth (8. 163f.), and, by the common ancestry of Atlas, he even is a distant relative:

> sic genus amborum scindit se sanguine ab uno. 8. 142

Therefore, Evander can be exempted from the epic's political animosity against everything Greek, and his name (if loosely understood by Romans as "good man") has, it appears, been aptly integrated into the friend-or-foe pattern of the *Aeneid*. Nevertheless, it takes Aeneas many lines (8. 129–145) to explain why in this case he does not mind turning to a Greek leader, *Danaum...ductor* (129) for help, even approaches him in person and not (as he approached King Latinus) through *legatos* (143–145). Why Vergil should at all introduce the Greek king in exile and his settlers, is a question worth asking. The answer will be given later in this Chapter.

A specific point may be brought up right away. For his plot-line the poet needed, as Chapter 4 has shown, a young hero (roughly corresponding to, but more idealized than, Patroclus in the *Iliad*) who could both be radiant (so as to attract Aeneas' – and the reader's – quasi-parental love) and vanish from the story (i.e., die) without leaving a gap in the cast of the main characters (as the death of Aeneas' real son, Ascanius-Iulus, would have done), though his death would set the stage for later revenge. Evander's son supplies such a figure. Thus, the encounter of Aeneas and Evander also has a long-distance effect within the work's composition.

On the other hand we observe that, considering the urgency of the strategic situation (and of Father Tiber's injunction at 8. 59), Aeneas' visit at Pallanteum, including an evening of sight-seeing, does not exactly speed things up; nor does Evander himself influence the events actively, providing as he does a small contingent of troops: twice two hundred horse, 8. 518f.; i.e. few, for so important a name. ("We have only tiny forces for military support", *nobis ad belli auxilium pro nomine tanto / exiguae vires*, 472f.). He can do no more than pass on oracular instructions (cf. the seer prophesying the fated events, *haruspex / fata canens*, 498f.) and send Aeneas on, referring him to the powerful but leaderless Etruscan army. Evander's relevance to the story will perhaps turn out to be ideological rather than dramaturgic, and his function in Book 8 might be found in a wider context of meaning rather than in the chain of action.

Such a finding, though at first sight surprising, would turn out not to be too unusual. On occasion, especially when a political purpose is involved,² the "dramatist" Vergil is known to relax his strict requirements of a tightly woven plot-line. A well-known example occurs in the same Book (8). Aeneas, like his Homeric model Achilles, receives a new set of armor before entering the fighting that will culminate in his avenging Pallas' death on King Turnus as Achilles avenges Patroclus' death on Hector. There is a difference: Achilles does need the new arms (after all, his own, used by luckless Patroclus, are now in the hands of Hector). No such technical necessity has fallen upon Aeneas: to motivate her gift, his frightened mother (370) only points to the Latins' general haughtiness (*superbos*, 613) and Turnus' specific fierceness (*acrem*, 614), i.e., to moral qualities.

Vergil's motive for imitating part of the *Iliad*'s sequence here lies outside his story-line. Homer had used the occasion to have Hephaestus, when manufacturing the new shield for Achilles, depict on it a wide spectrum of scenes from human life in general. Vergil is desirous of presenting another prophetic overview of Roman history and its presumed culmination in Augustus (8. 626–728). He seizes Homer's artistic device of the pictorially decorated shield to achieve his political purpose – but without firmly anchoring the occasion in the plot-line.

In fact Aeneas, when lifting the history-laden shield on his shoulder, displays – this effect is unintended by the author, one must assume – some of what Grönbech viewed as the funny side of this hero (*heroische Komik*)³ as well as his "heroic mulish-stubborness" (*heroische Maultier - Hartnäckigkeit*);⁴

> ignorant of history he enjoys the picture,
> shouldering fame and fate of his descendants.
>
> rerumque ignarus imagine gaudet
> attollens umero famamque et fata nepotum.   8. 730–731.

To provide his creator with an opportunity once more to crown Roman history with Augustus, Aeneas must feel joy (*gaudet*) about a chain of events (presented to him in the form of a "picture") the extended meaning of which transcends his knowledge (*ignarus*). This is, as we shall see in detail later, the second time in the same Book that a sectional perspective fills Aeneas with joy (*laetus,* 311, covers the past but not the all-important implications regarding the future which will be Augustan Rome). So there is reason to expect that in Book 8 the poetic *probabile* is repeatedly held in abeyance in favor of the political message.

Chapter 6

The expectation is confirmed by the Book's overall movement which proceeds in four major sections: (1) Troubled[5] Aeneas is reassured by Father Tiber,[6] who advises him, among other things, to go and conclude an alliance (56) with King Evander's Arcadians (1–96). (2) The lengthy description of Aeneas' visit at Pallanteum (a: 97–369; b: 454–596) is interrupted by (3) Vulcan's forging of the new arms at Venus' request (370–453). In the final section (4) Aeneas, after departing from Pallanteum, reaches a hill (604) from which the Etruscan army can be seen; but no contact is made. Instead, Venus delivers the new arms to her son, and the description (626–728) of the events pictured on the shield takes up the overwhelming part of this final section (597–731).[7]

A detail needs to be clarified so the reader will more easily fathom the disruptive composition in the final section. Against R. D. Williams (*ad* 8. 454–604), but with Servius (cf. *ad* 607) and CN (*ad* 585–607), I do not refer *huc* (606) to the Etruscan camp. Both *hinc* (603) and *huc* (606) mean the grove (*lucus*) sacred to Silvanus, the detailed description of which (597–602) would hang in mid-air if the context had no use for it. In truth Tarchon's camp is "not far from" the *lucus* (*haud procul hinc*, 603), whereas Aeneas and his men seek shelter in it (*huc...succedunt,* 606f.).

One can see that the action line (if what little activity there is in this uneventful Book may be called "action") is cut off at the point where King Tarchon and the Etruscan forces are within sight – the actual meeting of Aeneas and Tarchon as well as the conclusion of their alliance is postponed: these matters are not reported until Book 10 (146ff.). (The intervening Book [9] concentrates on Turnus' hostile activities and the threatened Trojan camp.) Rightly (though mistaken about Vergil's underlying literary purpose) Servius states *ad* 8. 607 "they take care of their horses and bodies; with enormous artfulness he left out what followed, intending to report it in Book 10", *et equos et corpora curant: ingenti arte quod sequebatur omisit, rediturus in decimo* (*scil., libro*). The cumbersome postponement reveals the preponderance Vergil assigns to the shield's political message: the latter is what the reader's attention is to focus on undivided. This finding can be taken as another clue that Book 8 may primarily be accommodating political aspects rather than tightness and probability of plot-line.

A final statement concerning the contents of the Book as a whole can be derived from observing Aeneas' route in 8. His trip *inland* to the site of future Rome is, geographically speaking, a *detour* – the Etruscan army which he is to pick up is waiting for its fated foreign leader, if no longer on the *sea shore* (8. 497f.), ready to sail, so at least not far from the coast (*prope Caeritis amnem,* 597; *haud procul hinc,* 603). And it is *by sea* that Aeneas will lead them to the battlefield (10. 147; 156f.; 164f.; 213f.). To put it pointedly: from his camp, Aeneas moves up the river to get to the sea. To understand Vergil's point in Aeneas' excursion, we may recall that the *Aeneid*'s hero has no direct connection to future Rome: Aeneas will only found Lavinium (today's Pratica di Mare, 16 miles south of Rome, as the crow flies); his son Ascanius-Iulus will found Alba Longa (near Castel Gandolfo on the Alban Lake, today the Pope's summer residence, 14 miles southeast of Rome); hundreds of years later, Romulus and Remus will leave Alba Longa and found Rome on the Palatine Hill. It must be attractive for Vergil (and welcome to Augustus) if the Julian ancestor from Troy is given opportunity to pay an early visit to that hilltop on which, in the time of Vergil's reader, Aeneas' greater descendant has his palatial residence and from which he, in accordance with and in fulfillment of the *Aeneid*'s prophecies, rules over the known world. Another Augustan location turns out to be preordained.

Evander's presence at the site of future Rome provides the premise for Aeneas to be received hospitably. But the hero also needs a motive for his excursion to future Rome. It is supplied by Father Tiber's advice of an alliance (56) – inefficient advice, we said, since the new ally can provide no more than 400 horse. Returning, then, to the question of the Arcadians' presence in the epic, suffice it here to say this much: the detour, resulting in Evander's hospitality (and directions), at least provides Aeneas with a good night's rest on (or near) the palace grounds of his greater descendant. Here may also lie the reason why Vergil makes Aeneas go *in person* (*me, me ipse meumque...caput*, 144f.) instead of having him send the usual ambassador, as, e.g., Ilioneus (*non legatos*, 143). More on this later.

One may of course maintain that Vergil anyway could hardly exclude from his account the longstanding Greek influence as evidenced still in his time by, e.g., the cult of Hercules in the *Forum Boarium*, at the trading post (where a water and a land route crossed) from which Rome had grown.[8]

But in this area, too, one may observe the Augustan adaptation. By having the Greeks settle on the Palatine under the guidance of Apollo (8. 336; the same Apollo who is the guide of Aeneas and, in Vergil's own time, of Augustus) and by making them piously welcome the Julian ancestor, Vergil uses the mythical tradition to dress the outcome of later history in the garb of initial voluntary compliance – the same way as he has Tarchon, eponym of the *Tarquinii*, piously make the Etruscan forces subject (*subiungere*, 8. 502, is the word used by the Etruscan *haruspex*) to the foreign, i.e., Trojan, leadership. (The same voluntary subordination, to cite a third case, is shown by King Latinus in Book 7, but there the pious intentions are frustrated by King Turnus' impious interference, as Chapter 7 will show.) In those early days at the dawn of Roman history

Chapter 6

when Aeneas arrived in Italy, all options were still open and, had all those involved only listened to the divine pronouncements, the Golden Age willed by Fate and eventually achieved under Augustus could (the poet seems to tell us) have had an early chance in Italy (albeit limited in time to the epic's narrative, considering later external as well as internal conflicts) at far less cost in human suffering.

To today's historian it must of course sound rather absurd that the Etruscans – who later conquered Rome and ruled the city for more than a century and who, e.g., in the account of Dionysius of Halicarnassus, though eventually defeated, gave Aeneas and his son a hard time, (D.H. 1. 64–65; cf. Livy 1. 2) – should be piously waiting for Augustus' ancestor to be their leader. But Vergil is not interested in "history" *per se*. To him, early history is rather like a quarry from which he chooses raw materials to shape and to fit into his pro-Augustan design. One need only think of the way his myth depicts opposition against the Julian founding father (Mezentius, Turnus – see Chapter 7 below) as godless sin, contemptuous of divine will, whereas cooperation with and acceptance of Trojan-Julian leadership (Tarchon, Evander and, at least initially, Latinus) is in each case presented as pious compliance with divine orders.

By now we may be in a position to formulate a preliminary approach. We saw that various ethnic elements (Etruscans; Greeks; Latins; Rutulians) which populated Italy in the times of its early history are duly mentioned in the epic but that their ranking takes place according to the contribution the author allows them to make (or not to make) to *his* concept of fated Julian leadership. Evander's position in Book 8 is no exception. The Book shows a peculiar composition: early on, its movement draws on converging divine instructions (Tiber, 51ff.; Apollo, 334ff.); it culminates in the Augustan message of the pictorial shield. Along this path, it is characterized by a lack of tightness in its story-line: river god Tiber directs Aeneas for help to a king unable to be of real help; the hero given new arms without loss of the old; his overall route amounting to a geographical detour; the imminent link-up with the Etruscan army prevented and postponed; Aeneas' uninformed joy (730). All these features cannot but induce the interpreter to wonder (and to investigate) whether Aeneas' earlier joy (311) and Evander's tales, as well as their walk together, may likewise point to a level of meaning beyond the facts of the story told, i.e., may possibly amount to another Augustan reference. If anywhere in the *Aeneid*, the eighth Book is the place to look for an "implied" political message.

As *Excursus (1)* at the end of this chapter shows, this statement proves true even for a section which usually is considered alien to Book 8: the story of Hercules' victory over Cacus the monster as Aeneas hears it from the mouth of King Evander. Customarily taken to be a Vergilian exercise in the hypothetical Hellenistic genre of small epic (*epyllion*) and an *aition* for both the *Ara Maxima* and the cult of Hercules in the *forum Boarium*, the section serves, as *Excursus (1)* shows, the general pro-Julian tendency of Book 8. On the one hand, it provides a mythical root for the residence of Augustus on the Palatine; within the plot-line, it prepares us (as Chapter 4 has shown) for Jupiter's emotional reaction to Pallas' imminent death in Book 10 (and, so, helps to direct subliminally the reader's sympathies in favor of Pallas and Aeneas); third, by placing Cacus' cave, against tradition, on the Aventine (8. 231) instead of on the Palatine, the section enables the Roman reader to understand the topography of early Rome which Vergil employs when making Evander the guide of Aeneas on their walk from Hercules' altar to the Arcadian king's residence.

(3) Aeneas' Landing at Future Rome: the Attraction of a *Fata Morgana*

Having secured a firm hold on the overall structure and tendency of Book 8, we may now trace Aeneas' movements at the site of Rome. The author supplies a key word even before Aeneas lands. Having rounded the last curve on his way up the winding river (*longos superant flexus*, 8. 95), Aeneas (moving now between what are today *Ponte Sublicio* and *Ponte Palatino*) has the Aventine to his right and can see the Capitoline Hill straight ahead. Between them, steeped in the light of the midday[9] sun, the southwest side (later defined by the Circus Maximus) and the western corner of the Palatine come more and more into view, eventually dominating the scenery on the right, while the Aeneadae "are rather speedily moving nearer to the city." Approaching the area of the Tiber Island's southeastern tip and of the oldest harbor[10] of Rome (i.e., the most likely landing site that would come to the mind of Vergil's contemporary reader), they "turn the bows toward the bank" (101). The decision to draw near and land (we observe the causal *asyndeton* at 100/101; cf. 7. 34/35) is based on their preceding observations,

> when from a distance they saw walls and a citadel and, here and there, roofs of houses,
> which today the power of Rome has raised equal to the sky – {where} then Evander had his weak little empire.

> cum muros arcemque procul ac rara domorum
> tecta vident, quae nunc Romana potentia caelo
> aequavit, tum res inopes Evander habebat.   8. 98–100

The key word of course is *nunc*, "today", indicating the primary time frame, which is that of poet and audience. The deficient (cf. *rara, inopes*) past is measured by the standard of the glorious present – a device used (imitated)

Chapter 6

also by other poets of the Augustan age. Propertius, in a regime-friendly poem (4.1. 1–4), unabashedly weighs the *maxima Roma* of his day against the "weed and hill" around here "before Trojan Aeneas", and Augustus' new temple for Apollo on the Palatine against the "refugee cows of Evander". It is the Julian line to which the new civilization is owed.

On the one hand, then, Vergil's reader is supposed in his mind to eliminate contemporary buildings in order to arrive at the scenery of the narrative. The resulting thought process amounts to "subtracting" individual structures from the city of his day. This also means, on the other hand, that the *Aeneid*'s text, in expressly referring to "today's" sky-scraping "power of Rome" (99f.), requires the reader to be aware of and identify contemporary monuments that are missing in the ensuing narrative description of Evander's *res inopes* (100), i.e. he is asked to have, while reading on, a precise picture of the imperial city before his inner eye.[11]

The poverty of ancient conditions renders today's splendor even more impressive. The word "power", *potentia*, covers more than sacred buildings. It makes one rather think of what nowadays is called the building program of Augustus as a whole. "He prided himself that he left behind in marble the city which he had taken over in brick", *gloriatus marmoream se relinquere, quam latericiam accepisset* (Suet. *Aug.* 28. 3). In Aeneas' visit, then, we encounter a section in which what is not mentioned but implied may be an important part of the poet's message and result in a compliment to the Emperor, unspoken but equally or perhaps even more effective than the depiction of his final victory and triumph on Vulcan's shield at the end of Book 8. We may be certain that this is what a contemporary resident of the city would understand.

The reader must not forget that Aeneas' decision to land is induced *visually* (*vident*, 99). The same relation between visual objects and motivation to land is used to describe Aeneas' fateful decision to enter the mouth of the Tiber (7. 29–34/35–36; see Chapter 7. Both times, the motivation is indicated by causal asyndeton). There it is the beautiful landscape which attracts him (a beauty known to Vergil's reader), and, consequently, he is joyful, *laetus*. Here, at Pallanteum, no especially attractive sight is at hand in the time of Aeneas. But in the day of Vergil's reader, the western slope of the Palatine which Aeneas and his men face just before and when landing is the newly created center of Augustus' self-representation. Its terraces (the *substructiones*) carry the area of his palace.[12] The wing of public function and of private rooms (on the left, when viewed from the river) is complemented by another one on the opposite side (parallel to the *Circus Maximus*), containing the two libraries. In the center of this arrangement (overall width about 165 yards)[13] rises (*surgebat*, Prop. 2. 31. 7; cf. Ovid,

Tr. 3. 1. 59f.), from the level of the upper terrace, the marble structure of the temple of Apollo (finished in 28 BC), celebrating (though vowed on an earlier occasion) the victory at Actium which made Octavian the sole master of Rome and its empire by eliminating (in official language) Rome's enemy Cleopatra and her unmanly instrument, Antony.

The shortest distance from the river bank (near the ruins of the *Ponte Rotto*) to the temple of Apollo is about 450 yards as the crow flies. The impressive sight was enhanced by the huge marble and gold (Prop. 2.31.1 and 3) colonnade (*porticus*) in front of the temple (on the lower level), itself probably based on wide substructures which extended the hilltop in the direction of the river.[14] The unifying concept, in which the ruler lives together in symbiosis with "his" god (a covered ramp allowed him private access; some ancient sources even indicate that the god's statue in the area of the temple bore Augustus' features)[15] follows Hellenistic patterns of "autocratic self-representation" (*autokratische Selbstdarstellung*).[16]

A few more features enriched the complex: to its left (looking from the river to the slope) the temple of Cybele, later (AD 3) to be rebuilt by Augustus (*R.G.* 19. 2), would be in full view. Though foreign, the Great Mother enjoyed highest favor since coming from Phrygia, homeland of the Trojans. (Aeneas' deceased wife Creusa, the reader recalls from Book 2, was held back in the Trojan land by Cybele, line 788.) Also, being considered the city's second founder after Romulus (though he declined the un-republican surname in favor of the more providential – "augural" – "Augustus", Suet. *Aug.* 7. 2), the new ruler lived where Romulus once had lived (Dio Cass. 53.16. 5), and Romulus' hut was kept in good repair on the Palatine (D.H. 1. 79.11; Plut. *Rom.* 204): a primitive thatched structure, supported by wooden poles (probably like the *capanne* unearthed there in modern times),[17] situated between his private quarters and the temple of Cybele.

Crowning the ensemble of (from left to right) temple of Cybele, residence, Apollo's temple, and libraries, there was the chariot of the Sun-god, representing the course of the sun (and suggesting the extension of Augustus' rule?), on top of the temple roof (as *acroterion* topping the pediment): truly, a sky-scraping (*nunc...caelo aequavit*) manifesto of *Romana potentia* (8. 99f.). It is in front of this temple that Horace has his chorus pray to the Sun-god that he may never look upon anything greater than Rome: *alme Sol,...possis nihil urbe Roma visere maius* (*C.S.* 9–12). One thinks also of the prophecy (*Aen.* 7. 100f.) that Roman rule will eventually cover everything under the "Sun on his way from Ocean to Ocean", *qua Sol utrumque recurrens aspicit Oceanum*. The timing of Aeneas' arrival is perfect. The Roman reader had to "subtract" the dazzling impression which the whole complex afforded from the river bank when exposed to the light of the noon (or early afternoon) sun (8. 97).

All this splendor would of course be inconceivable to Aeneas who was facing a bare hill with hardly any houses (huts), unaware (as so often) of the true reason why his creator would bring him to and have him disembark at this very site at precisely this time of day. No attractive *vista* (like the inviting landscape around the Tiber mouth [7. 25–36], discussed earlier) was offered to him by the *muros* and *rara...tecta* (8. 98f.) – the poet is calling on his reader's experience of a visual impression which would have been a *Fata Morgana*, (i.e., a mirage) to Aeneas.

The splendid view is also lost for today's visitor, who looks up to the bare hillside and the plastic roofing which protects the excavated grounds. Even the impressive height, rising from the river bank level, is diminished today because the immense modern embankments unduly lift the spectator's viewpoint. When, from the right (western) embankment just south of the *Ponte Palatino*, one studies the few ancient (2nd century BC) layers atop the vaulted mouth of the *Cloaca Maxima*, and then goes and compares their height with the low ground in front of *Santa Maria in Cosmedin* near the left bank, one may conceive an approximate picture of the rising perspective Vergil had in mind for Aeneas as well as for his reader. It is somewhat helpful to observe that the low-lying main road crossing the *Forum Boarium* today (the *Via L. Petroselli*) is about five to six feet higher than the ground level from which the podium of the adjacent rectangular temple of Portunus rises (formerly known as the temple of *Fortuna Virilis*). The same is true of the nearby round temple of Hercules (situated on the other side of the *Cloaca Maxima*), of which, when viewed from across the river, only the upper half with its modern roof is visible today.

Another (and probably more striking) substitute visual impression may be gained by today's reader if one positions oneself on the stairs at the southern tip of the Tiber Island. One sees, under the modern (straight) section of the *Ponte Rotto*, the mouth of the *Cloaca Maxima*. Raising one's eyes from the water level to the *Ponte Palatino*, one sees, behind and above it, the roof of the round temple of Hercules and, further in the background, the top part of the campanile belonging to *Santa Maria in Cosmedin*. Now the top storey of the campanile reaches up almost to the height of the podium on which the temple of Palatine Apollo stood. So the campanile may serve as a substitute impression of the view Vergil expected the reader to have before his eyes: standing on the steps of the island, one should picture the temple rising from a Palatine level equal to the top of the campanile.

Of course, there were embankments in this area in Vergil's time,[18] too, and they had been raised by several yards in the preceding century[19] when the rectangular temple of Portunus was erected on top of the filled-in grounds of an older temple (of the same god).[20] How much change again was brought about by the improvements done on river bed and harbor under Augustus[21] is hard to gauge for us; even harder is the question whether Vergil expects his reader to call to mind any of this particular work.

Are such detailed considerations really warranted by (and required for understanding) the message of Book 8? I would, while pointing to the text's repeated visual appeal, have to answer "yes" and, in addition, to point to what follows, beginning with the scene of the first encounter of the two parties. King Evander and a select body of his men are celebrating the festival of Hercules at the *Ara Maxima* (it too was restored in Augustan time; *aras*, 106, is a poetic plural as *montibus* is at 53, the last mentioned referring to the Palatine – cf. *Pallanteum*, 54 – as the former is resumed by the singular *hanc...aram*, 186, cf. 271 and Excursus 1). The specific information which must have struck the contemporary reader as strange is that the sacrifices took place in the grove (of Hercules) *outside the city*, *ante urbem in luco* (104).

Already the *pomerium* of Romulus is said to have included the altar of Hercules (Tac. *Ann.* 12. 24. 1f.). The "Servian" wall (allegedly built under Servius Tullius in the sixth century BC but today generally understood[22] to have been erected two centuries later) ran (in today's topographical terms) between the church *Santa Maria in Cosmedin* and the fountain as well as the Portunus temple on the opposite side of the *Via L. Petroselli*, parallel to the river.[23] This again places the altar just inside the city. For the crypt of *Santa Maria in Cosmedin* is to be identified with the inner parts of the altar.[24] Stepping down the steps to the crypt, one can today easily see the large blocks of tufa.[25]

For residents of Augustan Rome, then, it must have been an unlikely concept to picture their city's predecessor on so tiny a scale that even what they believed to be one of their oldest religious monuments (cf. *antiquissimum sollemne*, etc., Livy 9. 34.18 – the historical truth is, of course, very different) should not have been within its walls. A similar surprise is contained in the description of the city walls (*muros*,[26] 98) and, with them, the citadel (*arcem*, 98). Evander's city appears (with one notable exception, as we shall see) limited to the immediate area of the Palatine Hill.[27] Aeneas and his men, when landing, "approach the city" (*urbique propinquant*, 101); they plan to move in the direction of the Palatine Hill which is in front of their eyes. Before reaching it, however, they will find themselves invited to participate in the religious festivities *ante urbem* (104).

The first contact between the two parties is made by young Pallas. From

Chapter 6

the outset, his character is drawn in marked difference from that of his later killer, Turnus, though both are called *audax*, "bold" (8. 110 and 7. 409) when they appear for the first time. Turnus' "audacity" (cf. *audaci*, 9. 126) will later reveal itself as defiance of divine will (*nil me fatalia terrent...responsa deorum*, 9. 133f.). Pallas' "boldness" shows itself both in the courage with which he later faces his superior enemy (10. 449–451) and now in the fearlessness, grounded in *piety*, which bids him go and meet the newcomers alone so that the sacrificial action at Hercules' altar is not interrupted (*audax quos rumpere Pallas sacra vetat*, 8. 110f.).[28] Right from the beginning, the reader is made to feel that Aeneas is meeting a young follower of kindred values worthy of his attention (as Pallas' killer will be deserving of Aeneas' retribution). The *Aeneid*'s basic black-and-white pattern proves ever-present – and so is (explored in Chapter 4) the concomitant subliminal guidance provided for the reader's gut reaction. The higher Pallas' congeniality, the deeper the impending loss and pain of Aeneas – and the more intense the reader's sympathy for Aeneas' feelings and conduct.

It is important to remind ourselves of Vergil's own intentions, so we do not overstate the influence of his literary model, which in this case is Homer's *Odyssey*: at the opening of Book 3 we find aged Nestor sacrificing outside his city on the beach when Telemachos arrives. Nestor's son Peisistratos goes to meet him and questions him in much the same words with which Pallas addresses the arriving Trojans.

The Arcadians are presented as fearfully watching the two (8. 79) "high-boarded" (*celsas*, 107) boats glide towards them, driven by their "silent oars" (*tacitis...remis*, 108; the absence of splashing noise results from Tiber halting his current: *tacita refluens ita substitit unda*, 87; the easy reading *tacitos* in 108 misses the point).

Apparently the reader is asked to "subtract" the artificial embankments we mentioned earlier from his picture of the *Forum Boarium* so the boats are in view from the location of the altar. Nevertheless, Vergil's sense for theatrical scenery needs an elevation: the two high-ranking persons should meet on an equal level (Chapter 4 has shown that Pallas can on occasion be given precedence even over Aeneas; cf. *ipse...Pallas*, etc., 8. 585–591). Aeneas is standing on and speaking from the high stern (which is turned toward the shore) of his boat:

tum pater Aeneas puppi sic fatur ab alta   8. 115.

It would be unseemly to have noble Pallas talk up to him from a lower, i.e., inferior, position. So Vergil places the boy (cf. *pueri*, 12. 943) high on a knoll from which he can speak in corresponding fashion: *procul e tumulo...inquit*, 112f. Some may doubt that the poet's *topothesia* (a term Servius uses for fictional topography in the *Aeneid*)[29] should be based on a detail such as a hill actually existing in the area: the elevation may rather have a merely poetic existence due to the necessity of *decorum* (though it is of course easy to picture an ancient knoll in the elevated area on the left bank near today's *Ponte Palatino*).

While sacrificing in the sacred grove (*in luco*, 104), the Arcadians watch the boats approaching "amidst the shady wood" (*inter opacum...nemus*, 107f.) which presumably covers the area between them and the river (and perhaps beyond).[30] When Aeneas and Pallas set out together, they "leave the river" as well as "advance and enter the sacred grove":

progressi subeunt luco fluviumque relinquunt.   8. 125

Originally, Aeneas decided to land facing the city on the Palatine which he intended to approach (*urbique propinquant*, 101). Now Pallas takes him slightly to the right, off the direct route to the west corner of the Palatine, to reach *lucus* and *ara*, about 250 yards from the *portus Tiberinus* area (much closer if one pictures Aeneas as having landed slightly *before* reaching the area of today's *Ponte Palatino*).

Let the description of the first encounter suffice to acquaint us both with the precision and consistency Vergil employs in delineating details of his poetic topography and with the demand made on the reader to verify Aeneas' route in terms of actual distances or structures in his contemporary city. Modern readers who feel alienated by the epic's frequent "un-poetic" references to its Roman environment may wish to recall the ancient thesis (Donatus, p. 2, ed. Georgii) that a primary goal of the *Aeneid* is to give political support to Augustus whom Horace, in a made-to-order public poem (*C.S.* 50), identifies as "the famous blood (lineage) of Anchises and Venus", *clarus Anchisae Venerisque sanguis*, – to quote an official voice contemporary with the *Aeneid* or, more likely, influenced by it. Vergil does not write for "the world" but for Rome which *is* the world for him and his time. How much the sociological notion of a "central city state" applies to Rome can be a striking experience also for the reader of Augustus' *Achievements* (*Res Gestae*); the term comes to mind when he lists his largesse to the Roman plebs, his building activity in the city or even when he merely refers to his being "absent" and "present" (5.1., *scil.* from and in the city, rather than – perhaps – a senate meeting or Italy. See Brunt-Moore *ad. loc.*).

Chapter 6

(4) An Augustan Walk: Circling the Hill to Approach its Top

(a) *Poetically Blocking the Southern Access to the Palatine Hill so as to Cause a Detour: Differing Narratological Levels*

Having watched Aeneas landing as if attracted by a *Fata Morgana* with his eyes set on the future palace grounds of his greater descendant, we are now prepared to resume our original inquiry (suggested by the peculiar organization of Book 8) about possible ideological or political implications of his visit. After the second part of the Hercules festival with its songs, dancing and the renewed meal (*mensae grata secundae dona*, 8. 283f.)[31] has been completed, *divinis rebus... perfectis*, "all" (*cuncti*) move to the city, *ad urbem* (8. 306f.).

What the Roman reader would expect is that they roughly continue in the direction Aeneas and Pallas had taken when leaving the boats and heading for the *Ara Maxima*. (The reader does expect a correction to the left since their path to the altar, we then said, had taken them somewhat out of their way, viz. to the right of the straight line to the southwest corner of the Palatine.) For, less than 250 yards behind the altar, there began the nearest regular access route to the west corner of the Palatine, the so-called "Stairs of Cacus", *scalae Caci*, which would take one up between the "hut of Romulus" (and Cybele's temple) to one's left and Augustus' living quarters (continued by Apollo's precinct and the libraries) to the right.

Vergil does not mention this access. Instead, he has Evander and his guest walk almost 180 degrees clockwise around half the hill (a course which for some time takes them through the valley between the Palatine and the Capitoline Hill, i.e., through the so-called *Velabrum*) until they enter the plateau of the Palatine from the opposite side, i.e., the (north-)eastern access road. Why the detour? If the so-called Stairs of Cacus were too steep to climb for King Evander, "burdened with age" (*obsitus aevo*, 307), it would still have shown greater factual probability if the poet had granted him an (early) sedan chair than that he sent him on an extended late-evening (cf. 280) walk (*ibat*; i.e., *non vehebatur...sed ambulabat suis pedibus senex*, Don. *ad* 307). It may be worthwhile to take another sharp look at the route along which the old king takes his guest.

First a detail merits clarification. Who are "all", *cuncti* (306), who leave the altar for the city? First, of course, Evander himself, with Aeneas and Pallas at his side all the way (the three verbs in the imperfect tense in 307b–309, indicate extended action). Whether the (less important) others follow along or take a different route we are not told. Certainly not all of the Trojans (though all of the townspeople, of course) are headed for the city, for next morning Aeneas will go to see his men at the boats (546).

Earlier, though only Aeneas had been mentioned by name as coming with Pallas to the altar, King Evander addressed a plurality of Trojans (*amici*, 172), and his invitation to join the annual sacrifice and meal was not limited to Aeneas (plural imperatives 173 and 174). Consequently, he assigned seats to the "men" (*viros*, 176), and

> Aeneas has a meal together with the Trojan young men
>
> vescitur Aeneas simul et Troiana iuventus   8.182.

Since the whole chine of an ox is involved (*perpetui tergo bovis*, 183; see even the plural *taurorum*, 180), one might think that the crews of both boats have joined Aeneas and Evander for the meal – were it not for the formulaic character of these epic lines (180–183). It seems easier to assume that *Troiana iuventus* (182) points to a select group of young warriors forming Aeneas' retinue (among them, of course, the never-absent adjutant, Achates, cf. 466) – a group large enough to give decorum to Aeneas and small enough to be received and stay with their king overnight on the hill.

This explanation accounts both for the presence of *Troiana iuventus* (545) at next morning's sacrifice on the hill and their being distinguished by Vergil from the companions (*socios*) whom Aeneas, likewise on the next morning, goes to see again (*revisit*, 546) at the boats. It is also in keeping with the *Aeneid*'s aristocratic tradition that the common soldiery (though, of course, an object of their good leader's care and concern)[32] plays no part in important matters of politics. This makes it unlikely that Aeneas' and Evander's evening walk should be conceived by the reader as including a return to the harbor area and a stop at the boats. Consequently, we need not assume that the two kings walk directly along the river bank; rather they are free to move at some distance from (and, for the first part, roughly parallel to) the Tiber.

A second detail reinforces our awareness of possible implications entailed by the route the two kings take. Here a few words are necessary to outline the situation and its Julian links. On the next morning, Aeneas and Evander, accompanied by Achates and Pallas respectively, have an early (cf. *matutini*, 456; *matutinus*, 465) meeting in the middle (*mediisque residunt aedibus*, 467f.) between guest accommodations and the old king's living quarters. It would be tempting to identify the meeting place, on the basis of our present-day knowledge, in terms of Augustus' residence. That here is another manifestation of the Vergilian distinction between old and new, ancient and present (cf. 8. 99f.), is very likely. But this is not going to be my point now.

When Evander suggests that it is Aeneas at whom the Etruscan seer's fate-informed revelation (*fata canens*, 499) is aiming, and Aeneas whom fate (*fata*, 512) favors, even "whom the expressions of divine will demand"

Chapter 6

(*quem numina poscunt*, 512), Aeneas is (and so is Achates) overwhelmed by the immense task (521f.). But then his divine mother gives the sign (*signum*, 523; 534; of her promised gifts, *promissa*, 531; cf. 612): lightning, thunder, the sound of a trumpet and an apparition of the new arms in an unclouded part of the sky. This un-Aphroditean scenery grants Aeneas the encouragement and confirmation he needs: "I am demanded by Olympus", *ego poscor Olympo* (533; cf. 512). What better place than the residential hill of Rome's fated Julian ruler and what better agent could be found for this theatrical clap of thunder than the ancestral goddess of the Julian family? (Considering the fact that it was on this hill that another early member of the family, i.e., Romulus, received the bird signs which bade him found Rome here, one wonders whether the Roman reader saw even more continuity?) It is only consistent that Aeneas, encouraged, now voices the Julian claim both of justice (Turnus' punishment, *poenas*, 538) and of *clementia*, forgiveness, toward enemy peoples misled by their leadership. The latter takes the form of pity expressed for the poor (*miseris*) Laurentians' imminent suffering (537), exemplified by Homeric phrases that originally, in the *Iliad* (21. 301f.), described fleeing *Trojans*.[33] The tide is turning.

Aeneas' words take us directly to the detail in question. The miracle requires a human response in the form of a sacrifice. So Aeneas gets up from his seat

> and first wakens the sleeping altar with Herculean fire
> and happily approaches yesterday's Lar and the lowly
> Penates. According to ritual, Evander slaughters select
> two-year-old sheep, and so do, side by side, the young Trojans.

> et primum Herculeis sopitas ignibus aras
> excitat, hesternumque larem parvosque penatis
> laetus adit; mactat lectas de more bidentis
> Euandrus pariter, pariter Troiana iuventus.   8. 542–45.

Commentators tend to assume that *Herculeis* belongs to *aras* rather than to *ignibus*; "It is transferred *more Vergiliano*" (CN *ad loc.*). But then we have to assume also that "Hercules would naturally be one of Evander's household gods" (CN, reporting on Heyne) – an unlikely companion to the Arcadian king's *parvi penates*, considering Hercules' elevated position and palaeo-Julian function in the overall context. An alternative discussed (and rejected) by CN is Wagner's "another sacrifice at the Ara Maxima, as well as at home" – but the text does not say so; this would involve "Aeneas' going to a more or less distant place, which the Ara Maxima must have been".

The latter assumption is incorrect, as my reader knows: the *Ara* is only about three hundred yards away from the west area of the hilltop. Aeneas (or one of the men) could go down the *Scalae Caci* and fetch the fire within a matter of minutes. The long route around half the hill taken by the two kings the evening before would certainly carry the risk that the kindling fire might be extinguished before arrival. And the text equally admits the meaning (in fact, it is most naturally understood to mean) that Evander's altar on the Palatine is rekindled with "fire fetched from Hercules' altar" (cf. Cerda in CN: *ignibus ex Herculis ara sumptis*).

Besides, the last-mentioned possibility is the only one which satisfies the overall two-step structure of the passage. Stage I (*primum*, 542) is described in the lines quoted and translated above. Stage II (introduced by *post*) opens as follows:

> Thereafter he walks from here to the boats and sees his companions again,
>
> post hinc ad navis graditur sociosque revisit, 8. 546.

Therefore not the topography but the text in itself and alone does not allow the interpreter to split up the first stage by having it take place both at the *Ara Maxima* and at Evander's residence (so one would arrive at a total of three separate actions overall). The sacrifices described in lines 542–545 are performed exclusively before Evander's household gods on the Palatine hill (though with kindling fire fetched from the *Ara Maxima*). And it is from up here (*hinc*, 546) that Aeneas goes down to see his companions again – presumably via the same quick access route by which the fire had been fetched before: the (later) so-called *Scalae Caci*.

To return to and include our first detail: our result makes it likely that – apart from Aeneas, Evander, and Pallas who split away from "all" (*cuncti*, 306) – the others used the same route the evening before when they, on their way *ad urbem*, disappeared from the reader's sight, though Vergil's text makes it appear as if there is only one, the round-about, access route "to the city" (*ad urbem*, 306). (This does not necessarily mean that all went up to the hill upon entering the wall, as we shall see later.).

The topographical conclusion to be drawn from a detailed observation on *cuncti* (306) and *Herculeis* (542) is that Vergil considers the *Scalae Caci* access to the western corner of the Palatine as existent already in the days of his narrative. The question to be asked is this: why then does he pass it over in silence and why does his King Evander not use it? Recalling the poet's motive when making Aeneas land (101), we give the obvious answer: no additional Augustan propaganda value can be gleaned from letting Aeneas have a close-up inspection of the bare hillside. It is the panoramic view one experiences from the river bank which the author wished to utilize in order to conjure up a wide-angle, sun-lit Julian perspective before his reader's eyes. Consequently, when accompanying Aeneas on the detour he is being taken, the reader may do well to look out specifically for further

Chapter 6

evocations of Augustan landmarks. The walk has been politically focused right from the perspective of Aeneas' landing.

What is of highest interest for our overall investigation is not only the constant evocation of individual sites and edifices (later on we shall duly mention a number of them) but Vergil's technique in guiding his reader. The customary explanation of why the *Scalae Caci* are not mentioned is that "so baneful a creature as his Cacus" does not fit the site of the later royal residence.[34] Our findings about Vergil's attempt to give the Palatine an early air of chosenness confirm the thesis: Vergil could not settle the monster on the Palatine. But, we are forced to add, it is not only that he wished to exile the *name* of Cacus (and its bearer) and, so, had the monster reside on the Aventine. Above all, the southwestern access itself to the Palatine did not, beyond the original vista experienced by Aeneas, contribute any further to the *visual concept* the poet developed for his reader. (Nor did the *Circus Maximus* area which would have required Aeneas to be led by the alternative route, counterclockwise around the Palatine.) So the poet passed over the southwestern access in silence.

On occasion, the interpreter has to spend more energy on unearthing hidden premises than on illuminating the target passage itself. If we now trace the "political walk" proper (8. 306–369), we will be aware that topographical difficulties may result from ideological priorities. First of all it should be stated that the long detour cannot be explained as an easy alternative route for old Evander. Leaning on the two younger companions left and right for support (Don. *ad* 308), "he kept easing the burden of the way by speech on this and that feature" (309). In the same way as the poet's political intention induces him to be silent about the southwest access to the Palatine, so Evander is, in the final analysis, taking the circuitous route not because of his great age. Rather, the purpose for which Vergil presents him as decrepit is that the king appears motivated to slow the pace and talk about the landmarks as they may come into view. (Inconsistently but naturally enough, talkative Evander may make the detour even longer than necessary.)

That the two walkers (Pallas, though present, is no longer signified hereafter) are not pictured as walking up closely to every single place mentioned, is clear from the fact that marveling Aeneas "moved his quick eyes around over all objects". His eyes are "easily moving", *facilis* (310) – they cover more ground than his decrepit guide would physically be able to. Possibly, then, more distant objects may sometimes be mentioned in the order of their being *seen* by a turn of the head (or even of their being associated) rather than according to their close topographical vicinity.

Corresponding to Evander's communicativeness, Aeneas has to be fascinated by what he sees, *capiturque locis* – though he of course can't see what the reader is asked to call up before his inner eye. The situation is as anachronistic and unreal as if a twenty-first-century writer had a Roman soldier sail up the Thames or an early settler up the Potomac, letting the poor legionary or the fur-clad settler get excited about the flat landscape where today Big Ben and St. Paul's or the Jefferson Memorial and the Pentagon strike the visitor's eye.[35] Aeneas, on his part, happily begins to ask detailed questions and receives answers about individual "memorials of men past" (*singula laetus exquiritque ~ auditque virum monimenta priorum*, 311f.). His untimely happiness and talkativeness in pursuing local details appears so ill-motivated that the ancient commentator Donatus, always intent on tidy consistency, refers us back to the pressing military need that brought Aeneas to Pallanteum in the first place: he is happy and converses, we hear, because the old king had right away promised (cf. 170f.) help for early next morning. My reader is acquainted with Vergil's proneness, especially in Book 8, to let requirements of contemporary politics overcome consistency of plot and character. So we will rather recall the equally untimely, since similarly ignorant (*rerum...ignarus*, 730), joy and fascination which the Julians' ancestor displays about the incomprehensible "picture" (*imagine*) on Vulcan's shield when he is about to shoulder – to quote the author's information for his reader – "fame and fate of his descendants" (8. 730f.; *miratur*, 730 ~ *miratur*, 310; *gaudet*, 730 ~ *laetus*, 311). Such inconsistency of motivation is inherent in the task of writing a story that points beyond itself.

Concerning this walk (but also concerning the whole Pallanteum episode), there are apparently three levels of understanding which constantly run together in the narrative presentation but have to be kept separate in the reader's mind:

(A) The chronologically oldest layer offers a pre-Evandrian perspective as told in the Arcadian king's musings and recollections about times past (i.e., past to him, 314ff.). Here we list his story about Fauns and Nymphs and an uncivilized race of men making up the original inhabitants of the area, to be followed by the "golden centuries" under divine exile Saturnus; an age which in turn was supplanted by a tarnished period of war and greed, as reflected in waves of immigrants.

(B) The most recent immigrants (333ff.) are Evander himself and his Arcadians. Events touching them represent the aged king's own sphere of personal experience (the destruction of Cacus at the hands of Hercules would also fall under heading B).

(C) Interspersed are remarks and names incomprehensible to both Evander and Aeneas, but understandable only to Vergil's contemp-

Chapter 6

oraries who are acquainted with Rome's history and institutions down to the time of Augustus: "arx", "Capitolium", "forum Romanum", "Lupercal", and "Asylum". A term like "the elegant Carinae" (*lautis Carinis*, 8.361) draws on the reader's recent, even present-day experience.[36]

It is level C, especially in the context of Augustus' rule, of the *Romana potentia* of today, *nunc* (8. 99; cf. *nunc*, 348), which the poet is aiming at, and for the sake of which he is willing to incur all those inconsistencies we have pointed out, including those in the overall composition of Book 8. It is on this C-level that we should search for the meaning and significance of Evander's and Aeneas' walk, but not limit our investigation to the level of awareness and experience available to host and guest. After all, the *Aeneid*'s hero is involved in developments that surpass his intellectual scope.

And to the extent that Evander is seen to speak as the founder of the *Roman* citadel, even the information he gives on level A is interesting to Vergil the Augustan, for two reasons. On the one hand, his reader can learn more about the difference between earliest, lowly beginnings and today's sky-scraping city; on the other hand, there is the fact that another prehistoric instance can be reported of divine interest (in addition to Hercules' visit) in the area (i.e., Saturnus' residence), even of *aurea...saecula* (324f.). This golden age and the idea of peaceful rule over nations exercised from hereabouts (*placida populos in pace regebat* – sc. *Saturnus*, 325) is helpful in establishing a divine precedent for (and that is the divine character of) the rule of Augustus, under whom, according to Jupiter's prophecy (1. 291ff.), war will end and rough centuries will give way to gentle ones; and he is the one "who", according to Anchises' prediction,

> Caesar Augustus, race of the divine (Caesar), will found
> *golden* centuries *again* for Latium, all over the fields
> once ruled by *Saturnus*.

> Augustus Caesar, divi genus, aurea condet
> saecula qui rursus Latio regnata per arva
> Saturno quondam.   6. 792–4.

Level C, among other things, means a return of ideal conditions achieved once already, though imperfectly (since short-lived), in prehistoric Latium (cf. 8. 324f.). On level B Aeneas' return to his family's alleged home country (cf. *revehis*, 8. 37) initiates the chain of events which will bring back, eventually, a once existent (= level A) golden age. Its realization and fulfilment lie before the reader's eyes (level C) who can *see* daily the edifices of Golden Augustan Rome (cf. *aurea nunc*, 348). Of course, Evander cannot know that his reference to the past golden age in Latium under Saturnus (324f.) touches upon the prophecy about Aeneas' descendant. But his guest – and with Aeneas, Vergil's reader – has heard the prophecy from father Anchises' lips and therefore is in a position to envisage the long-range historical context.

If, then, pre-Evandrian conditions can produce implications for the time of Augustus, it must be even more attractive for Vergil to place the Arcadian settler-king himself firmly in a palaeo-Augustan setting, i.e., to grant to level B (representing the story-line of Book 8), too, premonitions of level C. This he achieves by letting Evander and his Arcadians, who arrived as the most recent wave of immigrants, be guided by Augustus' personal and political deity, known as such to the Roman reader from interventions in the *Aeneid* as well as from contemporary religion and politics. The description of Evander's mission stylistically culminates in the mention of C-level god Apollo (emphasized position at end of line and of sentence, 336). The ideological point (level C) being of higher priority, the reader should not be surprised that it is introduced before topography (= level B) requires discussing it.

The exile Evander, then, first professes himself to have come here driven by (to give the key words in translation) "my mother's, the Nymph Carmentis', formidable prophetic counsel", and by her "inspirer, god Apollo" (333–336). Next, the author's narrative continues:

> These words had hardly been said, then (*dehinc*) he advanced and pointed out both the altar {of his mother}...
>
> vix ea dicta, dehinc progressus monstrat et aram   8. 337

It is not, one observes, the walkers' arrival at the altar that occasions the information but vice versa, the story of Carmentis' Apollonian guidance causes Evander to advance (*progressus*) and point out (*monstrat*) the altar (*Carmentalem*, 338, picks up *Carmentis*, 336). The walking route (level B) here is adapted (adjusted) by Vergil so as to exemplify the "evidence" there still exists in his time of the exile's divinely guided mission and arrival. It is only consistent that the poet intervenes and intersperses another parenthetic level-C comment, pronounced in the time-frame of his contemporary reader: Evander advanced and pointed out

> both the altar and
> the gate which the Romans (*sc.*, still today) speak of by name
> as that of Carmentis, ancient tribute to Nymph Carmentis,
> the fate-revealing seer who first sang that
> Aeneas' descendants (i.e., the Romans) would be great
> and Pallanteum (i.e., the Palatine Hill) would be renowned.

Chapter 6

>   et aram
> et Carmentalem Romani nomine portam
> quam memorant, Nymphae priscum Carmentis honorem,
> vatis fatidicae, cecinit quae prima futuros
> Aeneadas magnos et nobile Pallanteum.   8. 337–341

Carmentis' gift of prophecy is connected to her name (she "sang", *cecinit*, 340; cf. *quae nomen habes a carmine ductum*, Ov. *F.* 1. 467). Fordyce (*ad* 8. 335f.) should not feel surprised that Vergil fails to exploit the situation for a long prophecy as Ovid (*F.* 1. 509–536) does. Ovid's passage anyway builds partly on the *Aeneid* (as well as on Propertius and also Horace). Vergil's method here has been all along *visually* to evoke the city of Augustus through Aeneas' eyes and his experience of Evander's little realm (cf. 8. 98f.; 310–312). Major prophecies would be out of place since diverting from a narrative concept where fulfillment of destiny is anyway optically demonstrated through appeal to the reader's eyes. Major prophecies are reserved for causal concatenations revealed in special situations, in Book 1 (Jupiter), 6 (Anchises), and 8 (the shield). "Renowned" Palatine, in all its present-day splendor, is both a sight and a political reality familiar to the reader.

 The altar of Carmentis (or Carmenta) was situated at the corner formed by the southern foot of the Capitol, on today's *Vico Iugario*, across from *S. Omobono*. On the same (northern) side of the street, its foundations located under the (northern) pedestrian crossing of today's *Via del Teatro di Marcello*[37] (or under that of the *Vico Iugario*[38] itself at the intersection of the two streets), was the *Porta Carmentalis*. At this point, it is unavoidable that we try to visualize the precise route. The distance covered so far by the two kings, then, corresponds to the length of today's *Via L. Petroselli* from *S.a Maria in Cosmedin* (i.e., the *Ara Maxima*) to a point just beyond the *Vico Iugario*; a little less than 500 yards – five minutes for an able-bodied walker, perhaps ten to fifteen for a man *aevo obsitus*. Their way *ad urbem* (306), then, has so far taken them along the outside of the city wall.

 Evander's city, which has its *arx* (cf. 98; 313) on the Palatine hill, is hemmed in (*claudimur*, 473) between "Etruscan" (i.e., until recently, enemy-controlled: 569ff.) river on one side and Rutulian threat to its wall (474; cf. 55; 146f.) on the other. But Vergil has granted the *parva urbs* (cf. 554) a bulging extension of its walls (for these, cf. *muros*, 98; *murum*, 474), protruding at least over part of the later *Forum Boarium* and of the *Velabrum* so as to include the gate named after Evander's mother. It is difficult to decide whether in Vergil's time the gate which closed the west end of the *vicus Iugarius* toward the river (the bank was about 150 yards further down) ran north-south (i.e., parallel to the Tiber) or east-west (i.e., perpendicular to the river) as part of a 'bend' of the wall (or even of an arm) extending from the south corner of the Capitoline in the direction of the river bank. Excavation results advocate the east-west direction.[39] At any rate, the gate as well as the street it guarded were so arranged as to narrowly include inside the city walls the temples of *Fortuna* and of *Mater Matuta* (located partly below today's S. Omobono). A different (older) alignment, masterfully reconstructed by Coarelli,[40] can still be verified: the predecessor(s) of the (two) temple(s) had been sitting just outside an (older) wall and outside the gate, i.e., the older city wall ran so as to exclude the older temple(s). Now the early wall – of which there is no archaeological evidence anyway beyond the immediate gate area – would hardly have followed the straight course of today's *Via L.Petroselli*. Rather (thinks Coarelli), it conceivably was bent away from the river inland so as to allow space for and to adjust to the *Velabrum*, the swampy expanse of water between Palatine and Capitoline. (Still, in Vergil's time, the river might on occasion inundate the area between Palatine and Capitoline as far as the *Forum Romanum*, even up to Vesta's temple, Hor. *C*. 1. 2.13–16.)[41]

Having stated this much, we are in a position to verify that Vergil apparently wishes his reader to think of the 'republican' wall (of the fourth century BC: we mentioned its scarce remnants earlier) when picturing the walk of the two kings, but not of an older fortification; for the *Velabrum*, which once served as the harbor, is not mentioned as an obstacle in the two walker's path. Nor are they presented as having adjusted their route so as to walk *around* the swamp – in which case a detour would be required: they would have to follow approximately the bending course of the *Cloaca Maxima* close to the *Lupercal* (which Vergil mentions only *after* they have *entered* the city, 8. 343) on their way inland and to return to the river along the *vicus Iugarius*.

These considerations confirm the earlier observation that Vergil does not wish his reader to ponder about an entrance into the city closer to the *Ara Maxima* (i.e., the *Scalae Caci* access). Rather, from the grove (the starting point where Evander began his explanations: *haec nemora*, 314f.),[42] they have made their way to Carmentis' altar and her gate as their first landmarks worth mentioning.

Vergil is again seen not to mind anachronism: construction of the *Cloaca Maxima* drainage system, serving the *Argiletum* and the *Forum Romanum* areas east of the *Velabrum*, is by tradition ascribed to the Etruscan king Tarquinius Priscus in the sixth century BC, and the drainage of the *Velabrum* itself (the oldest "harbor") in all likelihood took place even later. Nevertheless the two kings apparently manage to keep their feet dry (not to mention any greater discomfort one might incur while attempting to

Chapter 6

cross a swampy area on foot).⁴³ The reader is not asked to go further back into the past than Republican Rome when picturing to himself the *forum Boarium* in the time of Evander. (As a matter of fact, the area's last major remodeling, temples included, took place after the devastating fire of 213 BC; cf. Livy 24. 47.15–16; 25. 7. 5.) The *Aeneid*'s anachronistic picture is even more remarkable in light of the fact that Ovid vividly memorializes the former swampy character of *forum Romanum* and *Velabrum* (*F.* 6. 395–416).

However, that Vergil should mention the monuments of Carmentis is natural enough, not only because her altar (with *flamen*) and cult (though connected basically with childbearing) were intact in his day (their level-C relevance is of course also enhanced by Carmentis' prophecy); for on level B itself it appears appropriate and well-motivated that Evander should have his eminent guest enter the city through the gate named after his prophetic mother, servant of Apollo.

Here the Augustan reader can still in his own day think he is tracing Evander's steps and influence. The Roman audience found the story credible also because the gate just incorporates the temple of *Mater Matuta*; according to legend (Ovid, *F.* 6. 529–532), it was Evander's mother Carmentis who hosted and fed Ino-Leucothea, announcing (*o.c.* 6. 541–548) her new name *Mater Matuta* and her deification as well as deification for her son Palaemon-Portunus.

The temples of mother and son faced one another across the old harbor of the *Velabrum*. Vergil's silence on Portunus' and Matuta's temples, just passed by the two kings in the opening section of their walk, reveals his lack of interest in possible level B monuments for their own sake. This, though a conclusion drawn *ex silentio*, nevertheless can serve as a complementary confirmation of our interpretation which ties the poet's prevailing interest to the Augustan character of level C, as for instance documented in Carmentis' association with the tutelary deity of Augustus.

If we accept the above-mentioned excavation of the gate area as it is documented, the two walkers had to make a 90 degree right turn from the route followed so far, to be able to see Carmentis' shrine in front of them. In walking up to the altar (*progressus*, 8. 337), Evander would have the gate called after his mother to his right. For the *fanum Carmentis*, as entered in the excavation maps (identification is tentative), lies both inside and outside the city fortification, being part of the southern foot corner of the Capitoline hill. About the altar itself we have the contemporary eyewitness report of Dionysius of Halicarnassus. He, in the context of mentioning two altars (one of them dedicated to Evander at the Aventine), "saw" (ἐθεασάμην) them "set up, on the one hand to Carmenta at the foot of the

Before Founding Lavinium, Aeneas Inspects the Site of Rome

so-called Capitoline,[44] by the gates of Carmenta" (καὶ βωμοὺς ἐθεασάμην ἱδρυμένους, Καρμέντῃ μὲν ὑπὸ τῷ καλουμένῳ Καπιτωλίῳ παρὰ ταῖς Καρμεντίσι πύλαις, D. H. *Rom. Ant.* 1. 32. 2). If our hypothetical reconstruction of the walk so far is correct, the two walkers are, at this point, still outside the walls.

(b) *Extending the Detour: Testimonial to Rome's Two Founders (The Julians' Mission, I)*

So far, we have followed Aeneas and Evander (and Pallas, who, however, no longer receives any mention) from their starting point, the *Ara Maxima*, to their first stop. For the ensuing discussion, I here offer a sequential list of the landmarks Vergil mentions along the route:

(1) Altar (and Gate) of Carmentis (8. 337f.)
(2) *Asylum* (overgrown depression on the Capitoline; 342)
(3) *Lupercal* (cave where Romulus and Remus will be nursed by the she-wolf; 343)
(4) *Argiletum* (grove; in Vergil's time, an alley between *curia Iulia* (Senate House) and *basilica Aemilia*; 345)
(5) *Arx* (citadel; later the place of Tarpeia's treason; northern peak of Capitoline hill; *ad Tarpeiam sedem*, 347)
(6) *Capitolium* (southern peak of Capitoline hill, 347; seat of the city of Saturnus, 355 ff.)
(7) City of Janus (visible on the *Ianiculum* hill beyond the river, on the right bank; 358)
(8) *forum Romanum* (361)
(9) *Carinae* (in Vergil's time, elegant residential quarter on Esquiline hill, site of, e.g., Maecenas' home, 361, and of Vergil's own house next to the gardens of Maecenas: *vita Donati* 42).
(10) Evander's palace (on the Palatine hill; 359; 362; 363)

It is generally assumed without further discussion that the two heroes will right away pass through the gate of Carmentis once they have reached its vicinity. But to this interpreter it appears worthwhile in the first place to raise the question, do they enter Evander's city at this point of time? If we assume they do, Evander will be embarking on a strange zig-zag course, which has even caused commentators to question the soundness of the transmitted text:[45] next, they would move northeast on the *vicus Iugarius*, along the Capitoline, to see the *asylum* (342; the depression might best be viewed, on this side of the Capitoline, from the *Forum Romanum* area or from as close as possible to it). Then, they would go back south to the west corner of the Palatine near the *Circus Maximus* (the *Lupercal*, 343), only to recross the *Velabrum* once more in the opposite direction, toward the

277

Chapter 6

Capitoline's two peaks (*ad Tarpeiam sedem et Capitolia*, 347). The last-mentioned crossing, which includes approaching or pointing out the *Argiletum* (345) northeast of the *Forum Romanum*, would anyway afford them an adequate opportunity to catch a view (if it is to be taken from the east side) of the *asylum* valley between the two peaks of the Capitoline on their approach to the hill (*ad Tarpeiam sedem et Capitolia*, 347). Why does the *asylum* receive a separate visit or approach beforehand (342)?

Once already we have seen that topographical vicinity is not generally the organizing principle of the tour. This time, one may at least be sure that the *asylum* is indeed the "next" location (*hinc*, 342, whether understood in either its local or its temporal meaning) pointed out[46] by Evander: "the vast grove which fierce Romulus made his *asylum*" (342f.), i.e., the valley between the Capitoline's two peaks which Romulus used to receive refugees and dissatisfied elements from the surrounding area so he might enlarge the number of inhabitants able to bear arms in his endangered new settlement (cf. Livy 1. 8. 5f.). Within his own setting (i.e., on level B), of course, Evander himself "had no reason to draw Aeneas' attention to the *ingens lucus* (342) for its own sake".[47] The relative clause *quem Romulus acer asylum rettulit* is another intervention by the author, providing C-level information to *his* audience: Evander points out the place which to *us* Romans today represents the fighting spirit which allowed our city, even in its earliest stage, to survive in a threatening environment. The "next" location pointed out after the *Porta Carmentalis*, then, has been selected (though this need not be the only reason for Vergil's choice) because of the contribution it makes to the proto-Augustan perspective of Rome's history, not for its topographical vicinity. After all, founder Romulus (living roughly four hundred years after Evander) is central to the ideology of Rome's 'second' founder who considered the name Romulus for himself at one time, but dropped it in favor of 'Augustus' (Suet. *Aug.* 7. 2). Nevertheless (as we shall see later in this Chapter) Augustus jealously continued to maintain a sort of monopoly for himself in matters concerning Romulus.

There is another reason, likewise located on level C (and perhaps even closer to the ruler's own aspirations), why the *asylum* is mentioned. "Aeneas at the site of Rome" (to use Warde Fowler's title of 1917) has always fascinated scholars, not least because of the exciting possibility of tracing his route with the help of the ever-growing findings of archaeology. An important step, fully to be credited here, was made by Grimal (1948) who saw that "derrière la Pallantée d'Évandre, c'est Rome augustéenne qui apparaît".[48] Grimal seems to assume that the vicinity of the *names* of Apollo and Carmentis (in one and the same line, 336), "le rapprochement des noms de Carmenta et d' Apollon", is meant to trigger the reader's recollection of the nearby temple of Apollo and the theater of Marcellus – the latter soon (17 BC i.e., two years after Vergil's death, but certainly a gigantic construction site already in his lifetime) to be the site of some of the secular celebrations under the protection of Apollo and Artemis – as of a "vaste ensemble apollinien."[49]

The verbal association of collocated names may carry some weight, but one wonders if Grimal has fully fathomed the function and implications of the visual indicators for the reading of our text. So far, Vergil has led us a very direct route, by appealing to our eyes. Evander, after all, *points out* (*monstrat*) his mother's altar. The author has given no indication that the optical guidance should henceforth be discontinued.

If, as we were led to understand, the two walkers are still at (outside) the gate when the next step is being contemplated by Evander, the nearest viewing point for the *asylum* is found not (as assumed by Grimal) by turning right into the *vicus Iugarius*, but by going *northwest*, i.e., by setting out as if to round the Capitoline clockwise. One does not have to go very far. A distance of less than three hundred yards, in today's terms: as far as the *via Montanara* and the *Piazza di Campitelli*, which allows the first impressive glimpse of the ravine that ends up at the *asylum*, the hollow between the *arx* in the north (today occupied by *S.a Maria d'Aracoeli*) and the Capitol proper on the southern peak. The best access today is granted by the stairs of Michelangelo, the *"Cordonnata"*. Having reached the *Piazza del Campidoglio* and facing the *Palazzo Senatorio* (built on top of the remnants of the ancient *Tabularium*), one can still verify being in a hollow by reviewing the steps which lead up left (behind the *Palazzo Nuovo*) to *S.a Maria d'Aracoeli* and right (behind the *Palazzo dei Conversatori*) to the *Via del Tempio di Giove*. This much information may suffice for the modern reader. I in no way suggest that the aged Evander and his guest are supposed to have climbed up the hill. For a glimpse of the *asylum*, they only had to continue in the same direction for a few minutes on the level route they had pursued so far.

While having the two heroes move along on the Capitoline's west side, I am ready to claim that this understanding of the text was natural in the eyes of Vergil's contemporaries – not only for the philologist who wishes to remove at least one unnecessary leg from the seeming zigzag course pursued by Evander. For the alternative – looking for the depression *inter duos lucos* (Livy 1. 8. 5) from the *Forum Romanum* side – must have been difficult to visualize for Vergil's contemporaries, considering that there, on the east side of the Capitoline, the ravine had long ago been filled in by the Archives, i.e., the *Tabularium*, (re)built under the consul of 78 BC, Q. Lutatius Catulus. Impressive as today's remnants may rise from the *forum* level (even when viewed from the Palatine, the second floor arches may seem to reach as high as the *Piazza del Campidoglio*), the ancient building was taller.

Over the *substructio*, there rose the *Tabularium* proper,[50] of which the lower porticus (three out of eleven original arches)[51] is recognizable still in today's eastern facade. It was topped by another storey (or by a facade hiding the roof from view),[52] this one, too, decorated with columns and arches.[53] The building's west side, now replaced by the facade of the *Palazzo Senatorio*, faced the *asylum* depression (bordering on the temple of Veiovis). Still today, the top line of the *ancient* building, when traced along the side and compared to the rear façade facing the Piazza del Campidoglio, is as high as half the staircase which leads up from the piazza level to the entrance door of the Palazzo Senatorio: the *forum* was invisible from the *asylum* depression.

From these considerations it is clear that it would have made less sense for Vergil to expect his contemporaries to visualize the *asylum* from the blocked *forum Romanum* side – excepting the possibility that the *Tabularium* should be considered one of the sky-scraping (8. 99f.) edifices the poet wishes his reader to contrast with the modest past of King Evander's time. Considering, however, that Augustus' 'forerunner' Romulus is the focus here (a focus continued in the following line: *Lupercal*), it is unlikely that the target figure and the topography of his time ought to be obscured in Vergil's intention by a reference to a Republican, i.e., pre-Augustan, high-rise building. We shall have to deal with a similar but slightly different case soon.

So far, we have only demonstrated the probability that Vergil's contemporaries would naturally understand not the *Vicus Iugarius* side but the river side route along the Capitoline to be intended here (at *Aen.* 8. 342). We have not yet turned to the "Augustan view" which strikes the eye of someone who – this is true still in today's city and therefore can be described in today's terms – has moved along the *Via L. Petroselli* as far as its intersection with the *Vico Iugario* (where the street name changes to *Via del Teatro di Marcello*) and now looks ahead (across the ancient *forum Holitorium*).[54]

The closest and most massive building, begun by C. Julius Caesar (in rivalry with Pompey's theater – or by Marcellus when he was aedile) and completed by Augustus (D.C. 43. 49. 2), is the Theater of Marcellus on the left. Its impressive height (36 yards) and width (143 yards) makes it an ideal candidate for the skyscraping aspirations mentioned at 8. 99f., even if, in Vergil's own lifetime, the view was still that of a gigantic construction site. Though dedicated in 13 (or 11) BC, the theater was already in 17 BC, two years after the *Aeneid*'s author died, so far completed that it could be used for Augustus' Secular Games. It was named after the Emperor's nephew (his sister's son), son-in-law and potential successor, whose untimely death (23 BC) is commented upon in the *Aeneid* by a pretentious[55] piece of praise from the lips of Aeneas' prophetic father, Anchises

(6. 863–886. Marcellus' mother, i.e., Augustus' sister Octavia, is said to have fainted when Vergil read this obituary to her and to her brother, *vita Donati* 113–115). Augustus himself (among other measures) honored the dead by having Marcellus' golden image as well as a golden crown placed on a curule chair which was set among the magistrates in the theater (D.C. 53. 30. 6). The theater has been visible from as far away as the *Ara Maxima* and now dominates the scene ahead of the two kings to the left.

Next, though at this point still partially kept out of view by the bulk of the theater on the left and by the temple of Bellona on its right, there is the temple of Apollo, of which three columns (on its southeast corner) have been re-erected earlier in the last century. Again, we see an edifice that was being completed while Vergil was working on his epic, in the year 23 BC. In this case, the history of its construction and decoration prove to be of the highest political interest.

C. Sosius, *triumphator* 34 BC and consul 32 BC, took it upon himself to restore (or, rather, to replace) the old (431 BC) temple of *Apollo Medicus*. Having been pardoned after fighting on Antony's side in the battle of Actium (D. C. 5. 2. 4), Sosius is today seen by archaeologists to have adjusted the decoration of 'his' temple (customarily called the temple of *Apollo Sosianus*) to the changed political environment of the early principate.[56] His eagerness seems to have paid off, for he is listed among the *quindecimviri sacris faciundis*, the priests of Apollo who took part in the Secular Games of 17 BC. The temple was crowded with Greek artifacts and often served (as did the neighboring temple of Bellona of 296 BC on its right, seen from the *Porta Carmentalis*) for Senate meetings. Definitely, especially since being dedicated to the tutelary deity of the *Princeps*, Sosius' temple proved a worthy neighbor to the Theater of Marcellus – so worthy indeed that its dedication date was set so as to coincide with Augustus' birthday (Sept. 23).

The temple is neighbor also to another important building associated with the imperial family, the huge Porticus of Octavia (covering an area of 132 x 145 yards), built by Augustus himself (or by his sister with his support?) in the place of an older portico (of Metellus) and dedicated – in consonance with his family-oriented building activity and policy – to the ruler's sister (the mother of Marcellus; at this time his sister Octavia was still wielding more influence than his wife Livia). Inside were two temples, of *Iuppiter Stator* and of *Iuno Regina*, their ends connected by the *curia Octaviae* – another Augustan meeting place for the Senate.[57] There was also a library founded by Octavia to commemorate her son Marcellus. The grandeur of the whole complex is still communicated by the preserved

Chapter 6

entrance gate, restored under Septimius Severus. (The built-in brick facade has to be subtracted since it belonged to a later church.)

It is questionable whether the *porticus* could be seen from the *Porta Carmentalis* area, being covered from view almost completely by the theater and the two adjacent temples. As a matter of fact, the *Apollo Sosianus* temple was squeezed in so tightly that its southwestern corner was only seven yards from the theater, while the northwestern corner was running up against the portico.[58] Nevertheless, if on the right of the Bellona temple the view was unobstructed, Vergil's contemporaries should have been able to see the northeast corner of the *porticus Octaviae* (the eastern side would reach even beyond what is today the *Piazza di Campitelli*) from the *Carmentalis* gate area, even without advancing any further.

One would see much more of the portico if one walked, as the archaeological evidence suggested to us Aeneas and Evander did, somewhat ahead in order to see the *asylum* depression. Once more Vergil's route evokes in his reader a powerful level-C architectural presence of which the level-B characters Evander and Aeneas were as ignorant as sleepwalkers. Since the *porticus Octaviae* was probably built between 33 and 23 BC (perhaps dedicated after 27), its construction again takes us into the years when Vergil was working on the *Aeneid* and designed the route for the walk. It should be added that the three buildings which bear names connected with Augustus: Marcellus, Apollo, Octavia, formed the southern complex in the Emperor's revamping of the whole *Campus Martius* (he was helped in this undertaking by Agrippa). For understanding Book 8 of the *Aeneid*, it is enough for us to realize the uniformly Augustan prospect Vergil evoked in his contemporary reader.

There is one more instance of visual guidance which may escape the *Aeneid*'s modern reader who is unfamiliar with the ancient topography. The *Porta Carmentalis* since the times of the late republic opened onto a colonnade which led northwest toward the temples of Apollo and of Bellona. (It apparently ended at the *Circus Flaminius* and has thus even been understood to represent the *porticus triumphalis*.)[59] Still today, one can see two double arches along the *Via del Teatro di Marcello* on the northern sidewalk of the *Vico Iugario* and parts of the continuation northwestward, especially two travertine columns – the course leading to the right of the three re-erected columns of the *Apollo Sosianus* temple, i.e., put more precisely, to the temple of Bellona. This is in almost direct continuation of the northwestern direction taken by Aeneas and Evander ever since leaving the *Ara Maxima*. Today, one is offered an unobstructed view over the whole distance: from the entrance to *S.a Maria in Cosmedin*, i.e. the location of the *Ara Maxima*, all the way to the remnants of the colonnade, to the tall structure of the Theater of Marcellus and to the area of the Bellona temple, appearing to the right of the theater.

It seems most natural that a contemporary reader, not trained in archaeology, would understand Vergil as having the colonnade in mind when he sent the two kings on to look at the *asylum*. The colonnade also hugged the temple of Bellona on the right and must have reached even the *porticus Octaviae* – a location (*Piazza Campitelli* and beyond, in today's terms) where the *asylum* ravine comes more and more into view. In this area, then, somewhat more than 200 yards from the *porta Carmentalis*, on the Augustan street level (several yards below today's *Piazza Campitelli*) the "huge" (*ingentem*, 342) wooded saddle would be experienced as an impressive sight indeed. Taking his position at the corner of *Via del Teatro di Marcello* and *Via Montanara*, today's visitor still can catch a glimpse of the ravine between *S.a Maria d'Aracoeli* on the left and the Capitolium proper on the right.

Little did Aeneas know (his present guide did not possess the prophetic voice with which Anchises had spoken in Book 6) that, right where he was standing, a sight much more spectacular than that woody depression would one day be created by and for his glorious family – and that this future construction was the real reason why he now had to show himself interested (cf. 310f.) in staring happily (*laetus*) at an overgrown hillside ravine.

One may ask, should not the Capitol and the temple of Jupiter Optimus Maximus likewise be thought of as alluded to? After all, both are certainly within view here, the temple offering its western long side (and, possibly, *acroteria*).

I would consider the question off the mark and argue that, on the one hand, the Capitol, including the temple, is dealt with later (8. 347f.); on the other hand, the *asylum* being thematic here, the poet certainly thought about (and implied a possible solution for) the problem confronting his metropolitan reader: how to perceive and map out a likely route for the two walkers, which would lead them to viewing the *asylum*. This thought process would lead the reader to decide upon the *porticus Octaviae* vicinity. But the inclusion of any buildings (such as the Jupiter Optimus Maximus temple on the Capitol) unrelated to the route's immediate topographical and ideological context must appear haphazard to the poet's concept.

There is, as our text suggests, another (and this one, a valid) question: why would Vergil pick the visually less striking saddle for Aeneas to see and discount the more spectacular mountain peak (the *Capitolium* is, after all, closer to the spectators than the *Asylum*)? The question bares the core of Vergil's intentions. My answer: the depression between the two peaks was chosen not to raise the reader's interest in the Capitoline Hill – but to draw the two hikers (and the reader's attention) on toward the southern *Campus*

Martius and the Augustan edifices-under-construction. If the *Asylum* alone (without any visual ramifications) had been Vergil's intended focus, it would indeed have been sufficient to mention it later, along the way from the *Lupercal* toward the *Argiletum* or during their approach *ad Tarpeiam sedem et Capitolia* (347), in a purely narrative fashion. But by the polar way the two locations associated with Rome's first founder are presented here, they provide an apt narrative setting for some of the second founder's activity.

The route suggested above, then, not only removes two inexplicable extra laps from the three customarily assumed crossings of the *Velabrum* area between Capitoline and Palatine. Even if one assumes that the verb *monstrare* (343) need not always entail walking up closely to the object pointed out, those movements across the valley cannot be eliminated – though some may perhaps be somewhat shortened in the perception of the topographically informed Roman reader. Certainly, a grotto shown "under the cold (overhanging?) rock", *gelida monstrat sub rupe* (343), requires a rather close-up approach for inspection. Now, after our investigation, it is no longer necessary to assume that the two walkers *first* left the gate of Carmenta in a northeastern direction toward the *Forum Romanum* area for viewing the *asylum*, and *then*, walking (a mere turn of the head won't suffice here) along the sides of an acute angle, would have had to return south to view the *Lupercal* – only to go back north again.

It also makes more sense for the level-B narrative itself if Evander proceeds as follows: upon returning (from viewing the *asylum* depression), via or along the course of the triumphal colonnade and, this time, passing through (a fact which need not specifically be mentioned) the *porta Carmentalis*, he would go and point out the *Lupercal* where the twins Romulus and Remus were nursed by the she-wolf. The decision that the place was to be included in the tour at all is, of course, a level-C choice. After all, by mythical chronology the twins were born about four hundred years after the time of Evander. (One should not take offence that the two geographically distant places, *Asylum* and *Lupercal*, are mentioned within only two lines: they are connected by their reference to Romulus. At 361, two even more distant places, *forum Romanum* and *Carinae*, are mentioned in one and the same line.)

Let us recall that Vergil decided to be silent about a city entrance in the *Scalae Caci* area. His silence also determines the walkers' route so that Aeneas would set his foot on the southern *Campus Martius* before entering the city. This concept entails that the *Lupercal* cannot be approached until after the city has been entered through another entrance (i.e., the *porta Carmentalis*, about three hundred yards northwest of the *Lupercal*). In this way, too, the Palatine is showing two different faces: from the river, Aeneas sees the lofty site of Augustus' future residence; on the walk, he reviews from closer-to the fateful grotto at the foot of the Palatine. Though not found up to this day, the *Lupercal* is known to have been at the southwest corner of the hill. Dionysius of Halicarnassus reports that the cave from which the spring issues "is shown along the road to the *Circus Maximus* [i.e., the *vicus Tuscus* ?], built against the Palatine" (*Ant. Rom.* 1. 79. 5; cf. 32.3–5. See also Servius *ad Aen.* 8. 90: *ubi nunc est Lupercal in Circo*).

For the narrative on level B, there is a plausible reason why Evander would wish to include the *Lupercal*. Sensing the linguistic ingredient *lupus* = wolf in the name, ancient learned speculation could easily draw the parallel to Arcadian Pan Λυκαῖος, which offers the same association in Greek (λύκος = wolf). The connection makes it natural for the exile Evander to have set up a sanctuary for a divinity of his home country, the "*Lupercal*, named after the Parrhasian custom, as being that of Pan *Lycaeus*" (8. 344). The procedure is in line with the respect he pays to his mother's altar. (The Roman reader must apparently understand that the Latin name has been substituted by Vergil for Evander's Greek original.)

However, this piece of consistent level-B motivation should not deceive today's reader about the true motive which guides the author himself when introducing the sanctuary. Though topographically separated by a considerable distance, *asylum* and *Lupercal* are, as indicated above, united through the person of Romulus. The first was a model of his cunning statesmanship, the latter the place of his miraculous survival against all odds: Rome's 'first' founder grew up under supra-natural protection. (One may add that it was the religious occasion of the *Lupercalia* which led to his recognition and ensuing career, Livy 1. 5; Aelius Tubero in D.H. 1. 80.)

Viewed in these terms, it is not difficult to outline the level-C relevance of the recent route: Carmenta's altar and gate (tied together grammatically by *et...et*, 337f.) gave occasion to reveal the history of the Palatine as divinely predetermined. As far as symbolism is concerned, we may now add that it is much more appropriate for the Julians' ancestor to enter his family's future city through a gate which is associated with Apollo's prophetess than through an access connected by tradition with a cattle-stealing monster like Cacus.

Next Romulus, seen as the skillful guide to power of his threatened young state and as living under divine protection, shows himself a worthy and proven predecessor of Augustus, presumably Rome's greatest ruler ever. (The grammatical connection is established by single *et*, 343.)

Evander (as we indicated earlier) is integrated into the teleological web: arriving under Apollo's guidance, he was led by his piety to found the sanctuary which later protected Rome's founder. An indelible fixture in

Chapter 6

Italian mythology anyway, the Arcadian king is, in the *Aeneid*, assigned the teleological function of being fated history's trailblazer.

We may recall a parallel on this occasion. In Livy, Evander's founding of the *Lupercal* is narrated as a footnote, integrated into the context of *Romulus'* story (1. 5. 1–2). The same applies to the Hercules-Cacus episode and Evander's role at the institution of the cult of the *Ara Maxima*. The story is told by Livy (in a ring composition: 1. 7. 3b *Graeco* ~1. 7. 15 *peregrina*) as part of the religious practice of *Romulus*; Hercules' was the only foreign cult Romulus accepted. (It is misleading when Ogilvie characterizes Romulus' constitutional measures in 1. 8 compositionally "as an interlude between Cacus and the Rape of the Sabine Women".)

For our argument a welcome (though hardly necessary) external parallel, for the role the *Aeneid* assigns to Evander, is provided by Livy. Fate picked Evander so that he might prepare the road for greater ones who would follow him. The place of Romulus' survival will depend on Evander's piety as Hercules and Aeneas have relied on his hospitality (and piety). The second Romulus, at the end of the prophesied development, will (as will his court poet) keep the memory alive of the fated string of events. In addition to eighty-two unnamed temples he restored to splendor (in 28 BC), Augustus in his *Achievements* singles out a number of edifices he (at other times) took under his care and mentions them by name. The *Lupercal* is one of them (*R. G.* 19.1). His poet agrees with him in this emphasis.[60] Ultimately, it is not early-Rome romanticism but level-C teleology which again turns out to determine the selection of places shown by Evander to Augustus' ancestor Aeneas.

As a confirmation *a posteriori* one may take the fact that, a decade after Vergil's death, the *Lupercal* will be depicted on the panel left of the entrance to the "Altar of the Augustan Peace", in most prominent display, according to the modern re-figuration. The panel right of the entrance will be taken up by Aeneas, sacrificing the sow and its thirty piglets – a scene likewise appearing in the *Aeneid*'s eighth Book. The emperor himself and his family are seen on the side panel of the *Ara pacis Augustae*: for a usurper's self-esteem, the presumed roots of his "dynasty" can be more important than his own picture. Vergil had good reason for letting Aeneas inspect the *Lupercal*.

(c) *Monuments of the Julians' Mission, II: the Unsuspecting Ancestor Reaches the* forum Romanum *Grounds*

If even localities which can easily be explained within Evander's own sphere of personal experience (his mother's altar; his hometown god) point beyond him and ultimately serve the Augustan ideology of level C, it is difficult to think that there is no ulterior motive behind the selection of other places mentioned in the narrative. Yet just that may seem to be the case with the following example (8. 345f.) – "the grove of the accursed *Argiletum*", a narrow passageway leading, in the reader's time, to the suburb on the other side (northeast) of the *forum Romanum*. Its myth (based on popular etymology) makes Argus a guest of Evander who tried to overthrow his host, only to be killed himself by the Arcadians. Pious Evander nevertheless buried him for hospitality's sake, declaring the place "accursed" (*sacri*, 345 = *exsecrabilis*, Servius). Servius, apparently baffled by the king's telling of the story, concludes that Evander does well dwelling on the explanation "lest he become suspect to his guest" (i.e., to Aeneas), *ne apud hospitem veniat in suspitionem*. Even if awkward, this comment would restrict the motive for mentioning the *Argiletum* to level B itself. It also shows the difficulty the ancient commentators incurred when trying to explain (find a motive for) the mention of the *Argiletum*.

But Grimal,[61] noting that the arch of Janus once stood where the *Argiletum* issues onto the *forum* (and that, moreover, Janus is mentioned a little – twelve lines – later at 357), believes the story itself was introduced to facilitate mentioning the *Argiletum* (Vergil's text, however, lets Evander first point out the *Argiletum* and then tell its story). Its name, like the name of Carmenta earlier, would "irresistibly" evoke the arch of Janus, "one of the 'holy places' of Augustan policy", "l'un des 'lieux sacrés' de la politique augustéenne", l.c. (Closing the Gates of Janus was the symbol of the *pax Augusta*, cf. *Aen*. 1. 294; *Res Gestae* 13). With it, Augustus' building activity in the vicinity would come to mind.

Grimal is basically right but, again, his method of verbal associations – across twelve lines – perhaps proceeds more conjecturally than is necessary. We observe that the *Argiletum* is loosely attached to the preceding group:

And also, he points out the accursed grove of the *Argiletum*,
and calls on the place as witness and tells of the death of his guest Argus.

necnon et sacri monstrat nemus Argileti
testaturque locum et letum docet hospitis Argi.   8. 345f.

Necnon et is not as direct and weighty as the *hinc* used for the preceding and following sets of examples (342; 347). In Vergil's use, it rather can add something less important to a more essential preceding point (a use not sufficiently exemplified in the dictionaries). At 1. 707 (where also see Austin) *nec non et* introduces the lower-ranking Tyrians who enter Dido's palace after the important characters – *Cupido*, 695; *regina*, 697; *Aeneas*, 699 – have taken their places. The late-comers function as supernumeraries, showing admiration for what they see (*mirantur...mirantur*, 709).

Nor does *testatur* (he "calls on the place to tell its story", Fordyce *ad* 346) with necessity entail that they would walk close up to the place (as *progressus*, 337, did, qualifying *monstrat*, 337). As a matter of fact, an accursed place is hardly a *monumentum* (cf. 312) which the king would wish to take his guest to for close inspection as he did when he led him to the altar of his mother. It is therefore possible that Evander "points out the grove" from some distance (as one would anyway in the case of a somewhat extended wooded area, *nemus*, 345) and then perhaps specifies the spot (*locum*, 346) within the setting. Whereas at 337 it was the story he was telling that caused him to advance to the altar, at 345f. he possibly points out the locality *in passing* without approaching it closely and tells its gloomy story *while* simultaneously having in mind already, and heading for, the next target area, the Capitoline (347). So one would have to leave open for now the question of how closely the two walkers came to the Argiletum. On the one hand, telling the story (346) might take Evander all the way to the Argiletum, after first (345) pointing out the grove from a distance. On the other hand, he might cut short their approach at some point when reaching the *forum Romanum* area. More on this shortly.

One might, considering the casual introduction (*necnon et* is, after all, not merely a matter of stylistic variation) of the *Argiletum* section ("And he does not fail to point out..."), think of printing it in parentheses so that the series of connections between places would run as follows: *dehinc...et...et; ...hinc...et...; (necnon et...-que...et...); hinc...et...* (337–347). One might think of doing so, I say – were it not for the *hinc* at 347 (which cannot refer back to the *Lupercal* once the walkers have moved on to view the *Argiletum*) and for the contemporary reader's unavoidable reaction to Evander's act of pointing out. The reader cannot but wonder: how can one, while crossing the *Velabrum* area from the *Lupercal* in a northerly direction (the reader would naturally picture himself following the *Vicus Tuscus*), even see the *Argiletum*? To provide a positive answer to this question, the reader has to 'subtract' (the word understood as discussed in the context of 8. 99f.) from his perception not only the memory of the old *basilica Sempronia* which used to block a free view across the *forum Romanum* to its northern side, but above all its recent replacement, the new *basilica Iulia*, which was begun by C. Julius Caesar and completed by Augustus. And the same problem, of course, arises when Vergil's reader pictures Evander walking all the way over toward the *Argiletum*: again, the *Basilica Iulia* would have to be 'subtracted' to clear a straight approach.

It must be admitted that the actual size of the original Augustan basilica is unknown to us. What one sees today is the larger base area (*ampliato eius solo*, R. G. 20. 3; 110x55 yards) on which Augustus rebuilt the hall after the fire of 14 BC.[62] (It was rebuilt again, after another fire in AD 283, by Diocletian.) But it seems a safe guess that the first Julian plan already was larger than that of its predecessor, the *basilica Sempronia*.[63] The remains visible today are those of a three-storey building with five naves: a central hall (90x20 yards), surrounded by two concentric porticos.[64]

It should not strike us as odd that again – as before, in the case of the dynasty-related buildings on the southern *campus Martius* – Vergil neither identifies by name nor even mentions the basilica which in his day blocked the view his Evander demonstrates to Aeneas. Indirect praise (on the epic's large scale, Aeneas the ancestor is to cast light also on Augustus the present-day ruler: Donatus, p. 2), even praise *ex silentio*, can be more effective (and less embarrassing) where the reference is obvious and unmistakable. After all, the two walkers are here taking a first glimpse (more will have to be said later) of another core area of later Julian self-representation. Even Augustus himself, usually not shy about his achievements, fails to drop the name *Iulia* when (*R. G.* 20. 3) "modestly" mentioning that he completed what his adoptive father had almost finished, viz. "the basilica between the temple of Castor and the temple of Saturnus", *et basilicam quae fuit inter aedem Castoris et aedem Saturni, coepta profligataque opera a patre meo, perfeci*.

That silence can be used to proclaim the key word is shown by the continuation: after "my father", Augustus mentions his two (adopted and prematurely deceased) "sons", in whose names "the same" building was to be resurrected after the fire – in the case of his own untimely death, by his heirs: *et eandem basilicam consumptam incendio...sub titulo nominis filiorum meorum incohavi, et, si vivus non perfecissem, perfici ab heredibus meis iussi*, (l.c).

What, then, keeps Vergil's contemporary reader from himself verifying and reenacting Evander's observation is the obstacle[65] formed by the large and tall, visible symbol of his ruler's dynastic concept displayed on the *forum Romanum*. (Even if still under construction at the time of writing, the building would naturally be viewed as completed in a piece of poetry intended to instruct readers for years to come.) Though the basilica already in Vergil's lifetime clearly expressed the family goals, its mission became even more obvious later (and here the later development reinforces the interpretation of the early beginnings), after the deaths of Caius and Lucius (whose names, by the way, never stuck; the building always remained the *Iulia*): the basilica had all along represented the emperor's unlimited dynastic hopes, reaching out into the future even to the time after his own anticipated death (as the quotation shows).

The emperor's unexpected modesty (one may prefer to call it well-targeted restraint) in an overall context of self-praise (in *R.G.* 19–21,

Chapter 6

Augustus deals with his own building program) and the reticent understatement concerning obvious family claims find their counterpart in the poet's treatment of the *forum Romanum* (this level-C term is actually used at *Aen.* 8. 361). To illuminate the situation by a modern parallel, one might think of a poet who praises the view one may once have had of the Potomac from the La Fayette Park area (the view is blocked by the White House). Ignorant of the area he is surveying, Aeneas is about to stumble across the historical site where his family will be eternalized in marble.

The "basilica between the temple of Castor and the temple of Saturnus" is more strictly defined by the two streets which, running along its short sides, issue onto the *forum*; in the east, between the basilica and the temple of the *Dioscuri* (traditionally called that "of the Castors"), passes the *vicus Tuscus*, coming from the *Circus Maximus* and the *Lupercal* area (today covered approximately by the *via S. Teodoro*); in the west, between the basilica and the temple of Saturnus, runs (visible still today, at a much lower level than the *via della Consolazione* as the upper continuation of the present-day *vico Iugario* is called) the *vicus Iugarius,* which, coasting the Capitoline Hill, originated at the *porta Carmentalis*. (As a matter of fact, both streets have apparently had to adjust their course somewhat in order to accommodate the Augustan enlargement of the basilica plan.) If one wished to continue one's way eastward, there was (except for the *clivus Argentarius* which continued hugging the northern elevation of the Capitoline) only one street leaving from the other side of the *forum*, opposite the center of the *basilica Iulia* (i.e., the center of its long side facing the *forum*): this exit was the *Argiletum*.

The *Argiletum* was not only marked by the arch of Janus (mentioned earlier as part of Grimal's reasoning), but by its squeezed-in position between two important monuments. The *basilica Aemilia*, on its right (=southeast) when viewed from the *basilica Iulia*, had been rebuilt in the years 55–34 BC, originally with financial support from C. Julius Caesar,[66] but nevertheless by L. Aemilius Paullus, member of the basilica's founding family (with claims to Trojan origin). As Caesar did not object to the old family name, so Augustus allowed it to continue: a "republican" figleaf in an otherwise Julian environment.

On the other side of the *Argiletum*, to its left (=northwest) when viewed from the *Basilica Iulia*, there rose the *curia Iulia*, the senate house – today represented by a reconstruction, done in the 1930's, of Diocletian's restoration. No longer really a part of the old republican *forum*, the *curia Iulia* was more of an appendix to the *forum* of C. Julius Caesar, to the plan of which it was adapted, and on which its rear doors opened. Construction was begun after a fire in 52 BC and was completed by Octavian (dedication in 29 BC). The new orientation of Rome's power can be illustrated by two occurrences. At the opposite end of his own *forum*, Caesar had built the temple of the Julian family goddess, *Venus Genetrix*. Being a living god himself, he did not mind on one occasion receiving the senators in the *pronaos* while himself being seated in the *intercolumnia* (Suet. *Iul.* 78. 2).[67] The other event is that Octavian, upon completing the senate house, placed his own *Victoria*, stepping on a globe, inside at the far end of the senators' benches. "From now on she would be present at every meeting of the Senate!"[68]

Viewed next to its giant neighbors, the *Argiletum* amounted to not much more than a gap in the Julian building program – a narrow passageway, as insignificant among its neighbors as the *Asylum* in relation to the giant buildings of the *forum Holitorium* or the southern *Campus Martius*. If Vergil had thought rather of the quarter (likewise called *Argiletum*) than of the street which led to it, the blockade of the spectator's view would be complete.

Let the selective description given above provide an impression of what the ancient reader associated with the most recent section of King Evander's guided tour, from the *Lupercal* toward and past the (more or less) distant *Argiletum* to "Tarpeia's seat and the Capitol" (*ad Tarpeiam sedem et Capitolia*, 347; the last word being a poetic plural). No matter whether the reader pictured the two walkers on their way from the *Lupercal* arriving at the *forum* via the *vicus Tuscus* or – less probable, as will be confirmed later – the *vicus Iugarius*, or even by crossing the site of the future *basilica Iulia*, there was no chance of missing the Julian implications of the route. In recent years, archaeologists (for instance, Zanker 1987) have been less hesitant than literary critics in recognizing the claim to solitary power which underlies the republican facade of the Augustan age. So it seems appropriate for us to spell out in somewhat greater detail the framework of recent references which Augustan Vergil could count on in his audience when he had the Julian ancestor visit the *forum Romanum* (cf. 361), the political center of the old republic.

Interpretation of the following lines is fraught with difficulties. Having determined earlier that the *Argiletum* is possibly pointed out (*monstrat*, 345) from some distance, we consequently shall be open to taking *hinc* at 347 not necessarily in its local ("from this place") but in its temporal meaning: "hereafter", "next". This can relieve us from positing another circuitous movement which would have Evander first steer north (*Argiletum*), then west (Capitoline Hill; or, if the *Capitolium* is meant, southwest), then (south)east (northern access to the Palatine) again. On the other hand, at least a degree of physical approximation toward the

Chapter 6

Argiletum is quite plausible, and a circular movement is compatible with a guided tour, perhaps best explaining the series of visual pointers given in the text.

There are, as we shall see later, different ways of understanding line 347, depending partly on the meaning one accepts for *Capitolia*, partly on the determination of *Tarpeiam sedem,* and partly even on the function of *et*. One thing, however, we may this time be sure about: the old king takes his guest right toward the (foot of the) hill: *ad...ducit*, 347.

Commentators compare a section (8. 652f.) from the pictorial description of Vulcan's shield.[69] But this passage itself is not without difficulty, as Excursus 2 at the end of this Chapter shows. Lines 8.652f. most likely reflect the traditional dichotomy of the Capitoline's two summits: the citadel (*arx*) was the early city's defence bastion, whereas the other (southern) summit, the *Capitolium* proper, represented the religious center, being the seat of the Capitoline Triad, with the temple of Jupiter, Juno, and Minerva.

It is with a sharpened sense of the hill's dual character that we now approach line 8. 347:

Hereafter, he leads him to the Tarpeian seat and the Capitol,

hinc ad Tarpeiam sedem et Capitolia ducit.

CN think that "*sedem* apparently refers to the temple of Jupiter". Their understanding entails both that one takes *Tarpeiam* in the "mannered" way (or in Varro's meaning) discussed in Excursus 2 and that *et* is used epexegetically,[70] specifying: to the Tarpeian seat, "that is, the Capitol". This however seems unsatisfactory because it pegs on Vergil here that same tautological element our Excursus 2 rejects at 8. 652f.: both expressions, *sedem* and *Capitolia*, would, in CN's reading, refer to the Capitoline's southern peak.[71]

If a summary terminology seems called for, then it would be less offensive to accept a notion congruent with Livy's occasional hendiadys (noted in Excursus 2) which comprises the hill as a whole: Evander leads his guest "to the seat of Tarpeia (=the *arx*) and the Capitol (=seat of Jupiter)". The fact that *ad* is not repeated before *Capitolia* may be seen to favor this reading.

There is of course no *a priori* compelling reason why line 347 must be understood in the way that proved likely at the military situation of 652f. But it is enough if modern readers do not right away discount the distinction, between the two summits, which Excursus 2 finds not only expressly stated in Livy's strategic passages but also implicitly underlying the hendiadys the historian uses when dealing with the hill as a whole.

Moreover, Vergil does here not merely speak of the "citadel" (as Livy does in cases of his hendiadys) but his phrasing specifies, in a way comparable to Propertius at 4. 4. 29, "the domicile"[72] of Tarpeia (or even of her father Tarpeius), i.e., the northern summit. And, above all, preserving the distinction within the unit seems *a priori* more in keeping with the context of an eyewitness inspection of the two-peak hill which is just being provided by Evander to his guest.

Thus, though there is no strategic necessity here of distinguishing, Vergil nevertheless saw fit to hint at the two summits' differing functions. His reason for doing so is revealed in the next line (348) where, while nothing further is mentioned about the citadel, a modifier ("golden") is attached to *Capitolia*. Apparently, the poet wants his contemporary (cf. *nunc*, 348) reader to set his eyes on the southern peak, known for the gilded roof of the temple (restored by Augustus) of Jupiter Optimus Maximus (*aurea* provides a visual stimulus par excellence). At great cost, Augustus restored the temple around 26 BC. It is among those specifically mentioned by name in his *Achievements*. Vergil's focusing is only too understandable; for it is a special feature of the southern peak which his Evander is to single out and deal with in the second continuous speech (351–358) of the whole walk. It also is confirmed now that (as we noted), on the earlier part of the walk along the Capitoline's western foot, the temple of Iupiter Optimus Maximus was not yet to be thematic.

In passing we should observe that Vergil here (at 8. 347) is once more using unmistakable level-C terms (*Tarpeiam, Capitolia*), the meaning of which neither Evander nor Aeneas would be able to fathom. By now, the constant referencing to standards of Vergil's own time (see also *aurea nunc*, 348) has again and again proved disruptive to the fiction of level B: if Aeneas is supposedly fascinated by the places (*locis*, 311) and the memorials of earlier men (*virum monimenta priorum*, 312) he asks about, one wonders which precisely they are. From Aeneas' own sphere of experience (or experience preceding his own timeframe), there have so far been mentioned only "groves" (314: Aeneas the environmentalist? One sees the dissertations coming...); Carmentis' gate as well as altar; and the accursed *Argiletum*. (Both the *asylum* forest and the *Lupercal* grotto, chosen for their level-C relevance, had hardly any other than environmental fascination to offer in the setting of level B.) The majority of the places on the walk are of concern rather to Vergil's contemporary reader. Indeed, it looks as if ignorant Aeneas is sent to tour the area in order that the *audience* be fascinated by places which produce patriotic or Augustan associations.

It is time to determine more precisely, if possible, the area where Evander takes Aeneas *ad Tarpeiam sedem et Capitolia*. The following conditions

Chapter 6

apply: the area lies beyond the *Argiletum* which was an earlier item on the route; the walkers cannot have approached along the route of the later *vicus Iugarius* because that street coasts (and therefore already *is* "at", *ad*) the Capitoline;[73] their approach takes them off the course to their ultimate destination (the Palatine): it would not make sense to say "he leads him toward" if that has been their direction anyway. To avoid a full double crossing of the *forum Romanum* area (once across its short extension, to reach the *Argiletum*, the other time across its full length on their way to reach the Palatine), an alternative was formulated above, viz. that the *Argiletum* may be pointed out from some distance but not necessarily physically approached. Of course, if the reader finds the detour caused by a circular movement and twofold crossing of the *forum* not offensive, one may feel free to let Evander first steer all the way to the *Argiletum*, then – *hinc*, 347 – toward the Capitoline Hill. Under this premise, it may even seem somewhat easier both for the two hikers to view the *arx* first and to Vergil's contemporary to catch a glimpse of the golden roof of the temple of Jupiter Optimus Maximus – if that is what the author intends his reader to do. (See, however, later on.)

Anyway, Vergil's reader will picture the walkers, on their south-north route from the *Lupercal*, skirting (less likely: crossing) the *Basilica Iulia*'s short side along the *Vicus Tuscus* and reaching the *Forum Romanum*. Also approaching (or from a distance glancing at) the *Argiletum*, they will move southwest across the *Forum* and reach the road adjacent to the *Basilica*'s long side, i.e., the side facing the *Forum*, parallel to the lower *Sacra Via* of Vergil's day. (They may have stayed along the lines of this road all the time if they are pictured as not having approached the *Argiletum* physically).

They might stop at about the area where the road is closest – the distance is about twenty-two yards – to the southwest end of the *rostra*.[74] The orators' platform had been transferred to its present location by C. Julius Caesar in 45/44 BC. (Is the reader perhaps invited to take his position also right *on* the southwest corner of the *rostra*, when picturing the topographical implications of this section? Perhaps, but for a brief moment only: not all the points mentioned would be visible from the *rostra*.)

At this point, the reader, turned toward the hill, could, text in hand, verify: the *Argiletum* (turning his head right, he would see it across the *forum*, slightly behind himself); and, left of the senate house and the corner of Caesar's *forum*, the *arx* would appear behind the temple of *Concordia*. (The cella of the temple at that time did not have the huge – 50 x 26 yards – extension it received when, between 7 BC and AD 10, Tiberius was allowed to rebuild it in a shape worthy of Augustus' prospective successor. Nor did the medieval tower, still today affixed to the right side of the *Tabularium*, obstruct much of the view of the *arx*.) In front, there would be the *Tabularium* (blocking out the *asylum* depression, as discussed earlier); in front of its left half and extending beyond its left corner, the temple of Saturnus; and, left again of the temple of Saturnus, there rose the southern bulging extension of the *Capitolium* (with the temple of *Iuppiter Tonans* and, even if not fully visible from here so certainly in the reader's mind associated with the summit, the golden roof [348] of the temple of Jupiter Optimus Maximus). Finally, in turning his head just a little more to the left, Vergil's reader would see, next to (i.e., left of) the *Capitolium*, a section of the *Ianiculum* (cf. line 358): the *Forum* pavement level (still visible in the *rostra* vicinity), we said earlier, was so low as to allow the Tiber frequently to flood the *forum* area. Today, *we* have to discount the elevation of the *via della Consolazione* which allows us to see no more than the roof line of *S.a Maria della Consolazione* (or, if stepping back and taking our position closer to the *Argiletum*, we may catch a glimpse of the roofline of the high houses along the *vico Iugario*. If today's visitor wishes to see the top of the *Gianicolo*, he must take his stand behind and above the *Argiletum*, on the grounds of the *forum* and *via Salara Vecchia*, dug up by archaeologists during the final years of the 20th century).

Our consideration demonstrates that Vergil could be sure that his reader would find a position on the *forum Romanum* from which his imagination could verify the prehistoric local conditions alluded to in the epic's narrative. Taking into account that the two walkers are pictured as being on the move most of the time, the reader would find it even easier to visualize that their constantly shifting perspective allowed them to focus on one after another of the localities mentioned (and not mentioned) in the text. The reader, while tracing the route, would find himself in a thoroughly Augustanized, formerly republican environment – so much so that I feel tempted to say: at the center of the Augustan Empire.

This is no hollow statement. Near the front of Saturnus' temple, in fact at the northwestern corner of the semicircular *rostra* (a hundred feet from the approximate position we hypothesized), is the "navel of the city", *umbilicus urbis* (possibly identical[75] with the *mundus* which symbolizes an opening to the underworld). Even closer (near or at the southwestern end of the *rostra*, in front of the entrance stairs to the temple of Saturnus), there is the point which in 20 BC (in the year before Vergil's departure for Greece and, upon being taken back to Italy by his ruler, his death) Augustus decorated with the *milliarium aureum*, the gilded milestone from which the major roads of the empire were taking their measured departure.[76] The metropolitan reader would find that Evander and Aeneas were unwittingly skirting the geographical center of the Augustan empire.

Even though Vergil does not specifically refer to the Golden Milestone, the *milliarium aureum* may help us today to sense the specifically Augustan presence the poet was conjuring up at this point. Without realizing the political implication, which directs the reader's thoughts toward the architectural changes brought to the *forum* by Aeneas' living descendant (as well as by Augustus' adoptive father), we will not understand the level-C meaning of Evander's ensuing speech.

There was one particularly striking edifice that the Augustan contemporary would have at least partially to "subtract" (or could one see through its *intercolumnia*?) in order to visualize the *Capitolium* and, with it, the "golden" roof of the dominant temple of Jupiter Capitolinus (after the general restoration of temples in 28 BC, again to be restored by Augustus after the fire of 9 BC; cf. *R. G.* 20.1 and 4). This is the temple of Saturnus (mentioned above) on its high podium, right in front of his eyes. It deserves mention under the watchword *quae nunc Romana potentia caelo aequavit* (8. 99f.) because it had recently (from 42 BC on) been totally reconstructed (podium and all) by a new convert to the cause of Octavian, L. Munatius Plancus: "The work was probably finished a few years after the battle of Actium (31 BC), when Plancus, formerly a partisan of Antonius, was already on Octavianus's side."[77] The case is not dissimilar to that of C. Sosius, rebuilder of the *Apollo Sosianus* temple, and one may feel certain that it offers no exception to the rule that in these days dedications are executed by a member of the dynasty itself or a close associate.[78]

Behind the temple, there are *substructiones* carrying the *clivus Capitolinus*, the road up to the Capitoline which began in front of the temple's facade. Counting in the rising elevation behind the temple, one feels that Vergil did not expect his reader to picture the two walkers approaching the hill any closer than the *forum* side of the temple. This area (close to the southwestern end of the *rostra*) does, we said, allow a view of the Capitol's eastern top – bristling, in Evander's time (*olim*, "once", in striking asyndetic juxtaposition to *nunc*, "today", 8. 348) with forest-like thicket.

The confrontational comparison of "then" and "today" is emphasized twice again (*iam tum*, 349; *iam tum*, 350), establishing the most intense assertion so far of the narrator's time level within the time of the narrative, in our terms: of level C in level B. This stylistic feature (caused by the chiasmus *aurea nunc / olim...horrida*) should open our eyes to a possible level-C implication, especially when we see the narrator himself summarizing in advance the story Evander has to tell.

"Already then", in Evander's time, the poet instructs us (349 and 350), the awe-inspiring place, its cliff and forest, made the rustic inhabitants tremble. And Evander goes on to specify (351–354), in looking to the hilltop, that an unknown god lives (*habitat*) up there, whom his Arcadians believe to be Jupiter, seen by them often in person, when he brandishes his storm- and fear-inducing dark aegis. "How right they were!" is the reaction Vergil expects of his reader, who himself is familiar with the hill's relevance for the country's religion, old and recent. The modern reader will wish to be reminded of a few facts so we too can appreciate Vergil's points.

There is first the ancient temple of *Iuppiter Feretrius,* supposedly dedicated by Romulus when he offered the *spolia opima* (later defined as the spoils taken by a Roman *imperator*, in single combat, from the enemy's commander) after defeating the Caeninenses and their king (Livy 1.11; Plut. *Rom.* 16. 3–8; D. H. 2. 34. 4).[79] The temple was restored by Octavian ("at Atticus' urging", *Attici admonitu*, Nep. *Att.* 20. 3) ca. 32 BC. As a matter of fact, Augustus lists it not among the ones which he rebuilt (*refeci*, *R. G.* 20.1), like the temple of *Iuppiter Optimus Maximus*, but among those he "built" (*feci*, *R.G.* 19. 2). The temple played an important part in his ideology. History offered only two more cases of *spolia opima,* and in his own time Octavian jealously guarded the honor. The Senate had accorded the right to deposit spoils as *spolia opima* to his adoptive father C. Julius Caesar, if not to himself.[80] When M. Licinius Crassus in 29 BC laid claim to *spolia opima*, Octavian felt a "challenge to his position as Romulus' successor", and the claim was denied on the grounds that M. Licinius Crassus, only a proconsul at the time, was not in possession of full *imperium* (the war was not waged under his auspices).[81]

To illuminate the contemporary climate, it is worth looking a little deeper into Augustus' involvement with the *area sacra* (and especially with Jupiter) on the Capitol. Concerning the same issue, Livy (4. 20. 5–11) is walking a tight-rope, correcting (or interpreting) his own preceding narrative account and trying to weigh "all" his sources with regard to Augustus' personal "eyewitness" finding that indeed there had been no exception to the consul-with-*imperium* rule in one of the preceding cases of *spolia opima*. Octavian categorically stated that he himself had seen the title *consul* inscribed on the old linen corslet of the slain enemy, following the name of the victor, *Aulus Cornelius Cossus*. Both Augustus' concerns and Livy's diplomatic retraction are illuminated by Livy's historical narrative according to which (4. 20. 2) Cossus, in the triumphal procession, not only outshone his own commander (Dictator Mamercus Aemilius) but was, in the soldiers' songs, even equated with Romulus: *in eum milites carmina incondita aequantes eum Romulo canere* (l.c.). Though details of the Livy passage are hotly debated, one may at least safely maintain that the temple of *Iuppiter Feretrius* on the Capitol, then, in Vergil's time, was an important symbol of the unmatched (i.e., jealously guarded) superiority of Romulus' present-day successor.

Chapter 6

Second, there was, of course (as mentioned earlier), the national shrine of Iupiter Optimus Maximus (shared by Juno and Minerva, the other two members of the Capitoline Triad). Begun, according to tradition, under the Etruscan kings (Tarquinius Priscus) and dedicated by the newly established republic (509 BC), it burnt down in 83 BC, then was reconstructed in marble and dedicated in 69 BC. The statue of Jupiter, added a few years later, was of ivory and gold.[82] It, like the gilded roof (Plin. *N.H.* 33.57) is likely to form the reference to Vergil's *aurea* (*Aen.* 8. 348). But since it was located more to the *Campus Martius* side of the hill – its facade, however, looked south in the direction of the *forum Boarium* – it is not necessarily the first or only building that comes to mind when Vergil's reader pictures Aeneas looking up from the *forum Romanum* side.

A third temple of Jupiter, this one again of personal importance to Augustus, must not go unmentioned since it "must have stood...on the south-east edge of the hill overlooking the forum".[83] Already Norden[84] sensed a compliment to Augustus in Evander's words but did not fully fathom the poet's intention.

While in Spain in 26 BC, Augustus was almost hit by lightning (the torchbearer in front of his sedan-chair was killed). He responded by vowing a temple to Jupiter the Thunderer, which, of considerable size and completely of marble,[85] was dedicated on Sept 1, 22 BC. The emperor himself paid frequent visits to *Iuppiter Tonans*, and so did his Romans – so much so that neighboring Iupiter Optimus Maximus, up till then the chief god on the Capitol, complained to Augustus in a dream that he was losing worshippers to the new competition. Augustus responded by hanging bells on the gables of the new temple, thus indicating that it was intended to be nothing more than an entrance to the domicile of Iupiter Optimus Maximus (Suet. *Aug.* 29).

Whatever the truth value of the dream story, it confirms what the *Baugeschichte* implies: *Iuppiter Tonans* was of personal importance to Augustus – even more personal than *Iuppiter Feretrius* who guarded his ambition as *imperator*. *Iuppiter Tonans* had spared Rome's savior so he could survive to complete his achievements. In Vergil's presentation much more is involved than paying a compliment to the emperor for his recently-built temple. The double perspective of guide Evander explaining (*Aen.* 8.351–354) and author Vergil introducing the hill from a modern perspective (347–350) brings out into the open once more that it is not Aeneas' acquaintance with the divinely inhabited thicket on the hill (level B) that is the ultimate goal of our text, but the instruction of the reader (level C). The repeated, almost exclamatory words, "already at that time!", linguistically make sense only if they are complemented by "and not only in our time"; i.e., the reader's existing knowledge about Augustus' new temple for Jupiter the Thunderer up there is called up and appealed to by the writer. Even a detail like the Arcadians' alleged observation of Jupiter brandishing, with his right arm, the dark aegis and rousing up the rain clouds (353f.), cannot but have reminded the contemporary reader that the cult statue of Jupiter Tonans was holding a thunderbolt in the right hand (as did that of Jupiter Optimus Maximus).

What is the purpose of so obviously paralleling past experiences and present-day worship? The answer is simple and surprising. If Vergil can present a mythical tradition according to which the god of thunder was "already then", i.e., in prehistoric times, observed and recognized being active on the part of the Capitol which is seen from the *forum Romanum*, then Augustus' act of picking the site and building there a temple to the Thunderer had nothing arbitrary about it. On the contrary, the emperor's act only acknowledged and sealed the tradition. In other words, Augustus did not create a new place of worship *ex nihilo*. The poet provides the needed evidence and anchors the ruler's "enlightened" (i.e., consciously pious) response to being divinely spared by embedding it in a pre-determining frame of early "unenlightened" local worship.[86]

We now understand why the occasion was so important to Vergil that, for the second time only during the whole walk, he made Aeneas' guide speak in *oratio recta*. On a small scale, Evander's words (351–354) provide for Augustus' new temple what the *Aeneid* as a whole provides for Augustus' rule. To disengage the ruler from the troubled accidentals of recent history (which brought him to power), his family is repeatedly shown to have been divinely preserved and to stay in contact with age-old manifestations of divine will. The splendor of Augustan Rome, which forms the background behind the story of the walk, results from a providential plan which Vergil's poetry is fit to make transparent by projecting the present onto the screen of a mythical past.

As in the case of the *Lupercal*, Evander the "good man" (if his name be understood by Romans in such a non-original way) here again is the palaeo-Julian trailblazer – a literary character who adds prehistoric, divinely sanctioned depth to an institution of the author's own time. Our question, asked in this Chapter's opening pages, why Greek Evander plays such a prominent part in the eighth Book of the Roman national epic, is now answered as it was then: the undeniable historical fact of an early Greek presence in the *forum Boarium* neighborhood could be put to good use in demonstrating prehistoric, divinely inspired events precursory of the chosen Julian line and of the activities of its members.

The poet's introduction (8. 347–350) covers the contents of the first

Chapter 6

half only of Evander's speech. In the second half (355–358) the aged king, without further comment, moves on to another topic (set off by *praeterea*, 355), of twofold focus. The remnants of two cities are pointed out to Aeneas: one citadel on the Capitol, city of Saturnus (territory which Janus voluntarily yielded to him); the other – further left – on the *Ianiculum*, the hill beyond the river, city of Janus. Evander finally returns to offering some level-A information, the kind which Aeneas was presumably interested in (311f.).

Vergil rounds out the utterances of the guide by a stylistic ring: *virum monimenta priorum* (312) is chiastically referred to by *veterum...monimenta virorum* (356). Thus there is at least some surface consistency: the level-B guide starts out and ends with level-A information. Most of what lies in between, however, concerns level C, and all that follows his speech will be author's level-C narrative.

Seemingly unsurmountable difficulties have been caused by a single line:

The name of this one had been (i.e., before its destruction)
Ianiculum , of that one, *Saturnia*.

Ianiculum huic, illi fuerat Saturnia nomen. 8. 358.

How can anyone, standing (as has been assumed) in front of the Capitol, refer to a city on its top as "*that* one" (*illi* – usually said of the alternative farther removed from the speaker), while calling a city on the hill down the road (i.e., down the *vicus Iugarius*) and beyond the river "this one" (*huic*)?

The most ingenious "solution" was suggested by Grimal (1945). Adjusting geography to grammar, he postulated, in addition to the traditional prehistoric city of Saturnus on the Capitol ("that one"), a city of Janus on the other summit, i.e., on the *arx* ("this one") – without any hard evidence whatsoever. Assuming the two walkers to have skirted the Capitol by following the *vicus Iugarius* (a route we had reason to reject earlier), Grimal postulates two positions for them. In the first, Aeneas and Evander are in front of the *Tabularium* grounds, at equal distance from both the *Capitolium* and the *arx*. Consequently, the remnants of cities on these two summits can – according to Grimal – be equally denoted by "these": *haec duo...oppida*, 355; *hanc...hanc*, 357.[87] After moving on as far as the grounds of the (later) Arch of Septimius Severus, and before turning right toward the Palatine, they are seen by Grimal to be closer now to the citadel (*huic*, 358), but further away from the Capitol (*illi*, 358) which is behind them. Therefore (says Grimal) the city of Janus must be located on the *arx*.[88] The two walkers then only have to turn *right*[89] to walk in the direction of the Palatine (which they supposedly approach by joining the *clivus Victoriae* route; it hugs the hill, running south to north from the *Lupercal* area, then turning east).

According to the account given in this Chapter, however, Evander and Aeneas would not turn *right* in front of the Capitol, but *left*. Having, on their route northward from the *Lupercal* (343f.), directed their eyes (and perhaps even their steps) to the *Argiletum* (345f.), they next saw in passing the "seat of Tarpeia" (=northern summit, 347a) and then focused, with extended interest, on the Capitol (=southern summit, 347b–354). There can be no doubt that their attention has – counterclockwise – followed a semicircular movement. Looking, from their position on a line formed by *rostra vetera* and the western short end of the *basilica Iulia* (to use the terms of Vergil's contemporary reader),[90] in southwestern direction and continuing the leftward movement of their attention, they now see, next to (i.e., left of) the Capitol, along the extension of the *vicus Iugarius*, the *Ianiculum* hill beyond the river. (Today's visitor, we said, would have to take his stand on the elevated *via della Salara Vecchia* area and look across the *forum* to be able to see the *Gianicolo* beyond and above today's elevation of the *Piazza della Consolazione*.)

It is not only because the two mountain sites, *Capitolium* and *Ianiculum*, appear visually next to one another (one right, one left) that their hilltop cities can be addressed by the same demonstrative pronoun (*haec duo...oppida*, 355; *hanc...hanc*, 357): above all they share the same demonstrative pronoun because the remnants of either one are equally thematic the moment when Vergil steers the speaker Evander back to his original topic of *veterum...monimenta virorum* (356; cf. 312). It is also their level-A topicality which ties the two places together on an equal basis. The organizing principle of their connection is comparable to the one applied when *asylum* and *Lupercal*, though geographically apart, are tied together by their common level-C factor, i.e., the person of Romulus, Rome's first founder and Augustus' predecessor. Each time (as is also the case with *forum* and *Carinae*, 361) two places physically distant from one another are mentioned within a line or two.

So we find *Saturnia* and *Ianiculum* visually and linguistically juxtaposed in lines 355 and 357. But what about 358, where the physically closer one is called "that", the more remote one "this"? We must not forget that the circular movement of Aeneas' and Evander's visual attention keeps turning counterclockwise. The Capitol, earlier at the center of their extended interest, and, just before, sharing their attention with the hill beyond the river, is now at the point of vanishing both from their visual perception and their intellectual grasp as they continue turning leftward (being about to take their course to the Palatine). "That one" is the one dropping from the speaker's sight, "this one" is the one newly (or last, even if briefly) in focus. The moment the two walkers start leaving the Capitol in the direction of the Palatine, they also start having a better view across the *Velabrum* (i.e., the valley between Capitoline and Palatine), and ever more of the *Ianiculum* hill may come into view on their right than merely its southern parts (discounting again, as before, the *basilica Iulia* of the reader's day). The greater dominance of the *Ianiculum* over the Capitol may actually be an indicator that, upon completing their left turn movement, they now are setting out on their approach toward the Palatine.

Thus one should not take offense that an object more than a mile away can be called "this one". Evander used the same nomenclature, "here" (*hic*, 193) and "look at this rock" (*hanc aspice rupem*, 190) when his speech focused on the remnants of Cacus' cave across the valley on the hill opposite the speaker.[91] Being philologists, we should keep our eyes open for a change of focus or perspective rather than go into the business of moving mountains...

(d) *Monuments of the Julians' Mission, III: Crossing the* forum Romanum *Area, and Approaching the Palatine Hill via the Northern Access Route*

Evander's guided tour having come to an end, the perspective now definitely changes to the writer's own historical time. Not only are we going to hear that Aeneas and Evander saw[92] cows all over on the *forum Romanum* (361) – cows could be seen even on "the elegant *Carinae*" (361; i.e., the Western slope of the Esquiline), that fashionable residential area of Augustus' time (Maecenas had settled on the Esquiline Hill in grand style; already Pompeius had a house on the *Carinae*). Either term was apt to jolt the contemporary: the *forum Romanum* by its historical overtones and because of its recent (and still progressing) Julian transformation, the "elegant *Carinae*" by the unepically jocund and down-to-earth tone as well as because of the recent residential gentrification (Maecenas' estate covered the grounds of a former poor people's cemetery and the place of executions). The reader is being forced to look on the rest of the route again with the eyes of Vergil's contemporary. This design corresponds to the introductory reminder of the "Roman power" of "today" and its sky-scraping edifices (8. 99f.). The contrast of "then" and "now" is further emphasized by Evander's "poverty" (*pauperis*, 360) and his cattle (*armenta*, 360), so inapposite to the elegance of the *Carinae* – and to the architectural upgrading which the *forum Romanum* has undergone in Vergil's time. Whereas *lautis* may strike a note of social elitism, *Romano* in the same line (361) has a wider, a national, appeal.

In addition to forcing his reader to have the Augustan *Stadtbild* in mind when visualizing the rest of the walk, the "modern" names also serve as markers to indicate the route taken by the two walkers. Let us trace their steps first. Evidently, they cross the *forum*'s full length, then proceed on to the *Velia*, i.e., the saddle between (roughly) the Esquiline's hillside (=*Carinae*, today's *via Cavour* area) and the Palatine. The fact that they view the *Carinae* area speaks against Grimal's thesis according to which they use the *clivus Victoriae* and rather in favor of their walking up the *clivus Palatinus* which enters the Palatine from the *Velia*, i.e., from the north(-east). This route is perhaps further supported by the verb *mugire* (361, emphasized by the curious mix of sense perceptions observed earlier); the word offers one possible etymology for the ancient gate of the Palatine here, which presumably received its name from the lowing of the cattle: the *porta Mugonia*.

Now the precise location of this gate (though probably determinable with sufficient precision for understanding Vergil's purpose) has not been secured with ultimate certainty. It was situated on the right (i.e., the southern) side of the "upper" *Sacra via* for someone coming from the *forum*.

Dionysius of Halicarnassus says the *porta Mugonia* "leads to the Palatine from the *sacra via*" (φέρουσιν εἰς τὸ Παλάτιον ἐκ τῆς ἱερᾶς ὁδοῦ, 2. 50. 3), and according to Livy (cf. 1. 12. 3–8) the *porta Mugonia* (or *vetus porta Palati*) was located near the temple of *Iuppiter Stator* (which Romulus perhaps only vowed, but Regulus after 294 BC built). Plutarch tells us that the temple of *Iuppiter Stator* was "erected at the beginning of the *sacra via*, when one goes up to the Palatine (ἱδρυμένον ἐν ἀρχῇ τῆς ἱερᾶς ὁδοῦ πρὸς τὸ Παλάντιον ἀνιόντων, *Cic.* 16. 3). Still today one can verify, at the northern foundation of the Arch of Titus, the point where the Augustan pavements of the "upper" *sacra via* (= *clivus sacer* ?) and of the *clivus Palatinus* join. So these passages may seem sufficient for us to locate the *porta Mugonia* in this area.

But Coarelli places the gate so that it would almost face the bend where (between the temple of Romulus the son of Maxentius and the basilica of Maxentius) the street towards the *Carinae* turned off to the left;[93] in his words, "da situare di fronte al portichetto medievale antistante alla basilica di Massenzio."[94] To arrive at this conclusion, Coarelli not only has to let the *via sacra* begin at the temple of Romulus. He also has to accommodate the ancient information adduced above. But Coarelli's attempt to identify the existing temple of Romulus (son of Maxentius) as being in truth that of *Iuppiter Stator* runs into a difficulty. In the catalogues of the *regiones* as cited by him, the temple of *Iuppiter Stator* is listed (coming from the *Colosseum* area) after the *Meta sudans* and the temple of Venus and Rome, but *before* the *via sacra* (i.e., its beginning at the Arch of Titus, one supposes) and the basilica of Constantine (or Maxentius). However, the temple of Romulus which we see still today (usually attributed to the fourth century AD) would have to be listed *following* the basilica of Constantine and, therefore, can hardly be claimed for the slot of the "temple of *Iuppiter Stator*" – which traditionally has been sought at the (later) Arch of Titus.

Chapter 6

This sequence may be compared with another indication of the gate's location which is found in the route which Ovid's unwelcome book takes (*Tr.* 3. 1. 28ff.) upon arrival in the city (one must assume, at the very *milliarium aureum* mentioned earlier in this Chapter), trying to find its way to the library of Palatine Apollo. Since the book's route moves in the opposite direction, "*sacra via*" here must be understood as coming from the *forum* area; it possibly indicates the street's short arm along the temple of Vesta and the *regia* (the long arm of the *sacra via* being the one which starts at the foot of the *arx* near Caesar's *forum* [cf. 27] and skirts the *basilica Aemilia*, according to one hypothesis).[95]

The points passed by Ovid's book are: *fora Caesaris* (27); *sacra via* (28); temple of Vesta (29); *regia Numae* (30); *porta Palati* (31); (*sc., Iuppiter*) *Stator*, (32); then, the Palatine (32) and, finally, Augustus' palace which is first conjectured (35) and then confirmed (37f.) to be a "house of Jupiter". Special emphasis is given to the palace, its honors and its master (37–48); to the temple of Apollo, the portico of the Danaids and the library (59–64).

Now, after King Numa's palace has been mentioned (30), the book's guide

> from there on, directing their course to the right, said
> "this is the gate to the Palatine,
> here is (*sc., Iuppiter*) *Stator*", etc.
>
> Inde petens dextram "porta est" ait "ista Palati,
> hic Stator", etc. *Tr.* 3. 1. 31f.

Luck renders *inde petens dextram* by *at this point he turned right* ("an diesem Punkt wandte er sich nach rechts"), which would seem to amount to "at the *regia Numae*". But in his commentary, he annotates as follows: "*dextram*; an der heutigen *Via San Bonaventura?*" Now the *via San Bonaventura* climbs the Palatine just outside the Arch of Titus, parallel to – and only a few yards east of – the existing *clivus Palatinus*. Thus the comment proves helpful, for the Augustan pavement at the Arch of Titus suggests that to Ovid's reader the access to the Palatine was hardly at the *regia*. *Flecte vias*, Martial (1.70.9, cf. 5) advises his own book, apparently at the same location.

How then did Ovid's contemporary reader map out the route? Having passed the temple of Vesta on its right and the *regia* on its left, the street is next being joined from the left by the arm of the *sacra via* which has skirted the *basilica Aemilia* side of the *forum*; from the *regia* onwards, it gently curves to the right for about 200 yards in an almost semicircular movement until it reaches the area on which later the Arch of Titus was built. Therefore my translation is designed to allow for the possibility that the final right turn is made some time or distance after the *regia* has been passed, viz. at the *porta Mugonia*, at the foot of the *clivus Palatinus*. (It is natural that neither in Ovid's nor in Vergil's text are any more edifices mentioned for the stretch from the *regia* to the *porta Mugonia*; no building of great political or religious importance was there.) It is hard to decide whether *petens dextram* refers only to this sharp final turn or includes the street's preceding semicircular movement also. The circumstances speak in favor of the second alternative, especially in view of the fact that Ovid does not list contiguous buildings, but picks landmarks along the way.

Understood in either way, Ovid's account is not contradicted by TDAR's statement concerning the *clivus Palatinus*, "The existing street of imperial times...corresponds in general with the early one."[96] Consequently, we shall figure the two walkers doing their final sharp right turn at about the position of the later Arch of Titus toward the *porta Mugonia*, through which they pass to climb the hill. But first, we have to return to where we left them: to the *forum*.

The area had undergone important transformations in the recent past, both under C. Julius Caesar and, especially, under Octavian–Augustus in the years following his final victory at Actium.[97] As before, when Aeneas, coming from the *Lupercal*, faced the western end of the *forum* (the most impressive building the Augustan reader would register there was the *Curia Iulia*, the only edifice then clad in shining marble),[98] so now the poet positions his hero – or rather, his reader – in a perfect situation to view the New Architecture on the (south)eastern end of the *forum*.

In completing their left turn, roughly, in front of the *Rostra*, and starting to move east, the walkers leave the Capitol behind them. They will now follow the direction taken by the road along the *basilica Iulia* (the course of one arm of the *sacra via* running parallel, beyond the *forum* on their left, along the *basilica Aemilia*). The reader pictures them moving east either on the grounds of this road or of the *forum* itself. To the poet's contemporary it is immediately apparent why Aeneas should now walk toward and face also the other short side of the *forum*; it contains the buildings which complete what one feels tempted to call the "Julianization" of the formerly republican core of Rome.

Octavian had sealed the eastern end of the *forum* by another edifice in shining marble (the more impressive because situated on a raised foundation): the temple of *Divus Iulius,* his adoptive father – the first time a mortal in Rome received a temple. Though dominated by a statue (facing the *forum*) of C. Julius Caesar with the *sidus Iulium* (the comet which appeared after Caesar's assassination) mounted on its head, the temple also served the aggrandizement of Octavian himself (as did, we recall, the *curia Iulia*, which likewise was dedicated in 29 BC on the occasion of Octavian's triumph).

Not only was the temple adorned with Apelles' *Venus Anadyomene* (thus placing Caesar as a link in the chain which reached from Aeneas' divine mother to Octavian himself); there was more. Julius Caesar had, as mentioned before, relocated the old orators' platform, shaped as a *hemicyclium*, to an area at the northwestern end of the *forum*, near Saturn's temple (and Octavian built a rectangular enlargement in front of it, the length of which, about 27 yards, filled most of the *forum*'s western short side). The ships' beaks, signs of the republic's naval victory of 338 BC over the Antiates, were inserted in the wall so as to face the *forum*. Now Octavian built another platform, facing the old one, on the southeastern short side of the *forum*, in front of Caesar's temple. The claim[99] attached to the new *rostra Iulia* (as they were later called to distinguish them from the *rostra vetera*) was expressed by the ships' beaks (rams) attached to them: they belonged to the fleet of Cleopatra and Antony. Octavian's naval victory at Actium of 31 BC was to be considered equivalent to that of Antium three hundred years earlier. Supposedly, the state was saved on both occasions.

A personal feature is worth mentioning: since Julius Caesar had allowed Antony to do the refurbishing of the republican *rostra*, Octavian could draw personal satisfaction from the fact that Antony's defeated ships supplied the trophies for Octavian's own new *rostra*, and, beyond this, that the new *rostra* amounted only to a small effigy of the huge original which the victor displayed near Actium itself.[100]

Is it far-fetched to mention these facts in the context of dealing with Aeneas' and Evander's walk? I would say, No. For one, the shield of Vulcan, delivered to and reviewed by Aeneas the day (or two days?) after his walk with Evander, extols the victory of Actium in almost baroque exaggeration (8. 675–714). It likewise pictures (8. 714–728) Octavian's triumph of 29 BC (on the occasion of which the *Divus Iulius* temple was dedicated) in visionary terms which exceed reality at the time of writing (the temple to Palatine Apollo, mentioned 8. 720, was by that time not finished; some subject nations, mentioned 724–728, not yet – even never – conquered. But, we said earlier, Vergil writes also for future readers, not merely for the year in which he is actually writing). Above all the Roman reader, if he wished to trace the walkers' route, would do so in terms of the markers provided by the recent architecture. We, too, have to use them for our own understanding of the text. The reader is to conclude: so it is here that Aeneas passed through among grazing cattle long ago – here where his descendant has been (re-)building a new Troy. At this point more than anywhere else it becomes manifest why Aeneas has to complete the detour that took him to the site of Rome rather than go directly to the Etruscan army which he needed so urgently to relieve his threatened and isolated camp.

But the reader's contemporary associations were not confined to the new architecture alone. The temple of *Divus Iulius* was connected to Aeneas also in another way. To understand the connection, our time, drowning in its own forms of entertainment, faces the fact that Augustus himself wanted to be remembered for the extraordinary celebrations and festivals he gave. One need only look at the passages of his *Achievements* in which he lists the games and shows he gave for the city population to understand the long-lasting impact such events were designed to have (*R. G.* 22). The case in point here, however, is of the less vulgar kind.

The dedication of the temple of *Divus Iulius*, being part of Octavian's triumphal celebrations, was also celebrated by the "Troy" contest[101] (listed by Dio at the head of the triumphal shows) – a display of horsemanship Octavian liked to see practiced (*frequentissime*, Suet. *Aug.* 43. 2) by select noble young Romans. Once more Vergil obliged and provided the mythical "evidence" so that the ruler's present-day wish could appear anchored in past tradition: in Book 5, at the end of the warriors' games in honor of deceased Anchises, Aeneas asks for an appendix (*Aen.* 5. 545–603), in which the young Trojans (and Sicilians) give a display of the martial game on horseback. As two of the three leaders who head the groups of youths, there act Ascanius and his close friend Atys. The information loses its air of youthful innocence once the modern reader takes into account that Atys and Ascanius prefigure the related families of the *Atii* and *Iulii* of Vergil's time – the two branches from which Augustus claimed descent.

The contemporary readers or hearers, acquainted as they were anyway with the show through its frequent performances, could hardly miss the connection. On the one hand, Vergil explains the relationship of *Atys* and *Atii* (568; no explanation is any longer necessary in the case of Ascanius-Iulus and *Iulii*; Jupiter himself gave it to Venus – and to the reader – early on in the epic, 1. 267f.; 288). On the other hand, the author tells us that Ascanius later introduced the game into his city of *Alba Longa* (hometown of the Julian family); from there, *maxima... Roma* (5. 600f.) received and preserved it; "today" (*nunc*, 602, referring to occasions like that of 29 BC), the riding boys are called *Troia*.[102] Vergil's account is rich in offering "deliberate parallels"[103] to Augustus' own initiatives, down to the golden chains worn by the riding boys around their necks (*Aen.* 5. 558f.). It was such a chain which the ruler gave to a son of the aristocracy who broke a leg while participating in the *lusus Troiae* (Suet. *Aug.* 43. 2). So, the sight of the *divus Iulius* temple not only evokes dense present-day experience in the

Roman reader. Being a long-distance reader, he also has, by the time he reads Book 8, remembered the Julian/Atian climax of the contests in Book 5.

As elsewhere, one can observe how the poet, while imitating Homer (the funeral games for Anchises are modelled on those Achilles gives in honor of Patroclus in the *Iliad*), integrates his model into a quite different design of his own. Augustus will have been pleased by what looks like a belated addition to Anchises' belated funeral games (held a year after his death, but henceforth intended to be an annual event, 5. 46; 53; 59f.). If Aeneas in Book 8 was (as so often) unaware that he was approaching the site of a monument that would give cause for his son's contest to be celebrated later, for another famous deceased of the family, Vergil could count on it that the reader, who had lived through the years after Actium, would certainly make the connection back to the "today" of 5. 602. In other words, Aeneas' celebration of the "Troy" contest for his father Anchises comes to its literary and political fruition only when Aeneas visits the place which gave Augustus, descendant of Ascanius and Atys, occasion to celebrate the same contest for *his* (adoptive) father, C. Julius Caesar. As Octavian institutes a cult to his father in 29 BC, so, according to Vergil, did Aeneas.[104] The ancestor's walk is truly a political one.

In addition to the *curia Iulia* and the *Divus Iulius* temple, there was probably a third edifice which was dedicated on the occasion of Octavian's Actian triumph in 29 BC – and Aeneas should be facing it now. In the eyes of the reader who took his *Aeneid* with him to the *forum Romanum*, Aeneas (who, together with Evander, had the choice either of following the course of the later road along the *Basilica Iulia* or of crossing *the forum Romanum* grounds lengthwise; see figs. 11 and 12) may even be at the point of walking through it. This was the triumphal arch which the Senate had awarded Octavian after the victory of Actium, to be built on the *forum Romanum* (Dio Cass. 51.19.1).

Though we have no written record of the completion of the actual building itself, it seems unlikely that Octavian should have foregone the opportunity. The indirect tradition, represented by coins, points to at least two edifices, an earlier single arch and a younger triple arch. While older scholarly opinion often placed both arches at the southern side of the *Divus Iulius* temple (more precisely, between this temple and the one of Castor and Pollux),[105] Needergard, after newly researching the grounds, has concluded that in this place there never had been any other than the triple arch whose foundations are visible today. This one is to be equated with Augustus' arch which celebrated the return in 19 BC of the Roman standards captured by the Parthians in 53 BC.

The two foundation tables visible next to (east of) the middle foundations of the triple arch are shown by Needergard to belong to a later time and therefore cannot have supported the single arch of 29 BC. On the other hand, an inscription[106] found in 1546/47 on the *forum* near the remaining three columns of the Castor and Pollux temple (*CIL* 6. 873) supplies evidence that a building was dedicated here to Octavian in 29 BC. If that inscription does not fit the existing remnants, and no other foundations of an arch have been found, there may be room again for the replacement theory: the foundations of 29 BC may have been removed for, or covered by, those of the arch erected after 19 BC.

An alternative hypothesis, however, more recently presented with fresh force, should be mentioned: Coarelli[107] suggests that the earlier arch, too, had three archways and that it was this earlier one which stood on the foundations visible today between the temples of Caesar and the Dioscuri. Coarelli places the later ("Parthian") arch on the other (northern) side of the temple of *Divus Iulius*, between it and the *basilica Aemilia* (a location which is, however, not compatible with Needergard's review of the evidence). For verifying Vergil's literary intention the archaeological uncertainty is not crucial: either location would by Vergil's reader be viewed as lying before Evander's and Aeneas' eyes on their way across the *forum* to the Palatine.

So we do not today any longer feel sure where on the *forum* the triumphal arch of 29 BC stood – we only have reason to believe that it was dedicated together with the other two buildings. Since the triumphal celebrations, lasting for three full days, were the major public event of the twenties (and no other Augustan building was raised there until the second arch of 19 BC), Aeneas' crossing of the cattle-grazing area was, to contemporaries, certainly not as devoid of political overtones as it has been to some modern readers.

As a matter of fact, the political implications of Aeneas' visit to the *forum Romanum* area (cf. *Aen*. 8. 361) can hardly be overstated, as the role accorded to the *forum* in Octavian's policy shows. Already his father the dictator had (we said earlier) set the tone for turning the former center of the republic into a tool of autocracy: by removing the *comitium* and relocating the orators' platform; by reorienting the senate house (henceforth the *curia Iulia*) toward his own *forum Iulium* ; and by erecting the *basilica Iulia*. Octavian continued the trend: by finishing the *basilica Iulia*; by erecting the *rostra Iulia* in front of the *Divus Iulius* temple (as well as the temple itself, of course); by setting up his personal *Victoria,* standing on a globe, inside the *curia Iulia* (and another one on the roof); by having part of the Egyptian booty set up in the temple of *Divus Iulius* ; and by erecting his triumphal arch. (Both father and son let, we saw, the *basilica Aemilia* be restored under

Chapter 6

its old name: a token of Julian "republicanism".) Minor objects (as, for instance, a statue of Octavian himself on horseback in front of the *rostra vetera*) round out the overall picture.

Octavian's Julianization of the *forum* aimed at a systematic balance: a republican western short end and a dynastic manifestation on the eastern short side, facing each other.[108] The tendency is clear from the beginning: from now on, the safety of the state depends on the divine mission of the Julian family. The inscription of 29 BC which was found near the foundations of the later (Parthian) arch displays a dedication by Senate and People to "Imperator Caesar, son of the Deified Iulius" etc., defining the occasion as "the state having been saved", *republica conservata* (*CIL* 6. 873).

Tying the state's survival to the survival of his family remained Augustus' policy. Even if in later years he did not continue his adoptive father's obtrusive autocratic self-representation,[109] he allowed no one else to erect any building on the *forum* but himself and his prospective successors, who were members of his family:[110] his own second triumphal arch of 19 BC is followed, probably in 3 BC,[111] by an arch (portico) for his adopted sons (i.e., his grandsons) *Caius* and *Lucius* (both described not as the sons of his son-in-law Agrippa but as "grandsons of deified Caesar", *Divi nepotes*);[112] in 6 AD the prospective successor at that time, Tiberius, is allowed to rebuild the temple of Castor and Pollux (and later, in 10 AD, that of *Concordia*).

So the emperor's dynastically oriented building policy on the *forum* stayed consistent over the decades of his lifetime. This continuity allows us to include hindsight in weighing the importance which he must have ascribed to the first link of the chain. Both the temple of his deified adoptive father and the star of Venus mounted on the head of the statue point to the family's desired prominence, in politics the one, the other in myth. The latter betrays the same desire for divinely ordained, more-than-secular legitimacy which we verified in the scene of Aeneas arriving in Italy as depicted (in today's reconstruction) on the panel to the right of the entrance of the *ara pacis Augustae*. (The *Aeneid*, too, has Aeneas arrive in Italy under a divine plan, as will be discussed in Chapter 7.) This preoccupation can also be confirmed from Octavian's coinage. Contemporary examples are: after Actium (29 BC, mint of Rome), Venus is represented with spear and helmet, a shield nearby, with Octavian's head on the reverse; he himself appears, godlike and naked, with his foot on a globe, a scepter and an *aplustre* in his hands (Giard 1988, 66, 13–17; 19–20; with Plate I).

The epic poet's contribution to the dynastic concept which was imposed on the formerly republican *forum* must have been invaluable to the ruler. By shaping the myth, Vergil could actually tell the nation that the Julian ancestor had once been here – even more: *long before* Romulus (he, too, son of a divinity and a mortal of Trojan name) founded the city, and *long before* republican spirit freed the city from Etruscan suppression, the Julian leadership was already predetermined and confirmed in the divinely-arranged presence of the homecomer from Troy. (Before the son of Venus, as Book 8 instructs its reader, even the Etruscan power bowed its head in support.)

As in the case of the detour outside the *porta Carmentalis*, where Aeneas moved on ground Julianized in the reader's time, so the ancestor's visit to the *forum Romanum* serves Octavian's claims of his family's equivalence to (not to say: priority over) the republican element in Rome's history. Again we observe the poet supporting dynastic aspirations by supplying a connection of (pre-)historic dimension which other arts could perhaps express pictorially but not create and establish conceptually on their own. Here, too, the poet functions as the ideologue of the *princeps*.

The dynastic aspect applies also to the remaining part of the walk from the *forum* (361) to the area where the walkers can view the *Carinae* (361). Vergil's reader would picture them walking up the short end of the *sacra via*, between (in terms of Augustan times) the temple of Vesta on the right and, a few yards further up, the *regia* on their left.

The *regia*, originally palace of the kings and, in times of the republic, official seat of the *pontifex maximus*, had received an accretion in the temple of the deified dictator, which was built next to it. So (as Coarelli puts it)[113] even in death Caesar stayed forever connected to the office of high priest he had held in life. The building had been restored sumptuously in marble by Domitius Calvinus, a follower of Caesar's cause, in 36 BC.

Octavian himself neither touched nor assumed the highest religious office in the state until 12 BC, after the death of his adoptive father's successor – as the *princeps*, taking pride in his own modesty, tells posterity in his *Achievements* (*R.G.* 10. 2.). Though it would have been unprecedented if he had taken away the office from the chief *pontifex*, it must be said that Augustus was not free from occasionally doing the unprecedented. The royal aspects of the *regia*, revived by C. Julius Caesar's conduct, may have played a part in this act of self-restraint.[114] (Already Cicero joked ambiguously, when Atticus had gone to see Caesar at his official seat of authority, "You are said to have been seen at the royal palace", *visum te aiunt in regia, ad Att.* 10. 3a). But it is significant that, from Augustus onward, the chief pontificate stayed in the imperial house (eventually, in the fifth century AD, it was officially assumed by Christianity). Augustus himself already may be implying a touch of heredity when finally assuming "the priestly office which my father had held" (*R. G.* 10.1).

Equally (or even more) important for the Julian claim to leadership of the state was the temple of Vesta which lay just across the *via sacra* from the temple of *Divus Iulius* and from the *regia*. Augustus tied its cult and priestesses (they were supervised by the *pontifex maximus*) increasingly close to his own person. Since the *pontifex maximus* had to have his seat of office close to Vesta and on public property, the *princeps* in 12 BC even relocated the center of the cult by building a temple to Vesta on the Palatine and giving part of the palace grounds as a gift to the Roman people. Even if one is sceptical on the question whether *aedicula* and *ara* (CIL I, 2nd edition, nos. 213; 236; cf. p.317. 28) amount to a real temple, Ovid's testimony in the *Fasti* (4. 949–954) seems to assign to Vesta a share equal to that of Apollo, with Augustus being the third divinity residing on the Palatine. The involvement of the Senate leaves no doubt about the official weight given to the matter of Vesta's new location.

Augustus' lasting concern is understandable since Vesta's temple was said to hold, in its inaccessible inner shrine, the holy objects which Aeneas had saved from burning Troy (they were carried in his father's, Anchises', hands while Aeneas himself was carrying the old man, cf. *Aen.* 2. 717). In it were also stored the state gods of Troy and the *Palladium*, the effigy of Athena on which once the safety of Troy and now that of Rome herself depended.[115] Already at the time of Caesar the dictator (to cite one example), in 47/46 BC, a silver *denarius* was issued showing Venus' head on one side and on the other, together with the name *CAESAR*, Aeneas holding his father on the left arm and shoulder while his right hand, stretched forward, carries a helmeted figure with spear and round shield: the *Palladium*.[116]

As the cult and the priestesses of Vesta were supervised by the *pontifex maximus*, it was relevant to Augustus' intentions that, in the person of his adoptive father Caesar, the family had already had access to the high office before. One understands why, in his *Achievements*, he mentions the fact of his father's tenure of the office: *sacerdotium...quod pater meus habuerat* (*R.G.* 10. 1). So, as far as the Julians' image is concerned, Ovid appears right on target in having Augustus state that he was called upon to wage war as an avenger by "my father and Vesta's priest", *pater... Vestaeque sacerdos* (*F.* 5. 572f.). Similarly, Ovid speaks *pro domo* when he makes Vesta of all gods take responsibility for having lifted the dictator Caesar up to heaven, leaving behind only his "bare effigy" (*simulacra...nuda*) and "shade" (*umbra*) to be pierced by the daggers of the criminals who were out to pollute "the priestly head" (*pontificale caput*). After all, "he was my priest", *meus fuit ille sacerdos*, states Vesta (*F.* 3. 699–706).

The picture is rounded out by a section from the *Metamorphoses* (15. 745ff.). There Ovid has Caesar's soul (*anima*) raised to heaven by

"Aeneas'...golden mother" (*aurea... Aeneae genetrix*, 761f.), i.e., by "fostering Venus" (*alma Venus*, 844) herself; it is she who – wishing to protect "Aeneas' descendant" (*Aeneaden*, 804), the only survivor descended from Trojan Iulus (768) – tries to prevent the flames of Vesta from being extinguished by the blood of "Vesta's priest" (i.e., the blood of C. Julius Caesar):

> facinusque repellite neve
> caede sacerdotis flammas exstinguite Vestae!   *Met.* 15. 777f.

The whole section and, especially, the last-mentioned line, once more provide evidence of the Augustan (Julian) ideology which ties family pedigree (Venus, Aeneas, Iulus, Caesar), survival of Rome (Vesta's unextinguished fire) and state religion (highest priesthood) together into one formidable and awe-inspiring complex of dynastic leadership in the state.

These later passages allow us to gauge Octavian's original irritation about the act of Lepidus who, after the dictator's death, "exploiting the opportunity provided by civil unrest had occupied" the pontificate (*civilis motus occasione occupaverat*, R. G. 10. 2). So it is ironical (modern readers might be inclined to call it macabre) and politically significant that Vergil's Aeneas should now pass the spot where the objects once entrusted to him by the injunction of Hector's ghost would eventually come to rest:

> Troy entrusts to you her holy objects and her gods.
>
> sacra suosque tibi commendat Troia penatis.   *Aen.* 2. 293.

In Aeneas' dream, Hector even goes so far as to bring forth "powerful Vesta", *Vestamque potentem* (2. 296), together with the eternal fire (2. 297), from the inner parts of the house.[117]

The scene of the call to Aeneas in the night of Troy's fall is (and is meant to be) one of the most powerful in the whole *Aeneid*. Certainly, Vergil could trust that it was still present to the Roman (and long-distance) reader's mind by the time he read of the hero's visit to the site where, in his own time, the Vestal Virgins kept alive the eternal flame Aeneas brought from Troy. If, however, we find the Trojan ancestor himself ignorant (as so often) of the higher purpose behind the specific route on which he is being led by Evander, we must remind ourselves that his story is not told for his or its own sake but for the sake of giving a mythical underpinning to the political power structure which had arisen from the outcome of a civil war.

The rest of the walk is wrapped up quickly. Where are we to picture Evander's domicile? Is the reader to assume that, as has been thought, it lies on the side of the Palatine which faces the *Velia* and the *Carinae*? This view is based mainly on two premises: (a) that Augustus' palace lay in this

Chapter 6

area (a view contrary to *communis opinio* among today's archaeologists) and (b) that Ovid's *Tristia* (3. 1. 31 ff.) seem to lay no distance between the temple of *Iupiter Stator* and the palace.[118] But the words "while I admire details", *singula dum miror* (*Tr.* 3. 1. 33), need not mean that the walk has ended. They only indicate "that there was nothing to particularize in this residential quarter."[119]

In all probability, one should then go with a different interpretation of the path taken by Ovid's book. The book, we recall, after passing between the *regia* and the temple of Vesta, reaches the Palatine's top (the area of Rome's original founding, *Tr.* 3. 1. 32) via the Palatine gate and the temple of *Iupiter Stator*. It then confronts us rather unexpectedly with the "house of Jupiter" (37). Since clearly the palace of Augustus is to be understood here, today's archaeological information would of course point to the western corner of the hill. Corroboration of this view may be found in the *Metamorphoses* (1. 168–176) where the Milky Way is said to be leading away from the houses of the *plebs* and, before ending at Jupiter's palace, being studded left and right with the houses of the more influential gods. The whole arrangement is then called the "great heaven's *Palatine*", *magni... Palatia caeli* (176), obviously referring to and pointing out the location of Augustus' palace.

Taking into account the political orientation of Aeneas' and Evander's walk in the *Aeneid*, one is, when trying to locate Evander's fictional domicile, inclined to invoke Ovid's (likewise political) route and to think of the site of the Augustan palace complex. After all, Evander's tour seems to have partly supplied the model for the path Ovid's book takes. E.g., *Tr.* 3. 1. 34 imitates *Aen.* 8. 364f., allusively assigning to Augustus in relation to his palace the rank Hercules and/or Aeneas took in Evander's house.

However, one should not expect from Vergil's pen in the present context the obtrusive description by which the exile Ovid wishes to impress the ruler in order to gain mercy. In all three major Augustan areas: during the initial view of the Palatine's west corner (the future site of Octavian's palace complex) which originally attracted Aeneas' attention; around the theater of Marcellus and the *basilica Octaviae*; and on the *forum Romanum*; Vergil always relied on the *reader's* ability to identify the buildings in question, pointing himself only to the general fact that in his own day there were edifices that seemed to equal the sky, or mentioning the name *forum Romanum*. Vergil was not (as was Ovid in his desire to return to Rome) in the first place out to flatter and compliment Augustus, but to instruct the nation about the fated greatness of its present ruler.

There is another feature which can throw some light on the walk in *Aeneid* 8. Ovid, imitator of Vergil in *Tristia* 1. 3, but going out of his way to openly please and flatter Augustus, mentions the same three central areas of Augustus' building activity which we found in Aeneas' and Evander's walk. His book first sees *fora Caesaris* and *via sacra*; then palace, temple of Apollo, and library; thirdly, on the southern *campus Martius*, a temple "next to the neighboring theater" (scil., of Marcellus) where a library is connected with the *porticus Octaviae* (as was shown earlier in this chapter).

That the selection turns out to be the same as in *Aen.* 8 is the more remarkable since only the last two building complexes can be connected with a library (the alleged intention of Ovid's book is to find a home, i.e. a library, for itself in Rome where it might be admitted).[120] A conclusion then suggests itself: if Ovid, in wishing to find the emperor's ear merciful, deems it appropriate to touch upon the same three major areas of Augustus' building program as has Vergil before him, then the level-C value of Evander's guided tour did indeed consist in drawing attention to those same three areas of Julian self-representation as this chapter has identified them by tracking the route.

There may also be a sort of immanent logic (admittedly, sometimes a dangerous principle for an interpreter to invoke but one justified at the end of our investigation) that would induce the reader to think of the site of Augustus' residence when trying to locate Evander's domicile. Not only would the semicircular walking route around the Palatine Hill make good sense if it ended at the location which first struck Aeneas' eyes when he came up the river (*Aen.* 8. 98f., cf. especially *arcem*). Above all, it would be difficult to picture that Augustus' Trojan ancestor did visit the major building sites of the victorious Julian family but stopped on the eastern plateau of the Palatine without crossing over to the new and crowning glory of its western corner. After all, by staying overnight near the future location of Romulus' hut, of the temple of Cybele (the goddess of the Trojan home country), and of the temple of Apollo, he could give the emperor's residential grounds precisely the air of mythical predestination which the usurper desired and his poet appears to supply here as he does elsewhere.

These considerations still cannot give us certainty, but they are well compatible with other indications drawn from Book 8. Foremost one would mention, along with Aeneas' initial view of the Palatine's southwest corner, the close proximity of Evander's palace to the *Ara Maxima* (8. 542f.; explained earlier in this Chapter). Both circumstances, especially when considered together, make the reader inclined to locate the Arcadian king's residence toward the river side of the hill (i.e., on the *Germalus*) rather than toward the (north)eastern wall and its exposure to the din of Rutulian arms (474). Definitely the *arx* (98) of Evander's *res inopes* (100), visible from the river (98), must not be pictured as being expansive. But most decisive is that the portent of Venus, ancestral goddess of the Julians, which to Aeneas confirms his divine mission (*ego poscor Olympo*, 533), cannot be imagined as being watched from any other place than from the grounds of Augustus' (and Apollo's) residence. In similar fashion, Carmentis' prophecy that *Pallanteum* will once again be "renowned" (8. 341) is best taken to point to the leading family's divinely sanctioned homestead (whereas her prediction of future greatness for the *Aeneadae* pertains to the Romans in general). Would *auctor Apollo* (336) steer the pious trailblazer from Arcadia to a site on the Palatine unconnected to the god's (and his protégé's) future abode? After all, as Suetonius tells us (*Aug.* 29; cf. Dio Cass. 49.15.5), the god marked the site for the temple by lightning.

Returning from the implications to the final stretch of the walk itself, we can state that the route suggested above with the help of Ovid is in agreement with Vergil's text.[121] Following Evander's last words about *Ianiculum* and *Saturnia*, the two walkers "*kept approaching* the domicile of pauper Evander from below",[122] and they "*kept seeing* the cattle low on the Roman *forum* and the elegant *Carinae*". The imperfect tenses (*subibant*, 359; *videbant*, 360) point to extended activity, well compatible with crossing the *forum* and climbing the *clivus Palatinus*. Naturally, the old man would pause during the way up and, looking back, utilize the stops for pointing out the view of *Carinae* and Esquiline hill behind them. Their eyes would see more the higher their path was leading them. Today's visitor to the site is deprived of the early stages of the view above all by the basilica of Maxentius whose huge remnants conceal the lower parts of the landscape almost completely.

The long uphill walk is ended by a sharp caesura (*asyndeton*, followed by so-called *ut primum* with perfect tense, 362): "As soon as one had arrived at Evander's domicile", etc. Evander's welcoming words (362ff.) are of great difficulty. I can be persuaded neither that Aeneas is asked to show himself beyond human wealth and, thus, "worthy of (a) god" (cf. Seneca, *Ep.* 18. 12f. and 34. 11), nor that he should show himself worthy of his predecessor in the place, i.e., Hercules:[123] the poet's contemporaries would hardly understand why Augustus' ancestor, arriving on the threshold of the palace complex, should be seen to be referring to another great one, and not carry his meaning only in and for himself and for the Julian family.

A clue is given in the word play that Evander "led *huge* (*ingentem*) Aeneas under the roof of the *narrow* (*angusti*) house" (366f.).[124] The local hospitality is not of the kind that would be appropriate for an Aeneas: we are to think in terms of a god's visit paid to a mortal's house.

> Take it upon yourself, my guest, to despise riches
> and shape yourself, too, worthy of
> a god, and come not harsh toward

needy circumstances.

> aude, hospes, contemnere opes et te quoque dignum
> finge deo, rebusque veni non asper egenis.   8. 364f.

In Ovid's imitation (*Tr.* 3. 1. 34), we recall, the *deus* turns out to be Augustus himself. It would be natural to see (as R.D. Williams' commentary does) in Evander's words a hint at Aeneas' later deified status. It is not meant that he should show himself worthy of Hercules but that he should prove himself worthy of his own later status of a god (which he will hold like Hercules and which Hercules has already *earned* through his earthly conduct and achievements). Whether human Evander here speaks out of character in alluding to Aeneas' posthumous divinity or whether he possesses more foreknowledge than he will reveal on the next morning is perhaps an inappropriate question in an encomiastic context. But it may not be quite out of context to see here another level-C allusion, viz. to the modesty of Augustus' living quarters within the palace complex (a fact pointed out earlier in this chapter). What Evander wishes to convey, then, is: huge Hercules came under this roof, found room (cf. *cepit*, 363) in this "royal palace" (*regia*). You, likewise on your way to earn divinity, do the same.

This interpretation of the difficult lines 364–365 puts them in harmony with the surrounding text – and with the overall tendency of the section: if Venus' son, ancestor of future god Augustus, is asked to rest on leaves and on a bear's hide (368), the discrepancy with the real position assigned him (and his greater descendant) by the fated course of world history is so apparent that the truth shines forth even brighter.

Aeneas' visit to the site of future Rome serves a unified, consistent and demonstrable purpose.[125] The many references to contemporary monuments found in Book 8, when verified with the help of the archaeological evidence and reviewed in their Augustan setting (and meaning), confirm the epic's political tendency which Chapters 1 through 5 ascertained by way of literary analysis.

(5) Chapter 6, Summary of Results

In conclusion, here follows a summary survey of this chapter's results, under the two aspects of the sites visited and the ideological support given by the poet to the emperor.

First, the sites: southern *Campus Martius*; *forum Romanum*; Palatine Hill.

Vergil has Aeneas being led to view the grounds of three major *construction sites of Augustan Rome*, on which building activity was intense in the twenties BC:

Chapter 6

(1) Aeneas is granted a view toward the southern *Campus Martius* at the *forum holitorium*, where Vergil's contemporary reader would locate
   (a) the *Theater of Marcellus*, named after the nephew and potential successor of Augustus
   (b) the *Temple of Apollo Sosianus* (dedicated on Augustus' birthday; *cella* frieze celebrates Augustus' triumph)
   (c) the *porticus Octaviae*, built by Augustus' sister, possibly with the emperor's support, containing temples of Jupiter and Juno, as well as (probably) a *curia* for the Senate, and a library in memory of her son Marcellus
   (a)–(c) are each closely connected to the imperial family

(2) the *forum Romanum*, which is being Julianized in these years; Aeneas is led especially past the grounds of the following edifices:
   (a) the *basilica Iulia*, the *curia Iulia*, and the *basilica Aemilia* (the locations of the two last-mentioned alluded to by the name of the squeezed-in *Argiletum*)
   (b) the new *rostra Iulia*; located opposite the republican ones at the other end of the *forum*, they are equal in size to them and, so, of modest proportions; but, at the same time, they constitute a small effigy of the immensely larger *rostra* Octavian erected at *Victory City* near Actium.
   (c) the *Temple of Divus Iulius* (the emperor's adoptive father and the first Roman ever to receive a temple)
   (d) the *Arch of Augustus*, awarded after the Actian victory
   (e) the walk leads past the site of the *Temple of Vesta*, where ultimately (and still in the reader's day) the holy objects will be stored which Aeneas brings from Troy: the *Palladium*; the eternal fire; the state gods of Troy.

(3) Aeneas eventually arrives on the site of his greater descendant's future residence.

Second, after the sites:
the poet's special support of the imperial ideology:

(1) The ancient Arcadians' observation of Jupiter the Thunderer on the *Capitolium* shows that Augustus did not choose the site for the temple arbitrarily: the poet can supply the (pre-) historic peg which helps to attach the Emperor's founding act to a desirable divine background. (Stahl 1998 shows that Vergil follows the same procedure when, in Book 3, having Aeneas land at Actium.) Augustus seals a pre-existing tradition.

(2) A similar case concerns that part of Augustus' residence on which he built the temple of Apollo: he chose the site which the god himself had marked by lightning (Suet. *Aug.* 29).

Again the poet provides a mythical peg and precedent, not only by letting ancestor Aeneas spend a night on the same grounds, but also by letting him receive a special revelation up here.

On the next morning, Aeneas here experiences thunder in the sky and the apparition of the new arms which will lead him to victory. Following his divine mother's, Venus', showing of the arms, Aeneas offers a sacrifice on the Palatine, using kindling fire fetched from the *Ara Maxima*; once again the place of the Emperor's founding activity has not been picked arbitrarily or based on a recent decision alone: it had been sanctified by his ancestor's ominous experience at the outset of history (which itself had been preceded by the visit of savior Hercules).

In concluding, let us briefly return to Aeneas. When, on the morning after his arrival, looking down the *Stairs of Cacus*[126] toward the *Ara Maxima* and the area of his landing (the reader, too, had placed himself down there, when he pictured Aeneas' perspective at the time of landing), our hero may have wondered why on the previous evening his host had brought him up here by way of such an extensive detour. Vergil's contemporary audience would have had no difficulty answering his question.

It appears, then, that careful evaluation of the role played by stone monuments in the *Aeneid* can supply the interpreter with a tool which helps us to achieve greater objectivity and perhaps even to avoid errors which may result from uncritical application of modern literary concepts.

Chapter 6, Excursus 1: Hercules visiting Julian Territory

Separate consideration may be given to a section of Book 8 which has often been felt to be an anomalous addition, a display of Vergil's ability to compose a small epic (sometimes called an *epyllion*) within the major work. But, though even more difficult to integrate into the plot-line than some other sections, the story of Hercules' victory over Cacus cannot be wholly excluded from the present analysis. For it contains features and details which bear both on plot-line and on meaning, and in one case even on the poet's topography of early Rome.

To explain to (and justify before) his Trojan guest the local worship of non-indigenous Hercules (foreign gods are likewise not always welcome in the Augustan Rome of the reader's day), non-native (yet palaeo-Augustan) Evander tells the story of Cacus. The monster had stolen four bulls and four cows from the herd which Hercules was taking through the area on his way back to Greece after he killed Geryones. Cacus' death (the hero chokes him in his cave on the Aventine) adds a local feat to the famous cycle of Hercules' labors; it gives the so far unknown place some early, albeit parasitic, mythological publicity – a fact which possibly has motivated Vergil to choose Cacus the superhuman monster over Cacus the herdsman (Livy 1. 7. 5) and Cacus the brigand (D.H. 1. 39. 2). Pallanteum's elevation to mythical rank through the son of Jupiter is aptly exploited in the song presented a little later before Aeneas' eyes by the Arcadians. To some of the well-known labors (enumerated and enriched by some lesser known ones, 288–300), they

> above all add Cacus'
> cave and himself, breathing fire.
>
> super omnia Caci
> speluncam adiciunt spirantemque ignibus ipsum.   8. 303f.

To the reader it may seem odd that Aeneas should have to listen twice, in song and in narrative, to the same story, important as it may be to the young community. Evander's report emphasizes the relief Hercules brought the poor Arcadians from Cacus' assaults (188f.), and it ends with the establishment of the *Ara Maxima* (271–272), the service at which was provided by two local families.

Lines 268–270 merit a detailed discussion. That Evander should speak here of the "younger" ones (*minores*, 268 = "younger generations"?) observing the cult, though himself a contemporary of the events, seems to some to present a difficulty. It would be removed by taking lines 268–270 as a parenthesis pronounced by the author (printing a period at the end of line 270 with Hirtzel, against Mynor's text). This would (solving another difficulty) make Hercules (and not the two families mentioned in 269–270) the likely subject of the singular verb form *statuit* (271), i.e., ascribe to him the founding of the huge altar. This understanding also would allow Evander's words *hanc aram* (271) to refer back directly to the subject of the altar which formed, after *haec sollemnia* and *has...dapes* (185f.), the climactic third point he intended to explain to Aeneas (*hanc tanti numinis aram*, 186) by telling the story of Cacus' destruction.

That Potitius is said to be *primus...auctor* and the *domus Pinaria* takes the place of *custos*,[127] agrees with the ranking of the two families reported elsewhere, e.g., by Dionysius of Halicarnassus, who assigns the Pinarii τὴν δευτέραν τιμήν (1. 40. 4; cf. Livy 1. 8. 13). The story attached to the family names is based on popular etymology (Serv. *ad* 8. 269 and Serv. Dan. *ad* 270) and appears rather fantastic. However, the understanding of the difficult *auctor* offered by Serv. Dan. (*ad* 269: he too sees a difficulty) makes the Potitii not necessarily the founders of the altar or the cult but only the *condicio sine qua non* for the performance of the ritual. The ritual was, according to tradition, taught or even started by Hercules himself: Serv. *ad* 269; D.H. 1. 40. 2f.

This, then, is the alternative to taking *auctor* as "founder" (a meaning demanded, e.g., at 8. 134) which may suggest itself from Serv. Dan. *ad* 8. 270 (discounting the popular etymology): *Potitios dici, quod eorum auctor epulis sacris potitus sit*. Taking *Potitius auctor* (8. 269) and *domus...Pinaria* as in apposition with *minores* (*que...et* = τε...καί, cf. *Aen*. 8. 486; 4. 484f.), we may render as follows: "(beginning with) ancestor Potitius and the Pinaria... family", where *primus*, looking as usual to what follows,[128] helps to cover the period from the time immediately following the cult's inception down to the *minores* ("and the younger ones happily have observed the festive day"). In similar fashion, *ex illo* (268) bridges the time to the reader's present ("Ever since, the honor has been paid."). For *auctor* pointing to family origin in the *Aeneid*, see 4. 365 (Dardanus) and 7. 49 (*Saturne, ...tu sanguinis ultimus auctor*); as *auctor* at 8. 269, so *origo* at 7. 371 is intensified by *primus, -a*.

Evander is not in all versions the builder of the *Ara Maxima* (nor the founder of the cult). Livy (1. 7. 13) appears to make Hercules the builder of the altar and founder of the cult, obedient to the *omen* of Evander's mother, Carmentis. Since in the *Aeneid* Evander narrates the events, he would, if he was the builder, inappropriately have to speak of his own achievement while praising Hercules. It appears only consistent that, for setting up an altar considered to be "the biggest", the superhuman strength of Hercules himself should be credited by Vergil – as is done by his "followers", i.e., by Propertius:

'ara per has' inquit (*scil*. Hercules) 'maxima facta manus'   4. 9.68,

and by Ovid:

constituitque sibi, quae maxima dicitur, aram   *F*. 1. 581.

Taking 8. 268–270 as an author's intervention would do away also with a third offense one has found in the passage: "The Potitii are given an unexpected role" (Fordyce *ad* 268). There is nothing surprising in their being mentioned if it is the author who reminds his contemporary reader of the role the two families played (down to 312 BC, cf. Livy 9. 29. 9) in the cult before it was taken over by the state. We moderns are sometimes not aware that the time of reference in the epic is that of author and reader (often denoted by a *nunc* = "today", as at 8. 99), not of the events narrated. The poet takes the past to the reader, not the reader into the past.

The section of Book 8 which deals with Aeneas' visit to Pallanteum is, as was shown, richer in authorial interventions than other parts of the work. Nevertheless it should be noted that a major objection voiced against seeing lines 268–270 as part of Evander's speech could hardly override my argument. Servius (*ad* 268) finds Vergil's use of *minores* novel: it should, like *maiores*, be used only when the customary series of generation indicators (corresponding to our great-great-great-grandson and, in the other direction, -father) is exhausted. But Serv. Dan. *ad loc.* is willing to take Evander's high age into account and see in the *minores* of 268 his younger fellow Arcadians. This is a use which could be confirmed already from the late work of Ovid (see OLD *s.v. minor* [2], 3 c). At *Tr.* 4. 10. 41ff., he speaks of his regard for poets older than himself, most of whom he met in his own lifetime; then continues:

> And as I for the older ones, so the younger ones felt respect for me.
>
> utque ego maiores, sic me coluere minores.   4.10. 55.

But the fact that it would be linguistically possible to take *minores* as being Evander's younger contemporaries can hardly override the argument I have made for taking lines 268–70 as the author's comment for his contemporaries.

Not too much weight should be given to the fact that the poet's intervention at *Aen.* 8. 268–270 would in some way correspond to the opening statement of Evander's speech (185ff.; *honores*, 189 ~ *honos*, 268). The author may well, in rounding out the speech for his reader, himself with a comment go beyond the narrative situation. It is above all the altar which, serving as the concrete symbol of the religious context, helps to close the ring around the Aracadian king's narrative: *aram* (186) is (we said above) resumed by *aram* (271), prophetically (we observe the future tense) and triumphantly culminating in Evander's repetition of *maxima semper* (271; 272; genuinely Vergilian and reformulated by Prop. 4. 9. 67 and 68). But there is also the correspondence of the residents' relief at having been saved from the danger (*saevis...periclis servati*, 188f.) and the author's (in our interpretation) emphasis on the joyfulness (*laeti*, 268) of local worship and service ever since. The ring defines the story as the *aition* for worship and altar.

The story itself of Cacus as told within the ring (8.190–267) is a highly polished narrative of precisely defined sections.[129] It clearly presents itself as a genre specimen: an *aition*, we said, in the form of a miniature epic (*epyllion*), of Alexandrian learnedness (but with Italian references). In spite of its artistically autonomous character, it has been connected to all sorts of (mostly political) references: Cacus ~ Cleopatra; Hercules ~ Augustus;

Cacus ~ Turnus; Hercules ~ Aeneas; etc. Such interpretations are hardly based on the sequence of thought the text offers.[130] Showing the flaws of some arbitrary readings, Fordyce is right to ask the rhetorical question; "Would a tale of Hercules be expected by itself to make the reader think of Augustus?" (*ad* 8. 184–279, see especially p. 225f.).

Fordyce is methodologically correct in asking for a "pointer" in the text. However, the situation does not restrict us to saying "artistic purpose is justification enough". For one, we have seen that Hercules' visit to, and help for, Pallanteum elevates the place that later was to be Rome to a high 'connection' within mythology. After all, Hercules is the "true" son of Jupiter, as the Arcadians emphasize in their hymn: *salve, vera Iovis proles* (301). This goes well with the analysis we gave earlier of the Book's political goals: a prehistoric or mythical distinction of the area and of the hill on which Augustus built his residence, bestowed by the son of Jupiter. This gives the place a kind of preordained and chosen character (after defeating Cacus, Hercules stayed overnight on the Palatine, 8. 362f.). Viewed in the context of Book 8, this means that the area where Augustus built the temple of Apollo and is pictured as receiving the gifts of nations from all over the world (8. 720–727) has been set aside by special distinction even before Aeneas, the first of the Trojan-Julian dynasty, was sent here by divine instruction. This is as close as Vergil could go to giving the area a continuity of destiny where there actually was none. The ground had been divinely prepared.[131]

There is another reason why Evander should draw so impressive a picture of Hercules' fight with Cacus and express the Arcadians' gratitude to the hero so intensely. This reason lies outside the aged king's awareness and is motivated by the author's long-distance composition. In the tenth Book Pallas, ready to face Turnus in "unequal fight" (*viribus imparibus*, 459), prays to Hercules for success (460–463), invoking the hospitality which Hercules enjoyed at Pallanteum. Since Pallas knows of the savior's immense strength displayed in the fight with Cacus, it seems well motivated that he should invoke this guest of his father's for his own "immense undertaking" (*coeptis ingentibus adsis*, 461).

At this point in Book 10 (as Chapter 4 has shown) Vergil's far-reaching strategy in conceiving the Hercules episode of Book 8 becomes apparent in the five-fold use he makes of the father-son relationship; the most remarkable purpose being that (by having Hercules, the "*true* son of Jove", according to 8. 301, invoke his father Jupiter for help in Book 10 and having, as shown earlier, Jupiter, unable to help, turn his eyes away from the death scene) the author imbues his reader with sympathy both for Pallas "the boy" and for his fatherly avenger Aeneas; simultaneously the

Chapter 6

reader is being persuaded that Turnus, sinner against a tie sanctioned by the highest god, deserves harsh punishment.

Hercules the helper, as depicted in Evander's speech, then, does play an important part in Vergil's concept of the long-term development. We are neither restricted to artistic purpose alone nor to arbitrary conjectures about Hercules' standing for Augustus, etc. This does, however, not preclude that one or another minor feature may indeed entail a compliment to Augustus. If the *Salii* priests (usually connected with the cult of Mars, perhaps with that of Hercules at Tibur) are presented as singing Hercules' praises on the occasion (8. 285ff.), many a reader will recall that, hardly more than a decade earlier, in 29 BC, Octavian himself was by senatorial decree included in the traditional hymn of the *Salii* (i.e., was included among the gods that protect the state); in his own proud words (*R.G.* 10.1): *nomen meum senatus consulto inclusum est in Saliare carmen*. It is not incongruent with the spirit of the episode that the same priesthood whose hymn names the present-day guarantor of Rome's safety should be said to have praised in song the savior of the first Palatine community. The older a tradition, the greater its religious truth value – and the better the case for predestination.

In sum, then, Hercules' stay, the *aition* and his cult have been shown to serve, though indirectly, the same pro-Julian tendency and plot-line as can be demonstrated for the rest of Book 8. Augustus' (and Evander's) residence is being rooted in mythology, and the road is opened which will lead to Jove's emotional affliction about Pallas' killing – a strong subliminal influence on the reader's judgement later on. If the context lets us derive any guidelines concerning Aeneas' stay at Pallanteum, one would expect to see a similar tendency enacted.

Chapter 6, Excursus 2: *Arx* and *Capitolium* in *Aen.* 8. 652f.

Among the numerous pictorial representations which Vulcan creates on the shield he makes for Aeneas, the following is found:

> In summo custos Tarpeiae Manlius arcis
> stabat pro templo et Capitolia celsa tenebat   8.652 f.

In these lines Manlius, "guardian of the Tarpeian citadel" (i.e., as to be shown below, probably of the northern peak of the Capitoline, once betrayed by Tarpeia for love or for gold to Romulus' enemy, King Tatius), "was standing in defense of the temple" (sc. of *Iuppiter Optimus Maximus*, on the southern peak, i.e., on the *Capitolium* proper) "and held the high Capitol". This refers to a well-known scene, cherished by Roman historiographical tradition: in (or before) 387 BC, M. Manlius ("Capitolinus"), awakened by the cackling of Juno's holy geese, was supposedly able to save the Capitoline against the attacking Gauls.

What area is covered by the poetic plural *Capitolia celsa* at 8. 653? One should perhaps beware of OLD's general definition of *Capitolium* as "the Capitoline hill at Rome together with the *arx*, temple of Jupiter Capitolinus, etc." For, as indicated above, Roman tradition separates the *arx*, citadel of early Rome (northern peak), from the Capitol (southern peak). Both together make up the Capitoline Hill. TDAR gives (*s.v. Capitolinus mons*, with selected exemplifying passages) a good short account, saying "the official designation of the hill was Arx et Capitolium"; the diminishing importance of the defensive aspect and the growing importance of the religious center "led to the gradual application of the term Capitolium to the entire hill." For an illustration, helpful to clarifying Vergil's terminology, let us scan Livy's report about the Gauls' assault on the hill, including Dictator Camillus' measures and speech following the eventual Roman victory (Liv. 5. 38.10–5. 54).

Though he may occasionally speak of the (Capitoline) "hill so small", *tam exiguus collis*, 5. 40. 5, Livy usually employs a hendiadys, like *in arcem Capitoliumque,* 39. 9; *ex arce Capitolioque*, 44. 5, when speaking of the whole hill. The connection is so tight that the verb can be in the singular as when the detested idea is put forward that "citadel and Capitol will be abandoned", *arx quoque et Capitolium deseretur*, 51. 3. Correspondingly, an accompanying adjective can be in the singular: "Capitol and citadel being unharmed" is expressed by *Capitolio atque arce incolumi*, 53. 9; and so one can read that "Rome's citadel and (the) Capitol *was* in immense danger", *arx Romae Capitoliumque in ingenti periculo fuit*, 47. 1. People living on the hill are summarily described as those who lived *in Capitolio atque arce*, 50. 4.

What is interesting for us in these cases is that, even when he speaks of the hill as a unity, Livy nevertheless shows an awareness of the duality and of the difference between the two summits. This difference is naturally marked more strongly whenever the differing functions of the two peaks are addressed, as examples may show.

The young men of fighting age, when abandoning the town, are seen moving "to the Capitol and to the citadel", *in Capitolium atque in arcem*, 40. 1; the Gauls take precautions, concerned about a possible attack "from the citadel *or* the Capitol", *ex arce aut Capitolio*, 41. 5; a man approaching from the river (i.e., from the southwest) makes his way up "to the Capitol", *in Capitolium*, 46. 9; the house of Manlius was "in the citadel", *in arce* 47. 8; the Capitoline games were to be celebrated "because Jupiter Optimus Maximus had protected his own dwelling (i.e., the Capitol) and the citadel of the Roman nation", *suam sedem atque arcem populi Romani*, 50. 4; it is possibly in a distributive sense that "gods and Romans" (*dique et homines Romani*) may be said to hold "Capitol and citadel", *Capitolium...atque arcem*, 51. 3 (the temple of *Iuno Moneta* on the *arx* was built much later on the grounds of Manlius' former house); can the couch for Jupiter's meal be prepared "perhaps anywhere else than on the Capitol", *num alibi quam in Capitolio* ? (52. 6). One takes refuge by going "on the Capitol to the gods (= the 'Capitoline Triad'), to the dwelling of Jupiter Optimus Maximus", (*confugimus*) *in Capitolium ad deos, ad sedem Iovis optimi maximi*, 51. 9. But if the physical protection granted by the citadel is meant (rather than protection by the gods), the flight may be described by the words *in arcem confugerunt*, 38. 10. The Gauls below look up and around (*circumferentes oculos*), "to the temples of the gods and to the citadel" – the latter being the only place which offered the sight of war, *ad templa deum arcemque solam belli speciem tenentem*, 41. 4.

On occasion, however, the terms may appear almost interchangeable: at 46. 2, the narrative describes a man as descending *de Capitolio* (he later returns *in Capitolium*, 46. 3), but Camillus in his speech refers to him as having descended *ex arce*, 52. 3. Nevertheless our investigation has sufficiently demonstrated in Livy's usage the validity of the basic distinction between the two summits, i.e., between strategic defense and religious center. Awareness of this traditional distinction must accompany and guide us in analyzing the couplet (*Aen.* 8. 652f.) which one has adduced to explain 8. 347.

> On the top part (sc. of the shield) Manlius, guardian of the Tarpeian citadel, was standing in front of the temple and defending the towering Capitol,
>
> in summo custos Tarpeiae Manlius arcis
> stabat pro templo et Capitolia celsa tenebat,   8. 652f.

On the surface, the situation (i.e., the night in which the geese – or goose – saved the Capitol) is like the one described in Livy 5. 47. There Manlius was apparently not sleeping in his house on the *citadel* (reflected in Vergil's *Tarpeiae arcis*, the citadel once betrayed by Tarpeia), but on the *Capitol* itself when he was awakened (*excitus*, 5. 47. 4). For the Gauls had been climbing up the southern corner of the Capitol, ascending from the shrine of Carmentis (4. 47. 2. The steep route uphill may seem to be alluded to in the *Aeneid* passage by the adjective *celsa*, "lofty", "towering"). And Manlius, quickly reaching the spot where the first Gaul has emerged from the climb, uses his shield to push the man back down the cliff (4. 47. 4).

If we add that the temple of Jupiter Optimus Maximus (or, more precisely put, the left corner of its facade) pointed to the southern corner of the Capitol, we may think that we can verify from Livy the precise picture which Vergil's Vulcan produced on this section of the shield. In the left foreground one would see the climbing Gauls, about to reach the top; in the section's background right, the facade of the temple; between the two, confronting the first Gaul, defender Manlius.

However, the lines that follow in the *Aeneid* (8.655–658) prove that Vergil's picture of the situation differs from Livy's: there are more than one Gaul on top of the hill in the *Aeneid*, and they are about to (*tenebant*; Servius says that *paene* is missing) take possession of the *arx* (657); the warning geese, too, had announced a plurality of intruders (*Gallos*, 656); they were already *in limine* (656), which can only mean on the threshold of the temple (hardly of Romulus' thatched hut, 654).

That Vergil offers a version different from Livy's is confirmed indirectly by the comment of Servius whose sources had the Gauls attack either "by crossing thickets and rough rocks", *per dumeta et saxa aspera*, or even by way of mines (saps; *cuniculos, ad* 652).

Does Vergil then here distinguish between *Capitolium* and *arx* in the way Livy does when referring to the strategic situation? First, line 657 advises us to answer in the positive; also, it would amount to a mere tautology to say (652f.) that "the guardian of the citadel stood in defense of the high Capitol" if Capitol and citadel are not distinguished. Servius, it must however be noted, does not seem to make the distinction since he can say of the *Capitolium* that "this clearly is the city's citadel", *hoc arcem urbis esse manifestum est* (*ad* 8. 652). And his sentence "Manlius, guardian of the *Capitol*, drove the Gauls from the *citadel*", *Manlius, custos Capitolii, Gallos detrusit ex arce*, turns both Vergil's and Livy's strategic nomenclature around by 180 degrees, climaxing the trend of exchangeability the roots of which we saw already in Livy's non-technical passages. But Servius' confusion does not entail that Vergil himself likewise failed to distinguish citadel and religious center.

There is another word in the couplet *Aen.* 8. 652f. which has not been (and may not be) clarified sufficiently, viz. *Tarpeiae*. At first sight one may think of the "Tarpeian citadel" as that in which traitress Tarpeia lived (or which she betrayed) or perhaps where she was buried (Servius, explaining *Tarpeiam sedem*, 348; Plutarch, however, who does not distinguish the two peaks but speaks of the Capitol only or the λόφον ...Ταρπήιον, *Rom*. 17.5 and 18.1, says she was buried there and her remains were later removed so King Tarquinius could dedicate the ground to Jupiter – a clear indication of the *Capitolium* peak). Further, one may think of that which was under the command of her father, Tarpeius (*Sp. Tarpeius Romanae praeerat arci*, Livy, 1. 11. 6; Plut. *Rom*. 17. 2).

But in the second place the adjective may also refer to the rock or cliff (*rupem,* Livy 6.17.4; πέτραν, Plut. *Rom*. 18.1) from which criminals,

Chapter 6

murderers and traitors, were hurled to their deaths as a form of punishment. (Here the name may originate from a certain Tarpeius who supposedly proposed the law for this sort of execution.) And this cliff is usually assumed to have been situated on the southern rim of the *Capitolium* (though the location is not undisputed: one has also thought of the *citadel*).[132] However, the cliff can hardly be specified by the noun *arx* used in 8. 652 and therefore may be dropped from consideration in our context.

Thirdly, there is the inclination of poets, especially the Augustan and later ones, to widen and transfer, in their mannered way of using riddling speech, the application of the adjective. Propertius (3. 11. 45) with horror speaks of Cleopatra setting up her mosquito nets *Tarpeio...saxo*; certainly, he means the Capitol, not the cliff. At 4. 1. 7, he extends *rupes* to encompass all of the *Capitolium*, while simultaneously transferring the adjective *Tarpeius* to Father Jupiter (who in the early times was without a temple, residing on the "naked rock", from where he "thundered") on the Capitol:

And the Tarpeian Father thundered from the bare rock,

Tarpeiusque pater nuda de rupe tonabat.   Prop. 4. 1. 7.

(Thundering Jupiter may, as we shall see, be an imitation of a Vergilian reference.) At 4. 4. 93, the same poet has Tarpeia leave her name to the whole "mountain", *mons* – an extension beyond the specific use at the poem's opening (*Tarpeium nemus et Tarpeiae...sepulcrum*, 4. 4. 1). One may, conversely, feel tempted to argue in favor of a restriction in the use of the term *mons* here. In discussing C. Julius Caesar's plan of building a theater (at the *forum Holitorium*; see TDAR *s.v. theatrum Marcelli*), Suetonius (*Caes.* 44) speaks of *theatrum...summae magnitudinis Tarpeio monti accubans*. He certainly means the Tarpeian cliff, i.e., the southern edge of the hill only. On the other hand, Livy (1. 55. 1) speaks (outside the passages discussed above) of *monte Tarpeio* where the precise reference would be to the peak of the *Capitolium* (cf. Plut. *Rom.* 18. 1, mentioned earlier). In the light of the extensions, Livy's use here as well as the statement by Varro (rejected as false by TDAR) that the "mountain" (*mons*) was earlier (before being named Capitoline) called *Tarpeius...a virgine Vestale Tarpeia* (*LL.* 5. 41) is best viewed outside the technical tradition and the development following it which we exemplified from Livy's fifth Book. In Ovid, we find the same extensions again: Jupiter (after all the god of the *Capitolium*) holds "the Tarpeian citadel", *Tarpeias...arces*, *Met.* 15. 866 (*Tarpeias...arces*, referring to the *Capitolium*, is also found *Pont.* 2. 1. 57; 4. 9. 29). Nevertheless, the traditional dichotomy appears also in Propertius when he alludes to the precise topographical situation: Tarpeia laments her wounds while sitting on "the Tarpeian citadel", and her lament is intolerable to "neighboring Jupiter" (i.e., Jupiter on the *Capitolium*):

> et sua Tarpeia residens ita flevit ab arce
> vulnera, vicino non patienda Iovi.   4. 4. 29f.

Obviously, no reliable topographical indications can be drawn any longer from the non-traditional, extended use Propertius and Ovid occasionally make of the name. The question then is whether Vergil at *Aen.* 8. 652f. offers an example of this more mannered use (which would partly overlap with the alleged early use reported by Varro), or is closer to the meaning of the strategic report of Livy (and the topographic precision of Prop. 4. 4. 29f.). Since Vergil uses the adjective *Tarpeiae* to characterize the noun *arcis* and depicts a military situation – here and in the preceding lines Romans (*Aeneadae*, 648) are defending their freedom, *pro libertate*; Cocles, Cloelia, Manlius – one may wish to claim the epic poet here for Livy's side. This both does justice to line 657 and agrees with our earlier finding that, if taken otherwise, lines 8. 652f. would offer an awkward tautology. (Simultaneously we can say that the patriotic context of *Aen.* 8. 646–662 excludes any reference to the place of execution called "Tarpeian" cliff which we considered in the second instance above.)

Methodologically speaking, the archaeological evidence, combined with a philologically precise understanding of the text, has demonstrated not only the consistency of Vergil's topographical design (8.347 and 652f. are in agreement with one another) and the soundness of the transmitted text, but also the uniformly Augustan concept of Aeneas' evening stroll around future Rome.

Chapter 6, Excursus 3: "Reversed" Use of *hic* and *ille* for Literary Emphasis

Fordyce (*ad* 8. 357f.) shows himself dissatisfied: "But the use of *huic* and *illi* to refer to the more distant and the nearer object respectively is awkward." An excursus may be useful – even if no exact parallel can be found – to illuminate Vergil's use of *hic* and *ille* here from similar passages.[133] We may start from Forbiger's correct observation as reported (and endorsed) by CN (*ad loc.*), "that 'huic' is applied to Janiculum as being in thought nearer the speaker and consequently first named in the preceding verse."

For some readers, this statement needs elaboration. In the preceding context, the *arx* received about half a line (8. 347a), the *Capitolium* seven lines more (347b–354). So the one-sided emphasis was clear beyond doubt. But in the present case of *Ianiculum* and *Saturnia* one may ask, Is it really possible that the brief mention of the former at 358 is supposed to convey (and carry) Evander's greater and more vivid interest?

The question requires us to consider two areas. On the writer's plane, there is a problem (observed and stated earlier in this Chapter) which results from the complex composition. The narrative of level B (Evander and his time) is pervasively oriented toward the overriding interest of level C (the Rome of Augustus). The upshot of this orientation is that the number of pre-Evandrian monuments on fictional level A (presumably objects of Aeneas' interest, 8. 311f.) appears disproportionately small. Any additional evidence for level A which can be accommodated in the context of the walk must therefore be welcome to the author. The ruins of Janus' city represent just the kind of material the author needs to satisfy Aeneas' fictional interest. So Evander might be expected to place some emphasis on his latest example.

On the immanent plane, the aged king can be seen to round out the information provided for his guest by returning to his opening words (314ff.): the most important character he had mentioned there of Italy's early development was Saturnus whose civilizing influence had introduced the dispersed regional population to the orderly life of a civic community and its institutions (314–325). Pointing out the remnants of Saturnus' city certainly confirms Evander's opening description by supplying visible evidence (cf. *vides*, 356), and so helps to round out his guided tour. But it does not add anything new to the picture of Saturnus; his name does not even receive an attribute at 357: it is merely recalled as a known quantity.

Janus, however, is specially characterized as a familiar Roman deity by the common epithet *pater* (cf. Serv. *ad Georg.* 2.4) when he is newly introduced into the context, and (as Forbiger observed) he is given first place in line 357.[134] This arrangement in itself may announce a higher priority in Evander's attention, going well with the shift of perception due to the left turn Evander and Aeneas are completing at this time near the grounds of the later *rostra vetera*.

Now, for the use of *hic* to denote the intellectually closer object (though it may be more remote in space or time), convincing parallels can be cited.[135] Occasionally, the greater relevance of the more distant object is somehow or other indicated beforehand, and not always as briefly as in the case of Janus' epithet *pater*. As a matter of fact, if viewed as forming the concluding and confirming instance within the wider framework of pre-Evandrian monuments cited at 8. 356 and 312, then *Ianiculum*, too, can conceivably lay claim to a relevance which has been foreshadowed or even established long before its name occurs at 358.

Before turning to a few examples, we are now in a position to confirm that there is a linguistically marked step forward in thought-development from line 8. 357 to line 358. In 357, the two cities are viewed on an equal footing (except for the telling fact that Janus' city is listed first) as evidence of a time long gone by. Consequently, they may in this respect be represented by the same pronoun (in a way similar to *hoc nemus, hunc...collem*, just before, at 8. 351). Szantyr remarks: "Zwei verschiedene Objekte können umgangssprachlich durch doppeltes *hic* bei verschiedenen Deutebewegungen bezeichnet werden...in die hohe Dichtung führte sie [*scil.*, die Doppelung] Verg. (z.B. *ecl.* 4,56) ein", etc.[136] In 358, on the other hand, the city of Janus is singled out pointedly (*huic*), while that of Saturnus recedes from view (*illi*).

As far as supporting examples are concerned, the first-word-position taken by the reference word of *hic* (as *Ianus* precedes *Saturnus* at *Aen.* 8. 357) is generally substantiated by a long number of listings in *TLL*.[137]

When Diana has turned Actaeon into a stag and he begins to understand his situation, Ovid describes his dilemma as follows:

What shall he do? Shall he return home (and) to the royal palace,
or hide in the woods? Shame prohibits this, fear that.

quid faciat? repetatne domum et regalia tecta
an lateat silvis? pudor hoc, timor inpedit illud.   *Met.* 3.204f.

Actaeon is ashamed to show himself in the palace, and afraid to stay out in the wilderness (a dangerous place to be for a stag). "This", *hoc*, refers here not to the last-mentioned alternative but to the earlier one. In terms of topography, it refers – Actaeon is still out in the wilderness – to what is physically more remote (the palace), whereas "that", *illud*, points to his frightening present whereabouts. While he is considering the alternatives, his home (cf. *domum*) is, understandably, what ranks first in his (and the poet's) considerations.

Writing to her husband Ulysses, Penelope in Ovid's *Heroides* mentions what aged Nestor told her son Telemachus:

He reported that by your sword Rhesus and Dolon were slain,
and how this one was betrayed by sleep, that one by guile.

rettulit et ferro Rhesumque Dolonaque caesos,
utque sit hic somno proditus, ille dolo.   *Her.* 1.39f.

"This one", *hic*, refers to the first-mentioned (who, by the way, was killed later than the other). Why should Penelope give the Thracian King Rhesus greater priority in her thoughts? Because his death meant the greater danger to her daring husband: the spy Dolon was treacherously killed alone along the way (so to speak), King Rhesus among his men inside his own camp:

> You dared – o too, too forgetful of your close ones! –
> to touch the Thracian camp with nocturnal guile
> and to butcher so many men at once...
>
> ausus es – o nimium nimiumque oblite tuorum! –
> Thracia nocturno tangere castra dolo
> totque simul mactare viros,...   *Her.* 1.41–43

By ranking the two cases through *hic* and *ille* (as well as, in line 39, by a sequence which runs against the time line of killings), Penelope indicates which one causes her heart the greater anxiety. It is unfortunate that Ehlers in *TLL* lists the passage under *vera inversione* (*sc.,* of *hic* and *ille*), stating: *animo non propius est*.[138] What can be closer to Penelope's mind than Ulysses' danger? But then, our original passage (*Aen.* 8. 358) is misplaced in the same group by Ehlers.[139]

Mercury, in order to make Argus (guard of Io) fall asleep, plays the flute and tells him the story of Syrinx, the nymph with whom Pan fell in love (Ovid, *Met.* 1. 689ff.). Syrinx deceivingly resembled Leto's daughter Diana,

> and she could be taken for Leto's daughter, if not
> this one had a bow of horn, that one a bow of gold.
>
> et posset credi Latonia, si non
> corneus huic arcus, si non foret aureus illi.   *Met.* 1. 696f.

Ehlers states that *ille* here refers to the predicative noun.[140] Nevertheless one may feel surprise that *hic* does not point in the usual way to "the latter", the more so since "the latter" here is an Olympian goddess, by rank far superior to "the former" who is only a nymph. For discussing why *hic* here does not refer to the last-mentioned, a more general consideration is suggested by the context. It is the nymph Syrinx who holds center stage throughout the narrative and *therefore* is pointed out by *huic*.

Thus using *hic* and *ille* can help the author to convey where he wishes to place the long-range emphasis of his narrative. A case in point is the story of Daphne's *metamorphosis* into the laurel tree (Ovid, *Met.* 1.452–567). The god Apollo in close pursuit and the nymph Daphne, barely escaping, are compared to (in this order) a dog and a hare, the former believing he is about to seize his prey, the latter uncertain whether he is still free or caught already.

> Thus the god is fast and so is the maiden, – this one from
> hope, that one from fear.
>
> sic deus et virgo est hic spe celer, illa timore.   *Met.*1. 539f.

Again we see *hic* refer not to the latter word but to the one which is more distant in the sentence, and *TLL* lists this as another instance of "true inversion" of the two pronouns. The following line in the text, however, bears out that it is the pursuer on whom the narrative focuses (so naturally he is "this one" – as *Ianiculum* is at *Aen.* 8. 358):

Nevertheless the pursuer, helped by Cupid's wings,
is the faster one...

qui tamen insequitur, pennis adiutus Amoris
ocior est...   1. 540f.

Apollo's attribute *celer* (539) is here turned into the comparative *ocior* (541), indicating his advantage. The girl remains *illa* (543; 552), an object of the god's eyes (cf. *nitor*, 552), until the poet finally changes his emphasis: *her* (*hanc* takes first place in the line and in the sentence), even in her new state, Phoebus loves – *hanc quoque Phoebus amat* (553).

It is one of the shortcomings of the *TLL*-type methodology that it rarely looks beyond the immediate passage to the larger context.[141] In the present case guidance for the reader is provided not only through the continuation of *celer* by *ocior* and through the fact that *hic* is resumed in the following *qui*-clause. In the preceding comparison, the pursuing dog (mentioned first in line 533) is *hic* and the fleeing hare (mentioned last in 533) is *ille* (534). The parallel use of *hic* and *ille* in 539 and 534 can hardly be ascribed to chance but points to conscious arrangement which one hesitates to list, as does *TLL* for 539, under "*vera inversione*".

The solution to the puzzling linguistic phenomenon is found in Ovid's overall concept. Though ending with the *metamorphosis* of Daphne, the story in the first place does not focus on her but is one of revenge. Apollo, proud about having slain the Python, ridicules little Amor's use of arms (bow and arrows). Irate Amor (*Cupidinis ira*, 1. 453), claiming the greater glory for himself (*...tanto minor est tua gloria nostra*, 465), teaches the scoffer a lesson, by shooting a love-inciting arrow at Apollo, a love-avoiding one at Daphne.

What follows, then, is the story of Apollo's punishment, i.e., of his first love (*primus amor Phoebi*, 452), and the narrative, after a description of Daphne's virgin character (477–487), focuses on the situation and feelings of Apollo (490ff.). The reader sees Daphne *through the eyes of Apollo* (cf. *uritur* 496; *sperando* 496; *spectat* 497; *videt* 498; *vidisse* 500; *laudat* 500). His lengthy address (504–524), delivered while running after her, makes a fool of him ('Please, run more slowly...and I'll pursue you more slowly!'). Even in the section where Daphne is described (525–530) she is depicted not for her own sake, but as she appears to her frustrated lover: "Her beauty was enhanced by her flight", *auctaque forma fuga est*, 530. So there can be no

Chapter 6

doubt that the "inversion" of *hic* and *ille* (*illa*) at 539 (and 534) does reflect the narrative focus of the story and must here be ranked as a consciously employed means of literary emphasis.

Ovid's style is broader than Vergil's, we said earlier. For this reason the *Metamorphoses* can supply an easier way of illustrating the linguistic phenomenon under discussion. A more concise use is exemplified by a pre-Vergilian example from Sallust's *Iugurtha*. When the protracted efforts of the consul Marius succeed in taking a mountain fortress of Jugurtha by a ruse, the narrator is patently on the attacker's side, as terms like "finally" (*tandem*, *Iug.* 94. 3) and "our soldiers" (*militibus nostris*, 94. 4) reveal. So one is not surprised to see the Romans called "these" though they are not mentioned last:

...while all, Romans and enemy forces,...were fighting: for glory and empire these – those for survival,...

omnibus, Romanis hostibusque,...pro gloria atque imperio his,
illis pro salute certantibus,...   *Iug.* 94. 5

In its almost Thucydidean brevity, the passage is well comparable to *Aen.* 8. 358 where *huic* alone (likewise preceded by a brief advance signifier) conveys the focus of the author's interest.

The examples presented here suffice to demonstrate the broad use Latin authors can make of exchanged ("inverted") *hic* and *ille* for the purpose of emphasis. It remains to cite a Vergilian instance where the linguistic phenomenon supports the literary intention in a way comparable to Ovid's story of Apollo and Daphne. Such an instance is found in *Aeneid* 8.

An advance hint may be given by the use of *hic* which Evander makes in his narrative about Hercules' victory over Cacus. Though standing with Aeneas near the *Ara Maxima* in the (later) *Forum Boarium*, he nevertheless, in pointing to the distant Aventine Hill, scene of the fight he is about to describe, says *hanc aspice rupem* (190), and he describes the location of Cacus' cave by the words *hic spelunca fuit* (193).

In describing the morning after Aeneas was received on the Palatine Hill, the narrator spends ten lines on detailing how old Evander gets up and ready to see Aeneas (8. 455–464). The complementary description dealing with Evander's Trojan counterpart is unusually brief (one line), considering Aeneas' position in the epic:

And no less early did Aeneas move around.

nec minus Aeneas se matutinus agebat.   8. 465

The line is almost prosaic when compared to the ridiculous effect of raising Evander's morning toilette to the level of epic style ("and he puts the

Etruscan fetters around the soles of his feet", 458). The disproportion in literary emphasis means that the aged Arcadian king is here elevated for his role of being the author's mouthpiece, for soon, at the meeting with Aeneas, he will reveal the role which fate is holding in store for Aeneas as leader of the kingless Etruscan army (470–519).

Taking into account the author's intention in this section, one understands why Aeneas, though being the last-mentioned of the two, is referred to by *ille*, whereas *hic* is reserved for Evander:

> This one was accompanied by his son Pallas, that one by his companion Achates.
>
> filius huic Pallas, illi comes ibat Achates.   8. 466.

There is, of course, also the difference between son and side-kick in this line (Aeneas' son has for good reason been kept away, as was shown in Chapter 4), and the greater emphasis accorded to Pallas points to the end of the prophetic speech where father Evander offers that his son accompany Aeneas (514–517). Later, Evander faints (584) in premonition of Pallas' death. At the time of departure, our fourth Chapter found, Pallas' radiance is made to outshine even that of Aeneas (*ipse...Pallas*, 587) in order to raise the reader's concern for the young life which Turnus will so brutally extinguish.

Far from displaying a "rather negligent use",[142] line 8. 466 employs *hic* and *ille* in precise agreement with the literary intention of the context, in this respect truly comparable to the way Ovid uses the pronouns in the composition of his story about Apollo and Daphne. Recalling also the concise use of the pronouns in Sallust, we cannot feel free to dismiss the "inversion" of *hic* and *ille* at *Aen*. 8. 358 without checking for a possible poetic purpose. The result of this excursus suggests that the linguistic "abnormality" of line 358 rather serves as a pointer, designed to support the conclusion which the attentive reader draws from tracing the route (and the conversation) of the two walkers: it is at this point that Aeneas and Evander complete their left turn, away from the Capitol and toward the Palatine, and it is at this juncture that Evander adduces his final and confirming level-A example. At this moment, the *Ianiculum* beyond the river is indeed nearer to their thoughts than the hill which is physically close by. Thus it turns out that *huic* at 8. 358 is indeed sufficient to carry and convey the emphasis. And the excursus confirms that the tracing of the hikers' route in the text of Chapter 6 above is correct.

Chapter 6

Notes

[1] Norden (1903). A welcome more recent review of the *Aeneid*'s ties and references to Augustan art and architecture is found in Zanker (1988); though not all of his examples may appear conclusive to all of his readers, his result is: "The *Aeneid* and Augustan art are inextricably interwoven; the artist and his age cannot be separated or read apart from one another."

[2] See Stahl 1969, 351, n.1.

[3] Grönbech 1953, 32; cf. 38.

[4] Grönbech 1953, 37.

[5] The causes of Aeneas' concern (cf. *quae...cuncta videns*, 18f.) are outlined in 1–18.

[6] The Roman river's central position in Vergil's geography has been emphasized by della Corte (1972), see esp. his chapter 4.

[7] For a detailed analysis (emphasizing the episodic) of Book 8, see Bömer (1944; especially p. 322); also, Walsh (Introd. to Fordyce's commentary) XXV.

[8] Passages concerning Evander's position in Greek and Roman pre-history are collected in Bömer (1958), vol. 2, pp. 54f. The sequence of mythical immigrants, from Saturnus down to Evander, was fairly well established by tradition. See, e.g., Coarelli (1988 A), 107.

[9] and early afternoon: pluperfect in 97.

[10] i.e., the *portus Tiberinus*, and discounting the swampy *Velabrum*, once navigable, between Capitoline and Palatine. See Staccioli 1988, 34 (no. 9 on *tavola* 1). Coarelli 1988 A, 18–25 *passim* (map on pp. 104–105; map of the archaic harbor: p. 241). Since the beginning of the second century BC this harbor had lost its importance: a new one, the *Emporium*, was built down river from the Aventine.

[11] "Vergil lenkt den Blick seiner Leser auf das augusteische Rom, das sie vor Augen hatten." Binder (1971) 40.

[12] Not over-luxurious (certainly not in the private quarters) inside, it is true (Suet. *Aug.* 72.1; 73): the palace rooms have been found to be conservatively decorated. But Augustus' private refuge upstairs (his "Syracuse", Suet. *Aug.* 72. 2) quite undogmatically displays latest Egyptian taste, possibly acquired in the country of origin (and imported by a transplanted artist and his craftsmen). See Carettoni 1983, 86–93; color photographs opposite p. 81.

[13] Plans in Carettoni, o.c. 8; 10.

[14] In recent years, one has tried to integrate the statues of the portico (Danaus, with drawn sword, and his daughters, versus the sons of Aegyptos) into the Palatine's political context by maintaining varying associations with Antony, Cleopatra, Actium (see Lefèvre 1989, 12–16; Harrison 1998, 230–237). The assumed political symbolism of these sculptures is, of course, hypothetical and cannot be proved. Ovid, who in *Tr.* 3.1 is out to sing the praises of Augustus while detailing features of his palace on the Palatine hill and relating them to the Emperor's events, has no pro-Augustan comment whatsoever to offer when mentioning *Belides et stricto barbarus ense pater* (*Tr.* 3.1.62). For details, see Chapter 3, Section 2.

[15] Schol. Hor. *Ep.* 1. 3. 17; Serv. *ad Ecl.* 4.10 (without giving the location); the information is by no means certain.

[16] Zanker 1983, 24. The libraries also belonged to this tradition. Zanker mentions Pergamon and Alexandria.

[17] Photograph in Lugli 1970, 159, no. 198; drawing (reconstruction) in Coarelli 1988 B, 126.

[18] A cross section as well as a front view of the embankment in times of the republic can be seen in Coarelli 1988 A, 40. (On p. 39, an older photograph of the mouth of the *Cloaca Maxima*. A close-up photograph in Lugli 1970, 120 no. 69.)

[19] Livy 40. 51. 4 (179 BC). At that time (between 179 and 142) the *pons Aemilius* (of which remnants survive in today's *"Ponte Rotto"*) too was built.

[20] Coarelli 1988 A, 146f.

[21] Coarelli 1988 A, 22f.

[22] Lugli 1970, 25

[23] Evidence collected in Coarelli 1988 A, 35–41. The older hypothesis that the *Forum Boarium* was not protected by a wall but only by the river itself, has apparently to be discarded. Coarelli 1988 B, 16; cf. 1988 A, 65f.: "l' ara maxima era infatti, come il Foro Boario, all' interno del pomerio e delle mura, che in questa zona...passavano tra la facciata di S. Maria in Cosmedin e la fontana antistante."

[24] Coarelli 1988 B, 323.

[25] The location is, it seems, generally accepted, whereas its extension under the existing church (crypt) and/or the diaconal palace behind the apses is debated. See blueprint in Lugli 1970, 312. Different blueprint, with marking: G. Massimi 1953, tav. 3, cavo XIII. Description: Coarelli 1988, 323. I do not assume that Vergil expected his reader to think of the altar's shape in terms older than the second century BC restoration in *tufo dell' Aniene*.

[26] *muros*, a customary plural for a defensive wall, is later picked up by the singular *murum*, 474, but again by a plural at 592.

[27] The wall in *opera quadrata* on the southwest corner of the Palatine (sixth century BC, similar to one on the Capitoline) apparently must be understood as a retaining wall rather than an archaic fortification. See Coarelli 1988 B, 127. In the imagination of Vergil's contemporaries, it may well have seemed to picture a very old fortification.

[28] Servius' mistaken understanding (occasionally followed by modern critics) of *audax* as *virtus sine fortuna* (*ad* 8. 110; "ill-starred gallantry", Fordyce) and *fortis sine felicitate* (*ad* 9. 3) tends to gloss over the basic difference (contrast) by which Vergil separates the two death-bound characters. Of course, the pious friend of pious Aeneas dies innocent and so appeals to the reader's sense of pity. (See Chapter 4.) The positive or negative moral value of *audax* depends on the context, e.g., whether the boldness is displayed towards men or towards gods (and oracles). A comparable ambivalence, discussed in Chapter 2, is attached to *furor* and *ira*. A similar distinction is inherent in *superbus*.

[29] Servius *ad* 1. 159. Della Corte (1972, e.g., p. 85) has reintroduced the term into the modern discussion.

[30] In 7. 29f., Aeneas from the sea discovers a huge grove, *ingentem lucum*, "amidst" which – *hunc inter* – the Tiber flows.

[31] Servius *ad* 8. 283 and 1. 216 thinks of the meal's first (meat) and second (fruit) course. It would perhaps fit the situation better to recall here Hercules' wish (Serv. Dan. *ad* 8. 269) that he receive sacrifices both in the morning and in the evening, *ut mane et vespere ei sacrificaretur*. (Cf. *vesper*, *Aen*. 8. 280.) When Aeneas arrives around noontime, the sacrifices are done and Evander's men are sitting at table (*mensis*, 110). Whether the food served to the unexpected guests consists of leftovers from the meal or is newly prepared, remains open, in agreement with epic disregard for details of everyday life.

Chapter 6

[32] E.g., 1.197–209; *o socii,* 198.

[33] See Stahl 1981, 161.

[34] Small 31; Small herself (103; 105) goes so far as to make Vergil comply with Augustus' goals in relocating the monster on the Aventine: Cacus (in her interpretation, originally a seer; see her Chapter 1), she argues, would not have been allowed to co-exist with Augustan *augur Apollo* on the hill the Princeps made his religious center.

[35] On Aeneas "the tourist", see Grönbech 1953, 29.

[36] One has wondered how newcomer Evander can say that "we Italians" (331ff.) gave river *Albula* the new name *Thybris*. It is (though the name change must have occurred before Evander, of course, according to 7. 15 and other passages) much more natural to see herein another – parenthetic – intervention by the author himself, comparable to the parenthesis on *Potitii* and *Pinarii* verified in *Excursus 1* of this chapter at 8. 268–270. Likewise, the characterization "King Evander, founder of the Roman citadel", *Romanae conditor arcis* (313), is Vergil's shorthand for his contemporary readers, meaning something like "founder of the {early} citadel {which was a forerunner} of {what today is called the city of} Rome". (Rome the city, of course, was thought to have been founded by Romulus.)

The distinction made here would render it doubtful that Vergil "legt Wert darauf, den Griechen Euander als Italer auszuweisen (V. 331f.)" (Binder 1971, 114). Binder himself admits (1971, 112) that, wherever post-Evandrian names occur, "redet Vergil 'ex sua persona'". Vergil's strict separation of levels A, B, and C makes it equally doubtful that Aeneas (after all, *ignarus*, according to 8. 730), when looking at the shield, "sieht, dass kommen wird, was Carmentis vorhergesagt hat: *Aeneadas magnos et nobile Pallanteum,* und spürt die Verantwortung, die ihm für die Erfüllung der Prophetie zukommt", etc. (Binder 1971, 117). Binder's principle ("Prinzip", o.c. 141) is in danger of creating correspondences between the early part of Book 8 and the shield rather than verifying correspondences intended by the author.

[37] Staccioli 1988, 41; location no. 24 on his *Tavola 1.*

[38] Coarelli 1988 B, 318: "tracce della quale sono state viste al centro della strada moderna" (i.e., the *Vico Iugario,* in Coarelli's context); cf.16. See also G. Ioppolo's maps in his 1974/75 publication or in Coarelli 1988A, 395 and 239 (also: 235). Coarelli (1988 A, especially pp. 19; 34; 52; 234–242; 370ff.; 390ff.) discusses in depth the possible location, even the possibility of two gates: the older *Porta Carmentalis* (part of the 6th century BC wall), one gate of which may have to be identified with the *Porta Triumphalis,* and a younger one, built in the fourth century BC, incorporating the *area sacra* around today's *S. Omobono* in the city. On the difficulty of identifying the reference of Vergil's allusions, see the text below.

[39] See the drawings in Coarelli 1988 A, pp. 235 (by Ioppolo); 239 (by Ioppolo); 395.

[40] Coarelli 1988 A, 234–244.

[41] The *Campus Martius* area (beginning a little north of the *Porta Carmentalis*) was exposed to flooding up to modern times. Today's visitor to the city may form an impression by reviewing the modern high water marks affixed to the facade of *S.a Maria sopra Minerva* in the *Pantheon* area. The marks reach heights of several yards above today's street level. Equally informative are the marks on the south wall of the church *S. Rocco* on the *via di Ripetta* next to the location of the *Mausoleo di Augusto.*

[42] Cf. *nemus,* 108; 305; cf. the specific cases *ante urbem in luco,* 104; *hanc aram in luco statuit,* 271; also, Fordyce *ad* 7. 29.

⁴³ Epic style, of course, and personal dignity of the walkers forbid to mention such trivialities. In a post-convivial context, Ovid (*F.* 6. 405f.) is more realistic about the *Velabrum* in early times.

⁴⁴ TDAR, *s.v. Carmentis,* concludes from the evidence that "the shrine was...probably within the limits of the forum Holitorium". NTDR, *s.v. Carmentis, Fanum,* interprets Servius' "next to the gate" as "just inside it (*iuxta portam*, not *extra portam*: Servius *ad Aen.* 8. 337)." But Vergil has Evander first show the altar, then the gate (there is no reason to assume a *hysteron proteron* at 8. 337f.).

⁴⁵ "The text of Virgil is, however, unrevised here and hardly more than a series of jottings." Richmond 1958, 181.

⁴⁶ Of the two grammatical possibilities, "from this location, he points out" (cf. OLD *s.v. hinc,* 5a) and "from here, he {moves on and} points out", the first is excluded by the topography.

⁴⁷ Fordyce *ad* 8. 337ff., with further remarks on Vergil's mixing of time levels.

⁴⁸ Grimal 1948, 351. ("behind the Pallanteum of Evander, there appears the Rome of Augustus").

⁴⁹ Grimal 1948, 349 (a huge assemblage dedicated to Apollo).

⁵⁰ *Q Lutatius Q f Q n Catulus cos substructionem et tabularium...faciendum coeravit,* CIL VI, 1314. Coarelli 1988 B, 32; NTDR 376f.

⁵¹ Lugli 1970, 136.

⁵² Lugli 1970, 133, n.6.

⁵³ For a possible reconstruction, see Staccioli 1988, p. 92.

⁵⁴ For a quick survey of the buildings mentioned in the following section one may turn to Coarelli 1988 B, 272–277; Staccioli 1988, 203–208; Lugli 1970, 285; 294–313 (a good map is provided by Lugli in the folder at the end of his volume); TDAR and NTDR, *s.vv.*

⁵⁵ Stahl 1981, n. 29 on p.177.

⁵⁶ La Rocca 1988, 122–129; Zanker 1988, 68f.; description (and photographs) of the architrave representing a triumphal procession (in all likelihood, that of Octavian-Augustus, not of Sosius): Bertoletti 1988, 144f. with *Kat.* 41.

⁵⁷ Lugli 1970, 303. Doubts about Augustus' personal involvement in the building are voiced in NTDAR, *s.v. Porticus Octaviae* (p.317), in spite of Suet. *Aug.* 29. 4 and D.C. 49. 43. 8.

⁵⁸ The stone map of the time of Septimius Severus offers a good survey. See, e.g., Coarelli 1988 B, 273. Staccioli 203. On a circular building, which "virtually blocked" the passage between temple and theater, see NTDAR, p. 13, c. 1.

⁵⁹ Coarelli 1988 A, 397. Even if one does not accept all of Coarelli's conclusions about the triumphal gate, the evidence (including photographs) on the course of the colonnade as needed for our literary purpose is well documented on pp. 393–399.

⁶⁰ Norden long ago (1901, 273) saw Aeneas' visit at the *Lupercal* as "eine Huldigung für Augustus." The contrast of Augustus' splendid restoration and the "cold rock", *gelida...sub rupe* (*Aen.* 8. 343), of Evander's time becomes clearer if one reads Donatus' comment that *rupes* is used for "rocks unordered, precipitous, and rising naturally to immense height", *rupes dicuntur saxa incomposita et praerupta et erecta naturaliter in altitudinem immensam.*

⁶¹ Grimal 1948, 350.

⁶² Coarelli 1988 B, 68.

Chapter 6

⁶³ Cf. Coarelli 1988 B, 43; 58; Staccioli 54.

⁶⁴ Coarelli 1988 B, 68; a reconstructive drawing by G. Tognetti is shown in Staccioli, p.55.

⁶⁵ The modern reader may submit that Vergil's contemporaries may well have been able to see the *Argiletum* from the *Velabrum* area by just looking through the spaces between the columns (the *intercolumnia*) of the *basilica Iulia* (provided the *tabernae* did not prevent them). This would only strengthen my argument. For, by searching in his mind (or, *Aeneid* in hand, with his eyes) for a position allowing him to look through the *intercolumnia*, Vergil's contemporary would be even more aware of the Augustan basilica of his own time.

⁶⁶ Bauer 1988, 200; a reconstructive drawing of the facade facing the *forum*, after the Augustan rebuilding of 14 BC, *ibidem* pp. 204–205; Zanker 1972, 7.

⁶⁷ See also Gros-Savron 55f. and the blueprints in von Hesberg (1988), 114 and 115.

⁶⁸ Zanker 1988, 80; cf. 1972, 42. On the roof of the *curia*, Augustus likewise placed a Victoria on a globe.

⁶⁹ Binder (1971, 187) takes the connection for granted, and even believes that Aeneas, when inspecting on his new shield the pictorial representation of the Capitoline with Jupiter's temple (653), Romulus' hut (654), and citadel (652; 657), recognizes in it the bare hill to the foot of which Evander led him the day before.

⁷⁰ For this use of *et*, see OLD *s.v.*, 11.

⁷¹ One ought not to think that CN are in agreement with Servius who says (*ad* 348): *quae* (sc., *Tarpeia*) *illic sepulta Tarpeiae sedi nomen inposuit* (see also his comment on *Tarpeiam sedem*, 347: *duo haec...nomina postea monti indita sunt*). For Servius does not mention that she was buried on the grounds of the later Jupiter Optimus Maximus temple (Plut. *Rom.* 18.1), i.e., the *Capitolium*; in Servius' context, "there" can refer only to the citadel (*arcis proditione...illic*).

⁷² No indication is given here (as would usually be the case) by the context that *sedes* should be taken as "grave" (scil. of Tarpeia).

⁷³ Grimal (1948, 350) has Evander follow this route ("En suivant le *Vicus Iugarius*," etc.). This causes Grimal later to misunderstand the situation at 8. 357f. See also Grimal 1945, 61, n. 2. Binder (1971, 118ff.) accepts Grimal's route.

⁷⁴ These would be either the curved *rostra* (the so-called *hemicyclium*) (re)built by Antony for Caesar, or Augustus' own rectangular *rostra*, which on three sides prevent a view of the older ones; he built the latter one possibly between 14 and 12 BC after a fire, or even as early as 29 BC. See Coarelli 1985 A, 237–257 (see especially plan 47 on p. 246); Murray and Petsas (1989) 119–122; see also Giuliani-Verducci (1987) 47; Gland 65 (in favor of the late date, following the fire of 14 BC); and our discussion in the following Chapter.

⁷⁵ Coarelli 1988 B, 58: "*Umbilicus urbis* e *Mundus* sono dunque la stessa cosa." The remnants of the *umbilicus* visible today are a late (third c. AD) construction, but the underlying idea goes back to the origin of the city.

⁷⁶ Today, nearby Capitol Square serves as the point of departure for measuring distances from Rome.

⁷⁷ Pensabene 179.

⁷⁸ La Rocca 1988, 123f.

⁷⁹ The triumph is mentioned as the first on the *Fasti* of Augustus (dealt with later in this Chapter).

⁸⁰ Cass. Dio 44. 4. 3; cf. TDAR *s.v. Iuppiter Feretrius, aedes.*

⁸¹ Ogilvie *ad* Livy 1.10. 7. "Such military glory infringed a monopoly" (Syme 1974, 308). One may also compare the "triumphal monopoly" (*Triumphalmonopol*, Coarelli 1988 C, 73) Augustus developed for himself and members of his family.

⁸² Coarelli 1988 B, 30; Lugli 127–129.

⁸³ TDAR, *s.v. Iupiter Tonans*, p. 306. "On the southeastern brow of the hill overlooking the Forum Romanum", NTDR, p. 226. Richardson locates its foundations on both sides of the *via del Tempio di Giove*. If this is correct, one would wish to assume that Aeneas and Evander are now moving a few yards in a southwestern direction, parallel to the western short side of the Augustan *basilica Iulia*. The massive temple of Saturnus does not obstruct the view from here to the brow of the *Capitolium*.

⁸⁴ 1901, 273.

⁸⁵ von Hesberg 1988, 102: (the temple) "muss von auffallender Pracht gewesen sein."

⁸⁶ One hesitates to claim – as Binder (1971, 132f.) does – our passage, beyond its wording, for the concept of Augustus as Jupiter's incarnation or as Jupiter's representative on earth (cf. Horace, *C.* 1. 12. 49–57). On the other hand, Fordyce's comment *ad* 337ff., "this romantic account of Aeneas' sightseeing" and on Vergil's "antiquarian enthusiasm", misses the author's political message completely.

⁸⁷ Likewise, Binder (1970,134) understands that by *haec...hanc...hanc* (8. 355–357) "...Ruinen zweier Festungen gemeint sind, die unmittelbar vor den Betrachtern liegen."

⁸⁸ Grimal 1945, 57–62.

⁸⁹ See also Binder (1971, 135): "Euander wendet sich mit seinem Gast vom Capitol nach rechts," and Binder's overall argumentation on pp. 134–137.

⁹⁰ This is, one recalls, the older (smaller) Augustan basilica which had not yet forced a relocation of the mouth of the *vicus Iugarius* closer to the temple of Saturnus.

⁹¹ For readers interested in the specific use of *hic* and *ille* here under discussion, Excursus 3 at the end of this chapter provides more information.

⁹² For the mixed expression, they "*saw* the cattle *low*", see Fordyce *ad loc*. However, cattle when lowing take a distinctive posture, with head thrown back and whole body heaving. This can indeed be seen.

⁹³ Still today, the street to the *Carinae* is seen between the temple of Romulus and the basilica of Maxentius; at least the latter building was, of course, not yet in existence at the time of Augustus. Its enormous size may have forced a rerouting of the side street.

⁹⁴ Coarelli 1988 B, 79; cf. 87.

⁹⁵ On the difficulties of defining the course of the *sacra via* see Coarelli 1988 B, 78f.; NTDR, *s.v.*

⁹⁶ TDAR, *s.v. porta Mugonia*. Also, NTDR *s.v. Sacra Via*, p.339.

⁹⁷ Two instructive maps (by Gatti), indicating Caesar's and Augustus' buildings in the area, are found in von Hesberg 1988, pp.112 and 113 (*Abb.* 39 and 40).

⁹⁸ von Hesberg, 98. Zanker (1972, 40) adds the *basilica Iulia* as another marble building erected "in diesen Jahren".

⁹⁹ Here I follow Zanker (1972, 12ff.) whose study may be consulted for further details. See also Coarelli 1985, 308–324.

¹⁰⁰ See Murray and Petsas (1989) 119–122. Stahl 1998, 64–67. Augustus may also have drawn satisfaction from hiding Antony's hemicyclic *rostra* behind his own rectangular ones.

Chapter 6

[101] ἀγῶνές τε παντοδαποὶ ἐγένοντο, καὶ τὴν Τροίαν εὐπατρίδαι παῖδες ἵππευσαν, Dio Cass. 51. 22. 4.

[102] It appears doubtful that Vergil, by comparing the riders' movements to the courses of a labyrinth (5. 588–591), is undercutting his own story (and point) of the game's Trojan origin – as was recently maintained again by Binder (1985, 355f., quoting Constans). If indeed Vergil knew of an equation of Etruscan *truia* and "labyrinth", he may have, with equal or even more probability, intended to show how the labyrinthine movements of the Trojan game could have led Etruscans to accept the word *truia* for what the Greeks (and Romans) called "labyrinth". Vergil's method then would be similar to the way in which Book 2 introduces a tradition hostile to Aeneas only to supply a benign explanation (see Stahl 1981, 167); or in which Book 3 derives *palaestra* from Trojan origins (3.280 f.; see Stahl 1998, 60). The Trojan claim is the more remarkable as "nicht eine einzige Quelle kennt einen ausserrömischen lusus Troiae" (Dinzelbacher 1982, 153).

Let us exemplify Vergil's thought pattern from a wider context. In Book 8, the whole Etruscan might is (unhistorically) said to bow its head before the Trojan leader. Vergil's jealous assertion of Trojan-Julian superiority makes it doubtful that in Book 5 he could grant priority to an Etruscan name in a context which seeks to establish Trojan origin and precedence (see especially *primus*, 5. 596; *quo puer ipse modo, secum quo Troia pubes*, 599). Rather, the situation is the opposite: he "corrects" the "mistaken" derivation, by letting the Etruscan name for labyrinth be derived from the Trojan game (provided there really *is* more to lines 5.558–595 than a comparison). Scholarly interpretation easily tends to prove "complexité virgilienne" (Binder 1985, 356) or ambiguity at the cost of the work's own train of thought. The tight connection of *hunc morem* (5.596) and *nunc* (602) is not sufficiently taken into account by Dinzelbacher (his objection no. 3, p. 153).

[103] Briggs 274; cf. 282.

[104] Briggs 276.

[105] See, e.g., Zanker 1972, 42; overview of opinions in Needergard.

[106] The inscription plays no part in Needergard's reasoning. It (*CIL* 6.873 = *ILS* 81; quoted also in Ehrenberg/Jones under III 17 on p. 57, location stated: "Rome, Forum") "was found toward the southeast end of the forum in the sixteenth century, but the reports of it are confused and contradictory," NTDR *s.v. Arcus Octaviani*:

[107] Coarelli 1985, 258–301.

[108] The eastern short side had, of course, its own republican fig leaf. The rams on the new *rostra* were to symbolize the saving of the republic at Actium where the larger rams of Antony's fleet adorned the memorial erected by 'the savior of the republic'.

[109] For the artistic expressions of this presumed policy change, see Zanker 1988, especially Chapter 3 (cf. p. 85ff.: "A Change of Focus: Self-Glorification Gives Way to Religious Devotion"). On the question whether or not there really was a break in Augustus' career, see Raaflaub and Toher, XII–XIV. For the whole question of the Iulian changes on the *forum Romanum*, see Zanker 1972; 1987, 85–87; Coarelli 1985, especially 233–304; von Hesberg; Gros and Sauron, 63.

[110] Zanker 1972, 22f.

[111] Zanker 1972, 46. See also the re-naming of the Basilica Iulia (to be restored after a fire) after his 'sons' Gaius and Lucius, *R. G.* 20.3.

[112] Zanker 1972, 17.

[113] Coarelli 1985, 323.

[114] Bowersock (1990, 380) thinks it may have been "the splendor of the pontificate" that kept Augustus from seizing title and office. Bowersock has rightly emphasized the importance of the pontificate for the Augustan ideology. But the pontificate is only the coping stone. The groundwork for Augustus' central position in the state religion is laid already in the *Aeneid* which makes the Julian ancestor the carrier of Vesta and the Penates – the same state-saving divinities which Octavian is said to carry on his own ship against Cleopatra and Antony (*Aen.* 8. 679 ~ 3.12; cf. 2. 293 and 296).

[115] Cf. Cicero, *Phil.* 11. 24. A matter of some dispute was how, if the effigy had been stolen by Ulysses and Diomedes preceding the fall of Troy, Aeneas could have brought it with him. Some amazing solutions were developed, among them that Diomedes himself later took the *Palladium* to Lavinium and handed it over to Aeneas...

[116] On exhibition in Berlin, *Charlottenburger Antikensammlungen*. For a (not too clear) photograph, see Amersdorffer 75, n.112. (See also *BMC* No. 31ff.; Crawford no. 458.1.) An enlarged photograph, this one not very clear either, appears on p. 39 in Amersdorffer (text: on p.34).

[117] Are these the inner parts of *Anchises'* house? When, after the dream, the priest Panthus actually does bring the objects to Aeneas (*Aen.* 2. 318–320), Vesta is no longer specifically mentioned.

[118] Bishop 1956, 188.

[119] Richmond 1958, 180.

[120] That, in the end, Ovid's book – diverging from the route it has followed so far – is refused entrance even at the temple of Freedom (*Libertas*) near the senate house is an ambiguous climax which is apt to undercut the ill-fated intention of the preceding instances.

[121] From their viewing *forum* and *Carinae*, Binder (1971, 137) concludes – as we did above, for different reasons – that they turned right "an der Stelle, wo jetzt der Titusbogen steht." However, the *forum* area (one should note) they have seen already while crossing it.

[122] "they *went along uphill* to Evander's dwelling," Fowler 1917, 75, n. 1 (emphasis Fowler's).

[123] Binder 1971, 144.

[124] Binder 1971, 144.

[125] And the purpose is totally Vergil's own design: the guided tour is not found in Dionysius of Halicarnassus or any other author. See Walsh (in Fordyce) xv.

[126] The Hercules temple can today be well viewed from the Cybele temple area on the Palatine Hill.

[127] For this word cf. 4. 484, a meaning not specified in OLD.

[128] Stahl 1985, 26f.; Ch. II n.10, n.11, n.12; Ch. III n. 32.

[129] 190–199; 200–204; 205–211; 212; 213–216; 217–224; 225–232; 233–235; 236–240; 241–246; 247–250; 251–255; 256–261; 262–267.

[130] An example (with rich references to preceding literature) is an early article by G.K. Galinsky (1966), who throughout relies heavily on "parallels of imagery, language, symbolism and, partly, theme" (p. 51). As I documented in the opening chapter, such features can be cited usefully when seen as supporting the train of thought; but we leave the sphere of demonstrability if we ascribe to them independent

interpretative value, especially when analyzing a Book of admittedly problematic composition and when asking questions about its relations to other Books. Not dissimilar in method to Galinsky's interpretation is the one more recently offered by Morgan, who dismisses "the liberal, ambivalent Vergil of the orthodoxy" in favor of "a rather brilliant propagandist" (1998, 192).

[131] In passing it should be repeated that, of course, we are unable to say with certainty where on the Palatine Vergil pictured Evander's palace. It is true that in the poet's time Augustus had not been the only resident (though probably, at least after the battle of Naulochos in 36 BC, the most active real estate buyer and builder) on the hill. Yet to the poet's contemporaries the ruler certainly was the most prominent resident, his residential complex the most visible, the first to come to the reader's mind. More on the location Vergil had probably in mind in the next part of this Chapter.

[132] Coarelli 1985, 28: "'E anche possibile che la Rupe, che sappiamo visibile dal Foro, fosse sull' Arx."

[133] For some helpful remarks and examples, see *LS* s.v. *hic*, I.D.; *TLL*, s.v. *hic*, column 2715, lines 40ff.

[134] Whether *arx* in Ovid (*F*. 1.245f.) supports the reading *arcem* (usually preferred over the variant *urbem*) at *Aen.* 8. 357 I leave for the reader to decide.

[135] Luck's definition (*ad Tr.* 1.2.23f.) is too narrow for his own list of examples: "*hic* bezieht sich auf das im Satzgefüge Entferntere, dem Sprechenden aber *räumlich* näher Liegende" (italics mine). In the case of *Aen.* 8. 357f. (which he adduces), *hic* points to the *räumlich ferner* Liegende, viz. the *Ianiculum*.

[136] Szantyr 181 (paragraph 105, *Zusatz* b).

[137] *TLL*, s.v. *hic*, column 2715, lines 46ff.

[138] *TLL*, s.v. *hic*, column 2716, line 45.

[139] *TLL*, l.c., lines 39–41; see also the following example in the text above.

[140] "ille de '*nomine praedicat*.'", *TLL*, s.v. *hic*, 2715, line 70.

[141] For a critique of the methodological problem, see Stahl 1985 (e.g., among the passages listed in the Subject Index under "Shackleton Bailey" and "Housman").

[142] *usu neglegentiore*, *TLL* s.v., column 2716, lines 62–64.

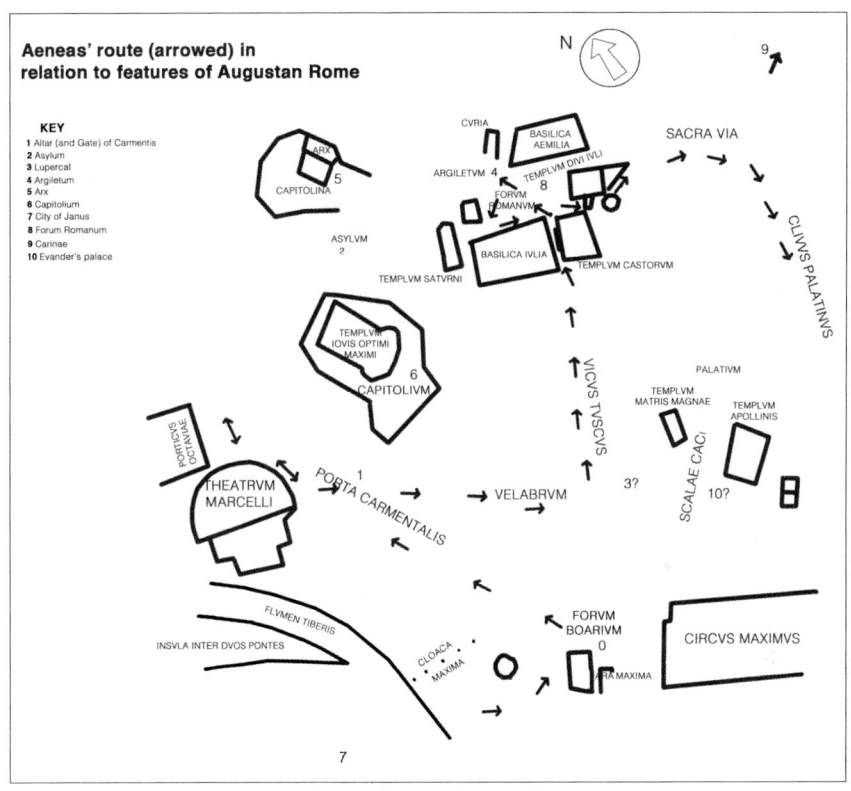

Aeneas' route (arrowed)

PART III

TESTING A CRITICAL METHOD BY REPEAT APPLICATION: THE ANCIENT AUTHOR GUIDES HIS READER

7

ALLOCATING GUILT AND INNOCENCE, II: TURNUS, THE IMPIOUS OPPONENT

One cannot hope to define adequately the initial impression the poet suggests of Turnus without first analyzing two aspects: first, the overall context and setting in which the Rutulian king is placed when being presented to the reader for the first time, i.e., the complex situation depicted in the opening narrative of Book 7; and second, the way in which Vergil makes Turnus react to this original situation or, rather, to elements contained in it.

Such a two-pronged procedure, when suggested in theory, may appear *a priori* appropriate and one may therefore expect that it be generally accepted. But the practice of interpreters has often been different, and they have built on loose assumptions that might easily have been confirmed or refuted by a close reading of the relevant passages. It is indispensable first to have clarity on specific points essential for understanding not only Vergil's concept of Turnus but possibly the intention of the whole *Aeneid* itself. After all, the opening section of Book 7 also opens Vergil's "Roman *Iliad*", i.e., the weightier (*maius opus*, 7.44) second half of his work, which comprises Books 7 to 12.

Much Vergilian scholarship rests on unverified intuition. This is especially striking when found in a scholar whose book has, over several decades and editions, exercised very great influence on Vergilian studies and contributed enormously to upgrading the picture of Turnus, from that of a country's enemy ("Staatsfeind") to one of a tragic hero. Pöschl started his interpretation of Turnus hundreds of lines into Book 7; apparently, he

Chapter 7

found nothing worthwhile reported before "the scene in which Turnus appears for the first time".[1] At that point, Turnus, in his dream, encounters the Fury Allecto and seems to succumb to her influence – a process that makes Pöschl feel increased compassion (*Mitleid*) for the hero, even lets him see "the innocence of his guilt" ("die Schuldlosigkeit seiner Schuld").[2] Without interpreting the evidence provided by Vergil in the earlier parts of the narrative, Pöschl informs us that husband-*in-spe* Turnus is, among other things, fighting "for his *rightful claim* on Lavinia", "für *sein Recht* auf Lavinia (VII 423)" (*sic*; italics Pöschl's).

The experienced reader of the *Aeneid* may be surprised that Pöschl, in his defense of Turnus, includes a supposedly "rightful claim" pronounced by, of all lower divinities, a Fury – a Fury sent, moreover, by Juno (enemy of Fate's plans and of future Rome) to "destroy the peace" that had come about in Latium between the newcomer Aeneas and the local King Latinus (*disice compositam pacem, sere crimina belli,* 339). One might perhaps expect that an alternative interpretation (though itself problematical) of the same dream scene would have won easier acceptance and greater influence than Pöschl's. E.g., Hornsby seems to think that Vergil rather inculpates the Rutulian hero "in the first appearance of Turnus in book VII". He maintains: "From his mad dream of glory Turnus never awakes",[3] thus assigning him an entirely dreamy career within the *Aeneid*, marked by lack of realism.

Given the confusion of the scholarly situation, it may be indispensable for us, too, to focus on the dream – but by placing it in its *context*, i.e., by analyzing the development that leads up to it.

1. Mastering the Logic of Events, Timing, and Circumstances

From the beginning, we must be careful to avoid a longstanding and widely repeated misconception (reflected also in Pöschl's appraisal) concerning Turnus' personal situation – a misconception that is bound to elicit sympathetic feelings from the reader: viz. that Turnus is the fiancé of Princess Lavinia ("Latinus' daughter Lavinia was betrothed to Turnus," etc., R. D. Williams *ad* 7.45ff.). For if, by Aeneas' arrival in Latium, Turnus is deprived of his promised future wife, a severe injustice is done to him, and his ensuing wrath can count on the reader's sense of fairness: through six books, he will be seen as fighting the wrong done to his heart and to his honor. In this case, a shadow would be allowed to fall on the purity of Aeneas' involvement with Lavinia (though not necessarily on Aeneas himself, except by implication). If, however, it turns out that there never was a betrothal (as this interpreter will argue), and if, furthermore, it was (as this interpreter will also argue) clear *before* Aeneas' arrival in Latium that Lavinia was *destined* not to be Turnus' wife, then the reader may arrive at the opposite judgement: Turnus, by the continued pursuit of his marriage plans, not only would appear to act like a brigand claiming someone else's rightful bride, but, by fighting Destiny, would allow doubts to fall on his religious morals. On the other hand, Aeneas' course of action can, under the latter assumption, not be subject to the blame of insulting a sacrosanct human bond.

The reader's reaction to the situation will largely depend on what (s)he understands to be the timing of events. It is only consistent (though not often observed) that Vergil places heavy emphasis on the temporal sequence. When embarking on the more important, "Iliadic" half (*maius opus moveo*, 7.44) of his poem and invoking Erato in a sort of "second proem" (on which more later on), the poet initially explores the state of affairs existing in Latium at the time "when the foreign army first landed its fleet on Italian shores" (37ff.). The description of events *before* the Trojans' arrival extends from 45 to 105a. At 105b a new dimension is being added to conditions as they had developed up to that time (the pluperfect *tulerat* points to the state of affairs reached and prevailing then). The new dimension is indicated grammatically by the so-called *cum inversum*, "when the Trojan youth tied their fleet to the grassy bank of the river". The repetition (39 and 105) of the temporal conjunction *cum*,[4] introducing identical content on each occasion, provides a firm setting for the description of 'pre-Trojan' happenings in Latium. The section also, being positioned between the Trojans' approach up the Tiber (25–36) and their first actions on land (107ff.), establishes a basis to judge the ensuing development. The reader will measure later events by the religious standards expounded in this introduction. For now, we investigate the meaning of the time frame.

After hearing (50f.) about King Latinus' divine ancestry and the loss – *fato divum*: pro-Trojan Providence has been at work already – of his male offspring, we learn that daughter Lavinia alone (*sola*, 52) was upholding the kingdom's future; i.e., she is viewed here as the royal heiress who, moreover, was *iam matura viro, iam plenis nubilis annis*, old enough to be married, both physically and legally (53). Consequently, many young men from Latium and all over Italy were striving for her hand. Among them was Turnus, distinguished by his beauty, ancestral power and – the queen's favor (whether because he was a relative of hers, as Servius reports and Dionysius of Halicarnassus asserts, or only because of the reasons here indicated by Vergil). "With marvelous desire" she "kept pushing (hastening)" (imperfect of extended action in the past) the idea that he "be associated as the son-in-law" (56f.).

Nothing whatsoever invites us to believe that the queen's emotional thrust (*miro...amore*) in continuously promoting the marriage has taken her anywhere near her goal. As far as King Turnus' situation is concerned, he is clearly listed as one suitor competing among others (*petit*, 55 ~ *petebant*, 54), and no hint is given that his prospects were favorable ones (the decision on questions concerning the succession to the throne lies, of course, with the king not with his consort. In fact, no solution to the suitors' competition was within reach: *petebant* is imperfect of duration again.) On the contrary, an emphatically placed "but" (*sed*, opposing *properabat*, *petit* and even *petebant*) shows that fulfillment was denied to the endeavours of all and any of the interested parties:

> But portents of the gods, by various frightening appearances,
>   were standing against it.
>
> Sed variis portenta deum terroribus obstant.   58

A "flashback" (Williams; 59–105) explains the religious obstacles to Lavinia's marriage: a swarm of bees in a sacred laurel-tree is taken to indicate that a foreign leader and his army will rule the kingdom from the acropolis. And fire, catching Lavinia's hair during a religious ceremony and spreading, is interpreted as meaning fame for the maiden but war for her people. Deeply distressed by the two portents (*portenta deum*, 58 ~ *monstris*, 81), King Latinus seeks guidance from a third, well-established[5] supra-natural source (*mirabile dictu*, 64 ~ *visu mirabile*, 78 ~ *modis...miris*, 89). He consults the oracle of his father Faunus and receives the following answer:

> Don't strive to join your daughter in marriage with a Latin,
> my progeny, nor entrust her to the marriage (chamber) at hand!
>
> ne pete conubiis natam sociare Latinis,
> o mea progenies, thalamis neu crede paratis;   96f.

The second alternative appears, as already Servius saw, specifically to refer to King Turnus who is not a Latin in the narrow sense (i.e., not a Laurentine),[6] but, as 367ff. show, a free Rutulian not subject to Latinus (cf. *libera*, 369). The reference to Turnus is valid no matter whether at 97 one supplies *natam* or takes *crede* as "trust". *Paratis* here means "at hand" ("ready without the trouble of seeking", CN *ad loc*.; "to hand, available" OLD, s.v.1) rather than "prepared" ("vorbereitet" transl. Binder); the latter might perhaps be applicable to the queen's "preparations", but certainly not to King Latinus: he is nowhere shown so far to have conceded or entered any binding commitment concerning the sought-after (cf. *quaesitas*, 423) marriage of his daughter, *iam matura viro, iam plenis nubilis annis* (53). If he had already made a prior decision in favor of Turnus, it would be absurd of the oracle to still address both alternatives (*ne*, 96...*neu*, 97) and to reject them both. Moreover, at 270, Latinus shows that the religious obstacles (*monstra*, 270 ~ *monstris*, 81) have been binding on him. Even the Fury in Turnus' dream cannot point to a broken promise but only to Latinus' constant refusal (*abnegat*, 424 is durative, "has been (keeps) denying") of Turnus' request.[7]

Faunus' answer to Latinus continues as follows:

> A son-in-law will come from abroad, who by his blood
> shall carry our name up to the stars, and by his stock our descendants will
> watch all nations being made subject and ruled
> as far as the Sungod on his path can see from Ocean to Ocean.

> externi venient generi, qui sanguine nostrum
> nomen in astra ferant, quorumque a stirpe nepotes
> omnia sub pedibus, qua Sol utrumque recurrens
> aspicit Oceanum, vertique regique videbunt.   98–101

Being a local echo of a far grander prophesy (viz., Jupiter speaking to Venus about "Trojan", *Troianus*, Augustus[8] who will limit the empire by the Ocean, the fame by the stars", 1.286f.), Faunus' pronouncement is easy to classify for Vergil's contemporary reader: Latium is about to face Augustus' ancestor, and Latium will, upon being upgraded (more on this below, *ad* 219ff.) by Trojan-Julian blood, become famous when Aeneas' stock (cf. *quorumque a stirpe*, 7.99) eventually will rule the world. *Turnus' marriage plans are in conflict with Rome's Julian future*, i.e., with the course of fate: *portenta deum...obstant* (58).

At this point one may (as has indeed been done) object: why should Turnus think of giving up his hoped-for bride to his rival Aeneas and not rather uphold his own claims? Why give in and cede the maiden to an invader from abroad? The question is, as Vergil's composition shows, asked wrongly (because it uses Turnus' mistaken perspective, viz. that of rivaling suitors who stand on an equal footing).

Following the quotation of Faunus' oracle (96–101), the reader is given a curious piece of information. Though the oracle had spoken to him in silent night (*silenti nocte*), King Latinus "did not keep the contents to himself but, flying far and wide, *Fama* (104; here = personified 'tidings', 'news', cf. 3.121; 7; 392) already (*iam*) had (pluperfect) carried them through the Ausonian (=Italian) cities, when" (the Trojans landed).

Why does Vergil explicitly wish his reader to know that the old king did not keep his mouth closed (*non ipse suo premit ore Latinus*, 103)? Beyond Servius' charming answer (*ad* 7.103), *quo a se repelleret generos*, in order to keep the suitors away from himself   I ask my reader to recall that the sub-clause about the Trojans' landing ("when", *cum*, 105) picks up the earlier "when"-clause (*cum*, 39) of identical content and thus concludes the report

Chapter 7

on the conditions and timing of the events (37ff.; details below) in Latium prior to (or: at) the Trojans' arrival. In particular the pluperfect *tulerat* (as well as the temporal adverb *iam*, 104f.) shows that the process of spreading the oracle had already come to its end (the cities in Italy were informed) when Aeneas and his men landed.

Recalling the earlier information (54f.) that Lavinia's suitors came from "all over Ausonia", *e...tota...Ausonia*, the reader concludes now (and this will be confirmed later when we interpret Turnus' dream at 420ff.) that among the "Ausonian cities"(104f.) informed by *Fama* was, of course, neighboring Ardea, the town of King Turnus. (The hypothesis of Faunus' oracle being located near Ardea is, under this aspect, not an unwelcome one[10] though in no way necessary for our understanding.) Vergil's sharp compositional distinction between conditions in pre-Trojan Latium on the one hand and Trojan arrival on the other, then, has severe consequences for the reader's view of Turnus' behavior. (I am speaking here of the conscientious reader who is not content with a vague impression gained from superficially scanning the text.) *Turnus must have known already before Aeneas appeared in Latium that the gods were against his becoming Lavinia's husband* and thus the heir (the term the Fury will use, 424; see also 52) to the kingdom. Persisting in his aspirations (this would be valid whether or not the old king had promised him his daughter's hand – which, as we saw, he had *not*) will make Turnus a rebel against the will of the gods. His actual hostility against Aeneas is, in degree of criminality as well as in chronological order, secondary because his first offence is: he has violated the pronounced will of destiny.

I emphasize *"pronounced"*[11] will because we observed how Vergil stressed both the binding character for *all* of Italy (*omnis...Oenotria tellus*, 85) of Faunus' oracle and the special religious legitimacy of Latinus, who, as "Father" (*pater* 92) of the country (on this term, see also Chapter 8) exercises the function of the *sacerdos*: he *himself* (i.e., in person: *ipse* 92) has, in ritually correct fashion (*rite* 93: in Rome, an indispensable condition for a successful religious action) performed the numerous requirements of the consultation, when receiving the divine injunction.

Vergil's explicitness in emphasizing that the oracle was so widely spread has proved a fact hard to get around for those who wish for a pitiable, innocent-since-uninformed, Turnus. The assertion that "On the divine level, he [scil. Turnus] is quite simply alone from the beginning" (Thomas 1998, 292) requires some creative reading: "Nor does Vergil anywhere tell us that Latinus informed him of it (scil., the prophecy): Rumor circulated it." "Rumor" instead of "news" in a case where *Fama* has spread the actual information (*haec responsa* and *monitus...datos* are the gammatical objects of *tulerat* 102–105)? If Turnus held the divine tidings emanating from the all-Italian oracle to be a mere "rumor", he was obliged to seek clarification (as he fails to do at 9.122–37, but Father Anchises dutifully does at 2. 689–91). After all, it was old King Latinus himself who saw to it that the oracle from "silent night" was divulged. In view of the handshakes exchanged "so often" (*totiens* 367) one can hardly assume that Turnus was excluded from religious communications. Turnus "has no personal *autopsy*" (*sic*; my italics). Should Vergil, to convince Thomas, have reported that Latinus sent the Rutulian king a certified autograph of his dream minutes? Thomas employs the same type of gap-finding and -filling when his theory leads him to define the actual ending Vergil wrote to his epic as "the closure it lacks" (2001, 281). "The question is not whether the prophecy occurred, but whether Turnus is ever helped by divine signs" (Thomas). It would be correct to say that Turnus refuses to observe "divine signs". At any rate, a so-far unconvinced reader will, at the time he reads Turnus' dream (7.421–23), no longer be able to doubt that Turnus does know the contents of the oracle – if the reader is willing to pay attention to the text.

This clarifies the nature of Turnus' defiance (and helps to explain the old king's later curse): he sins in spite of knowing better, disregarding authoritative information issued by a widely acknowledged divine source. No wonder that, when facing his final trial, he will be fully aware that the gods are against him and that Jupiter is his enemy (*di me terrent et Iupiter hostis*, 12.895). The sympathy that some readers have expressed for an innocently fierce Turnus who refused to give up his alleged fiancée to a foreign invader – this sympathy does not flow from the moral or religious situation or from the facts as the *Aeneid* tells them. From the beginning the poet's design of the time frame denies King Turnus any chance of being innocent.

The point is of utmost importance for understanding Vergil's concept of political (allied with the religious in Augustan time) and personal guilt. The opponents of Aeneas may not always fully comprehend that they are challenging the fated course of history and that they therefore are, like any opponent of the Trojan-Julian House in the *Aeneid*, guilty to an almost cosmic extent of the word. However, Vergil will in the end usually make sure that they are (and feel) guilty also within their own little sphere and according to their own environment's code and range of moral (religious) concepts. A good example in point is, as we saw, Dido. In her case, however, the question of guilt is presented almost obtrusively. With Turnus, initially more is left to the reader's observation of clues embedded in the text. Why this is so may be shown by a preliminary hypothesis.

Since Italy is supposed to feel reconciled to living under a heaven-sent

Julian leadership residing at Rome, and Turnus is in the *Aeneid* the highest representative of those Italians who are independent from King Latinus, Augustan Vergil will not condemn the hero outright from the beginning. He will even – here we again encounter his masterful psychagogy – veil or mask the hero's original sin to a degree that it takes an active participation on the part of the reader to verify the truth about guilt and innocence. Many a reader has found it easy to feel the same sympathy for Turnus that the poet's endearing detail engenders for the Italian host in the section usually called "the gathering of the clans" (7.641 ff.). But in both cases the seemingly appealing traits, while downplaying latent unattractive features, simultaneously serve the poet's political goal of not alienating the Italian reading public from his Julian message. The writer's problem of keeping his Italian audience while more and more revealing the negative qualities of its representative will be solved by increasingly isolating and separating self-seeking Turnus from his miserable (cf. 8.537; 12.452) and misled people. But the basic guiding statement on right and wrong is contained already in the opening section of the "Roman *Iliad*".

And it is here, too, that the standard of measuring Aeneas (a standard we observe subliminally being impressed on the reader's mind ever since Book 1) is unobtrusively reconfirmed and reinforced for the new line of action beginning in 7. For inculpating one of the two chief adversaries largely means exculpating the other. Julian Vergil would never have endorsed the version adopted by Livy, according to which Turnus starts hostilities because Lavinia, earlier pledged to him as his bride, subsequently was withdrawn and given to foreigner Aeneas: *Turnus rex Rutulorum, cui pacta Lavinia ante adventum Aeneae fuerat, praelatum sibi advenam aegre patiens simul Aeneae Latinoque bellum intulerat* (1.2.1). Furthermore, there occur no portents in Livy's version, no oracle by Faunus – and, consequently, no divine clarification of the situation for Turnus preceding Aeneas' arrival. Vergil has doubly taken care to keep the Julian ancestor clear of the charge of bride-stealing: there is no earlier betrothal to Turnus but, on the contrary, an earlier oracular injunction to all of Italy. The poet indeed seems to have mastered the logic of timing and circumstances.

Thus our initial immanent interpretation, of the emphasis which the opening of *Aeneid* 7 places on matters of timing, receives indirect corroboration from the treatment Livy gives the same matter in the version adopted by him.

To throw Vergil's creative thrust into sharper relief it will be useful to extend the comparison beyond Livy to one or two other ancient versions offered by the tradition available to us. But before doing so, we should return to the "second proem" (of which we so far have utilized only line

7.39) and verify how firmly embedded the results of our interpretation are in the framework of announcement and execution set up by the author. That is, lines 45b–106 should be seen also in relation to the whole introductory announcement (37–45a), which is clad in an invocation of the Muse.

This invocation, paralleling the one early in the first Book (1.9), indicates the beginning of the work's second half, considered the weightier one of the two by the poet. It deals with "terrible wars" (a poetic plural, 41), which, beyond the battlelines and kings driven to face death (42), involve "the Etruscan host" (fighting on Aeneas' side) and "all of Hesperia (*totam...Hesperiam*) forced under arms" (43f.). This is a highly stylized and somewhat exaggerated characterization. The (allegedly) *total* extent of geographical range and population involvement (cf. *totam* and also the catalogue of Italian nations at 7.641ff.) causes the poet to say that he is now creating "a greater series of events, a greater work" (*maior rerum mihi nascitur ordo, maius opus moveo*, 44f.); the latter term, picking up *totam*, should not be freely understood to be "his greater commitment" (Fordyce *ad* 37–45), but a comparison with the scope of the earlier action: *Iliad* versus *Odyssey*, so to speak. This does not preclude a hint at the majesty of the achievement.

The announcement is bipartite (37–40; 41–45a), with either part being marked by an invocation: *Nunc Age,...Erato* (37) and *tu, diva, mone* (41). Whereas Part II, as we saw above, widens the view so as to include Etruria and all of Hesperia, Part I is limited in its geographical scope to "ancient Latium" (*Latio antiquo*, 38), an area much smaller than the Latium of the reader's day. And whereas Part II announces that the poet will "sing..., sing" (*dicam...dicam*, 41f.) of horrible war, Part I, again on a much smaller scale, will "explain" (*expediam*, 40) pre-Trojan conditions in ancient Latium, etc. Parts I and II are related to each other like announcement of the *Vorgeschichte* and of the history of the war itself, indicating an arrangement of events suggestive of Thucydidean stringency.

In verifying which sections of the ensuing narrative are being announced here, it is easiest to start with Part II, the *horrida bella* that form the main content of the "*Roman Iliad*", as the work's second half is often called. Full-scale war is what Juno aims at and what she formally achieves by herself breaking "the iron gates of war",

belli ferratos rumpit Saturnia postis 7.622.

She has to commit this act herself since the responsible human leader, Latinus, refuses to declare war on the Trojans. When leaving their towns with their troops, the "kings excited to war" (*bello exciti reges*, 642) should

Chapter 7

each be understood to "enter the war" on their part (cf. *init bellum*, 647). Later still, Turnus will give (display) the signal for war, *belli signum* (8.1), on the Laurentine acropolis. Since most of Book 8 is filled with Aeneas' search for help at Pallanteum (at the site of future Rome) and in Etruria, even with the production by Vulcan of Aeneas' shield, no act of war is actually committed before Book 9 where Turnus, by sending his spear into the air (as Octavian [-Augustus] will do when starting war on Cleopatra), signals "the beginning of battle", *principium pugnae* (53), and leads his men to attack the Trojan boats. However, since the assault is divinely voided, some may see the first act of war happen as late as the excursion of Nisus and Euryalus (9.314–449) or even the attack against the Trojan camp itself (9.503ff.).

Whatever the reader's decision in determining the outbreak of actual hostilities, hardly anyone will deny that Juno's act of opening the Gates of War constitutes the change from Peace to War. After all, the poet has here antedated the act (the Gates of Janus being opened) by which in his own time (*nunc*, 7.602) the beginning of war was declared. So he uses the occasion to mention some of the campaigns Augustus had undertaken (or, at least, was thought to plan; lines 604ff.). The greatest compliment to the Emperor – who was so proud of having closed the Gates or War twice during his rule (*R.G.*13) – lies, of course, in the fact that it is Juno, divine representative of his ancestor's enemies, who pushes the gates open. It is no small literary achievement for pro-Julian Vergil to have associated the land-taking Trojan newcomers with peace, their reluctant host country and its population with war. This point will be of interest to us soon and should be registered in passing now: it clearly fits into the pattern of allocating guilt and innocence we verified concerning Turnus and Aeneas.

The war itself, of course, must be separated from the development that leads up to it. This development, in itself, may contain some initial hostilities that, without being part of the greater war, may turn out to trigger the chain of events. Such a precursory hostile encounter is actually part of Vergil's picture,[11a] and we watch it being enthusiastically welcomed by warmongering Juno. Satisfied with Allecto's, the Fury's, incendiary work, she says:

> The causes for war are established, and hand-to-hand combat with arms is taking place.
>
> stant belli causae, pugnatur comminus armis,   7.553.

This fighting is the last link in the series of events covered by Part I (7.37–40) of the announcement: "...and I shall recall the beginnings of the first combat", *et primae revocabo exordia pugnae*. Far from being "a variety for '*prima exordia pugnae*'", (CN; see also Fordyce *ad loc.*), these words here literally mean "the beginnings of the first fight". They point ahead to the fighting that develops from the wounding of Sylvia's stag, the fighting so enthusiastically welcomed by Juno (7.553) as we just saw. The words are picked up, with the usual precision of Vergilian referencing, at 542: just before reporting back to Juno, the Fury (we read) left Hesperia "as soon as...she had brought about the deaths of the first fighting, *primae commisit funera pugnae*. (The initial deaths in the first combat have been reported immediately before this, 533ff.)

However, it is not only the end, but also the start of the first fighting that is covered by the wording of the announcement in line 40b. For when Ascanius' dogs pick up the scent of Silvia's stag, the poet comments: "this was the first cause of the sufferings < to come > (and kindled the farmers' minds with war)", *quae prima laborum causa fuit*, 481f. The episode is encircled by corresponding phrases.

Thus the whole section (7.475–539) which describes the initial outbreak of fighting (before open war is declared) is clearly covered by the announcement of line 40b. And since this is the third in a series of peace-destroying (cf. 339) actions performed by Juno's hellish helper, the two preceding actions (pushing Queen Amata to counteracting Faunus' oracle, 341–405; inciting Turnus to war, 406–474) as well as Juno's monologue and her orders to the Fury (285–340) must likewise be seen as subsumed under the announcement of line 40b. In short, the words "I shall recall the beginnings of the first fight" (40b) comprise the full development that leads up to voiding the peaceful understanding reached just before between Trojans and King Latinus at 285 (*pacemque reportant*).

This leaves, if Vergilian composition is meaningful and self-consistent, lines 37–39 (and the words "I shall explain", *expediam*, in 40a) to announce the section of the narrative that is contained in lines 45b–285. Three points are offered: (a) kings (*qui reges*); (b) times of events (*quae tempora rerum*); (c) condition or state of affairs (*quis...status*); all three (and certainly not only (c) though it is linguistically most closely connected) pertain to ancient Latium, *Latio antiquo*, and all three are seen in reference to the time "when the arriving army first landed its fleet on Italian shores" (39). The precise temporal reference of the "when"-clause is, of course, of lesser importance to the *reges* (first resumed in the opening of the narrative: *rex arva Latinus et urbes*, 45), for Latinus and Turnus are kings (cf. *regum*, 316; 442) both before and after Aeneas' arrival. Likewise, the state of affairs of Latium can be described preceding Aeneas' arrival (45ff.) as well as following it (e.g., Latinus' palace and the ancient Latin customs reflected in its set-up, 170ff.) because *status*, by definition, is a condition continuous and extended in time.

Chapter 7

Matters are somewhat different concerning *tempora rerum*. Following Servius, though not his philosophical reasoning, I take *rerum* with *tempora* rather than with *status*, because the timing of events, *rerum*, is neither arbitrarily changeable nor can it be said, as in the case of "kings" or "state of affairs", that it does not make much difference whether an event is reported [i.e., takes place] earlier or later in the narrative. For the timing of events (and human reactions to them: e.g., to the portents) is what gives Vergil's version of the story-line its unalterable individuality and determines the reader's interpretation of the characters. We saw earlier that the "when"-clause of 39 has its precise temporal reference in the other "when"-clause of equal contents at 105f. ("when the Trojan youth tied their fleet to the grassy dam of the river bank"). If we now observe again that, at the second occurrence, the "when"-clause is correlated to a main clause in the *pluperfect* (*tulerat*, 105), we can confidently state that here apparently is a case where the *tempora rerum*, as announced at 37, have come to bear on the presentation. Thus we may conclude that the two "when"-clauses, though seemingly identical in content, have slightly different functions: the earlier one is more general since it helps to characterize a *period* (kings, timing of events, existing conditions) in Latium's history, viz. at (around) the time of the Trojans' arrival. The second, in referring back to the first, picks up the exact temporal sense *only*: this had been the temporal sequence of events, now completed, (up to) the moment the Trojans arrived.

Since our earlier interpretation of lines 45b–106 showed the timing to be vital for evaluating Turnus' (and, indirectly, Aeneas') behavior in moral and religious terms, it is no small confirmation for us to see that Vergil has given its due place to the time element also among the topics announced in Part I of the invocation of the Muse. We moderns easily overlook the difference between *tempora rerum* and *status*, inured as we are to stopgap verbosity. Comparing announcement and ensuing narrative brings out the nuances and compelling correspondences of ancient composition devised according to the rules of rhetoric.

In regard to semantics, let us say that *tempora* here (at 37) means not so much, as in an often quoted passage from Lucretius (5.1276), the successive "seasons" (experienced by different metals as they come into or go out of fashion or use), but rather the stages of development undergone (here by Latium), as in Horace's *tempora si fastosque velis evolvere mundi* (*sat.* 1.3.112). Horace points out (op. cit. 111) that injustice existed before justice, that law arose from lawlessness; i.e., he is saying "if you wish to study (explain) the empirical history of mankind from stage to stage".[12] If, at *Aeneid* 7.37, "history" appears too comprehensive and general a term, then "sequence of events" certainly catches what Vergil's announcement *quae tempora rerum* seeks to bring into focus for his reader.

Pointing out the exact correspondence between announcement and ensuing narrative, our investigation has yielded another insight into Vergil's lucid architecture. The result entails a warning to literary critics. Far from being free to develop our own lines (and preferences) of interpretation, we again face the eventual inescapability which the author's text and its intention subtly impose on the reader's mind. The fact that the reader may ultimately arrive at only one *valid* interpretation means, as we shall see, a large step on the road to accepting the material consequences that flow from the interpreted text. The issue of inescapability will return on the higher level when the reader experiences his own inability to take a position outside the political conviction and ideological creed so persuasively offered by the author.

In returning to our comparison of other ancient versions different from Vergil's, we may now proceed with an even greater certainty that observance of the time sequence is a primary tool in bringing out the tendency pursued by Vergil.

Beyond Livy, one may usefully adduce M. Porcius Cato and Dionysius of Halicarnassus. In the latter's version (1.57), King Latinus abandons a war with the Rutulians he already has on his hands, when he hears that the Trojans (called "Greeks" in D.H.; cf. 1.61) have invaded the coastal strip of his empire (i.e., south-east from the mouth of the Tiber). In the night before the battle with the new enemy, a divine dream admonishes Latinus to take the newcomers in as co-dwellers with his own people: for they would mean "great benefit for Latium and a common good for the Aborigines" (as Latinus' subjects are called in D.H.). Let us add that Aeneas has a corresponding dream in the same night, in which the Penates advise him to approach Latinus and to suggest that Latinus grant the "Greeks" land for a settlement and use them as allies rather than view them as enemies. The next morning, a parley comes about between the two leaders, and the instructions given in the dreams are implemented. Among other things, Aeneas offers his people's services in defending Latinus' country and conquering that of his enemy (1.58.3; cf. 59.1, a more equal basis).

Thus, we may again state the differences in order to illuminate the uniqueness of Vergil's design. Whereas in the *Aeneid* Latinus' dream forms the climax in a series of portents and, by informing him of his nation's future, continues the epic's overall 'metaphysical' orientation (the fated mission of Aeneas' stock), the two dreams in D.H. are more tailored to solving an immediate emergency posed by problems on hand (though Dionysius, it must be said, in general knows enough about oracles accompanying Aeneas' course). In fact, like many a dream in ancient literature, Latinus' vision seems to have a simple psychological explanation (a corresponding statement can be made about that of Aeneas): feeling one enemy behind his back and having to battle against a new one in front next morning, he naturally dreams that it would be "great benefit" for him if he could turn the new one into an ally against the old. The unnamed "local divinity" (τις...ἐπιχώριος δαίμων, 57.4) provides both a handy literary wrapping for Latinus' difficult situation and a smart road out of the military dilemma, but this *daimon* can in no way be compared to Vergil's all-Italian (*omnisque Oenotria tellus*, 7.85) oracular information center.

Most illuminating, however, for the reader of the *Aeneid* is the fact that, in the *Roman Antiquities*, up to the meeting of the two leaders the name of Turnus ("Tyrrhenos") has not been mentioned at all — and will not be mentioned until much later (64.2). By then, the Rutulians have been subdued, Aeneas' city (Lavinium) is built, Aeneas has married Lavinia, the two nations have fused to become "Latins". It is only in the context of another, new Rutulian uprising that Turnus' name comes up. Described as "a deserter" (τῶν αὐτομόλων τινά, 1.64.2), pushed on by his aunt Amata ("Amita"), wife of Latinus, he joins the rebels. His complaint is that, in the matter of Lavinia's marriage, the father-in-law has "passed over" (παρελθών, 1.64.2) the relative in favor of the foreigner. No word here (as in Livy) that Lavinia had first been pledged to Turnus, then been married to Aeneas. No word either (as in Vergil, *Aeneid*, 7.55f.; 406ff.) about his being the king of the Rutulians, beautiful and powerful through his ancestral line. And no divine injunctions to give Lavinia to a foreigner for dynastic or fate-inspired reasons. Rather, the two leaders Aeneas and Latinus have set a practical example (πρῶτοι ἄρχουσι μίξοντες, 1.60.1) of intermarriage to their peoples who were themselves eager to enjoy the mutual benefit.

Thus Vergil's design stands out again (except for the one feature that Lavinia was *not* promised to Turnus beforehand – a feature shared by both of them). And it is by introducing Turnus the unsuccessful suitor of Lavinia so early, even before the decisive oracle is pronounced, that the *Aeneid* subsequently manages to assign him the position of a rebel against the gods. Methodologically speaking, Livy and Dionysius have supplied us with valuable alternatives to Vergil's plot, but they have – to repeat – not given us the decisive interpretative criteria which only the immanent analysis of the *Aeneid*'s text could yield. With this in mind, we shall be cautious about accepting the thesis that Rumor spreading Faunus' oracle represents a "bridge passage"[13] or that the oracle itself is introduced also to mitigate Latinus' impropriety displayed in his offering his daughter to a complete stranger.[14] Both arguments, one ancient and one modern, risk underrating the tightness and economy of Vergil's story-line and plot structure as well as the pro-Julian viewpoint chosen in delineating the main characters. Obedience toward the divine will as practiced by Latinus, even blind obedience (as we would probably call it), is the highest virtue in dealing with the god-sent palaeo-Julians, not upon facing them but even before facing them.

The last writer to be reviewed in our comparative survey is the earliest in time, M. Porcius Cato. To demonstrate this alternative variant requires going into great detail. The reader interested in the result only is advised to skip the following pages and go directly to the summary on p. 370.

Cato's "Origins", *Origines*, though composed more than a century before the *Aeneid*, are generally considered to form an important step in consolidating the vulgate version of the Aeneas story.[15] And though the few fragments preserved from the first book are hardly sufficient for reliably reconstructing its train of thought, the remnants can be highly significant for delineating further the choices open to (and those made by) Vergil when he designed his own version.

Both in Dionysius and in Livy, we recall, Latinus, though initially upset about the invasion of his territory, comes to terms with the newcomers, and together the new allies face the hostile Rutulians. In Vergil, there is no initial uneasiness at all toward the Trojans but a divinely prearranged welcome. However, whereas the aged and powerless king *in the long run* stays loyal (returns) to Aeneas, his people will side with Turnus and the Rutulians. In Cato, Latinus (not separated from his people as far as can be determined) is reported both to fight (presumably first) with Aeneas against the Rutulians and (presumably later) with Turnus against Aeneas and the Trojans (Wörner's reconstruction). At a first glance, it may appear as if Vergil managed to create a more consistent version by separating the pious king from his unruly people. (He has, as we shall see, achieved much more than mere consistency.) Also, the fragments tell that Aeneas, immediately upon arrival (*simul ac venit ad Italiam*, fr. 11), received Latinus' daughter Lavinia in marriage (the reason for Turnus to start war against both Aeneas and Latinus), and that Aeneas' men ravaged the country (*cum Aeneae socii praedas agerent*, fr. 10) near "*Laurolavinium*" (the reason why both Latinus and Turnus fight against the *Aeneadae*).

Scholarship has usually tried to eliminate supposed *Widersprüche* by whittling away at alternative data; by denying authenticity to one of two contradictory testimonial passages – sometimes even when they are handed down to us by the same ancient source; by arranging a more acceptable time sequence for events where the given simultaneous or serial occurrence seemed unthinkable. As one editor[16] justified his own resulting story-line:

"*sic explosis discrepantiis et obscuritatibus narratio in probabilitatem quandam revocata est.*" One wonders whether "a degree of probability" may not be found by traveling a different road.

For the sake of widening our awareness of the range of options open to Vergil – but not so much for the sake of contributing yet another facet to Catonian scholarship and *Quellenforschung* – let us here hypothesize that Cato in the first Book of his *Origines* offered two versions not one. Phenomenologically speaking, a survey of the main representatives of our tradition does reveal a potential for two different major versions of the alliances formed upon Aeneas' arrival in Italy. (Livy actually mentions two variants: *duplex inde fama est*, 1.1.6. In the one which he discards Aeneas has first to defeat Latinus before receiving peace, *pacem*, and the status of a relative, *affinitatem*. But this minor variant is not what I am aiming at here. I mean the larger constellation that also involves the Rutulians.) In both Livy's preferred version and in Dionysius of Halicarnassus, the threat of a battle between Aeneas and Latinus is real; the war is, however, averted by a parley (favored and furthered by divine influence in Dionysius): it looks as if an alternative outcome of the story-line is indicated but not actualized. What if, so far not realized by us, there once did exist two versions of the relations between Aeneas and Latinus (and the Rutulians), a 'confrontational' and a 'harmonious' one?

In the case of prevailing confrontation, Aeneas would have to fight against the combined armies of Latinus and Turnus as in frs. 9 and 10 of Cato (and in Vergil where friendly Latinus loses control over his hostile people). In the case of a harmonious settlement, Aeneas would (marry Lavinia and) join forces with Latinus and his people against the Rutulians and Turnus – as in Cato, fr. 11 (and in Dionysius).

What leads this interpreter to his hypothesis is the fact that those modern reconstructions which try to accommodate and incorporate as many of the preserved data as possible in a single Catonian story-line, are so utterly unconvincing. E.g., a marriage of Aeneas with Lavinia, to which Turnus reacts (*propter quod Turnus iratus*) by waging war against both father-in-law and son-in-law (fr. 11), appears, at least to me, incompatible with a (following!) war of both Latinus and Turnus *as allies* against Aeneas (fr. 10). For why should Turnus, if he started the war because Latinus gave Lavinia to Aeneas, later be willing to support the same Latinus when the daughter, the cause of his wrath, was no more available than before? There is a serious flaw in motivation in this version (basically the one of Klauser and Wörner).[17]

Equally implausible appears the reason given for Latinus' switching sides. Aeneas' men are said to have supplied the *casus belli* by looting King

Latinus' territory – after he concluded friendship with Aeneas, and *after* Aeneas married Lavinia![18] It seems unlikely that, because of looting, Latinus would have abandoned daughter and alliance to approach his daughter's disappointed and enraged former suitor.

But, apart from this improbable behavior, the wording of fr. 9 does not – I am sorry to contradict "allgemeiner Ansicht"[19] – suggest that any period of time at all intervened between arrival and looting (*Aeneam...ad Italiam venisse et propter invasos agros contra Latinum Turnumque pugnasse*, where *invasos agros* is usually taken to be identical with the occasion *iuxta Laurolavinium cum Aeneae socii praedas agerent* of fr. 10a).[20] The account is not unlike the opening situation in Livy (*...Troiani...cum praedam ex agris agerent*, 1.1.5) and, to a degree, Dionysius (1.57.1f.) – which should not be constructed to mean that it has been carried back into the text of Cato's fragments from either author.

One reason why the looting (and the ensuing war) might be assumed to take place late in the development of Trojan-native relations could be found in the geographical location of its occurrence near (fr. 10a) "*Laurolavinium*" – the late name which, apparently we are asked to accept,[21] of course stands for Lavinium, the city of Aeneas, named by him (as Roman tradition tells) after his wife Lavinia. Ergo, the conclusion runs, in Cato's version Aeneas was already married to Lavinia and had built his city when the (first) war (of three) started.

The inference does not hold. For, whereas it is true that Servius (the source of fr. 10a) freely substitutes the late name of Laurolavinium for the original and older Lavinium in Cato's text,[22] he does not share the traditional belief that the city was named after Lavinia, Aeneas' wife. In commenting on *Aen.* 1.5 (*dum conderet urbem*), Servius discusses three possible identities of the city founded by Aeneas: Vergil might be pointing to *Troia*, the camp-like settlement Aeneas founded immediately upon reaching Italian soil. (As authorities for the name *Troia* he mentions Livy [cf. 1.1.4] and Cato [fr. 4]). At the other end of the development, Vergil might be pointing to the final goal of Roma. In between, Servius thinks, *Laurolavinium* might be a candidate for the city founded by Aeneas. (We see he does not necessarily call Aeneas' settlement by the simple name Lavinium.) At 7.31, Servius, after mentioning Aeneas' first, camp-like settlement near Ostia, tells us that "later he built a huge camp in Laurolavinium, traces of which can still be seen" (*postea enim in Laurolavinio castra fecit ingentia, quorum vestigia adhuc videntur*). But we also hear (*ad* 7.158) that, from the original camp, Aeneas will transfer his *imperium* to "*Lavinium*" – a mention of the traditional name of Aeneas' city, which Servius will himself employ when it is mentioned in Vergil's text itself (at 1.270).

At 7.170, Latinus' city is called "*Laurolavinium*" by Servius, and this is in line with his concept of the name's origin. For, in Servius' thinking, the "*Lavinium*" part of the name has nothing to do with the king's daughter. Standing apart from the mainstream of tradition, Servius explains (*ad* 7.59, *laurus erat*) that "when, after the death of his brother Lavinus, Latinus enlarged Lavinum, he called it, after the laurel tree he found (there), '*Laurolavinium*'". *Latinus post mortem fratris Lavini cum Lavinum amplificaret, ab inventa lauro Laurolavinium id appellavit.* (In spite of several variant readings, the text is convincing as printed in Thilo-Hagen).

The last-quoted sentence is all that is needed. There is no necessity for us to assume with Schröder that Servius, when he employs the name of Laurolavinium in a Catonian context, is thinking of the city Aeneas built and named after his wife Lavinia. He might rather be pointing to the city of King Latinus.

Our consideration not only frees us from assuming that Cato supposed the raids to have taken place *after* Aeneas' marriage and the establishment of his city. It also allows us to understand fr. 9a (and, along with it, 10a) in its natural prima facie meaning suggested above: there was no extended period of time between landing and looting; in addition, we may now be reasonably certain that the looting was conceived by Cato as having taken place in the area (not of Aeneas', but) of King Latinus' city "*Laurolavinium*".

What the clarification attempted above does, is, alas, to open the discrepancy between two groups of Catonian fragments even further. This may be felt to be a negative result when viewed in the light of scholarship's traditional attempts to combine as many fragments as possible into the 'reconstruction' of a single-strand story. Methodologically speaking, however, we should understand that, in the case of two groups of conflicting testimonia, the evidence clearly favors the hypothesis of two original versions over that of one original single-strand version (to be recovered by 'eliminating' contradictions). The questions that must be asked immediately are, of course: which of the two versions did Cato consider the true (in his sense, historic) one? And: why did he offer the other version along with it?

It is, of course, difficult to find an answer to the first question because we do not know the line of argument Cato pursued. But we can form an idea of what our source (Servius, in almost all pertinent fragments) considered the historical truth; or even, in the best case, considered Cato's conviction of what was true.

The latter case is possibly once evidenced by the words *secundum Catonem historiae hoc habet fides* (*sic*. Schroder, *fidem*. fr. 9a) – Servius' expression of what he understood Cato to have believed to be reliable historical fact. The words introduce the report on Aeneas having had to fight both Latinus and Turnus "because of invasion of the fields", *propter invasos agros*, etc. This context goes well with fragment 10a about the looting near Laurolavinium and the ensuing hostilities. The parallel fragment of the same version (omitting the initial looting), 10b, is introduced by an expression of Servius' conviction that the historical truth (*si veritatem historiae requiras* – as opposed to other versions about Turnus' death as reported by less reliable commentators of the *Aeneid*) about the matter under discussion can be found in Livy and Cato.

That is, the combination of fragments 9a; 10a; 10b supplies us with a version that Servius considered both to be historically true himself and to be Cato's account of what was historically true. It should not come as a surprise to us that these fragments together do combine into a consistent story-line, which can be summarized as follows:

Upon landing in Italy and looting the fields near King Latinus' city, Aeneas and his men have to fight the combined armies of Latinus and Turnus. Latinus dies on the acropolis, Turnus flees and secures the help of Mezentius (the Etruscan king). In a second encounter (*secundo proelio*, 10b) Turnus dies; Aeneas, though apparently victorious, disappears. Finally, in a third encounter (*tertio proelio*, 10b), Ascanius kills Mezentius. What gives this version its consistency and grand sweep is the continuous and progressive fighting. Starting out from nothing (they have to loot – for necessities, we assume), the Trojans have to fight it out on Italian soil all the way through over three nations (Aborigines, Rutulians, Etruscans) and with two generations of their own (Aeneas, Ascanius) participating: a heroic and, for warrior mentality, glorious tale – but also one of little human appeal in the eyes of men who would wish to see more in the *Aeneadae* than bloody invaders and conquerors of Italy.

The second version (if Cato did write two versions) of Aeneas' arrival in Italy would correspond to the 'harmonious' one of our earlier, hypothetical distinction. Such a story-line is indicated in fr. 11 where Aeneas receives Lavinia as his consort *immediately* (*simulac*) *upon arrival*. It is hard for any reader to picture such *blitz* congeniality and on-the-spot royal family relationship without the kind of religious influence to which we see the mind of King Latinus being exposed, as preparation, in the *Aeneid*. (The motive of Dionysius, that Latinus has a war on his hands with the Rutulians, is absent.)

The wedding of fr. 11 goes well together with the information offered by fr. 8 that the Trojans "received" (*accepisse*, the same word as in fr. 11, *accepit uxorem*) a piece of land from Latinus (though, of course, one might argue that land assignation, unlike the stronger kinship ties of

Chapter 7

marriage, does not so strongly preclude a hostile turn in relations at a later time).

The methodological question to be raised here is: if, as we showed, the alternative, 'hostile' story-line was considered to be historically true by Cato (and Servius), how can, among that of others, Cato's authority (*Catonis auctoritas*) be invoked for the land assignation? The key possibly lies in the context on which Servius is commenting and in his slightly awkward diction in this passage. At *Aen.* 11.316, King Latinus suggests granting a piece of land to the Trojans. Servius comments that Donatus erred (*erravit*) in locating this land along the River Ufens; he himself prefers to follow Livy's, Sisenna's and Cato's authority. "For Cato in his *Origines* says that the Trojans received the land from Latinus which lies between Laurentum and the Trojan camp" (and he goes on to mention the size of the area). *Cato enim in Originibus dicit Troianos a Latino accepisse agrum, qui est inter Laurentum et castra Troiana*. We can now see that Servius stated his main objective, i.e., the correction of the mistaken location as given by Donatus, in the subordinate relative clause. The clause itself is grammatically dependent (but considered fact: indicative *est*) on the higher ranking sentence offered by the accusative-cum-infinitive ...*Troianos...accepisse...* That is, here Cato's authority is being invoked for the location, not for the fact of land assignation. Conceivably, the sentence has been taken from an overall context which, in the *Origines*, was clearly marked as an unhistoric alternative to historic truth.

The same consideration must be made concerning fr. 11, with good reason. For Servius, again our source, himself indicates that the opening narrative (of fr. 11) leads to a story-line different from the one he himself set out before, in commenting on other passages of the *Aeneid*. Using a strong "but" (*sed*), he returns to the chain of events as he presented it earlier (*ut supra diximus*). That is, here Servius himself indicates (though only in passing) the existence of two versions in Cato – or, at least, of an incompatibility to be bridged (or, rather acknowledged) by *sed*.

Why does Servius, in what is today numbered as fr. 11 of Cato, depart from his own earlier testimony? Again, the context he is commenting on contains the key for us.

The scene of *Aen.* 6.760ff. is in the underworld. Deceased Anchises foretells the future to visiting son Aeneas. At this moment, he is pointing to a young man (*iuvenis*) in whom he asks Aeneas to recognize his *postuma proles*, a son to be born from his future consort Lavinia. (This son, the first issue from mixed Trojan and Italian blood, 6.762f., will be Silvius, first of the Alban kings. The Julians themselves, stemming from Ascanius, are from 'pure' Trojan background.) To Aeneas, as to the reader, *Lavinia coniunx* (764) is an unknown entity (though we know, ever since Creusa' death and prophesy in Book 2, that Aeneas will remarry, viz. a *regia coniunx*, 2.783). So it is only appropriate that Servius closes his reader's knowledge gap by filling in the circumstances of time and place: "as Cato says" (*ut Cato dicit*), "the moment Aeneas came to Italy, he received Lavinia as his consort." But this does, of course, again not necessarily mean that in this comment we encounter the version Cato considered the correct one in his own context.

Apart from the contradiction (indicated by *sed*) to Servius' own earlier report which we already mentioned, we should now see where this 'harmonious' opening leads. Perhaps to our surprise, we find ourselves close to the *Aeneid*'s story-line. "Because of this" (i.e., the development leading to the marriage, I understand) "enraged, Turnus undertook war(s) both against Latinus and against Aeneas after he had secured support from Mezentius" – *propter quod Turnus iratus tam in Latinum quam in Aeneam bella suscepit a Mezentio impetratis auxiliis.*

The distribution of forces resulting from this constellation, then, is that we find Latinus on Aeneas' side, both of them fighting against the allies Turnus and Mezentius. No wonder that Servius hastens to recall his earlier statement (*ad Aen.* 4.620 = Cato, fr. 10a), reconfirming (*ut supra diximus*) that Latinus died in the first war (i.e., not on the side of Aeneas but as an ally of Turnus if the pronouncement is to be covered by the words *ut supra diximus*; though the opposite would not be impossible: in this version, Latinus might well die "in the first battle" while fighting for Aeneas. See Servius Danielis *ad* 1.259); in the second war, Turnus and Aeneas perished; in the third, Ascanius killed Mezentius. Servius' reader has been led back on track.

What are we to make of the crossed and enraged suitor Turnus in Cato? It is too easy to assume (with Schröder)[23] an interpolation from Livy: "...scheint aus Livius (1,2,1) interpoliert zu sein". For in Livy, we saw, *Turnus, cui pacta Lavinia ante adventum Aeneae fuerat*, has reason to be so upset: a pledge made to him was broken. The broken pledge, we saw on the other hand, is a matter that Vergil keenly avoids – both to keep Aeneas' image clean even of indirect fault and to lay the ground for Turnus' guilt. So one should not rashly impute to Cato a Turnus, "den man sich bei Cato (ähnlich wie in der späteren Tradition) mit Lavinia verlobt vorstellen muss", "whom in Cato (as in the later tradition) one has to picture as being betrothed to Lavinia".[24]

In this situation, it is illuminating that the author of *Servius auctus* (Servius Danielis, SD), who *ad Aen.* 1.259, tells roughly the same story (under the sloppy attribution *sicut historia habet*), is more detailed on the motive of

Turnus "who before these events had hoped Lavinia would be his wife", *qui ante Laviniam sperabat uxorem*. The word "hoped" (or even if one translates "expected"), being so far away from the certainty of "having been promised", seems to pull us directly into Vergil's story-line, especially so if we read that the Aeneas of SD was well received by Latinus because recognized as Venus' son and the protégé of fate. However, SD's story differs from Vergil's in a decisive point: right away, Aeneas does marry Lavinia, *filiam eius Laviniam duxit uxorem* – as he does in Cato, fr. 11, but is prevented from doing in the *Aeneid*.

It cannot be excluded, then, that in the *Origines* of Cato there was also a version that painted a favorable local response to Aeneas' arrival in Italy. When compared to its alternative of Aeneas and Ascanius the irresistible conquerors, it makes – as does the *Aeneid* – the newcomers appear in a more appealing light: the outbreak of war is due more to Turnus' intransigence or, at least, personal grievance than to any bellicosity peculiar to the *Aeneadae*. Clearly, such a version would be music to the ears of the Julian family. But from Cato's pen?

Before answering this disturbing question, let us cite another, corroborating case of two versions ascribed to Cato by tradition. It, too, concerns the Julians, or, more precisely, their Trojan ancestor, Ascanius-Iulus, son of Aeneas and Creusa of Troy.

In fr. 9e we read that, because of his outstanding virtue, Ascanius was not only believed to be a son of Jupiter but even called "little Jove", "*Iolus*" – a name that was later changed to "*Iulus*", "from whom the Julian family sprang, as [L.?] Caesar…and Cato in his *Origines* write." Clearly, here is possibly some mixing-in of Julian family historiography, and the question must be: how much of this was in Cato's own text? The minimum assumption would limit the Catonian part to merely mentioning the change of name or to the clause "*a quo Iulia familia manavit*" whereas the maximum latitude would attribute the whole fragment to Cato (etymology is an area not alien to Cato's interests, as, e.g., is revealed in Book 1 of the *Origines* by the etymology at fr. 14).

Consensus will hardly be reached. But can one deny the minimum fact that the report touches on the change of name from Ascanius to Iulus (via *Iolus*)? With or without the express relative clause *a quo Iulia familia manavit*, there is no denying the fact that Cato is here reported to have dealt with the name of the ancestor on which the Julians later were known to base their exclusiveness (then by asserting that Iulus was the great-grandson of Jupiter through Venus). This fact itself has contributed considerably to scholarship's refusal to consider fr. 9e genuine.[25] In addition to the Julians' lacking prominence in Cato's time, one has asked: what interest could

Cato have in helping them to prominence? "on ne voit pas ce que pourrait être Iule sinon l'ancêtre de la *gens Iulia*. Or Caton n'a aucune raison de s'intéresser à cette famille, qui d'ailleurs est loin d'occuper au milieu du IIe siècle un rôle de premier plan dans la vie politique romaine."[26] So Cato had no reason to say what he is reported to have said: the fragment must be spurious.

Let us turn to the other fragment that deals with the same Ascanius (9a). The text is taken again from Servius when commenting on the change of name from Ascanius to Iulus (*ad Aen*. 1.267). In doing so, Servius summarizes the whole story of the three wars the *Aeneadae* had to face in Italy (the 'hostile' version in our earlier distinction); at the end of the last war, Iulus kills Mezentius. "And after the killing of Mezentius Ascanius began to be called Iulus after the down of his beard" (in Greek, ἴουλος), "which began to grow at the time of the victory"; *et occiso Mezentio Ascanium Iulum coeptum vocari a prima barbae lanugine, quae ei tempore victoriae nascebatur.*

This matter-of-fact etymology seems to tell a story (a case of *adaequatio nominis ad rem*, so to speak). Apparently Cato wished to demonstrate that, by the end of the third war, Ascanius had just and barely grown up so as to take his dead father's place, and had acquired enough strength to defeat the older Mezentius. While recalling from our earlier considerations that fr. 9a seems to carry Cato's endorsement as historical truth (*secundum Catonem historiae hoc habet fides*), we cannot but ask: what kind of razor-blade philosophy lurks behind this down-to-earth etymology? We wonder even more when we compare it to its high-flying alternative of "little Jupiter"! Is it perhaps so that the mutual exclusiveness of the two versions exists by design in Cato's *Origines*?

It is certainly to be admitted that Cato had no reason to help the Julians to political prominence (that they themselves did not desire to become prominent in Cato's time is a potentially dangerous *ex silentio* conclusion, resting as it does on the absence of coins and similar clues). In fact, Cato would be the last we would suspect of pandering to the vanities of the privileged. After all, in the military contexts of his *Origines* he is even said to have cut out the names of the generals involved in the events. He is known to have set rustic manners against a senatorial life style. How do we picture the man's reaction to a family claiming a "little Jove" their own? (Provided he ever did encounter such a preposterous claim – this must remain hypothesis.) What we know of him would suggest that he would cut them out (like the generals' names) – or, since two mutually exclusive versions have been handed down to us by tradition, that he cut them down to size: not Jove, but whiskers, my friends. Does anyone feel tickled?

Chapter 7

We return to the question whether there could have been a pro-Julian version of Aeneas' arrival in Italy from Cato's hand. Our answer now: yes, there may well have been, but it is doubtful that the version was music to the ears of contemporary Julians. For Cato, if he did write such a version as the fragments display, did not publish it without its alternative which painted the Trojans as ruthless conquerors, hardly a blessing to the native Italians. To his unbiased and down-to-earth mind, the 'natural' (one may also call it 'realistic') psychological reaction and ensuing development following the arrival of land-taking invaders would be (as it would very likely be to today's historian) that the natives react by closing ranks in defense against the outsiders. And he might well feel that special interests are involved in a presentation that makes the newcomers heaven-sent guests in the eyes of the nation next to the shore, bringers of a peace that is disturbed by troublemakers beyond a nearby river. (He would probably have found it easier to agree with Dionysius' version which does not downplay the military value the Trojans represent to a Latinus who is already pressed by a pre-existing war with his neighbors beyond the river).

Cato's exact intention, in writing double versions of events, lies beyond certain knowledge for us, since we do not possess his train of thought in Book 1. But, unusual as my hypothesis is within the range of Catonian scholarship, I ask my reader to consider it on its methodological merits: it does accommodate contradictory evidence, and it does not proceed by the simple means of discarding any evidence that resists a one-way explanation.

Returning to, and considering, our larger context, the investigation into Cato's first Book was done for the purpose of understanding the range of options open to, and actualized by, Vergil. We can now see much more clearly that his design picked up the 'harmonious' alternative, the one friendly to the Julians. From the background of options we have established so far, it is not difficult to show the stringent consistency which he forced himself to observe in developing the plot-line further.

At this point, however, my reader may wish to voice a question: granted that Latinus initially is friendly toward the *Aeneadae, what about his later failure to continue his support?*

But first let us summarize. To deliver its message, the *Aeneid* draws certain advantages from the options we have so far seen actualized by its author. By choosing the 'harmonious' version (in which King Latinus welcomes the foreigners in his kingdom) over the 'natural' or 'realistic' one (in the latter one the incoming *Aeneadae* face a united native opposition and conquer the resistance of three Italian peoples one after another), he frees Aeneas from the odium of being an unwanted invader. By making Latinus, in so acting, obey divine orders, he has Aeneas' arrival removed from the sphere of chance human encounters. At the same time, he has – this was earlier shown to be the function of the key section 7.45–105 – the natives informed of the long-range divine intentions that necessitate Aeneas' arrival on Italian soil: Aeneas' stock (= Augustus) will rule the world from hereabouts. At this point, the 'harmonious' version (as opposed to the 'natural' or 'realistic' one), by turning 'supernatural', also becomes ideological (in this case, 'idealistic' is hardly the appropriate complementary term to 'realistic'). Almost unnoticeably, the core idea of the *Aeneid* is being invoked: Julian leadership and the will of Destiny are one and the same. Lines 7.45–105 are a key section also for the reader (and Roman citizen) to receive instruction: he can measure the actors in coming events by the standard of their compliance with the portents, especially the widely distributed oracle of Faunus. If the reader cares enough to find out, the moralising colors of black and white are clearly distinguished.

In one matter Vergil (Buchheit believes this is the poet's own invention)[27] develops the option he chose even further: by having (7.206f.; 240; details later) Aeneas' ancestor Dardanus originally emigrate from the vicinity of Aeneas' landing site, the poet not only takes the potentially degrading label of "refugee" finally from Aeneas' shoulders, but grants the Julians' ancestor, by allowing him to be a home-comer, an original right to the soil he is disembarking on. Shaping a myth can hardly come closer to creating a legitimizing imperial ideology than it does here.

The story about the homecoming of Dardanus' descendant has a counterpart in the result that flows from Vergil's "neutralizing" (as I would like to call it) of King Latinus (too old to be a warrior, he can no longer, as in Cato, fight for one side or the other). For by objectifying Latinus Vergil is able to upgrade this character to be a guiding figure for the reader of the *Aeneid*. While bestowing on him the quality of religious obedience, the dignity of royalty and priesthood as well as the respect enjoyed by age, Vergil concentrates in Latinus the features required on the Italian side for a pro-Julian version: land and legitimate ruler have been waiting for the long-lost race to come home and take possession of their own.

This situation is given its compositional complement in the figure of irreverent Turnus: making King Latinus friendly toward the *Aeneadae* but powerless creates conditions for Turnus to be powerful and hostile – and wrong since he refuses to share wise Latinus' inspired views about the newcomers. (But love for Lavinia and an uncontrollable temper are features that will make him, in spite of being guilty in the objective sense, interesting enough initially to preserve the reader's, especially the Italian reader's, openness toward him).

Chapter 7

Once more Vergil takes his design a step further. He repeats the feature which he newly introduced into the story, viz. that of a split between the ruler and his subjects. Only this time it is the king – the tyrant, we should say – who travels the wrong road, not his people. While the Etruscans (under their substitute leader Tarcho and in expectation of a prophesied and desired leader from abroad, *externos optate duces*, 8.503 – again Aeneas, of course) are being characterized by a "just fury" (8.494) and "just wrath" (8.501; see the details in Chapter 2, Section 2) against their cruel former master, the ruler himself is introduced to the reader as *contemptor divum*, despiser of the gods (7.648). And it is this criminal figure with whom Turnus associates himself by offering him protection against his tortured people (8.443)! Truly, "guilt by association" is another psychagogical guidepost Vergil offers his reader. While the plot may thicken and perhaps become less transparent through increasing complexity, the allocation of black and white, guilt and innocence, is never in doubt to a reader who entrusts his judgement to, and draws his standards from, the poet's parameters. As far as our specific interest in the conception of Vergil's Turnus is concerned, the work's dramaturgy leads us to the same result to which the timing of Faunus' oracle and of Aeneas' landing has led us before: Turnus, being the chief opponent of the Julians' ancestor in the *Aeneid*, is by design denied any chance of being innocent.

At this point, however, my reader may wish to voice a question. Granted that Latinus initially is friendly toward the *Aeneadae* and, thus, to be rated 'good' on the ethical scale set up for his reader's use by Vergil, doesn't he later on allow himself to be swayed by the combined opposition of his wife, his people and Turnus so as to drop the reins (7.600) and fail Aeneas? Should this behavior not transfer his rating to the 'guilty' side?

Indeed it does. Feeling no longer able to resist Turnus' fervor for war, Latinus immediately predicts *poenas* (7.595), paid in blood, for the intransigents and *triste...supplicium* specifically for Turnus who "will worship the gods with prayers (too) late" (7.596f.). This shows that Latinus is aware of the godless turn affairs are taking – an important condition for determining his guilt. (The words also, of course, outline to 'deaf' Turnus his own 'guilty' status.)

One may sympathize with an elderly man who, instead of (perhaps vainly) attempting to face down overwhelming opposition from those closest to his heart, chooses the easier route of letting things drift and of himself withdrawing into passivity. But Vergil – as with other characters unsupportive of the Trojan-Julian cause – will exact a full confession of guilt from Latinus' lips. Much later, when trying to dissuade Turnus from entering a single combat with Aeneas, Latinus diagnoses his own earlier moral failure. In the first two lines quoted below he admits that he had been well instructed how to act:

> By divine sanction I was forbidden to marry my daughter to any
> of the old suitors,
> and all gods and men were announcing this to me.

> me natam nulli veterum sociare procorum
> fas erat, idque omnes divique hominesque canebant.   12.27/28

Latinus is referring to the situations described in 7.45–105, the key section for the reader's standards of judgement. Our earlier interpretation of 7.96–97 may be indirectly confirmed by the fact that in Book 12 again there is no mention whatsoever of any special favor granted to Turnus by Latinus, he still is no more than a suitor, *natam...petentem*, 12.42. At the early stage, Latinus turned down all suitors alike, including Turnus, in agreement with divine advice (*nulli...procorum*, 12.27; *ne...conubiis...Latinis,...thalamis neu...paratis*, 7.96f.). It was only later that he caved in when, after offering his daughter to Aeneas, he ran into the combined opposition of his wife Amata and her nephew Turnus. At that point, he allowed personal relations to prevail over obedience to divine orders:

> Defeated by my love for you, defeated by blood relationship,
> by the tears of my saddened wife, I broke all ties:
> I snatched the promised bride from my son-in-law, I took up impious arms.

> victus amore tui, cognato sanguine victus
> coniugis et maestae lacrimis, vincla omnia rupi:
> promissam eripui genero, arma impia sumpsi.   12.39–41

One would be gravely mistaken if one understood the deprived son-in-law here to be Turnus. The three words *arma impia sumpsi* alone, found in the same line as and running parallel with (not counter to) *promissam eripui genero*, forbid such a misunderstanding. For Latinus never took up arms against Turnus (not to mention "impious" arms).

On the contrary, in confessing that he "broke all ties", Latinus is by no means referring to family ties but to divine ties, imposed on him by, among others, his father's, Faunus', oracle. In this similar to Turnus, Latinus eventually and against better knowledge set personal desire over divine guidance. As Turnus proves his wrong orientation by associating himself with, and hosting, criminal Mezentius, *contemptor* of gods, so Latinus displays the wrong attitude when giving up his resistance against Turnus. Guilt is being incurred by (and that is, allocated to) the opponent of Aeneas' cause, *once again*. And guilt is being confessed in the end. (On the political ramifications of Latinus' pivotal role, see section 1 of the *Epilogue*.)

Chapter 7

We have glanced far ahead from the portents that set the stage in the opening section of the "Roman *Iliad*". But without being aware of at least some of the implications that will bear on later parts of the work, one cannot lay bare the technique the poet employs of early correlating his reader's mind to a network of references that help pre-set reactions to later events. As in Book 2, there is an early "learning process". Based on the appeal emanating from an old king who is obedient to divine hints, the process establishes habits of measuring good and evil that secure sympathetic feelings as well as a reverent attitude toward the Julian cause. Insubordination toward a god-sent race must be detested, as must be the view that they are a bunch of bellicose invaders – as, e.g., irreverent Juno, tutelary goddess of Turnus, prefers to think (10.65f.), before herself being subjected to an exemplary learning process. By the time of her utterance, however, the reader has long learned to know better than she does. May the topic of reverence and right attitude take us, well-prepared, back to the time preceding Aeneas' landing on Italian soil (7.1ff.).

Reverence has (we should be aware) been recommended to the reader ever since the first line of Book 7 where the poet, claiming to speak as a representative of his contemporaries (*nostris*, 7.1), pronounces that "eternal fame" was given to "our shores" by the fact that Aeneas' nurse died here! In our own time (*nunc*), he continues, reverence (honor) is being paid to her resting-place, and "in great Hesperia" her name signifies (the location of) her bones.

Apart from giving an *aition* for the promontory of *Caieta*, the section (7.1–4) is well designed to stimulate the reader into thinking: if so much honor is given to Aeneas' nurse alone, what amount of reverence and veneration would be appropriate on the occasion when the Julians' Trojan ancestor sets his foot on Italian soil! Clearly, a straightforward recommendation to his contemporaries by the poet might have to be so high-flying as easily to appear pompous. So it is better to prepare the reader for the right attitude by giving him the advance guidance a less elevated case (Aeneas' nurse) allows, and to leave the appropriate verbal expression to a god – the river god Tiber who later on will welcome Aeneas 'home' (cf. *re-vehis*, 8.37) in the appropriate fashion that some mortals (e.g., Turnus) have failed to display, i.e., he is speaking from equal to equal:

> Born of the race of gods, oh you who carry back for us (for our benefit)
> the Trojan city from the enemy and preserve eternal Pergamon,
> you, long expected by the Laurentian soil and the Latin fields:
> here your home is certain for you, certain (do not give up) the
>   gods of the house ...

> O sate gente deum, Troianam ex hostibus urbem
> qui revehis nobis aeternaque Pergama servas,
> expectate solo Laurenti arvisque Latinis,
> hic tibi certa domus, certi (ne absiste) penates;   8.36–9

To the attentive reader, it will come as no surprise that, among gods available, Tiber should be the one to welcome Aeneas in Latium. For Vergil has, as Rehm once pointed out,[28] systematically made this river the goal of Aeneas' travels: "Eine zentrale Stellung nimmt in der Aeneis der Tiber ein".

The ghost of Creusa in Book 2 (782); Aeneas himself, when looking to the future (3.500); Ascanius, making offerings at his grandfather's grave (5.83); Venus, requesting that her son reach "Laurentine Tiber" (5.797); the Sibyl, predicting to Aeneas "war, horrible war" on Italian soil (in these words foreshadowing the poet's "second proem", 7.41) and a "Tiber foamy with much blood" (6.87) – they all have raised our expectations towards the moment of Aeneas' arrival in Latium. The tragic irony at the opening of Book 7 of course consists in the fact that, whereas the reader is immediately allowed to identify the river (*Tiberinus*, 7.30), Aeneas does not yet know that this estuary, to whose beauty he feels attracted, means the end of his travels.

Here we are dealing with another structural topic developed in the opening section: that of mood and emotionality. Following the reverential tuning of the reader (7.1–4) and the last escape experienced by the *Aeneadae* (Circe's land, 5–24), there now follows the establishment of an emotional bond between Aeneas and the new land (25–36).

Vergil has here, in good epic tradition, utilized a seemingly objective landscape description (*ecphrasis*) to lead the reader into the subjective realm of the hero's innermost soul. If the Tiber has a beautiful (*amoeno*, 30) flow and the birds sing and fly in the grove (*lucoque volabant*, 34), one asks: 'beautiful' to whose observing eye? The birds flying – watched by whom? The answer, anticipated at 29f. (*Aeneas...prospicit*) and hidden in the logical *asyndeton* between lines 34 (to be ended by a colon) and 35, is: by Aeneas. "<Ergo> he ordered his men to bend the course and turn the bows to the land, and joyfully he followed the shady river" – as "joyfully" as once he and his men departed on what they thought was the last short leg of their travels, from Sicily to Italy: *laeti* (1.35).[29]

The same technique is used when, after Juno's storm, the miraculously quiet harbor on Libya's coast comes, feature by feature, into view (1.157–169), followed by *asyndeton*. "Into this harbor...Aeneas...enters for shelter" (*subit*, 1.171~*succedit*, 7.36). It is used in the storm itself, for the detailed scene of destruction is painted for a desperate observer. The words *talia iactanti* (1.102); *mirabile visu* (111); *fidum* (113); *ipsius ante oculos* (114); *apparent* (118); even the names of companions Ilioneus, Achates, Abas, Aletes

(120f.); all require the complementary viewer (Aeneas) whose heart is torn by what his eyes must watch.

The most striking model of such epic technique is the description of the exquisite natural beauty displayed by Calypso's island in the *Odyssey*: so beautiful that "even an immortal, coming to visit" (and this points to Hermes, the god who indeed visits and views it), "might gaze when he saw it and feel joy in his heart. There then he stopped and gazed, the slayer of Argos, conductor of souls" (*Od.* 5.74ff.). The point, however, is not Hermes' reaction but rather that all this divine beauty is not able to attract the eyes of a *mortal* being who longs to be home with his loved ones: Odysseus was not found here but sat far off on the shore, given to "tears, groans and pains": "Shedding tears, he kept looking out over the barren sea" (*Od.* 5.82–84).

A similarly strong emotion, though not of contrast to, but of agreement with, nature's beauty, is indicated in Aeneas' motive of ordering his men to change course and approach the river: we are to feel that he is what he can be so rarely: *laetus*.

The section (25–36) has two compositional references, one concerning Turnus (*fluvio...amoeno*, 30; *flumine pulchro*, 430; more on this later), the other concerning Aeneas' own tragic present ignorance. For all the joy resulting from entering the river mouth is – at least for the reader – vain and wiped out immediately (37ff.) when the poet, in his own voice, utters the "second proem" we discussed earlier and, in it, himself repeats the Sibyl's ominous words (6.86 7.41) of the horrible war, *horrida bella*, Aeneas will face. The fact that we readers know what Aeneas does not yet know, viz. that this presently happy man is about to face another war of Iliadic proportions, is certainly apt to secure him our sympathy.

The tension of joyful mood and overhanging threat increasingly encroaches upon the reader, who, upon watching the omens and King Latinus' prudent response in the key section 45–105b, wearily keeps checking for signs of sinister foreboding in an unexpectedly friendly (friendly for Aeneas, that is) development.[30] The first concrete signs of impending conflict will come early in the form of geographical indications that may easily escape the modern reader's ear.

Upon landing on the river bank, the *Aeneadae* turn to rest and food (7.107ff.). It is now that the dreadful prophecy once given by the harpy Celaeno (3.255ff.; mitigated by Helenus, 3.394; cf. 365ff.) comes to a rather benign fulfillment, according to the less pessimistic (*sperare*, 126) aspect ascribed here to Anchises. So it is with relief that Aeneas now recalls his father's words

ibique memento
prima locare manu molirique aggere tecta.   7.126f.

Allocating Guilt and Innocence II: Turnus the Impious Opponent

He can turn his attention to the new land, for the end of their travels and of the sufferings connected with them has come. "Therefore come on and let us, <tomorrow> at the first sunlight, happily (the key word again!) search out what area this is, which men inhabit it, where the tribe's city is, and let us, from our harbor, go into different directions. But now let us make libations to Jove, invoke Father Anchises in prayers," etc. (130–134).

It is perhaps explained by his eagerness that, already before beginning the extended sacrifices to a vast number of divinities (old and new, his father and mother among them, 139f.) and even before the joyful festivities on the occasion of the final landing and impending settlement (146f.), Aeneas should give out such detailed plans about next morning's excursions. What surprises the reader is that the actual execution of the plans is described in much the same words over again, 148–150: *primo...lumine solis*, 130 ~ *prima*[31]*...lampade*, 148; *vestigemus*, 132 ~ *explorant*, 150; *loca...homines... moenia gentis*, 131 ~ *urbem...finis...litora gentis*, 149; *diversa*, 132 ~ *diversi*, 150.

After so much preparation, it is disconcerting that, at least at first reading, these reconnoitering excursions in different directions appear to be of no consequence, for the time being. Only in the next, second step (*tum*, 152) Aeneas decides to send ambassadors to King Latinus.

Why would the poet wish to be so detailed (*diversi ~ diversa*) in reporting a seemingly subordinate undertaking? A reader acquainted with Vergil's systematic way of writing will doubtless expect that premises are being laid down here for future action. A clue can be found in the information brought back by the scouting parties, viz. "that these are the stagnant waters of the source of river Numic(i)us; this the river Tiber; that here the brave Latins live" (150f.). That is, the scouts on their trips in different directions had contacts with ("brave") Latins subject to King Latinus, with people on (up) the river Tiber (settlers of King Evander at Pallanteum? cf. 9. 244), and with people near the Numic(i)us – approaching the area of the Rutulians under their King Turnus.

Several passages in the *Aeneid* mention either one or both rivers in connection with the Rutulian tribe. At 7.793ff., the poet gives the list of Turnus' manifold followers (among them the fighters from Ardea and the *Rutuli* in the wider sense, 795). He goes on to characterize the inhabitants (perhaps the same as before) by the areas they inhabit: those

> who plow your glades, Tiber, and the sacred banks of the Numicus,
> and work the Rutulian hills with the plow, etc.

> qui saltus, Tiberine, tuos sacrumque Numici
> litus arant Rutulosque exercent vomere collis   7.797f.

Chapter 7

The extension of the Rutulian tribe toward the Tiber (and, perhaps, even beyond) is indicated by the similar wording used at 11.318f., where Latinus considers bestowing a stretch of land near the Tiber (*est antiquus ager Tusco mihi proximus amni*, 316) on the *Aeneadae*:

> The Aurunci and the Rutulians put the seeds in the ground (there) and with the plow work the hard hills,
>
> Aurunci Rutulique serunt, et vomere duros
>   exercent collis...

In this passage, though, one must assume that the land the Rutulians work is not theirs but that they have it on loan from Latinus (*est...mihi...ager*, 11.316). Servius suggests that Latinus emphasizes the harshness of the area – see also *asperrima*, 319 – to make the give-away palatable to his audience (which includes Turnus, 362; 376. Latinus is speaking before the *concilium magnum* of his chiefs, 11.234).

According to Evander, ruler of Pallanteum, the Rutulians even roam threateningly as far as his settlement (i.e., the site of future Rome). He explains to Aeneas that on the one side his settlement is circled "by the Etruscan river" (i.e., the Tiber), but

> on the other, the Rutulian presses us and raises the din
>   around the wall with his arms.
>
> hinc Rutulus premit et murum circumsonat armis.   8.474

These passages alone, geographically imprecise as they are, give us a sense of the area covered by Rutulian influence. We can see that Aeneas' ambassador Ilioneus, when asserting before King Latinus that Apollo ordered the *Aeneadae* to go to

> Etruscan Tiber and the sacred fords of Numicus' sources
>
> Tyrrhenum ad Thybrim et fontis vada sacra Numici,   7.242

expresses claims that directly touch on Rutulian-held territory.

To the Roman reader, Numicus was "holy" (here and at 7.797) because on its banks Aeneas' mortal body disappeared after his final battle with the Etruscan King Mezentius and the Rutulians (D.H. 1.64.1) – a tradition alluded to by Vergil himself when he has Jupiter remind his consort that *Aeneas Indiges* (12.794) is destined to rise to heaven. Vergil, of course, in his own version, arranges the deadly encounter of Aeneas and Mezentius in such a way that not Aeneas but Mezentius dies; Aeneas' death will occur following three years of rule in Latium, 1. 256ff., after he has built his city, i.e., Lavinium. And Lavinium, in historical times head of the Latin League, was known to any Roman for its cult of the Penates (*sacra publica populi*

Allocating Guilt and Innocence II: Turnus the Impious Opponent

Romani deum penatium, quae Lavini fierent, Ascon. ed. Kiessling-Schoell, p.18f.). In fact, the consuls, on such important occasions as taking office or leaving for war, used to sacrifice to Jupiter not only on the Capitoline hill but also to *Iupiter Indiges* at Lavinium. Members of the priesthood of the *Laurentes Lavinates* could be found all over the empire.[32] Thus, by merely mentioning ("holy") river Numicus, Vergil raises well-defined associations in his reader.

To appreciate fully the impact of the seemingly innocent news Aeneas' scouts bring back about Tiber and Numicus (7.150f.), the reader has to recall the Sibyl's prophecy to Aeneas about the horrible war to come to Italy:

> and I see a Tiber foamy with much blood.
> You will not lack another Simois nor Xanthus nor another
> Greek camp; another Achilles is already born in Latium,
> he too son of a goddess.
>
> et Thybrim multo spumantem sanguine cerno.
> non Simois tibi nec Xanthus nec Dorica castra
> defuerint; alius Latio iam partus Achilles,
> natus et ipse dea;   6. 87–90

The New Achilles, of course, will be Turnus (and by eventually defeating this Achilles, Aeneas will become a sort of super-Achilles himself and be able to make up for his awkward inferiority evidenced long ago toward the real Achilles of Homer's *Iliad*.)[33] The Sibyl is alluding to the scenes of fighting, most pernicious to the Trojans, in Book 21 of the *Iliad* when river Xanthos (= Skamandros) tried to stop the attacker Achilles (and the gods who helped Achilles) and had to call in his "brother" (and tributary) Simoeis, *Iliad* 21.308ff. In the Sibyl's prophecy, the Tiber seems to take on the role of the new Xanthus. So we can hardly go wrong in understanding the new Simois to be represented by the smaller Numicus (though not a tributary of the Tiber) – the moment we watch, at 7.150f., Aeneas in Latium being acquainted with the names of two rivers, one of them being the Tiber mentioned by the Sibyl.

Aeneas himself, it is true, in his happiness of finally exploring the promised land, shows no awareness of the dismal aspect contained in his scouts' reports. Probably we are to think that he has not yet added up one and one, so to speak. For the happiness (*laeti*, 130; 147) he communicates to his men is based on (*quare*, 130) the retrospective aspect that the sufferings of their travels are over (*laborum...finem*, 117f.; *exitiis positura modum*, 129). He does not yet look ahead to the negative aspect of the future. His ignorance of the country's rivers (see also *adhuc ignota...flumina*, 137f.) may again suggest a degree of intended tragic irony.

But we, the readers, cannot miss the frightening undertone: the geographical information communicated at 7.150f., while signaling to Aeneas his target area (cf. 7.242), to us indicates, even delineates, the battlegrounds prophesied by the Sibyl in Book 6. The author has transmitted to us that sense of fearsome foreboding and the helpless sympathy sometimes expressed by the tragic chorus or felt by the audience when watching a tragedy unfold on stage.

Up to this point, one may speak with a certain confidence about the contacts Aeneas' scouts have made. "Den ganzen Südwesten Latiums denkt sich Vergil von Turnus beherrscht." ("all of southwestern Latium Vergil pictures as ruled by Turnus.")[34] Controversy arises as soon as one attempts to be geographically precise. Almost every single one of the – often small – rivers that cross the Roman Campagna on their way to the sea has, at one time or another, been claimed by scholars to be the Numic(i)us. Recent decades have seen a redirection of *communis opinio*. For long the Rio Torto that flows between Lavinium (today: Pratica di Mare) and Ardea was a favorite, elaborately defended by, among others, B. Tilly.[35] Recent years have seen a concentration on the Fosso di Pratica which rises east of Pratica di Mare, winds round the former acropolis on its north side and then moves west and to the sea.[36]

This tendency should perhaps be viewed in the wider context of the excavations of Lavinium. By "Aeneas' arrival in Latium" scholars frequently meant the route by which worship of Aeneas had reached Rome. The statuettes found at Veii and similar 'evidence' seemed to establish that he was an immigrant from Etruria.[37] Castagnoli responded to the thesis of Rome's Etruscan foundation by pointing to evidence at Lavinium: e.g., the oldest phase of the sanctuary of the thirteen altars, part of "una netta ascesa culturale" in the early half of the sixth century BC, occurred "in pieno parallelo con Roma",[38] and the excavations at Lavinium are seen by Castagnoli as proving direct Greek influence here and at Rome, as against the thesis of Etruscan mediation.[39]

Among the sites excavated, it was especially the "tomb of Aeneas" outside Lavinium (about half a mile south of Pratica di Mare) that gave wings to scholarly imagination. If this was the tomb seen and described by Dionysius of Halicarnassus (1.64.4f.), then the Fosso di Pratica must be the long-searched-for Numicus. The tomb[40] consists of a 7th-century grave to which a *heroon* was added (attached) in the 4th century (the whole covered by a mound, today removed, and surrounded by trees "worth seeing", D.H.). To the river on which Aeneas allegedly died (if the identification is correct) today one measures a distance of half a mile (800m). Closer by, i.e., less than an eighth of a mile (little more than 200m) west of the *heroon*, a body of water is found, stretching about an eighth of a mile from north-west to south-east, and measuring half its own length at the point of its greatest width.[41] Neither river nor pond is visible from the low-lying site of the *heroon* because the rough road that crosses the fields here in a southerly direction (passing the thirteen altars on its right and branching out a path to the *heroon* on its left) is elevated. From the top of the mound one could certainly see pond and river.

Since our sources[42] tend to place the site of Aeneas' death as well as his tomb in the immediate neighborhood of, i.e., right upon, the river, the relatively long distance of half a mile between shrine and river has naturally been seized upon as a counterargument to the equation Fosso di Pratica = Numicus.[43] One scholar has replied that the Numic(i)us in antiquity did not have "einen genau begrenzten Lauf" (a precisely defined course),[44] and pointed to Vergil's *fontis stagna Numici* (7.150), together with Servius' comment *nam Numicus ingens ante fluvius fuit, in quo repertus est cadaver Aeneae et consecratum...* That the river took its course to the sea through wide areas of marshes or swamps is well evidenced.[45] The other difficulty we mentioned, viz. that *super* in Livy's statement (*situs est...super Numicum flumen*, 1.2.6) means literally 'on the river', not 'near the river',[46] has been countered by the translation "jenseits" ("beyond").[47]

Whichever way one may decide to deal with the set of problems touched upon above, the difficulties faced by the interpreter of the *Aeneid* are enhanced by the fact that Vergil wrote poetry, not history. In an (often controversial)[48] book entitled *"La Mappa dell' Eneide"*, della Corte has borrowed Servius' term *topothesia* (*ad Aen*. 1.159)[49] to denote the poet's freedom in dealing with what is usually known as topography.

A severe problem for all attempts at geographically locating the Numicus is thought to be, as Rehm once put it, "dass sich der Fluss in der *Aeneis* weiter nördlich zu befinden scheint" (that in the *Aeneid* the river appears to be farther north).[50] This (if accepted) would hang together with the fact that Vergil alone[51] among our ancient sources has relocated Aeneas' landing point farther west, from the shore area near Lavinium to the mouth of the Tiber. The question then arises: how many features did he relocate along with the disembarkation point? Della Corte has flatly spoken of Vergil's "'tiberizzazione' dell' Eneide".[52] This may be exaggerated, but a verifiable instance as, e.g., the transposition of the prodigy of the white sow and its 30 young ones from the site of future Lavinium (D.H. 1.56)[53] to the Tiber (*Aen*. 8.43ff.; 81ff.; cf. 3.389ff.) can hardly be overlooked. An extreme assumption of Vergilian telescoping was made by Carcopino, who distinguished between the real Numic(i)us (which he equated with the Fosso di Pratica) and the "Numicius de Virgile"[54]

Chapter 7

(identified by him as what is today the *Canale dello Stagno* which drains the salt marshes near Ostia). The latter one is said by Carcopino in the *Aeneid* to take on features of the 'real' Numicus.

A position like Carcopino's opens the door to speculation (though some details may appear persuasive: e.g., the close neighborhood of Tiber and Canale as a parallel to the closeness of Simois and Xanthus may remind us of the Sibyl's prophecy).[55] He, like many scholars before and after him, has also – to mention one of two more cases that concern the context of Book 7 – felt free to assign a specific location to the city of King Latinus. Vergil's own indications are sparse. We saw that Aeneas' scouts departed in "different directions" from their location near the mouth of the Tiber. The description of Latinus' palace contains a hint of a location near the sea (*ereptaque rostra carinis*, 7.186) which goes well with the *navalia* of 11. 329 (for the meaning of the word, cf. 4. 593). Today, most scholars seem to follow Dessau[56] in assuming that the ancients did not believe in the historicity of "*Laurentum*" – a name that, as we showed earlier, does not occur in the *Aeneid*. Wissowa[57] had, even before Carcopino's first edition (1919), pointed to such Vergilian periphrases as *Laurentis tecta tyranni* (7.342) or *Laurentis regia Pici* (7.171). No convincing archaeological identification has so far come forth. The same skeptic reserve should be applied regarding our third point of reference at the opening of Book 7, viz. the site of Aeneas' camp – which some scholars have tried to identify with archaeological areas of Ostia.[58]

What, then, does result for the interpreter of the *Aeneid* from all of this? That Vergil would make his Aeneas land on the Tiber rather than on the Numicus is only too understandable. The Julians' ancestor *had* to use the major gateway to his family's future world capital, to the site of which he was, after all, scheduled to pay a historically foreshadowing visit in Book 8. As the carrier of the Julians' fated mission, he had to be shown in an anticipatory move towards the goal of history, which the (first) proem had defined in a stylistically pointed arc: *Troiae...ab oris* (1.1) to *altae moenia Romae* (1.7). So significant a predecessor could hardly any longer be allowed to sneak in through the back door of the Fosso di Pratica (or Rio Torto) and perhaps take a bumpy return trip overland to Pallanteum. We must not forget that the cult of Aeneas never really took hold in Rome but was at home in Lavinium. To 'naturalize' the Julian ancestor at Rome, Vergil therefore, after setting up the founding father's first camp at the mouth of the Tiber, put him in *direct* contact with the site of Rome and, especially, with his greater descendant's residential district on the Palatine hill (Book 8). The conclusion the reader is invited to draw, then, is that Lavinium is, historically speaking, not a goal but a detour: a waiting station on the route to Alba Longa (historically, the Julians' hometown) and Rome. This is why elderly Tiber himself, *deus ipse...Tiberinus...senior* (8.31f.) – and not an anonymous divine voice or one of the *Penates* as in Dionysius (1.56) – tells Aeneas what the prodigy of the white sow means, and why Tiber gives the prodigy a subordinate position in a context that sends Aeneas up the river to Pallanteum, i.e., to the site of future Rome.

If then, at the end of a long investigation, we summarize the meaning of the information brought back by Aeneas' scouts at 7.150f., we may discern two spheres. The first is that of a background which we modern readers necessarily miss when reading the passage. To Vergil's contemporaries, the Numic(i)us meant a whole network of religious associations, reinforced, e.g., by annual sacrifices which the Vestals, guardians of the city's hearth and of the *Penates* at Rome's Vesta temple, offered at Lavinium. The second sphere is the place Vergil assigns the information in the development of his plot. Assuming that he does not change existing geography (i.e., does not transpose a river closer to the Tiber), it seems more natural to assume that by the Numicus he means the more western of the two rivers, i.e., the Fosso di Pratica, and not the Rio Torto. For this makes the distance to be covered by the scouts in one day – followed by the hurried (*haud mora; festinant*, 7.156) departure of the ambassadors to Latinus – somewhat easier to manage. One should not object that 'poetic license' allows the poet (10.687f.) to have Turnus, when being carried away in a boat from Aeneas' camp, saved by being swept home all the way to Ardea – 20 miles along the coast! For this is clearly marked as a case of divine interference for which there is a well-known Homeric model. What remains for us to state, then, is that in lines 130–151 Vergil has established a first contact between Aeneas' men and Rutulians ruled by Turnus (as well as with subjects of King Latinus). We shall see that, as in the case of Latinus divulging the oracle (7.103f.), so this contact will come into play later on, although at present the reader is not being illuminated about the long-range purpose these two pieces of information serve. They are part of what I call "the logic of circumstances".

For now (i.e., concerning the situation Aeneas faces on the day after the landing when receiving his scouts' reports) the information is sufficient to permit Aeneas the choice of picking a counterpart for official contacts. We are not expressly told that, for identification, he relies on Anchises who taught him about the coming war as well as "the Laurentian people(s) and the city of *Latinus*", *Laurentisque docet populos urbemque Latini*, 6.891.

In choosing the *augusta...moenia regis* (sc. *Latini*, 153), he seems to follow his father's information: not Turnus' Ardea, but Latinus' city (its presumed name *Laurentum*, we said, does not occur in the *Aeneid*, but only that of its

Chapter 7

inhabitants, the *Laurentes*; cf. 12.547) appears appropriate. Going over the last twenty or so lines once more, we see that "walled city", *moenia*, is the label twice employed for Latinus' city (at 131 and, elevated by the epithet *augusta*, 153), but that once so far the technical term for "chief city" (*urbem*, 149; cf. 167) has been used. Turnus' city is not categorized until later when it receives the less distinguished label *muros* (well characterizing the acropolis of Ardea) together with (409, in apposition) the term *urbs*: the latter is apparently used with regard to Ardea's prosperous past, now lost (*sed fortuna fuit*, 413), i.e., to its being the chief city of the Rutulians. For the future chain of events, let us then keep in mind that, though a first contact between Trojans and Turnus' Rutulians has apparently taken place (150), the counterpart chosen by Aeneas is the king of the *Laurentes*.

Aeneas' next step, executed in highly formalized terms, is to send an embassy to King Latinus "to demand peace for the Trojans", *pacemque exposcere Teucris* (155) – a request that we shall see fulfilled at the end of the new section: "and peace is what they carry back (*sc.*, to Aeneas)" *pacemque reportant* (285; cf. *donis*, 284, corresponding to *dona*, 155, and so likewise helping to close the compositional ring).

But Aeneas himself (*ipse*, 157) stays behind to engage in the first stages, ritual as well as practical, of building the first Trojan settlement, a fortified camp, on Italian ground. The execution (*moliturque locum, primasque... sedes...aggere cingit*, 158f.) corresponds to the working *he* recalled of Anchises' guiding announcement (*prima locare manu molirique aggere tecta*, 127), thus once again demonstrating the son's strict observance of the father's advice. The verb *moliri* is the same once used of the Carthaginians building their new city before the eyes of an admiring (and grieving) onlooker, viz. Aeneas (1.424; we may also compare *optare locum tecto et concludere sulco*, 1.425, with *humili designat moenia fossa*, 7.157). Finally he can do for his own people what he was denied so long (cf. his pain about *arva...Ausoniae semper cedentia retro* at 3.496). His "Odyssey" is finally over, and nothing will turn him away from what he is doing now.

Aeneas' building activity throws a certain ambiguity on the embassy. When King Latinus exclaims "I wish only Aeneas *himself*...would come here", *ipse modo Aeneas...adveniat* (7.263ff.), the reader knows what Aeneas "himself" is meanwhile doing: *ipse humili designat moenia fossa* (157)!

That is, Aeneas starts fortifying a piece of land while his ambassadors are on their way to ask the owner's permission. Vergil does – understandably – not dwell on the precarious legality of Aeneas' action. (Dionysius of Halicarnassus allows his Latinus an outburst of reproaches against Aeneas' marauding behavior.) Besides it is, for Vergil, probably subordinate to higher-ranking considerations:

Allocating Guilt and Innocence II: Turnus the Impious Opponent

(1) "Ideally", on the level of Fate, no complications should be expected between Fate-sent Aeneas and Latinus, obedient to the local oracles. (On this level, it will be only through Juno and Allecto that complications arise.)

(2) The ancestor of the Julians is too royal a being to negotiate in person with a local king. (Powerless and pauper King Evander in Book 8 is granted an elaborate exception which only confirms this rule 8. 127–45. Queen Dido's standing was heightened by the undeniable role Carthage would one day play in Rome's history.) Though the high moral qualities of the Latin race will make them a welcome ingredient for the new mix of nations, the reader is not allowed to forget that the Trojan (in Vergil's time, Julian) component is the superior one, divinely destined to yoke the aimless Latin (and Italian) horses to the chariot of Troy's revival in future Rome. The charioteers are provided by the *Aeneadae*, down to Vergil's own time.

The different ranking of the two nations is indicated, after an initial glance at 98–101 (see above), on occasion of the first official contact, though primary emphasis goes to the positive qualities displayed by the *Laurentes*: the ambassadors encounter the Latin youth outside the gates practicing their martial skills (the Latins, however, report the unknown Trojans to their king as "huge", *ingentis...viros*, 167f.: no equality perceived here!). The detailed description of Latinus' *curia* (a temple, 170–191) ascribes to Latin indigenous tradition many a religious practice, political institution, martial tradition, that may be recognized by the Roman reader as being part of his own life still. The question whether the temple depicts Augustus' residence (Servius) or better fits the Capitoline Hill (see Fordyce) is otiose since it tends to obscure the passage's function of elevating the rich Latin patrimony preserved in "today's" Rome (where the Senate meets in a *curia* built by the leading man).

To the many parallels one has observed between Books 1 and 7, we may add (as indicated above) that, whereas Aeneas negotiates through an envoy (Ilioneus, in both cases), the other side is both times represented by its highest authority: Queen Dido in Book 1, King Latinus in 7. But the dramaturgically different sequences should not be dismissed easily. While in Book 1 Aeneas is eventually revealed in highest splendour (a radiance more shining than that emanating from the Carthaginian queen) and the tragedy of misunderstandings will take place inside her city, Book 7 never sees Aeneas inside King Latinus' walls: the conflict occurs "earlier". This hangs together with the different timing accorded by the poet to Juno's actions. In 1, her storm drives – in geographical term – Aeneas to Carthage. What follows happens through Venus' fears for her son (Dido falls in love, Book1) and through Juno's intervention (in a storm, she causes Aeneas and Dido to seek protection in the same cave, Book 4). In 7, Juno will prevent any direct encounter at all from taking place between Aeneas and Latinus, by sending Allecto to incite Amata, Turnus and Ascanius' dogs. For Aeneas' elevated rank, one may also adduce Dido's long hesitation in her chamber on the morning of the hunt (4.132–135). Nevertheless, she eventually will go out *before* Aeneas arrives. By waiting for him outside until he "himself joins his suite with hers", *ipse...agmina iungit*, 4.141f., she has ceded the more kingly position. The simile of Apollo, 4.144, is given to arriving Aeneas. In Book 1, it was she who was compared to Apollo's sister, Diana – before Aeneas appeared. These examples are sufficient to demonstrate the high importance Vergil attributes to questions of "status" (as we say today) – in correspondence to rules of status increasingly observed by Aeneas' descendant in Vergil's own time.

The envoys are received with greatest respect by the Latin king (192ff.): their city and race are known to him. The voluntary obedience to laws should recommend his own people's hospitality to the Trojans. Rumour has it that the Trojan ancestor Dardanus emigrated from Corythus' city in Italy (the reader knows that this is true from the revelation, about the race's double root, given to Aeneas by the Penates at Crete, 3.163ff.).

Ilioneus, though responding to the king in similar terms of respect, is firm (and becomes firmer in the course of his speech) about the Trojan position: they have come here not by any chance but on purpose (*consilio* 216), after the loss of their empire, "which the Sungod once, when coming from the end of the sky, saw as the greatest" (217f.) – a nice compliment by the poet to Augustus' family and its alleged hometown.

> Jove is the beginning of our race; about Jove as its forefather
> exults the Dardanian crew; our king himself comes from Jove's
> supreme race: Trojan Aeneas has sent us to your threshold.
>
> ab Iove principium generis, Iove Dardana pubes
> gaudet avo, rex ipse Iovis de gente suprema:
> Troius Aeneas tua nos ad limina misit.   7.219–221

At first sight, these lines look like a mere confirmation by Ilioneus of the rumour reported by Latinus. But a closer look reveals more: beyond being a confirmation, the tricolon reaches a climax not mentioned before by Latinus. The emphasis "our king himself", *rex ipse*, does not make sense if it does not set Aeneas "himself" apart from his Jove-descended race (if he were only to be subsumed together with the others, we would perhaps expect "he too" but not "he himself"). What separates Aeneas from the rest of his race that sprang from Jove's union with Electra (a union which, we have just been reminded, took place back here in Italy, 206f.) is, of course, the fact that he is the direct grandson, through his divine mother

Venus, of supreme Jove, *Iovis de gente suprema* ("Son of the goddess, *nate dea*", Helenus the seer addresses him 3.374). The seemingly unsuspicious confirmation of Latinus' information through Ilioneus contains a firm hint: the returning descendant of Dardanus is more visibly blessed, has a higher claim on divinity than all others descended from the original emigrant: in Aeneas and his men Latinus faces a chosen branch of the race. Their divinity has been reconfirmed and reinstated in *this* generation.

There is a discrepancy between the alleged ancient power of Troy (its war with "savage Mycenae", *saevis...Mycenis*, 222, is stylized into an intercontinental conflict of Europe and Asia, in good literary tradition) and the present suppliant situation of the Trojans (and also, of course, in view of their future worldwide mission). Ilioneus asks for a "tiny place", *sedem... exiguam* 229, to settle the gods of their forefathers, together with peaceful acceptance on the shore and "air and waves open to all". This sounds modest but is incompatibly small regarding the political task of one day ruling the world.

> We won't disgrace your kingdom, and neither will your reputation
> be light or (and) the gratitude for so great a benefaction cease,
> nor will the Ausonians regret having received Troy in their lap.
>
> non erimus regno indecores, nec vestra feretur
> fama levis tantique abolescet gratia facti
> nec Troiam Ausonios gremio excepisse pigebit.   231–233

After his father's, Faunus', announcement of a foreign "son-in-law who, by his blood, will lift our name to the stars" (96f.; the poetic plural *generi* perhaps includes Aeneas' people with their leader) – a claim the old king will endorse again immediately, cf. 270–272 – Latinus now hears the same message of the foreigners' superiority from Aeneas' ambassador. The wording is remarkable. Together with the *modest* assurance "you won't regret it" (231–232), there comes the promise of future excellence for the Italians (*Ausonios* – this term transcends Latinus' territory), expressed in terms of breeding (*gremio excipere*, more direct than *sanguine* at 98 and 271): by accepting the Trojans in their midst, the Italians will be biologically upgraded!

Behind the humble request for a "peaceful shore" stands the biological superiority of the future masters: the Trojan-Julian House (and, presumably, some other families with them) will fertilize the indigenous race. According to ancient views of male and female contribution in producing progeny, the female merely nurtures the seed provided by the male. Thus Ilioneus leaves no doubt about the role to be played by Italy in the Trojan-Julian projection of the future. We should not forget that the Trojans have left (with one notable exception) their women behind in Sicily. Of course, Italy's role in Rome's history will be more active, rather that of a fiery warhorse, manly in character, that needs the charioteer. That is why it will be represented through unstable and unruly King Turnus. Carthage, on the other hand, could never have been represented, in Vergil's Augustan scheme, by a king. An "unstable" (cf. 4.569f.) female like Dido was required for Roman thought.

We saw earlier that the suppliant request (*rogamus*, 229) represents, as far as the hard facts are concerned, hardly more than a hollow gesture since it has been preempted and voided in advance (at least, in our modern eyes) by Aeneas who is now prophylactically fortifying his camp (7.158f). In similar fashion, Ilioneus amplifies his request by adding the overriding viewpoint of Fate (234) and of Apollo's orders (241f.) that "urge" the Trojans to settle "at Etruscan Tiber and the holy fords of river Numicus" (242), i.e. (we said), on the Rutulian territory of Turnus. Vergil's text is, of course, not as explicit as I have been just now in naming names (line 242 is today easily read as mythical topography rather than as territorial politics). It would be incompatible with Augustan ideology to represent the Emperor's forefather as a straightforward conqueror rather than an invited guest.

This is the other side of the coin. On the one hand, the oracles, especially the one given by Faunus, make Turnus in his persistence a rebel against divine authority rather than a defender of fiancée and home country. On the other hand, Destiny's will exculpates Aeneas, even justifies the threat of using arms in "defending" (doubtless the appropriate term in Vergil's eyes) his divine mission. One may compare arguments advanced by ancient – and modern – historians about Rome's allegedly involuntary conquest of the Mediterranean or, to stay within the *Aeneid*, Aeneas' *involuntary* assault on King Latinus' city in Book 12 – an attack undertaken only because of Turnus' perfidy and resulting in forcing Turnus back to the battlefield and to the forsaken terms of the duel. Thus, though perhaps strange to our eyes, it lies within Vergil's Augustan concept that Ilioneus makes his prospective host aware of Aeneas'

> powerful right arm
> whether someone has experienced it in (the) loyalty (*sc.* of an
>   alliance) or in war and arms
>
> dextramque potentem,
>   sive fide seu quis bello est expertus et armis.   234–235

He goes on to inform Latinus that many nations (*multi...populi*, 236) have tried and wished to associate "us to themselves". The humble tone (*nos...sibi*, 236ff., is, of course, more flattering than *se...nobis* would be) is continued in the next lines

Allocating Guilt and Innocence II: Turnus the Impious Opponent

don't despise us because we voluntarily
carry the ribbons in our hands and utter words of request

> ne temne quod ultro
> praeferimus manibus vittas ac verba precantia   236–37

But the discerning reader, knowing of Aeneas' anticipatory taking of the land, will see the ambiguity of "don't despise us because of our miserable appearance". The specific "don't despise" rests on the wider background of "don't underrate us", i.e., "don't be mistaken" ("let there be no mistake"). The word *ultro*, "voluntarily", "at our own initiative", signals that they might well be able to act differently but prefer to observe ritual form. The potential threat is, of course, though unveiled in 234–238, softly embedded in a suppliant overall context. Even the *parva...munera* (243f.) that demonstrate good will in spite of miserable conditions must thus, precisely by their "smallness", appeal to Latinus' (and the reader's) benevolence and *misericordia*.

Ilioneus' speech, being a masterly stroke of Vergilian dialectic, has a general lesson for us. It helps to verify Aeneas' conscientious observance of rules regulating interstate communications. Where a different subsurface constellation ("invader" versus "invaded") might suggest itself, the reader is prevented from pursuing this line of analysis by the superimposed divine order:

> it was the oracles of the gods that drove us, by their
> orders, to seek out your land
>
> sed nos fata deum vestras exquirere terras
> imperiis egere suis   239–40

Who is the reader to blame the Trojans, especially since they received additional guidance from the "huge orders" of Apollo, *iussisque ingentibus urget Apollo* (241)? He, after all, is the god who, by lightning, has indicated his desire to have a temple on Rome's Palatine Hill in the area where Aeneas' greater descendant has chosen to have his residence today. In weighing the claims of both sides, we also should not forget that the reader's heart, by the time the *Aeneid*'s second half opens, is firmly beating for Aeneas and his party. It is, at least for the final landing and eventual taking of land, not necessary for Vergil to establish afresh his hero's credentials (as he did with the prayer during Juno's storm in Book 1) or imbue the reader with sympathy (as did the fall of Troy in Book 2). A new appeal for sympathy and partisan spirit from the reader will not be necessary until later, when Pallas' death will have to be avenged.

In his silent reaction as well as in his reply (249–273), Latinus primarily refers to Faunus' oracle: this must be the announced foreign son-in-law;

this one (a wording consonant with the oracle as pronounced at 99f. though not a literal repetition), he concludes,

> will have a progeny excelling by virtue and one that, by its powers, will occupy the world
>
> huic progeniem virtute futuram
> egregiam et totum quae viribus occupet orbem   257f.

Again (cf. 231–234) the biological superiority is provided by the newcomer not by the natives. If the reference to 99f. is correct, then these words allude to the Julian family (derived from Ascanius-Iulus) rather than to the future mix of Italians and Trojans. However this may be, Latinus happily (*laetus*, 259) grants the Trojan request, expresses desire for Aeneas' presence as a guest and ally, and wishes to shake hands with him:

> part of the peace will be for me to have touched the ruler's right hand
>
> pars mihi pacis erit dextram tetigisse tyranni   266

Since the handshake will never come about, some may argue that *pax* did not come about either. I doubt that with Vergil the breaking of intended peace here will weigh less heavily than the breaking of a formally concluded one would. For confirmation, we shall adduce lines from this same book later on in this chapter.

In obedience to the oracle, Latinus amplifies his grant by offering his daughter (268ff.). In doing so, he quotes the original wording of the oracle (270ff.). He also mentions that, by an oracle of his father's shrine, by very many *monstra* (cf. 81; 58), he is forbidden to give his daughter to a man "of our nation". In saying as much, he makes it abundantly clear that he has never acceded to any of his daughter's many suitors, and that Turnus in particular never has been given any assurance by the man whose son-in-law he hoped to become. Interpreters talking of Turnus' "rightful claim" on Lavinia or of his betrothal to the king's daughter cannot invoke Vergil's text for evidence.

The other side of the coin is that the peace which Aeneas' envoys asked for (155) and received (*pacemque reportant*, 285) expresses the will of Destiny (soon to be crossed) and bears the author's stamp of approval.

This concludes Vergil's masterful arrangement of timing and circumstances. A new phase will now open with divine and human reactions of discontent.

2. Engaging the Guilty Mind

'All is well that ends well'. The final words of a long section (*pacemque reportant*, 285 ~ *pacemque exposcere Teucris* 155) appear to invalidate all the fears that have been with the reader ever since the Sibyl's prophecy and the "second proem". But, as in a well-composed tragedy, it is just at the moment when the desired good fortune seems guaranteed that evil misfortune, here in the person of irreconcilable Juno, enters the scene and falls upon its victim: a still ignorant Aeneas, who, just because of his ignorance, can still be characterized by the familiar key-word: *laetum*, 7.288.

Juno's monologue (293–322) has often been linked to the one she utters before causing the storm against Aeneas in Book 1 (37–59).[59] It is one of the structural parallels, like the speeches ambassador Ilioneus gives before Queen Dido and before King Latinus or like the two proems which, together, emphasize the epic's division into an Odyssean and an Iliadic half. One grasps the work's unity of design when recognizing that the leading opponents are the same: pious Aeneas – happy here in Book 7 as he and his men were there (1.35) before the catastrophe – and fate-defying Juno. As, in Book 1, she tries to undercut the Fates' will (*sic volvere Parcas*, 1.22), so in 7 she complains – albeit with considerably stronger frustration – about "the fate of the Trojans, opposed to our fate!" (7.293f.). Her choice of words, ascribing to her own personal desires the character of destiny, shows that she has not changed (see also the words: "my wishes finally lie worn out?!", 297f.). That fact is also revealed in her choice of another inappropriate paradigm: Mars could destroy the Lapithae, Diana the city of Calydon (in Book 1 it was Minerva punishing Ajax) – but *I*, "the great consort of Jupiter" (308; in 1.46 it was " *I*, Queen of gods and Jupiter's sister and consort"),…am defeated by Aeneas", *vincor ab Aenea* (310). Subjective, vain, almost 'human' in her ambition and resentment – this is Juno.

It is worthwhile recalling these well-known parallels in order to prevent *a priori* a misunderstanding like Pöschl's (quoted at the opening of this chapter) from being perpetuated further: nothing pronounced by this intransigent goddess or her hellish assistant Allecto may be claimed to represent the poet's own position. In calling in the underworld Fury,

> if I can't bend the gods above, I shall set the underworld in motion,
>
> flectere si nequeo superos, Acheronta movebo,   7.312

Juno relies on a monster whose heart, the poet himself tells us, is interested in "grim wars, outbursts of wrath, ambush(es) and harmful crimes" (325f.); and Juno's orders to Allecto include the following:

> destroy the peace that has come about (*sc.*, between Aeneas and Latinus), sow the seeds of war;
> would that the young want, demand and simultaneously snatch up arms.
>
> disice compositam pacem, sere crimina belli;
> arma velit poscatque simul rapiatque iuventus.   339–340

Chapter 7

Besides, her uninformed fear (333f.) that the Trojans might cajole King Latinus into giving them his daughter in marriage misses the fact: it was Latinus who spontaneously offered the marriage (7.268–73) in accordance with his father's oracle. The Trojans did not even have to ask.

If ever the reader may be sure, then it is here: no one influenced by or associated with this false suspicion and such hellish plans can be said to have a "rightful claim", as Pöschl, referring to Allecto's words at 7.422, wishes us to believe King Turnus has on Lavinia.

Since we already have, earlier in this chapter, dealt extensively with the subdivisions of which the overall section (286–600) is structurally made up, we can now immediately turn to the apparent victims of Allecto's influence: Queen Amata (341–405), Rutulian King Turnus (406–474) and the hunting dogs of Aeneas' son, Ascanius (475–539). For the purpose of the present chapter's central inquiry, it is appropriate to start (and finish) with Turnus.

After (*postquam*, 7.406) creating havoc at King Latinus' city, Allecto moves on to Ardea, where Turnus lies in deepest sleep (*iam mediam nigra carpebat nocte quietem*, 7.414; cf. *somnum*, 458; *placida...nocte*, 427), i.e., no disturbing news has reached him of what has been going on elsewhere. Allecto transforms herself into old Calybe, priestess at the local temple of Juno. (The temple was well-known to Roman readers: it was to Ardea that the *decemviri* went at the height of the war with Hannibal in 217 BC to attain help from Juno against Carthage.)[60] Therefore, when she appears to Turnus in his dream, Allecto represents a familiar figure, causing (at least initially) no disquiet to the dreamer.

In her opening words (421–437), Allecto tries to bring home to Turnus the (alleged) ingratitude of King Latinus who has failed to grant (actually, he is said to have been denying, *abnegat*, 424) him the marriage with Lavinia. The course of action "Calybe" recommends is twofold: Turnus is to burn the Trojan leader (the poetic plural aims at Aeneas) and his ships (*Phrygios...duces pictasque exure carinas*, 430f.), and he should confront King Latinus with a threatening ultimatum concerning the marriage (*rex ipse Latinus...Turnum experiatur in armis*, 432ff.).

The initial reaction of the dreaming king (435–444) is anything but awed. He mocks the priestess (*vatem irridens*, 435); tells her not to raise such false fears (*ne tantos mihi finge metus*, 438); that it is her senility ("age incapable of truth") which "in vain plagues you with worries" and, "among the arms of kings, deceives you with false fear", *falsa...formidine* (442). He even tells her as much as to go off and dust the statues of the gods and take care of the temple. "Men will take care of wars and peace, men, by whom war must be handled." He is certain that "royal Juno has not forgotten us".

The dreamer must be absolutely certain of being in control of the situation if he feels he can afford to accuse a seer of false fear (the juxtaposition *falsa vatem formidine* looks like *a contradictio in adiecto*, so one might here diagnose a Sophoclean-type misreading of the situation). Allecto's change of costume as well as her message has resulted in her not being taken seriously by her intended victim. What is one to make of the Fury's inefficiency?

A key is provided in Turnus' matter-of-fact response, given in a condescending tone: "It has not escaped my ears, as you believe it has, that a fleet has entered the waters of the Tiber" (436f.). In other words, "Calybe" has not told him anything new – he has been living with this information for some time already, without feeling disquieted by it.

If Turnus received the news about the Trojans' presence on the Tiber not first from Allecto, when did he receive it? It must have been at some point of time before the dream, i.e., we are crossing the border from dream back to waking life. Is it possible that "Calybe" alias "Allecto" is part of Turnus himself, a poetic externalization of (daytime) concerns that flare up again during sleep, taking on a life of their own by appearing in the garb of Juno's priestess (after all, a person familiar to the dreamer)? Is the god-sent dream, then, nothing but an epic convention that helps the author to introduce facts of empirical psychology into his poetic presentation?

The answer to the question is important for the reader's judgment of Turnus' behavior: is he helplessly overwhelmed from the outside by supernatural powers (Pöschl's "innocence of his guilt"; cf. Thomas 1998, 285, with note 36), or does he – not unlike Dido, as demonstrated in Chapter 5 – autonomously choose to follow ready tendencies or desires inside his own breast? Since the understanding of the *Aeneid*'s second half hinges on this issue, it is worthwhile to break off here and look for additional examples of the poetic technique which an ancient reader, especially a reader of an epic, might recall and be accustomed to in such a case. The primary candidate for our search must, of course, be Vergil's great model, Homer.

Unsurprisingly, 'divine influence in Homer' has been the object of intensive research with occasionally contradictory results. To a considerable degree, the source of the contradiction is Homer's text itself. A figure such as Helen may exemplify the inherent ambiguity. When, upon hearing about the imminent duel of her two husbands, she feels homesick and does not want to return to the bed of her second husband (Paris), she is shown in a dialogue with Aphrodite (*Iliad* 3.383ff.).

The goddess of love appears in the character of a familiar servant

Chapter 7

woman (familiar as Calybe is to Turnus), who draws to Helen an attractive picture of Paris waiting at home. Recognizing the goddess in the human garb, Helen first resists but then yields to the goddess's threat that she might find herself between the two fighting sides. Of course one may theorize that Helen originally was a local goddess herself and therefore in Homer may dare to contradict another goddess. But it may be equally or even more convincing to understand that the poet has externalized Helen's inner situation and thoughts. Helen, still feeling attracted to her second husband, first fighting her inclination but then, when being threatened by the irate goddess, giving in for considerations of safety – this is a perfectly consistent sequence of empirical psychology.

No doubt men in early times used to ascribe strong impulses to divinities outside them. But there is no doubt either that epic in its mature art could use the divine apparatus also to depict poetically an inner conflict on the human level. When, in the first Book of the *Iliad*, Achilles is insulted by King Agamemnon, he feels the urge to kill the leader of the Greek army but is undecided whether to proceed or to control his anger (1.188ff.). When he draws his sword, Athena appears and, in a conversation, advises him of the orders from Hera (the goddess promoting Greek victory): verbal abuse? – yes; fighting? – no. Since Athena was *visible only to him*, Achilles must, standing as he was with his sword drawn for twenty-six lines (194–220), have appeared to an outside observer like a paradigm of indecision. (As a matter of fact, at 2.241 a fellow-warrior reproaches Achilles for lack of "gall", χόλος, – the same "gall" Achilles felt but thought of suppressing at 192.)

In similar fashion, matricide Orestes, in Aeschylus' *Choephori* (1048ff.), being the only one able to see the avenging Furies, must give witnesses the impression of being out of his mind. The Chorus quite empirically diagnose that, as a consequence of his deed, "a confusion (ταραγμός, 1056) is falling on (his) mind". Thus drama may be added to our evidence, which shows the scenery of supranatural forces used for the externalized presentation of inner problems.

There are more cases in Homer where divine intervention occurs without invalidating empirical causality, and they are not limited to the psychological sphere. When Athena diverts an arrow aimed at Menelaos so as to prevent serious injury (4.130ff.), the missile penetrates three different layers of his armour but only grazes his skin. Menelaos himself, in perfectly empirical deduction, seems to ascribe his survival to the high quality workmanship of his armour (4.185ff.). When Apollo punishes Agamemnon for his arrogance by sending a plague, he first (1.150ff.) directs the arrows from his silver bow against roaming dogs and against the mules, before shooting the humans: Homer makes the archer god almost scientifically observe the empirical progress of an infectious disease – rather as Camus would have an approaching plague announce itself first through rats coming out of the sewers to die openly in the streets before the disease strikes humans.

The fact that in the *Iliad* divine causation and empirical causality may occur simultaneously and parallel to each other, might have induced scholars to ask whether a similar phenomenon can be observed in the *Aeneid*. Concerning Allecto, we should first consider the broader range of experience that lies outside the sphere of dreams. Of highest interest – in addition to Dido- are, of course, the other two cases in which Allecto, ordered by Juno, is said to cause disturbances: Queen Amata's revolt and the unhappy hunting trip of Ascanius.

Whereas Latin Amata and Rutulian Turnus actively oppose King Latinus' alliance with the fate-sent newcomers, there is no such evil scheming in the Trojans' contribution to the breaking of the peace (475–539): Ascanius (Aeneas' young son – by no means Aeneas himself!), carried away by his well-known (cf. 4.156–159) and innocent boyish hunting ambition (*eximiae laudis successus amore*, 7.496), wounds a stag, an extrordinarily impressive specimen of its race (483). As it turns out, the stag is a pet, cared for by the daughter of a local family of herdsmen. Father Tyrrhus and the girl's brothers react in the crude fashion of tough country people (*duros...agrestis*, 504): they gather, picking up primitive 'arms', to go after the culprit. Evidently, we again have entered the sphere where guilt and innocence are being allocated, and, considering the uncivilized reaction of the natives, the question arises: can there be more innocence than is displayed in little Ascanius' desire for praise? To our surprise, the answer comes in the affirmative.

This is where Allecto enters the framework of the story. For Ascanius was not searching specifically for a stag. He was hunting small game "by snares and by running down" (CN; *insidiis cursuque feras agitabat Iulus*, 478) when Allecto incited the hunting dogs to "sudden rage" and gave "their noses the well-known scent" (*et noto naris contingit odore*, 480), so that they went in hot pursuit after the stag.

Two things are remarkable here. First and in the context of our investigation about divine causation and empirical causality, it must be said that, similar to the outbreak of the plague in Homer, Allecto does not alter anything in what one would consider the normal course of events: hunting dogs, when picking up a "known" scent, usually go after the game. In Vergil, too, divine intervention does not automatically do away with natural process.

Secondly, immediately after the words describing the dogs' behavior, there follows the author's statement "this was the first cause of the sufferings and it inflamed the rustic minds for war" (481f.) – a statement which, as we showed earlier in this chapter, both refers back to the announcement given in the "second proem" (*et primae revocabo exordia pugnae*, 7.40~*quae prima laborum causa fuit*), and leads, after the first hostilities, to the summarizing words (*sc., Allecto*) *primae commisit funera pugnae*, 7.581, triumphantly welcomed by Juno: *stant belli causae*, 7.553.

Thus, at the very beginning of Vergil's chain of events (*prima...causa*) we do not find Ascanius so much as his dogs: it is their behavior which leads to affecting the "rustic" (482; 504) minds of the natives. Since dogs can hardly be expected to show moderation, it seems that Vergil assigns responsibility for the outbreak of hostilities to the uncivilized reaction of the natives. Such a procedure, though verified by us before when we considered the time sequence of oracles and arrival of the Trojans, would seem remarkable in view of the versions we considered earlier of Cato, Livy, and Dionysius of Halicarnassus. All three of them, when reporting the outbreak or imminent threat of hostilities, assigned the cause to the circumstance that Aeneas' men had been ravaging the countryside (an accusation in the *Aeneid* raised by Juno, 10.78). The question arises: has Vergil changed the 'historical' tradition he inherited to the extent that he does not allow any guilt at all on the Trojan side? Already we have seen that, at least so far, his cause of war must be called a "hunting accident" rather than human failure on the part of Ascanius.

As it turns out, Vergil will in the end allow some Trojan contribution to the outbreak of hostilities – but he will veil it. Next, however, Allecto, instigator of war, is (after working in Ascanius' dogs) shown to shift her influence exclusively to the Italian side. When Sylvia's screams (*vocat, conclamat*, 504) succeed in immediately calling the country people together and making them take up their primitive arms, this is ascribed to Allecto: "for the savage [Fordyce's rendering of this word] plague is hiding in the silent forest" (505). Again one may state that Allecto, in hiding, does not interfere with empirical causation, especially in view of the fact that the herdsmen's *ira* (508) is mentioned. The only seemingly active intervention Vergil grants her is that she, on the roof of the stables, blows the horn (*cornu*, 513; *bucina*, 519) and thus gives the sign (*signum*, 519) to which the area's "indomitable farmers", *indomiti agricolae* (521), react by gathering for (formal) fighting. Here, too, one may easily understand an allegory; especially so since the customary instrument, *bucina* (see also *pastorale signum*, 513) is being used: Allecto stands for the extraordinary fervor with which the trumpeter calls to battle (and his call is received).

Allocating Guilt and Innocence II: Turnus the Impious Opponent

One can hardly found a thesis of divine causation on a loud but customary trumpet call.

But one can say that, by the shift in Allecto's targets (from the rage of Ascanius' dogs to the farmers' heated reaction), the reader is guided to locate responsibility for the ensuing confrontation on the Italian rather than on the Trojan side. In agreement with this impression, the Trojans are presented as <u>reacting to</u> the Italian military deployment by *for their part, too*, sending help to Ascanius from the camp:

> nec non et Troia pubes
> Ascanio auxilium castris effundit apertis. 7.521f.

From sticks, poles and other makeshift 'weapons' (506–510), the escalation has now reached a formal military confrontation of battle lines (*derexere acies*, 523; etc.).

It is at this late point that Vergil will – implicitly – admit a Trojan contribution to the actual outbreak of fighting, and thus pay tribute to the tradition my reader found represented by Cato, Livy and Dionysius. Almo, the eldest son of shepherd Tyrrhus (i.e., the eldest brother of Silvia), is struck down by a "whirring arrow" (531) in (front of?) the first line. Only a reader who actively searches for an answer to the question "which side launched the first shot?" and who will take into consideration that Almo's death is the first hostile action reported by the poet, will arrive at the conclusion that it was a *Trojan* archer who opened the actual hostilities. Vergil does not explicitly tell us so.

Here we have, once more, become aware of a technique which, while not exactly suppressing 'historical' truth as handed down by tradition, does not take pains either to record expressly actions which may throw an unfavorable light on the Trojans. From Book 7, my reader recalls another example: Vergil did not emphasize the fact that Aeneas was appropriating a territory at the same time as his ambassadors were being sent out to ask the owner's permission. In view of this awareness, the somewhat cryptic lines that follow immediately upon the report of Almo's death are not without special interest:

> All around, bodies of men <were stretched lifeless>, and
>   <among them> elderly Galaesus,
> while offering himself as a mediator for peace; he was second to
>   none in his sense of justice,
> and once the wealthiest in Ausonian fields.

> Corpora multa virum circa seniorque Galaesus,
> dum paci medium se offert, iustissimus unus
> qui fuit Ausoniisque olim ditissimus arvis. 7.535–37

One will hardly assume that the self-appointed mediator was killed by Italians of his own side, but must conclude here that the Trojans caused the death of a man characterized by highest justice still in his final hour. Do the "many corpses" perhaps likewise belong to Italian fighters (and thus point to a Trojan first attack)? This cannot be clearly answered, but there is certainly no praise to be earned from the killing of a just man who tries to prevent an unholy war. So, in the end, any reader who is not careless may find at least some indirect indication in Vergil's presentation denoting a Trojan contribution to the outbreak of hostilities.

Yet how pale is this indication when compared, e.g., to the indignation the reader is made to feel when – *vice versa* – another "whirring arrow" (*stridens...sagitta*, 12.319), likewise from an anonymous hand, puts mediating Aeneas temporarily out of commission and allows Turnus to resume hostilities! The truce that is violated in Book 12 is, objectively speaking, well comparable to the "peace", *pacem*, that Aeneas' ambassadors had "carried back" to the camp from King Latinus the day before Ascanius' hunting excursion (7.285). Or, if Book 12 seems too far away from Book 7, how pale is the indication of possible Trojan guilt in the opening of hostilities when compared to the clear-cut condemnation of both Queen Amata's and King Turnus' opposition to the arriving Trojans! In analyzing Vergil's technique, we must not forget that, when reading about Ascanius' outing and its unhappy consequences, the reader's expectation has, by two impressive antecedent cases, been set to find the fault with the natives – even if the Trojans at the camp should be committed to the "peace" as insecurely as the subjects of King Latinus (in fact they come out with the defensive intention of assisting Ascanius). To realize the full extent of Vergil's bias, one must verify the emphasis and prominence the poet has given to Amata's and Turnus' behavior.

As it has turned out, allocation of innocence or guilt is closely connected with the degree to which supernatural forces might be understood to either invalidate (override) natural processes or leave their functioning intact. So far, both Homer and Vergil (and, in the case of Orestes, Aeschylus) have been shown at least on occasion to endorse the latter alternative. Considering the history of human understanding, this alternative, we said, possibly represents the poetic utilization of a feature displayed by early religion: namely, that man ascribed to external forces (considered divine) what he found hard to deal with and to control in himself. This does not mean that, whenever poetry employs such forms of presentation, the poet in his own thinking (as has been assumed of Homer) is still tied to that early form of belief. On the contrary, the fact that he employs it to represent inner processes in an externalized fashion conducive to epic narrative rather suggests that he himself has long left that early stage behind and expects his audience to have done likewise. Our hypothetical consideration may be disappointing for a certain branch of Homeric scholarship but it is necessary for understanding Vergil's view (and handling) of elements which he and his readers considered ingredients of inherited tradition. Again, we must say that here we are speaking of the educated reader. Unsophisticated minds were not denied a literal understanding.

If, with the foregoing considerations in mind, we turn to Queen Amata's condition, we immediately observe that, even before Allecto attacks her, she, "afire", is "boiling" with (being boiled by) "feminine worries and outbursts of wrath" about the Trojans' arrival and Turnus' marriage.

femineae ardentem curaeque iraeque coquebant   7.345; cf.344.

To a Roman ear, this is not at all a complimentary description since feminine emotion only too often points to the absence of that desirable rational behavior which is supposedly a characteristic of male self-control. (We recall the different reactions Vergil assigns Aeneas and Dido after Mercury's visit in Book 4. If Amata decides to talk, we should be careful not to attribute cool objectivity to her words.) The durative imperfect *coquebant*, along with the durative participle *ardentem* – together a curious mix of metaphors, shows that we are dealing with a condition, a state of mind and not with a momentary fit or transient mood.

So we may not be too surprised when seeing that the snake, thrown at Amata by Allecto and rolling over her body "without touching (it)", *attactu nullo* (350), does not seem to change her condition though the stated purpose is "that, in a state of fury imparted by the monster, she confuse the whole house" (348). As a matter of fact, it is difficult to picture the presence of the monster when it turns into Amata's golden necklace or into the ribbon of her hair – objects that must have been with her, in their usual place on her body, anyway. The first stage (*prima lues*, 354), in which Amata is not yet seized *toto...pectore* (356), is wholly consistent with the state of *femineae...curaeque iraeque* (345) described before Allecto's onset: "in the usual custom of mothers", *solito matrum de more* (357: so far, no change from normal experience here!), she turns to husband Latinus, complaining about his lacking of pity for daughter and mother (– and even for himself, *tui*) and painting the picture of another Paris about to abduct another Helen (i.e., Lavinia). Clearly to the reader of the epic, Amata is wholly mistaken about Aeneas' character and intentions. Her complaints are touching and perhaps understandable but they are also *femineae* – carried away against the oracles by unfounded worries to the degree that her view of reality is false. Her picture of Aeneas resembles the one fostered by misguided

Chapter 7

instigator Juno who, we recall, wished to prevent that "the *Aeneadae* could cajole Latinus with a marriage" (333f.) – whereas in truth the initiative had come from Latinus, on the basis of the oracles, 7.268–273. In similar fashion, Amata's thoughts also do not reflect what the reader knows to be the correct view of the present state of affairs.

It is important that we are aware of Amata's mistaken and anxiety-driven perspective, so that we view the continuation of her argument in proportion, when she invokes Latinus: "What of your scrupulous (inviolable) guardian responsibility?" *quid tua sancta fides?* (365). *OLD* is right (*s.v. quis* 1, 12) in printing this question not in isolation but together with the two lines which precede it. For Amata is continuing her argument, not introducing a new point. Feeling that her husband is relentlessly abandoning their daughter (and, implicitly, herself, the mother, along with the daughter) by handing her over to a pirate, she concludes that Latinus has betrayed his "sense of duty towards others" (another well-documented meaning of *fides*, cf. *OLD s.v.* 8, coming close to "protection" or "guardian care" which *L&S* list *s.v.* under II.B.2). As her next words reveal, she suspects a change in Latinus' attitude between the past and now: "What of your old (former) concern for your close ones...?" *quid cura antiqua tuorum* (etc.)? (365; the masculine form *tuorum* grants an impact of greater generality to her own and her daughter's alleged plight.)

Of course, she is mistaken as she has been before. Latinus, directed by divine orders and informed of the splendid future that awaits the homecoming *Dardanidae* in their (and his) land, has done the right thing. Amata, crossed in her own, supposedly safer, marriage plans within the circle of kinship, is both angry (*irae*) and concerned (*curae*, 345) to the degree that she wrongly accuses Latinus of lacking *cura* (365). The reader, though (we said) not without sympathy for the mother, has long ago (7.96ff.) registered Latinus' pious obedience to and observance of divine will.

The connection of line 365 and lines 363f. has had to be clarified here in detail because a longstanding misinterpretation tears the first question of line 365 away from its context and makes it refer to Turnus – Turnus who is mentioned by Amata not before line 366 and, after that, is made the topic of lines 367–370. Taking *quid tua sancta fides* as pointing to an earlier promise allegedly made by Latinus to Turnus (a meaning of *fides* excluded by the context of our passage alone), the misinterpretation puts Vergil's Turnus in the place of the deprived fiancé whom we, earlier in this chapter, found connected with the name of Livy. Incorrectly CN remark on the first question in 7.365: "The sense is obvious, 'what has become of your solemn pledge' etc.", and similar is Fordyce' mistaken translation "What of your pledge solemnly given?"

Allocating Guilt and Innocence II: Turnus the Impious Opponent

Having offered my reader a logical and contextual understanding of line 365a, I now proceed to discuss the slightly changing viewpoint of 365 and 366.

> What of your scrupulous guardian responsibility? What of
> your old (former) concern for your close ones
> and your right hand so often given to kinsman Turnus?
>
> quid tua sancta fides? quid cura antiqua tuorum
> et consanguineo totiens data dextera Turno?   7.365–366

One can see that Turnus' name is attached to tuorum, "your close ones", (i.e., Lavinia and Amata in the original context of "daughter" and "mother", 360 and 361) like an afterthought – slipped in here (*et*, 366) and then expanded upon under a different perspective in 367ff. He is out of place in line 365, at least in 365a, if one should wish to take 365b as the beginning extension – *tuorum* – which would then – *et* – be explicated by 366. But 365b is still concerned with Latinus' neglected obligation (*cura antiqua*) to his own, and so is 366. A sharp break occurs not before 367, since lines 367–70 then, abandoning the accusations against Latinus, introduce and develop the new point: Amata's counter-suggestion that Turnus' family background would fit the oracle.

"Latinus had doubtless promised Lavinia to Turnus before the portents mentioned vv. 58 foll." (CN ad 366). "Doubtless"? It would be strange if for such an important fact the reader would have to rely on the words of a woman whose perspective is demonstrably not that of the author. "*data dextera*: there is an inconsistency between these lines and 54ff., where there is no suggestion of betrothal and Turnus is only the suitor favored by Amata." This comment by Fordyce seems at least to leave the door open that "54ff." may be correct, without however indicating that what he calls "an inconsistency" may be due to Amata's distorted view of reality.

Let us take a closer look, keeping in mind both Amata's wishful thinking about a marriage of Turnus and Lavinia and the king's strict adherence to the forbidding oracle. ("Before the portents", to repeat and take issue with CN's words, Turnus had, as we showed earlier, anyway been nothing more than one suitor among others.) What does a "right hand, given so often to kinsman Turnus" mean under these circumstances?

The phrase can hardly mean that the handshake pledged Lavinia to Turnus. If that were to be the meaning, why repeat the solemn act "so often"? Because Turnus felt unsure about the future and needed weekly reassurances? That appears absurd. It is much more likely and natural that the king on many an occasion shook the hand of his wife's nephew (or even his own nephew, if one prefers the connection through

Pilumnus rather than the one through Venilia), while acknowledging him as "a relative" (*consanguineo*) and nothing more. Since, on the one hand, Allecto will play on the fact that Turnus' military prowess protected Latinus' peace (7.426; the peace which Latinus had enjoyed for so long, 7.46), and since, on the other hand, Tiber mentions (8.55) constant war between Arcadians (at the site of future Rome) and "Latins" (represented by Turnus – no uncommon inconsistency here either, especially if we keep in mind the material collected on Vergil's use of "Latin" in note 6 above), there is ample reason for Amata to use the word *totiens*, "so often", at 7.366 – but the implication that these handshakes should amount to an agreement on a marriage would still be totally and exclusively hers, resulting from her wishful thinking. All this, unnecessary to say, tells us nothing about the feelings of King Latinus, who so far has set – and will set almost up to the end at 7.600 – pious obedience over personal inclination. His self-reproach about having ultimately dropped his resistance (cf. 12.29ff) was mentioned earlier by us.

Breaking away from her accusations against her husband, Amata, almost like another Iocasta, ventures to give Faunus' oracle about the son-in-law from abroad a rationalizing twist that would favor her own wishes: any man not subject to "our sceptre" would go for a foreigner according to her sophistic interpretation, and Turnus would seem especially qualified since his family's origin (i.e., Acrisius' daughter Danae from Argos) points "right" to "Mycenae", *mediaeque Mycenae* (367–372).

The queen's misguided words reveal more than she can know. Vergil's reader is supposed to shudder at this woman's unholy suggestion that the bride whom Fate has destined for Aeneas be given to a man who can be connected to the city of Agamemnon, conqueror of Troy! We have not forgotten Ilioneus' recent words of the "storm" which emanated from "savage Mycenae" (*saevis effusa Mycenis*, 7.222) and devastated the fields of Troy. Amata's wishful and willful understanding of the oracle would lead to consequences that far exceed the scope of her subordinate mind. But, like other opponents of the Trojan-Julian destiny, she is found guilty within her own little sphere, too. As with Turnus, her first offence is against the gods whose pronounced will she falsifies by replacing the word "foreign" (*sc.*, son-in-law) with "of foreign origin". In Vergil's design, prospective mother-in-law and son-in-law are of a feather.

"[Allecto] does not create the passions which are let loose; the causation is not imposed externally", etc. As far as quoted, R. D. Williams' comment (*ad* 7.323f.) outlines a thesis with which our own observations are in agreement, at least for the initial phase of Amata's behavior. The basically metaphorical character of Allecto (standing here for human rage) is revealed in equal clarity in the transition to the second stage. The process is doubly characterized, both mythically and psychologically (7.373ff.), the two aspects being contained in two parallel subordinate clauses which are followed by a common main clause: "When (*ubi*) (a), having tried in vain with these words, she saw Latinus continue his opposition and (b) the serpent's infuriating poison, having slipped deep inside her intestines, invaded her completely, then (*tum vero*) the unhappy one, excited by exorbitant phantasies, moved in rage and frenzy all over the city." The reader is reminded of Dido's twofold motivation by (a) Aeneas' presents and (b) Amor's presence (*pariter puero donisque movetur* 1.714; see Chapter 5).

While the divine cause (a) has become even more pale and unimaginable than at 346ff., the empirical chain of cause and effect (b) is thoroughly convincing in itself (again, no supernatural power is needed): when being turned down by her husband, Amata becomes "furious" – and will take things into her own hands, no longer thinking of the obedience a Roman *matrona* has to observe towards the decisions of the *pater familias*: she clearly is measured by standards known to Vergil's reader. When not yet totally (*necdum...toto...pectore*, 356) possessed by rage, she observed the decorous behavior expected of mothers (*solito matrum de more*, 357) and turned to her husband's authority; when her plea proves unsuccessful, she now yields totally (*totam*, 375) to rage, leaving the bounds of decency (*sine more*, 377). Thus, though her unhappy state is acknowledged (*infelix*, 376), the poet does not withhold moral judgement (we registered comparable features in his description of Dido).

The fact that Vergil does not withhold moral judgment, neither here nor, as we shall see, on the occasion of the behavior displayed later by the queen, should warn us not to take the comparison of fury-driven Amata to a top, whipped by boys, as relieving her from being responsible for her actions. The passage has been discussed often, especially by R. J. Rabel[61] who (apart from finding an unconvincing reference that allegedly ties 1.83 and 7.378 to each other) gives a summary on the literature and advances an interpretation of his own, based on Cicero, *Fat.* 42–43. According to the Stoic philosopher Chrysippus, as the top or the roller moves only when struck but then the roller continues on grounds of its own *volubilitas*, so a sensual impression impacts the mind (I leave out the complicated details of this Stoically conceived process); but it is within human power to assent: *nostra...in potestate* (ἐφ' ἡμῖν). According to Rabel, Vergil, like Chrysippus, would not see Amata impelled by an outside force.

Difficult as Chrysippus' comparison (and Cicero's report on it) appears, we might (provided that Vergil here does pick up a piece of Stoic theory) argue that Amata's basic condition (the *volubilitas*, of the cylinder), before

Chapter 7

the impact of her husband's refusal, was characterized by a pre-existing, boiling-hot emotion of anger and worry rather than an irascible "feminine" nature alone: *femineae ardentem curaeque iraeque coquebant* (7.345). The second stage, then, would be her express assent of giving herself over to rage, and R. D. Williams' formulation (*ad* 7.323f.), "She allows herself to become the plaything of Allecto", would preserve the amount of moral autonomy implied here.

Without risking my reader's disaffection by overstating "multiple correspondences",[62] I point to four basic references:

(1) Amata is "excited by exorbitant portents (portentous visions)", *ingentibus excita monstris* (376)[63] as the top, flying under the whip, *torto volitans sub verbere* (378), is "driven under the lash", *actus habena* (380) by excited boys, *intenti ludo* (380);

under the impulse, Amata (2) moves "all over the city", *immensam...per urbem* (377) as the top moves "in a wide circle", *magno in gyro* (379), or "in curved spaces", *curvatis...spatiis* (381);

(3) her movement is "frenzied" and "frantic" (*furit lymphata per urbem*, 377) as the top is "(repeatedly) flying to and fro", *volitans* (378), in ever new bursts of movement whenever "the blows give it thrust", *dant animos plagae* (383).

(4) A fourth detail, not mentioned before by the narrative, is added within the simile itself: the marvelling bystanders, fascinated by what they see but do not understand, *stupet inscia...manus mirata...* (381f.).

This fourth detail is reflected, along with the other three, (3) no less swiftly than that movement (*non cursu segnior illo*, 383; i.e., *volitans*, 378; *magno in gyro*, 379; *curvatis spatiis*, 381) she

(1) is driven (*agitur*, 384 ~ *actus*, 380 ~ *excita*, 376)

(2) right through the city (cities, *urbes*, 384 ~ *per urbem*, 377; *medias*, i.e., away from the palace, 384 ~ *magno*, 379 ~*immensam*, 377); and

(4) the fierce (=instigated?) people (*populosque ferocis*, 384 ~ *manus mirata*, 382; if *urbes* and *populos* are instances of genuine plural the extent of Amata's movement is wider after the simile [384] than before [377]).

In 383 bf., then, the author himself, more precise than some of his interpreters, tells his readers what the simile serves to illuminate: (3) the erratic swift movement over (2) wide areas before (4) a crowd of stimulated onlookers, performed under (1) the influence of (false) portent-like perceptions: the emphasis of the passage lies on the visual impression offered by a frenetic expanding movement (we readers, too, are onlookers) more than on philosophical definition of a driving force.

The passive form *agitur* might suggest to some that Amata no longer has a free will but is Allecto's toy. Yet one might argue that this expression

Allocating Guilt and Innocence II: Turnus the Impious Opponent

is taken over from the simile of the whip-driven top (*actus habena*) and does not exclude the possibility that Amata, with her well-targeted intentions, still has some influence on the movement.[64] Being completely (*totam*, 375) given over to her worries, she emancipates herself from her husband's guidance and will employ her rational powers in the service of her rage.

In the following lines, Vergil describes the third stage of her fury ("yes, even..." *quin etiam*, 385), saying that she undertook "a greater religious crime" and "a greater fury". This clearly implies that her preceding fury likewise must be considered a crime (though a lesser one), *nefas*. The stages of the climax are indicated by (1) *prima* (354), *necdum...toto...pectore*; (2) *ubi nequiquam..., tum* (373ff.); (3) *quin etiam...maius...nefas maioremque...furorem* (385ff.; cf. also 377).

The new crime is not at all involuntary (and thus ends all interpretative speculations on Amata's actions being involuntary or heteronomous or outside accountability): *in order* at least to delay (*moretur*) if not to prevent (*eripiat*) Lavinia's marriage to Aeneas, Amata takes her daughter to the mountains, *pretending* (*simulato*: the meaning is clear *cum pace* Fordyce) to fulfill the will of Dionysus *(numine Bacchi*, 385).

The poet's (narrator's) abhorrence at the crime he has to report is so great that he himself (apart from the first "*euhoe Bacche*" which is Amata's exclamation) invokes the god in direct address (389–391), as if to call Dionysus' attention to the blasphemy by reporting directly to the god and, thus, distancing the poet from what he reports (this is a more context-bound understanding of the Latin text than seeing in it a mixture of *oratio recta et obliqua*).

The queen's behavior proves infectious: the Latin women leave their homes to join her in the wilderness. Clearly, they are caught by the spirit of Bacchic revelry, and one may (cf. CN) indeed assume that Amata is, not unlike another Pentheus, in the end herself overwhelmed by the power she intended to control for her own purposes, when we see her, eyes suffused with blood, swinging the torch and singing of Turnus' and Lavinia's wedding – her true intention coming out, the criminal convicting herself, so to speak. Her distorted moral judgement is revealed in her appeal to the (allegedly) "pious minds" of her fellow-revellers to follow her "if concern for maternal right is vexing you again", *si iuris materni cura remordet* (402). This is absurd. She has left the "customary decent behavior of mothers" (*solito matrum de more*, 357) long ago and turned to indecency (*sine more*, 377). It is quite consistent that she should now ask the mothers to throw off the ribbons of the *matronae* and start the orgies with her (403). In her mind, *ius maternum* has lost its tie to the norms of the (Roman) community.

How does the final line of the section,

Chapter 7

> Allecto drives the queen from all sides with the goads of Bacchus
>
> *reginam Allecto stimulis agit undique Bacchi*   7.405

go together with Amata's initial manipulation of Bacchic religion for her own purposes? It may indeed seem best to see (with CN and Servius) the queen fall victim to the power she misused. But let us not forget that in her 'mad' song and in her address to the revelers, as well as in her appeal to their allegedly "pious minds" (401) and to a "maternal right" (402) she "herself" (*ipsa*, 397, sets her off from the others) still adheres to her identical initial intention of marrying Lavinia to Turnus and not to Aeneas ("she sings of her daughter's and Turnus' wedding", 398). In other words, under Allecto's influence she even now does not do anything that would lie outside her original, human motivation. 'Bacchus' is a fitting poetic garb to describe the alleged working of Juno's fury-causing helper. Another (more convincing) possibility of interpreting lines 384–385 is that they conclude the Amata episode on the level of myth by which it is opened (341–343), thus preserving the superhuman narrative frame. This is an adequate understanding since the narrative now continues on the mythological level with the grim goddess (*tristis dea*, 408), her local task achieved, flying on to Ardea.

This is consonant with the earlier result we drew from the section that took its beginning from Ascanius' dogs. Vergil does not invalidate the chain of cause and effect when introducing Allecto – and he makes it clear several times that the workings of his Allecto do not do away with human responsibility and guilt. The question we shall have to ask, then, is: if mythical and epic 'Allecto' does not change or overrule normal natural processes – why introduce her at all? The answer will be clearer after we have also finished dealing with the Turnus episode.

Earlier we observed that, in Homer, divine causation and empirical causality may occur simultaneously and parallel to each other. In the case of the Rutulian king to which I now return, it was Homer who supplied the model for Vergil. Walsh[65] points out that in both *Iliad* 2 and *Aeneid* 7 the king (Agamemnon there, Turnus here) has a divinely-sent dream which incites him to action; later on, each book offers a description of the king's military contingents (the so-called Catalogue of Ships and the Gathering of the Clans), introduced by almost identical invocation of the Muse by the two poets (*Il.* 2.484ff.; *Aen.* 7. 641ff.). Considering the structural similarities, it is advisable to take a close look at the dream in *Iliad* 2.

On the surface, there seems to be divine causation only. The supreme god Zeus experiences a sleepless night (2.2) because he has, against the wishes of his consort Hera (a strong supporter of the Greeks), to fulfill a

Allocating Guilt and Innocence II: Turnus the Impious Opponent

promise he gave the sea goddess Thetis, mother of Achilles, the greatest Greek hero. He has promised to let the Greeks suffer defeat at the hands of the Trojans until the Greek leader Agamemnon restores the honor of her son Achilles whom he has insulted. Zeus solves his problem (2.5ff.) by sending "baneful Dream" to sleeping Agamemnon with the false message that on this day he can take Troy since Hera has won over all the other gods to her pro-Greek, anti-Trojan position. The idea of "Zeus' will" (1.5) is that Agamemnon, instead of taking Troy, will maneuver himself into a hopeless situation from which only Achilles can save him. (This is first achieved when, in Book 9, Agamemnon, finding himself defeated and bottled up in his own camp, sends an embassy to Achilles' tent, asking for his help.)

So far, events may seem to be running consistently as required by the context of the divine level. But there is an empirical aspect to all of this, and it is surprisingly simple. If Agamemnon insults and antagonizes his strongest warrior so that he withdraws from fighting, it is only natural that the Greek side should suffer defeat. "Zeus' will" (1.5), i.e., to support the Trojans at the cost of the Greeks, viewed in this way, reflects and expresses part of empirical reality. I say "part" because events on the battlefield do not always follow the intentions of the highest god. By inventing ever new delays and diversions of "Zeus' will", the poet manages to draw a picture of the vicissitudes of fighting as they occur in the real world where each side experiences its ups and downs. And even when the audience expects the decisive Trojan push against the Greek camp to be imminent, there will still occur another (and another) reversal: when, in Book 13, Zeus turns his eyes away from the battlefield, he no longer expects interference from any of the other gods (13.1–9). But his brother Poseidon takes the chance to afford the Greeks an opportunity to push back the Trojan onslaught. And, seeing Poseidon work down there on the battlefield, Hera, on the upper level, decides to support her brother by putting Zeus, her husband, out of commission for a longer period: visiting him on the top of Mount Ida, she seduces him and puts his mind to sleep (Book 14, 153ff.).

Thus the reversals on the battlefield each time seem to result from divine causation. On earth, however, the events may manifest themselves both empirically and supernaturally. Poseidon, though taking on the human shape of well-known priest Kalchas when encouraging the Greeks (13.45), is nevertheless recognized as a divinity by mortal Aias, son of Oileus (66f.); when appearing as an unknown old man (14.136), Poseidon nevertheless raises his voice to a superhuman volume (147ff.). This ambiguity may be compared to our earlier observation that Menelaos, when saved by Athena from a missile, himself ascribes his survival to the excellent workmanship of his armor.

Chapter 7

A similar empirical component can be seen in Agamemnon's dream and in the events that surround it. One has to understand his situation. While he was still quarrelling with Achilles, Nestor, his aged and highly respected adviser, had warningly implored him to "let go your wrath in a benevolent attitude toward Achilles who is a strong bulwark for all the Greeks against the evil war" (1.283f.). But Agamemnon's response (1.286ff.) had been far from conciliatory. In fact, his continuing nagging had made things worse. The king's own behavior contributed to the loss of his army's "strong bulwark".

The audience may be sure that, during the days following the quarrel, the Greek leader himself was not too happy about the way he had conducted himself in the assembly. On the morning after the dream, he publicly, before the whole army, states his regret about the quarrel; and though, in truly royal insolence, ascribing its causation to Zeus (as he later will likewise ascribe the cause of his delusion to Zeus, among others, at 19.87), he at least admits as much as "and I was the first to be angry" (2.378). The occasion, however, to him is a trivial one: "We, I and Achilles, fought because of a girl" (377). He is far from realizing – or admitting – that he himself is responsible and has to pay for insulting the god Apollo by insulting his priest (father of the "girl").

Agamemnon's behavior, both at the time of the quarrel and on the morning after the dream, displays a desire to be right and an inclination to avoid self-criticism by admitting as few errors as possible. The dream, occurring in between, some time after the first and in the night before the second event, fits the pattern very well. Its main point suggests that the dreamer pursues a line of wishful thinking. If the dream tells Agamemnon that he can take Troy this very day, this would be the ideal solution to the king's problems: he could show the world that he can reach the goal of this war (which by now has been dragging on for almost ten years) without relying on the help of Achilles; his leadership would appear truly sovereign and independent of others.

The wishful character of the dream is further enhanced by the fact that the messenger of the good prospects is none other than Nestor – the same councilor who had warned against antagonizing "bulwark" Achilles, and whose advice, Agamemnon soon realizes, was correct and good. Since Nestor (in the dream) seems to make an about-face (after all, he advises attacking the Trojans without Achilles being present to help), the king may consider his own earlier actions justified. If this dream-Nestor even refers to Zeus ("a more interesting complexity", as Kirk *ad* 2.20–1 calls it; on the surface it seems – as happens in dreams – to break the illusion), the better so: after all, Nestor himself is only mortal, but Zeus is the divine authority and guarantee which backs kings and their dignity against intransigent "subordinates" (like Achilles, as Agamemnon indicates at 1.174f.; cf. 2.26f.).

The important role Nestor plays in Agamemnon's thinking (he is the one "whom Agamemnon honored most among the elders [councilors]", 2.21), can be inferred also from the fact that, upon awakening from the dream, the king first convenes a meeting of his elders – by the ship of *Nestor* (2.53f.). The irony of the situation is complete when the real Nestor, impressed by the king's dream (and his own role in it?) announces that, if any other Greek would report such a dream, "we certainly would call it false" (2.81). But, the man "who claims to be by far the best of the Greeks"[66] being the dreamer, one should go ahead and call the soldiers to arms. The adviser's skepticism is overcome by awe of royal authority.

So far, it has been shown that the Zeus-sent dream is perfectly compatible with the dreamer's frame of mind and personal experience. However, one would appreciate a closer indication that there is a carry-over from his own daytime concerns into his dream – comparable to, say, Penelope's worries before she falls asleep which then are addressed by the dream apparition of her sister Iphthime (*Od.* 2.787ff.; 804ff.). Such a carry-over is found in "Nestor's" opening words to sleeping Agamemnon:

> You are asleep, son of fiery-hearted, horse-taming Atreus?
> A counsel-bearing man should not be asleep all night long,
> to whom troops have been entrusted and who has so many
>   concerns on his mind.   2.23–25

These lines precisely depict Agamemnon's daytime concerns: the responsible (cf. "entrusted") commander in chief should not fall asleep but ponder his worries and find a solution (=counsel) to the problem of how to protect his threatened army. The opening words of "Nestor" reflect the burden of the dreamer's own conscience. Again, it turns out, divine causation in Homer can take place without overriding the empirical psychology and without abdicating personal responsibility. From the viewpoint of the human level, the divine apparatus appears as a poetic externalization of internal problems (and their wishful solution) – similar to the dialogue between Achilles and Athena which externalizes Achilles' inner conflict.

The double aspect of divine origination and empirical explanation is explicitly discussed in the seventh book of Herodotus' *Histories* on the occasion of another dream apparition, which (according to the commentary of How and Wells) is "modelled after" Agamemnon's dream in *Iliad* 2. At the center of the story is the insecure young king of Persia, Xerxes, subject to conflicting influences from his environment. Following his uncle's, Artabanos', warnings, he gives up his plans of conquering Greece.

Chapter 7

In the nights following the renunciation, he is visited in his sleep by the threatening figure of a man – the reader of the preceding books easily identifies the apparition as the spirit or ambition of Persian expansion, to the historian an example of insatiable (though perhaps fatefully inescapable) greed, unbecoming mortal men.

Frightened, Xerxes seeks his uncle's advice concerning the presumably divine apparition, even asks him to sit on the throne and sleep in the royal bed in the king's place, so Artabanos may see for himself. The uncle is skeptical: "But these things, my boy, are not divine. For the dreams that wander toward men are such as I can instruct you – I, being many years older than you." The empiricist's voice is being heard here, bearing down on his young nephew with the full weight of life-long experience. "Especially these dream visions are in the habit of wandering <toward men>: things one is concerned with during daytime." (τά τις ἡμέρης φροντίζει, 7.16.).Though leaving, on principle, room for truly divine dreams, Artabanos concentrates ("especially these visions") on the kind that amounts to a carry-over of daytime concerns. And Xerxes has recently during daytime been occupied with the campaign against Greece.

So Artabanus is unconcerned, even outlines conditions (not to be explicated in detail here) under which he will acknowledge a divine origin of a dream. When sleeping in the king's bed in the king's clothes, he is visited by the apparition which addresses him as follows: "So you are that man who dissuades Xerxes from campaigning against Greece...?" (etc., 7.17). Screaming loudly, Artabanos jumps up and tells Xerxes to revert to his original plan of campaigning against Greece (7.18).

Even considering the possibility that metaphysical necessity (the apparition mentions τὸ χρεὼν γενέσθαι, 7.17.2) is at work here, it is surprising that empiricist Artabanos should convert himself from a warner to an advocate of the campaign. For, according to his own theory, he should expect his daytime concerns to reappear in his dreams, especially so in the face of the fact that he had in advance pondered the question whether the apparition would or would not address him, too. Considering the catastrophic outcome for Persia of the actual campaign (in anticipation compared by Artabanos to his knowledge of earlier such Persian campaigns ending in disaster which are recounted in the *Histories*), we may adapt and vary what we had to say earlier about Nestor's compliance with Agamemnon's dream: the experienced adviser's skepticism is overcome by, or succumbs to, a non-rational, awe-inspiring impression. In both Homer and Herodotus it would have been wiser for the councillor to stick to his immediate reaction.

As far as the dream in *Aeneid* 7 is concerned, there is no warning adviser who would reverse the original opinion. Here, the warning is authoritatively given by Faunus' oracle (7.96–101), the information (*Fama* 104f., cf.3.121; 7.392) is spread by Latinus (103f.), and it remains immutably valid (though unheeded as in Herodotus and Homer). The change effected is solely on the mind and soul of the main character, from a condition of peaceful sleep to criminal, mad desire for war, *scelerata insania belli* (7.461). This concentration is, of course, not an essential difference from Homer and Herodotus. After all, it is Agamemnon who counts, not Nestor; Xerxes, not Artabanos. What the historian contributes beyond the epicist is the explicitly empirical explanation of dreams given by Artabanos, a theory which is borne out by the author's narrative. Herodotus has made it quite clear in the early parts of the book that young Xerxes is exposed to conflicting influences (Mardonios, the Aleuadai, etc. versus Artabanos), which the reader then recognizes in the young man's nightmarish dreams. In the *Iliad*, we likewise recognized Agamemnon's daytime worries in his dream. But one cannot point to a passage in the epic that would actually pronounce such a theory.

If Herodotus' presentation can be viewed as drawing on that of Homer, then one should also say that, in the section discussed here, the historian has hardly added anything fundamentally new to the concept. Artabanos' theory expressly does allow for occasional divine causation, but, in a skepticism based on long experience, he demands that an empirical explanation be tried first. Thus the double motivation which appears in Homer (Zeus sends the dream; Agamemnon dreams of his daytime worries) is split up into alternatives by Artabanos (though one must say that, for Herodotus himself, metaphysical necessity may simultaneously lurk in the background, here as always (ἐχρῆν γὰρ Κανδαύλῃ γενέσθαι κακῶς, 1.8.2).

Returning, then, from history to epic, one may feel reassured in asserting that the *Iliad*, too, maintains a consistently empiric perspective on Agamemnon's dream (in addition to the divine). Thus our excursus on Herodotus has brought to light no contradicting evidence but supportive parallels only. Moving on to Vergil and back to our original question – namely what the educated reader would think when reading of King Turnus being set upon by Fury Allecto – one may confidently assume that the educated reader as well as the poet was acquainted with Homer's and Herodotus' presentation (in philosophical terms a comparable position, fitting the case of Amata, had, as we saw, more recently been reconfirmed by Cicero, *Fat.* 42f.) and therefore did not expect the victim's responsibility to have been put on hold or held in abeyance. As far as the ancient reader's anticipation is concerned, literary tradition suggests to him that in the dream he will encounter Turnus' very own thoughts in spite of the Fury's intervention. There is no *a priori* reason why the case of Turnus should be structurally different from, say, Amata's wrath or from Ascanius' dogs picking up the scent of the stag (or from Queen Dido's process of falling in love). Empirical causality and psychology can be expected to remain intact.

The preceding sentence may take us back to Turnus' dream and our earlier question whether perhaps "Calybe" alias "Allecto" is part of Turnus himself, a poetic externalization of his troubled condition. A positive answer seems to be suggested by his self-assured response, which indicates that she does not reveal any information to him that he does not know already. Since our excursus has meanwhile shown that the literary tradition favors a psychological interpretation, we should now try to see how far an empirical approach is required for understanding Turnus' dream. If Allecto/Calybe proves to voice thoughts of the dreamer himself, any assumption of heteronomy may have to give way to one of autonomy and moral and religious responsibility. The dream would be the point where Vergil might, as he does in the case of Amata or the native Italians, be engaging the guilty mind (the topic to which Section 2 of this chapter is dedicated): the reader could measure Turnus' character by the way he now reacts to the circumstances set up in the opening scenes of Book 7 (dealt with in Section 1 of this chapter).

> Turnus, are you going to tolerate that so many toils have been wiped out[68]
>   to no purpose,
> and that your kingdom (=scepter) is transferred to Dardanian settlers?
>
> Turne, tot incassum fusos patiere labores,
> et tua Dardaniis transcribi sceptra colonis?   7.421–422

"Calybe's" opening words are very revealing. They seem to indicate that Turnus' military support for Latinus did not primarily spring from kinship obligation or alliance duty but was motivated by the hope of reaching a specific goal. If the hope were to go unfulfilled, his toils would have been "to no purpose", *incassum*. Especially the numeral "so many" (toils) points to a long series of acts which should qualify the doer for the desired reward.

The next line is more to the point. Should "your" kingdom go, in legally valid fashion, to the immigrant? The possessive pronoun "your" makes, objectively speaking, no sense at all for, as far as the reader of Book 7 can determine, Latinus' "sceptre" has never been awarded to Turnus (on the contrary, the old king has stuck strictly to the forbidding oracle his father, Faunus, gave him). "Your" cannot be spoken meaningfully in the perspective of the Fury, either. She can only use this word meaningfully if she wishes to allude to Turnus' own innermost thoughts. "Yours" – or, in his perspective, "mine" – can apply to Latinus' kingdom only as an expression of Turnus' personal hopes and projections – there is no support in the real world for use of the possessive pronoun. The same must be said about the word *transcribere* which refers to legal transfer (assignment). A sceptre which is not legally owned by Turnus cannot be in danger of being legally "made over" (Fordyce) to someone else – except in his imagination: "Legally, this ought to be my kingdom, not to be made over to the Dardanian settler." Pöschl clearly misread Vergil when, from this very line we have been discussing here, he derived Turnus' "*Recht* (*rightful claim*; Pöschl's cursive) auf Lavinia".[69] The "Fury", it turns out, is giving voice to the ambition of Turnus.

The perspective of lines 421–422 is so consistently that of Turnus and his threatened hopes that the opening vocative *Turne* almost functions like the self-address which characterizes a soliloquy. Not dissimilar from the case of Agamemnon ("A general with your worries should not be asleep!"), "Calybe's" words do not even admit any other than an empirical-psychological understanding. They amount to the suggestion that recent developments may cross out the dreamer's longstanding hopes and plans. The simplest explanation of the situation is that dreaming Turnus is on the verge of synthesizing pieces of information which, registered during daytime apart from each other on different occasions, did not appear to pose a threat then. This would also explain why the Fury's appearance has, so far, had nothing formidable about it, quite contrary to Allecto's nature as called upon by Juno. "Calybe" is a familiar person, a longstanding fixture in Turnus' daily life.

> The king continues to deny you the marriage and the dowry
>   sought with your blood,
> and the heir <to succeed> to the kingdom is being sought from abroad.
> Come on now, ridiculed, offer yourself to dangers that go unrewarded –
> go now, scatter down the Etruscan lines, cover the Latins with peace!
>
> rex tibi coniugium et quaesitas sanguine dotes
> abnegat, externusque in regnum quaeritur heres.
> i nunc, ingratis offer te, inrise, periclis;
> Tyrrhenas, i, sterne acies, tege pace Latinos.   7.423–426

The last two lines reveal Turnus' distorted view of his own situation. If he protects the peace of Latinus' kingdom – then Latinus ought to give him the kingdom! If Latinus doesn't, he is ungrateful, and Turnus will be an object of ridicule. It is, of course, Turnus who, by allowing only one form of reward, wrongly and mistakenly classifies himself as ridiculed. There is no objective indication in the epic that Latinus ever slights him (though he may severely reprimand him for his unholy actions, 7.596f.). Still in his address in the twelfth Book, Latinus treats him with greatest respect (*o praestans animi iuvenis,* etc., 12.19f.) – though still then clearly describing his position as that of the suitor not yet rewarded, "you who strive for our daughter and for a connexion with us through marriage" (*natam et conubia nostra petentem*, 12.42). Though a lot has meanwhile changed in Latinus' attitude and behavior toward Aeneas, nothing has changed in the status of Turnus ever since the poet's first words about the eminent suitor at 7.54f.: *multi illam...petebant..., petit ante alios pulcherrimus omnis Turnus...*

Once more we must state that, in pronouncing this line (425), the Fury expresses Turnus' own feelings. Especially *ingratis* and *inrise* fit no one else's perspective, while the sarcasm of *i nunc* shows the potential, not yet realized, of giving up allegiance or even of forcefully asserting his alleged claims or merits.

Lines 423–424 not only document to the reader King Latinus' continued compliance with his father's, Faunus', oracle (7.96–101). In Turnus' thoughts, reflected in Allecto's wording, Latinus' piety is turned into arbitrary, autonomous refusal: *rex...abnegat.* Disregard for divine injunctions comes to light also in the fact that the oracle's wording is being alluded to, but it is twisted. Whereas the oracle spoke of a "son-in-law from abroad" (whose descendants would raise the Latin name to the stars), Allecto, playing on Turnus' ambitions, modifies this to "an *heir* from abroad is being sought for the kingdom". Here she reveals that Turnus' primary motive for desiring Lavinia is the political position (the "dowry", 423) he can earn from the marriage: to become heir to Latinus' throne, (in Servius' understanding) ruler himself by virtue of his marriage. We recall that Latinus' male descendant(s) had died early (a circumstance arranged "by fate of the gods", *fato divum*, 7. 50), and

> alone a daughter was upholding the house and so great a realm,
>
> sola domum et tantas servabat filia sedes   7.52

– a daughter who was, moreover, ready for marriage both as far as physical maturity and as far as her legal age was concerned (7.53). The same result regarding Turnus' motive flows from the words "the dowry sought after with your blood" (7.423; the blood lost through wounds on the battlefield, not the kinship relation is meant here, as 425f. show). His military prowess has been of service to Latinus only as a means of getting closer to the Latin throne.[70]

With *quaeritur* (424), the words *a Latino* must be supplied to define the agent. This once more makes it appear as if Latinus is seeking a son-in-law from abroad at his own, free initiative – a suggestion which is the more impious as it mocks the original wording of the prophecy (*externus*). The dreamer's concern, as addressed by Allecto, is not about a divinely ordered mission and founding of a fated race, but about a possible sell-out concerning the position of prince consort or heir to the throne.

What weighs heaviest when the reader judges Turnus' thoughts is that the oracle is known to him for "Allecto" can play on its wording (*externus*). In his own soul now we find confirmed what we concluded when asking why Vergil let the old king spread far and wide the oracle which he had heard in "silent night" (7.103–105): Turnus knew before Aeneas' arrival in Italy that Lavinia was destined not to become his wife. Nonetheless, he did not care to heed the divine voice so as to scale back his political ambition: his decision was made long before the dream.

The importance we ascribed, when investigating the "logic of circumstances", to the spreading of the oracle "through the Ausonian cities" (7. 104f.), has now been confirmed. Turnus, too, received that information then; that is why a mockery or parody of the prophecy can now be offered to him to appeal to (and raise the heat of) his feelings.

For the interpreter, a slightly different conclusion is perhaps even more relevant. The Fury is trying to incite Turnus to action by making him recall a piece of information he received (as the reader is able to verify) a considerable time before the present dream. This definitely makes "Allecto" an extraverted poetic presentation of Turnus' personal concerns. The fact that Vergil saw to it (7.103–105) that attentive readers would be aware of the empirical way in which the information was acquired, even prevents them from understanding the dream, too, in any other but an empirical way. It is only short-distance readers (like Pöschl or Thomas) who will, while starting from "the scene in which Turnus appears for the first time", tend to see here an innocent victim being overwhelmed by a force outside himself.

On the other hand, some may ask why Vergil makes it so complex – almost misleading is the impression created by the appearance of the Fury – for his reader to get to the bottom of Turnus' impious soul? Perhaps he wanted to give those who in the first place wanted to find a positive picture of Italian "patriotism" without going into the moral details a chance to see their hope fulfilled (after all, he is not very open or obtrusive either when describing the Trojan contribution to the outbreak of hostilities, as we saw). This would perhaps keep the naive Italian reader from feeling antagonized by an *a priori* sacrilegious Turnus. The fact, however, that the information was received in waking life before the dream (a feature immediately to be repeated as we shall see, and therefore undoubtable), together with the other fact that Allecto's language depicts Turnus' own feelings, leaves no doubt that we are dealing with empirical, not merely

Chapter 7

mythical psychology. At the same time, the poet's artistic desire is being served: to observe (but at the same time utilize for his own agenda) epic convention as offered by his greatest model, Homer.

From the conditions of the dream, one can even determine the amount of information so far available to Turnus. If the "heir" from abroad is still "being sought" (*quaeritur*, 424), then the right son-in-law has apparently not yet been found; if Latinus is still seen to "deny" (*abnegat*, 424) the marriage, then the possibility of marriage must still be open, no decision must yet have taken place. Taking this together with the narrative statement that Turnus

> was already enjoying deep rest in black night,
>
> iam mediam nigra carpebat nocte quietem,   7.414

i.e., is not troubled by any disquieting information, we can see that he (or "Allecto") is unaware of the latest development at Latinus' city (a development which has driven Amata to disobedience already), viz. that the king has meanwhile officially committed his daughter to Aeneas, in whom he has recognized the prophesied "son-in-law from abroad" (7.268ff.). *The speaking Fury, as far as the state of her information is concerned, does not exceed the knowledge available to her victim* – another clear indication that "Allecto" stands for Turnus himself.[71] (Even Juno at this point hardly knows more, 7.333f.) The confinement of "Allecto" to Turnus' state of mind (and of information) even leads to a break in the character of Allecto: though coming right from Latinus' city, *after* (*postquam*, 406) creating havoc there, she reveals nothing whatsoever to Turnus about the disturbances already effected – though her presumable goal of inciting Turnus to action could be reached much faster by letting him know right away that meanwhile Latinus personally has offered Lavinia to Aeneas.

Up to line 7.426, the "Fury" has employed sarcasm to impress on Turnus the idea that his loyalty toward King Latinus has not paid off; i.e., we see doubts being sown in Turnus' mind about the appropriateness of the course he has been following so far. What is needed next is that these doubts (and the new course of action resulting from their acceptance) be dressed in the garb of legitimacy. This is done, climactically, in two steps. In the first, "Calybe" ascribes her appearance before, and message for, sleeping Turnus to the "orders" (*iussit*) of the "all-powerful (*omnipotens*) daughter of Saturn" (428). Of course, there is no way that Juno may objectively be called "all-powerful". But, if she were, Turnus would be justified in changing his course – justified since being ordered by unlimited heavenly power, and, consequently, free from religious guilt. The *epitheton ornans* is used poignantly. The second step: after ordering (429–431) the deadly attack on

Aeneas and his boats, and before exhorting (432b–434) Turnus to confront Latinus, "Calybe" claims "The great power of the gods orders this", *caelestum vis magna iubet* (432a) – thus suggesting even a heavenly consensus!

In the *Iliad*, too, "false Dream" claimed a consensus: allegedly, Hera (Juno's Greek counterpart) had won over all the other gods to her anti-Trojan position, so they all would favor Agamemnon's cause. But behind similar appearances a fundamental discrepancy is revealed: the dream's promise, if fulfilled, would lead Agamemnon to military victory and personal rehabilitation; for Turnus, the dream's fulfillment would result not only in gratification of his desires but, beyond that, in a breach of loyalty and disobedience towards clearly expressed divine will (Agamemnon does not know that taking Troy this very day would violate Zeus' will). A matter of (im)prudence and damaging consequences in Homer, in Vergil the dreaming king's behavior, viewed objectively, involves the question of moral and religious responsibility.

Turnus' mind, however, does not respond to objective religious and moral requirements, but to the relative immediacy of impending loss as perceived by him. If his interests should be threatened and active interference would help them, then the alleged divine consensus would offer a (to the reader, specious) moral and religious justification of action. So far, however, he does not yet feel pushed to take that last step.

Before closing in on Turnus' reaction, let us briefly recapitulate that the course of action suggested by Juno through Calybe is twofold:

(A) Turnus is to arm (*armari*, 7.429) himself and his Rutulians and to lead them into the field (*in arva*, 430), and to burn Aeneas and his fleet. Even this seemingly factual order (we are now in a position to add) contains allusions to Turnus' state of mind and, thus, is revealed to be a poetic externalization: *laetus*, "happy" (430), appeals to Turnus' delight in fighting (or even to the fulfillment of his hopes through war), while the attribute *pulchro*, "beautiful", of the river "on which the Phrygian leader has settled" (430f.), reveals an emotional bond of the young Rutulian king to the landscape of the Tiber. Here we find the compositional reference to line 30 in the section 7.25–35. As Aeneas (without knowing that he had reached the end of his travels) felt attracted by the natural beauty of the landscape and therefore ordered his companions to enter the river, so Turnus is open and attached to the river's beauty. Again "Allecto" is found to play on the Rutulian's own feelings.

(B) May King Latinus himself,
if he does not agree to granting [you] the marriage and to
obey your word,
feel and finally experience Turnus in arms!

Chapter 7

> rex ipse Latinus,
> ni dare coniugium et dicto parere fatetur,
> sentiat et tandem Turnum experiatur in armis.   7.432–434

The lines just quoted have (apart from the difficulty offered by *fatetur*, for which see Fordyce *ad loc.*) suffered from the general misunderstanding of Turnus' status in the *Aeneid*. Assuming that Vergil pictures (which he doesn't, as we documented earlier) Turnus as betrothed to Lavinia, Heyne in his commentary took *dicto parere* as "keep his promise" (*promisso stare*), thus saddling King Latinus with a moral flaw and supplying Turnus with the kind of "rightful claim on Lavinia" which Pöschl and others believed they found. It is surprising how the rules of correct Latin can occasionally be overruled in favor of a preconceived interpretation.

The phrase *dicto parere* (7.433; cf. *dicta dedit*, 471), stronger than "agreement" (Horsfall *ad loc.*, translates "declare he heeds your bidding") in the *Aeneid* usually indicates the situation where a subordinate follows the request pronounced just previously by a higher-ranking character (Latinus and his ambassador Venulus, 11. 242; Venus and her son Cupid, 1. 689; 695). The wording at 7. 433 implies that King Turnus in the hypothetical encounter would, for the first time, assume the role of superior toward the Latin King. The *dictum* Turnus would order him to obey is contained in *dare coniugium* (in direct speech: *da mihi coniugium*).

To (A) war against Aeneas (*armari*, etc., 429f.), the Fury adds (B) war against Latinus (*in armis*, 434) as her second suggestion. Once more again, this suggestion lays bare Turnus' unholy plan to marry a maiden who is divinely destined for another, divinely fated, suitor and so become himself the forefather of the ruling dynasty. Beyond this, the fact that the suggestion originates in Turnus' own soul (rather than in "Calybe's" scheme) is revealed by the word "finally" (*tandem*, 434). The Fury has no reason to say "finally". It is Turnus not she who has been waiting for a long time to receive Lavinia's hand from her father, and it is Turnus whose patience may "finally" come to an end and be replaced by the urgency of an ultimatum. "Finally" also means that the Rutulian king has by now waited long enough and, so, earned the right to state his claim in terms befitting a man of action. No doubt, "Calybe" again stands for Turnus himself.

Turnus' reaction is, we said, not one of piety or obedience, but reflects his personal sense of urgency. At present, he does not see any reason to be concerned: "Don't make up fears so great for me", *ne tantos mihi finge metus* (438). "And Queen Juno has not forgotten me", *nec regia Juno immemor est nostri* (438f.) – the latter sentence meaning that his options (including the one to fight) are still open. The "fears so great", of course, result from implications of "Calybe's" speech: the oracle about the foreign son-in-law (alluded to

418

in 424) could be fulfilled by the arrival (alluded to in 422) of the "Dardanian settlers": in that case Turnus would be deprived of his innermost hopes.

But Turnus at present remains cool to Calybe's suggestion: "The news that a fleet has entered the waters of the Tiber has not, as you believe, escaped my ears." The possibility of an agreement between Latinus and Aeneas (which actually has taken place already, culminating in Latinus' offer of Lavinia's hand, 7.268ff.) seems so far-fetched to the Rutulian that, when the idea is presented, he ridicules the divine messenger, as we saw, as senile and deluded by false fear, *falsa...formidine* (442, with *vatem* forebodingly interposed between these two words, as we observed): the danger addressed by "Calybe" is not real in the eyes of Turnus. He could not be more mistaken, of course.

The option of war or peace is, he feels, completely his:

Men will take care of wars and peace – men by whom war must be handled.

bella viri pacemque gerent quis bella gerenda.   7.444

What is the basis of Turnus' self-certainty? His hint to Calybe that she has not given him any news makes us recall our earlier investigation into the possibly empirical character of dreams in epic. With empirical psychology meanwhile proven intact both in Homer and in Vergil, we are now prepared to deal with the more specific question: when did Turnus receive the news of the Trojans' arrival which he holds up to Calybe? If the point of time can be fixed, one gains further proof of Allecto's empirical character.

At this point, we can draw on the preparatory excursus on Vergil's geography. Our question, when investigating the set-up of circumstances, was: "Why would the poet be so detailed...in reporting a seemingly subordinate undertaking?" The undertaking in question was that Aeneas, upon landing, was said to send out scouting parties in three different directions (*diversa*, 7.132; *diversi*, 7.150) but then (*tum*, 152) to utilize only the contacts made by one of them, viz. by sending an embassy to King Latinus. The result of our detailed geographical investigation was "that in lines 130–151 Vergil has established a first contact between Aeneas' men and Rutulians ruled by Turnus (as well as with subjects of King Latinus)", and, referring to Vergil's systematic way of writing, we then stated that, "as in the case of Latinus divulging the oracle (7.103f.), so this contact will come into play later on", etc.

For the reader willing to follow patiently Vergil's long-range composition (instead of focusing only on Turnus' first appearance in Book 7) the reference is highly rewarding. It shows that the dreamer's dismissal of Calybe's information as old hat does indeed go back to waking life. In other words, one may understand that in his dream Turnus considers the possibly damaging implications of earlier daytime information but rejects the implications as unfounded. Consequently, he can likewise reject the course of action (A: war against Aeneas; B: war against Latinus) that would result if those implications were to appear cogent. All this is purely combinatory guesswork taking place in the mind of (dreaming) Turnus, uninformed of recent events in the real world (which would prove "Calybe" true).

Up to this point (7.444), then, the possibilities outlined in the dream remain mere possibilities and do not pose a threat to be taken seriously. In agreement with the benign outcome of Calybe's presentation is the introductory description of Allecto "taking off" (*exuit*, 416) her "grim shape and limbs of a Fury" *(torvam faciem et furialia membra*, 415), "transforming herself" (*sese transformat*, 416) into the familiar character of the old priestess. We may compare the development so far to what we called "stage I" in Amata's rage where she, until turned down in the conversation with her husband, stayed well within the bounds set for the behavior of a *matrona* (*solito matrum de more locuta est*, 357).

It is only consistent that, the moment the dreamer comes to accept a conclusion different from his first, relaxed response, Allecto should throw off the guise of Calybe and reveal herself as the Fury she is: angry about Turnus' condescending words (*Talibus Allecto dictis exarsit in iras*, 445), she hisses, erects two snakes in her hair, cracks her whip, etc. But by now we can see in her hardly more than an allegory of Turnus' rising fury, especially when watching the change *he* undergoes:

> But a sudden trembling seized the young man's limbs while he was
>
>   still speaking:
> his eyes turned stiff.
>
> at iuveni oranti subitus tremor occupat artus,
> deriguere oculi: 7.446f.

His trembling is the first expression that the fear he refused to accept before (*metus*, 438) is getting hold of him: soon (*pavor*, 458) it will overwhelm him.

In terms of empirical psychology, Allecto revealing her true shape amounts to the dreamer being enraged when putting two and two together, so to speak: "What if this combination *were* correct?", "What if the 'son-in-law from abroad' (424), object of the prophecy which Latinus disseminated (7.103ff.), and the Trojan leader (430f.) with whose scouts some of my people had oral contact (7.150) are identical?" That this *is*, after all, the correct interpretation can be seen from an accompanying feature. The Fury exercises her full force and pushes Turnus back "while he is still hesitating and seeking to say more", *cunctantem et quaerentem dicere plura* (449) – "more" can only be in the vein of his preceding refusal of her message: as she cut him off from speaking (*oranti*, 446), so now he resists (cf. *cunctantem*), in vain, the conclusion that would state his loss – the blow dealt him behind his back. The sudden (*subitus*, 446) change of his condition, highlighted by the onslaught of fear, is inescapable.

It is with splendid consistency that Vergil now (452f.) makes Calybe ironically throw back in Turnus' face his own words (440; 442) about her presumed senility and the "false fear" raised by her: for the danger she outlined then is no longer unreal to him – and, therefore, the option of peace on which he had insisted (*bella viri pacemque gerent quis bella gerenda*, 444) is no longer open.

> In my hand, I carry war – and death.
>
> bella manu letumque gero.   7.455

Death (*letum*, 455) has taken the place of peace (*pacem*, 444): this is one of those half-lines in the epic to the precision of which no meaningful addition can be imagined.

With these words, the Fury "hurled her firebrand at the young man and fixed the torches deep in his chest" (456f.): an action which if taken literally, is as hard to picture as the Fury transforming herself into Amata's necklace and ribbon (7.351ff.). But the corresponding development of the dreamer, added by asyndeton, is only too well within human experience: immense fear wakes him from his nightmare, his body sweating all over (458f.). The fear, *pavor* (458), of course is the actualization of that possibility of fear (*metus*, 438) which he earlier pushed away in so imperious a fashion. The sleep, *somnum* (458), now interrupted, is the same "middle of his rest" which he enjoyed "in black night" (414) at the time of Allecto-Calybe's appearance (415ff.). Beginning and end clearly mark the intervening episode as one of sleeping and dreaming, thus setting the frame for a possibly empirical understanding of the dreamer's thought processes. Similar to, but more complex than Agamemnon in *Iliad* 2, Turnus asleep has continued to process daytime information. The set-up leads us to the same result as the content.

His first waking action is that he, out of his mind (*amens*), calls for arms and searches for arms all over the house.

> There rages the love of iron and the criminal, insane lust for war
>   – and wrath in addition.
>
> saevit amor ferri et scelerata insania belli,
> ira super.   7.461f.

Turnus loves to fight anyway; and his wrath (programmatically introducing the Homeric feature of the *alius...Achilles*, 6.89) is easily explained: he is more than upset because, as he has (correctly) concluded in his dream, Latinus has obeyed the oracle and offered Lavinia to Aeneas behind his back. It is the third feature, the "criminal" (or "impious") "insanity of his desire for war", which contains the moral condemnation pronounced by the author. This straightforward negative characteristic follows both from Turnus' earlier conduct (against Faunus' well-published prophecy, he continued to maintain a claim on Lavinia and, i.e., the Latin throne) and from his willingness even to fight if pious Latinus should adhere to the oracle and, consequently, should disregard his wishes. His initial hesitancy toward "Calybe's" advice did not at all (we saw) result from pious observance of divine will but from two related components: on the one hand, he did not yet see any real threats to his interests, and, on the other, he was understandably not eager to face the sudden loss of his political hopes.

The unambiguous verdict of Turnus' moral and religious shortcomings (7.462) prevents us from accepting Pöschl's (and his followers') idea of "the innocence of his guilt" or to see, again like Pöschl, a tragic feature indicated by the ensuing (7.462b–466) simile which compares Turnus' rage to boiling water that leaves a cauldron in the form of steam. In whichever way the details are taken (to this interpreter, the simile seems best to fit Turnus' second reaction, leading up to the full outbreak of his so far latent rage), there is no way of deriving from the simile a moral tone different from the one pronounced in the direct description (458–462a) of his rage that precedes and is illustrated by the simile, or from the following description which seems to take (*ergo*, 467) the boiling over as the first step toward war, "under pollution of the peace."[72]

Turnus now does pick up "Calybe's" advice in both of the parts (denoted A [cf. 430] and B [cf. 434] by us before):

he was coming (he said), a match for both Trojans and Latins.

se satis ambobus Teucrisque venire Latinisque   7.470

So there is no doubt about his hostile intentions (*iuvenum* and *arma parari*, 468, refer back to *armari* and *pubem*, 429) when he announces the march "to King Latinus", *ad regem...Latinum*, "under pollution of the peace", *polluta pace* (467). This translation is more appropriate than "now that peace had been violated". Williams *ad loc.* takes the words as pointing to "the serene state of peace that existed", now defiled by Allecto's poison. But, after the detailed description (460f.) of Turnus' criminal lust for war, it would make no sense to exculpate him now when he is setting out on his war, by pointing back to Amata's rebellious acts. Above all, an important part of Allecto's action is still to come: the clash between Trojans and local shepherds, resulting in the deaths of Almo, Galaesus and others (7.532; 535; cf. 375).

It is true, the peace violated may seem to be the peace of the land, between Latins and Rutulians. But it is hard to see why Vergil would speak of a "peace" between Turnus and Latinus if, in his account, there never had been a hint of a possible political disagreement between the two before. And the peace in question cannot be the peace of the Latins either, which Turnus has so far guaranteed by giving them protection (426). The most plausible assumption is that Vergil wants his reader to think of the peace that had come about, in agreement with the fated future, between King Latinus and Aeneas' ambassadors (*pacemque reportant*, 285, *pacemque exposcere Teucris*, 155; cf. *pacis*, 266). It is this peace which Juno wanted to be destroyed by Allecto and replaced by war:

disice compositam pacem, sere crimina belli   7.339

Turnus' *scelerata insania belli* (on the mythical level instigated by Juno's hellish helper) is aiming at both Latinus (to make him either comply with Turnus' ambitious wishes, 433, or to conquer him, 434) and at Aeneas (with Latinus either obeying and joining Turnus or, if not obeying – *parere*, 433 – forcefully eliminated). Therefore, the religious term *polluta* in *polluta pace* well fits the violation of the holy peace entered by oracle-conscious Ilioneus and pious Latinus. In this way, the campaign of the Rutulian young army can be seen to fulfill also the specific instruction given by Juno to Allecto:

Let the (native) young crew desire, demand and simultaneously seize arms!

arma velit poscatque simul rapiatque iuventus!   7.340

The distorted viewpoint of Turnus is revealed in his order (469) "to protect Italy", "to drive the enemy from the territory". To Vergil's reader, Aeneas and his men have been introduced as a blessing for Italy, not an "enemy"! Even if Turnus should really think of Aeneas as an enemy rather than a rival for (or obstacle to) his personal ambition, he does so in contradiction of the divine voice, i.e., by willfully reinterpreting the given situation. His invocation of (and promises to) the gods after giving his orders (*divosque in vota vocavit*, 471) means that he is misleading his troops: against their country's destiny, they are serving the cause of a personal vendetta. It is significant that the motives of his followers (473f.) are stated as admiration of Turnus' beauty and youth, of his royal forebears, of his military deeds: not one, it turns out, is attracted to him by features such as "justice" or "piety" – features on which Aeneas' authority is, in Vergil's account, based *par excellence*.

Thus the investigation into Turnus' nightmare (as well as into Agamemnon's dream and Artabanos' dream theory) has led us to the same conclusion we were forced to draw in Section 1 of this chapter, when we compared Vergil's timing of events with different versions found in other authors. By design, Vergil denies Aeneas' adversary any chance of being innocent. Whether asleep or awake, Turnus pursues his personal ambition, indifferent to considerations concerning pious obedience, the fate of his misled people, violation of peace. Under the appealing surface of youthful impetuousness and military valour, the criminalization of the political opponent is as consistent and pervasive as is the demoralization ascribed and attached to Dido, symbol of the country's enemy, and as is the elevation of the ruling family, be it in mythical times or in the author's own period.

In a brief summary, we can now answer the question why at all Vergil introduces Allecto if she does not transcend empirically verifiable causality, either in the case of Turnus or in those of Amata and Ascanius' dogs. One, important, reason was revealed in his imitation of his model Homer, who liked to dress mental processes in the garb of a conversation between human and superhuman. This is a sufficient reason, considering Vergil's artistic goals.

But there is another dimension, too. Already in Book 4 we saw that Juno (and with her, Venus) does not exercise power over Dido before she has herself fallen from her own ideal of *pudor* (4.91; cf. 27 and 55). On the other hand, Juno's interference serves as a clear signpost to the reader: now the forces hostile to Aeneas and his family's historic destiny are taking over again. The presence of Juno makes it easy for less sophisticated readers to classify the strand(s) of action initiated under her guidance as hostile to the world order of Fate and Jupiter, so they cannot go amiss in interpreting the events and details at hand.

Beyond the help in classifying phenomena of the narrative, the mythical figures of Juno and Allecto may offer some readers a chance to accept the contents of the *Aeneid* with greater ease. I mean those who, while not penetrating the epic's fine print of moral and religious judgement and motivation, may find it easier to picture "their" Italian hero Turnus overwhelmed and subjected by a seemingly irresistible supra-human force. Until our own day, a wide audience, by reading the epic in this way, has found it palatable.

Throughout Book 7 the strands of moral white and black (when unraveled from their poetic wrapping) have been attributed so consistently that, once the reader traces them, there is no contradiction with the poet's well-known comments on the final gathering of Aeneas' opponents at

Latinus' court. After Allecto has worked on three different parties, Juno dismisses her and takes on herself the final task of forcing open the Gates of War (7.601–622, dealt with earlier in this chapter).

On this occasion, three different parties have combined to exercise pressure on King Latinus. The parties are: (1) the (male) relatives of the women who were led into the mountains by Amata (580f.); (2) the fighting shepherds (573f.; with them, they have the corpses of the men who became victims of the Trojans' first strike: young Almo, eldest son of Tyrrhus, and justest of all, elderly Galaesus, struck – as we learn now – in the face by the Trojans when trying to mediate for peace, *paci*, 7.535f.); and, of course, exploiting the explosive situation, there is (3) Turnus:

> Turnus was there, and, in the middle of the passion and the charges
> of homicide,
> redoubled the terror: the Trojans (he said) were being invited to
> (participate in) the kingdom,
> the Phrygian race being mixed (with the Latin): he was being driven
> from the threshold.

> Turnus adest medioque in crimine caedis et igni
> terrorem ingeminat: Teucros in regna vocari,
> stirpem admisceri Phrygiam, se limine pelli.   7.577–579

Again one can see that, in mentioning once more the ugly killings of Almo and Galaesus, Vergil does not suppress the Trojan share in the outbreak of the initial hostilities (though he does not emphasize it either). These deaths, occurring (as we saw earlier) when confrontation seemed no longer avoidable and in the absence of Aeneas, are surely deplorable also in the narrator's perspective. But to use them to reinforce the inspiration of terror and to build up the opposition to the fulfillment of Faunus' oracle is a heinous sin which the author will soon characterize as such (596f.). Moreover, the three lines about Turnus quoted above end on a climactic note: upon fanning the passions and presenting the fated events (the Trojans' arrival; their admission to the Latin blood) as a calamity for the land, he finally reveals his most urgent motive (it is the same as before, in the dream): *he* would lose the prospect of himself filling the vacuum on the throne.

That he feels he is driven from the "threshold", *limine*, does not so much point to "the threshold as symbol of welcome and friendship" (Williams *ad loc.*) but to its function of offering entry into the royal house. The persistent suitor is turned away while having (he feels) one foot almost in the door. The term "threshold" goes well with the preceding narrative in which Latinus was shown to have made no concessions at all about his daughter to any suitor.

In making the loss of his own political prospects the high point of his speech, Turnus confirms what his earlier slogan of "protecting Italy" (scil., against the Trojan "enemy", 7.469) suggested. The war which is going to start under his leadership is Turnus' private war for his personal ambition, with no consideration of the possible cost in blood and sorrow to his misled people. In our second chapter, we have already dealt with the voices of the widows and orphans who, later on, will curse Turnus and his war (11.215–219; in the words of Drances, 362f.: *pacem te poscimus omnes, Turne...miserere tuorum*; at 361, Drances addresses him as *causa malorum*).

Strict observation of the text, then, takes us much closer to those earlier interpretations which saw in Turnus the enemy of his own country than to the more or less innocent victim of the Fury recent decades (and methodologies) have predominantly claimed he is. Vergil's success in guiding an un-preoccupied (and attentive) reader is the more striking as naturally the sympathies of an audience would favor the natives when they, feeling threatened, close ranks, but not the foreigner whose men caused the first deaths in the initial confrontation. Thus some may find 'interpretations' appealing which view Aeneas' party as destroyers of a bucolic peace. Vergil's reasoning, however, inescapably runs in the opposite direction: the crime lies with him who violates the divinely ordered peace that had just come about between King Aeneas and King Latinus. Though the last sentence may seem applicable to the Trojans also (who launched the first strike), it must be recalled from the structure of Book 7 that this was a skirmish on a low level, unauthorized by any leader. The question of responsibility arises when a leading figure utilizes the situation to start a full-scale war. The two aspects are kept well apart in the composition of the narrative.

The consequences for a view of the epic as *Menschheitsdichtung*, "mankind poetry" (or, perhaps, "poetry of the human condition") are dire. Here is a work of art which chooses to represent the political opponent as an uninhibited egotist devoid of ethical and religious responsibility and, on the other hand, heaps human virtue and sensitivity as well as the unearthly glow of Providence on its main hero. The hero's predominant function (as the oracles keep telling) is to found the world-dominating line from which the author's present-day ruler has sprung (Book 7 is especially rich in references to, and its editorial viewpoint is firmly planted in, the time of Emperor Augustus: 3; 92; 412; 602–615; 616; 643). Such a work, far from opening the eyes of its audience to the concerns and basic situation of humanity in general, by its clever design tends to limit the reader's human sympathy to the party-in-power (or: 'destined'-for-power), while raising moral disdain for the political adversary to an accepted and un-reflected practice. The power of poetry over the reader's soul has, like rhetoric before it, been firmly pressed into serving one political party, *i.e.*, the party that rose victorious from the murderous recent civil war. If Vergil is declared a *Menschheitsdichter*, the term "Mensch" will have to be reserved for, restricted to, the ruling class and its adherents.

The political bias is (at least for the part of the modern audience aware of, and prepared to acknowledge, the fact that there is a bias) again placed and hidden under the protective umbrella of objectifying religion when the three groups of Aeneas' opponents in Latinus' city are censured in an editorial intervention:

> At once they all demand the unspeakable war – against the portents,
> against destiny, under perversion of the will of the gods.

> ilicet infandum cuncti contra omina bellum,
> contra fata, deum converso numine poscunt. 7.583f.

Latinus alone withstands the crowd's demands and is compared to the unmoved rock beaten by the surf (586–590). But since he lacks the "power to overcome the blind [i.e., un-illuminated by the portents and by Faunus' oracle] intention" and things go Juno's way, he feels "broken by fate" (*fatis*, 594 – as if he surmises that fate has set war before Aeneas' success). He threatens the offenders, especially their leader Turnus. His people, misled rather than actively guilty, receive his compassion – *o miseri* – rather as the author in his own voice deplores the coming destruction of the Italians before Aeneas' onslaught in a simile which pities the "poor farmers", *miseris agricolis*, sensing the coming storm (12.452f.), or as Aeneas deplores the deaths the war will inflict on his opponent's people, *miseris...Laurentibus* (8.537). Pity for the suffering adversary is another human quality the author's design reserves for those who follow the oracles. In vain one will search for such generous sympathy in Turnus and his associates.

> You yourselves will pay with your accursed (sacrilegious) blood the penalty
>   for this outrage,
> you poor ones. But for you, Turnus, (o shameful event!) for you
> the grim death penalty will be waiting, and too late you will worship
>   the gods with prayers.

> ipsi has sacrilego pendetis sanguine poenas,
> o miseri. Te, Turne (nefas!) te triste manebit
> supplicium, votisque deos venerabere seris. 7.595–597

Clearly the mouthpiece of the author (cf. 7. 583f.), Latinus gives the same verdict which the attentive reader of Book 7 must arrive at. Religious (*sacrilego*; *nefas*) and judicial (*poenas*; *supplicium*) terminology gives Latinus' words the high rank of a dire prophecy, easily understood (and accepted) by the reader because of the king's pious ways and priestly function. In the opening section of Chapter I, it was explained how Turnus' behavior makes the death blow from Aeneas' hand look not only deserved but required (in terms of the author's concept, of course). The present chapter has confirmed in detail that the criminal and sacrilegious aspect of his mindset is a given, right from the outset. To restate the point: already in Book 7 Turnus displays a conduct which, in religious terms, merits (requires) the death blow he receives at the end of Book 12.

As far as our overall interpretation is concerned, the earliest of the four strands that lead up to the death of Turnus offers an important antecedent to the picture of the Rutulian King as it is painted in later books (as previewed in the opening chapter). By no means should he be seen as someone who has incurred guilt unwittingly, along the path of war, perhaps while being carried away in the heat of battle to commit atrocities (as, for instance, carrying around on his chariot the cut-off heads of his enemies, 12.511f.). Our third and fourth chapters already revealed the extent to which he proceeded deliberately in reserving for himself, and killing, the young warrior son of Evander for the vengeful purpose of teaching the aged king a lesson by causing him pain. Book 7 demonstrates that criminal and sacrilegious behavior is ingrained in Turnus, that he is guilty from the very beginning, an original sinner.

This result rules out the element of chance in his career. All the instances of less than heroic conduct in Books 7 to 12 are part of a particular personal pattern. It does not help modern defenders of Turnus if one (unsuccessfully, in the eyes of this interpreter) tries to doubt or defuse one or another later case, since a crime deserving the death penalty can be observed already in the Roman *Iliad*'s opening episode. A wide arc (reinforced along the way by further occurrences of impious and less than honorable behavior) reaches from King Latinus' curse in Book 7 to Turnus' execution in Book 12. This far-extending arc is most important for the interpreter when verifying Vergil's concept of Turnus. In turning against the *Aeneadae* (and inciting the Italians to follow him), and especially, in doing so in spite of the oracles, Turnus (in this respect like his tutelary goddess, cf. 1.17–23) *knowingly* infringes upon the metaphysical idea expressed in the *Aeneid*.

So there can hardly be any doubt that, in confronting the divinely ordained course of history, Turnus is guilty in an even higher sense than when, later on, killing Pallas or evading the contracted duel. He also is more guilty than Dido. She did not know (except from what she had heard when Aeneas spoke of the oracles and portents that guided his travels) that she was trying to obstruct the course of fate – however much she tried to force the gods' hands in repeating the sacrifices for a better outcome (4.63). What she intended to gain, after all, was to find gratification of her personal love, an essentially private desire (though not without consequences for her public image and for her city). Turnus tried to usurp a public position which (he knew, 424) was being kept vacant for the carrier of a divine mission.

Our opening chapter outlined four strands in the second half of the epic which all come together (and individually result) in the death of Turnus as it is narrated in the work's final scene. At that time, we addressed, but did not investigate in detail, the fourth (i.e., on the epic's time line, the earliest).

Now, after following Vergil into the depths of Turnus' impious soul, it can be stated that the reader experiences the strongest accusation against the Rutulian king first. Throughout Books 8–12, the reader will expect the death of Turnus, according to Latinus' dire words *te Turne, (nefas!) te triste manebit supplicium,* "for you, Turnus, (o shameful event!), for you the grim death penalty will be waiting!" (7.596f.).

Already before the climax of the fourth strand, the aged king's prediction to his people,

> you yourselves will pay the penalty for this with your sacrilegious blood,
>
> ipsi has sacrilego pendetis sanguine poenas   7.595

has come true in the devastating crescendo of the last two Books. Now, when at the very end of the work Aeneas, in avenging the death of Pallas, executes the duty solemnly imposed on him by Pallas' father (11. 177–81) and pronounces that "Pallas...is exacting the penalty from your criminal blood", *poenam scelerato ex sanguine sumit* (12.949), the observant reader realizes that simultaneously those dire prophetic words of Latinus,

> for you, Turnus (o shameful event!), for you the
> grim death penalty will be waiting,
> and too late you will worship the gods with prayers
>
> te Turne, (nefas!) te triste manebit
> supplicium, votisque deos venerabere seris.   (7.596f.)

have also found their fulfillment. Only Juno, who slyly tries to argue that Turnus' piety was established by his earlier offerings to Jupiter (10.620), could propose that Turnus might "pay the penalty with *pious* blood", *pio det sanguine poenas,* 10.617. But her subjective, egotistic perspective has from the opening (1.16–33; 46–49) been set in counterpoint to the plans of fate which the poet's voice advocates throughout.

Turnus himself, on the other hand, is obviously aware of those dire consequences predicted by the old king: he invokes the Shades (*Manes*), "since the disposition of the gods above is hostile towards me", *quoniam superis aversa voluntas* (12. 647). This insight into his doomed condition has been with him long before he experiences the terrible Dira (914) which (in the narrator's voice) is dispatched "whenever the king of the gods sends horrible death...or frightens *guilty* cities with war", *si quando letum horrificum ...deum rex molitur, <u>meritas</u> aut bello territat urbes* (12. 849f.). When he finally faces Aeneas and no longer runs away, Turnus' reply to his challenger again acknowledges his condition :

> It is the gods that terrify me, and (especially)
> Jupiter who is my enemy.
>
> di me terrent et Jupiter hostis.   12.895

Vergil must have felt it necessary that Aeneas' opponent, besides being a treaty-breaker and a less than heroic killer on the battlefield, also be presented as conscious to the end that his actions violated the grander scheme of Destiny (which is already revealed to the audience early on by Jupiter, Destiny's speaker [1. 261f.] and overlord [1. 278f.]), in short: that in opposing Aeneas, the proto-Julian, Turnus was guilty, and guilty beyond the secular sphere. By contrast, the inquiring reader may gauge the blessing that the arrival and leadership of the Julian ancestor meant for the nations of Ausonia. Again one comprehends that (and why) Augustus ordered the work to be published, even posthumously and without the finishing touches being applied by the poet himself.

Notes

[1] "Die Szene, in der Turnus zum ersten Male auftritt" (1964 2nd ed., 168 = 1973, 122. The first edition appeared in 1950). These are the opening words of Pöschl's chapter on Turnus, still echoed, in unfortunate methodological continuity, decades later by Schenk (1984, 27) when he opens his detailed investigation (aiming to refute Pöschl's thesis of a "tragic" Turnus): "Die erste Szene, in der Turnus mit einer göttlichen Macht konfrontiert wird, is die Allecto-Szene im 7. Buch (406–474)." Schenk, however, later on does include in his considerations earlier sections of Book 7 (see, e.g., pp. 370ff.). In comparable fashion, Renger (1985; she, too, wishes to modify Pöschl's thesis) still fails to exploit fully the opening narrative of Book 7 for interpreting Turnus' dream (see especially pp. 22f.; 37; 43).

[2] op. cit. 1964, 172 = 1977, 124.

[3] Hornsby 1970, 137; cf. 136.

[4] The repetition at 105 reinforces our understanding at 39, where the customary translation of the juxtaposition *cum primum*, "as soon as", is inappropriate, while "the moment when" would be at least ambiguous; "when first", "the first time that", even "when originally" all cover a meaning that allows the condition or action addressed by the main clause to exist or take place simultaneously with, or even to have begun before, the action described in the *cum* clause.

That is, specifically, the *cum primum* clause in such cases does not necessarily depict an action that is (totally or partially) antecedent to the content of the main clause. Cf. Ter. *An.* 1–4:

> Poeta quom primum animum ad scribendum adpulit,
> id sibi negoti credidit solum dari,
> populo ut placerent quas fecisset fabulas.
> verum aliter evenire multo intellegit;

Here the juxtaposition *quom primum* is employed, *mutatis mutandis*, comparably to the well-known use of single *cum* in, e.g., *non tum cum emisti fundum Tusculanum, in leporario apri fuerunt* (Varro, *R. R.* 3.3.8).

For the more general use of juxtaposed *cum (quom) primum*, meaning "when first", "when for the first time", see Cic. *Ver.* 5; 45 (misquoted in Lewis and Short); Ter., *Hec., alt. prol.* 33. Against *OLD s.v. cum* 2, *quom*, 1.d., and *OLD s.v. primum* 2, compare *OLD s.v. primum* 2 3 and the material in Lewis and Short *s.v.* 2. *cum*, I.C.1.a (p. 492).

⁵ The oracle's vast (cf. *omnis*, 85) influence and the ritual procedures employed in consulting it (85–91) are described in the present tense (hardly a continuation of the historic present of 81ff; cf. 7.601ff.), *so as* to remind the reader (a) of the oracle's existence in his own time (though unknown to us: Rehm 1932, 76ff.; Boas 1938, 133ff.; Tilly 1947, 103ff.; with *hic et tum*, 92, cf. *hoc et tum,...more*, 616f.) as well as (b) of its presumed role in long ago predicting Italy's Julian destiny. When returning to the narrative (*hic et tum*, 92), the poet replaces the usual priest, *sacerdos* (86), with "Father (*sc.* Latinus) *himself*" (*pater ipse*, 92) – thus giving religious legitimacy to the aged king's illuminating dream beyond his son-father relationship with Faunus, by having him serve in official ceremonial function. Far from merely adding local color, lines 85–91 *a priori* establish the obliging authority for *all* Italians (here again line 85 and its hammering redundancy come into play) of the prophecy about to be issued to Latinus.

⁶ Vergil's use of *Laurens* and *Latinus* is inconsistent. Fordyce points out (*ad* 7.47) that the word *Laurens*, when predicated of the nymph Marica (she is, as Servius *ad* 7.47 informs us, usually located farther south than Latinus' settlement, viz. at Minturnae near the mouth of the Liris on the *Via Appia*) seems equivalent to "Latin". King Latinus called his people "*Laurentes*" after the holy laurel tree on the acropolis of his city (7.69–73). Thus the word is being used precisely (in its restricted sense) when Turnus is said to give out the sign for war "from the Laurentian acropolis" (*Laurenti Turnus ab arce*, 8.1; the collocation of words emphasizes his crime since the *arx* was fated to be Aeneas' place to wield power over the Laurentines, 7.69f.; cf. Renger 1985, 24). But when compared to Lausus, son of Etruscan tyrant Mezentius, Turnus himself may be called Laurentian (7.650; around this time, he has actually taken over Latinus' reins in the Laurentian city!). And since Latinus' settlement is initially to be recognized by the reader as the leading, or the key, city of the area, we find the nymphs of the Tiber (8.71) and the river itself (5.797), even the area of future Rome (7.661f.) called "Laurentian". This wider use of the name extends as far as forming the counterpart notion to the Trojans: *ambas / Laurentum Troumque acies*, 12.136f.

If *Laurens* in the *Aeneid* thus can cover much of the meaning normally (i.e., in historical contexts later than the *Aeneid* myth) reserved for the adjective *Latinus*, it does of course not obliterate the basic distinction between the Laurentines and the Rutulian people of Latium whenever such a differentiation is needed, as at 7.96f.

Chapter 7

Correspondingly, as 'Laurentian' can have a wider meaning, so 'Latin' in the *Aeneid* (which excludes the idea of the Latins being a fusion of Trojans and Aborigines found in other authors) need not refer to all of Latium but can be restricted to the city of King Latinus, i.e., take on the meaning for which we moderns might expect the word *Laurens*: when trying to interpret Faunus' oracle in favor of Turnus, the queen says "but if a son-in-law for the Latins (*Latinis*) is sought from a foreign race..." (7.367). The "Latins" here are she and her husband Latinus. Even when she, like a bacchant, is driven "right through the cities and proud peoples" (7.384; this can, of course, be a mere poetic plural denoting her husband's city and people alone) – although at 7.45, too, Latinus' kingdom is described by a plural, *arva et urbes* – and calls upon the "Latin mothers" (*matres...Latinae*, 400), the confusion she creates is still limited to the "whole House of Latinus" (407), and this "Latin" uproar does not, as lines 409ff. show, involve the Rutulian city of Ardea where King Turnus is lying soundly asleep.

The same restricted use of the adjective *Latinus*, that may or may not include other Latin peoples under Latinus' rule (cf. *magno e Latio*, 7.54) but excludes Rutulian Turnus, is confirmed also when at 7.470 Turnus distinguishes between himself, the Trojans and the "Latins". Precisely in this sense "Latins" applies to Faunus' oracle at 7.96f.: *conubiis...Latinis* concerns possible sons-in-law from Latinus' realm, while *thalamis... paratis* points to Rutulian Turnus. The distinction is inherent also in 7.150f., where, starting from Aeneas' camp, the "Latins" are found in directions different from Rivers Tiber and Numicus (the latter river later on, as we shall see, connected with Turnus). In the narrow sense, Latinus' city is called "the towers and houses of the Latins" (7.160). Here *Latini* appears equivalent to the *Laurentis* of 7.63 or to the use in 7.342 where the Fury Allecto, before moving on to Turnus' Ardea (cf. *postquam*, 7.406), first goes for "Latium and the high houses of the Laurentian ruler (= Latinus)."

[7] Thus Vergil's text beyond any doubt excludes even any compromising half-promise on the part of Latinus, as, e.g., the conjecture "...könnte Latinus mehr oder minder feste Zusagen gemacht haben" (Renger 1985, 22). Even C. Bailey's formula (*OCD*, 1970 *s.v.* Turnus), avoiding terms like "betrothal" or "fiancé", is not supported by the text he is referring to ("*Aen.* 7–12"): "He (*sc.* Turnus) was the accepted suitor of Lavinia, daughter of Latinus..., but Latinus subsequently betrothed her to Aeneas", etc. The interpreter of the *Aeneid* must be aware that Vergil's portrait of Turnus is fundamentally different from, say, Livy's (1.2.1). See below. *Latinum contra stare* (7.373f.) is valid all the way.

[8] For the identity see Stahl, 1985, Ch. V, n. 46 (p. 340).

[9] I fail to see how Williams comments on 7.103: "As Servius explains, Latinus might have kept quiet in order to preserve the present arrangement for Lavinia, but he did not". Any "present arrangement" stems from Williams' not Servius' (or Vergil's) pen.

[10] See Fordyce *ad* 7.82f.; CN *ad* 7.82; Tilly 1947, 103ff.

[11] For details, see note 5 above.

[11a] M. Hubbard suggested that this analysis shows how Vergil may consciously have used Thucydides as his model. There was early fighting (Leukimme, Sybota, Poteidaia) but this was not yet The War. See Stahl 2006, 301–20, for a brief summary.

[12] See Kiessling-Heinze *ad loc.* and Stahl, 1974, 29 ("wenn man die empirische Geschichte der Menschheit von Stufe zu Stufe studieren will").

[13] Gransden 1984, 51.

[14] Schlunk 1974, 10f.

[15] See, e.g., Ogilvie *ad* Livy, Books I–V, p. 34.

[16] H. Peter, 1914, CXXXII.

[17] Quoted by Schröder 1971, p. 93.

[18] "Doch wird diese Eintracht gestört, da die Begleiter des Aeneas auf Beute ausgehen und die Äcker (des Latinus) verwüsten (F 9a.10a.)". W.A. Schröder 1971, 91. The first six words of the quotation have no foundation in the Latin text. See also the reconstructions by Klausen and Wörner (quoted Schröder 93); by Ogilvie (commentary on Livy I–V, p. 34); Buchheit 1963, 87 ("später"). Schröder's reconstruction of Cato's "récit" has been accepted by Dury-Moyaers 1981, 84f.

[19] Schröder 1971, 117.

[20] For mere identification of fragments it is best to use Peter's Teubner edition (1914, 2nd edition) by number only. For a more detailed discussion, however, it is advisable to quote from Schröder's meritorious edition, because he identifies parallel tradition (found under the bottom line in Peter) by small letters.

[21] See Schröder 1971, 132.

[22] Schröder 1971, 113.

[23] Schröder 1971, 133.

[24] Schröder 1971, 131f.

[25] Schröder 1971, 124: only the change from Ascanius' name can claim to be Catonian, "da die Iulii Caesares sich nach Ausweis der Münzen erst seit Mitte bis Ende des zweiten vorchr. Jahrhunderts von Venus und damit Iulus ableiteten" etc. Slightly differently Ogilvie (*ad* Livy 1.3.2) on the claim "that Iulus was another name for Ascanius. This was an old claim, already found in Cato (fr. 9 P.). But the *gens Iulia* in the second century was of little influence and it was only in the closing years that it revived and began to exploit its claims for political ends."

[26] Perret 1942, 570.

[27] 1963, 165: "Vergil als Urheber".

[28] 1932, 56; cf. 49; 86f.

[29] Stahl 1969, 352.

[30] Tragic overtones have been studied by K. Reckford (1981).

[31] One can verify the emphasis in this line by comparing 4.6: *postera Phoebea lustrabat lampade terras*.

[32] Wissowa 1915, 28; for ancient passages concerning Aeneas' death on the Numicus, see Fordyce *ad* 7.150. The context explained above precludes the conceit that by the New Achilles Vergil points to Aeneas (R. Thomas 1998, 280f.). M. Hubbard suggested the possibility that *Latio* at 6.88 might even be a *dativus incommodi*, i.e., born to the detriment of Latium.

[33] See the conclusion in Stahl 1981, 174.

[34] Rehm 1932, 28.

[35] 1947, Chapter IV (66ff.); cf. 1959, 195.

[36] For close-up maps see "Enea nel Lazio" 1981, 164; Castagnoli 1972, I, at end of volume.

[37] A succinct *Bestandsaufnahme* may be found in Galinsky 1983, 37ff.

[38] Castiglioni 1977, 345.

[39] Castiglioni 1977, 345.

[40] Picture and plan in Galinsky, 1983, 60; 61; Dury-Moyaers 1981.

[41] For a map, see "Enea nel Lazio" 1981, 163.

Chapter 7

⁴² Collected by Ogilvie, *ad* Livy 1.2.6.

⁴³ Cornell 1977, 81.

⁴⁴ Galinsky 1983, 44.

⁴⁵ Castagnoli 1972 1; 91; 92.

⁴⁶ Cornell 1977, 81; *OLD s.v.* (*adj.*) A 2.b (and A 5.a) decides in favor of "on the bank".

⁴⁷ Galinsky 1983, 44.

⁴⁸ See the reviews by B. Tilly, *Gnomon* 47, 1975, 362–368, and N. Horsfall, *JRS* 63, 1973, 306–307.

⁴⁹ Della Corte 1972, 85 and *passim*.

⁵⁰ Rehm 1932, 44.

⁵¹ Boas 1938, 53; cf. Rehm 1932, 44; Tilly 1947, 1; Castagnoli 1972, 94; della Corte 1972, 121; 151.

⁵² 1972, 245; cf. 236 and *passim*.

⁵³ For ancient parallels, see Rehm 1932, 488; for the relocation, o.c. 47–49. Fordyce *ad Am.* 8.

⁵⁴ E.g., Carcopino 1968, 431 (*bis*).

⁵⁵ Carcopino 1968 2, 673f.

⁵⁶ CIL XIV, 186ff.; for a comprehensive discussion, see Castagnoli 1972, 85ff.

⁵⁷ Wissowa 1915, 25.

⁵⁸ See, e.g., Tilly 1947, 9ff. For a critique of Carcopino's assumptions which connect Aeneas' new Troy on the Tiber in Vergil with an intent of popularizing Augustan policy, see R. Meiggs, *Ostia Antica*, 2nd ed., London 1973, 46.

⁵⁹ see, e.g., Büchner 1961, c. 374.

⁶⁰ Coarelli, *Lazio*, 1985, 286, with a description of the (probable) site (today hardly verifiable because of the neglected state of the excavations).

⁶¹ 1981, 27ff.

⁶² See D. West's term in "Multiple Correspondence Similes" (1969).

⁶³ *monstrum* is well chosen: it covers both the mythical sphere of Allecto-sent, false prodigies and the mistaken fantasies Amata has expressed toward her husband.

⁶⁴ M. Hubbard has pointed out that, comparably, *coactus* at Hor. *C.* 1.16.14 (Prometheus being forced to use animal parts in addition to the insufficient clay) "refers to the constraint imposed by the limiting possibilities of a situation", *NH, ad loc.*). So Amata would see no other way to execute her intentions than by leaving palace and city.

⁶⁵ In Fordyce 1977, XVII.

⁶⁶ The same claim is of course made by Achilles (*Il.* 1.244; 412).

⁶⁷ For the position of the Artabanos story in the concept of the *Histories*, see the brief outline in Stahl 1975, 30f. On the fact (not applicable in the *Aeneid*) that both advisors, Nestor as well as Artabanos, later retract their consent and return to their original warning position, see Stahl 2012, 142–150.

⁶⁸ *fusos* is explained by Donatus *ad loc.*: "*...labores effundi, hoc est non paulatim sed semel interire.*" He adds: "*funditur enim quicquid uno impulsu contemptum traditur terrae.*"

⁶⁹ Pöschl 1964, 174.

⁷⁰ Our translation of *quaerere* here is minimal. One might well use the occasional meaning of "earn", which would make the expression of Turnus' claim more solid, though, objectively speaking, no more valid.

[71] This is in agreement with the epic tradition as investigated in our excursus above: Dream-Nestor is not aware that the plans of the real Zeus are radically different from those he announces as being those of Zeus (*Il.* 2.35ff.).

[72] At this stage of the investigation my reader may now be willing to accept Heyne's comment on *polluta pace* 467: "*violata jam: sc. consilio, conatu et voluntate Turni.*"

8

EPILOGUE

(1) Vergilian Coordinates: Priest-King Latinus

A reliable gauge for verifying that Vergil's coordinates have been ascertained correctly in the preceding chapters offers itself in the vacillating figure of priest-king Latinus. Here a long-distance reference comes into play, of the kind we observed e.g. in Queen Amata's words when she revealed to the reader more than she was aware of (a Vergilian technique similar to 'tragic irony'). Reinterpreting Faunus' oracle about the "son-in-law from abroad", she hoped to qualify Turnus by pointing to his family's Greek extraction "right from Mycenae" (*mediaeque Mycenae*, 7. 372). Little was she aware that this name means the strongest blame possible in the eyes of any person acquainted with the *Aeneid*'s metaphysics. As recently as 7. 222f. Ilioneus had reminded Amata's husband of the devastation issued from Mycenae (*Mycenis*). And at 6. 838ff. the shade of Anchises, mouthpiece of the Trojans' fated cause, had presented Rome's conquest of "Agamemnon's Mycenae", *Agamemnoniasque Mycenas*, as an act of avenging the Trojan forefathers (*ultus avos Troiae*).[1] The reader will measure the queen's wishful interpretation not only by the objective wording of the oracle itself, but also by pronouncements (in-)compatible with it made by other characters.

A similar case of long-distance reference we saw in Aeneas' final pronouncement at the epic's very end, when he, in killing Turnus, states that Pallas is exacting "the penalty from your criminal blood", *poenam scelerato ex sanguine sumit* (12. 949). Yet, while concentrating on the punishment of a specific crime (the un-heroic killing of the "boy" Pallas), Aeneas is unaware that he simultaneously is executing punishment for another crime that violated a higher order.

The reference takes the reader back to Book 7, where Turnus is characterized by his love of the sword and his criminal insanity of war, *scelerata insania belli* (461), and where King Latinus, while himself still in agreement with the oracle's orders, predicts punishment for Fate's opponents paid with their sacrilegious blood (*ipsi has sacrilego pendetis sanguine poenas*, 595), and the death penalty specifically for nefarious Turnus: *te, Turne, nefas, te triste manebit/supplicium* (596f.). In Aeneas' last words two strands, the poet's condemning narrative in Book 10 culminating in his prediction of Turnus' resentful death (503ff.; his resentment is saved for the epic's very last line: *indignata*), and the pious king's dire prophecy, coincide, compositionally and ideologically.

The condemnation of Turnus took place while Latinus was still putting up resistance to Turnus' war party and before he dropped the reins of his rule, *rerumque reliquit habenas* (7. 600). Vergil's narrative says that he had no *potestas* to overcome (*exsuperare* 7. 591) the blind undertaking (*caecum... consilium* 591f.) of the rebellious groups.

There are several specific grounds on which Latinus blames himself later (12. 29f.): for giving in to his love for Turnus, to the blood relation and the tears of his wife, Amata, for having broken "all bonds", for having snatched the promised bride from the son-in-law, for having taken up "impious arms". Above all of them ranks the violation of divine law, *fas* (12. 28), which had forbidden him to give his daughter to any of the "old" (*veterum*, 12. 27) suitors. One wonders what he could have actively done? Might he have ordered any remaining loyal Latins to forcefully (and, in all likelihood, unsuccessfully) prevent Rutulians and Latins from breaking the peace and making war on Aeneas? Or might he (since he blames himself for having torn the bride from her rightful fiancé, i.e., from Aeneas 12. 31) have tried to snatch Lavinia from the Bacchants and then sneak her out of the palace and into the Trojan camp? Or should he, in spite of his age, have taken up arms himself against Turnus? All these possibilities, when drawn out into their ramifications, in the end seem just that: possibilities, ineffective in the real world. What remains is the fact that he had not right away given (but only offered) Lavinia to Aeneas, but then withdrew, allowing Amata and Turnus time to continue pursuing their goal.

So, his self-reproach of having taken up "impious arms" must primarily refer to his passive consent to Turnus' aggression against Aeneas, opening for Turnus hope of still winning Lavinia and the throne of Latium, in spite of the oracle. Here lies the break with Latinus' earlier obedience to the oracle. After all, it had been he who had refused to open the Gates of War (7. 616ff.), fleeing such ugly ministry, *foeda ministeria*, by hiding –the same way he hid after his curse against Turnus (7. 600). Both times, the author endorses the aged king's (he usually is called *rex*) responsible (but powerless) concern for his country's mistaken course by specifically calling him *pater* (593; 618; so earlier, when piously consulting his father's oracle 7.92, and again, on the occasion of his remorse, 11. 469ff.).

The term *pater* had long been a republican honorary title of a statesman caring for his people. In the *Aeneid*, it is usually reserved as *epitheton ornans* for the Julian ancestor, Aeneas, but also marks special occasions, as when, at the solemn conclusion of the treaty for the war-deciding duel, the author calls him "Father Aeneas, origin of the Roman race", *pater Aeneas, Romanae stirpis origo* (12. 166). A subordinate may address him, *in absentia*, "best Father of the Trojans" (*pater optime Teucrum* 1. 555). The conclusion is that Vergil in his Latinus figure lays out clearly for his reader the coordinates of what is acceptable and what is not acceptable conduct in a ruler who deserves to rule. Again, the poet may with his nomenclature be giving support to Octavian-Augustus, who already early in the twenties BC in an extremely adulatory ode of Horace (*C.* 1. 2) was invoked as god Mercury and asked to return to heaven late only, but to stay down here as "avenger of (Gaius Julius) Caesar", *Caesaris ultor* (44), and to allow himself to be addressed as "Father and Princeps", *pater atque princeps* (50), he, the Romans' "leader" (*duce* 52), while forgiving the Romans their sins of having made (civil) war on him. In view of Augustus' ambitions as reflected by the compliant turncoat (theorists, forgive!) Horace, Vergil's depiction of Latinus' split loyalties, and especially of his desertion of the *pater* ideal, is hardly apolitical. The predominant position the concept held for decades in Augustus' wishful self-portrait is documented once more in his *Achievements*, where he, at the very end (35.1) and shortly after (34.2) mentioning the honor of being called Augustus, climactically lists the crowning event of his career: "In my thirteenth consulship the Senate, the equestrian order, and the whole people of Rome gave me the title of Father of my Country (i.e., *pater patriae*), "and resolved that this should be inscribed in the porch of my house and in the Curia Julia" (i.e., the senate house) "and in the Forum Augustum below the chariot which had been set there in my honour by decree of the Senate" (33.1; tr. Brunt/Moore).

In returning to the story-line after illuminating the contemporary weight of Vergil's terminology, one must then assume that, after twice (7. 586ff.; 618f.) vainly refusing to lend his authority to the breach of the divinely ordained peace which he himself had piously offered to Aeneas (7. 259ff., cf. 285), Latinus, in his reversal into passivity, went along with Turnus' activities. At 8. 17, when an embassy is sent to Diomedes for help, both Turnus and Latinus appear as the senders of the message: (the answer to the question asked)

> would appear clearer to Diomedes himself
> than to Turnus the King and to King Latinus
>
> manifestius ipsi
> quam Turno regi et regi apparere Latino.   8. 16f.

Here Latinus seems to co-operate with Turnus' bellicosity – though Vergil gives his reader an indirect glimpse only at his new position. The

Chapter 8

opening scene of Book 8 (8. 1ff.) predominantly belongs to Turnus and his like.

Later on, too, Latinus is seen to be on terms with Turnus (e.g., 12. 19ff.) as well as still serving his former official functions; his tendency is, as before, to speak in favor of having peace with the *Aeneadae*. When, in despair over the loss of human life (11. 231), he calls the *concilium magnum* (234), he suggests that an embassy to Aeneas "carry in their hands before them the branches of peace", *pacisque manu praetendere ramos* (332; a reversal of roles, cf. 7. 154f.) and expresses that he should have summoned the council earlier (302f.).

The passage most revealing about his change of heart is in his last speech to Turnus, if again by implication only. Then, fearing for the younger king's life, he tries to keep him from meeting Aeneas in single combat. It is true he snatched the promised bride from the rightful son-in-law (i.e., Aeneas, 12. 31; at 11. 105, the Latin negotiators ask Aeneas to spare the man "once called his host and father-in-law"; for the plural, cf. 7. 98). But even now he has not actually turned Lavinia over to Turnus who is still seen, as he was early in Book 7, in the status of a suitor (*petentem* 12. 42; cf. 7. 54). What follows from this is that – and the result agrees with the situation of a prospective duel – Latinus, by retiring and procrastinating, had indeed been opening an opportunity for Turnus to try whether he could defeat Aeneas in military combat. In case of victory Turnus would have (one may reasonably surmise) been awarded the hand of Lavinia. Clearly, Latinus did incur guilt by his inactivity and passive indulgence toward Turnus, which 'postponed' the action required by Faunus' oracle; so his self-reproaches are, after all, only too understandable.

If details of his volte-face concerning Aeneas are not spelled out explicitly in the epic, we should remember what was said earlier, in Chapter 7, about Vergil's way of shaping the figure of Latinus. From a forceful adversary, himself at exactly the right age in life for fighting, and actively participating in war (as he appears in Cato), Vergil has made him into a wise, aged priest king, whose piety bids him welcome the Julians' ancestor on Italian soil. After having served this function, he, to a degree, resumes the role we found him to play in the 'confrontational' tradition, but he is, in the *Aeneid*, assigned a background position as far as the action is concerned – so all the vigor and responsibility of opposing Aeneas' fated mission can fall on Turnus and his associates, types like Messapus, eager breaker of the treaty (*avidus confundere foedus*, 12. 290) or the despiser of gods (*contemptor divum*, 7. 648; cf. 8. 7), Mezentius.

There is no way, then, for the interpreter to use Latinus' example to find excuses for Turnus. By the opening of Book 8,

Epilogue

when Turnus displayed the sign of war from the Laurentine citadel,

ut belli signum Laurenti Turnus ab arce extulit, 8. 1f.

it is manifest who has taken over and who has stepped off the stage, according to Vergil's design. After first outlining the circumstances and portents surrounding Aeneas' arrival and after next depicting the pious obedience of Latinus and the uninhibited as well as sacrilegious reaction of self-seeking Turnus, Vergil now shows the Rutulian king criminally setting out on the path of his personal war against Fate-sent pious Aeneas.

The ramifications observed in Latinus' later conduct reinforce the results of our earlier investigation into the changes Vergil made in the traditional figure of the Latin king: in the *Aeneid* too old to fight, he carries the divine voice and, associating with the *Aeneadae*, is a guide for the reader – whereas Turnus is seen as hosting and associating with atheist Mezentius. Now we can go further by saying that, as long as peace seems to have a chance, Latinus presents a positive foil against which the reader can measure Turnus' impious aggressiveness. Once the hopes for peace are gone and war is breaking out, Latinus is held in the background and the reader's attention is focused, on the Italian side, on the wild and impetuous energy of Turnus. In Vergil's overall dramaturgy (if this term is allowed in analyzing an epic), then, good king Latinus (as long as he stays 'good') also serves to contrast with, and thus to emphasize, Turnus' basically sacrilegious attitude and character.

What all this amounts to is the thorough *Verteufelung* (diabolization) of the Julian ancestor's political opponent. The author clearly wants his reader to be on the side of peace and piety, i.e., of Faunus' oracle as well as of Aeneas and his men (which also means: on the side of Aeneas' now ruling 'descendant' – only a few years after his murderous civil war activities!). By oracular announcements, by editorial intervention, and by repeated references to the Age of Augustus, the *Aeneid* anchors its contents in a system of values which extends beyond the time of myth into the Roman reader's own day (in Book 7, see Rome's continued – *nunc*, 602 – rite of declaring war). And as the reader's present-day ruler identifies himself as a pious and objective force above chance partisanships (in his *Res Gestae* Augustus himself represents the republic; his civil war opponents, left nameless, are characterized as a "faction", *R.G.* 1), so Vergil identifies Augustus' forefather with objective Fate and the will of Jupiter. He withholds from Aeneas' adversary even the (genuinely) patriotic stance of defending his homeland, instead pushing him into a corner as a religious outcast, who eventually forfeits all claims on the Roman reader's sympathy.

That might is right is an old maxim of the powerful (Thucydides has the Athenians claim it toward the inferior Melians, 5.105.1f.),[2] so one would not be surprised to find its application in Vergil's imperial poetry. That the powerful is considered divinely blessed is, in the post-Hellenistic world, perhaps not unexpected either. But that the successful usurper and victor of a bloody civil war is depicted as a product of Fate's will as pronounced and prophesied since the earliest time of myth is a special achievement of Vergil's poetry; so is the concept which classifies the political adversary as an adversary of the country's religion. It took a special historical event (the final turn from republic to one-man rule) and the support from a brilliant mind (Vergil's explanation of Octavian's rise to power as divinely ordained long before the dawn of Rome) to enshrine this apotheosis of a Roman ruler over fellow Romans – a concept which, in varying shapes, was to find re-manifestations over centuries. The more cogent the system, the further away the *Aeneid* is from being an all-embracing *Menschheitsdichtung*. But the more urgently also the question arises: where does man, where does the individual, find consideration if the system can depict the political opponent, the non-complying individual, in terms of a sacrilegious criminal? It would be worthwhile to view the thought-pattern, which Vergil created for his *Aeneid* to justify Augustus' rule (and whose coordinates are revealed so translucently in the two sides of wavering King Latinus) in a wider historical context.

(2) Outlook: Occidental Footprints of Vergil's Augustan World Order
But that cannot be done here. I have to limit myself to a pastiche of smidgens. The preceding chapters have demonstrated that the *Aeneid* is much more intricately and inseparably interwoven with the Augustan state and its dynastic design than was widely believed in the later 20th century (19th-century European scholarship found it easier to think in hierarchic-nationalistic terms). Again archaeology is able to confirm this bond further. Augustus' own forum, dedicated in 2 BC, was decorated, on one side, with the statues of eminent republican citizens; on the left side (viewed from the entrance), members of the Julian family were represented. Aeneas held a prominent position among them in the exedra. He was shown leaving Troy with Anchises, who holds the state gods, on his shoulder and little Ascanius at his hand.[3] The emperor himself is said to have been the author of the inscriptions on the statues' bases. Evidently, Vergil's divination (or, perhaps: his 'inspirer') had set the tracks right. Vergil's footprint shows here 17 years after his death. No wonder that Augustus took care to see the *Aeneid* published in more timely fashion than its author had planned.

What Vergil was also able to foreshadow only (considering that he died in 19 BC) but did foreshadow, was Augustus' 12 BC 'election' to the office

Epilogue

of chief priest of the state, *pontifex maximus*. Augustus in his *Res Gestae* (10) makes a point that he had refused to accept the venerable office before his predecessor's death (i.e., partly still in Vergil's lifetime); but his desire to make it a hereditary privilege of the Julian dynasty is revealed: "the office which my father" [scil., C. Julius Caesar] "had held" and that "my predecessor" (unnamed; it was the former fellow-triumvir Lepidus) "had seized on the opportunity provided by civil unrest" (scil., following Caesar's death). Suggested conclusion for the citizen-subject who reads the inscription: by rights, the office should have passed directly from my father to myself. (In fact, the office would from now on stay with the emperors until the fourth century AD. See below.)

Vergil was able to support the claim. In the *Aeneid* Helenus, surviving seer-son of King Priam, cedes not only any claim to the kingship of Troy and its future fame to Augustus' ancestor ("you go ahead and carry huge[4] Troy to heaven"). He also advises Aeneas on religious practice, instructing him to veil his head at sacrifice upon arrival at his destination – a practice to be continued by the "descendants" (*nepotes* 3. 409: catchword in the *Aeneid*, meaning Vergil's contemporaries; cf. Jupiter at 12. 835f.). On the "Altar of the Augustan Peace," Ara Pacis Augustae (dedicated *ca.* 13–9 BC), Aeneas, arriving in Italy, is depicted with his head veiled in a scene of sacrificing.[5] And sure enough, a widely spread type of statue shows Augustus with his head veiled as the sacrificing and praying *togatus* – his favorite pose apparently already in the twenties BC,[6] at the time Vergil was working on his *Aeneid*. Once more Vergil can be seen to have drawn up the mythical blueprint of Augustus' dynastic and religious policies. (Or was the blueprint perhaps Augustus' own, and the poet only complied?)

The schema would apply far beyond the Age of Augustus. The concept of the divinely ordained state under priestly guidance, which demands the individual's submission and which in the *Aeneid* is so persuasively raised to the lofty heights of myth, lived on for centuries in Latinized Europe, and with it, the words and construct of the poet. Here is not the place to dwell on Vergil's *Nachleben*, which, under various aspects and intentions (on occasion, as Excursus 1 of Chapter 2 has shown, with the ulterior purpose of reinforcing a certain understanding of the *Aeneid*) has filled compendiums in recent years.[7] Only one or two more but significant points can here be noted in the unending succession of reuse.

A basic fact may remind the reader that the *Aeneid* was venerated and survived into the Middle Ages not so much because of its poetic or philological valuation but because of its connection to Augustus. Philologists used to (and still do) praise Vergil for his meticulous Latin rendering of the Homeric and other Greek models he had chosen to incorporate in

Chapter 8

his epic[8] (the great commentaries of Norden or Pease can bear witness to this tradition, as does the comparative work of Knauer) – an area of investigation that, when practiced exclusively, may (as was shown earlier) run the risk of closing its practitioners' eyes to historical Vergil's political message. Notably, panegyric epics of later centuries, in Latin or in the vernacular, even when praising non-Roman emperors, could actually be closer to the political spirit of their Vergilian model (one may, for instance, think of Camões' *Os Lusíadas*).

Christianity's welcoming reception of Vergil was rooted not only in his Fourth Eclogue and its prediction of the birth of a child (easily marking the poet out as *anima naturaliter Christiana* to compensate for his pre-Christian lifetime). This side of Christian reception found its peak in Vergil guiding Dante part of the way in the Divina Comedia. It is also in large part due to the poet's praise of Emperor Augustus, because Augustus ruled during the lifetime of Jesus. The *pax Augusta* helped to improve communications all over the provinces, and, so, facilitated spreading the Christian message. For the faithful it was an easy step to believing that Augustus was the god-sent ruler, since he was thought to be the enabler of spreading Christianity.[9] A curious late outgrowth of the 'sanctified' Augustus was touched upon earlier. Obviously born from the desire to compensate for Augustus' pre-Christian lifetime is the story of the Mother with Child appearing to Augustus on the Capitoline Hill, pagan Rome's religious center. The event is still commemorated *in situ* by a 12th-century AD altar in St Helen's chapel in the church Santa Maria d'Aracoeli, where the Tiburtine Sibyl revealed to Augustus that the successor greater than he would be a child… No wonder, then, that even the battle of Actium, wondrously described by Vergil on the shield of Aeneas in Book 8, could be integrated into the Christian context. (It is worth recalling that Propertius' Apollo had already addressed the victor of Actium as "the world's savior", *mundi servator*, 4.6.37).

Augustus, elected Pontifex Maximus legally by an all-Italian electorate, the size of which had never assembled at Rome before (a point he proudly makes in his *Achievements* 10), 'reunited' in his person the duties of ruler and chief priest for the good of the state (at Rome he did avoid officially becoming a god himself in his lifetime, the mistake his 'father' had made). To him, the event healed one of the last religious infringements caused by the civil war, finally completing the divinely ordained political mission the Julian family had served ever since Aeneas. Devastating consequences caused by a temporary deviation from Fate's will are demonstrated in the *Aeneid*, too, both concretely in Turnus' "criminal insanity of war" (7. 461) and ideologically by the two sides of priest-king Latinus, his initial obedience and ensuing doomed disobedience to Faunus' oracle. The Pontifex Maximus, during the Republic an honor for meritorious citizens of high standing, necessarily changed its character under the rule of one man who saw public prayers for his health undertaken periodically by consuls or priestly colleges by decree of the Senate (*R.G.* 9), his name incorporated into the song of the Salii priests (for the wellbeing of the state), and his person "by law" (*per legem*) declared "inviolable for ever" (*sacrosanctus in perpetuum*, 10.1). Besides, his influence in religious matters was guaranteed even further by membership in the leading priestly colleges (7.3).

By taking over the role of chief priest and by making the people's wellbeing dependent on his own, Augustus skillfully consolidated his grip on Roman religion as he had done on the state: as "the first citizen" (*princeps*, 13; 30.1; 32.3) he could increasingly claim to be pre-eminent not so much through holding a magistracy but in a non-autocratic, consultative mode by "influence" (*auctoritas*) only (34) – the latter feature prominent already in Vergil's Aeneas, a king who is never compelled to rule by force, and in essential matters may consult a council (*delectos populi ad proceres* 3. 58), as Augustus would do officially in his later years (his *concilium*); so once more the poet can be seen in his epic for the emperor to have prefigured the ideal that Augustus himself coveted and later painted for his public image.

It was Emperor Gratian (359–83 AD), Christian orthodox zealot, who dissolved the unifying Augustan model. Vergil had supported it (as well as warning the Latins of the inherent danger in case of human failure) by creating a mythical antecedent in the ambivalent figure of priest-king Latinus. When Gratian dropped the (now, pagan) title of Pontifex Maximus, he hardly foresaw the consequences of giving up the unifying concept. In the fifth century the popes appropriated the orphaned title ('pontiffs') and, so, acquired (and handed to their successors) a potentially powerful name (and tool), drenched in Roman imperial tradition, for claims of spiritually based authority over secular power. The earliest clash, not yet on the papal level, ended with the victory of the spiritual side, when in 390 Emperor Theodosius, denied communion because of his Thessalonica massacre, did penance before bishop St Ambrosius in Milan.[10]

The split of nomenclature, then, foreshadowed what later developed into the conflict of state and church, as notorious and complementary instances of which one may cite two events: the humiliation of excommunicated Henry IV before Gregory VII at Canossa (1099), and Pope Pius' VII abduction (1809) from the Palazzo Quirinale in Rome by Napoleon's soldiers and his later relocation by Napoleon to Fontainebleau. (During their long-lasting feud, Pius had excommunicated Napoleon.)

Chapter 8

On the secular side, the *pater patriae* idea, in its un-republican function as first used by Vergil (dealt with in the earlier part of the present chapter), having survived into the 19th (and even 20th) century, acquired worldwide interest. Emperors of the Holy Roman Empire naturally had continued the traditional nomenclature of the ruler honored and beloved by his subjects. To mention a few examples: the pompous memorial of Emperor Francis I in Vienna, dedicated in 1846, bears among its many decorations an inscription, "for Emperor Francis I, ... Father of the Country, Augustus", IMP FRANCISCO I...PATRI PATRIAE AUGUSTO" (etc.). A local ruler, too, Cosimo il Vecchio de' Medici of Florence, was designated *pater patriae* by the Signoria, and Peter I of Russia was named Father of the Country – as was Josef Stalin on his 70th birthday.

In this European context Vergil's scheme, though it yielded its metaphysical foundation (the divine origin of Rome's ruling dynasty and of its secular power) to Christian theology, did not lose its secular influence. Aeneas (together with biblical figures) as favorite ancestor for ambitious European families has been the object of M. Tanner's study. So, the *Aeneid* could still help to give voice to imperial ambitions, sometimes in unlikely places and situations. It is hardly surprising that last century's European dictators found a welcome model in Augustus' ruthless rise to power 'for the good of his country' (though apparently Mussolini felt even greater affinity to Caesar, Hitler to Pericles). Vergil's Fate-ordained ruler to whose nation Jupiter has allotted "empire without end" (etc.), *imperium sine fine* (*Aen.* 1. 279), and whose empire (limited "by the Ocean", *Oceano*, 1. 287) prefigures that of the *Roi Soleil*, appealed to the territorial ambitions of Fascism and Nazism. And where der Führer and il Duce themselves might not go into too much of the *Aeneid*'s historical detail, their "wissenschaftliche" (and journalistic) followers often were only too willing to do so. Let one historical *curiosum* conclude the selection of Vergilian footprints. On the castle in Prague, an unidentified volume on display in a glass case shows on its frontispiece the portrait of Emperor Matthias (1612–19) framed by an oval listing his titles: MATTHIAS D. G. ROMAN [sic] IMPERATOR SEMPER AUGUSTUS (etc). ("Matthias by the Grace of God Roman Emperor always Augustus", etc.). The subscription, alluding to the *Aeneid*'s line about Augustus,[11] "who bounds his empire by the Ocean, his fame by the stars" (*imperium Oceano, famam qui terminet astris*, 1. 287), deals with the problem that Matthias' dry-land empire was not limited by the Ocean, by replacing "Ocean" with "countries": *Imperium terris famam qui terminet astris*. Vergil's blueprint of the Augustan world order, as select footprints of the *Aeneid* show, has surely helped to paper the walls inside the pre-Enlightenment and pre-democratic European box.

(3) A Socio-linguistic Misunderstanding?

The Roman[12] (and, also, strands of the European)[13] tradition suggests that, on the one hand, the panegyric epic poet pays homage to his patron (including perhaps the latter's family) and, on the other hand, that the socially higher-standing patron gains prestige from the poet's endeavor. Is this interpreter right in grouping the *Aeneid* among such company? After all, following a lecture he gave at a Mommsen-Gesellschaft convention, he was accused of having made "Vergil a mercenary of Augustus."[14] The poet's relationship to his sponsor (Vergil died extraordinarily rich, after all) has long touched a raw nerve among Latin scholars, the more so, since Vergil himself mentions toward his patron, Maecenas (right-hand man of Augustus and promoter also of the emperor's cultural policies), "your ungentle orders, Maecenas", *tua, Maecenas, haud mollia iussa* (G. 3. 41. Vergil is referring to his ongoing work on the *Georgica*).

Today there is, in spite of ancient testimony,[15] a tendency to discount the possibility of officious directives given to the Augustan poets. (This involves a tricky sociological as well as moral problem which should perhaps command less attention than the primary question of how far the poets' texts must count as politically oriented.)[16] Some interpreters will argue in favor of mutual respect and of the poets' intellectual – and moral – "independence", rather than resume that unpalatable line of court-inspired literary production, which prevailed largely unquestioned before World War II (and even World War I) when and wherever Augustus, the first European emperor, was held in high esteem. In an award-winning book, entitled "Promised Verse", P. White, a pronounced representative of this tendency, being critical of what he calls "a habit of thought", i.e., "the political interpretation of Augustan poetry" (which, being "anachronistic", "has to be combated head-on"),[17] asks the question: "If Augustus did not lay down the lines to be followed, how did these and other motifs related to him come to engross such an important place in contemporary poetry?" Apart from stating that our information "does not suggest that he intruded on their work any more than did other members of the elite" (a statement which, sixty years earlier, might have worried a historian like Syme), "The answer seems to be that the poets elaborated an Augustan thematic by themselves, independently both of Augustus and of one another."[18] So, can the tricky sociological problem be considered neutralized by referring to forms of communication in "upper-class society" and "relations between friends" rather than "relationships of authority"?[19]

There may be problems in the approach pursued by White for adequately appreciating the art of the *Aeneid*; they would lie first in the overall concept of literature: does a critical evaluation, building on "thematic," "theme," and "motif," suffice to account for the work's coherent rhetorical organization and thoroughly traceable sequence of thought, which, according to ancient information, had been established before versification started? We have dealt with this overarching aspect earlier.

So we are supposedly dealing with independent initiative and voluntarism, not pressure, and, in addition (White tells us), Horace and Vergil "had personal contacts with Augustus that would have disposed them to write about him positively."[20] A fine line is being drawn here, considering the fact that Augustus took an active interest in the epic's progress, as well as that, in the end, he saw to its publication. In between he had, as in the case of the (completed) *Georgics*, parts of the epic about his mythical ancestor read to himself *in statu nascendi*, even repeatedly asked to see interim parts. What is the probability that there were no hints, suggestions, leading comments, 'directives'? Did Vergil entirely on his own take aim so well that Ovid (when addressing the emperor) could call the epic "*your* Aeneid"? It means disregarding (and diverging from) the context of *Trist.* 2. 533 when White suggests that Ovid may here "have in mind the rescuing of the poem by Augustus after Vergil's death."[21] Just before, at line 530, Ovid had spoken of poets who sing "part of them your family's" [=Aeneas'], "part your own deeds", *parsque tui generis, pars tua facta canunt*. But not to worry about imperial directives: according to White, Vergil's "friendship with Augustus was close enough that offers of advice would have been natural".[22]

For objectivity's sake, a case concerning Horace may serve as an introductory illustration. Binder[23] draws an interesting parallel: as academic presentation of the past often is connected to the modern-day scholar's political convictions, so the *mores maiorum* could be manipulated according to the interests of the regime which invoked them. In this area (Binder maintains) contemporary writers could (and were supposed to) help form the ideology of the Princeps. Among examples of cooperation between power and poet, Binder cites Horace's call for the restoration of dilapidated temples (*donec templa refeceris, C.* 3. 6. 2, etc.) and Augustus' claim of having done just that in 28 BC (*duo et octoginta templa...refeci, R.G.* 20). Of course, Horace does not raise a new demand but he reacts ("reagiert"), viz., "to a programmatic promise of Augustus" ("auf ein programmatisches Versprechen des Augustus") from the time before or right after Actium. "Augustus for his part could claim to have fulfilled the "demand" of the poet...". ("Augustus konnte sich seinerseits darauf berufen, die 'Forderung' des Dichters...erfüllt zu haben.")

Since White's optimistic view of the Augustan poets' independence can so easily be balanced by a less idealizing scholarly position, it appears desirable to take a more detailed look at his methodology and to ask whether his study really closes the door to "Augustan interpretation" – the answer being essential for standards of scholarship dealing with the Age of Augustus.

To return to the detail of Maecenas' *haud mollia iussa*: First, one should at least mention that his detailed investigation leads White to conclude that the word *iubere*, in the context of what he terms a "literary request",[24] tends to lose at least some of its peremptory force. So he grants, especially in pronounced imperatives, a much lower probability to the possibility of "duress, pressure, or the like"[25] exercised on the Augustan poets than traditional scholarship has done. White does, however, consider (and then deny) the possibility that in one of two key Propertian passages prodding or encouragement by Maecenas has taken place.[26]

This is Prop. 3. 9. 52, where the elegist, addressing his patron, says that "my talent will grow under your orders," *crescet et ingenium sub tua iussa meum*. Though White acknowledges the rising order of the topics mentioned by the poet here (the climax being, after gigantomachy and beginnings of Rome, an epic on Augustus' victory over Cleopatra, including the suicide of Antony), he allows no more than that "Propertius is imagining possibilities rather than fielding requests." According to White, there anyway was (in case there was a request) no emphasis placed on the Augustan topic: either Maecenas urged all three epics or "... Propertius was simply volunteering three examples of what he might try. It forces the text to isolate the last as the only poem specifically asked for." Does it really "force the text"?

White's suggestion does not appear convincing, in view of (to repeat) the stylistic climax (2:3:4 lines) and the chronology observed by Propertius in listing the three topics, from times of myth to the history-crowning triumph of Augustus. Why would the poet, while trying at least to buy some time with his *recusatio*, put Augustus' triple triumph at the end unless that culmination point is the suggested topic to the height of which his talent has been invited ('commanded'?) by the *iussa*, and to which (he intimates) it might eventually "grow" (via a long – and unlikely – 'learning curve' over a gigantomachy and an epic on early Rome)? The climax ending in Augustus is the more remarkable as it is (in, to White, a "confusing lurch") specifically added to the love poet's preceding refusal of a Thebais and an Iliad as epics unbecoming the follower of Callimachus, master of the chiseled small form.

How strong really was the pressure felt by Propertius to produce for the regime, may (without mention of the specific word *iussa*) be seen in the way he deals with the problem in Elegy 2. 1,[27] where he says to Maecenas that he is not (scil., unlike Vergil) able "to found Caesar's glory on his Phrygian forefathers" (42), but (17–38) he would, if he were able to, write an epic on the military feats of your Caesar, *tui...Caesaris* (2. 1. 25), and do so for the sake of Maecenas. And what about his (alleged, and quickly retracted) desire to rise to writing an epic on the battles of "you, my leader", *mei...ducis* (2. 10. 4), "O Augustus", *Auguste* (2. 10. 15)? Or the seer-poet in 3. 4 blessing the arms of "god Caesar", *deus Caesar*, and his prayer that Venus eternally preserve the precious descendant of Aeneas (and the following assurance that he himself will for the rest of his life, *exitus...vitae*, dedicate his post-love-poetry existence to philosophy, 3. 5)? Is one, in spite of the *recusationes* and retractions, really to believe that "Augustus was a poetically exciting idea",[28] and that there are no "trademarks of directions from without"?[29]

In view of Propertius 2. 1, Elegy 3. 9 does not at all suggest *a priori* that we should rule out the possibility of "duress, pressure, or the like," when we now return to the core passage of the debate, i.e., Vergil's much discussed utterance to Maecenas about "your ungentle orders," *tua, Maecenas, haud mollia iussa* (G. 3. 41), which impel the poet to write the *Georgics*. Already in Eclogue 6. 9 Vergil had, for the purpose of a *recusatio*, adduced the god Apollo's (6. 3) orders to fend off Varus' request for an epic: *non iniussa cano*, what I am writing now, I am writing under divine orders, i.e., commissioned by an authority against whom there is no refusal possible for a human. *Iubere*, here in the derivative litotes *non iniussa*, is seen to express that irresistible kind of higher directive which Varus, too, will have to respect (without feeling offended).

Though no Palatine Hill Tapes are available to us to prove the point, it would seem naive and unworldly to assume that Augustus or Maecenas employed language like "*iubeo te scribere de*" etc. This point is easily conceded to White. The favored young poet from the area of provincial Mantua would in all probability understand and know how even a hint (if not a request) dropped by the powerful "friend" had to be taken.

The situation is too different to allow extrapolating from "the relations of friends" taking place among (nearly) equals "in upper-class society," which White uses as his starting point. Maecenas, even in the role of "the great friend" (White, referring to *G.* 3. 41, Prop. 3. 9. 52, and other passages) is hardly close enough to bridge the social abyss. Tacitus would probably be more skeptical (since realistic) than White with regard to the Augustan poets' mutual relations with the powerful: "A gift from him who can give orders carries with it the force of necessity" (*merces ab eo qui iubere potest, vim necessitatis adfert, Ann.* 14. 14. 4).

On the other hand, as Maecenas has originally picked Vergil not for his social rank (but for his potential as a poet to be taken under his – or Octavian's – wing), so Vergil himself does not fill the shoes of those writers who in their publications drop the names of their sponsors (or 'great friends') for the purpose of self-aggrandizement. Turning a patron's *"rogo"* into a *"iubes"* can raise the poet's importance in the eyes of the reading public, as White points out: "The urgency of the request advertizes the value of the work." Would Vergil go over Maecenas' head and mention a future work on Octavian for his, the poet's own, publicity? This seems unlikely.

What intensifies the meaning of "order" at *G.* 3. 41 is, of course, the addition to *iussa* of *haud mollia*. One does not have to understand that Maecenas was ungentle in pronouncing his directive. Even if the speaker on the receiving end, i.e., Vergil, should perceive it merely as harshly pronounced (rather than as the realistic "irresistible"), then the addition of *haud mollia* would suffice to make his reader sense a degree of "duress, pressure, or the like"[30] denied by White.

But what makes *G.* 3. 41 stand out further above other passages is the existence of a parallel. At *Aen.* 9. 804 Jupiter sends, through Iris, severe orders, *haud mollia iussa*, to Juno, to keep her from supporting Turnus inside the walls of the Trojan camp. Unwelcome as the orders are to her, she nevertheless "does not dare" counteract them: the unwelcome *iussa* must be extremely binding if even a rebellious character like Saturnian Juno decides she cannot disobey them!

Going back to *G.* 3. 41, one can hardly rule out categorically the possibility of pressure or active influence. Vergil has just outlined his plan for an epic relating to Caesar Octavianus (a plan which, according to Kraggerud's convincing analysis,[31] envisions the *Aeneid*); but, for now (*interea*, 3. 40), he will pursue his *Georgics*, i.e., Maecenas' *haud mollia iussa*. Even if one sees the orders not as a command to write the Georgics but as an injunction to finish them before (cf. *interea*) Vergil may go on to what he would prefer much more to write, viz., an epic relating to Caesar Octavianus, it cannot be denied that the poet feels he is under duress not of his own making or choosing: *tua* puts the responsibility for the *iussa* squarely in Maecenas' court.

Talk of *"iubere* as being a conventional term in such contexts" may then on occasion veil more of the reality than it unveils. White maintains that, compared to its (peremptory) "dictionary partners *imperare* and *praecipere*," in *iubere* "the nuance of command which it conveys is significantly weaker than in other Latin verbs meaning 'order' or 'command.'"[32] This is hardly confirmed by the evidence in Vergil, where in ninety cases *iubere* is the preferred word for commands or orders, including military orders. (Of *praecipere*, I count fourteen occurrences; of *imperare*, five. Overall, forms of *iubere* are found far more than a hundred

Chapter 8

times in Vergil.) Again, the devil appears to hide in the detail. Even in the case of Dido's demand (*dic*, 1.753)[33] for the narrative of Aeneas' sorrowful experience, Aeneas' reluctant response (*infandum, regina, iubes renovare dolorem*, 2.3) reacts to the fact of which both are aware, viz. that the savior's imperative has compulsive power over the just recently saved.

Especially the perfect passive participle, mostly in the plural form *iussa* (taking up twenty of the instances, with two cases of *iussis* to be added), is always an expression of "order," "command," issued by an unquestioned (in only one case an arrogated) authority: "let us follow where the commands of the gods are leading us", *divum ducunt qua iussa sequamur*, *Aen*. 3. 114; cf. the "lordly commands of high-minded Jupiter", *iussa superba / magnanimi Iovis*, 12. 877f. Shall one assume that *tua haud mollia iussa* at *G*. 3. 41 (not counted in the number given above) is the only exception? (The submissive *iussis* of *E*. 8. 11 would hardly support such special pleading.)

It follows that one is not entitled categorically to place the *iussa* of *G*. 3. 41 into a different class from those *iussa* experienced by Propertius (the essential specific difference being that Vergil is a willing rather than a recalcitrant recipient of the *iussa*). And one can safely go one step further. Since the poet's mind "undertakes nothing sublime without you," *te sine nil altum mens incohat* (*G*. 3. 42), we may be sure that, as he writes the *Georgics* under Maecenas' orders, he won't write the much more ambitious (and *altum*) epic on Caesar Octavianus' ancestor either without any directives from the literary patron – or from even higher up. In the case of the *Aeneid*, it is even harder to discount as irrelevant or not pertinent the information supplied in Donatus' *Vita* (31; in all likelihood based on Suetonius' access to Augustus' correspondence): Augustus repeatedly demanded from the poet an outline or sample of his production, in Powell's wording (in his forthcoming paper), "an initial sketch (*prima carminis* ὑπογραφή) or any substantial section (κῶλον) of the *Aeneid*". After reading, would there be no leading comment or directive from the demanding recipient (who is, after all, the ruthless recent usurper of the empire)?

It is again the philological detail which advises against accepting the recent trend wholesale, and against narrowly demarcating the wide avenue of official influence or 'inspiration'. In spite of White's meritorious investigation, individual Latin contexts seem to prevent the establishment of a universal rule derived from generic, non-literary assumptions about social relations, by "subordinating discussion of the poems to discussion of their social background."[34]

It turns out that viewing parts of Augustan poetry as written to order may not miss the mark. Here I return to the other, the overarching, aspect of White's underlying litcrit methodology. Speaking of "motifs" (206)[35] or "an Augustan thematic" (206) or "the theme of primeval Rome"(186), or even of Augustus as "a poetically exciting idea" (207), runs, in the case of the *Aeneid*, a serious risk: by extracting data from their literary context, and by assembling them into a conglomerate of generic poetical topics, one is in danger of infringing the artifact's political individuality.

For instance, White sees "imperial symbolism" at work "in the poets' vignettes of Rome" (188). But visiting Aeneas sees the Capitoline not only as "a numinous spot where relics of a long-extinct settlement were visible" (186), but (we must complete White's comment) the god that gives the place its numinous character is *Iuppiter tonans* to whom Augustus built a temple there for having saved him personally during a severe thunderstorm (see Chapter 6)!

Speaking of "the poets' vignettes of Rome" (188), "the theme of primeval Rome" (184), "the motif so popular around 20 BC" (185), and holding Augustus' "campaign of public works" (187) responsible for the "theme's" frequent elaboration (Augustus "influenced the poets not by any direct approach to them", 187), excludes, at least for Book 8 of the *Aeneid*, too much of the dominant dynastic Julian context: neither "imperial symbolism" nor "the nationalism in his building program" (188) hits the mark – instead, rather, "Julianism," if not outright "Augustanism," would be the shoe that fits here.

The fact is that, what White calls the "theme" of "primeval Rome," should not (at least not in the *Aeneid*), and cannot, be isolated because it is fully integrated into the poet's overarching contemporary agenda and perspective of Julian family interests. This perspective aims at confirming the fated character of Augustus' position in Roman history, by having his ancestor touch on places like Actium and the grounds of edifices at Rome, which will be of signal importance to Augustus' very own policies. The function of a "theme" or "motif" should be appreciated only as integral part of the larger context, which it serves. This has been illustrated, e.g., in Chapter 6 by the twisted travel route Vergil has designed for his hero in order to take him to future Rome and the Palatine hill. That twisted travel route clearly gives priority to the fated political success of Augustus (Aeneas' visit shows that already since primeval time Rome and the Palatine have been destined to be the headquarters of his descendant's world rule) over considerations of poetic *probabile*.

White thinks (as quoted above) that "the political interpretation of Augustan poetry" is a "habit of thought". He limits his search mainly to poetry demonstrably ordered or suggested by Augustus or an intermediary. Even in these narrow confines (as our investigation of individual passages has shown) the universal validity of his thesis is subject to doubt. But within these parameters Vergil, it turns out, was firmly committed to presenting the latest Julian to the world as the choice of Providence and the only choice for Rome, with no alternative possible or even thinkable. Certainly, the *Aeneid* itself provides evidence of the poet's service in promoting his ruler's ideology and political goals. The epic's political commitment is so strong that the question of how far its components were or were not suggested, ultimately appears (as was said at the opening of the section) of secondary importance. What counts is the poet's complete loyalty and dedication to Augustus' concept of the Julians' divinely sanctioned leadership. Excluding, on the basis of general socio-economic considerations, the possible historicity of relevant events reported in the *Vitae* proves premature without a thorough analysis of the individual work's own peculiar coordinates and message. The issue of Vergil's "dependence", which has been nagging Latin scholars for such a long time, can hardly be considered solved by White's work.

This also has a bearing on the topic of propaganda inherent in my book's title. "Augustus laid bare a wealth of material which no poet had mined before, and it was irresistible. The worst consequence of reading Augustan poetry as propaganda is that it hinders us from studying this material critically."[36] It appears that the concepts of "critical" employed by White and by the writer of these pages are (as so often happens in present-day Vergilian scholarship) mutually exclusive.

(4) Conclusion

What then is one left with at the end of a long road, after one approach after another has turned out to be a cul-de-sac?

The attempts to 'de-Augustanize' (to use a term which originated in the Harvard school) Vergil have proved unsuccessful, including the one reviewed last that attempts to disallow the possibility of imperially inspired directives and, in particular, the peremptory value of *iubere*.

The thesis of the "gentle", compassionate, even Christianized Vergil has not held up either, in view of the fact that Vergil's often cited 'compassion' for human suffering proves partial in being employed even for propaganda purposes to win sympathies for the Trojan side. No bereft Italian mother is granted an artfully articulated wailing voice as is the Trojan mother of young Euryalus. (Servius *ad* 9. 479 observes that her speech contains "almost all the parts Cicero placed in his rhetorical instructions on raising the emotion of pity", *nam paene omnes partes habet de misericordia commovenda a Cicerone in rhetoricis positas*). When the Italians' suffering is pitied it is with the author's intent of baring the ruthless character of their leader, King Turnus, who sacrifices them for his self-serving war. The poet's sarcastic apostrophe (commenting on a man who is punished by being torn to pieces by four-horse chariots) "had you only kept your promise" (8. 643), reveals him as the unscrupulous political realist, as does his praise for Mummius, "distinguished by slaughtered Greeks" (6. 837).

Next: 'derivatives' in classical scholarship, which attempt to secure the *Aeneid*'s message from antecedent poetic "models" or from later imitations and references (instead of seeing such models as integrated in the poet's own overriding train of thought), too often, it has turned out, miss the text's meaning when (and because) they implicitly deny the poet a voice capable of clearly articulating and communicating his message himself. They can, therefore, methodologically speaking, have no privileged interpretative claims over the precise reading of the text itself.

Likewise, New Criticism's (to use again the customary name of this vaguely defined movement) way of establishing inter- (intra-, extra-) textual references on the basis of recurring words or phrases proved arbitrary whenever those 'references' are determined without observing the contexts they serve. The fact that assaults on cities are described in some overlapping vocabulary cannot mean that pious Aeneas' last-resort attack on the city of treaty-breaking Latinus in Book 12 is under the author's lens morally equivalent to the nefarious Greek assault on Troy as he painted it in Book 2.

Fragmentary 'interpretations' that disregard continuity, coherence and consistency of the *Aeneid*'s plot-line by breaking off chunks of the overall edifice (of the type 'the final scene of the *Aeneid*') have failed to demonstrate the existence of an anti-imperialistic undercurrent or second "voice" (not to mention "further voices") in the epic. Likewise, alleged cases of sub-surface "Vergilian ambivalence" (polysemy, multi-referentiality, allusiveness, 'unintentionality', etc.) often turn out to be additions arbitrarily (even wishfully) superimposed on the clear and cogent logic of the author's sequence of thought.

Let the examples recalled here suffice as a selection from what have turned out to be dead-end methodological attempts to open an escape route from Vergil the Augustan partisan. As explained in the opening chapter, this trend originated in post-World War II Germany with Pöschl's book on the *Aeneid* that was, at least partly, designed to make amends for his Nazi past, then found a wide echo in the U.S. in the works of Putnam and others. In the U.S., Pöschl's symbolic interpretation easily mingled with contemporary New Criticism, which seemed to open the prospect of an anti-imperial, more humane Vergil.

A potentially fruitful alternative to the 'theory'-related methods cited in the present summary should at least briefly be considered. It might offer itself in the edifying interpretations (these days rather unfashionable) of the past century that accept the *Aeneid*'s political message head-on, but then ascribe to it a 'wider' or timeless implicit meaning for humanity. Beauty may, here as elsewhere, have been in the eye of the interpreter. We should recall that this approach goes back to the "Roman values" (*römische Werte*) movement of the earlier 20th century, emphasized by R. Heinze in Germany. Underpinned by the concept of *Römertum* (roughly, "Romanness"), the 'Roman virtues' (*Römertugenden*), such as *fortitudo, disciplina, magnitudo animi, pietas, conscientia, cura*, could easily be 'interpreted' as being in harmony with contemporary ideology.[37] But under the influence of Syme's condemnatory view of Augustus and the anti-dictatorial mood in continental Europe after World War II, this road for a long time appeared closed.[38]

For a return to the old, it would obviously help to view Vergil in not-too-close association with Syme's autocrat: "Augustus is mentioned only three times in the *Aeneid*, though at important junctures," Galinsky tells his reader.[39] Why "only three times"? And why "mentioned" instead of "excessively glorified" (Galinsky later on more appropriately uses "hailed")? And does contemporary political partisanship appear only or even predominantly when Augustus is mentioned by name? To mind comes the politically-motivated travel route of 'Odyssean' Aeneas in Book 3; e.g., that Vergil's Aeneas leaves a victory monument near Actium where Augustus left the greatest victory monument he built outside Italy (and partly copied at Rome). The poet clearly supports Augustus' post-Actium propaganda, without mentioning his name. Judging strictly by occurrences of Augustus' name would unduly limit, and understate, the epic-wide homage Vergil pays (as the preceding chapters have demonstrated) to his ruler.

Galinsky feels that, on the topic of values, he shares and is guided by the lens of the "1990s" as opposed to that of "our forebears...in the 1930s". "And we have also come to realize the need for true values, guiding ideas, and a sense of direction".[40] This need of ours is apparently thought to be served by "Augustan culture" that "was inspired by ideas, ideals, and values".[41] Also, for taking this position, a more positive view of Augustus is welcome, which would distance[42] him from the association with Hitler and Mussolini ("...genuine leadership goes beyond the accumulation of power.").[43] "Not only did the political dispensation founded by Augustus last for almost two hundred years" (a sign of "genuine leadership?"),[44] but the Augustan culture, too, "transcended its times".[45]

In a section entitled "Transcendence", the reader is informed that Vergil uses the Augustan ideas "as a springboard for meditations on humanity and heroism. The Augustan ideas are extended to the point where the scope of these meditations becomes universal."⁴⁶ "Extended" or, rather, "extrapolated" by the interpreter?

In the values-seeking approach a desire is revealed for a non-partisan poet whose sense of compassion enlightens his reader about features of the basic human condition. It is the same desire that, we found, often underlies the theory-based readings and their sweeping generalizations. And because in that case the devil was repeatedly found to be hiding in the neglected detail, it should be checked whether the same might be true here.

> Few other heroic epics show so consistently the grief of the non-combatants and the pathos of the premature death of the young. The end of book 6 is a prime example.⁴⁷

Now: the end of Book 6 bemoans the premature death of young Marcellus, son of Augustus' sister Octavia (she reportedly fainted when Vergil read that moving passage at court) and, as Augustus' son-in-law, potentially his successor... If this is Galinsky's "prime example", should one not add a qualification by inserting two words, scil. the premature death of the <Trojan/ Augustan> young?

For, as a rule, those young whose death receives most elaborate poetic evocation of sorrow and appeal to the reader's sense of compassion die on the Trojan side: one need mention only Polydorus, Troilus, Palinurus, Nisus and Euryalus, Pallas (Lausus is honored by his slayer's, Aeneas', noble reaction which pays tribute to Aeneas' humanity). King Turnus, by contrast, at his death receives not a single word expressing pity, not even the respect that the poet pays to Turnus' heroic stand-in, Mezentius, who bravely and knowingly faces the deadly blow. (No wonder that the *Aeneid*'s ending has frustrated all those who have, with the latter-day tools of literary criticism, wished to dress up King Turnus as Vergil's lamentable and representative victim of Roman imperialism.) Vergil's partisan humanity stands in stark contrast to his 'model', Homer, who locates his most appealing scene (Hektor, death-bound, taking leave of his wife and little son, *Il.* 6. 369–493) not on the Greek but on the Trojan side.⁴⁸

The result of our glance at the 'Roman values' philology turns out to be the same as our conclusion about the theory-derived attempts to find in the *Aeneid* a non-partisan – or even a regime-critical – poet of the human condition in general. The result must be the more disappointing for either side to the extent that a closer look at Vergil's alleged humanity has revealed that even his readers' human capacity of feeling sympathy for suffering and sorrow is rhetorically manipulated and utilized for advancing sympathy for a political faction – and that only a few years after the horrible atrocities in which Vergil's emperor himself and his side had played a leading part. Vergil's implicit refusal to grant the same massive voice of compassion to the defeated side should be truly "disquieting" or "disturbing" to bi- (and multi-) vocalists – to use catch-terms they apply to passages that don't fit their desired picture of Vergil and of his, by their (non-Augustan) standards, less than attractive hero (e.g., pious Aeneas the 'priest-butcher').

In the end Vergil stands before us the trail-blazing, loyal supporter, the unconditional defender of Aeneas' latest descendant as the legitimate, because fated, heir to the kingship of Priam's Trojan empire. This is the conclusion at which a consistent, detailed, and linguistically precise reading of his epic arrives. It turns out that the ancient commentator Servius was right in asserting that Vergil's *intentio* is "to imitate Homer and give praise to Augustus based on his ancestors", *Homerum imitari et Augustum laudare a parentibus* (*ad Aen.* 1, p. 4).

Unavoidably, the question arises about the underlying premises of scholars' basic disagreements over the epic's message. In the case of *römische Werte* philology and similar trends, one can easily picture how the habits of European hierarchic tradition facilitated acceptance of the divinely sanctioned societal order propagated in the *Aeneid*. For receptive minds, it has apparently not been difficult to succumb to Vergil's seemingly objective and ethical rhetoric. But this nevertheless also presupposes a certain degree of willingness to consent, a deep-rooted feeling of affinity on the part of readers. Here the factor of personal subjectivity in scholarship comes into view.

Subjectivity may play an even greater role in all those interpretations of the later 20th century that tried to find a Vergil who would undermine the unequivocally Augustan message of his work, by encoding in it a 'deeper meaning', pronounced by a 'second voice' below the imperialistic 'surface', a voice (or voices) whose echoes supposedly can be located with the sonar of literary theory only – a type of approach that in its 'sophistication' is deemed not accessible to minds trained and acting logically.

Of course, one should not wish to take away from others "their" preferred Vergil – as long as they openly state their underlying assumptions. Problems for scholarship do arise when, as is so often the case, a preferred interpretation is connected with a claim to scholarly objectivity – which renders it subject to verification. Here then the question must be asked: Do perhaps these interpreters harbor a (possibly, subconscious) desire for the object of their research to echo and reflect their own views and feelings, or do they feel the urge to identify with an author because the author's own unadulterated message or position appeals to them? As a rule, the first alternative appears to prevail. But in either case, it cannot be discounted that such emotional identification with Vergil reveals a considerable degree of subjectivity. The author of the present volume was once met with a (well respected) Vergilian scholar's statement: "If you are right, we might as well throw away our Vergil right away."[49] "Our Vergil" – who would be "we"? Apparently, a community of scholars who find in the *Aeneid* a sufficient number of features acceptable to them.

Interpreters striving for objectivity will feel uncomfortable in view of this type of scholarship, since its representatives appear not ready (or, perhaps, even unwilling) to accept the *Aeneid*'s prima facies as offering the poet's genuine message. It has turned out that their desire to verify a message acceptable to them is fulfilled only at the cost of excluding and suppressing essential ingredients, among them the *Aeneid*'s political aim as it is documented throughout by, among the other indicators investigated in this book, its guiding prophecies, its plot-line and by the numerous tendentious references to the historical reality of the thirties and twenties BC.[50] An intrinsic reading of the epic has verified and refined the understanding offered by Vergil's contemporary Propertius (as sketched in my Prologue) as well as the general tendency of the surviving ancient commentators, Servius and Donatus. If the present volume has been successful in approximately (the scholar should never be sure of complete success) determining and restoring the *Aeneid*'s original message, disrobed of the accoutrements later centuries have (wishfully) added, its author would feel that he has made a useful contribution to Vergilian scholarship. Beyond that, he hopes to have raised awareness of the moral dilemma inherent in uncritically endorsing persuasive Vergil's terms of right and wrong.

Notes

[1] On the topic of Rome taking revenge on the Greeks for Troy's fall, see Stahl 1999.

[2] The Athenians' Machiavellian position must not be assumed to be an expression of Thucydides' own view (see Stahl 2003, 159–72). Vergil would never question the validity of Augustus' (and Rome's) power position.

[3] Blueprint of Augustus' Forum: Zanker 1987, 197, fig. 149. Versions of Aeneas fleeing with father and son: Zanker 204, fig.156a; 212, fig. 163. Parody of the endlessly reproduced scene: three monkeys with dogs' heads (mural painting from Stabiae), fig. 162.

[4] 3. 462; "huge" Troy: contrasting with backward-looking, nostalgic little toy-Troy that the resigned Helenus has built in Epirus. For Aeneas' visit to (Augustan) Buthrotum/Epirus see Stahl 1998, 44–46.

[5] Photograph: Zanker 1987, 207, fig. 157. The victims are different in both scenes.

[6] Zanker 1987, 106f., with fig. 104; 127f.

⁷ See the bibliography under Farrell, Ziolkowski.

⁸ "Homer speaks for himself, the philologists speak for Vergil and prove that he is a great poet..." (Homer spricht für sich selbst, die Philologen sprechen für Vergil und beweisen, daß er ein großer Dichter ist...), Grönbech 1953, 37.

⁹ The complex "Augustus and Christianity" has been thoroughly documented by Dahlheim 2010, 370–84.

¹⁰ "Superstition had won the first round of what was to prove a long battle for humanity and enlightenment." J. M. Roberts 1990, 285.

¹¹ For the identification see Stahl 1985, Chapter V, note 46.

¹² In the wake of White (see next section) and others, Goldberg (1995) has attempted to provide Ennius with a social upgrade by disputing the epic poet's (economic) "dependence" (120) on a number of sponsors. A key passage is a section of the *Annales* quoted by Gellius (*N.A.* XII 4), which, according to a widely accepted identification by Aelius Stilo, paints a self-portrait of Ennius as the Good Companion of a higher-ranking aristocrat (like M. Fulvius Nobilior, consul in 189 BC and hero of Ennius' epic Ambracia). Goldberg finds here a kind of social equilibrium, "the first open partnership between aristocratic and poetic interests" (121ff.). But the companion "on call" (*vocat*), "content with his lot", *suo contentus* (G. translates "modest"), hardly excludes the role of a subordinate. In Gellius' understanding he behaves as should the companion of a man of superior family and fortune, *hominis genere et fortuna superioris*. Goldberg may be asking more of the passage than it is able to deliver.

¹³ Noteworthy examples are Ariosto's *Orlando Furioso*, which includes the love story of Ruggiero and Bradamante, supposedly the founders of the d'Este family; Camões' *Os Lusíadas*, dedicated to King Sebastian (resulting, perhaps together with his service in the Far East, in a small pension from the king); Spenser's Faerie Queene, celebrating the Tudor dynasty (and earning him a small pension from Elizabeth I).

Glei (VE 894) estimates the number of Neo-Latin epics since the Renaissance as "far more than one thousand", not counting short epyllia . "...most deal with historical persons or events, among them classical, medieval, and (the biggest group) contemporary subjects, often panegyric in character".

¹⁴ "Sie haben Vergil zum Söldner des Augustus gemacht!", W. Stroh, in an uncontrolled outburst, delivered at the top of his voice. Later, in a small circle, he justified his harangue with the presence at the lecture of high school teachers who must not be allowed to leave the convention under the un-contradicted impression the lecture might had given them. Prof. Stroh provided an illuminating, though unintended, insight into the Vergil of the education industry.

¹⁵ Most recently, A. Powell has in a forthcoming paper critically reviewed the Suetonian-Donatan *Life* of Vergil, endorsing, under the historian's lens, the historicity of a number of reported biographical events.

¹⁶ The following remarks expand on what I have said in Stahl 1998, xxvf.

¹⁷ White 1993, 96.

¹⁸ White 1993, 206.

¹⁹ White 1993, 70.

²⁰ White 1993, 206.

²¹ White 1993, 301f. note 10 ad p.110. The Ovid passage was already earlier shown to be a painful thorn in the side of 'anti-Augustan' readers (see Chapter 4, note 363).

[22] White 1993, 115.
[23] Binder 1987, 29.
[24] White 1993, 266.
[25] White 1993, 268.
[26] White 1993, 134f.
[27] On elegy 2. 1, see Stahl 1985 (apparently unknown to White), Chapter VI, pp. 162–71.
[28] White 1993, 207.
[29] White 1993, 206.
[30] White 1993, 268.
[31] Kraggerud 1998. See especially 8–15.
[32] White 1993, 267.
[33] White 1993, 267.
[34] White 1993, 19.
[35] The following page numbers are taken from White 1993.
[36] White 1993, 207.
[37] For an instructive detailed survey see P. L. Schmidt in DNP 15/2, 314–22, where the name of E. Burck is foregrounded repeatedly; his publications of the nineteen-thirties and -forties (not accessible to me) apparently are completely suppressed in his collected writings of 1966/81 (Schmidt o.c. 317).
[38] The *Werteforschung* of scholars grouped around Haltenhoff, Heil, and Mutschler (Dresden) can, in view of their critical approach and essentially sociological analyses, (see their 2003 Einleitung, Vf,; 2005 Einleitung, VIIIf.) hardly be viewed as a revival of the old idealizing, edifying, and nationalistic (nationalsocialistic) movement.
[39] Galinsky 1996, 247.
[40] Galinsky 1996, 5.
[41] Galinsky 1996, 8.
[42] This distancing is briefly expressed by, among others, Galinsky (1996, 4).
[43] Galinsky 1996, 4.
[44] "We have witnessed that 'ideology' and 'propaganda' are inadequate foundations for lasting political systems" (Galinsky 1996, 5) – a sentence in its generality hardly incontestable.
[45] Galinsky 1996, 4 (my italics).
[46] Galinsky 1996, 239.
[47] Galinsky 1996, 247.
[48] Stahl 2001, 86–89.
[49] "Wenn Sie Recht haben, können wir unseren Vergil ja gleich wegwerfen" (A. Wlosok, responding to a lecture by the author). The same scholar, in an untitled (but headed in handwriting "meine Confessio Vergiliana") publication (1983), claims to offer a historically correct interpretation against Putnam's negative portrait of Aeneas (49). She finds Vergil's political message ("politische Botschaft") in the horrible war Aeneas has to wage in Latium. The poet "has made 'die grauenvollen Kriege' – horrida bella...and, along with them, war as such in any case ('und mit ihnen den Krieg schlechthin') the dominant theme of the *Aeneid*'s second half". She sees emphasis placed "again and again on the victims of the war and the sufferings of those afflicted. To them goes the sympathy of the narrator. To them the reader's compassion is being directed" (50). That it is predominantly sympathy for those suffering on the

Chapter 8

Trojan/proto-Julian side, to whom her 'reader's compassion is being directed', apparently escaped Wlosok's attention (here another compliment is due to Vergil's rhetorical psychagogia). In concluding, Wlosok states that the *Aeneid*'s call to peace ("Friedesappell"), beyond its contemporaries, applies to "all readers of all times" ("allen Lesern zu allen Zeiten", 51). *Pax Augusta/Romana* for all at all times? Still in the late 20th century, it was apparently not easy to look outside the European tradition. The occidental hagiography of Vergil proves unshaken.

The U.S. Vergil Society, a community of considerable scholarly merit, after for a brief period thanking its members for their annual contributions with the words "Thank you for your interest in Vergil", has quickly returned to the old formula "Thank you for your love of Vergil" (my italics): giving in to pressure of its membership? The object of scholarship as an object of affection? Whereas Thucydides (or Tacitus) is unquestionably granted praise for providing insight into the darker side of human nature, a barrier has been erected against recognizing in Vergil the skilful, often more veiling than revealing, propagandist – the kind of propagandist whose function and preponderance in contemporary society is being deplored so bitterly today. – For a glimpse at the theme 'Vergil and the education industry' see also note 14 above.

[50] A. Powell has, in the brilliant first chapter of his *Virgil the Partisan* (2008), illuminated the danger of a methodology that, by limiting itself to investigating Vergil's architecture and his relationship to his literary sources, by circular reasoning *a priori* precludes consideration of any other possible aspect, especially that of a work's political dimension. See also Chapter 2, Section 3 above.

BIBLIOGRAPHY (WORKS CITED)

WORKS CITED BY ABBREVIATION

CIL *Corpus Inscriptionum Latinarum*, Berlin, 1853–present.
CN *The Works of Virgil with a Commentary*, edd. Conington, J. and Nettleship, H., 3 vols., Hildesheim, 1963.
DNP *Der Neue Pauly. Enzyklopädie der Antike,* edd. Cancik, H. and Schneider, H., Stuttgart, 1996–2003.
L&S *A Latin Dictionary*, edd. Lewis, C.T. and Short, C., Oxford, 1879.
NH *A Commentary on Horace Odes, Book 1*, edd. Nisbet, R.G.M. and Hubbard, M., Oxford, 1970.
NTDR *A New Topographical Dictionary of Ancient Rome*, Richardson, L., Baltimore, 1992.
OLD *Oxford Latin Dictionary,* Oxford, 1982.
R.G. *Res Gestae Divi Augusti: The Achievements of Divine Augustus*, edd. and trans. Brunt, P.A. and Moore, J.M., London, 1967.
S *Servii Grammatici qui feruntur in Vergilii carmina commentarii*, edd. Thilo, G. and Hagen, H., vol. I, Leipzig, 1881. Vol. II reprint, Hildesheim, 1961.
TDAR *A Topographical Dictionary of Ancient Rome*, Ashley, T. and Platner, S.B., Rome, 1965.
VE *The Virgil Encyclopedia*, edd. Thomas, R.F. and Ziolkowski, J.M., Oxford, 2014.

EDITIONS, COMMENTARIES, HANDBOOKS, TRANSLATIONS

Austin, R.G., ed.
    1964 *P. Vergili Maronis Aeneidos Liber Secundus*, Oxford.
    1966 *P. Vergili Maronis Aeneidos Liber Quartus*, Oxford.
    1967 *P. Vergili Maronis Aeneidos Liber Sextus*, Oxford.
    1971 *P. Vergili Maronis Aeneidos Liber Primus,* Oxford.
Binder, G. and Binder, E. edd. and trans.
    1991 *Dido und Aeneas. Das 4. Buch der Aeneis*, Stuttgart.
    2008 *Publius Vergilius Maro: Aeneis*, Stuttgart.
Della Corte, F., ed.
    1984–1991 *Enciclopedia Vergiliana*, vols. I–V, Rome.
Donatus, Tiberius Claudius
    1905/1906 *Interpretationes Vergilianae*, ed. H. Georgii, 2 vols., Leipzig.
Eden, P.T., ed.
    1975 *A Commentary on Virgil: Aeneid VIII*, Mnemosyne Suppl. 35, Leiden.
Fairclough, H.R., ed. and trans.
    1916 *Virgil: Eclogues, Georgics, Aeneid I–VI*, vol. I, Cambridge, Mass. Rev. 1999 by G.P. Goold.

Bibliography

    1918   *Virgil: Aeneid VII–XII, The Minor Poems*, vol. II, Cambridge, Mass. Rev. 1934.

Forbiger, P.
    1875   *P. Vergili Maronis opera, Pars III*, 4th ed., Leipzig.

Fordyce, C.J. and Christie, J.D. edd.
    1977   *Aeneidos libri VII–VIII*, Oxford.

Giard, J.-B.
    1988   *Catalogue des monnaies de l'Empire romain I Auguste*, Paris.

Gransden, K.W., ed.
    1976   *Aeneid Book VIII*, Cambridge.
    1991   *Vergil: Aeneid Book XI*, Cambridge.

Hardie, P., ed.
    1994   *Aeneid Book IX*, Cambridge.

Harrison, S.J., ed.
    1991   *Vergil: Aeneid 10,* Oxford and New York.

Heyne, C.G., ed.
    1800   *P. Virgilii Maronis Opera*, 3rd ed., 6 vols., Leipzig.

Hirtzel, F.A., ed.
    1900   *P. Vergili Maronis Opera*, Oxford.

Horsfall, N., ed.
    2000   *Virgil, Aeneid 7, A Commentary*, Leiden.
    2003   *Virgil, Aeneid 11, A Commentary*, Leiden.
    2006   *Virgil, Aeneid 3, A Commentary*, Leiden.

Ladewig, T., Schaper, C. and Deuticke, P. edd.
    1973   *Vergils Gedichte*, 3 vols. in 2, Berlin.

Maclennan, K., ed.
    2003   *Virgil, Aeneid VI,* rev. Harrison, S.J. London.

Merguet, H.
    1912   *Lexikon zu Vergilius mit Angabe sämtlicher Stellen*, Leipzig. Reprint, Hildesheim 1960.

Mynors, R., ed.
    1969   *P. Vergili Maronis Opera*, Oxford.
    1990   *Georgics*, Oxford.

Norden, E., ed. and trans.
    1957   *P. Vergilius Maro. Aeneis Buch VI,* 4th ed., Darmstadt.

Page, T.E., ed.
    1894/1900   *The Aeneid of Virgil*, 2 vols., London. Reprint, London 1962.

Pease, A.S., ed.
    1935   *Publi Vergili Maronis Aeneidos Liber Quartus*, Cambridge, Mass.

Perret, J., ed. and trans.
    1977–1980   *Enéide*, Paris.

Szantyr, A., ed.
    1965   *Lateinische Syntax und Stilistik*, Munich.

Thilo, G. and Hagen, H. edd.
    1881–1902   *Servii Grammatici qui feruntur in Vergilii carmina commentarii*, 3 vols., Leipzig.

Wacht, M.
    1996   *Concordantia Vergilia*, 2 vols., Hildesheim.

Warwick, H.H.
 1975 *A Vergil Concordance*, Minneapolis.
Wetmore, M.N., ed.
 1961 *Index verborum Vergilianus*, 3rd ed, Hildesheim.
Williams, R.D., ed.
 1960 *P. Vergili Maronis Aeneidos Liber Quintus*, Oxford.
 1962 *P. Vergili Maronis Aeneidos Liber Tertius*, Oxford.
 1967 *Vergil*, G&R New Surveys in the Classics 1, Oxford.
 1972/1973 *The Aeneid of Virgil*, 2 vols., London.

SECONDARY LITERATURE
Amersdorffer, H.
 1976 *Antike Münzen aus der Sammlung Amersdorffer*, Berlin.
Barchiesi, A.
 1984 *La traccia del modello: Effetti omerici nella narrazione virgiliana*, Giardini and Pisa.
Bauer, H.
 1988 "Basilica Aemilia", in Heilmeyer, W.D. et al. (edd.), *Kaiser Augustus und die verlorene Republik: Eine Ausstellung im Martin-Gropius-Bau, Berlin, 7. Juni-14. August 1988*, Mainz.
Bertoletti, M.
 1988 "Architekturplastik des Apollo-Sosianus-Tempels", in Heilmeyer, W.D. et al. (edd.), *Kaiser Augustus und die Verlorene Republik: Eine Ausstellung im Martin-Gropius-Bau, Berlin, 7. Juni-14. August 1988*, 140–148, Mainz.
Binder, G.
 1971 *Aeneas und Augustus: Interpretationen zum 8. Buch der Aeneis*, Meisenheim am Glan.
 1985 "*Lusus Troiae*: L'Enéide de Virgile comme source archéologique", *BAGB* 44, 349–56.
 1987 *Saeculum Augustum, I, II, III*, Darmstadt.
Bishop, J.H.
 1956 "Palatine Apollo", *CQ* 6, 187–92.
Boas, H.
 1938 *Aeneas's Arrival in Latium: Observations on Legends, History, Religion, Topography and Related Subjects in Vergil*, Aeneid VII, 1–135, Amsterdam.
Bömer, F.
 1944 "Studien zum VIII. Buche der Aeneis", *RhM* 92, 319–69.
Bowersock, G.W.
 1990 "The Pontificate of Augustus", in K. Raaflaub and M. Toher (edd.) *Between Republic and Empire: Interpretations of Augustus and His Principate*, Berkeley.
Boyle, A.J., ed.
 1993 *Roman Epic*, London.
 1996 "The Canonic Text: Vergil's *Aeneid*", in *id.* (ed), *Roman Epic*, London, 79–107.
Braund, S.M.
 1997 "Virgil and the Cosmos. Religious and Philosophical Ideas", in Martindale, C. (ed.) *The Cambridge Companion to Virgil*, Cambridge, 204–21.

Bibliography

Briggs, W.W.
    1975   "Augustan Athletics and the Games of *Aeneid* V", *Stadion* 1, 267–83.

Brinton, A.C.
    2002   *Maphaeus Vegius and his Thirteenth Book of the* Aeneid, London.

Broch, H.
    1945   *The Death of Virgil*, trans. J.S. Untermeyer, Berkeley.

Brunt, P.A. and Moore, J. M. (edd. and comm.)
    1967   *Res Gestae Divi Augusti*, Oxford.

Buchheit, V.
    1963   *Vergil über die Sendung Roms*, Heidelberg.

Büchner, K.
    1961   *P. Vergilius Maro: Der Dichter der Römer*, Stuttgart.

Buckley, E.
    2006   "Ending the *Aeneid*? Closure and Continuation in Maffeo Vegio's *Supplementum*", *Vergilius* 52, 108–37.

Burck, E.
    1979   "*Vergil's Aeneis*" in *id.* (ed), *Das römische Epos*, Darmstadt, 51–119.

Carcopino, J.
    1968   *Virgile et les origines d'Ostie*, 2nd ed., Paris.

Carettoni, G.
    1983   *Das Haus des Augustus auf dem Palatin*, Mainz.

Castagnoli, F.
    1972   *Lavinium. Vol. 1: Topografia generale, fonti e storia delle ricerche*, Rome.
    1977   "Roma arcaica ed i recenti scavi di Lavinio", *PP* 32, 340–55.

Clausen, W.
    1987   *Virgil's* Aeneid *and the Tradition of Hellenistic Poetry*, Berkeley.
    2002   *Virgil's* Aeneid*: Decorum, Allusion, and Ideology*, Beiträge zur Altertumskunde, 162, Munich.

Coarelli, F.
    1985   *Roma*, Rome.
    1988A   *Il Foro Boario. Dalle Origini alla fine della Repubblica*, Rome.
    1988B   "Rom: Die Stadtplannung von Caesar bis Augustus", in Heilmeyer, W.D. et al. (edd.), *Kaiser Augustus und die verlorene Republik: Eine Ausstellung im Martin-Gropius-Bau, Berlin, 7. Juni-14. August 1988*, Mainz.

Connolly, P.
    1998   *Greece and Rome at War*, London.

Conte, G.B.
    1986   *The Rhetoric of Imitation: Genre and Poetic Memory in Virgil and Other Latin Poets*, trans. and ed. C. Segal, Cornell Studies in Classical Philology 44, Ithaca.

Conway, R.S.
    1932   "Vergil and Octavian", *CR* 46, 199–202.

Cornell, T.J.
    1977   "Aeneas' Arrival in Italy", *LCM* 2, 77–83.

Cova, P.V.
    1983   "La Fortuna di Virgilio nelle prima metà del Novecento", Estratto da *Virgilio nostro Antico*, Commune di Calvisano, 99–130.

Crawford, M.
　1974　*Roman Republican Coinage*, London.
Cucchiarelli, A.
　2002　"A Note on Vergil, *Aeneid* 12.941–3", *CQ* 52, 620–2.
Dahlheim, W.
　2010　*Augustus: Aufrührer - Herrscher - Heiland. Eine Biographie*, Munich.
Della Corte, F.
　1972　*La mappa dell'* Eneide, Florence.
Dinzelbacher, P.
　1982　"Über Troiaritt und Pyrriche", *Eranos* 80, 151–61.
Dury-Moyaers, G.
　1981　*Enée et Lavinium à propos des découvertes archéologiques récentes*, Collection Latomus 174, Brussels.
Farrell, J.
　1997　"The Vergilian intertext", in Martindale, C. (ed.) *The Cambridge Companion to Virgil*, 222–38.
　2001　"The Vergilian Century", *Vergilius* 47, 11–28.
Farrell, J. and Putnam, M.C.J., edd.
　2010　*A Companion to Vergil's* Aeneid *and its Tradition*, Chichester and Malden.
Feeney, D.
　1991　*The Gods in Epic. Poets and Critics of the Classical Tradition*, Oxford.
Feugère, M.
　1985　"Nouvelles observations sur les cabochons de bronze estampés du cingulum romain", in Bishop, M.C. (ed.), *The Production and Distribution of Roman Military Equipment*. Proceedings of the Second Roman Military Equipment Research Seminar, BAR International Series 275, Oxford, 117–41.
Fowler, D.
　1998　"Opening the Gates of War: *Aeneid* 7.601–40", in Stahl, H.-P. (ed.) *Vergil's* Aeneid: *Augustan Epic and Political Context*, London and Swansea, 155–74.
Fowler, W.W.
　1917　*Aeneas at the Site of Rome. Observations on the Eighth Book of the* Aeneid, Oxford.
Fraenkel, E.
　1954　"*Urbem quem statuo vestra est*", *Glotta* 33, 157–9.
Galinsky, G.K.
　1966　"The Hercules-Cacus Episode in *Aeneid* VIII", *AJPh* 87, 18–51.
　1981　"Vergil's *Romanitas* and his Adaptation of Greek Heroes", *ANRW* II, 31.2, 985–1010.
　1983　"Aeneas in Latium: Archäologie, Mythos und Geschichte", in Poeschl, V. (ed.) *2000 Jahre Vergil: Ein Symposion*.
　1988　"The Anger of Aeneas", *AJPh* 109, 321–48.
　1996　*Augustan Culture*, Princeton.
Ganzert, H.
　2000　*Im Allerheiligsten des Augustusforums*, Mainz.
Giuliani, C.F. and Verducci, P.
　1987　*L'area centrale del foro Romano*, Florence.

Bibliography

Glei, R.
1991 *Der Vater der Dinge: Interpretationen zur politischen, literarischen und kulturellen Dimension des Krieges bei Vergil,* Trier.

Goldberg, S.M.
1995 *Epic in Republican Rome,* New York.

Griffin, J.
1985 *Latin Poets and Roman Life,* London.

Grimal, P.
1948 "La promenade d'Evandre et Enée à la lumière des fouilles récentes", *REA* 50, 348–51.

Grönbech, V.P.
1953 *Der Hellenismus Lebensstimmung. Weltmacht,* Göttingen.

Haltenhoff A., Heil, A. and Mutschler, F.-H. edd.
2003 "*O tempora, o mores! Römische Werte und römische Literatur in den letzten Jahren der Republik*", Beiträge zur Altertumskunde, Band 227, Munich.
2005 "*Römische Werte als Gegenstand der Altertumswissenschaft*", Beiträge zur Altertumskunde, Band 171, Munich.

Hardie, P.
1993 *The Epic Successors of Virgil,* Cambridge.
2001 "A Virgil for Vietnam", *TLS* June 15, London.

Harrison, E.L.
1984 "The *Aeneid* and Carthage", in Woodman, T. and West, D. (edd.), *Poetry and Politics in the Age of Augustus,* Cambridge, 95–115.

Harrison, S.J.
1988 "Augustus, the Poets, and the *Spolia Opima*", *CQ* 39, 408–14.
1998 "The Sword-Belt of Pallas: Moral Symbolism and Political Ideology", in Stahl, H.-P. (ed.) *Vergil's* Aeneid: *Augustan Epic and Political Context,* 223–42.

Heinze, R.
1965 *Vergils Epische Technik,* 5th ed., Darmstadt.
1993 *Vergil's Epic Technique,* trans. Hazel Harvey, David Harvey, and Fred Robertson, Berkeley.

Hesberg, H. von
1988 "Die Veränderung des Erscheinungsbildes der Stadt Rom unter Augustus", in Heilmeyer, W.D. et al. (edd.), *Kaiser Augustus und die verlorene Republik: Eine Ausstellung im Martin-Gropius-Bau, Berlin, 7. Juni-14. August 1988,* Mainz.

Hesberg, H. von and Panciera, S.
1994 *Das Mausoleum des Augustus: der Bau und seine Inschriften,* Munich.

Hornsby, R.A.
1970 *Patterns of Action in the* Aeneid: *An Interpretation of Vergil's Epic Similes,* Iowa City.

Horsfall, N.
1973 "Corythus: The Return of Aeneas in Virgil and his Sources", *JRS* 43, 68–79.
1995 *A Companion to the Study of Virgil,* Leiden.

Hübner, W.
1970 *Dirae im römischen Epos. Über das Verhältnis von Vogeldämonen und Prodigien,* Hildesheim.

1994 "Die Dira im zwölften Buch der Aeneis: eine Klarstellung", *Eranos* 92, 23–8.

Inwood, B.
1985 *Ethics and Human Action in Early Stoicism*, Oxford.

James, S. L.
1995 "Establishing Rome with a Sword: *Condere* in the *Aeneid*", *AJPh* 116, 623–37.

Johnson, W.R.
1976 *Darkness Visible: A Study of Vergil's* Aeneid, Berkeley.

Kallendorf, C.
1999 "Historicizing the 'Harvard school': Pessimistic Readings of the *Aeneid* in Italian Renaissance Scholarship", *HSCP* 99, 391–413.
2004 Review of *Maffeo Vegio: The Short Epics*, introd., ed., trans., by Michael C.J. Putnam, with James Hankins, *Vergilius* 50, 216–22.

Kallendorf, C., ed.
1993 *Vergil*, New York.

Kirk, G.S.,
1985 *The Iliad: A Commentary vol. 1*, Cambridge.

Kleinknecht, H.
1963 "Laokoon", in Oppermann, H. (ed.), *Wege zu Vergil*, Darmstadt, 426–88.

Klingner, F.
1967 *Virgil: Bucolica, Georgica, Aeneis*, Zürich.

Knauer, G.N.
1979 "Die Aeneis und Homer. Studien zur poetischen Technik Vergils mit Listen der Homerzitate in der Aeneis", *Hypomnemata Heft* 7, 2nd ed., Göttingen.

Knight, W.F.J.
1933 "*Animamque superbam* and Octavian", *CR* 47, 169–71.

Kraggerud, E.
1987 "Perusia and the *Aeneid*", *SO* 62, 77–87.
1998 "Vergil Announcing the *Aeneid*. On *Georg.* 3.1–48", in Stahl, H.-P. (ed.) *Vergil's* Aeneid: *Augustan Epic and Political Context*.

Kronenberg, L.
2005 "Mezentius the Epicurean", *TAPA* 135, 403–31.

LaCerda, I.L.
1628 *P. Virgilii Maronis Aeneidos sex libri posteriores argumentis, explicationibus, et notis illlustrata*, Cologne.

La Rocca, E.
1988 "Der Apollo-Sosianus Tempel", in Heilmeyer, W.D. et al. (edd.), *Kaiser Augustus und die verlorene Republik: Eine Ausstellung im Martin-Gropius-Bau, Berlin, 7. Juni-14. August 1988*, Mainz.

Laird, A.
2003 "Latin Sans Frontières", review of *Roman Constructions. Readings in Postmodern Latin*, by D. Fowler, *CR* 53, 244–6.

Lefèvre, E.
1983 "Vergil: *Propheta Retroversus*", *Gymnasium* 90,17–40.
1989 *Das Bildprogramm des Apollo-Tempels auf dem Palatin*, Konstanzer Althistorische Vorträge und Forschungen, Heft 24, Konstanz.

Bibliography

Lloyd, C.
    1999   "The Evander-Anchises Connection: Fathers, Sons and Homoerotic Desire in Virgil's *Aeneid*", *Vergil* 45, 3–21.

Long, A.A.
    1986   *Hellenistic Philosophy* (2nd edn.), Berkeley.

Long, A.A., ed.
    1971   *Problems in Stoicism*, London.

Luck, G., ed.
    1967   *Tristia*, Heidelberg.

Lugli, G.
    1970   *Interario di Roma Antica*, Milan.

Lyne, R.O.A.M.
    1983   "Vergil and the Politics of War", *CQ* 33, 188–203.
    1992   *Further Voices in Vergil's Aeneid*, Oxford.

Mackail, J.W.
    1965   *Virgil and his Meaning to the World of Today*, New York.

Martindale, C., ed.
    1997   *The Cambridge Companion to Virgil*, Cambridge.

Massimi, G.
    1953   *La Chiesa di S. Maria in Cosmedin*, Rome.

Miller, J.F.
    2009   *Apollo, Augustus, and the Poets*, Cambridge.

Monti, R.C.
    1981   *The Dido Episode and the* Aeneid: *Roman Social and Political Values in the Epic*, Mnemosyne Suppl. 66, Leiden.

Morgan, L.
    1998   "Assimilation and Civil War: Hercules and Cacus", in Stahl, H.-P. (ed.) *Vergil's* Aeneid: *Augustan Epic and Political Context*, 175–98.

Murray, W.M. and Petsas, P.M.
    1989   *Octavian's Campsite Memorial for the Actian War*, TAPhA 79 Part 4, Philadelphia.

Mutschler, F.-H.
    2003   "Caesars Kommentarien im Spannungsfeld von sozialer Norm und individuellem Geltungsanspruch", in Haltenhoff, A., Heil, A. and Mutschler, F.-H. (edd.) *O tempora, o mores! Römische Werte und römische Literatur in den letzten Jahrzehnten der römischen Republik. Beiträge zur Altertumskunde*, Munich, 71–91.

Nedergaard, E.
    1988   "Zur Problematik der Augustusbögen auf dem Forum Romanum", in *Kaiser Augustus und die verlorene Republik*. [Exhibition catalogue] Antikenmuseum Berlin. Staatliche Museen, Preussischer Kulturbesitz: 224–39. Kat.104–109, Berlin.

Nethercut, W.R.
    1968   "Invasion in the *Aeneid*", *G&R* 15, 82–95.

Norden, E.
    1901   "Vergils *Aeneis* im Lichte ihrer Zeit", *NJA* 7, 249–82; 313–34.

Ogilvie, R.M., ed.
    1965   *A Commentary on Livy Books 1–5*, Oxford.

Oliensis, E.
 2001 "Freud's *Aeneid*", *Vergilius* 47, 39–63.
Otis, B.
 1964 *Virgil: A Study in Civilized Poetry*, Norman.
Parry, A.
 1963 "The Two Voices of Virgil's *Aeneid*", *Arion* 2, 66–80.
Pascal, C.B.
 1990 "The Dubious Devotion of Turnus", *TAPA* 120, 251–68.
Pensabene, P.
 1984 "Tempio di Saturno: architettura e decorazione", in Bietti Sisterni, A.M. (ed.) *Lavorie e studi di Archaeologia*, vol. V, Rome.
Perkell, C.G.
 1991 "*Dorica castra, alius Achilles* (*Aen.* VI, 88–90)", *Maia* 43, 195–8.
Perret, J.
 1942 *Les origines de la légende troyenne de Rome*, Paris.
Peter, H.
 1914 "M. Porcii Catonis Origines. Ex Libro I", in *Historicorum Romanorum Reliquiae*. Vol. I., Leipzig, 55–64.
Pöschl, V.
 1962 *The Art of Vergil*, trans. G. Seligson, Ann Arbor.
 1964 *Die Dichtkunst Vergils*, Darmstadt; 3rd ed. Berlin, 1977.
 1981 "Virgil und Augustus", *ANRW* II, 31.2:709–27.
Powell, A.
 2008 *Virgil the Partisan*, Swansea.
 2013 "Anticipating Octavian's Failure: from Tauromenium to the Death of Cleopatra", in *id.* (ed.) *Hindsight in Greek and Roman History*, Swansea, 171–91.
 (forthcoming) "Sinning Against Philology? Historical Method and the Suetonian-Donatan Life of Virgil", in *The Ancient Lives of Virgil*, Hardie, P. and Powell, A. (edd.).
Putnam, M.C.J.
 1965 *The Poetry of the* Aeneid: *Four Studies in Imaginative Unity and Design*, Cambridge, Mass.
 1981 "Pius Aeneas and the Metamorphosis of Lausus", *Arethusa* 14, 139–56.
 1985 "Possessiveness, Sexuality and Heroism in the *Aeneid*", *Vergilius* 31, 1–21.
 1995 *Vergil's* Aeneid: *Interpretation and Influence*, Chapel Hill.
 1998 *Vergil's Epic Designs: Ekphrasis in the* Aeneid, New Haven.
 2006 "Horace to Torquatus: 'Epistle 1.5' and 'Ode 4.7'", *AJPh* 127, 3: 387–413.
Putnam, M.C.J. and Hankins, J., ed. and trans.
 2004 *Maffeo Vegio: Short Epics*, Cambridge, Mass.
Quinn, K.
 1968 *Virgil's* Aeneid: *A Critical Description*, London.
Quint, D.
 1993 *Epic and Empire*, Princeton.
Raaflaub, K. and Toher, M., edd.
 1990 *Between Republic and Empire: Interpretations of Augustus and his Principate*, Berkeley.

Rabel, R.J.
    1981   "Vergil, Tops, and the Stoic View of Fate", *CJ* 77, 27–31.

Reckford, K.J.
    1961   "Latent tragedy in *Aeneid* VII 1–285", *AJP* 82, 252–69.
    1981   "Helen in *Aeneid* II and VI", *Arethusa* 14, 85–99.

Rehm, B.
    1932   *Das geographische Bild des alten Italien in Virgils Aeneis*, Philologus Suppl. 24. Heft 2, Leipzig.

Reinhold, M.
    1988   *From Republic to Principate: An Historical Commentary on Cassius Dio's Roman History Books 49–52 (36–29 BC)*, APA Monograph Series No. 34, Atlanta.

Renger, C.
    1985   *Aeneas und Turnus: Analyse einer Feindschaft*, Studien zur klassischen Philologie 11, Frankfurt am Main.

Richmond, O.
    1958   "Palatine Apollo Again", *CQ* 52, 180–4.

Roberts, J.M.
    1990   *The Penguin History of the World*, London.

Schenk, P.
    1984   *Die Gestalt des Turnus in Vergils Aeneis*, Beiträge zur Klassischen Philologie 164, Königstein.

Schlunk, R.R.
    1974   *The Homeric Scholia and the* Aeneid: *A Study of the Influence of Ancient Homeric Literary Criticism on Vergil*, Ann Arbor.

Schneider, B.
    1985   *Das Aeneissupplement des Maffeo Vegio*, Weinheim.

Schröder, W.A.
    1971   *M. Porcius Cato. Das Erste Buch des Origines: Ausgabe und Erklärung der Fragmente*, Beiträge zur Klassischen Philologie 41, Meisenheim am Glan.

Schwenn, F.
    1915   *Die Menschenopfer bei den Griechen und Römern*, Religionsgeschichtliche Versuche und Vorarbeiten 15.3, Giessen.

Segal, C.
    1990   "Dido's Hesitation in *Aeneid* 4", *CW* 84, 1–12.

Small, J.P.
    1982   *Cacus and Marsyas in Etrusco-Roman Legend*, Princeton.

Staccioli, R.
    1988   *Roma entro le mura*, Rome.

Stahl, H.-P.
    1969   "Verteidigung des 1. Buches der *Aeneis*", *Hermes* 97, 346–361.
    1974   "Peinliche Erfahrung eines kleinen Gottes: Horaz in seinen Satiren", *A&A* 20, 25–53.
    1975   "Learning through Suffering? Croesus' Conversations in the History of Herodotus", *YCS* 24, 1–36.
    1981   "Aeneas – An 'Unheroic' Hero?", *Arethusa* 14, 157–77.
    1985   *Propertius: "Love" and "War". Individual and State under Augustus*, Berkeley.

1990	"The Death of Turnus: Augustan Vergil and the Political Rival" in Raaflaub, K.A. and Toher, M. (edd.) *Between Republic and Empire: Interpretations of Augustus and his Principate*, 174–211.
1998 A	"Editor's Introduction", in *id.* (ed.) *Vergil's* Aeneid*: Augustan Epic and Political Context*, London and Swansea, xv–xxx.
1998 B	"Political Stopovers on a Mythological Travel Route: From Battling Harpies to the Battle of Actium", in *id.* (ed.) *Vergil's* Aeneid*: Augustan Epic and Political Context.* London and Swansea, 37–84.
1999	"Griechenhetze in Vergils *Aeneis*: Roms Rache für Troja", in Vogt-Spira, G. and Rommel, B. (edd.) *Rezeption und Identität. Die kulturelle Auseinandersetzung Roms mit Griechenland als europäisches Paradigme*, Stuttgart, 249–73.
2001	"On the Sadness of Silence in Ancient Literature", in *The Language of Silence*, Jaekel, S. and Timonen, A. (edd.), Turku, 86–104.
2002	"Sneaking it by the Emperor: Ovid Playing it Both Ways" in Amden, B. et al. (edd.) *Noctes Atticae: 34 Articles on Graeco-Roman Antiquity and its Nachleben. Studies Presented to Joergen Mejer on His Sixtieth Birthday March 18, 2002*, Copenhagen, 265–80.
2003	*Thucydides: Man's Place in History*, London and Swansea (Enlarged edition of 1966 German monograph).
2006	"Narrative Unity and Consistency of Thought: Composition of Event Sequences in Thucydides", in Rengakos, A. and Tsakmakis, A. (edd.) *Brill's Companion to Thucydides*, Leiden, 301–34.
2011	"The Sword-Belt of Pallas: Holding a Quill for the Critic? Vergil, *Aeneid* 10,495–500", *Würzburger Jahrbücher* 35, 7–31.
2012	"Herodotus and Thucydides on Blind Decisions Preceding Military Action" in Foster, E. and Lateiner, D. (edd.) *Thucydides and Herodotus*, Oxford, 127–53.

Stahl, H.-P. (ed.)
    1998   *Vergil's* Aeneid*: Augustan Epic and Political Context*, London and Swansea.

Suerbaum, W.
    1981   *Vergils* Aeneis*: Beiträge zu ihrer Rezeption in Geschichte und Gegenwart*, Bamberg.
    1999   *Vergils* Aeneis. *Epos zwischen Geschichte und Gegenwart*, Stuttgart.

Syme, R.
    1974   *The Roman Revolution*, repr. of 1962 ed., London.

Tanner, M.
    1993   *The Last Descendant of Aeneas. The Habsburgs and the Mythic Image of the Emperor*, New Haven.

Tarrant, R.J.
    1997   "Poetry and Power: Virgil's Poetry in Contemporary Context", in Martindale, C. (ed.) *The Cambridge Companion to Virgil*, Cambridge, 169–87.

Thomas, R.F.
    1998   "The Isolation of Turnus", in Stahl, H.-P. (ed.) *Vergil's* Aeneid*: Augustan Epic and Political Context*, London and Swansea, 271–302.
    2001   *Vergil and the Augustan Reception*, Cambridge.

Thome, G.
  1979 *Gestalt und Funktion des Mezentius bei Vergil, mit einem Ausblick auf die Schlußszene der Aeneis*, Europ. Hochschulschriften Reihe 15, Klassische Philologie und Literatur 14, Berne.

Tilly, B.
  1947 *Vergil's Latium*, Oxford.
  1975 review of F. della Corte, *La mappa dell'*Eneide, *Gnomon* 47, 362–8.

Trillmich, W.
  1988 "Münzpropaganda", in *Kaiser Augustus und die verlorene Republik: Eine Ausstellung im Martin-Gropius-Bau, Berlin, 7. Juni-14. August 1988*, Mainz, 474–528.

Webb, N.C.
  1978–80 "Direct Contact Between the Hero and the Supernatural in the *Aeneid*", *PVS* 17: 39–49.

Weinstock, S.
  1971 *Divus Julius*, Oxford.

West, D.
  1969 "Multiple Correspondence Similes in the *Aeneid*", *JRS* 59, 40–9.
  1998 "The End and the Meaning. *Aeneid* 12. 791–842", in H.-P. Stahl (ed.) *Vergil's Aeneid and Political Context*, London and Swansea, 303–18.

White, P.
  1993 *Promised Verse*, Cambridge, Mass.

Williams, G.
  1983 *Technique and Ideas in the* Aeneid, New Haven.

Wistrand, E.
  1984 "Aeneas and Augustus in the *Aeneid*", *Eranos* 82, 195–8.

Wlosok, A.
  1976 "Vergils Didotragödie: ein Beitrag zum Problem des Tragischen in der *Aeneis*", in Görgemanns, H. and Schmidt, E.A. (edd.) *Studien zum antiken Epos*, Meisenheim am Glan.
  1983 "Estratto", in *L'essenza del ripensamento sul Virgilio*, Mantua.
  2001 "Viktor Pöschl", *Gnomon* 73, 369–78.

Wörner E.,
  1884–6 "Aineias". *Mythologisches Lexikon* 1,1, 157–91, Leipzig.

Zanker, P.
  1972 *Forum Romanum: Die Neugestaltung durch Augustus*, Tübingen.
  1983 "Der Apollontempel auf dem Palatin: Ausstattung und politische Sinnbezüge nach der Schlacht von Actium", *ARID* Suppl. 10: 21–40.
  1987 *Augustus und die Macht der Bilder*, Munich.
  1988 *The Power of Images in the Age of Augustus*, trans. A. Shapiro, Ann Arbor.

Zetzel, J.
  1997 "Rome and its traditions", in C. Martindale (ed.) *The Cambridge Companion to Virgil*, 188–203.

Ziolkowski, J. and Putnam, M.C.J., edd.
  2008 *The Virgilian Tradition. The First Fifteen Hundred Years*, New Haven.

Ziolkowski, T.
  1993 *Virgil and the Moderns*, Princeton.

INDEX

Abas 375
Aborigines (of Latium) 359, 365
Acestes 190
Achaea 63
Achates 203, 267–8, 335, 375
Achievements see *Res Gestae*
Achilles 10, 15, 24–5, 33, 41, 49, 63–4, 110, 113, 135, 153–4, 167, 175, 189, 211, 255, 308, 379, 394, 407–9
Acrisius 402
Actaeon 331
Actium xii, 118, 126–7, 129, 132, 171–2, 234, 236, 252–3, 261, 281, 296, 305–6, 308, 310, 318, 444, 448, 453, 456
Aegeon 137–8, 143
Aegyptus 118, 126–8
Aelius Tubero 285
Aemilius, Mamercus 297
Aeneas 1–3, 5–14, 16–19, 21–8, 33–65, 68–76, 78–9, 82–7, 90, 93–6, 109–26, 130, 132–55, 163–76, 183–7, 190–208, 210–20, 222–33, 236–46, 251–74, 277–8, 280, 282–4, 286–90, 293, 295–6, 298–301, 305–6, 308–9, 311–20, 322–4, 329–30, 334–5, 348–9, 351–68, 370–92, 395–9, 400, 403, 405–6, 414–20, 422–30, 437–59
  as Dardanian 15, 386, 412–3, 419
  as Julian ancestor 3, 5, 9, 21, 23, 138, 147, 153, 286, 288, 354, 372, 382, 430, 438, 441
  as new Achilles 25, 41, 49, 139, 173, 379
  as *pater* 29, 439
  as *pius* 20, 45, 51, 54, 135–6, 121, 142–4, 148–9, 169, 185, 195, 212, 225, 237, 239, 242, 441
Aeneidos Liber XIII see *Supplement*
Aeolus 195, 212
Aeschylus 240, 394, 398
Agamemnon 90, 189, 211, 225, 394, 402, 406–11, 413, 417, 421, 424, 437

Agrippa 54, 282, 310
Ahenobarbus, Domitius 88, 93–4
Aietes 75–6
aition 33, 258, 322, 324, 374
Ajax 21, 42, 47, 90, 391
Alba Longa 257, 383
Alban Lake 257
Aletes 375
Alexander 90, 129
Alexandria 59, 129, 224
Allecto 2, 6, 73, 187, 207, 212, 216, 348, 356, 385–6, 391–3, 395–7, 399, 402, 404, 406, 411–7, 419–25
alliteration 22, 24–6, 37, 144
Almighty 228
Almo 397, 423, 425
Altri 89
Amata/Amita 2, 8, 14, 18, 23, 25–6, 39, 187, 189, 357, 360, 373, 386, 392, 395, 398–406, 411–2, 416, 420–1, 424–5, 437–8
ambiguity (and ambiguity-seeking) 26, 30 n.16, 65–6, 70, 77–8, 80–1, 85–6, 101 n.65, 102 n.81, 103 n.120, 131, 142, 150, 158 n.71, 253, 342 n.102, 343 n.120, 384, 389
ambivalence 63, 65, 78
anagnorisis 52, 58
anagnorisma/-os see *anagnorisis*
Anchises 36, 38, 42–4, 56–7, 60, 63–4, 68, 79, 85–6, 114, 136, 150–1, 163, 165, 167, 176, 201, 215, 232, 235–6, 254, 265, 272–4, 280, 283, 307–8, 312, 353, 366, 376–7, 383–4, 437, 442
Andromacha 74
anima naturaliter Christiana 234, 444
Anna 193, 219, 222–3, 239–41
Antiates 306
Antigone 183
Antony, Mark 128, 223, 252–3, 261, 281, 306
Antores 143

475

Index

Anxur, 135
Apelles 305
Aphrodite *see* Venus
Apollo 3, 4, 126, 129, 133, 139, 166, 175, 192, 223, 225, 229, 233–4, 236, 238–9, 257–8, 260–2, 266, 273, 276, 278–9, 281–2, 285, 312, 315–6, 319, 323, 332–5, 378, 386, 388–9, 394, 408, 444, 450
    Leucadian god 130
    Palatine, 128, 262, 304, 306
    Sosianus (temple) 281–2, 296, 318
Apollonius Rhodius 207, 217
Appian 171
Apsyrtus 75, 242
Ara Maxima 259, 263, 266, 268–9, 274, 281–2, 286, 319–21, 334
Ara Pacis Augustae 286, 310, 443
Aracoeli, S.a Maria 234, 279, 283, 444
Arcadian(s) 20, 132, 139, 254, 256–7, 264–5, 271, 273, 287, 297, 299, 318, 320, 322–3, 402
Arch of Augustus 318
Arch of Titus 303–5
Ardea 353, 377, 380, 383–4, 392, 406
Ares *see* Mars
Argiletum 275, 277–8, 284, 287–8, 290–5, 301, 318
Argos 376, 402
Argus 287, 332
Ariadne 183, 231
Ariosto, Ludovico 65
aristeia 110–1, 121, 132, 134, 141–2, 153
Aristotle 183–4, 227
Ars Amatoria 204
Artabanos 409–11, 424
Artemis 164
Ascanius/Iulus 18–19, 34, 53, 90, 92, 114, 136, 139, 164, 166–7, 176, 190–200, 203–7, 223–4, 231, 242, 254, 257, 307–8, 357, 365–6, 375, 386, 390, 392, 395–8, 406, 412, 424, 442
Asconius 379
Asia 40, 387
Assisi 234
Astyanax 74–6

Asylum 272, 277–80, 282–5, 291, 293, 295, 301
Athena *see* Minerva
Athenian(s) 442
Atys 307–8
Augustus xi–ii, 1, 3–4, 6, 34, 43, 58–9, 61, 66–8, 82–3, 86, 121, 127–9, 131, 150, 166, 171–2, 175, 177, 185, 197, 209–10, 221–4, 228–9, 231, 233–4, 236–7, 243, 251–5, 257–61, 263, 265–7, 272–4, 276, 278, 280–2, 285–90, 293–9, 301–2, 304–5, 307–8, 310–9, 322–4, 330, 351, 356, 371, 385–6, 430, 439, 441–50, 452–4, 456–8
    Caesaris Ultor 61, 171, 177, 439
    Emperor xi, 1, 3–4, 197, 426, 444
    Octavian xii, 3–4, 6, 59, 61, 127–8, 171, 177, 185, 210, 223–4, 236, 261, 291, 296–7, 305–11, 313–4, 318, 324, 356, 439, 442, 450–2
    Memoirs 172
    See also de-Augustanizing
Aulestes 20, 22
Ausonia 351–2, 384, 430
Ausonian(s) 38, 72, 351–2, 387, 397
Austin, R.G. 91, 151, 193–4, 199–200, 219, 226, 232–3, 241
Aventine 259, 270, 276, 320, 334

Bacchants 438
Bacchus 204, 406
baldric 52–3, 87–95, 115
Barchiesi, A. 63–4, 77, 82, 86
Basilica
    Aemilia 290, 304–5, 309, 318
    Iulia 288, 290–1, 294, 301–2, 304, 308–9, 318
    Octaviae 314
    Sempronia 288–9
Bellona 281–3
Big Ben 271
Binder, G. 69, 94, 193, 350, 448
Bishop, J.H. 88–91
Bitias 62, 93, 146
bivocal(ism) 68, 122, 130
Boyle, A.J. 24–5

476

Index

Briareos *see* Aegeon
Britain 90
Broch, H. 65, 180 n.34.
Brunt, P.A. 265, 349
Büchner, K. 167
Buckley, E. 77–9
Burck, E. 167

Cacus 258–9, 266, 270–1, 285–6, 302, 319–20, 322–4, 334
Caeculos 135
Caesar, Caius Julius 3, 60–1, 69, 88, 139, 166, 170–1, 177, 185, 236, 243–4, 280, 288, 290–1, 294, 297, 304–6, 308–13, 328, 368, 439, 443, 446, 449–50
Caieta 374
Callimachus 449
Calvinus, Domitius 311
Calybe 392–4, 412–3, 416–22
Calypso 376
Camers 19
Camilla 6, 11–13, 15, 22, 26, 29, 39, 47, 62, 133, 151, 153, 164
Camillus 325–6
Campus Martius 170–1, 282, 284, 315, 317–8
Camus, Albert 395
Canossa 445
Capitoline 168, 234, 259, 266, 275–80, 283–4, 288, 290–4, 296, 302, 324–6, 328, 379, 385, 444, 453
Carcopino, J. 381–2
Carinae 272, 277, 284, 301–3, 311, 313, 316
Carmen Saeculare 129
Carmentis 273–8, 293, 316, 321, 326
Carneades 215
Carthage 34, 183, 185–6, 191–2, 194, 196–7, 201–2, 204, 208, 211, 224–5, 227–30, 237–8, 240, 385, 388, 392
Carthaginian(s) 384
Cassandra 47
Cassius, Dio 170, 307–8, 316
Cassius, Lucius 60
Cassius, Parmensis 61
Castagnoli, F. 380

Castel Gandolfo 257
Castor 289–90, 308–10
Cato, Marcus Porcius 359, 361–71, 396–7
Catullus 152, 173
Catulus, Quintus Lutatius 279
Charon 146
chauvinism, male- 230, 242
Choephori 394
Chorus 394
Christianity 444, 454, see also *anima naturaliter Christiana*
Chrysippus 215–6, 403
Cicero 55, 87, 213–6, 244, 311, 403, 411, 454
Circe 375
circular reasoning 64–6, 73, 76–7, 97 n.10, 104 n.136, 122, 157 n.53, 227, 462 n.50
Circus Flaminius 282
Circus Maximus 260, 270, 277, 285
clementia/clemency 43–4, 51, 65–6, 82, 122, 176, 268
    Caesaris 44, 244
Cleopatra VII 127–8, 223, 244, 261, 306, 322, 328, 356, 449
Clivus Argentarius 290
    Palatinus 303–5, 316
    Victoriae 303
Cloelia 329
Clonus 92
Coarelli, F. 275, 303, 309, 311
Cocles 329
Cold War 235
Colosseum 88
compassion 7–9, 12, 17, 22, 38, 41, 43, 64, 67, 96 n.7, 121, 125, 145, 152, 155 n.6, 163–4, 167, 191, 193, 218–9, 234, 236, 239, 244, 245 n.15, 348, 427, 454, 457–8, 461 n.49
Connolly, P. 88–90, 93–4
Conte, G.B. 70, 122–6, 128–30, 135, 164, 197
Conway, R.S. 168
Corinth 63, 183
Cornelia 222, 232
Corythus 386

477

Index

Cosimo il Vecchio de'Medici, 446
Cossus, Aulus Cornelius 297
Crassus, Marcus Licinius 237, 297
Creationist(s) 235
Crete 386
Creusa 232, 261, 367–8, 375
Croesus 141, 223
Cucchiarelli, A. 87, 91
Cumae(an) *see* Sibyl
Cupid/Amor 184, 199–200, 203–4, 207, 223–4, 231, 239, 287, 333, 403, 418
  as Eros 207
Cura Iulia 277, 290, 305, 308–9, 318
Cybele 261, 266, 315

Danaid(s) 54–5, 87, 89, 119, 127–9
Danaus 119, 126–8,
Dante 5, 234, 444
Daphne 332–5
Dardanus 3, 371, 386–7
Darwinist(s) 235
Daunus 38–9, 44, 51, 64, 115, 176
De clementia 172
De fato 214
De spectaculis 170
'de-Augustanizing' Vergil's poetry 16, 36–7, 40, 120, 122, 125, 157 n.53, 454
Decembrio, Pier Candido 69
Della Corte, F. 381
Delphi 94, 128, 199, 205
Demoleos 93
diabolization 441
Diana 129, 133, 164, 192, 225, 331–2
Dido 2, 13–5, 23, 27, 38, 45, 47, 49, 56, 126, 146, 164, 173, 183–4, 186–208, 212–4, 216–33, 237–44, 287, 353, 385–6, 388, 391, 393, 395, 399, 403, 412, 424, 428, 452
Diocletian 289–90
Diomedes 9, 12, 82–3, 137, 228
  as Tydeus 153
Dionysius of Halicarnassus 258, 276, 285, 303, 320, 349, 359–63, 365, 370, 380, 383–4, 396–7
Dioscuri 290, 309
Dira(e) 35–7, 430
Divina Commedia 234, 444

Divus Iulius, temple 253, 305–9, 312, 318
Dolon 331
Donatus 1, 51, 55, 84, 86, 91, 115, 134, 173, 176, 252, 265, 271, 289, 366, 452, 459
Donatus, Tiberius Claudius 172
Drances 8–11, 15, 27–8, 42, 426
duplicity 253

Egypt, 127, 185
ekphrasis 11, 118, 120–2, 128, 132, 375
Electra 386
Elissa 232
Epicureanism 212
Epirote(s) 63
Erato 349, 355
Esquiline 277, 302–3, 316
Etruria 355–6, 380
Etruscan(s) 20, 45, 139, 142, 170, 258
Euphrates 236
Euripides 164, 183, 240, 284
Euryalus 6, 67, 91, 166
Eurystheus 88
Evander 10, 40, 44, 50–1, 95, 111–5, 164–9, 172–6, 257–60, 266–79, 282, 284–9, 291–6, 298–302, 306, 308–9, 313–7, 319–24, 330, 334–5, 378, 428
  as Father 55–6, 60–1, 112–3, 115, 117–9, 121, 124, 163–4, 169, 176, 335
  as King ix, 10, 46, 53, 55, 90, 109, 111, 143, 165, 174, 254, 256, 259, 263, 266–7, 269, 280, 291, 377, 385
  as pious 287

Fairclough, H.R. 94, 193
fama 351–2, 362, 387, 411, 446
Farrell, J. 235
Fascism 65, 446
Fasti 312
Fata Morgana 262, 266
Fate 3, 6, 7, 12, 33, 147, 212, 218, 224–5, 238, 258, 286, 348, 385, 388, 391, 402, 424, 437, 441–2, 444, 446
  as Destiny 349, 371, 388, 390, 430
  as Providence 349, 356, 454
father-son relationship 61, 114, 116–7, 136, 163, 166–7, 172, 176, 178 n.6, 323

Index

Fauns 271
Faunus 17, 27, 133, 350–2, 354, 357, 360, 371–3, 387–9, 402, 411–2, 414, 422, 425, 427, 437, 440–1, 445
Feeney, D. 35, 125, 135
feminism 184
Feugère, M. 90
fides punica 194, 242
Florence 446
Fontainebleau 445
Fora Caesaris 304, 315
Forbiger, P. 329–30
Fordyce, C.J. 152, 274, 288, 321, 323, 329, 355, 357, 385, 396, 400–1, 405, 413, 418
Fortuna 11
Forum 280, 291, 301–6, 310, 442
  Augustum 67–8, 439
  Boarium 257, 259, 262, 264, 274, 276, 298–9, 334
  Hilitorium 280, 291, 318, 328
  Iulium 309
Fowler, D. 253
Fowler, W. Warde 278
Fraenkel, E. 194
Freud, Sigmund 81–3, 85
Fufetius, Mettius 168
furor/fury 46–9, 56, 73–4, 83, 135, 399, 405
  as *impius* 46, 129
Fury *see* Allecto

Galaesus 397, 423, 425,
Galinsky, G.K. 65, 456–7
Ganymedes 185
Gauls 128–9, 325–7
Gellius 243
'gentle Vergil', *see* Vergil, as gentle
Georgics 235, 448, 450–2
Georgii, H. 265
Germany 455–6
Geryones 320
Giard, J.B. 310
Glei, R. 126
Golden Age 30 n.16, 65, 67–8, 105 n.152, 106 n.158, 121, 209, 211, 258, 272

Golden Milestone see *Milliarium aureum*
Gratian 445
Greece 185, 199, 295, 320, 409–10
Greek(s) 9, 58, 63, 75, 153, 258, 359, 406–9, 459
Gregory VII 445
Grimal, P. 278–9, 287, 290, 300, 303
Grönbech, V.P. 255

Haemonides 133
Halaesus 110
Hannibal 242, 392
happiness 124, 249 n.79, 271, 379, and see *laetus*, *laetitia*
Harrison S.J., 120, 124, 128–30, 135–7, 145, 148, 152
Harvard school 35, 41, 65, 68, 70, 72, 77–8, 80, 86, 135, 148, 454
Hector 33–4, 41, 74, 90, 110, 133, 153–4, 255, 313
Hecuba 202
Heinze, R. 88, 90, 93, 456
Helen 199–200, 203, 393–4, 399
Helenus 34, 45, 376, 387, 443
Henry IV, Holy Roman Emperor 445
Hephaestus *see* Vulcan
Hera *see* Juno
Heracles/Hercules 90, 143, 163, 167, 174, 257–9, 262–4, 266, 268–9, 271–2, 286, 314, 316–7, 319–24, 334
Hermes *see* Mercury
Herodotus 223, 409–11
Heroides 331
Heroon 380–1
Hesperia 186, 237–8, 355, 357, 374
Heyne, C.G. 418
Hieronymus 89
Hippolyte 88
Hippolytos 164
Hirtzel, F.A. 320
Histories 409–10
Hitler, Adolf 446, 456
Homer xii, 1, 9, 20, 41, 77, 82, 89–90, 110, 135, 138, 169, 175, 183, 189, 209–14, 255, 264, 308, 379, 393–5, 398, 406, 410–1, 416–7, 419, 424, 457–8

Index

Mercury 184, 186, 188–91, 193–5, 198–9, 201, 216, 218, 228–30, 232, 238–9, 242, 332, 376, 399, 439
Messapus 3, 12, 20, 22, 36, 440
Metamorphoses 69
metaphor 14, 51, 116–7, 120, 130, 138, 144, 240, 399, 402
Methodological Intermezzo 6
Mezentius 3, 14, 40, 45–6, 53, 62, 84, 94, 109, 111, 116–7, 138, 140–5, 147–9, 151–2, 154, 164, 173, 258, 365, 367, 369, 373, 378, 440–1, 457
Milan 445
Milky Way 314
Milliarium aureum 295–6, 304
Milton, John 65
Minerva/ Athena 213–4, 292, 298, 312, 391, 394, 407, 409
Mitleid(en) 167, 348
Mommsen, T. 446
Mummius, Lucius 63, 236, 455
Murranus 26
Muse 355, 358, 406
Mussolini, Benito 446, 456
Mutschler, F.-H. 60
Mycenae 200, 221, 387, 402, 437
Myopia 148

Nachleben 443
Napoleon 445
Naxos 183
Nazism 65, 446
Nedergaard, E. 308–9
nefas 55, 87, 92, 119, 121, 123–4, 127–8, 149, 158 n.54, 159 n.76, 405, 427, 437
Neoptolemus 93
Neptune 195
nequitia xii
Nero 170–1
Nestor 189, 264, 331, 408–11
New Criticism 120–1, 124, 126, 130, 455
New Historicism 80
Nikopolis 252–3
Niobe 128–9
Niphaeus 136
Nisus 6, 67, 166, 357–6

Norden, E. 298, 444
Numa 304
Numantia 208
Numic(i)us 3, 377–9, 380–3, 388
Nymph(s) 36, 192, 226, 271

Ocean 351, 446
Octavia 281–3, 457
Octavian *see* Augustus
Odysseus *see* Ulysses
Odyssey 33, 165, 213–4, 264, 355–6, 384
  as Roman 1
Ogilvie, R.M. 286
Oileus 407
Olympus 111, 268
Opis 12, 29
oracle(s) 2–3, 5, 13–14, 17, 27, 30 n.5, 32 n.30, 36–7, 70, 97 n.15, 133, 201, 223, 240, 337 n.28, 350–4, 357, 359–60, 371–3, 383, 385, 388–9, 390, 392, 396, 399–402, 411–2, 414–5, 418–9, 422, 425–8, 431 n.5, 432 n.6, 437–8, 440–1, 445
Orestes 240, 394, 398
Origines 361–2, 366, 368–9
Orion 142–3, 195
Ornytus 153
Orodes 142
Ostia 363, 382
Ovid 5, 69, 75, 88, 127, 131–2, 137, 177, 204, 243, 260, 274, 276, 304–5, 312, 314–7, 321–2, 328–9, 331–2, 334–5, 448

Page, T.E., 121
palaeo-Augustan 153, 273, 319
palaeo-Julian 268, 299, 361
palaeo-Roman 183
Palatine 126, 128–9, 131, 229, 254, 257, 259–63, 265–6, 269–70, 274–5, 277, 279, 284–5, 291, 294, 300–4, 306, 309, 312–9, 323–4, 334–5, 382, 389, 450, 453
Palazzo dei Conversatori 279
Palazzo Nuovo 279
Palazzo Senatorio *see Tabularium*
Palinurus 457

Palladium 312, 318
Pallanteum 18, 165, 175, 254, 256, 260, 263, 271, 316, 320, 322–4, 356, 377–8, 382–3
Pallas 37, 40, 45, 50–3, 58–60, 64, 71, 76, 85, 89–94, 109–19, 121–4, 126–7, 130, 132–4, 138–40, 143–5, 147, 151, 154, 164–70, 172–6, 225, 259, 263–7, 269–70, 277, 323–4, 335, 389, 428–9, 457
    as Aeneas' young ally 20, 56, 72, 75
    as new Patroclus 175
    as Prince 92, 163
    as *puer*/boy 10, 39, 44, 51–2, 54–7, 110, 121, 173, 175, 323, 437
Palmus 142
Pan 285, 332
Panaetius 208–9
Pandarus 62
panegyric (by Vergil, of Augustus) 65, 106 n.158, 224, 236, 447
Panthus 133
Paris 185, 393–4, 399
Parthia 236–7
Parthian(s) 308–10
partisan perspectives
    of characters in *Aeneid* 14, 142, 145
    of Vergil 28, 63, 67, 81, 117, 135, 140, 157 n.53, 234, 236–7, 389, 455–7, 462 n.50
    and modern readers 48, 233, 235, 457, 462 n.50
Pascal, C.B. 16
Pater Patriae 67, 439, 446
Patroclus 64, 110, 154, 254–5, 308
Paullus, Lucius Aemilius 63, 94, 171, 290
Pease, A.S. 218–20, 444
Pedia, lex 173
Peisistratos 264
Peleus 64
Penates 359, 375, 378, 383, 386
Penelope 331–2, 409
Pentagon 271
Penthesilea 47, 91
Pentheus 405
Pericles 446

Perseus 63
Perseverance in Religion (Vegius) 76
Persia 409–10
Perusia 171–2, 234
pessimism 65, 70, 102 n.82
Peter I (of Russia) 446
Phegeus 93
Phoenician(s) 187, 190–1, 202, 221, 225, 239
Piazza del Campidoglio 279–80
Piazza di Campitelli 279, 282
pietas/piety 50–2, 60–1, 76, 82, 123, 136, 146, 148, 150–2, 176, 197, 212, 216, 231, 264, 285–6, 414, 418, 423, 429, 440–1, 456
    as filial 38
    as human 143
Pinaria 320–1
Plancus, Lucius Munatius 296.
Plautus 87
Pliny the Elder 89, 129, 169–70
plot-line 2, 11, 33, 70, 116, 143, 156 n.33, 185, 202, 211, 251, 254–6, 259, 319, 324, 370, 455, 459
Plutarch 303, 327
Poetics 183–4, 227
Polites 113, 119
Pollux 308–10
Polydorus 457
Polymestor 200
polysemy 63, 253, 455
Pompeii (House of the Faun) 90
Pompeius Magnus 280, 302
Pompeius, Sextus 234
Ponte Palatino 259, 261–2, 265
Ponte Rotto 261–2
Ponticus 218
pontifex maximus 209, 311–12, 443–5
Pope(s) 257
    Pius VII 445
Porta Carmentalis 274, 278, 281–4, 290, 311
    Mugonia 303, 305
    Palati 303–4
Porticus Octaviae 282–3, 315, 318
Portunus 262–3, 276
Portus Tiberinus 265

Index

Pöschl, V. 13, 36, 115, 167, 195, 347–8, 391–3, 413, 415, 418, 422, 455
Poseidon 407
Potitius 320–1
Potomac 271, 290
Powell, A. 180 nn.33–4, 248 n.54, 249 n.87, 250 n.89, 452, 460 n.16, 462 n.50
Prague 446
Pratica di Mare 257, 380
Priam 25, 33, 45, 47, 64, 113, 119, 123, 165, 200–1, 211, 233, 238, 443, 458
probabile 200, 453
propaganda 81, 98 n.15, 129–30, 172, 223–4, 253, 269, 454, 456, 461 n.44
Propertius xi–xii, 40, 67, 86–7, 126, 131, 133, 171, 173, 176, 194, 218, 221–2, 233–8, 244, 260, 274, 293, 321, 328–9, 444, 449–50, 452, 459
Proserpina 243
psychagogia 109
pudor 29, 45–6, 221, 223, 227, 231, 240–1, 424
Putnam, M.C.J., 14, 41–2, 50–1, 59, 61, 73–7, 86, 120–22, 125–6, 130, 146–50, 152–3, 455
Pydna 63
Pygmalion 186–7, 191–2
Pyrrhus 25, 113, 123
Pythia 141
Python 333

Quellenforschung 362
Quinctius (consul) 145
Quinn, K. 117, 167–8
Quint, D. 59, 66, 80–6, 150
Quirinale 445

Rabel, R.J. 403
readers, long- and short-distance: *see* long- (and short-) distance readers
reception of Vergil 66, 68, 86, 101 n.63, 235, 251, 444
recusatio 449–50
Regia Numae 304
Rehm, B. 375, 381
Remus 257, 277, 284

Res Gestae 4, 61, 66, 172, 265, 286–7, 293, 307, 311–2, 439, 441, 443–4
revenge 36, 50–51, 59–62, 64, 72, 76, 82–3, 85, 100 n.46, 104 n.146, 105 n.153, 106 n.157, 109, 115, 117, 120, 127–9, 152, 160 n.84, 171–2, 176–7, 242–3, 254, 333, 459 n.1
Rezeptionsgeschichte 68, 77
Rhamnes 91
Rhesus 331
Riefenstahl, Leni 67
Rio Torto *see* Numic(i)us
Roi Soleil 446
Roman(s) 20, 53, 90, 136, 139, 145, 177, 206, 224
Romania 90
Rome 3, 6, 18, 33, 51, 109, 127–8, 130–1, 152, 164, 171, 183, 185–6, 195–6, 200, 202, 208–9, 212, 215–6, 224–5, 229, 238, 244, 253–61, 263, 265, 268, 272, 276, 278, 284–6, 291, 298–9, 301, 303, 305, 307, 310–15, 317, 319, 324–5, 329–30, 348, 351–2, 354, 356, 378, 380, 382–3, 385, 388–9, 402, 437, 439, 441–2, 444–6, 449, 453–4, 456
Romulus xii, 257, 261, 263, 266, 268, 277–8, 280, 284–6, 297, 301, 303, 311, 315, 324, 327
rostra 253, 294–6, 301, 305–6, 309–10, 318, 330
Rutulian(s) 3, 6, 19, 21–2, 36–7, 71, 117, 254, 258, 359–62, 365, 377–8, 383–4, 417, 419, 423, 438

sacerdos 133, 159, 312, 352, 431 n.5
Sacra via 294, 303–5, 311
Salii 445
Sallust 334–5
salto mortale (by critics) 66
Santa Maria della Consolazione 295
Santa Maria in Cosmedin 262–3, 274, 282
Sarpedon 117, 163–4, 167
Saturnus 271–3, 277, 289–90, 295–6, 300, 331
Scaevola, Q. Mucius 209

Scalae Caci 266, 268–70, 275, 284
Schneider, B. 69
Schröder, W.A. 364, 367
Scipio, Aemilianus 208
Scopas 129
Secular Games, *Secular Hymn* 244, 280–1
Segal, C. 126
Senate 67, 169, 253, 265, 277, 281, 290–1, 294, 297, 308, 310, 312, 318, 385, 439, 445
Seneca 75, 171–2, 211, 316
Septimius Severus 281, 300
Servius 1, 38, 51, 53–4, 113, 123, 166, 170, 176–7, 218, 231, 252, 256, 263, 265, 285, 287, 322, 327, 349–51, 358, 363–7, 369, 378, 381, 385, 406, 414, 454, 458–9
    Servius Danielis 367
Servius Tullius 263
Shades *see* Manes
short-distance readers *see* long- (and short-) distance readers
Sibyl 25, 49, 120–1, 134, 175, 375–6, 379–80, 382, 390, 444
    Tiburtine 234
Sicilian(s) 307
Sicily 117, 185–6, 190–1, 196, 375, 388
Siegerrecht 42
Silvanus 256
Silvia/Sylvia 357, 396–7
simile 13–17, 27, 32 n.30, 71, 74, 110, 120, 136–8, 142–4, 154 n. 3, 159 n.79, 173, 195, 197, 246 n.28, 386
Similienapparat 69
Simoeis 379
Sino 44
Sisenna 366
Skamandros *see* Xanthos
Sosius, C. 281, 296
Spain 208, 298
Sparta 200
Speer, Albert 67
Staatsfeind 347
Stadtbild 302
Stahl, H.-P. 65, 166
Stalin, Josef 446
Stoa 208

Stoic Philosophy *see* Stoicism
Stoicism 33, 35, 99 n. 32, 141, 208–10, 212–6, 228, 239, 248 nn.48 & 50, 403
subliminal(ity) 6, 8, 9, 163, 175–7, 201, 259, 264, 324, 354
Suetonius 316, 328
Supplement (of Maphaeus Vegius) 68, 70, 73–4, 76–7, 79–80
Sychaeus 191, 200, 205, 207, 220–1, 226, 240–1
Syme, R. 65, 171, 447, 456
Syrinx 332

Tabularium 279–80, 294–5, 300
Tanner, M. 446
Tarchon 256–8
Tarpeia, Vestal xi, 221, 277, 291–3, 301, 324, 327–9
Tarpeius 293, 327–8
Tarquinius Priscus 275, 298, 327
Tarquitus, 135–6, 138–9, 147
Tartarus 40, 243
Tasso, Torquato 65
Tatius, King xii, 324
Telemachos 264, 331
Tertullian 88, 170
Teucrian(s) 188
Thames 271
Thero 94
Theseus 183
Thessalonica 445
Thetis 407
Thomas, R.F. 14–6, 28, 36, 65–7, 70–4, 77, 80, 86, 135, 138, 149, 197, 352–3, 393, 415
Thome, G. 168
Thucydides 172, 441
Thybris 54
Tiber 3, 36, 110, 116–7, 224, 254, 256–60, 262, 264, 267, 274, 295, 349, 359, 374–5, 377, 379, 381–3, 388, 393, 402, 417, 419
Tiberius 294, 310
Tiburtine 11
Tigurini 60
Tilly, B. 380
Tisiphone, Fury 75

Index

Tolumnius 19, 20, 22
Tristia 131, 314
'Triumvirate, Second' 3
Troia 363
Troilus 457
Trojan(s) 5–6, 9–10, 12, 14, 20, 23, 25, 34, 36, 44, 49, 70, 81–2, 115, 133, 136, 141–2, 148, 153, 175, 184, 187–9, 191, 193–4, 196–8, 202, 212, 216, 218, 233, 239, 242, 261, 264, 266–8, 307, 349, 351–2, 355, 357–9, 361, 365–6, 370, 379, 384–93, 395–9, 407–8, 419, 422, 425–6, 431, 437, 439
Trojan War 253
Troy 1, 5, 9, 26, 33–4, 47–9, 56, 58, 83–4, 110, 113, 117, 133, 135, 141, 153, 163, 165, 368, 385, 387, 389, 402, 407–8, 417, 442–3
Turnus 5–29, 33–67, 69, 71–5, 78–80, 82–5, 92–6, 109–28, 134–6, 138–52, 154, 163–4, 166, 169, 174–6, 199, 201, 207, 210, 212, 216, 228, 230, 236, 239–40, 244, 255–8, 264, 268, 323–4, 335, 347–62, 365–80, 383–6, 388–90, 399–402, 405–6, 411–30, 437–41, 451, 454
  as impious 14, 37, 47, 257
  as King 1–3, 5–7, 45, 92, 109, 111, 141–2, 159, 199, 201, 207, 239, 244, 255, 350, 352–3, 377, 388, 392, 398, 411, 418, 454, 457
  as new Hector 175
  as Tyrrhenos 360
Turullius, Publius 61
Tyrians 287
Tyrrhus 395, 397, 425

Ulysses 74–5, 90, 331–2, 376
Umbro 135

Varro, 91, 292, 328–9
Varus 450
Vegius, Maphaeus 65, 68–80, 235
Veii 380
Velabrum 266, 274–7, 284, 288, 302
Velia 303, 313
Vellus Aureum 75, 80

vengeance, *see* revenge
Venus 9, 21, 24, 45, 69, 74, 79, 88, 137, 139, 166, 184–6, 191–2, 198–200, 202–6, 208–9, 212, 217–8, 222, 224–5, 229, 236, 256, 265, 291, 303, 306–7, 310–3, 316–7, 319, 351, 368, 375, 385, 387, 418, 424, 450
Vergil xi–xii, 3–6, 9–13, 16–7, 19–29, 33–7, 39–43, 46–55, 57–84, 86–7, 89–96, 109–10, 113, 115–17, 120–5, 127–55, 163–77, 183–5, 193–4, 199–202, 204, 206–10, 212–6, 218–9, 221–2, 224, 226–8, 231–7, 239–44, 251–60, 262–89, 291–311, 313–27, 329, 334, 347–54, 356–63, 367–72, 375–86, 388–90, 393, 395–400, 402–3, 405–6, 411–3, 415, 417–9, 423–30, 437, 439–49
  as gentle 59, 61, 132, 135, 156 n.32, 167–8, 454 (*see also* compassion, humanity)
  as new Homer 1, 117, 209
  as (non) partisan 28, 48, 63, 67, 81, 117, 145, 234, 455, 457
  see also partisan perspectives, of Vergil
Verteidigerinnen 127
Verteufelung 441
Vesta 211, 275, 304, 311–4
Via del Teatro di Marcello 274, 282
Via del Tempio di Giove 279
Via della Consolazione 290, 295
Via L. Petroselli see *Forum Boarium*
Via S. Bonaventura 304
Via S. Teodoro 290
Via Salara Vecchia 295
Vico Iugario 274, 280, 282, 290, 295
Victoria 11
Victory City 252, 318
Vicus Tuscus 285, 288, 290–1, 294
Vietnam 65–6
Villanova 89
Vitae 454
Vitruvius 88
Vorgeschichte 164, 355
Vulcan 10, 33, 79, 86, 141, 211, 251, 255–6, 260, 271, 292, 306, 324, 327, 356

West, D. 15, 193, 231
White, P. 447–54
White House 290
Widersprüche 361
Williams, R.D. 16, 18, 48–9, 92, 115, 134, 167, 226–8, 241, 256, 317, 348, 350, 402, 404, 422, 425
wishfulness (in scholarly interpretation) 31 n.30, 67, 97 n.10, 120, 154, 161 n.98, 169, 455, 459

Wlosok, A. 42, 184, 199, 227, 233, 241
World War II 447, 456
Wörner, E. 361–2

Xanthos/Skamandros 379
Xerxes 409–11

Zanker, P. 68, 291

INDEX LOCORUM

Vergil

Aeneid **1**. 92, 83; 278f., 209; 292ff., 211; 298ff., 186; 302ff., 187; 540f., 333; 565f., 189; 567, 190; 572ff., 191; 574, 193; 630, 198; 659f. and 677ff., 203; 683–8, 204; 717–22, 205

2. 10–13, 217; 23ff., 409; 34f., xii; 293, 34 and 313; 354, 49; 314–17, 48; 538f., 113

4. 27 and 28f., 221; 59, 223; 84f. and 91f., 224; 141f., 225; 169–73, 226; 220f., 228; 281 and 305f. and 310–13, 230; 328f., 206; 342f., 56; 347, 233; 547, 240; 550ff., 241; 696f., 243

6. 87–90, 379; 792ff., 272; 853, 42

7. 52, 414; 58 and 96f., 350; 98–101, 351; 126f., 376; 219ff., 386; 231ff., 387; 234f., 388; 236f. and 239f., 389; 242, 378; 251–4, 201; 266 and 275f., 390; 312 and 339f., 391; 339, 423; 340, 393; 345, 399; 365f., 401; 405, 406; 414, 416; 421f., 412; 423–6, 413; 432ff., 418; 444, 419; 446f., 420; 455, 421; 461f., 421; 470, 422; 521f., 397; 535ff., 397; 553, 356; 577ff, 425; 583f., 427; 595ff., 427; 595, 429; 596f., 7 and 429; 797f., 377

8. 1f., 441; 16f., 439; 36–9, 375; 98ff, 259; 115, 264; 125, 265; 142, 254; 182, 267; 303f., 320; 337–41, 274; 345f., 287; 347, 292; 474, 378; 538, 7; 540, 7; 542–5, 268; 546, 269; 358, 300; 364f., 317; 465, 334; 466, 335; 652f., 324 and 326; 730f., 255

9. 133f., 36; 759, 10; 760, 49; 560f., 146

10. 431, 133; 438, 111; 443, 113; 450, 112; 460, 174; 473, 117 and 164; 492, 113; 493f., 115; 494f., 113; 495b–498 and 499f., 118; 503–05 and 507, 116; 513ff., 134; 516f., 174; 519f., 167; 532f., 114; 550 and 552, 135; 599f., 136; 604f., 139; 607–10, 137; 649f., 140; 811f., 144; 825–6 and 827–8, 151; 829f., 152; 900, 145

11. 17, 7; 53, 173; 81f., 168; 173f., 112; 169–71, 169; 178f., 50; 215–19, 8; 318f., 378; 376, 10; 442, 10; 515f., 11; 522–25, 12; 688f., 153; 841f., 12

12. 4–9, 13; 30f., 17; 27f. and 39ff., 373; 70, 39; 79f. and 109, 18; 242f., 19; 447f., 21; 482f., 22; 568, 24; 572f., 24; 600 and 638–40, 26; 678–80 and 694f., 28; 797, 21; 895, 35 and 430; 913f., 37; 936ff., 38; 937f., 40; 938–41, 42; 941–44, 52; 943 and 948, 59; 945–49, 55; 948f., 56; 950–52, 62; 951, 83

Index locorum

Other authors

Augustus
Res Gestae 2, 172; 3. 2, 43

Dante
Divina Commedia **1**.106–08, 6

Ovid
Ars Amatoria **1**. 73f., 127; 229f. and 359f., 204
Fasti **1**. 581, 321
Heroides **1**. 39f., 331; 41ff., 332
Metamorphoses **1**. 539f. and 696f., 332; **3**. 204f., 331; **15**. 777f., 313
Tristia **3**. 1. 31f., 304; 61–2, 132; **4**. 10. 55, 322

Propertius
Elegies **2**. 6. 41f., 238; 7. 20, 237; 31.15, 134; **4**. 1. 7, 328; 131f, 87; 4. 29f., 329; 9. 68, 321; 11. 36 and 67f., 222

Sallust
Iugurtha 94. 5, 334

Vegius (Maffeo Vegio)
On Perseverance in Religion 1. 5, 76